ARCTIC JOURNAL

To: my sweet
Sister Hazel, 2011

Love ya + hope you
enjoy this book.
Happy Reading
my Dear.

Love From: Sister
Linda ♡ ☺

ARCTIC JOURNAL

A Fifty-Year Adventure
in Canada's North

Bern Will Brown

NOVALIS

© 2003 Novalis, Saint Paul University, Ottawa, Canada
Cover: Allegro 168 inc.
Photos (front cover): Bernard Willett Brown
Author photo (back cover): George Mayer
Layout: Gilles Lépine and Richard Proulx
Interior paintings and photographs: Bernard Willett Brown

Business Office:
    Novalis
    49 Front Street East, 2nd Floor
    Toronto, Ontario, Canada M5E 1B3
    Phone: 1-877-702-7773 or (416) 363-3303
    Fax: 1-877-702-7775 or (416) 363-9409

E-mail: cservice@novalis.ca
www.novalis.ca

National Library of Canada Cataloguing in Publication

Brown, Bern Will, 1920-
        Arctic journal : a fifty-year adventure in Canada's North /

Bern Will Brown. -- Combined ed.

Previously published in 2 volumes.
Includes index.

ISBN 2-89507-384-8

    1. Brown, Bern Will, 1920–. 2. Missionaries–Canada, Northern–Biography.

3. Catholic Church—Missions–Canada, Northern. 4. Oblates of Mary Immaculate–
    Canada, Northern–Biography. I. Title.

BV2813.B76A3 2003   266'.2'092   C2003-904362-2

Printed in Canada.

We acknowledge the financial support of the Government of Canada through the
    Book Publishing Industry Development Program (BPIDP) for our publishing
    activities.

5 4 3 2 1   07 06 05 04 03

NOVALIS

CONTENTS

FOREWORD

The Canadian Arctic has been undergoing tremendous changes in the last few decades. As old-timers say, "The North is not what it used to be." Indeed, it is not. The howling of the wolves has been replaced by the thunderous noise of snow machines. The limitless and unobstructed spaces of the tundra are now dotted with power lines. The gentle wake of the native canoes has become the tidal wave of the white man's powerful outboard motors. The serenity and limpidity of the northern sky is now streaked by the exhaust of jet planes. The teepee of the Dene people in the middle of the forest has folded up to make room for the frame house located on a street, heated by fuel oil, and electrified by diesel generators.

The land in its vastness, its beauty, its harshness, its isolation and its peace has shaped men and women who had to become ten feet tall to survive, a people somewhat outside time and walking to the beat of their own drum. They too are changing. In the past, the North shaped people; today, it seems that people want to shape the North.

Bernard Brown came to the North at a strategic time. The past was still present at his coming. The future was already being sketched on the canvas of history on his arrival. He had the chance to experience both the past and the future in the present of his life.

Very few people had the chance to taste the North in all its flavour, as Bernard Brown did. The land, the people, his work among the native people, his travels, his encounters, his adventures are served to us in the literary style of a diary that pricks the imagination while satisfying the legitimate curiosity of the reader.Bernard Brown is a master story-teller. The land, the people encountered, the events of everyday life, the joys and miseries of the North are the occasion for him to reveal the mysteries of a way of life which is rapidly vanishing. One can sense upon reading each page that Bernard Brown has been deeply marked by his experience. In the treatment of his subjects we see his knowledge, admiration, respect, attachment, dedication and love of land and people.

With its lively style, its simplicity of presentation, its wealth of information, and its authenticity of experience, this book will delight the reader. On turning each page, one will have the impression that the mystery of the North is slowly revealed.

Most Reverend Denis Croteau, O.M.I.
Bishop of the Diocese of Mackenzie–Fort Smith

INTRODUCTION

The year was 1967, and I had only just been appointed Commissioner of the North West Territories. It was Canada's Centennial, and celebrations were going on all over the nation. It was during this period that I first met Bern Will Brown, the leader of a crew of N.W.T. Voyageurs taking part, along with crews from throughout Canada, in the hundred-day, 3,283-mile Centennial Voyageur Canoe Pageant.

Affectionately known as "The Padre of the Logs," Bernard has lived in Northern Canada for some fifty years, while pursuing a rich life, first as a missionary and builder of churches, missions and cabins, and also as a trapper, photographer, artist, pilot and writer, not to mention a multitude of other services to his community and friends.

During my fifteen years associated with the Territories I spent a lot of time visiting and travelling with Bernard. While dropping into Nahanni and Colville Lake, I noticed the innovating style of the A-frame log churches that he built, and I marvelled at the speed and the very low cost at which he had completed them.

On a visit to Colville Lake during the Christmas holidays in 1965, I was surprised to see his collection of ten thousand pictures depicting life on the land. Several years later, on one of my regular visits to the settlement, I noticed a painting that he had done from one of his slides and I asked him if he would sell it to me. As a missionary, he had painted a number of beautiful pictures for several of the churches he had served, and I don't think that it ever occurred to him what they would be worth, or that, indeed, he should sell any of his work.

After much persuasion on my part, he agreed not only to sell me the painting, but to loan the photo he had used to develop the idea for the painting. I recall saying to him, "Bernard, you have a keen eye for detail, and, if you ever decided to commit to canvas what you have seen and learned from many years of living off the land with the Dene and Inuit of the Arctic, you could and would be making a great contribution to the people of this vast land and also mankind." I knew of no other person in the North at that time who had lived as long on the land as he had, with those magnificent people of the Arctic, and who possessed the God-given ability to record for posterity an authentic impression of life in the Arctic.

Bernard was not in the North for personal gain, and it took some time before he would agree. Of course, the rest is history. His picture of his powerful huskies and his companion, Philip Stenne, was unbelievably three-dimensional. It was used on the cover of the 1970 Centennial Report of the North West Territories Government and on the Hodgsons' annual Christmas card that year. During my twenty-eight years producing annual reports, never did I receive as many compliments for our format as that year.

I knew a good thing when I saw it, and during each visit to Colville Lake I would buy as many of Bern's paintings as I could for the N.W.T. Government. Some were given to distinguished visitors; the majority, however, adorn the walls of government offices or are in The Prince of Wales Heritage Centre in Yellowknife.

In 1975 I took HRH The Prince of Wales to Colville Lake to meet Bernard and his wife Margaret in order to show him what it was like living close to the land. The idea behind developing the Colville Lake settlement by the then Father Bernard Brown was to keep the native people on the land to de-centralize this area.

His life at times has been very difficult and no doubt lonely, but I know of nowhere else in this great country where one can be closer to his Maker and at peace with himself. While at times he may have been misunderstood, never have I seen him turn anyone away.

If he had chosen to live in southern parts of North America he could have succeeded at almost anything he chose to put his hand to, as he is that type of person. The difference between him and a lot of people who talk about making a contribution to their country is that many just talk, while Bernard lives and does it. He is indeed a man above men.

STUART M. HODGSON
FORMER COMMISSIONER OF THE NORTH WEST TERRITORIES

PREFACE

In my travels spanning over half a century in Canada's north, I've met many people whose lives were more noteworthy than mine. They had great stories to tell, and did tell them, but failed to put them in print. And now they're gone.

In the preface to the original *Arctic Journal* (volume I), I wrote: "From the day I arrived in the north in 1948 I've faithfully kept a daily journal which now fills up our fireproof safe. If this log Mission burns down, these pages at least will be saved."

After completing the manuscript of volume II, my wife, Margaret, and I were south on our yearly vacation when on October 11, 1999, a young vandal broke into the Mission and stole the safe. He took it by sled to a friend's cabin, where they proceeded to chop it open. Angry at finding no money in the safe, they threw the contents, over fifty years' worth of my daily journals, into their woodstove and burned them! The precious books I was so worried might perish if the house burned down were in the end the only thing here to be consumed by fire. Luckily this book was written before this terrible vandalism happened.

Since my high school days in Rochester I've been an avid reader of books about the north. This self-education enabled me to fit into the northern scene with ease when I arrived at the age of twenty-eight. I was well prepared for what lay ahead. The only thing that frustrated me was the lack of detail in most of these books. I wanted to know the names of the people the author met, the distances they travelled, the way they did things. I now have over 600 books on the north in my library; I often said to myself that if I ever wrote such a book, I would include as much detail as I could. So I wrote this book just the way I like to read them. The number of names in the index will attext to this.

In 1948, northern Canada still retained its northern character; most of this character has been lost in the intervening half century. Although I wish I had been born earlier, I am thankful that I was not born any later.

These pages paint a picture of one man's experiences in the north. They are coloured by my background and the type of work I was committed to doing. They don't pretend to be outstanding or heroic, they simply fill a gap in the history of the north. They tell it like it was in the second half of the twentieth century; in doing so, they commit to permanent print the names of many who might otherwise have been forgotten.

I was lucky to belong to an organization, the Oblates of Mary Immaculate, that could and did assign me to a variety of postings, from the Crees of Lake Athabaska to the Eskimos of the Arctic Ocean. (I use the term "Eskimo" deliberately as many of these people, including my wife, often refer to themselves this way.) If I had stayed in the same place for 50 years, I doubt this story would have been as diverse and interesting as I hope you find it to be.

I've covered a lot of ground in this book, mostly frozen, and I've met many interesting characters. In telling this story I am saluting some great northerners and recording for history a glimpse of their unique lives.

BERN WILL BROWN
COLVILLE LAKE
APRIL 10, 2003

1

GETTING THERE

It was six hours since I had left Fort Norman, Northwest Territories, heading north on the broad, frozen expanse of the Mackenzie River. The settlement had still been asleep at 6 a.m. when I pulled out. I was glad there were no eyes to witness my embarrassment when my toboggan overturned coming down the steep bank, throwing me into the snow. Luckily I'd clung to the head-rope, so I didn't lose my dog-team. As usual, these five huskies were keen to run at the start, but they didn't know that we had fifty-three hard miles ahead of us, with no trail to follow, or they would have conserved their energy. All my previous trips with them had been close to the settlement.

The lead dog, Fox, picked his way across the mile-wide river around broken ice slabs pushed up by the current at freeze-up time. This rough ice was hard on the oak sled boards. Once we had crossed to the west side of the river the going became easier, as the protected water here had been free of moving ice when it froze. We more or less followed the shore, occasionally cutting across to the many small willow-covered islands. At this latitude in January it's not really daylight until 11 a.m., but the dogs seem to run better at night anyway. It may be the wolf blood in them.

About noon I stopped for lunch, but we weren't near any brush I could use to kindle a fire. I sat on the curved head of the toboggan and pulled a huge ham sandwich from inside my shirt. Brother Médard had made it for me that morning and had advised me to keep it next to my wool undershirt so it wouldn't freeze. Nonetheless, it was frozen so stiff that I gave up gnawing on it and gave it to the dogs. I had better luck chewing on a dried whitefish. The temperature was forty-four degrees below zero, Fahrenheit.

After our ten-minute lunch break, we continued on with Fox breaking trail in about six inches of powdered snow. Having just passed a major landmark called Bear Rock, I estimated we were now ten miles out of Fort Norman, with twenty-five left to go before we would reach Pat Tourangeau's cabin where I hoped to spend the night. By 2 p.m. the hazy sun had disappeared, leaving us in semi-darkness. The dogs were tiring, which meant that I had to get off the sled more often to run behind and crack the whip.

As the miles lengthened my hopes of getting to that heated cabin faded. I began to worry about spending the night in the open without a tent or stove. Fox was weary, too, and began wandering off course. I had to keep correcting him with shouts of "Cha" for left and "Gee" for right. Precious time and energy were being wasted on this zigzag course. My spirits dropped with the temperature. Realizing at last that yelling directions at my leader was futile, I got off the sled, put on my snowshoes and started walking ahead of the team. I had to rethink this arrangement when Fox, eager to keep up, began stepping on the backs of my snowshoes and tripping me. I solved this problem by swinging a willow switch behind me, keeping him at a respectful distance.

We were now moving in a straight line – but at a much reduced pace – through a curtain of falling snow that enveloped us in a cold gloom and drastically limited visibility. I had to keep that vague left bank of the river in sight or we could end up travelling in circles without knowing it. As it was, we seemed to be moving in an eerie void with no horizon, land and sky blending in a solid whiteout. Only the harness bells and creaking snowshoes penetrated the silence.

I shuffled on, mile after mile, ever wary of stepping into over-flow that would be invisible until I got my feet wet; moose-hide mukluks absorb water like blotters. The fear of thin ice was uppermost in my mind. We were walking on snow-covered ice, beneath which flowed one of the world's greatest rivers; where the current was swift the ice could be thin. I kept straining my eyes hoping to spot a faint light from a cabin window up ahead, but it never materialized out of the mist.

This was my first trip by dog-team of any consequence and it was turning out like nothing I had expected. Now that I was on my feet walking, the cold didn't bother me, intense as it was. In fact, I soon overheated and my breath rimmed my wolverine parka hood in heavy frost. Still, after a few hours my legs were getting tired and I was hungry.

Worse than the physical discomforts, however, were the doubts and fears that preyed upon my mind. Was I really sure of the route I was taking? Could I have passed that cabin without seeing its light? Had they left and was the cabin now unoccu-pied? Could one actually get lost on this frozen river? If I didn't reach the cabin, could I make it through the night on this open trail? Questions like these occupied my mind as we plodded on, mile after mile.

My rest periods became more frequent. When I took time out to sit and rest on the head of the toboggan the dogs flopped down too, and every time I resumed the march it became harder to get the dogs up on their feet to follow me. By 7 p.m. I had to give in to fatigue and admit to myself that we weren't going to make it to the cabin; we would be forced to spend the night right where we were. The logical place to make camp was above the river-bank among the trees, but the banks were so high and steep that climbing them was impossible. My only alternative was a ravine which cut a gap in those insurmountable walls and seemed to offer some protection. When we got there I found the mouth of this ravine blocked by a ten-foot drift of snow, over which we tumbled in the dark. The dogs landed on top of each other, pre-cipitating the first dog fight of the day. I had a hard time breaking it up even with the help of the whip handle. This added exertion left me panting as I sat on the end of a drift log, contemplating the dismal prospects of the campsite in which I was to spend the night.

Taking my axe from the sled I splintered kindling off the drift log, the only piece of firewood in sight. Still wearing my snow-shoes I tramped down the snow and carefully arranged my precious kindling in the shape of a teepee, which I then lit. By the light of the feeble flames reflecting off the white walls of snow surrounding us, I unharnessed the dogs and chained them to the small green willows that stuck up through the snow. Next I placed my supper of a frozen whitefish and bannock near the fire to thaw. Returning from the sled with my arms full of gear I was dismayed to see my supper disappearing in great gulps down the throat of Mustache, the wheel dog. Another mistake: I had chained him too close to the fire. I moved him back without scolding him, thinking that if I had been in his place I'd have done the same. Then I set out another fish and bannock.

The fire was heating up steadily and I was beginning to luxuriate in its warmth as I sat close to it on my bedroll. Then, just as I extended my bare hands toward the welcome warmth and gazed into its crackling embers, I got the "Uh – Oh!" impression that it might be sinking. It was. As I watched, fascinated yet powerless, my precious source of heat and light gradually hissed its way below the surface of the snow and out of sight like some doomed ship at sea, leaving me in the dark again with a half-frozen supper. It was another lesson on life in the North: never build a fire on top of snow!

Not knowing how far I might have to dig down to solid ground, but estimating it would be farther than I could dig with a snowshoe – and not having much firewood anyway – I had to do without that essential part of any night on the trail. After gnawing at what grub was partially thawed, I turned to the next item of business: preparing a bed for the night.

How I envied the huskies: they had gulped down their frozen fish and were now contentedly curled up in the snow, snug as bugs in a rug. As for me, I lacked a tent for shelter or even spruce boughs to insulate me from the snow. The only hope I had of passing the night in any degree of comfort was that my as-yet-untried eiderdown sleeping bag would really be "proof against cold down to forty below," as the four-star guarantee claimed. Using a snowshoe for a shovel I dug out a niche in the wall of snow. That it resembled one of those tombs in the catacombs wasn't reassuring.

I spread the sleeping bag out on this icy shelf anyway and climbed in, parka, mukluks and all. One more mistake to add to my list of follies: my clothes were damp from melting snow and perspiration. Nevertheless I zipped the bag to the very top and pulled my head inside. As I lay there trying to sleep I could feel an ominous cold creeping up from my feet. I couldn't help mentally reviewing stories I had read of people in the Far North succumbing to sleep in the cold, never to awaken. So, though I prayed for sleep, I began to fear it. My sleeping bag became a shivering bag.

During that painful night I had plenty of time to review the events of the day that had ended in my present predicament. I asked myself if this was to be the life ahead of me at age twenty-eight. Did I know what I was getting into when I volunteered for the northern missions? Would the oil refinery workers and air force personnel at Norman Wells ever guess what it had cost me to come and conduct a service for them? Wasn't my left foot getting numb, or maybe frozen?

With the first faint glow of approaching dawn I was up and harnessing the dogs. I gave no thought to a fire or breakfast. I felt only a compelling urge to get away from the frigid ravine. And then, as I led the team down onto the river's ice again, I saw what appeared to be a dim light from a cabin window a half mile across on the opposite shore. It couldn't be! But it was. Throughout that miserable night I had been less than a mile away from the comforts of a warm cabin.

It wasn't just one tough break that had produced this adventure. My lack of experience in driving dogs – and a poor team at that, as I later found out – my lack of knowledge of the route and of camping out in winter alone, all had combined to produce this nightmare trip. I should not have been sent out on this trip without a veteran companion. I was learning the hard way.

As soon as my team caught the sound of the Tourangeau dogs barking they fairly flew over the snow toward them. At that moment a Canadian Pacific DC-3 airliner passed low over us on its landing approach to the Norman Wells airport twelve miles away. I could see faces in the windows and imagined their comments:

"Look down there, a dog-team, probably a trapper . . ."

"This cold doesn't bother that breed."

Would they have believed anyone who said: "You're wrong. That's a young missionary priest from New York State who's been in the country less than three months. He just spent the night in a snow bank across the river and nearly froze to death!"

❋ ❋ ❋

I was born in 1920 in Rochester, New York, and raised with two younger brothers nine miles north on the shore of Lake Ontario. Our home, named "Hearthcliff," sat on a bluff fifty feet above the beach. My mother, of French and Swiss stock, was extremely devout and made it a habit to attend daily Mass. My father, of English and Irish ancestry, was also one of three brothers. He was attracted to the outdoors and loved fishing and hunting. Living only a few feet from the water, we learned to swim early in life. We also had a canoe, a sailboat and an outboard motor. By age twelve I was running a muskrat trapline and catching the odd skunk! I took a mail order course in taxidermy.

About this time in my life I got very interested in art, for which I was showing some talent. My parents had me enrol in a Saturday class for beginners where I began with graphite sketches, then pen and ink, water colour, and finally oil. I liked it so much that I was spending every spare minute in my room painting. Some of those early works still survive.

As soon as I could handle a high-powered rifle, Dad took me with him on his annual fall deer hunts in the Adirondack Mountains. In the summer of 1936, when my brother Justin was fourteen and I a year-and-a-half older, we spent forty-six days paddling seven hundred miles in Ontario, Canada. The following summer we used a birchbark canoe on a trip farther north in the Province of Quebec. When I got into high school I began reading all the books about the Far North in the Rochester Public Library. I also enrolled in night school classes at the Mechanics Institute where I learned sketching from life. I was told I had a natural talent for art.

Like most boys my age, I wasn't sure what I wanted to do with my life. For some time I thought I might follow in the footsteps of my uncle, Dr. William Paul Brown, a medical doctor. So I hitchhiked up to Dartmouth College in Hanover, New Hampshire, and spent a week with a pre-med student. I was attracted to this college because of its ski team, but I soon found out that if I pursued a medical course I would have little or no time to ski!

In my last year in high school Dad had me enrol in a special civilian flying course conducted by the U.S. Army at the University of Rochester. Their long-range plan was to have flying instructors ready in case the United States joined World War II. Although I did get my private licence that year and then went on the following year to take their advanced acrobatic course, flying as a career didn't appeal to me.

During my four years of high school at Aquinas Institute, one of the Basilian Fathers who ran it suggested to me privately that I might be a candidate for the priesthood. Prompted no doubt by Mom's example and by her words, the idea had been germinating in my mind. One day Dad surprised me by saying that if he had to do it all over again he would have become a priest! Luckily for me he didn't. Still, the very atmosphere in our family was conducive to the idea. We five often said the rosary together, especially if we were driving in the car. We never missed Sunday

Mass. Several relatives were priests or nuns. As a remote preparation – just in case I decided that way – I signed up for both Latin and Greek in high school.

To get an idea of what might be involved I wrote to the Jesuits, who were in charge of the Catholic missions in Alaska, asking them how long their scholastic course took to prepare a person for priesthood. Their answer was staggering: a minimum of thirteen years after high school graduation! This meant that I would already be in my thirties before going north as a Jesuit. The idea was preposterous. Then I found out that a French order called the Oblates of Mary Immaculate had charge of all the Catholic missions in the Canadian Far North. So I wrote to them. Their answer was a bit more reasonable. They required their candidates to take two years of college in Buffalo, a year of novitiate in Massachusetts, two years of philosophy in Newburgh, New York, and four years of theology in Washington, D.C., culminating in ordination, for a total of nine years after high school. Although this course was four years shorter than the Jesuits', I would still be twenty-seven before I could hope to get into the North. These two religious organizations controlled all access to the northern Catholic missions on our continent. There was no alternative.

My big problem was my inherent hatred of school. I was close to finishing twelve years behind a desk and the very thought of suffering another nine years seemed beyond my endurance. I disliked school work so much I absolutely refused to carry books home to do homework except just prior to final exams when I crammed for a couple of nights. Luckily I managed to pass all my grades without failing.

On one of our hunting trips into the Adirondacks I met Nelse Defendorf at Keene Valley, who told me of a recent winter's trapping in Alaska. He spoke of workers needed in Ketchikan, Alaska, to man pressure hoses to wash down gold – no prior experience necessary. This idea so fired my imagination that I talked a classmate, Bernard Gallagher, into joining me after graduation for a trip to Alaska.

In that summer of 1939, as we started hitchhiking west with fifty dollars between us, America was in the dying throes of the Depression. Near Erie, Pennsylvania, a mini-hurricane left the roads blocked with fallen trees and we got a week's work as loggers. From Indianapolis we delivered a new school bus to Fort Scott, Kansas. At Cheyenne, Wyoming, we worked at the annual Frontier Days Rodeo prodding stock into chutes and later, on horseback, herding cattle back to their home ranch. From there we took a job chauffeuring a party through Yellowstone Park. We picked cherries in the State of Washington for Japanese-American farmers and finally bummed a ride with a trucker into Seattle. We had less than a dollar between us, but we had successfully reached the west coast.

Our plan now was to accept any kind of work on a ship heading for Alaska or, failing that, to stow away. As it happened there was a longshoremen's strike tying up all northbound ships along the Seattle waterfront. After three nights spent in this sleazy dock area we were so hungry and discouraged we hitchhiked to the site of the Grand Coulee Dam being built on the Columbia River and got some work shovelling gravel. Our dreams of Alaska were fading behind us.

As the summer wore on and the longshoremen's strike was still unsettled, we decided to head back east for home. En route we spent an exciting week with the Flathead Indians on a reserve in northern Montana. A couple of young bucks our age took a liking to us and let us use two of their horses to corral some of their buffalo with them.

From there we found so few cars on the roads we were forced to ride the rails. We boarded one of a string of boxcars with 129 Depression hard-luck types who were following the harvests for work. I was surprised to see women among them. This train kept rolling on day and night for three days, stopping only briefly now and then to take on coal or water. Luckily we met two professional hoboes named Lefty and Dick who took us under their wing and showed us some tricks of the trade. First of all, they had us climb up on top of a car loaded with lumber. By lying flat up there we went undetected when the railroad police, called bulls, drove everyone else off the train. They would all run ahead and again reboard as the train pulled out. We were left undisturbed, but we had to suffer a lot of traffic from fellow travellers who were moving back and forth over the cars to get to those that held ice for refrigeration. This melting ice was their only source of drinking water. And when there was no side wind the engine smoke blew over us in a shower of black cinders.

Later in the week, when the train began stopping at small towns, Lefty and Dick showed us how to go into a restaurant, order a meal and then, before it was served, go into their washroom, clean up and leave by the back door. Then we would work both sides of a street asking housewives for specific items of food for a stew we would cook up at the local hobo jungle. When we finally arrived at Minneapolis we tried to wash up using the trickle of water leaking from the refrigeration cars. Evidently we didn't do a very good job because when we tried to get into the local YMCA they refused us as being too dirty. We hitchhiked from there back to Rochester. It was the end of August and, although we hadn't accomplished our objective, we were a little wiser for having wrestled with life in the raw and having come out unscathed.

So now I found myself back home with my future unresolved, but I was in time to enter the juniorate class at the Oblate College in Buffalo if I so desired. My parents were urging me to give it a try. I finally phoned them and told them I was coming. For some reason I didn't want to admit to my buddies that I was entering a junior seminary, so I told them I was going to the Air Cadet College in Pensacola. Deep down I felt that I wouldn't persevere in the Oblate Juniorate and I didn't want to burn any bridges behind me. On the other hand I thought that I might regret it later in life if I didn't at least give the religious life a try. I said my goodbyes and hitchhiked to Buffalo.

I found myself in the juniorate with six other candidates, but before the year was out I was the sole survivor! This was a surprise, as I thought I would be the first to leave. I got home for the summer and continued my flying. In Buffalo again for my second year of college I had three new classmates, older men who had quit the business world to study for the priesthood. We four went through the next eight years together.

Once we began our novitiate in Tewksbury, Massachusetts, the following year, we could no longer go home for visits. Clad in cassocks, we entered the very strict phase of our training, a strictness that would persist right up to ordination. Our days were regulated by bells that woke us in the early morning, called us to chapel, to classroom, to work, to meals and back to chapel again. Our mail was censored both coming and going. We had no spending money, no newspapers or radio and smoking was forbidden under pain of instant dismissal. The next year, when we were taking our two years of philosophy in Newburgh, we met some of the army cadets from the military academy at West Point who admitted that our regimen was far stricter than theirs.

From the outset I had been very open about the fact that I had joined the Oblates to go north. I was accepted under this understanding with the promise that I had "a good chance" of getting this assignment if I persevered. Oddly enough I was the only candidate wanting to go in that direction. The rest of my classmates had their sights set on warmer climes.

Initially my superiors merely smiled at my unusual preference for the North. Yet as the years ground on and I persisted in my resolve I was looked upon as being odd. When I got down to my final year of theology in Washington some became downright hostile. I couldn't understand this attitude in view of their wide use of the Arctic in pictures to attract recruits.

"Brother, be sensible," said my superior as I sat stiffly before him in his office a few months before ordination. "You simply don't realize what this foolish idea of yours could lead to. The Oblates working in that frozen field are all Frenchmen. They're different from us. Very puritanical. I've heard they wear cassocks even in the shower! They speak only French. You wouldn't be able to talk to them or know what they were saying about you. And have you thought about those long winter nights that last for six months? Nothing to do? No one to talk to? You'd go stark, raving mad."

The pressure was on and every means was used to get me to change my mind about going north before I wrote my mandatory letter to the Superior General in Rome indicating my preference in a world-wide field of possible assignments. When my superior suspected that his harangues were not producing the desired effect on me he attempted to reduce my hopes to zero by adding that he would send an accompanying letter along with mine with an emphatic veto! It seemed as though I had run up against another type of longshoremen's strike blocking my way to the North.

At this point in my life my spirits were at a low ebb. As a good religious I had been trained to accept any assignment given to me by my superiors. In fact I had taken a vow of obedience to do just that. I knew deep down that I would honour this vow, but the idea of spending my life in Japan or Brazil or even in the States seemed as difficult a future to contemplate as would be that of submitting to nine additional years in classrooms. Possible, but painful. The focus of my dreams had never wavered from a life in the North.

And then, like an answer to prayer, my liberating angel appeared in the person of Bishop Joseph Trocellier, O.M.I. He was head of the Western Arctic's Mackenzie Vicariate and happened to visit our scholasticate. I lost no time in getting an interview with him and expressing my views. The result was that he not only encouraged me to persevere in my plans to go to the North, but promised that he would write his own letter to the Superior General requesting my services in his area of the Northwest Territories. The battle had been won and I could approach ordination with an untroubled mind. Although this did not dispel a frosty atmosphere around the scholasticate, I was at peace. I was heading north.

2

THE NORTH AT LAST

What a great feeling of liberation it was to get away from the grey walls of that institution. My youngest brother, Thomas, drove down to Washington in his car and took me back to Rochester for my first visit home in seven years. As we rode along, side by side, reviewing the news of the past few years, he suddenly informed me of a momentous decision: he had decided to join my religious congregation!

This was a complete surprise as I thought he was happily engaged in a profitable plastics business. After he had graduated from the Merchant Marine Academy at King's Point, New York, he spent several years on ships in the South Pacific and when he returned home Dad had helped him start his own business called "Tom Brown Associates." And now he was telling me he wanted to quit this lucrative career to follow in my footsteps! I had to admire his enthusiasm in tackling the long ordeal I had just completed. Without wanting to discourage him, I had to admit that I couldn't go through it again. Besides, I had been driven by a great desire to go north which motivated me and which he didn't share.

During the previous year our middle brother, Justin, had paid me a visit at the scholasticate to tell me of his desire to join the Christian Brothers and devote his life to teaching. He had graduated from the Merchant Marine Academy at St. Mateo on the west coast and after his tour of duty on supply ships in the

South Pacific had enrolled in the Mackay School of Mines in Reno, Nevada. He had spent a winter mining near Fairbanks, Alaska, and had a pilot's licence from the U.S. Navy.

When we talked over his qualifications I thought he would be a valuable addition to the Oblate Brothers in the North who were operating all kinds of transportation along the Mackenzie River. I advised him to forget the Christian Brothers and contact Bishop Trocellier. Once he did this he was quickly accepted and sent up to Fort Resolution in the Northwest Territories to begin his novitiate. So Justin actually got into the North ahead of me. Now, with our younger brother planning to join us, it looked like all three of us would soon be members of the same religious family.

That summer passed very pleasantly amid family and friends at Hearthcliff. We often sat out on the front lawn evenings, watching the boats come into port at sunset and the northern lights begin to appear across the lake over Canada. I imagined them reflecting off the land of ice and snow that would soon be my new home.

My hitchhiking days were over. When I left Rochester at the end of that summer I was driving a new two-ton truck loaded with medical supplies for the northern missions. After a week I reached the end of the road north at Edmonton. From there I continued via the Northern Alberta Railway (NAR) with the truck on a flatcar and myself in the Pullman. This train, dubbed "the muskeg express" by locals, was an adventure in itself. Rolling cautiously on narrow gauge tracks and pulled by a venerable steam locomotive, it took two days to reach the end of steel at Waterways, Alberta. Much of the roadbed lay on spongy muskeg and derailments due to tipping were frequent. The single coach car in which we travelled was lit by kerosene lamps swinging overhead and heated by a pot-bellied, coal-burning stove. Bunks were folded up out of the way during the day.

The cast of characters riding that train fit into the scene perfectly: Indian women with babies tied in blankets on their backs, grizzled trappers in mackinaws, moccasin-clad bush people who carried either half-pound tins of Ogden Fine Cut Tobacco to roll cigarettes, or empty tins for cuspidors if they were chewing Copenhagen Snuff.

Also on board was a fellow Oblate missionary, Father Pat Mercredi, born at Fort Chipewyan and now serving several mission stations along our route. When he heard that I was interested in art he just had to show me the paintings he had done on the walls of his church at the settlement of Philomena. It was dark at midnight when we reached that spot and we were already in our bunks, but Father Pat had the engineer make an unscheduled stop so we could scramble up the bank and with the aid of a flashlight see his paintings. The friendly conductor gave us ten minutes and then a blast from the locomotive whistle sent us scurrying back down to our car. The muskeg express resumed its clickety-clack progress north into the night. Actually I was less impressed with the missionary's artwork than I was with his ability to stop and hold a train.

Arriving at Waterways, we were met by a truck which took us the final three miles to Fort McMurray and the mission. This NAR rail line was supposed to go on to McMurray, but some said it was never completed so that they could still charge "construction rates." The area didn't impress me too favourably. The most southern mission in the Mackenzie Vicariate, it was not nearly northern enough in its atmosphere for me. I was to become very familiar with it when, ten years later, I would spend four years here.

While my truck and its precious load of medical supplies went on north from here via a Northern Transportation Company barge, I was given a lift by a commercial fisherman, George McInnes, in his Anson aircraft. I was seated on my suitcase in the tail of the plane when I happened to notice that this tail section was held by only three bolts. I inched forward beyond that dividing crack and got out my rosary, although if the tail did separate it wouldn't help any to be in any other part of the plane. At any rate, on a wing and a prayer we landed in Fort Smith. I had reached the Northwest Territories at last.

Fort Smith was the unofficial capital of the Territories, the seat of the civil administration with offices for all government departments. It was also the headquarters of the vast Mackenzie Vicariate which stretched as far north as people lived, and the home base of Bishop Joseph Trocellier, O.M.I., who presided over it. His enclave was a small community in itself, with the mission building housing about twenty Oblates, the convent accommodating some sixteen Grey Nuns of Montreal, the cathedral church, a three-storey hospital, two schools, warehouses and garages, stables, an ice house and even a morgue! Twenty miles out of town was St. Bruno's cattle ranch. Fifteen miles down river was the Brothers' sawmill.

The dedicated Grey Nuns cared for the sick – mostly natives suffering from tuberculosis – taught school, did the cooking and laundry, the sewing and a host of other tasks that kept them occupied from early morning until late at night. And they did it all with a smile while dressed in their uncomfortable starched habits. When they did finally retire to their tiny rooms in the hospital attic they often suffered through sleepless winter nights due to the cold. One of the nuns told me she always took the small rug off the floor and put it on her bed before retiring.

For their part the Brothers kept busy operating the large farm that enabled this whole complex to be self-supporting. They had milk cows and beef cattle, horses, chickens and turkeys. They cut enough cordwood to heat all the buildings and they milled enough lumber to put up all their buildings in Fort Smith and many others farther north. This was the supply depot for all the missions down river. During the short summer these Brothers used their boat, the *Sant'Anna,* and its barge to move all the supplies needed to operate the various missions down to the Arctic Coast. At Tuktoyaktuk they transferred freight to their forty-ton schooner, *Our Lady of Lourdes,* for distribution to coastal missions. A nightly short wave radio "sched" linked all the missions to this control centre at Fort Smith and requests for aid never stopped pouring in.

As soon as I arrived I was greeted by Oblate missionaries scurrying about in black soutanes with felt shoes sticking out the bottoms and bushy beards sprouting at the tops. The priests could be distinguished from the Brothers by the size of the crucifix stuck in their cinctures. Those of the Brothers were smaller.

"Comment ça va?" and "Bienvenue!" greeted me from every side as I started using my untried high school French. I was taken immediately into the bishop's office where he sat plump and jovial behind his pectoral cross and, through a haze of pipe smoke, queried me in a thick French accent about my trip. His immediate concern was the whereabouts of my new truck and its load of supplies. I assured "His Excellency" it was safe aboard a barge which would land in two weeks' time – barring a sudden freeze-up. The short interview over, I was shown to an even shorter room on the third floor where I lugged my suitcase and unpacked. I had no idea if I were moving in for good or merely passing through, but at least I had my foot in the door to the real North.

I had entered a world unlike any I had known before and hour by hour I was discovering its secrets. One thing I quickly learned was that the bishop was not the boss in that house; it was a bell hung strategically in the main stairwell which invariably snapped one to attention when it spoke. It had a spring-loaded clapper activated by a rope on the ground floor, and it spoke with an urgent firehouse clang that could stop a conversation in mid-sentence – or a deep sleep in mid-snore. The mission personnel's day was regulated by it from its first four-alarm summons to prayer at 4:50 a.m., until it sounded for night prayers at 8:30. Nobody liked it, but everyone respected and obeyed it.

Not assigned to any duties except to say Mass at the convent in the early morning, I found my days free to walk around and get acquainted. I had played the guitar since I was a kid, so I became popular in the TB ward from the minute I first yodelled a cowboy tune. And over at school I got instant recognition the minute I started drawing animals on the blackboard. I even wandered next door to visit the Mercredi family. My Dad was a great one for visiting people and I think I inherited that trait.

Our Oblate community assembled for meals three times a day in the basement refectory of the hospital. This ritual was presided over by the bishop, who sat at the head of the table, said the grace and blessed our food. Following a short reading from Scripture the bishop then gave us his *"tu autem Domine miserere nobis,"* which was a signal we were allowed to talk during this meal. We all answered, *"Deo Gratias"* – Thank God – and dug in with gusto amid some encouraging *bon appétit*'s. We ate all the courses out of our soup bowls "to save on water" – dishwater, I guessed. Following the meal we trooped into chapel together for a short prayer and following supper we congregated in the mission's upstairs recreation hall. There I was quickly initiated into the card game called cribbage, which I was told was a sine qua non of life in the North. They were right. It is *the* northern card game and I have been playing it ever since.

My International truck arrived in Fort Fitzgerald and I drove it over the sixteen-mile portage road to Fort Smith and helped unload it into one of the vast warehouses. Every day we watched fascinated as the local RCMP, the Royal Canadian Mounted Police, drove a two-ton truck into our pasture with a load of prisoners to dig up and carry away sod. They said that they were making a nine-hole golf course near their barracks. I couldn't help but think of the description of that game given me by Bishop Turquetil of Hudson Bay who had ordained me. "Golf," he said, "is a game with a three-foot stick with a small white ball at one end, and a damn fool at the other."

The members of the mission at Fort Smith didn't participate in any outdoor games as such, but on the big feast days we all piled into a freight truck and drove out to the Brothers' wood shack for a picnic. No one saw any need to take up golf. The seasonal buffalo hunt would be considered a sport by many, but to us it simply meant a lot of hard work – not the pulling of the trigger – but the skinning and butchering. Some of those brutes weighed over two thousand pounds. We weren't hunting for ourselves but for the children in our hostels and the patients in our hospitals and we needed a lot of meat to be sent as far north as Aklavik. I helped a little by bringing down an old bull with my .270 Winchester, an ordination gift.

Hunting the sharp-tailed grouse on their fall migration south, however, proved to be more of a challenge. You could pick them out of the tops of dead spruce with a .22, if you were a good shot. I can remember unloading fifty at the hospital kitchen and feeling relieved that it would be the Sisters' job, and not the hunters', to pluck them.

Father Mansoz was the oldest veteran at the mission and we were celebrating his seventy-fifth birthday. Following the banquet I was sitting with him in his room puffing on one of the White Owl cigars that were traditionally passed out. I had not acquired the tobacco habit yet and I put the question to this wise old missionary as to whether or not I should smoke? He replied that he thought maybe if I smoked a pipe it would provide some soothing companionship later on during the hard times and added, "Zer har zo mini tings ve kin not do, zee?" Then he got to reminiscing about his life in the North and how it had passed so unbelievably fast, saying, as he gazed out the window, "Zo mini tings to do yet. But zey tell me too hold now. Me, I feel just start, but zey say zit quiet, you do nuf already." Some forty-five years separated us and yet he predicted I too would be seventy-five before I realized it. He was right.

October's gold had given way to November's white. In spite of the similarities to the scholasticate I had just left I caught myself beginning to like this place – not everything, that's true. I really was not getting enough sleep, and I was getting very little out of the daily spiritual reading in French. The food was monotonous, either buffalo or whitefish, which showed little inspiration in its preparation. What compensated for these drawbacks, however, was the uplifting spirit of the place. One could not help but notice the open, generous and friendly atmosphere that hung over this religious community like a benediction. They were poor and it showed, but that didn't dampen their enthusiasm. Our

quarters were cramped, often cold and dark, but no one complained about it. No one expected anything better, so no one was
disappointed. Everyone had his own job to do and took a special
pride in doing it well for the common good. There didn't appear
to be any weak links in the chain, no discord, no problems that
couldn't be solved.

In short, it was a small, insular community of happy, dedicated religious people living a communal life in the ideal sense of
that word. Few in the outside world knew we even existed and
unfortunately that existence was to be short-lived. Fifty years
later they would all be gone, the mission turned into a museum,
and most of the other buildings torn down. Looking at that
empty space today one might find it hard to imagine the activity
that once flourished there.

On the 4th of November I was back in the bishop's office and
he was saying, "Fadder Brown, I'm a not a certaine justa yet
where I'm a gonna puta you, but ina meantime how you likea
visit your brudder Justin ata Fort Res (Fort Resolution)?" The
bishop had gone through the Italian scholasticate at San Georgio
and had a very musical combination of Italian and French
accents.

The following morning found me aboard the Canadian
Pacific Airline's DC-3 for the eighty-mile hop over to Fort Resolution on the shore of Great Slave Lake and to a reunion with the
younger brother who had beaten me into the North by a year. I
found him out behind the mission with a sledge hammer and
wedges, splitting four-foot lengths of firewood. We had a month
to fill each other in on our recent experiences, but to do this we
were allowed no special visiting privileges. Justin was going
through his year of strict novitiate training prior to taking his
first vows. We got together where and when we could.

The Fort Resolution mission was a smaller version of the one
I had just left at Fort Smith, with the addition of a large boarding
school for native children. The Chipewyan Indians living there
were still following their traditional lifestyle of hunting and trapping. Here I was excited to see my first dog-teams in action. I

joined Justin and his Oblate community in most of their daily religious exercises. The one that started the day at 5:15 in their dimly lit chapel is the most memorable. The usual prayers were followed by the standard half-hour of meditation, during which one of the good Brothers behind us demonstrated various types of northern snoring, outstanding for both variety and volume.

During the day when I couldn't be with my brother I took advantage of the chance to visit around the settlement. Fred Camsell, less well-known brother of Charles,* was the Postmaster. He told me of his yearly trips to Winnipeg for an education when he was a boy, and of his going to work for the Hudson Bay Company at Fort Rae in 1889. Joe Lirette was a "free-trader" and told me of wolves he had killed that weighed over 200 pounds.

Perhaps the most notorious local character was another trader by the name of George Pinsky. One of his little trade tricks was to give change to his customers – who paid with paper money – by tearing off a smaller portion of the bill to insure that the balance would be returned to his store. As a result a lot of the local bills were either sewn or taped together. I kept one as a souvenir. George sold me a half-dozen oranges at a fabulous price and invited me to return in the evening for a game of bridge. I never did get back to join in a bridge game and Justin didn't get to eat the oranges, as he was scrupulously observing one of the rules that forbids eating between meals and that directs that all gifts be shared with the community.

While at Res I was invited by the superior, Father Mokwa, to spend a couple of nights at the Brothers' wood camp ten miles away and act as chaplain. This occasioned my first ride in a dog-sled capably driven by Brother Petrin. I was amazed at both the power and speed of these draught animals and the intelligent way their leader obeyed the voice commands of the driver behind me.

---

* Charles Camsell, born at Fort Liard, N.W.T., in 1876, was Deputy Minister of Mines and from 1935 to 1946 he was Commissioner of the N.W.T. He was also the Chief Factor of the Hudson Bay Company.

When we pulled up in front of the rough-hewn log cabin bunk-house, out came a big, burly French-Canadian in a stocking cap and full beard. "My soul, comment ça va?" he shouted, and I knew I was meeting the most widely known and best-loved Brother in the Territories – the loud, jovial, cross-eyed Brother Henri Latreille, known simply as "Frère Hon-ri."

For the next two days that cabin rocked with his outrageous stories and laughter as he cooked for a half-dozen woodcutters. Following my early morning Mass for the crew, I was free to help the Brother with his many chores. He chopped the firewood needed to heat the cabin and fuel the cook stove and introduced me to the standard northern torture instrument called a Swede saw. He also had me help him visit a gill net set under the ice and to appreciate losche liver, one of the special northern delicacies, comparable to moose nose and beaver tail. We also checked the snares he had set for snowshoe rabbits.

To add excitement to these experiences we were visited one night by a pack of timber wolves who were trying to get at our sled dogs. They kept up a frightful chorus of howls as they circled our cabin in the dark. I would have been a hero if I had shot one and driven them off, but although I stayed up half the night I could not get one in my rifle's telescopic sight.

Back with Brother Justin at the Res mission I was full of enthusiasm after my brief bush experience and eager for more. We speculated on what the future held in store for each of us in this wild and exciting Northland and whether we couldn't manage to be stationed together after he had finished his novitiate and made his profession. What we couldn't have anticipated at the time was the accident that would befall him the following spring. While he was repairing the church roof, his safety rope broke and he fell thirty feet, breaking both ankles and injuring his spinal column. The local doctor put him in a cast, but when gangrene set in he was sent to Edmonton where he spent the next three months in hospital. It ended in his having to leave the North and give up his plans of becoming an Oblate Lay Brother. He never expressed any bitterness over this turn of events, accepting it all as the will of God. Dad, with his characteristic humour, would later tell people that he had two sons who were priests and one who fell away from the church!

Back in Fort Smith I was again in the bishop's office recounting my visit with my brother when he suddenly interrupted my small talk with something important. "Fadder Brown, I tink I finda justa spot for you – Forta Norman. Lots ah missionaries starta dere. Watta you tink?" I thought it was a great idea and heartily accepted my first official "obedience" in the Mackenzie Vicariate.

Although I had to leave the bustling mission at Fort Smith behind me, I had been lucky to experience it firsthand at its glorious peak.

3

FORT NORMAN

On December 3rd, 1948, I was on board Canadian Pacific Airlines (CPA) DC-3 Mainliner, piloted by Captain Ken Dewer, as it winged its way north over the frozen Mackenzie River with stops at Hay River, Fort Simpson and Wrigley. It was dark when we finally landed at Norman Wells, the northern terminus of the line, and stepped out into minus forty-five degrees Fahrenheit. While the ground crew scurried about putting wing covers on the aircraft for the overnight stay, the local RCMP escorted the stewardess away and we, the passengers, were taken to the CPA boarding house capably run by a matronly woman known affectionately as "Ma."

The next day I made the final flight to my destination, Fort Norman, aboard a Waco biplane flown by local bush pilot Mike Zubko. We sat down on skis in deep snow on Plane Lake a mile behind the settlement where Father Jean Denis, O.M.I., my new superior, met me with his dog-team. After we had thrown my baggage into his sled he offered to let me drive the team back to the mission. Borrowing his heavy mitts, I stood behind grasping the sled handles while he rode in the cariole. Careening down that steep, twisting trail into town, I fell off not once but twice, to his great amusement. Evidently dog mushing was not as easy as it looked.

Brother Médard, blood-brother of Frère Henri, welcomed me warmly when we got to the mission. Not as tall or as overpowering as his older brother, the clean-shaven Médard was more rotund, but he had the same jolly manner, the same heavy Quebec-French accent.

As soon as I had my parka off (as was the custom in those days, I wore my cassock underneath), I was given a tour of the building. The first thing I noticed was the height of the door jambs. Those early Frenchmen who had built it must have been very short, as they had allowed only a five-and-a-half-foot clearance for the doors. My two companions could walk through them erect, but I had to be careful to duck my six-foot frame. This two-storey mission had been built in the last century of squared spruce logs dovetailed at the corners, chinked with mud and straw and covered inside and out with hand-hewn boards. Once the logs had been covered on both sides in this way you could not see if the chinking was falling out, and to a great extent it had. The mission had been whitewashed on the outside, apparently to make it resemble a proper frame building. Inside, the boards lining the walls ran vertically and were painted – pink!

I was taken across the common room where accordion doors opened to reveal the chapel hidden behind them, unheated except during services. To the right of this were two smaller rooms, the first being a seldom-used parlour, the second the room of Father Denis. Along the left side was the room of Brother Médard and the kitchen. This opened up in back to a closed-in porch which he called a *tambour*, where he stacked his kindling. There was a second floor containing a library and three bedrooms, but this area was left empty and unheated during the cold months. To gain access to it, you had to go through the ground floor confessional, an arrangement I could never understand.

Out behind the mission there was a carpenter's workshop, a privy, several warehouses and a small garage for the tractor – all built of logs, of course – and five doghouses, to each of which a dog was chained. A hundred feet to the north of the mission stood the church dedicated to St. Teresa of Avila. It had been built of the same spruce logs, but its interior displayed the inspired work of many missionaries over many years. It becomes more impressive when one considers that all the lumber used had to be whipsawed from logs, then planed by hand. The altar and the two doors leading to the sacristy contained intricate fretwork that was truly marvellous. All of the walls were decorated with designs and pictures painted right on the boards with a mixture of local fish oil and coloured powder from France. The Gothic windows contained glass that had been three years in shipment from Montreal by York boats over perilous portages.

This building was a living monument to the missionaries who had laboured here over the span of nearly a century, beginning in 1859 with Father Henri Grollier. The one who spent the most time on it, however, was Father Xavier Ducot, who had arrived in 1876 with only two axes, three saws and eight nails! He spent forty years here. When in 1964 I heard that it was to be demolished, I tried my best to avert such a tragedy, wrote to the Superior General in Rome and volunteered to shore it up and skid it back out of the way to preserve it. Alas, my ideas of preservation were out-voted and it was torn down.

Like almost all settlements in the Territories, Fort Norman had grown around a trading post, in this case one placed strategically at the confluence of the Bear and Mackenzie Rivers. An imposing 1,750-foot outcrop of limestone called Bear Rock rises steeply from the Mackenzie a few miles down river. To the west the first ranges of the Rockies loom on the horizon.

The whites in town numbered about twenty-five and represented the same organizations found in most northern settlements. Besides the Church and the Hudson Bay Company, there were civil servants working as police officers, and one or more nurses, schoolteachers, game officers and Indian agents. Fort Norman was unique, however, in that it employed nearly a dozen men working for the Royal Canadian Corps of Signals who had handled communications up and down the Mackenzie River since the end of World War II.

There were some 200 natives living at the Fort, sometimes in town and sometimes out in the bush. They called themselves *Dene*, meaning simply, "the men." When they were met by

Alexander Mackenzie in 1789 they were dressed in clothing made entirely from the skins of the snowshoe rabbit, so he named them Hareskins, or the Hare tribe. Apparently when this type of clothing gets infested with lice it is almost impossible to delouse. The Eskimos noticed this when they first met them and called them *Iklilik*, "the lousy ones," a name they still use, although I doubt the Hare Indians are aware of it. Father Emile Petitot, who travelled extensively among this tribe in the 1860's, described them as a talkative people, "homely and friendly as children."

Although this tribe was still to some degree dependent upon their traditional hunting and trapping for a livelihood, their mobility had been curtailed the previous year when the government put up the first of many day schools. Previously their children had been educated in the mission-run boarding schools in Fort Providence and Aklavik. The problem with a day school was that the mothers would have to stay home to take care of the children instead of accompanying their husbands on their trap lines. Then the men did not go out as far or stay out as long, with a resulting loss of the fur harvest. When the people predicted this outcome the Department of Education told them not to worry because they would be given rations to compensate. Thus there began the era of crippling welfare in the Northwest Territories.

In the bush the people lived in tents, but in town most of them had constructed log cabins which were strung along a flat bench of land below the mission and the barracks. Each family had its dog-team tied outside. All had been baptized Christian in the previous century, with the exception of one old man who still practised the ancient rites of the medicine man whenever he could secure a client. Respiratory infections were endemic and many were carrying active tuberculosis. Death was common. Life was harsh and often brief, but the Church held out a promise of a better life to come and the missionaries who carried this message were held in high esteem.

Back at the mission I was assigned the parlour as my bedroom and lost no time in moving in. Even at midday I needed the light of a Coleman gas lamp in order to work, as the single-paned window was darkened by an inch of frost. A wind charger mounted outside was connected to a bank of six-volt wet batteries in the root cellar under the kitchen floor. These were perpetually undercharged, however, so electric lights were used only on special occasions.

On the morning following my arrival I was roused from sleep by Brother clanging a hand-held brass bell and singing out the traditional "*Benedicamus Domino*" – Let us bless the Lord! – to which I managed an unenthusiastic "*Deo Gratias*" – Thank God! I struggled to unzip myself from my sleeping bag. Swinging my feet out onto an icy linoleum floor I fumbled with a match and lit a candle. Through a cloud of condensation from my breath my wristwatch told me it was 4:50 a.m. The water in my basin was frozen solid. Thoughts like "we could probably be living just as comfortably in a tent" raced through my mind. I quickly dressed in my cassock and moved out into the common room where the heater, having been goaded by a can of fuel oil that Brother used to saturate the wood, was roaring its defiance at the cold.

I was just beginning to feel some heat when Father Denis rushed out of his room and opened the chapel doors. A new wave of frosty air swept across the room. The cold be damned! We three got down on our knees to recite the traditional Oblate morning prayers in French, followed by the breviary in Latin. At fifteen-minute intervals Brother rang another bell, mounted outside, to call the faithful to morning mass. Several old cronies shuffled in and sat on the floor by the stove in silence.

Following the Mass and the thanksgiving afterwards the chapel doors were closed behind us and I was introduced to the pious old souls who had braved the forty-five-below temperature to honour their God while the rest of the town slept. We shook hands, but I couldn't communicate with them. It was readily apparent that I would be practically useless here as a missionary until I could speak the language. And, as my companions were speaking French, I would need to master that language as well.

Our early morning spiritual exercises were followed by breakfast, presided over by Brother Médard in the small kitchen. It consisted of porridge and homemade bread. I soon got into the routine of spending the rest of the morning studying the Hareskin language, tutored by Father Denis. Lunch followed the Angelus at noon, after which I got some exercise outdoors, either hunting ptarmigan on snowshoes or driving the dogs to bring in a load of firewood.

At five in the afternoon the chapel doors were again opened so that we could pray the rosary together before the Blessed Sacrament. At six we took our third meal of the day in the kitchen, after which we played either cribbage or chess. Night prayer at 9 p.m. capped our day. Brother stoked the fire with a couple of large logs and we retired. We were following a schedule that was identical in every detail in all the forty-some missions throughout the Vicariate and very close to the one that had regulated my life for the past nine years. Our Oblate predecessors had been doing the same things at the same hours in this same house since way into the last century. It was, as Tevye said in *Fiddler on the Roof*, "Tradition!"

Others before me had studied the Hareskin language, but, oddly enough, they had left no grammar behind them. During my scholastic years I had studied French, Latin, Greek and Hebrew, all with the aid of grammars. Now I had to make my own. It was particularly difficult because, with the exception of a dozen words taken from the French, this language in no way resembled any I had studied. In only one way was I helped, and that was in the construction of their sentences which followed the Latin: the object came first, followed by the adjectives and adverbs, with the verb at the end.

The first sentence that I memorized was *"Dene ke'en tanedi?"* "How do you say that in Hareskin?" Armed with this one question I spent many an hour visiting the natives and marking down the names of anything I could point to. The nouns were hard enough to memorize, but the verbs were murder. One reason for this was that the verbs changed with the particular type of action described. For example, if you said you were going on foot or by boat or by aircraft, the verb for "going" changed with each mode of travel.

Another difficulty for the missionary was the absence of words to describe abstract ideas, especially those needed to explain Christianity. *Grace* was translated as "that which makes a man's heart strong." *Sacrament* came across as "God's medicine." For a newcomer like myself it was extremely difficult to separate a sentence into individual words. The problem was caused by a combination of the language's own elision and poor enunciation by the native speaker. One particular woman was the exception to this rule and when she visited the mission Father Denis would say, "Now just listen to her speak. You can hear every word."

And there are a lot of them. Father Petitot, who was the most gifted linguist to work among these people, estimated they may have some 600,000 words! He was also convinced that a language so rigidly structured, so grammatically correct as this could not possibly have been invented by an illiterate race of nomads. God created the earth, why couldn't God create a language, he argued. Later the renowned ethnologist Diamond Jenness summed up his study of eleven native Canadian tongues by saying: "The most primitive Indians of Canada, those of the Mackenzie River Valley, possessed the most complex language."

The French language was infinitely easier – no comparison – and aided by Brother Médard I made rapid progress in it. Trouble arose, however, from the fact that the brand of French he was speaking, the Quebec patois, was unacceptable to a Frenchman from France like Father Denis. This occasioned some heated arguments during meals and prompted our superior to keep a French dictionary on the table. At one meal Brother asked me, "Comment vous dites 'steam' – en Anglais?" (How do you say 'steam' in English?). I answered, "*Vapeur,*" and Father Denis threw up his hands in despair! One thing he couldn't stand was *Franglais.*

Once the Mackenzie River is frozen over, it becomes a poor place to set a gill net for fish, and that makes Fort Norman a difficult place to get dog food during the winter. Brother resorted to all kinds of tricks to keep the five mission dogs fed, like never putting soap in the dishwater so he could mix rolled oats in it later for dog food!

The nearest fish lake, called Taketue, lay twelve miles to the east and Brother had built a tiny, two-bunk log cabin there years before. He used to walk there on snowshoes to visit a gill net he had set under the ice. Now he suggested we drive the dogs up there and set a net.

When we arrived there the first thing we did was cut the two longest green spruce poles we could find. After trimming them neatly we tied them end-to-end, making a single pole forty feet long. Laying this pole on top of the ice where the net was to be set, we cut holes through the ice at both ends. Then we moved the pole on in a straight line from the second hole and cut a third. Finally we had a series of holes forty feet apart spanning the two-hundred-foot length of the net.

Next we tied the end of a long cord to our pole, which we then pushed through the first hole and under the ice toward the second hole. It was like pulling thread under cloth with a needle. The ice was thin enough that we could see the pole, so we had little difficulty using a forked stick to push the pole from hole to hole until we pulled it out at the last one. Now we had the cord under the ice from the first to the last hole, and all we had to do was attach the net to one end and pull it under. Brother had the net piled neatly at the first hole with rocks for weights attached to one side of the net and floats attached to the other. While I pulled on the cord he paid out the net, one side of which immediately sank to the bottom so that the net was in a vertical position. We secured both ends to a cord tied to a rock on the bottom and a forked green willow above the ice. The job took us about an hour and a half and worked without a hitch. It is one of those northern jobs that can be learned easily if one has a veteran to demonstrate how. We retired to the snug cabin and spent the evening playing chess.

The next morning we pulled out the net to see what we had caught. We opened the two end holes with the long-handled ice chisel and tied the long cord, called a *te-klu*, to one end of the net. Then we pulled the net out onto the ice dragging the *te-klu* back under the ice in its place. After taking a couple dozen whitefish and pike from the net we reset it by pulling it back with the *te-klu*. We piled snow around each end hole to minimize freezing, put the *te-klu* back in the cabin and left for home. During the winter we tried to visit this net once a week and, as I got more proficient at it, I went out alone sometimes and returned to the mission the same day. It was a welcome break from studying.

❄ ❄ ❄

Soon Christmas, the big feast of the winter, was upon us. Because the Mass (*Christ*-mass) is celebrated at midnight, the natives gave it the name *Tewe-yati* – "the night we pray." A few teams came from as far away as Fort Franklin on Great Bear Lake, some eighty miles east. They usually brought haunches of Barren Land caribou and large trout, food that was scarce around Fort Norman.

Others came in from the foothills of the Rockies to the west and were known as the Mountain Indians. I happened to be out on snowshoes one afternoon hunting ptarmigan along the river-bank when I ran into one of those families coming in for Christmas. They were covered with frost and moving painfully slowly when they stopped to shake my hand. Leading the procession was the father with a child on his back and a rifle in his hand, breaking trail on snowshoes. His wife was following in her traditional position about five paces back with the baby of the family wrapped in a blanket on her back. She was followed by two teenage daughters on snowshoes that were trimmed on the front tips with ptarmigan feet, good luck amulets.

Next in line was a team of four pitifully thin dogs straining in tattered harness ahead of a heavily loaded birch toboggan driven by two teenage boys. Bringing up the rear was another team of three dogs driven by the eldest son. When I asked him if he had a lot of meat he pulled back the canvas cover of his sled to reveal two children in their sheepskin parkas, asleep. As we stood there trying to communicate in the few words of their language I knew, the dogs curled up and the snow started drifting over them. It took a couple of cracks of the dog whip to bring them to their feet again to resume the last mile of their five-day trek into the settlement. I stood there fascinated as they got under way again, the sleds creaking along and a fog of ice crystals enveloping them. Gradually they dissolved in the distance and the wind went to work erasing their track, an apt symbol of their unrecorded passage through time. We can only guess where they came from as the drifting snows of a thousand cruel winters have wiped out the trails behind them. The Holy Family itself, en route to Bethlehem, couldn't have had a tougher trip than the one this family took to celebrate Christmas.

For two days before the big feast the Brother kept a roaring fire going in the big church to thaw it out. I paced the floor of the mission's common room, memorizing a sermon in English for the Midnight Mass which traditionally attracted all the whites in town. Father Denis would deliver another in the native tongue. When that night arrived and I was on my feet speaking, some might have misconstrued a few tears in my eyes as an expression of overwhelming emotion when, in fact, my feet were slowly freezing in tight Christmas moccasins. In spite of the temperature inside, the old church was crowded to the walls and the congregational singing was enough to raise the roof.

Three days later the children's Christmas tree party was held in the mission and some seventy adults crowded into that room to watch the fun. I had some fun myself watching an old-timer turn one of our electric lights off and on while exclaiming, "*Monla duye*," which could be loosely translated as "Those white men are amazing." A few days later, at midnight on New Year's

Eve, with the temperature slipping to sixty below, the town erupted in crackling gunfire in the traditional salute to the New Year – 1949.

On the 4th of January I had the rare pleasure of doing something strictly ministerial, performing a baptism. By now it was becoming obvious to me that such occasions would be few and far between. I could keep myself busy all right, but not doing things that are considered priestly. So why all the years of theology? To prepare me for what? The endless stream of native visitors who occupied Father Denis' day in idle conversation were not discussing theological problems. They were talking about hunting, trapping and the weather. I wondered to myself if I could stand a lifetime of such banal conversations? Where were the challenges of yesteryear, when our missionaries wrestled with the devil himself to win pagan souls to Christ? Now ministry seemed to have evolved into a simple holding pattern to maintain the status quo. Pioneer men of the cloth in the last century had rounded up and branded all the sheep. All that remained for their successors was to keep the flock from straying. We were all well aware of the privations and hardships of our black-robed predecessors, but surely they must have been compensated for their trials by the satisfaction of seeing their spiritual achievements? Perhaps I was arriving on the scene a hundred years too late?

❊ ❊ ❊

Why is it that the North seems to be so populated with the type of person we call a "character"? Perhaps there are just as many in Edmonton or New York, but they are lost in the crowd. Perhaps it's the free spirit of the North that encourages people to be eccentric. Whatever the reason, I was running into an unusually large number of characters in the Territories.

Some of the most noteworthy characters have worked for the Hudson Bay Company. Among these were the three Gaudet brothers whose combined service among the Hareskins spanned a century. Now only Tim survived and he was spending his retirement years at Fort Norman. Tall, but slightly stooped, with a handlebar mustache drooping under a strawberry nose and with a heavy gold watch chain swinging from his vest, Tim represented the stereotypical HBC veteran. He often came to the mission at night to engage us in a game of rummy. His distinctly different French-Canadian accent must have resembled that spoken by the authentic *coureurs de bois* who in the early years manned the Company's York boats.

Besides possessing the skills needed by a successful trader, Tim was also skilled in the arts of bush life, like snowshoe-making. Everyone working in the bush needs several different sizes of snowshoes. I needed a pair, but I wanted to learn to make my own. So Tim guided me through all the phases of construction, from the proper selection of a white birch sapling, through the splitting, cutting and bending stages, to the final insertion of the *babiche* (webbing). The project was so successful that I went on to make several pairs. One pair, six feet, six inches long and used in deep snow, is now over forty-five years old and I'm still using them. The satisfaction I got from walking on shoes I had made was worth all the labour involved. Some years later I was invited to teach this skill in a high school workshop – to young natives!

In the opening chapter I described my first painful dogsled trip to Norman Wells. After Easter I made a second one, but in the meantime I had learned to handle the dogs better. The days were longer and I made it to Pat Tourangeau's cabin with no trouble. Now he, his wife, Cecilia, and their eight kids were living in their log warehouse because the timbers holding the sod roof of their main cabin were rotting and they feared they would collapse. Pat was prevented from making these repairs on doctor's orders to take it easy, following the results of a chest X-ray that indicated he might have TB.

In fact he stayed indoors all that winter doing light housework while his robust wife took his dog-team and ran his trapline, even shooting a moose. Late in the spring Pat received a second letter from the Department of Health apologizing for an error. They had read the wrong X-ray and there was absolutely nothing wrong with Pat! Upon receipt of this news the first thing Cecilia did was to pin Pat to the floor to demonstrate how strong she had become during his winter hibernation. And then she ordered him outside to tackle the wood pile.

On the following morning of my trip I hitched up at Pat's cabin and ran the remaining twelve miles into Norman Wells, where I was again welcomed by the Imperial Oil refinery manager, K. Murray Mackenzie. The refinery itself was mostly dormant during the winter, with a skeleton crew keeping essential units heated but processing little crude. Although only forty-odd air miles separated Norman Wells from Fort Norman, their atmosphere and living styles were worlds apart. Here at Norman Wells I was quartered in a modern frame bungalow, steam-heated to around ninety degrees. The first thing I did was to remove my wool underwear. I ate T-bone steaks in the mess hall and my dogs ate almost as well. There was no wake-up bell and everyone spoke English. I held a daily service in the recreation hall and spent the rest of the day visiting the employees and their families.

Another character emerged from this group in the person of Hamar Nelson, a bachelor and part-time employee. Essentially a loner used to trapping and prospecting, Hamar was forced into the company of fellow humans from time to time to earn a new grubstake. When he emigrated from Scandinavia he landed on the shores of Hudson Bay and from there he moved west alone with his dog-team across the Barrens. He claimed that all he took with him for dog feed when he left Baker Lake was a sack of arctic hare skins and a case of tallow. Every night he would heat some tallow and dip a hare skin in it for each dog. When he passed Coppermine the Eskimos there dubbed him "The Lone Traveller."

He did a lot of prospecting in the mountains west of Norman Wells. He would disappear into those hills in the late fall and nobody would hear anything of him until he reappeared again in the spring. He would paddle in on a raft or a skin boat with a few sled dogs. He wouldn't tell anyone where he had been nor show his rock specimens. While recuperating at the Wells he would go back to work for the refinery. Depending on his physical condition he would go on some strange diets, sometimes eating nothing but vegetables for a few weeks, then straight meat and then again, all liquid.

I greatly admired this northern veteran and took advantage of my visits to the Wells to learn basic survival techniques from him. He showed me how to crimp the ends of a tent's stove pipe sections so that an eddy was created in the draught to trap the sparks. Then they didn't fly out the top and burn holes in the tent. He was the first person I had met in the North who knew how to build an igloo and I wasn't satisfied until we went down on the river and he demonstrated their construction. I'd go down every afternoon with a snow knife and build one until I got it right. No doubt there were some people watching who thought I was as odd as my instructor.

Back at the mission in Fort Norman I again tackled the study of the Dene language, which became more interesting as I began to put words together to form intelligible sentences. The closest satellite community to the Fort was at Willow Lake about thirty miles north-east, where a half-dozen of the Norman natives had built cabins. One of these Hareskins with the improbable name of Colin Campbell had a cabin there in which his wife had died the previous year. Following native custom he moved out of it and I was able to buy it for the mission for fifty dollars. I went up there by dogs, spent a few nights, and made plans to convert it into a chapel. Another project that emerged from the melting snowdrifts was an eighteen-foot round-bottomed cabin cruiser that had been lying out behind the mission for years. I decided to re-caulk its hull, overhaul its twenty-horsepower inboard Kermath engine and launch it as soon as we had open water.

Day by day, as the sun rose higher, the snowbanks sank lower and ice on the inside of the mission's windows lost its grip on the glass and fell off, letting in that blessed sunshine. Our spirits rose with the temperature. Soon we could see patches of bare sand on Windy Island a mile across the river, followed by the cheery sight of ducks and geese landing there. When the west wind carried their raucous clatter across to us, how it activated our salivary glands!

Father Denis and I waited till the town was asleep one night and then we stole across with the dog-team pulling the toboggan loaded with a light canoe. Arriving at the open water near the islands we put the dogs in the canoe, ferried them to dry ground and tied them up. We were surrounded by migrating waterfowl who seemed to sense the range of our shotguns.

There was a flock of several hundred Canadian honkers on open water to the west of our island and I decided that the only way to get into range was to paddle upstream above them and then, lying unseen in the bottom of the canoe, drift down into their midst. This plan worked perfectly right up to the point where I could hear their cackling all about me, but when I tried to extricate myself from under the thwarts I was seized with the worst charley horse of my life. Before I could regain control of my leg muscles there wasn't a bird left within range. In fact I didn't bag my first goose until we had expended all our shotgun shells on ducks. Luckily I brought a goose down with my .22 as it flew over.

There was no darkness that night, neither was there any sleep for us. Yet when we retreated across the river before the town woke up we carried with us enough birds to brighten our table for the next month.

The term *break-up* means little to the person who has never passed a year in the North, but to those who have, it is a magic word that separates winter from summer and denotes everything that breathes new life into the land. The month was May and the white-knuckled grip of winter was finally broken. The smell of spruce permeated the balmy air as small birds reappeared in their branches and sang their cheery songs. People left their parkas at home and put on rubber boots to get out of their dark cabins and into the sun to greet one another. As Thoreau observed, "the winter of man's discontent was thawing as well as the earth."

The winter's drifts of snow melted and ran down to the river, quickly lifting its burden of ice forty feet above its winter level. Finally one day, without trumpet or fanfare, this whole frozen surface of the mighty Mackenzie began to move north. The break-up had begun! And as word raced from cabin to cabin the whole population assembled along the bank to watch in fascination. The spectacle was irresistible, drawing even the recluses we had scarcely seen all winter. Everyone was in a festive mood, greeting neighbours with words that meant, "Hurrah! We've survived another one!"

What dynamic forces of nature were at work before our astonished eyes: chunks of ice the size of houses, churning and tumbling, gouging tons of earth from the bank we were standing on. After the first day of ice had passed a more interesting spectacle hove into view: huge spruce trees, some standing upright in the press of ice, marched by in stately review, followed by intact cabins that must have slid down some crumbling cutbank, and then someone's scow, undamaged, on top of a huge cake of ice. The crowd cheered! It was like watching a parade and no one wanted to go home in case he should miss something.

Gradually the amount of ice began to thin out, but its place was taken by more trees and logs. Finally the floating ice completely disappeared and was replaced by a sea of wood stretching from bank to bank. We saw pass by huge, hundred-foot timbers that must have come all the way from the Liard River or even the Peace from above Fort Smith. All were on their way to the salt waters of the Arctic Ocean where wind and tide would scatter them from Herschel Island on the west to Cape Parry on the east. The show went on night and day for nearly a week before the river could free itself of this burden of ice and wood. And then, suddenly one morning, we awoke to find it reflecting a clear, blue sky without a stick to mar its glassy surface. The break-up was over. It was summer.

4

A VISIT
TO THE ESKIMOS

"The banana boat is coming!" The cry went around town the day after the ice went out. And sure enough, there she was, rounding the bend up river, Captain Streeper's *Stewart Lake* from Fort Nelson. Always the first boat to arrive after break-up, it was carrying a load of fresh food which he sold right off the deck. The captain did a land-office business for a day and then shoved off and followed the retreating ice down river, stopping at each settlement.

The passing of the *Stewart Lake* indicated that all was clear up river, so we could embark on the annual harvest of firewood. Brother and I launched the mission's twenty-two-foot freighter canoe, which was pushed by a nine-horsepower motor called in the North a "kicker." We went up river twenty-five miles to drift back collecting logs as we went. We were looking for long, straight logs that would make a good raft. They were found stranded on small islands and sandbars by the recent high water. We would go ashore with the Swede saw, cut off the root end and roll them into the water, where we lashed them together. Soon we had a stable log platform upon which we put our tent and cook stove.

It was great to be out working in the sun except for one draw-back – the mosquitoes. Justin and I had encountered mosquitoes on our canoe trips in Eastern Canada, but nothing like this. Their size and ferocity were remarkable enough, but their sheer number was unbelievable. They followed us around in a cloud and if the citronella juice we were using discouraged them from biting, nothing prevented them from penetrating our eyes and mouths. Head nets might have helped if we had had them. All we could do was drape our kerchiefs over our heads. Brother didn't seem to be bothered by them as I was, so I supposed that one built up some immunity to them over years of exposure. At least in our tent at night our mosquito bars (nets we hung over our sleeping bags) protected us from them. In spite of this nuisance we brought back a raft of about thirty cords of wood, enough to heat the mission and church for another year. We landed them at the foot of the village and from there Brother skidded them up into the mission yard with his tractor.

Having completed this job, I was free to launch the refurbished cabin cruiser I had re-christened the *Nayuka* – Northern Lights – and to give it a shakedown cruise. From what I heard, it had been built in Vancouver and given to Bishop Breynat to be used to visit the missions along the Mackenzie. I soon learned why he had abandoned it at Fort Norman some twenty-five years earlier. Its barrel shape not only made it tippy, but it drew a lot of water, a disadvantage in navigating a river full of sandbars. The inboard engine, however, seemed to run fine, so I decided to use it to visit my outpost mission at Norman Wells. A twenty-two-year-old native, Alphonse Menako, joined me as first mate.

We had a good trip down river to Norman Wells where I was surprised to find that the Royal Canadian Air Force had moved in, swelling the population by two hundred souls. They were part of the 408 Squadron at Rockcliffe, near Ottawa, and were occupied photographing all of the Western Arctic to correct the existing maps. They gave me a Quonset hut (which got its name from Quonset, Rhode Island, where they were prefabricated), across from the new canteen and dining room. I divided it into a chapel and living quarters behind. The Imperial Oil refinery was now operating at full capacity, so the town was abuzz with activity. With aircraft taking off and landing continuously, trucks roaring up and down the dirt roads, people coming and going, Norman Wells was a far cry from the sleepy Fort Norman I had just left.

Genial Wing Commander Roy Woods, in charge of the Air Force personnel, enlisted my help to keep his men occupied on the days when bad weather prevented them from flying. One thing we did was start a leather craft shop. We organized tours of the abandoned Canol (Canadian Oil) camp across the river. The Americans undertook the Canol project during World War II to get oil from the Norman Wells field across five hundred and ninety-eight miles of muskeg and mountains to a refinery at Whitehorse in the Yukon Territory, to fuel the Pacific fleet. To do this, five thousand U.S. servicemen built a four-inch pipeline west and a supply depot to service a new road.

With the completion of the pipeline and the end of the war in 1945 the entire project was abandoned and all the buildings, vehicles and materials left to be sold by Imperial Oil. There were streets of Quonset huts and warehouses jammed with parts and equipment. One building held nothing but chains for vehicles, another tires and another tack for the horses flown in for the officers, horses which were now running loose somewhere in the vicinity. Two huge nose-hangars stood empty on the airstrip. Neatly lined up in one field were countless new radiators for the Caterpillar tractors, while in other lots stood rows of Jeeps, weapons carriers, trucks, drag lines and buses. One huge thousand-seat mess hall had a gaming room off one end equipped with crap tables and other gaming devices. Here, tacked to the bulletin board, was a list of all the female kitchen staff with their monthly VD ratings after their names like combat decorations.

Outstanding in all of this was the large two-storey log building put up for the officers, which boasted a huge fireplace incorporating in it a stone from each state in the Union. On the days off I took groups across the river in *Nayuka* and then, using a

Jeep, drove them on a tour of all these buildings, sometimes going as far as mile thirty-six on the Canol Road to the Carcajou River pumping station. If nothing else, those tours taught some Canadian Air Force men a lesson in the wastefulness of war. Too bad the American taxpayers couldn't see what had happened to 137 million of their tax dollars.

My work at Norman Wells was exciting and not without its rewards in the spiritual field. I would have liked to have spent the entire summer there, but my youngest brother Thomas had engaged himself as a deck hand on the mission supply boat and I had permission to join him. He wanted to see firsthand this country that had so captivated his two brothers. Alphonse and I were on our way back upriver when we met the *Sant'Anna* around Bear Rock and I jumped ship to leave my companion to continue on alone to Fort Norman.

Stepping on board that venerable old diesel tug pushing its precious one-hundred-and-fifty-ton barge of supplies for the Arctic missions was like stepping into the last century. I was immediately surrounded by French-speaking religious in cassocks or wimples, the everyday costumes of the Oblates or Grey Nuns, unchanged since the 1800's. Right next to my brother to greet me was a living legend, Bishop Gabriel Breynat, O.M.I., who had retired in 1943 and was now making his farewell visit to many of the missions he had founded in the last century. And whom should I spy out on the fantail peeling spuds but "My soul!" himself, Brother Henri! The entire boat and barge was full of heroic characters, as though calculated to add just the right background to this historic voyage. For once I was in the right place at the right time.

The *Sant'Anna* was more than just a supply boat: it was a floating monastery observing all the canonical hours,* regulated by the ship's brass bell and serving as a water-borne cathedral for the daily pontifical Mass celebrated by His Excellency. I had no

---

* The canonical hours are the prayers mandated by the church for its clergy and religious to be prayed at designated times during the day.

sooner met everyone on board when Brothers Sareault and Dabrowski up in the wheel house brought us into the dock at Norman Wells to take on fuel. Soon we were on our way again downstream under the midnight sun as Thomas and I leaned on the rail and talked of the family and of our plans for the future.

The next morning after Mass and breakfast we glided through the picturesque Ramparts section of the Mackenzie River under a warm, cobalt sky. An hour later we were nosing the barge into shore at Fort Good Hope and were met by Father Alexis Robin, a veteran of over forty years at this post, and his assistant Brother Roger Mahé. All hands, including able-bodied passengers like myself, pitched in to unload the year's supplies for this mission. The Sisters walked up the hill to visit the most famous of all the churches in the Territories. Brother Joseph Kearney had started its log sills in 1865 and when he died there in 1918 it still wasn't completed. Its colourful interior wall decorations made it the most impressive building along the entire length of this great river.

At that time a travelling magician by the name of Nemo was visiting Fort Good Hope, accompanied by his wife and a pilot flying the same old Sikorsky Amphibian aircraft used by the famous African explorers Martin and Johnson. We all crowded into the mission common room that evening to witness a thrilling magic show. When Nemo tried to leave the next morning, however, his aircraft didn't have power enough to break clear of the river's glassy surface and get airborne. He was forced to taxi all the way to his next port of call, Arctic Red River, about two hundred miles farther north.

When we pulled into that settlement the following day Bishop Breynat's successor, Bishop Trocellier, also arrived in his little scow, *Notre Dame de Fatima*, piloted by Brother Petrin. So we again found ourselves gathered with the natives, crowded into this mission's common room that night to watch Nemo in action. Bishop Trocellier was astounded when the magician removed his wristwatch without him being aware of it. Amazingly, Nemo could do this despite the fact that he had two bandaged fingers, caused, he said, by bailing the leaking hull of their Sikorsky the day before. When they took off the next day to fly over the mountains into Alaska we wondered if they would make it.

As the *Sant'Anna* continued north and approached the Arctic Coast the temperature dropped. Only two rooms on board were heated: the engine room, so noisy one couldn't carry on a conversation, and the galley, where we congregated to listen to old Bishop Breynat tell stories of the North he had known. Soon the steep banks of the Mackenzie fell away as we entered its flat delta, a maze of a thousand small lakes and channels with no navigational markers. Our two Brothers handling the wheel, however, knew from experience how to steer us safely up the Peel Channel where, out of the rain and fog, loomed Aklavik. The waterfront was crowded with the Eskimos' schooners and there were Eskimos themselves in parkas, just as we had always pictured them. We had suddenly entered an entirely different kind of North.

On the bank to greet us were a half-dozen Oblate Fathers and Brothers, plus a dozen Grey Nuns with a hundred and fifty children from the hostel. No doubt the forty-some tuberculosis patients from the hospital would have been there too, if they had been allowed to leave their beds. In spite of the bad weather, a warm welcome awaited us as we neared the shore. Soon the gangplank was lowered and the *Sant'Anna's* passengers streamed down into the welcoming crowd to begin a three-day visit.

Although this large mission complex had a lot of interesting features, like its huge permafrost ice cellars, I was more fascinated by the Eskimo people themselves who were in town from their winter traplines to trade their furs. They immediately impressed me as a very happy and outgoing race of people, far less reticent than the Indians. They all seemed to be fluent in English and everywhere I went I was invited to partake of a cup of tea or any food they had on the table. I had found the Indians reluctant to do this unless I knew them well. My own explanation for this was a gut feeling that the Indians were very conscious of their different lifestyle, especially in the preparation of food, while the Eskimos didn't seem to care. If it was good enough for them, it was good enough for a white man. I like that attitude.

I walked over to George Peffer's trading post and he showed me drawers full of the cash he was using to buy white fox pelts. I paid a visit to Canon Montgomery, brother of the famous English General "Monty." He graciously toured me through the Anglican hostel and hospital, ending up in his cathedral that featured a beautiful, large painting of a native Christmas scene behind the altar. Unfortunately it was completely destroyed by fire years later. When I related this visit to my fellow missionaries I got some disapproving comments, which surprised me. Apparently there existed a deep-seated rivalry between these two missions that bordered on hostility. I was told that if the people saw me visiting the "opposition," they might conclude that we had capitulated. Apparently my fraternal overture was slightly ahead of its time.

Our arrival in Aklavik anticipated by a day the official visit of Canada's Governor General, Lord Alexander of Tunis, who was touring the Arctic in a Canadian Air Force Canso, or Catalina Flying Boat. The local Administrator, L.A.C.O. Hunt, was in a dither trying to get some four thousand feet of boardwalk built in time to cover the quagmire left after melting snow and incessant rain. When the distinguished guest arrived, however, he was driven around town in a Jeep and never used the new sidewalks. The spectators did, nonetheless, and I stood with the crowd, camera in hand, across the street from the one-room shack marked RADIO STATION CHAK, where the local dignitaries presented him with gifts of furs and native sewing.

As this was not her last port of call, not all the freight brought down river by the *Sant'Anna* was off-loaded at Aklavik. We still had freight for Tuktoyaktuk on the Arctic Ocean, from which point it would be carried east by the mission schooner *Our Lady of Lourdes*. As we backed off the beach at Aklavik not only was our barge floating higher, but there were many empty bunks as some of the missionaries, including the old bishop and all of the nuns, had left the ship. In a haze of rain we zigzagged through Schooner Channel and finally got back on the broad Mackenzie. It was smooth sailing down past the reindeer station until we reached the open waters of the Beaufort Sea at Kitigazuit. Here the ocean, driven by a west wind, was running an angry sea and the rain turned to driving snow. It was only the 16th of July. The Brothers prudently decided to run into shore to tie up and wait out the bad weather.

Within the previous twelve months three six-hundred-foot towers had been erected in a triangle several hundred miles apart to test a new navigational system called Loran. As luck would have it, we had landed within a mile of one of these stations manned by 120 Royal Canadian Air Force radio technicians. The Commanding Officer was most hospitable and gave us a tour of his new installation. He quite candidly admitted to us that he was experiencing some trouble from a few of his men who were making and drinking alcohol in spite of regulations. In the kitchen he pointed to a tell-tale ring mark on the stove top that fit exactly a brass fire extinguisher hanging on the wall. Someone had ingeniously converted this cylinder into a portable still, filling it with mash, putting it on the hot stove after hours and then drawing off the spirits through its rubber hose. The C.O. was sure he could catch them red-handed and expected to administer a stiff military penalty.

Our host also mentioned that the Governor General had stopped at the base, but that he had unfortunately forgotten to bring the mail for which they had been waiting over two months, an unpardonable sin in the North. The C.O. confessed that morale was low on the base as a result. Anyone could understand that: no spirits followed by no mail! Just how low we couldn't guess until a week later when we heard that all the windows in his quarters had been smashed by rocks and he was forced to evacuate his wife and children, the only family on the base.

The following day the Brothers unhitched the barge from the front of the *Sant'Anna* and put it on a long tow-cable behind.

With this arrangement we were able to cross the open stretch of ocean and get safely into the harbour at "Tuk." The flat horizon here on the Arctic Coast was broken only by a few pingos[*] farther inland.

The settlement was strung out along a protected gravel beach dominated by the Hudson Bay Company store and warehouse, the police barracks and the mission church and mission warehouse. The few Eskimos around had set up tents for the summer and tied their sled dogs to long chains laid out on the muskeg.

Father Jean Franche, the resident priest, gave Thomas and me a tour of his buildings, showing us the huge polar bear hide in the sanctuary of his church, a yard-long section of mammoth tusk in his attic, as well as an old whaling dart gun no longer used. His team of huskies seemed to be huge compared to sled dogs upriver and looked as if they might have had some St. Bernard bred into them.

Thomas and I joined the Brothers unloading the barge into a large warehouse. Brother Auguste Josset, the engineer for the forty-ton *Our Lady of Lourdes,* was on board his boat riding at anchor just off shore and ready to transfer this freight to the missions along the Arctic Coast as far east as Cambridge Bay and Bathurst Inlet.

As soon as we got our barge unloaded, Thomas and I ran around the settlement with our cameras like tourists. The more I saw, the more I wished I could be assigned to an Eskimo mission like this. The land was treeless, covered with gravel and practically flat to the horizon. I could imagine how desolate it would look in winter, yet it possessed a peculiar charm hard to describe. The native people were unusually outgoing and hospitable and welcomed us into their tents. In short, I liked Tuk so much that I wished I could stay, but the sea was calm and the Brothers were

---

[*] Pingos are a phenomenon of the severe and prolonged Arctic cold which, by exerting extreme pressure, forces large cone-shaped mountains, consisting mainly of ice and gravel and covered with moss, to rise above the otherwise flat land.

anxious to get back into the protection of the river, so we shoved off, empty at last.

Because of the contrary current, our return voyage upstream on the Mackenzie was slower in spite of our shallow draught. When we reached the Sans Sault rapids above the Ramparts we were barely moving ahead until the Brothers attached an outboard motor to the transom to give us a little extra push. All too soon we were nearing my home base at Fort Norman. This trip left me with a new-born desire to go farther north in the Vicariate, to work among the Eskimos. I hoped, too, that my youngest brother Thomas, who had experienced this adventure with me, would himself catch the spark and volunteer for this North country. He didn't, however: I wasn't to see him again until his ordination in Washington six years later when he asked for and received an assignment – to Brazil!

5

GREAT BEAR LAKE

By the last week of July I was back in the mission at Fort Norman observing punctually all the canonical hours as if nothing had happened, as if I had never crossed over the Arctic Circle nor seen the Eskimo lands under the midnight sun.

I plunged into the daily routine with renewed vigour, especially my study and practice of the Hareskin language. I hadn't really stopped this study during my absence, as I carried my notebook dictionary with me.

Mission life was far easier in the summer: no need to worry about feeding a fire. I had moved upstairs into a spacious room and Brother's well tended garden was producing all the fresh food we had lacked during the winter.

This was the season for visitors, most of them travelling on the river. They were a welcome diversion, except for one who put us on our toes, so to speak. This was the Oblate Provincial, Reverend Father Jean-Louis Michel, O.M.I., Vicar of Missions, an ex-army officer coming on his yearly inspection tour to insure that we were living according to the precepts of our Holy Rule. We were being especially vigilant so as not to give reason for a reprimand, but I slipped up and immediately drew fire. I had doffed my cassock in order to join the local boys for a game of softball on the town flat. When it finished I had loitered about two minutes too long before getting back into clerical garb. Such conduct, I was informed, would not be tolerated.

The Provincial (whom Brother Henri referred to as "Le Cap-itaine") took advantage of his visit to drum up candidates for the boarding school at Fort Providence. Delivering the sermon at the High Mass on Sunday, he dispelled a vicious rumour to the effect that no children were being sent from this settlement because the hung fish being fed to them at the hostel were rank. "Nonsense!" he thundered in Hareskin, which he had mastered during his early years at Fort Good Hope. What he didn't realize, however, was that the reason no children from Fort Norman were cur-rently attending either that hostel or the one at Aklavik was that the local Pastor, Father Denis, was dead set against it on the grounds that all his problem parishioners were former residents of these venerable institutions. The school at Providence had been in continuous operation since 1867 and there were quite a few old grads living at Fort Norman. Those who come back from Providence with any education, argued this missionary, show an aversion to the trapping life and, while assuming an air of supe-riority around town, turn out to be loafers, brew-hounds and trouble-makers. Needless to say, he didn't voice this opinion in front of our distinguished visitor. Still, this studied assessment sounded alarming to me. I wondered what the result would be now that the government had built a day school right in Fort Norman?

With the freight delivered to Fort Norman Mission by the *Sant'Anna* came about five hundred board-feet of spruce shiplap from the Brothers' sawmill near Fort Smith, destined for my project at Willow Lake. One of the locals by the name of Paul Wright volunteered to help me, so we loaded up the freighter canoe and ascended the Bear and then the Willow Rivers. He handled the nine-horsepower Johnson in the stern while I stood in the bow with a long pole, as the water in September is very shallow. It was amazing how we navigated that fast water barely deep enough to float us.

We unloaded the canoe in the deep grass in front of the run-down log cabin and began a week of renovations that trans-formed it into a neat and efficient outpost mission. I had always loved carpentry. When I was seventeen I had thrown the bed out of my room at home and put in double bunks which I made from pine trees I had felled. In the scholasticate I was appointed to the position of house carpenter. The heaviest part of my baggage coming into the North had been a wooden box of carpenter's tools. Now I had a chance to use them and I lost no time putting down a floor and building a set of bunks and an altar inside the cabin, while outside I built a stage for storing fish and put in solid posts for tying dogs in winter. The finishing touch was a cross nailed to the peak of the roof.

I was amazed at how much satisfaction I got working with my hands like this. The reason was evident: I could see the results immediately. More important tasks like studying the language were slow to show results and were not rewarding. When we shoved off to return to Fort Norman, that little cabin behind us filled my heart with pride; I couldn't wait to return by dog-team and occupy it.

On the 9th of September the Brothers from Aklavik came up river with their boat the *Immaculata* and its barge, a miniature version of the *Sant'Anna*. The purpose of this yearly visit was to pick up a load of potatoes from Norman and Good Hope for the hostel and hospital in Aklavik in exchange for cash to help cover the Fort Good Hope Mission's expenses for the year. It was a fortunate arrangement, for the once-a-year donations at Christmas were not enough to support them for even a month. Bishop Trocellier was urging each mission to work at something to help meet its own running expenses.

I took advantage of this trip to return to Norman Wells and the hustle and bustle of that busy little town. Its storage tanks were just about full and the photo detachment had photographed pretty well all the Western Arctic from the air. The boys of the Signals Corps, however, had added something new, the low-power radio broadcasting station CFNW, 1240 on the dial. It was located six miles up river at their beam station. They suggested I put a religious message on the air Sundays, so I began going up there by boat once a week to broadcast a half-hour sermon. The missionary life held many surprises and unexpected opportunities; it was getting hard to predict what I would be doing from week to week.

Those American Quonset huts were often referred to in the North as "igloos." A few of them found their way across the river from Canol. Sections of the half-moon-shaped structures could be bolted together easily to any desired length. There was one very long one near my chapel which had been used as a curling rink until a better one was built and this one abandoned. It occurred to me that the people of Fort Norman would welcome such a shelter since they had no facility for indoor winter sports. The Imperial Oil Refinery manager was only too happy to donate it for such a worthy cause.

Now that I had it the problem was how to get it to Fort Norman. First it would have to be completely dismantled, no easy task if I had to tackle it alone. When I discussed this project with Commander Woods he saw no difficulty as he had plenty of air crew only partially busy. Before I knew it the whole building was neatly piled in stacks and the nuts, bolts and wiring boxed and ready for shipment. All I needed was the ship. After a phone call to Frank Broderick, President of Northern Transportation Company in Edmonton, a giant barge was put at my disposal for a free lift to Fort Norman.

At this juncture I sped ahead to Fort Norman to call a meeting of the Community Club to discuss the project and insure the necessary volunteers to off-load the material. Where I had met with nothing but cooperation at the Wells, I now found myself up against innumerable objections from those who should have been most eager to see the project succeed. The upshot was that, when the barge did arrive, no one showed up to help Brother and me to unload it. Nor was it ever rebuilt. The sections lay in the field between the mission and the barracks until the elements completely destroyed them years later. Whether they were used or not, I'm sure the good Lord rewarded the charity of our neighbours to the north, while teaching me the lesson that unsolicited gifts are not always appreciated. No doubt we are allowed to fail now and then to keep us humble.

That fall at Fort Norman I was to experience my first freeze-up in the North. Although not nearly as spectacular as break-up, it was a seasonal weather mark that abruptly put an end to summer and signalled the onslaught of another winter. In anticipation, we set about all the tasks that must be done at that season; like getting all the vegetables into the root cellar under the kitchen floor, the potatoes in bins, the carrots buried in boxes of sand and cabbages hung from the ceiling. Then we cut up the driftwood gathered after the ice went out in the spring, and re-banked the mission buildings with dirt.

In late October all the small lakes were frozen and there was enough snow to use the dogs in harness, so Brother and I went out to Taketue and set the net again. By mid-November the Mackenzie was running loose pans of ice that had formed in backwater eddies up river. As the days wore on and the sun swept a steadily lowering arc in the southern sky, the ice floating by on the river got thicker until it covered the surface from shore to shore. On the 21st it stopped and froze together, signalling the end of freeze-up. About a week later we were down on its surface with long ice saws cutting and hauling ice, our winter's water supply, which we stacked outside the back door. With the completion of this job I was free to do a little travelling again.

Loading up the cariole and harnessing the dogs, I took off full-speed out the back road and over the bank of the Great Bear River, where the trail pitches down at a breakneck angle onto the frozen river. There were no more hazards the rest of the thirty-five miles to Willow Lake, where about thirty natives who had been camped here since open water welcomed me. Although I was enjoying the comfort of my new cabin, one thing disturbed me: in the summer I had given a new gill net to Sheriah on the promise that he would hang some stick fish on my new stage for my dogs, but I found the stage empty and Sheriah was camped at Whitefish Lake another twenty miles north. The next day I went on to his tent and camped with his family, returning the

following day with a good sled-load of whitefish which fed my
team for the week I stayed there.

The return trip to Fort Norman went smoothly enough with
the dogs running well pulling an empty sled, so after a while I sat
in the cariole and watched the miles slip by. The sun disappeared
and the moon came up on a calm night with ice fog filling the low
valleys.

Nearing home, we slipped down onto the frozen surface of
Great Bear River and were half-way across when Fox, the lead
dog, suddenly stopped. I thought that he had tired and wanted
to quit, so I got out of the sled and walked up to him with the
whip in my hand. He was crouched on the edge of open water!
Deep and dark as it was, the white steam just above it made it
invisible from a distance. The Bear had opened up during the
time I was at Willow Lake. I cautiously retreated, called the
leader to me, and had him follow me as I walked down along the
shore and out onto the Mackenzie, making a wide, three-mile
detour to avoid crossing the Great Bear River entirely.

I owed my life to Fox that night. Other lead dogs would have
plunged right in and swum for the other shore before I could
have gotten out of the cariole. The Bear is deep at this point; I
doubt I could have touched bottom, and with the ice so thin
along the edges, it would have kept breaking off had I tried to
pull myself up onto it, soaking wet. If I had given up the struggle,
the swift current would have carried me down and under the
thicker ice of the Mackenzie. All the elements that night were
right to lull the novice into a false sense of security: the balmy air,
the moonlit landscape, the cheerful ringing of the harness bells
and the comfort of the cariole, which in an instant could have
become my coffin. Suddenly I had a new respect for sled-dogs in
general, and this lead dog in particular. With these thoughts rac-
ing through my mind I broke out in a nervous sweat. For twenty-
two years following this incident I drove dogs in every kind of
weather and terrain, but I believe that this was my closest brush
with death.

The Mounties in Norman, like all the detachments of the RCMP in the North, had a crackerjack team of sled-dogs, two teams in fact, because the member of the Force on patrol always had a native special constable travelling with him. The latter's job was not limited to the patrols. He fed and cared for the dogs and kept them exercised and in top running form. I happened to be visiting the barracks next door to the mission one evening when Corporal Gordon Brown was busy in the kitchen baking bannock and beans which he would put outdoors immediately to freeze. He was preparing trail grub for a patrol to Fort Franklin on Great Bear Lake and planned to leave December 9th with Special Constable Alfred Lennie. This looked to me like a golden opportunity to get inland and see the famous Bear Lakers myself, with the permission of my superior, Father Denis, of course. When I broached the subject to him the next day he was only too willing to let me absorb the punishment of a trip that usually took him three days – on snowshoes mostly – and left him lame for a week. I had the idea that if I could increase our dog-power I might be able to ride most of the way, so I purchased two older dogs the next day from Jack Hardy for twenty-five dollars apiece.

As planned, the three of us pulled out of Fort Norman on the 9th of December in the dark, Alfred in the lead with the corporal following and myself bringing up the rear. This was the first experience my dogs had of following other teams. The sight and smell of all those other canines just up ahead excited them and they pulled like mad. In fact, the first three of my dogs were so close to the back of the Mountie's sled that they kept getting their harnesses mixed up and I had to apply the brakes to keep them in line; when I let up on the brake the dogs up front would get tangled again, I would have to turn the toboggan over on its side to stop the team and then walk up and fix their harnesses. As a result I had the brake on most of the first twelve miles before we stopped to make fire for our first mug-up of tea.

In little over half an hour we were on our way again, but my dogs didn't seem as anxious as before to overtake the teams ahead. A few more miles and the police teams gradually pulled ahead and out of sight. I didn't see them again until we pulled into their noon lunch fire. Before I had eaten they left, but I wasn't worried about following them as their trail was fresh in a couple of inches of loose snow. Nevertheless, I ate as quickly as I could because I knew how short the daylight was at that time of year. When we resumed the chase it wasn't long before one of my newly acquired dogs started playing out, flopping down on the trail and bringing the whole team to a halt. I took him out of harness and let him follow behind, hoping he would keep up, as he had only himself to drag along. Yet soon there was no sight of him. Thinking that he had simply decided to bed down somewhere along the trail behind us and get some rest, I thought no more about it. Some weeks later someone brought me his collar and told me that was about all that the wolves had left of him. At the time, however, I had no idea we were being trailed by wolves and I doubt that we could have done anything about it even if we knew.

By three o'clock it was dark again and I hadn't seen my companions since noon. The second dog I bought played out and I had to let him out of harness as I had his brother, but he followed closely behind. This wasn't all that difficult at the speed we were now making and perhaps he sensed the menace following. At any rate, the team began to stop altogether at any little rise in the trail and I was obliged to get off the sled and start running behind, cracking the whip whenever they looked like they were about to stop. After about ten miles of this I was ready to drop too, but I couldn't, as the only tent we had was up in Alfred's sled. When the moon finally rose we were simply walking and I was praying that those guys up ahead would quit for the day and camp. At one spot they left an encouraging message written in the snow. It said, "Not far." Still, it sure seemed far; when we dragged ourselves into their camp it was 9 p.m. and they were already asleep in the tent. Unhitching my dogs I chained each one to a tree and distributed frozen fish, then I re-lit the fire in the tent stove, cooked my own supper and ate in silence as my travelling mates fell back to sleep after a short greeting.

I was anticipating a deep, dreamless sleep myself as I finally got into my sleeping bag, but the troubles of the day pursued me into the night. In spite of the youthful spring in my twenty-nine-year-old legs, the hours I had been on them running that day had overtaxed them and a series of painful muscle spasms kept jerking me awake during the night. They are often called charley horses, but in this case charley *dogs* would be more appropriate. As I lay there that night, reviewing all the events of the day, I determined simply to raise a first-class string of dogs; otherwise I would be endlessly repeating the miseries of that day.

Around 6 a.m. Alfred was starting a fire by candlelight, bringing in snow to melt for morning coffee and in general rattling pots and pans to indicate that it was time to rise and shine. It seemed to have been an awfully short night and I felt like doing anything except tackling the second leg of our journey to Great Bear Lake, but remembering the long American tradition of toughness and perseverance goaded me into action. I might be on my knees, but a "Remember the Alamo" spirit would force me to fight to the end of the trail which, in this instance, was Fort Franklin.

After breakfast of rolled oats and bannock we struck the tent and harnessed up in the dark, using flashlights. Thinking Fox deserved a break after working in the lead position all of the previous long day, I put him in the number four position and put N.T. in the lead. This was a mistake, I quickly learned, for when the police teams moved out and before I could untie my sled Fox bit through the traces on both sides of him, allowing my first three dogs to take off without me. Evidently he didn't like the demotion and quickly changed his position from number four to number one. I soon caught up to Corporal Brown who had stopped and was holding the first half of my team. After some temporary splicing with rope from the sled wrapper I was again on my way behind my full team. I soon noticed, however, that my dogs had lost the zip that they had had the previous morning. There was no need to use the brake at all today as my companions pulled steadily ahead and out of sight. Evidently the long run of the day before had left my dogs as stiff as me and I hoped that they wouldn't play out, forcing me to run behind them again.

When I caught up to the corporal and his special constable, they were just finishing their lunch around their noon fire. As I moved in, they moved out, assuring me that I would have no trouble following their fresh trail to the lake. It would have been nice to stretch out and luxuriate before that warm fire and linger over my noon meal, but the fear of going on alone along a strange trail in diminishing light drove me to get on the way again as soon as I could. To make matters worse, I hadn't covered many miles before a light snow began to fall. When I came upon their afternoon tea fire they were long gone, so I didn't stop.

As the light decreased, the falling snow increased and the trail became less distinct. We were moving ahead at a slow dog-trot while the muffled tinkling of the bells did little to dispel the gloom surrounding us. What I wouldn't have given for a fresh team of dogs or at least to have seen the cheerful blaze of a camp-fire up ahead, but no light relieved the darkness. Even the moon was hidden as we plodded along, mile after weary mile, in ever-deepening snow.

Then around supper time the black spruce began to get smaller and their numbers to thin out and the stretches of open tundra grew larger. I reasoned that we must be approaching the windswept shores of the big lake. We passed a rather large Quonset hut half-buried in snow. I thought it must belong to the Northern Transportation Company which operated boats in the summer connecting the Mackenzie River with Port Radium on the east shore of Great Bear. At last we ran beyond the trees alto-gether and the trail was blown out. Fox began to wander so I stopped him. Perhaps we were already on lake ice. Was Fort Franklin to the left or right? It was supposed to be only four miles away, but I couldn't distinguish any lights or sound to direct us. They said that there was open water all winter long around the inlet of the river. How close were we to it? In this darkness we could run into it with no warning.

As I sat on the edge of the sled and rolled a cigarette to pon-der my predicament, the dogs dropped in their tracks and curled up, apparently content to spend the night right there. As much as I wanted to complete that last four miles and get into a heated cabin for the night, the risk that I would take to do it didn't seem worth it. Finally prudence won out and I turned the dogs around to backtrack to that Quonset hut. I dug down to the door with my snowshoes and found it unlocked. Inside there was all I needed: a huge barrel stove, some firewood and a spring cot and mat-tress. This was as far as we'd go this day. I dragged my gear from the cariole, lit a candle, built a roaring fire and thawed some sup-per, thanking God for the protection of this old hut. After eating I threw my sleeping bag on the cot, blew out the candle and climbed in to sleep thirteen uninterrupted hours.

Late the next morning I was awakened by the sound of voices outside. I got up and went to the window to see a group of natives talking together, looking around in the snow for tracks, pointing in various directions, while about a dozen dog-teams were drawn up behind them. My dogs were completely drifted over with snow and invisible, and they were still so played out that they didn't even get up to bark at the intruders. So the posse, evidently out looking for me, didn't know I was in the hut till I opened the door and yelled at them. Then they all crowded in to shake my hand, showing genuine relief that they had found me alive, for when I didn't show up the night before rumours spread that I must have gone into open water nearby. Now we all formed a triumphal procession across that last four miles to the settlement.

Great Bear Lake is a mighty body of water: in fact, with its eleven thousand square miles it is the biggest within Canada and even has its own tide. It straddles the Arctic Circle and stretches from a heavily timbered south end up into the edge of the Barren Land toward Coppermine. The natives who have inhabited its shores for at least the last five thousand years are closely related to the Hareskins living around Fort Norman and go by the name of Bear Lakers. I counted 174 of them living there at that time. Sir

John Franklin, the British explorer, had built a fort at the site of the present settlement in 1824 and passed that winter there, but the North West Company operated a trading post at the same location since 1799.

If Fort Norman was remote and isolated, Fort Franklin was desolate by comparison: no road, no mail, no electricity, no school or nursing station, no white people, just the Hudson Bay trading post run by a Métis and surrounded by a dozen rough log cabins and a scattering of tents. A school had been started the year before, but it was boarded up for the winter. Near it stood the weather-beaten log cabin put up by one of the missionaries some twenty years earlier. It was to this "mission" that I was taken on my arrival. After digging a huge snow drift away from its only door I stepped down into a dark room about fourteen by sixteen feet that contained a small cast iron box stove, a few rough benches and a tiny altar clinging to the corner wall. A door in the back wall led into an eight-foot lean-to addition containing a cook stove and a bed. Outside and mounted on two poles nailed to the corner logs was a ship's bell. Twenty feet away there was a small log warehouse containing an axe and a Swede saw. If one word could describe the whole set-up, it would be poverty.

Church mice are notoriously poor and I moved right in with some of them to share their life for the next month. Not that I was disappointed in what I found there; after all, Father Denis had not painted a rosy picture. Still, there was not one pleasant surprise; everything was stripped to the bare necessities. That's the picture that stays in my mind of a mission outpost in the North. It was bound to be an interesting adventure. I chained up my dogs and moved in.

First things first: I needed a fire immediately and some of the Bear Lakers were right there with an armful of kindling. The dogs needed to be fed and another native appeared with a sack of herring. The temperature in that little mission might have been perpetually chilly, but the cooperation I got from the people was heart-warming. In fact, someone brought me fish for the dogs every night I was there. As they needed exercise I started going every day for at least one load of firewood. There was hardly a tree within sight of the Fort and to find dry wood I had to go at least three miles. Try as I might, I simply couldn't melt the ice on the inside of the mission's windows and I couldn't keep a fire going all night. As long as I stayed in my feather robe I kept fairly comfortable. The trouble was that the mice must have felt cold and tried to share my warmth during the night, for they scampered over my sleeping bag looking for an opening. Charity stopped right there. The temperature hovered around forty below, and the wind off frozen Bear Lake seemed to blow night and day, leaving drifts so hard one could walk over them without leaving a trace. Fort Franklin was an exposed place to begin with, but that constant wind made it even worse.

Following the same custom as at Fort Norman I offered a Mass every morning early and it was well attended. Then I cooked some breakfast and did the chores; took the dog-team for a load of firewood which I then bucked up with the Swede saw, walked out on the lake to the community water hole for my two buckets, said my breviary and studied my grammar. A visit from Chief Francis Eya was part of this daily routine. From him I heard a report on the daily happenings in the community. Afternoons I found time to walk around visiting and practising the language. Occasionally I stopped in at the store to pick up a few items and chew the fat with Fred Loutit, the trader.

Fred came from mixed native and white ancestry around Great Slave Lake and had been at Fort Franklin for the past eight years. He lived alone, not by choice but through circumstances which he was ever on the lookout to change. An introvert and a hypochondriac to boot, he found it difficult to visit around or make new friends. There was, however, one ray of hope on Fred's horizon. He discovered in his yearly ration of water-glassed eggs that some of them bore the names and addresses of the farmers' daughters out in Alberta where they were produced. Fred wrote to these girls and, if he got an answer, he would visit them with matrimony in mind when, every few years, he got out to civilization. So far his efforts had not borne fruit, but he had some splendid prospects lined up for his next trip outside. I'll bet his district manager never realized how important that yearly supply of hen fruit meant to this trader. One didn't joke about eggs to Fred.

As Christmas approached I became aware of the problem of fitting everyone into the mission's small room for the popular Midnight Mass. I decided to say the three consecutive Masses allowed at Christmas and divide the people up into three groups, each group assigned to a different Mass. The idea looked good on paper, but its execution failed when everybody showed up for the first service and stayed right through all three.

It was standing room only, wall-to-wall and out the open door. And I had to be careful where I put my feet when turning from the corner altar, as the children covered the floor under me. All the faith in that great expanse of wilderness was distilled into that one roomful of fervent Christians whose prayers that holy night must have penetrated the vault of heaven. I felt a sudden realization of my usefulness as the Lord's instrument in orchestrating this humble song of praise on the anniversary of His birth. Later years saw me presiding over much larger congregations in more elegant surroundings at this midnight service, but I doubt any of them approached the genuine fervour of this Christ-mass.

A few days later we reached the century's half-way point, ushering in the New Year, 1950, with a barrage of rifle fire directed at the starry sky. I stayed on until we had celebrated Epiphany, the feast of the Three Wise Men, on January 6th. Then on the morning of the ninth, a month to the day since leaving Fort Norman, I harnessed my team and headed back.

Luckily I had a companion for the trip: Jimmy Cleary, known locally as Egoneetsi, a knowledgeable veteran of the trail who drove a splendid team of six huskies. All that day he broke trail ahead of my team, which seemed to have learned to harbour their strength as we never got separated. By nightfall we had reached the half-way point, a height of land dividing Great Bear Lake from the Mackenzie Valley called Nadanatli, where I had camped with the police on the trip out. This time it was much colder, however, and we carried no tent. Egoneetsi showed me how to construct a fire using full tree-length dry poles that could be pushed in together gradually to keep the fire going all night, and how to dig down to the moss with snowshoes and cover this sleeping pit with spruce boughs while the excavated snow was piled up behind to reflect the heat back on us.

With this arrangement we slept warm outside in the forty-below temperature, getting up only once or twice to push the fire logs together. The following day we got into Norman in fine shape. Neither of us had gotten out of our sleds the whole way. I was amazed at the ease of this trip compared to the ordeal going out, in spite of deep snow on the trail all the way and the much lower temperature.

6

A NEW OBEDIENCE

On my return to the mission at Fort Norman I resumed the orderly life with my two companions. Progress in the Indian language continued under the tutelage of Father Denis, while I persisted in trying to converse with Brother Latreille in French.

About once a week Brother and I would go out to Taketue with the dog-team to visit the nets. Other afternoons we might work in the wood lot closer to home to cut green birch for holding the fire at night. These trees attracted snowshoe hares and Brother showed me how to set snares for them, an essential skill in this country. If a person got stranded in the bush for any reason, he could always manage to use one of his shoelaces for a snare and keep from starving.

Brother had a sense of humour that thrived on minor disasters. Once, while the three of us were sitting at the kitchen table, Father Denis asked for the food in a metal pot sitting behind Brother on the hot stove. Brother picked it up gingerly in his callused finger tips and handed it to Father Denis, who as quickly dropped it with an appropriate exclamation in French, sending Brother into gales of laughter.

Two years previously the Army came through Fort Norman on a training exercise called "The Muskox Expedition." After spending a night at the mission, they left a barrel of fuel oil behind to lighten their load. Once when I was sitting in the common room practising my Hareskin on two local braves, Brother

woke up from his short siesta and shuffled out, leaving behind a
cloud of smoke from the large pipe clamped between his store
teeth. Noticing a chill in the air, he retreated to the kitchen and
emerged with a tin can of this fuel oil. Opening the door of the
wood stove he threw the fuel in on the hot coals with a flourish.
Some of it shot right through a crack in the side of the stove and
across the moccasins of our visitors. The stove not only roared to
life, but the line of fire quickly followed the path of oil and the
two natives were startled to see their moccasins burning. While
they ran outside to plunge their feet in a snow bank Brother collapsed into a chair laughing so hard he had to hold his ample
stomach while tears rolled down his cheeks. I was equally
amused by the humour of the situation, but our native friends
apparently were not, for they failed to return. Later we had some
fun kidding them about this incident, because their word for the
devil is *eketsele* – "burned feet."

It was now the end of January, time for me to visit my outpost
parish at Norman Wells. I was joined by the RCMP and a French-
Canadian trapper by the name of Henry Cadieux. We made good
time until we were opposite the Tourangeau cabin and started
across the river. This freeze-up had been particularly violent and
acres of slab ice had frozen in upright angles resembling tank
traps. We were forced to walk ahead of our teams with axes trying to break off the worst chunks, but even then our oak toboggans took hard punishment and some of the dogs were torn out
of their harnesses. We were glad to reach shore and camp for the
night with the Tourangeaus.

We continued next morning on toward the Wells and six
miles down the road reached the Royal Canadian Corps of Signal's beam station, where a few Army signalmen were stationed.
One of them, Johnny Bell, had raised four fine-looking grey
huskies with an eye to eventually driving them in harness and
getting a little outdoor exercise. He told me that they had already
learned to pull his sled and he asked if I would mind if he accompanied me back to Norman with them. A week later I came out
of the Wells alone and stopped to pick up Johnny for his first

dogsled trip. It was mid-afternoon by the time he was all set to go and we started up river. The weather looked fair when we left, but as we were crossing the frozen Mackenzie at Tourangeau's a light snow began falling and the wind rose. Up to that point Johnny's team seemed to have no trouble following me closely, but soon they lost their initial steam and began to lag behind. As my stops to let him catch up became more frequent, I became aware of the responsibility I had accepted when I agreed to accompany him on his first trip.

The elements conspired against us as the snow got heavier and daylight dimmed. It was dangerous to get out of sight of my companion, as he had no lead dog and the trail I was making in the fresh snow was quickly obliterated by the wind. We had barely made twenty miles when I decided to call it quits and do the prudent thing – camp for the night. Luckily I carried a tent with me and we were able to get up off the river and into the timber where we set it in the protection of the spruce.

When we woke the following morning the flapping of the tent indicated that the wind had not died as we had hoped. Once we got down on the river to resume our trek we realized just how strong it was and how poor the visibility was in the falling snow in spite of the daylight. No matter: I felt confident we could make the twenty-five miles to Fort Norman and we started off at a good clip. With Johnny's team close behind the first ten miles were reassuring, but then they began to tire and the gap between us lengthened. It was just about the worst weather we could have picked, with a howling head wind at thirty below, blowing snow stinging our faces, and no visible trail to follow. Nor was there any protection anywhere along this route. We might just as well have been out somewhere in the Barren Lands. Indeed, the high banks of the Mackenzie funnelled the winds against us like a giant venturi. We were soon reduced to a crawl, with me driving ahead a few hundred yards and then waiting for Johnny to catch up. Darkness caught us still a long way from our goal and, as much as I hated to do it, I had to admit to my companion that we would have to camp another night.

We finally found a ravine where we could get up over the river's bank and into the spruce to set up the tent again. We were both stumbling around in the semi-darkness, axes in hand, chopping down dry spruce trees to fuel our tent stove when a curious accident befell us both almost simultaneously. Both our axe handles broke and the heads went flying into the deep snow, impossible to find. Now we were reduced to breaking up small, dry branches with our hands. And to top that off we had no dog feed for this unscheduled second night on the trail and I had to sacrifice the steak and bacon I was bringing back as a special treat. As we lay in the tent that night I tried my best to convince my young companion that this was not your typical dogsled trip, but that a combination of bad weather and bad luck had worked against us.

The morning of our third day broke clear and calm and the storm was over. When we got our teams hitched up and down on the river's surface again I was in for the biggest surprise of the trip. We had actually crossed the river the night before and camped on the east side without knowing it. Ten easy miles and we were into the Fort at last, but Johnny had had enough of dogsledding. He took his dogs back in an aircraft and never made another trip.

As for me, I couldn't afford that luxury, and after a night's rest I took Brother out to Taketue and returned the same day. The more our dogs were used, the better their stamina and speed. Besides, I was learning how to handle them. There's a lot of dog psychology involved. For one thing, being too "palsy-walsy" with your team, feeding them tidbits at odd hours and playing with them, tends to lessen their respect for you so that when you crack your whip behind them it does not produce the desired result. On one trip back from Taketue I was behind the police special constable when he stopped his team, tied his sled to a tree and proceeded to give each of them a few solid cracks across the rump, indicating to them that he was not pleased with their performance. They got the message and when we resumed I couldn't keep up with him.

On the other hand there were some drivers who were convinced that only wicked dogs worked well in harness. One such was Pat Tourangeau who kept his team tied back in the bush where they had no contact with humans and who used to beat them with a chain. He paid a high price for this treatment, however. One spring day when he was returning to his cabin in his hunting canoe while his dogs were running loose along the river bank, his children saw him coming and ran to greet him, but four-year-old Norman fell and the dogs were immediately upon him, tearing his flesh and literally scalping him before Pat could help. In fact it was Pat's wife, Cecile, who ran out with the .30-.30 and shot most of the dogs on her child before they quit. Norman had to be flown to Edmonton on a mercy flight to save his life, but he was left badly disfigured.

I never did understand cruelty to dogs, but I had to admit that the natives got a sterling performance out of almost any emaciated team they happened to be driving. Sometimes I watched fascinated while travelling behind such a team; mile after mile the driver would throw a short stick at each dog in turn and then retrieve it again as the sled passed it. They were kept perpetually scared and straining in their harnesses. And they were wicked too. Once a native was driving his team behind me for several hours until finally I slowed and his leader got close enough to sink his teeth into my leg. I never let a team get that close to me again.

During the next two months I made two more trips downriver to Norman Wells and then in early April I set out again for Great Bear Lake to spend Easter with the people out there. Alfred Lennie again went with me and we each carried a heavy load of freight for the Hudson Bay store. Mine consisted mostly of rifle shells and cigarette papers. It was almost balmy weather compared to our trip out in December, as the sun was high and the days long. In spite of our loads we both rode all the way over a well-worn trail.

In a letter to our bishop following my first stay in the Fort Franklin mission outpost I had suggested that we put up a better building out there, and he agreed. With this prospect in view I enlisted the help of the Bear Lakers in getting a dozen of the largest trees in the area cut and skidded into place. We located a small stand of very old spruce on the crown of a hill adjacent to a lake a mile away, some of which were nearly two feet in diameter at the base. Being green, they were very heavy and we had to use as many as twelve dogs to skid one of them into town.

Following the religious services of Good Friday and Easter Sunday I organized a kind of winter carnival or sports day that took place out in front of the settlement on the frozen surface of the lake. It included marksmanship, an ice chopping contest, snowshoe and dog-team races, followed in the evening by a drum dance. It was a first for the people of Bear Lake and, although I had some difficulty in getting them to understand and participate in the events, once underway they all enjoyed them.

The Hudson Bay trading post at Franklin was supplied once a year by boats coming up the swift waters of the Great Bear River. If shortages occurred during the winter they had to be supplied from the sister post at Fort Norman and brought in by dog-team. When it was time for me to return to Norman ten teams had been hired by Fred Loutit to go and bring back 300 pounds of supplies each, so we all went together. It made an impressive convoy. I was amazed to notice that a few young bucks had apparently joined the group at the last minute like stowaways, having no equipment but the parkas on their backs. They either jumped from sleigh to sleigh or ran behind. At the half-way point on the ridge at Nadanatli we all slept in the open around a huge fire. Just before arriving at the Fort they stopped again to make fire, which puzzled me as we were so close to our destination, but I learned that they customarily changed into their best clothing and dressed up the dogs with their embroidered *tapis,* or blankets, before they made their grand entrance. I went ahead to the mission and later watched them all drive their teams into the Hudson Bay fenced compound, where they left them unattended while they went into the store. A few minutes later all ten teams of dogs rushed at each other in a king-sized pile up of snarls and flying fur that brought most of the villagers out of their cabins. Certainly everyone knew that the Bear Lakers had arrived in town.

Brother had a welcome surprise for me. The previous summer I had acquired a large husky bitch from Aklavik and during my absence at Bear Lake she had had four nice pups, three of them males. This was the beginning of a much-improved team of dogs for the mission. Unfortunately I lost one of the males when he was six weeks old. He bothered his mother as she was eating and she snapped at him, inadvertently breaking his jaw. I was forced to shoot him and learned from the incident that pups should be weaned and separated from their husky mothers as soon as possible. This bitch, Vicky, nonetheless went on to produce many fine litters of pups and I was soon driving the ideal team of blood-brothers.

As it got warmer and the snow melted, the trails would support the dogs only at night when they froze. At this time of year two steel runners called leashes are attached to the bottom of the oak toboggans to facilitate their running on the frozen trails at night and to prevent wear and tear on the toboggan bottoms. Thus equipped, I made one last trip out to Willow Lake and returned on the first of May, at which time the trails were becoming so bare of snow it became difficult to travel by dogsled. According to my notebook I had accumulated a total of 1,247 miles by dogs since fall. I was slowly growing out of my greenhorn status.

Mail travelled in and out of Fort Norman by Norman Wells on a weekly schedule, weather permitting, aboard a Canadian Pacific Airlines' Norseman, equipped with either skis or pontoons. The mail had become very erratic recently and the townspeople were complaining and writing letters of protest, but to no avail. Then two attractive nurses were assigned to the nursing station and the situation changed dramatically; mail delivery had never been so good. Funny, but no one had thought of this effective solution to the problem before.

Another ten years in the field had expired for Father Denis and he was again eligible for a vacation to his home in France. He was replaced temporarily by a French-Canadian veteran of the North, Father Maurice Beauregard, who now joined Brother Médard Latreille and me at Fort Norman. I decided that he, as a new member of our religious community, deserved a welcoming duck dinner. So as soon as the first feathery migrants appeared I positioned myself down along the river's bank at the crack of dawn and, suitably armed with our twelve-gauge shotgun, waited. It wasn't like the previous spring over on Windy Island when we saw huge flocks of migrating birds, but I did manage to bag two mallards which I bore triumphantly back to the mission where my two companions were still asleep. I intended to carry them into Brother's room as a wake-up surprise, but in my enthusiasm I miscalculated the height of his doorway and the resulting impact dropped me to the floor like a pole-axed steer. Brother woke up in a typical fit of laughter as I lay stunned on the floor grasping my proud trophies.

Brother had the floor of the room over his kitchen covered with his seed potatoes, which proceeded to sprout. As soon as the large field behind the mission was dry enough he had it ploughed and disked ready for planting. The next chore was to cut up the seed potatoes so that each section had a sprout sticking out a couple of inches for a head start. Care was taken that the rows were absolutely straight and a measuring stick used to separate the sprouts evenly. The more I thought of the week of back-breaking work ahead of us, the more I thought that there must be an easier way of doing it. I began tinkering with an old stone boat, cutting two holes in its floor, attaching small plough-like wooden fins in front and two more behind, the idea being that this contraption pulled behind our tractor would allow two men to sit on it alongside boxes of sprouts which could be placed in the ground through two floor openings. The fins in front opened a furrow and those behind closed it again. We used it and it worked! In fact we planted the whole field in a day while the three of us sat down. I felt like a budding Cyrus McCormick.

Following another break-up and the passing of Streeper's "banana boat," we again went up river and gathered our yearly raft of firewood, but this year on top of the logs we added bags of sawdust from Cleve Cinnamon's sawmill. Our idea was to use it to preserve ice through the summer for drinking water.

At that time Father Denis returned from his two-month furlough in France, carrying a precious bottle of French cognac. This he placed ceremoniously on the kitchen table in order to introduce us to an after-dinner drink he called *pause-café*. After our first meal together he demonstrated just how a touch of the powerful liquor was to be added to a cup of coffee. Brother, however, got his directions all backwards and added a dash of coffee to a cup of cognac which so infuriated our superior that he removed the bottle to the safety of his room, thus ending our experiments with *pause-café*.

It was now the right time of year to set the annual barrel of Mass wine, over which Brother presided with loving solicitude. The dried muscatel grapes were delivered annually by the *Sant'Anna* and came in twenty-pound boxes. These were dumped into an oak barrel half-full of clean water and placed upstairs in a warehouse where it was kept warm by the long, sunny days. Brother went up there several times a day to stir this mash with a paddle and after twenty-one days the liquid was ready for bottling. Church regulations on Mass wine are very strict: no sugar can be added, and the alcohol content may not exceed thirteen per cent. The superior got suspicious after sampling this batch and sent a small bottle of it out to the University of Alberta for analysis. Evidently he failed to identify exactly what he was sending, as the report back suggested that his horse may be diabetic!

"Summertime and the livin' is easy" is especially true of the North. The mission was warm again and I could move upstairs to my summer bedroom where I was out of the traffic. Under the midnight sun the garden in the side yard soon produced lettuce and radishes and our meals became more varied and flavourful. My formal lessons in Hareskin ceased, for I could now carry on a fair conversation as well as deliver a sermon in the language. French was the common language of exchange among my three companions, and I was no longer ignorant of the trend of the conversation going on around me. So, all things considered, life was a lot easier as I entered my second summer at Fort Norman. The trouble was, the more acclimatized I got, the more I realized that it couldn't last. There were now three priests living where normally there was only one. One or two of us would have to go, but which, and to where? This uncertainty prompted a sharp lookout upriver, from which direction we were expecting the arrival of the man who held our destinies in his hands, Bishop Joseph Trocellier.

Our anticipation mounted as his little motor scow, *Our Lady of Fatima,* piloted by Brother Petrin, hove into view one day in July and pulled into shore. We priests could hardly contain our feelings of suspense as the bishop proceeded casually with his pastoral visit. Father Denis had made no secret of the fact that he had offered himself for the new foundation and permanent posting at Fort Franklin. Father Beauregard didn't seem to have any preference, while I prayed that I wouldn't be sent anywhere south of where I was.

We each had our private interview with His Excellency. During mine he told me how pleased he was with my progress during my first year-and-a-half in the country. I think he was taking his time to size each of us up and make up his mind where we could each best serve his Vicariate. He kept us hanging until the eleven o'clock High Mass on Sunday when, during his sermon, he announced the new obediences to the whole population: Father Denis was to take charge of the mission at Fort Providence, Father Beauregard was to take over this mission at Fort Norman and Father Brown was to proceed to Great Bear Lake and build a new mission at Fort Franklin!

There it was. Everyone knew at once and after the Mass we exchanged congratulations. No mention had been made of Brother Médard Latreille, as he was considered a permanent fixture at Norman and was perfectly happy with that. I would have been happy to have him go with me to Franklin, but I realized, too, that a Brother skilled in carpentry would be more helpful. To fill that gap the bishop told me that he was lending me Brother Maurice Larocque from the mission at Fort Simpson to help get me started. Apparently this whole idea of building a new mission at Bear Lake had not been planned very far in advance. In fact no material had been ordered for it, but the bishop advised me that he was having lumber destined for a new church at Fort Wrigley sent on down to Norman to be taken up the Great Bear River by the Northern Transportation Company. I was anxious to see the plan for the mission at Franklin, but there was none; the bishop told me to make the plan myself. I appreciated his confidence in me, but this looked like a big order if not an impossibility for someone so inexperienced in construction. Anyway I had my orders and immediately got to work with pencil and ruler to work something out. Before I had anything to show him, however, the bishop got away downriver.

"Father Beau," as he was affectionately called, would now have not only the Fort Norman Mission to look after, but the parish at Norman Wells, not to mention the outpost at Willow Lake. We decided to go down to the Wells together in the *Nayuka* so that I could show him our Quonset chapel and introduce him around. En route I kept working on my plan for the new building at Fort Franklin. While at the Wells one day we talked with Wing Commander Roy Woods who commented on the trouble he was having from all the smoke in the air from recent forest fires. He was about to send a Canso aircraft to Fort Good Hope to pick up a crew of fire-fighters and he invited us to go along. This gave us the opportunity to catch up with the bishop again. I was particularly anxious to show him the plan I had made and get his approval. It showed a two-storey frame building thirty feet wide by sixty long, topped by a steeple. One side of the main floor would be the chapel, twenty feet wide and running its whole length, while the side facing the lake would be divided into a common room, kitchen, office and bedroom. The upstairs would contain a storeroom and a spare bedroom. The bishop gave it a cursory glance and pronounced it "excellent," with the proviso that I have enough lumber to do it as planned. He wasn't sure how much he was diverting from Fort Wrigley.

I had expected that we would go over every square foot of my plans, cancelling or at least revising many of my lines, but here I was walking away with a carte blanche permission to do what I could with whatever material I received. I was reminded of my Dad's comment to guests when he was showing them the log bunks I had built in my bedroom when I was seventeen: "Yes, Bernard built them out of his own head and had wood left over!"

Father Beau and I ran down the hill to reboard our aircraft and fly back to the Wells, not anticipating the ride we were in for. The pilot had lowered the nose wheel once he was on the water so as not to damage the hull of the amphibious Canso when he nosed into the riverbank at Fort Good Hope. When he backed off, however, there was so much mud stuck in the nose wheel well that he couldn't retract the wheel fully and we were forced to take off with it stuck partially down. Both of us were up in the pilot's compartment and the spray of water shooting up through the open hatch drenched us as we tried to plug it with our jackets. Once airborne, the geyser quit, but, with a full load of fire-fighters and a glassy river, that takeoff run seemed to go on for minutes. Now the captain radioed ahead to Norman Wells to stand by with fire-fighting equipment: he would be forced to land on the gravel runway and wasn't at all sure that his nose wheel wouldn't collapse on touchdown. Father Beau and I got busy with our rosaries and, thank God, we made a safe landing amid a cheering crowd led by the Wing Commander, who stated publicly that no aircraft of his could possibly crash with two chaplains on board!

When we got back to Fort Norman we found Brother Larocque had already arrived from Fort Simpson. A slightly built French-Canadian, Brother Larocque was as quiet and retiring as the Latreille brothers were fun-loving extroverts. It didn't take him long to size up the plans and make a mental note of the material involved. While he gathered up what tools the Norman mission could lend us, I purchased a twenty-two-foot freighter canoe and a nine-horsepower Johnson outboard from one of the natives. Our lumber had already been transferred from the *Sant'Anna* to the *George Askew*, a stern-wheeler that plied the lower half of the Great Bear River for the Northern Transportation Company. Brother and I soon followed in my canoe, loaded to the gunwales, with a local native hired as pilot.

All my earthly possessions were in a trunk on board, but my most precious baggage was the memory I carried of my first two years in the North. I had learned to like both the country and its people and would have been content to go on living at Fort Norman had the bishop so decided. The fact that it had been my training ground both in learning to cope with northern living and in acquiring two languages meant that this post held a special place in my heart. I was grateful to Father Denis for all the hours he had spent patiently explaining the complexities of the Hareskin language, and I would miss the humour of Brother Médard that brightened the dark days. Perhaps if we had had some sort of farewell banquet I could have put these thoughts into words, but as it was we simply packed up and went our separate ways. There was no one on the bank to wave us off as we pushed out into the current of the Mackenzie and a little lump in my throat told me that the first chapter of my life in the North had just ended.

7

BUILDING
AT FORT FRANKLIN

The Great Bear River, about seventy miles long, empties Great Bear Lake into the Mackenzie River. It is fairly straight, clear and fast, with nine miles of shallow water running over mostly flat limestone at the half-way point commonly referred to as "the rapids." The lower segment of the river tends to be wider and therefore shallower, with a less distinct channel, while the section above the rapids is narrower and deeper, with a much swifter current.

In order for the Northern Transportation Company to get supplies to its Crown affiliate, Eldorado Mine on the east side of Bear Lake, the Company had built a portage road around the rapids and maintained a fleet of trucks there supervised by Andy Brass. It also maintained an airport named Bennett Field after Bill Bennett, President of Eldorado. It was strictly a summer operation getting the mine supplied, mainly with diesel fuel, for the coming winter, and taking out the thousands of small bags of uranium concentrate on the back haul destined for further refining at Port Hope, Ontario. A substantial steel ship, named *The Radium Gilbert* after Gilbert LaBine who discovered the mine, plied the two hundred miles of open water on Great Bear Lake connecting the mine with the river boats. Besides this activity there was a Colonel Yukamin with a crew of Army Engineers constructing a road to connect the portage with Bear Lake, a project rumoured to cost a million dollars, but never completed or used.

It was into this beehive of activity that we pointed the nose of our canoe on the 18th of July and slowly pushed our way up to the foot of the rapids the first day. Emptying the boat and pulling it out, we set a tent and camped for the night while I enquired about the possibility of getting a truck to take us across the portage the next day. The following morning, after Andy helped us across the portage, we resumed our voyage above the rapids. Now we were seeing this beautiful river in all its rugged glory, careening off rocky points, twisting and turning in the summer sun, its clear depths moving with schools of arctic grayling, its placid eddies reflecting the tall spruce overhead. We were heavily loaded and our guide had to take advantage of every slack backwater behind the bars and little points to keep us advancing. Out in the centre of the stream we would have made no progress at all. Toward the end of the day as we approached Great Bear Lake the trees along the bank became more stunted and twisted and the temperature dropped noticeably. Some of the banks were solid with ice that would last all summer. Finally we passed the Quonset hut where I had found shelter the winter before and then the Northern Transportation Company dock and then we were out onto the lake itself. Fort Franklin was clearly visible four miles to the left. In no time at all we were across the bay of Keith Arm and I was moving into the mission cabin.

We were visited immediately by seven carpenters who had been sent in by the Department of Public Works to finish the two-storey school they had begun last summer. As they had a cook as well as a good supply of grub, they invited us to take our meals with them, a welcome and unexpected stroke of good luck.

I was free to put up the new mission anywhere I thought suitable, because the land was not yet surveyed nor did we have any lease. The fact that the school was now going up on the east end of the settlement, a few hundred yards farther out than our present site, indicated that the town would probably expand in that direction. I would have preferred to build in the heavy timber at the west end of town where we would have been on better ground off the permafrost, but it now appeared that such a site would be practically isolated. Brother Larocque was pleased with the huge logs we had cut and hauled at Easter. The spot where they had dropped when the snow melted seemed to be as good as any on which to begin construction. However, the Northern Transportation Company had off-loaded our lumber some three hundred yards away, and this meant that we would have to spend the first week with our canoe hauling this material up to our building site. Chief Francis Eya rounded up five capable workers who were willing to help us at a salary of $125 a month, and we got to work.

The foundation for our building had to be those twelve thirty-foot spruce trees which we flattened on the top side with axes. As we were building on permafrost, it wouldn't have helped to pour cement footings under them, which we didn't have anyway, so we simply levelled them with some gravel and flat stones. On top of these mud sills went the four-by-six-inch fir timbers I had taken from the ill-fated Quonset curling rink. Once we had an insulated double floor laid we had a nice flat platform to work on and the walls went up quickly under the expert supervision of Brother Larocque. Besides the pesky flies, the weather gave us the most trouble that summer: it rained on us every working day but seven. We could carry on in spite of the weather, but when we ran short of nails and certain other vital materials it became evident that I would have to make a trip down to Fort Norman in the canoe.

Several of the Bear Lakers jumped into the canoe with me to visit friends down there and we had a dandy roller-coaster ride, not stopping at the rapids, but going straight through in five hours. En route I made a lucky hit with my .270 when I shot a large sandhill crane in the neck and killed it. The natives told me they never kill this bird, called a *deleho*, because its death would bring on a three-day rain. I replied that, with all the rain we had been getting, they wouldn't notice it. Brother Médard was delighted with it and not only cooked it, but invited Bud Boyce, the Game Warden, to join us for this special treat of "Bear Lake goose." All declared it to be delicious. It was.

It didn't take me long to find the material needed at Franklin and I engaged a river pilot to return with me. At the appointed hour the following morning this chap failed to show up, so I decided to go it alone. Aside from shearing a few pins en route, especially at the lower stretch of the river, I made it through to Bear Lake without incident. Like so many disappointments in life, the guide's absence turned out to be a blessing in disguise: I made five trips down to Norman for supplies that summer and never needed a guide.

When we got to the peak of the roof the question of the belfry came up. I showed Brother a picture of one in a photography magazine I was reading that had a little of the Byzantine onion design about it, a tiny cupola at the top of which I could imagine a beacon. Brother started the wheels of his computer-like brain and with only his steel square to go by, cut out every piece of wood for that tower on his table saw on the ground. Not only that, but when assembled on the roof every piece fit perfectly. This amazed me and made a big impression on the professional carpenters working on the school. They immediately donated enough copper sheathing to cover it. Gleaming in the sun like solid gold, the spire of the new mission church was indeed a beacon in the wilderness, a sight any missionary would be proud of.

I was up on the roof one day when a stranger walked up to the building and, doffing an incongruous brown derby, introduced himself as "Mr. Roy Gravel, age fifty-three, your new teacher at your service." I had met many characters in the North, but Mr. Gravel would soon top them all. He moved into the school immediately, even though it was unfinished, and joined us at table to share with us in a most candid manner the amazing vicissitudes of his past life. Our meals were now spiced with true-life episodes not unlike those of a soap opera. If we gained one character in town, we lost another when the Hudson Bay Company suddenly replaced Fred Loutit with a young white boy named Bob Williams. So where before there had been none, now there were three whites in Fort Franklin: Gravel, Williams and myself.

When I made my last trip by canoe to Fort Norman on the 16th of September I brought back that mission's five sled dogs: two older dogs plus Vicky and her three pups. Suddenly I needed a good supply of fish for dog food and, because I could afford little time from the critical job of getting the mission closed in before freeze-up, I decided to hire one of the Bear Lakers, equip him with nets and place him somewhere to fish for me. John Takazo agreed to take on this job and suggested the best place for a fall fishery would be at a bay called Klowahtah, forty-five miles out along the south shore of the lake. We picked the first flat calm day, which happened to be the 22nd of September, and set out in my freighter canoe loaded with Johnny's family, his dogs, tent and a small hunting canoe.

Keith Arm of Great Bear Lake has few islands and the only one on our route was down the lake about thirty-five miles. Although it is marked "Manitou" on the chart, Johnny told me that its real name was Gorabee and that a monster by that name had drowned there when he attempted to swim the lake. The island had formed over his carcass. He added that Gorabee's home in the nearby rocks still existed, but as it was inhabited now by bears no native would dare go near it. I don't think Johnny would have made a stop there had he been in charge of the boat, but as I was manning the kicker, I pulled into shore, much to his consternation. He wouldn't even step on shore himself, but, seeing that I was determined to see Gorabee's home, insisted that I carry the rifle.

I had no trouble finding the entrance to the cave in a limestone outcrop some two hundred yards up from the water, hidden behind a few scraggly spruce. Its opening was approximately the size of a normal cabin door, but inside it opened into a room about sixty feet long by fifteen wide with a ten-foot ceiling and was completely empty. I could visualize the place being used as a safe haven by prehistoric cave men; there being so few caves in this country, this one must have been found and used by them.

That fall I wrote to anthropologist Dr. Richard S. MacNeish of the National Museum in Ottawa about this unusual cave and he came down the following summer to investigate it. After borrowing my canoe and a few shovels he hired some men and went down there. He returned a few days later, however, empty-handed. The floor of the cave which would contain the artefacts he was interested in was now covered with tons of rock that must have fallen from the ceiling during the ages, and he had neither the time nor the funds to dig it all out. He added, however, that he thought I was the first "European" to see this cave and he intended to give it my name. Well, most explorers in the North get a lake or mountain named after them, but I was quite willing to settle for a hole in the ground. Yet I was to be denied even that honour. The following year I was in the Yellowknife library looking over the Journal of the Franklin Expedition, especially the map they had drawn of Great Bear Lake in 1826. The cave was clearly marked!

Johnny and family appeared to be genuinely relieved to see me return to the canoe unharmed. I could not understand how an age-old story such as this could still be exerting an influence on these people in the mid-twentieth century.

I left Johnny and his family off at Klowahtah equipped with four gill nets and sixty large trout hooks. Once a week I went back to get a load of fish and when I finally moved him back to the settlement on October 17th he had taken a total of 2,650 herring and 105 trout. Although this was a good start on my winter's dog feed, I still had to set nets for herring near the mouth of the river after freeze-up.

While Brother and I were using every scrap of material we had to get the mission closed in before the cold weather set in, the Department of Public Works crew were putting the final touches to the interior of the school and had plenty of material left over. They not only gave me enough bricks to build a chimney, but enough lumber to add a ten-foot extension for storage.

They had installed at the school a five-ton Lyster diesel engine attached to a generator, which the teacher was supposed to keep running. Mr. Gravel, however, acknowledged a complete ignorance of anything mechanical. Indeed, he protested that he had been hired to teach, not to fill the shoes of an engineer, and absolutely refused to accept responsibility for keeping that huge engine running. Therefore, by default, I was approached with the proposition that if I would accept this responsibility a line could be strung over to the mission, giving me power also. I jumped at the offer.

In the meantime Brother Larocque had received a letter from his superior at Fort Simpson informing him that he was to return as soon as possible to continue his work with a crew building St. Margaret's Hospital there. Although we now had the new mission building sealed on the outside so that it could be heated, it was practically an empty shell inside; I was hoping he might be allowed to stay on and continue helping me. In fact I had written the bishop suggesting this, but having no answer in reply, I had no choice but to let him return to his post. The Public Works crew had engaged a boat to take them part way down the Great Bear River where they were to be picked up by an aircraft at Bennett Field. When they left on October 12th, Brother Larocque left with them. Two months later, when I got the first batch of mail following freeze-up, there was a letter from the bishop giving me permission to keep Brother with me for the winter!

Now I was alone again in the little log cabin doing my own cooking and looking forward to the day when I could move into the new mission next door. One of the irritants I never got used to in the old cabin was the mice. To discourage them I had brought back a cat I named Charlie-ho on my last trip from Norman. He was probably the first cat the natives had seen in Fort Franklin and they were very wary of him, calling him a *nontaja,* or baby lynx. If he didn't actually kill many mice he certainly kept them below the floor boards and off my bed at night. And then came the day we were surprised by the visit of a short-tailed weasel who emerged from a mouse hole in his white winter pelage, a magnificent ermine. To Charlie-ho he, however, must have appeared like a huge albino mouse who had chased him recently in a nightmare and he retreated to my lap completely demoralized. Actually I was glad to see this professional killer, as I knew he could pursue mice right into their dens.

I had boasted about Charlie-ho's hunting ability to the natives and they were impressed. One such was the widow Guykazo, who lived in a tent with her four children a hundred feet from my cabin. They all slept together in a bed of spruce boughs on the floor, covered by a huge feather blanket, and the mice bothered them at night so she asked to borrow Charley-ho. I lent him out on the condition that they keep their sled dogs well tied while he was in their employ. Two days later I walked over there in the evening to see how he was doing. They were all in bed and gave me only vague answers as to Charlie-ho's whereabouts, but I could hear a muffled "meow" coming from inside a covered fifty-pound Klim can. Lifting the lid I peered down into it with the aid of my flashlight and there was Charlie-ho, in water up to his neck!

As I pulled him out and dried him off, Guykazo spilled the whole sordid story. Apparently the first night Charlie-ho had kept them awake running over their sleeping bag chasing mice. The second night the mice were laying low and, with no activity, Charlie-ho felt the fall chill creeping in as soon as the fire went out. So he tried to crawl under the blankets with them, which scared them out of their wits. The eldest son, Bekoya ("The Brain"), got up and put this "lynx pup" into the empty Klim can, covered it, and went back to bed. Charlie-ho's "meow" now sounded like the roar of a lion in the empty can, so Bekoya got up again and proceeded to dampen the sound by pouring a bucket of water on him. Charlie-ho went back to the mission with me.

I now spent my days alone over in the new building. The cat kept me company as I built a partition upstairs for a bedroom and then a few shelves, to which I would give a coat of varnish before returning to the log cabin at night. I installed my

Electrohome radio up in the new building as soon as I had a shelf built for it and it was powered by one of those large A-B battery packs that lasted a year. It had an effective short-wave band and the best station was the American Armed Forces station AFRTS coming out of Los Angeles, to which I kept it tuned all day as I worked. One evening I couldn't find Charlie-ho before I returned home, so I had to leave without him. The next day I had trouble keeping my station tuned and also noticed water on the floor under the battery, which I presumed was getting old and maybe leaking. I dried it up and re-varnished the spot as well as the shelves.

All that day I had not located Charlie-ho and began to suspect that he had slipped outside and fallen prey to the roaming huskies. The third day I was again up in that room, working with the radio blaring, when it went off the station. I re-tuned it and stood there looking at the dial, wondering what the trouble could be, when I again lost my station and I thought I could actually see the dial move! Suddenly I got a creepy feeling that made me blink and wonder what the devil was wrong. I re-tuned AFRTS and got down close to watch the needle. Nothing happened. Five minutes later when my back was turned I not only lost my station, but the BBC suddenly came on. This had never happened before. I pulled the radio out from the wall and out jumped Charlie-ho! I could hardly believe it. Apparently, with the battery removed from its niche in the back of the radio, the cat had curled up in there. When I pushed it against the wall to varnish in front of it I had unwittingly trapped him inside – for three days! All the tubes were covered with hair. The amazing thing was that he never uttered even one little "meow."

In the meantime my neighbour in the brown derby, the schoolteacher Mr. Gravel, had started his class of first-graders full of enthusiasm, of which he certainly needed a generous amount, for none of them spoke any English. He was riding high on a wave of initial enthusiasm so characteristic of many civil servants who come North, his head exploding with a thousand ideas of projects for the people. Typical of them was his

feather-marketing scheme. He had read somewhere that the milliners of Paris paid high prices for feathers and was horrified to
learn that most of the feathers plucked locally were scattered to
the four winds. He intended to put a stop to this needless waste
immediately and sent out word that the feathers of all birds
plucked should be sent to him for safe-keeping and eventual sale.
Later, to prevent loss of feathers in transit, he offered to pluck the
birds himself in a special room upstairs in the school designated
"the feather room." When Colonel Yukamin had closed his camp
at the end of summer he sent tons of grub over to Franklin to be
distributed by the teacher. Thus began the weekly handouts
called "rations" every Friday, and it was soon noticed that the
feather-producers got the lion's share of this booty. The feathers
in the feather room got deeper and deeper over the next two
years until Mr. Gravel left, at which point a small ladder was
needed to scale the plywood barrier put up over the door to contain the fluffy mass inside. Unfortunately he was never successful in making a deal with the Paris milliners. His successor inherited a lot of feathers.

Baby-sitting the diesel generator at the school turned out to
be a more time-consuming job than I had anticipated. For one
thing, its fuel tank had to be refilled every eight hours and when
it was allowed to run out, the jets had to be bled in order to get it
started again. It was bolted to a concrete slab directly connected
to the school's cement foundation, with the result that when it
was running normally the school had a rhythmic vibration not
unlike that of a huge ship at sea. As long as he could feel that
steady throbbing the teacher knew that all was well, but when it
stopped he was soon pounding at my back door.

I solved the fuel problem by installing a forty-five-gallon
drum in place of the ten-gallon one it had come equipped with.
The panel of dials proved an irresistible temptation to Mr.
Gravel, however, who loved to change the ohm setting whenever
he thought the voltage was low. I would notice it immediately
over in the mission, as my lights would get bright, then dim
again. The result was that he gradually burned out all his bulbs

and started borrowing mine. Finally we got down to my last bulb and he was reduced to using a gasoline light while his huge electric plant, strong enough to light the entire village, rumbled on, hour after hour, powering only the small electric blower in his oil furnace and my one light bulb. In spite of seven thermostats distributed throughout the school, all of which he had turned up full, he complained of the low temperature and was convinced they weren't working. So he had me disconnect them and put in a single switch on the furnace that turned the heat on full-throttle. Once it was on I don't think he ever turned it off.

All Hudson Bay posts were equipped with a telegraph key which the managers operated daily using Morse code. In this way they were advised of changes in fur market prices or possibly a frost in Brazil which would necessitate an immediate mark-up in coffee prices. Mr. Gravel got a message out advising the Department of Education that he was out of light bulbs and we were amazed to see an aircraft land on skis loaded with nothing but bulbs. This was an event, for we got only three aircraft during the entire year.

In no time at all the school was ablaze with light and so was the mission, but soon the whole process began repeating itself; Mr. Gravel fine-tuning the ohm meter and gradually burning out all the bulbs until he put us both in the dark again.

Shortly after that the generator committed suicide when the set screw on the fan at the end of the exciter loosened and cut through the end of the armature wiring. I thought maybe he could keep warm by burning wood instead of oil in his furnace, so I converted it for him, but without the fan to circulate the heat throughout the building only the furnace room was warm. The only alternative was to take the small oil stove from the stout house out behind that had heated the rations and move it and the rations upstairs into the living room. We had no flue to which we could connect the chimney, so we removed a pane of glass from the window and stuck the chimney outside. Egg crates were piled to the ceiling on either side of the room and a dozen desks were lined up in the centre while Mr. Gravel moved his bed into the kitchen just off his new classroom.

Everything worked like a charm until one night a terrific wind out of the north-east blew directly into the stove pipe which was sticking horizontally out of the window, causing a mild explosion that drove the damper into the wall across the room, filled the school with smoke and changed the paint scheme from white to grey. Yet these minor setbacks didn't quench the enthusiastic Mr. Gravel, who carried on with his classes by the light of a gas lamp, bundled in an overcoat, a sporty pair of earmuffs added under his brown derby.

After these trials, however, it occurred to me that Charlie-ho would make an ideal companion for our teacher, especially during his long evenings in the feather room. So when Mr. Gravel's birthday came around I put a large red ribbon on the cat and presented him to the teacher as a precious gift. He was received with open arms. The following week I was informed that Charlie-ho was thriving on the canned lobster found in Colonel Yukamin's grub supply and demonstrating genuine affection for his new master.

"It's uncanny how our temperaments are synchronized," Mr. Gravel confided to me one day. "He senses my every mood. When I've had a good day and feel in a playful mood, we chase each other around the rooms, and when I'm down in the dumps he retires to the top of the egg crates and lets me brood in silence. Next to a wife he's the best companion I could have!" I congratulated myself on having brought these two characters together. One evening, however, when I was cooking supper there came a knock at the door and when I opened it Mr. Gravel shoved Charlie-ho into my arms with the announcement, "Here, take him, I'll explain everything later."

The following day I got the whole, sad story. "Something strange has happened to the finely-tuned rapport between us," confided my neighbour. "We have fallen out of sync. I had a discouraging day with the kids and Charlie-ho insisted on playing with me, and when I threw off this depression and felt like a romp with my companion he hid himself and wouldn't have a thing to do with me! We just couldn't go on living together like this. One of us had to go."

After digesting this tale of domestic strife and feeling like a marriage counsellor, I tendered what sympathy I could and promised I would study Charlie-ho and try to figure out his problem. Actually what I did was to pawn him off on Bob Williams, who quickly objected to him for an entirely different reason. Perhaps because of the stress he had been under at the school for the past few weeks Charlie-ho lost control of his bladder during his first night at the Hudson Bay manager's quarters and left an ugly stain in the middle of the new beige rug. The young manager, thinking only of the reaction this spot would trigger from the district manager on his next inspection trip, took it as a personal insult and before he had regained his composure took the poor culprit outside and executed him with a .30-.30.

Charlie-ho was gone but not forgotten as Fort Franklin's first cat.

8

PRACTISING MEDICINE

Ten days after Brother Larocque left I had the upstairs bed-room in the new mission completed and began sleeping there, although I was still cooking and eating in the old log mission. It took me another month to complete the new kitchen. What gave me the most trouble was the large kitchen cabinet with its built-in sink and row of drawers, particularly difficult for a novice cab-inet-maker. The fact that it is still in use after more than forty years is surprising.

This carpentry work was as fatiguing as it was confining and I would have preferred to be out of doors driving the dogs. When a man is still in his twenties he has enough energy in his legs to make him want to run it off now and then, almost needing to release it in a burst of speed. As soon as there was snow on the ground I was often drawn to the window to watch a team of dogs run by. How I would have loved to join them, but the work fac-ing me inside was pressing and I realized that I would have no one to help me. Besides the bedroom and kitchen, I needed the chapel area completed in time for Christmas.

Early in November Great Bear Lake was frozen over. By mid-month some daring hunters had crossed to the south shore over five miles of ice and spotted an advance herd of caribou a few miles inland. Chief Eya gave me all the details and invited me to join a mass hunt scheduled for the following day. The temptation was too great to resist and I immediately got busy preparing my gear. Yetsa's daughter Rosie had spent most of the summer embroidering a new set of seven moose-hide harnesses for my dogs, so this was all ready and Albert Menako had sewn a new moose hide on my new oak toboggan. I had just to add a few ropes and rings. By midnight I put the sled and harness outside ready to go in the morning.

I had never participated in a caribou hunt and looked forward to this adventure with keen anticipation. I was not to be disappointed. At first light the settlement came alive with the chorus of eager sled dogs being put into harness. As we fell into line on the trail leading across the lake, there were over twenty teams strung out leaving a trail of ice fog in the forty-below air. After covering the first five miles across the thin ice of the bay, we hit the south shore in a tight group, every team nose-to-tail with the next, moving ahead at a fast trot. We began to climb slowly through a partly open parkland of small spruce, heading directly into the sun which was rising at an oblique angle behind the haze on the horizon.

The first sign we got of the herd ahead was the change in attitude of our dogs, raising their heads to sniff the air and quickening their pace. It was another mile before we could actually see the cloud of vapour up ahead indicating caribou beneath. Soon we were close enough to see the quarry, a vast herd of thousands of animals covering a wide muskeg where they had been feeding.

Now the fun began. As there was practically no spruce of any size to tie the sled head rope to, the trick was to tip the toboggan over on its side, creep up and sit on its head, rifle in hand, and try to prevent the dogs from dragging you ahead. You shot over their heads, hoping that you wouldn't hit one accidentally as they jumped and barked in their harness.

Some of the hunters stopped short and began to fire immediately while others wanted to get into closer range or couldn't stop their teams and kept their heads low as the shells fired from behind raced overhead at the targets. It was a wild, chaotic scene, surpassing anything I had imagined, with over a hundred crazed huskies filling the frosty air with their howls while twenty high-powered rifles spat out fire and the poor caribou raced about in utter confusion. The strange part of it was that I alone couldn't fire a shot! In turning my sled on its side, my rifle, still in its case, got caught between the sled's backboard and a "niggerhead,"* snapping the stock in two just behind the trigger guard. When the firing died down there were still plenty of animals within range of my telescopic sight and I wondered to myself if I could fire by holding the two sections of the broken stock together. I couldn't go back empty-handed. No matter the risk I just had to try it.

First of all I found a small spruce to tie the sled to and then, by cradling the barrel in a branch, I fired. Although the stock jack-knifed with the recoil, the bullet sped true to its mark and the caribou dropped. I quickly dispatched three more, two of which were hobbling on broken legs. With the help of my dogs I skidded all four carcasses together and began the less exciting work of skinning and butchering.

My hunting companions were spread out all over the muskeg doing the same thing, as the surviving members of the herd continued digging up and feeding on the caribou moss at a respectful distance. I tied the head rope of my sled to the rack or antlers of a large bull I had killed, thinking that this would restrain the dogs, but when a pair of yearlings ran by at close range they lunged after them, dragging my bull behind, and I had to drop my knife and jump on the bull's back to stop them. After that I tied them in a circle with the lead dog's trace snapped to the sled.

In an hour's time everyone had his toboggan loaded with meat with the hides tied on the top prepared for the triumphal trip home with the first meat of the season. As I pulled out with my load I could see several wolves creeping up on the kill site from the outer muskeg. I learned later that some of the hunters

* The unfortunate term *niggerhead* is used commonly in the North to designate the clumps of moss that stick up a foot or two all over the muskegs. They usually measure about two feet across and may be formed by frost heave.

had killed more animals than they could take away and intended to return for this meat the following day, but a sudden, violent west wind took all the ice out of the bay and by the time it had re-frozen the wolves had cleaned up everything. The lesson that should have been learned was not to kill more than you could keep, but I was to learn that those who live off the land are not necessarily conservationists. A case in point came up about two weeks later when Sonny Naedzo asked me if I would go with him to bring in the meat of a dozen caribou he had shot about fifteen miles away. I figured that my dogs needed a good thirty-mile run if they were to get in shape for the trip to Fort Norman, so I went with him. We had gone about half-way when we ran into another bunch of caribou. Sonny opened fire on them and soon we had two sled-loads of meat right there. Sonny never did go back for the animals he had originally shot.

I had just gotten into the mission after this trip when some-one came to tell me that old Lucy Trakazo was sick. When I asked what kind of sickness, they said she couldn't pass water. I imme-diately began to think of what I could substitute for a catheter which I didn't have. If I could only locate a piece of plastic tube it would work. I had heard that in similar circumstances the natives had successfully used a swan's hollow wing bone. Before I could locate something, however, another person ran in to say that she had died.

This wasn't the first death I had had at Franklin. During the past summer twenty-one-year-old Jimmy Tucho was running a slight temperature and complaining of a sore throat. I began injecting him with a daily dose of 2 cc's of penicillin at the mis-sion. I had been warned not to engage an aircraft unless it was a case of life or death two years before, when I had stopped at Edmonton en route into the country. Dr. Faulkner at Charles Camsell Hospital, who had charge of Indian and Northern Health Services, had told me that aircraft medevac charters were very costly. I had this warning in the back of my mind as I con-tinued to treat Jimmy, who showed no sign of improving. Finally I could wait no longer and, although my patient didn't look at all near death, I had Bob Williams send a message to pilot Pappy Hill at Norman Wells. He lost no time in flying over in the CPA Norseman and landing out in front of the settlement on floats. Because there was no dock and the shore rocks could easily damage the floats, he waited a couple of hundred feet from shore. We took Jimmy out in a canoe, but before we could get him into the aircraft, he died.

Before I had left home to come North my uncle the doctor gave me some practical advice regarding most of the first-aid problems I might encounter in the North. He also gave me a copy of the latest *Merck Manual* (a handy medical reference work for diagnosis and treatment). Another friend, Jane Hasselwander, gave me her student nurse's dissecting instruments. Before I left Fort Norman the nurse there gave me a box of medicines and bandages she thought I might need at Franklin. Nonetheless, I found myself up against a bad health situation that would have taxed the skills of a bona fide medical doctor. I don't think that it is exaggerating to say that the natives of Fort Franklin at that time were riddled with tuberculosis. I noticed this right away in winter by the amount of blood spat along the trails in town. The worst cases had found their way out to the Charles Camsell Hospital, where they had died, and this reinforced the conviction that a visit to hospital was a one-way trip. Perhaps if some curable individuals had been evacuated first and then returned cured, it might have encouraged others to submit themselves for treatment before they were terminally ill.

Assisting at a childbirth in the role of midwife was a challenge I didn't look forward to, but it was inevitable. One night I was awakened to go to the cabin of Sonny Naedzo whom I had married to Georgina Cleary the previous October. During the next hour she delivered a healthy baby with little help on my part. After tying and cutting the umbilical cord I waited patiently for the placenta to be expelled. The book said it should come out in about fifteen minutes, but said little about how much pressure should be used on the cord to help in the process. After a half-hour I became worried and exerted more pull on the cord. It was amazingly tough and I had no fear of breaking it, but I was apprehensive about pulling out more than just the placenta, if that were possible. I think I was sweating more than Georgina when it finally emerged an hour after the birth.

In mid-winter I was successful in getting a Dr. Gray to fly down from Aklavik Hospital with a portable X-ray machine. He landed in a De Havilland Beaver aircraft equipped with skis and we set up the X-ray in the Hudson Bay store, as it alone had electricity. I acted as interpreter for the doctor as he gave Chief Eya a little pep talk on rounding up everyone in the settlement for their first X-ray. It was after supper when they began coming in to stand in line, stripped to the waist, to get their picture taken, after which I was charged with the task of giving them shots for smallpox and diphtheria. By midnight we had processed 75, but 100 had failed to show up and the doctor was very perturbed and vented his dissatisfaction at me saying, "What's the matter with these people? Don't they realize TB is decimating them? The government has gone to a lot of expense flying me down here for this clinic, but I can't hold this aircraft here another night. How are we going to get them in here?"

Although I was doubtful about the outcome, my only suggestion was that the two of us go about the village pounding on doors and urging the laggards to get up to the store. After this midnight invitation we went back to work and by four in the morning our total had risen to 126. Yet I realized that those who were spitting the most blood did not show up. Others believed the rumour that it was that devilish X-ray machine itself that gave a person tuberculosis. Most of the 50 who never came to the clinic reasoned that if they did have the disease they might as well die right there among their family and friends than off in some strange land.

Because of this reluctance of the natives to go outside for help, I wrote several letters to Dr. Faulkner requesting a periodic visit from the nurse in Fort Norman. Finally Miss Beckham flew in for a trial visit. She was a sight: an Englishwoman of generous proportions, hidden behind a mask of white powder and red lipstick, a combination guaranteed to scare the living daylights out of a group of people who had seen few if any white women and who had no knowledge of these aids to beauty. I escorted her about the village to see my current patients and she was a sensation wherever we went. The adults were as tongue-tied in disbelief as if I were showing off a winged monster from Mars, while the children scrambled screaming under the beds. Poor Miss Beckham couldn't understand the reception she was getting and I found it difficult to be candid with her and simply mumbled something about the people not being used to visitors. Unfortunately her visit accomplished very little and she never returned. In one way I couldn't blame her. No one wants to waste her time without accomplishing anything, especially the professional person.

On the other hand, you can't blame the Bear Lakers either. To be confronted with such a formidable specimen of an alien race takes some getting used to. Perhaps if I had been able to remove her makeup and perfume and rub a little fish oil on her face so she smelt "right" it might have helped. I don't suppose there was anything we could have done about her curly red hair. She and Dr. Gray were certainly dedicated and capable members of their profession, but they just didn't understand the people they were sent to help.

When December rolled around and we hadn't had any mail since summer I decided to run in to Fort Norman with the dogs. Sonny Naedzo went with me. Both our teams were in good shape and they needed to be, because the snow was deep and no one had broken a trail yet this winter. I carried a small tent and we pitched it both nights, leaving it set the second night for the return trip. Brother Médard welcomed me back at Norman with his customary good cheer and Father Beauregard was pleased with the sled-load of fish and meat I brought. It took me a few days to read all my mail and then I had to answer the important ones, for there was no telling when I'd get the next chance to send mail out. Furthermore, it was time to get the Christmas cards on their way.

One thoughtful woman in Edmonton had sent me a parcel containing a head of lettuce and three tomatoes which arrived frozen solid. I considered them a complete loss, but Brother Médard insisted he knew of a technique to thaw and save them. When his process failed and they turned black he made a salad out of them anyway and put them on the table to watch our reaction, which provoked his typical gales of laughter. I had missed his humour at Franklin and it was good to be back in an Oblate community in spite of the regulatory bells, the early rising and the frosty windows. Yet deep down I was no longer at ease there because I kept thinking of my Franklin mission, of the plans I had for celebrating Christmas with my people there and of those who were critically ill. Before returning I got a good supply of medicine from the nursing station. The return trip was the best I had made – thanks to a splendid performance from my seven huskies – except for a frozen chin, the result of forty-below temperatures.

I had just gotten back into the mission after unharnessing my dogs when someone ran in to announce another death in the village. This time it was the oldest member of the Betsedea family, Cecile's mother Yahon. If this weren't enough to cast gloom on this family, I soon learned that Rosie Yetsa had succumbed to tuberculosis while I was away. Neither death was any surprise, and I had given both the Sacrament of Extreme Unction (since revised as the Sacrament of the Sick) before I left. It was particularly tragic in the case of Rosie because her parents wouldn't accept any medicine for her – not to mention evacuation to a hospital – so her doom was sealed. Nor did the future look any better for this family: four of its living members were spitting blood.

My long days of carpentry resumed as I continued to put up partitions and hang doors in an effort to have the chapel ready for Christmas. I hired Johnny Neyalle to help handle the four-by-eight sheets of plywood, which speeded up the work considerably; it also helped that I no longer had to go over to the old mission to cook my meals. When the big feast rolled around everything was ready. There would be no more trouble trying to stagger the congregation for the three Midnight Masses: now there was plenty of floor space even though we didn't have benches, and the barrel stove threw all the heat we needed. I had hung accordion doors across the altar end of this large room so that with them closed the room served as a rec hall. We brought in a spruce tree and trimmed it. Underneath I put a pile of presents I had gotten from the States in the mail at Fort Norman.

On Christmas afternoon after the gifts had been distributed to the children I introduced them to some traditional games of my culture, like pinning the tail on the donkey (I drew a caribou), musical chairs, candle lighting, as well as nail driving, a balloon dance and a contest to see who could whistle first after eating five soda crackers. Not everything turned out as I had planned however. As a special treat I had made a bucket of ice cream, but the reaction was *"Ellagu!"* – "It's cold!" – and they held their dishes over the stove until it was melted before eating it. I had even planned on having games outside for the adults and in anticipation had put flags out on the lake for the dogsled race course and targets for the shooting events. The fifty-below temperature and stiff wind, however, postponed these events until Easter. An inside drum dance and stick game was substituted, and everyone agreed that it was the best Christmas ever.

As the last days of 1950 ticked into eternity I couldn't help but feel thankful to God for all its blessings, but especially for the new mission, so spacious yet so easy to heat. I used to shudder walking by the old log building, remembering how dark and cold it was. In preparing a year-end report for the bishop I notified him that the cost of building the new mission at Fort Franklin came to exactly $7,829.22, including the materials, the transport and the labour. Although the job wasn't completed I didn't anticipate needing any more material to finish. I sweetened my letter by enclosing a U.S. cheque for $2,000 ($2,200 in Canadian funds) from Aquinas Institute, the high school from which I graduated in Rochester. It represented the result of a paper drive they had organized for the missions.

Among the letters I had received at Norman was one from Bishop Trocellier dated early November, in which he told me that a "good American" in Toledo, Ohio, was giving him a four-passenger Aeronca aircraft. He then went on to describe a trip he made to Rochester on which he visited my parents and noticed on the wall of my room my pilot's licence. As I was the only missionary he had who was trained to fly, he added, "If you are able to pilot that machine you may have it and then get away from dogs." Now I had to write him: Thanks, but no thanks. I had enough of flying to realize that it was not as much fun as driving dogs and a lot more dangerous.

The bishop did receive the aircraft and sent another missionary to the States to get licensed in my place, but I never regretted my decision. At that time, in that place, dogs were the best means of transportation.

Now that the new mission at Fort Franklin was built it was time to give it an official name. I had great devotion to the Carmelite nun, Thérèse of Lisieux, who had not only been canonized by the Church but named Patroness of Missions. Since the parent mission at Fort Norman carried the name of the "big" St. Teresa of Avila, it was fitting that the new daughter mission on Bear Lake be named after the French St. Thérèse, who was affectionately known as "The Little Flower." The bishop granted my request and it was official: Mission St. Therese.

9

TRAGEDY
AND TABOOS

Gone were the leaden skies, the endless fall of snow and the dark days of November and December; we were now into the clear, bright days of January. The atmosphere was clean and the air sharp as temperatures stayed down around forty below zero. The frozen surface of Great Bear Lake sparkled in the New Year's sun as it sailed higher and higher over Rocher Clark, a mountain on the far southern horizon. Now I no longer needed a gas lamp to see if I were sawing a board straight. The sunlight poured in through the mission's new windows, most of which faced south toward the lake.

The bluer skies were a promise of the fine weather to come with spring, when I hoped to be outside enjoying them, not still inside, harnessed in my carpenter's apron. To speed that day I enlisted help for the outside work so that I could finish the inside work faster.

First I gave a contract to Isidore Yukon and Victor Beyonnie to cut fifteen cords of firewood at eight dollars a cord. Then I hired Francis Baton to drive my dogs five hours a day, six days a week at seventy-five cents an hour, to bring this wood in from the bush and to visit my nets. Now I could devote myself entirely to the carpentry and at the same time my dogs would be working and kept in fine shape for the long hauls. Just like athletes, sled-dogs must be continually exercised in order to run well.

By mid-February it was time to go into Fort Norman again for the mail. Luckily, Jimmy Cleary, who the winter before had taught me the right way to camp out at night, accompanied me, along with Victor Menago. I drove my seven dogs and had the sled loaded with a hundred and fifty herring and three hind-quarters of caribou. Vicky and her three pups were in the team now and they pulled their hearts out. I couldn't get over the pace they set and kept up, hour after hour.

That night we camped in my tent which we set at the height of land right on the old burn where there is plenty of dry wood. The next morning I left the tent set for our return trip and put thirty-five herring in a gunny sack high in a spruce. That day we ran into a dozen caribou on a small lake and they would have disappeared into the bush at the far end had not Jimmy resorted to the old trick of firing over their heads into the trees beyond, causing them to wheel around and come back down the lake toward us. As they passed broadside both Jimmy and Victor opened fire on them with no effect. When they got down to the other end of this lake Jimmy was able to turn them once more with a shot into the timber ahead of them. I had not fired at first because of the small calibre of my rifle, a .22, while my compan-ions carried the standard .30-.30. When I saw no hits after the first pass, however, and they were coming back again I decided to give it a try. So all three of us joined in firing at them when they passed the second time. Again, none of them dropped and this time they were not fooled by a third shot over their heads to turn them. They kept on going up and into the bush as we looked stu-pidly at each other.

Then Victor thought he saw one of them go down in the deep snow off the lake, so we drove our dogs up there and, sure enough, we found one dead caribou. As we butchered it there was lots of speculation about which of us had hit it, but when a .22 long slug was found in the heart, speculation ended. The lowly .22 calibre rifle had proved more effective than the big guns. This fresh kill not only provided the ultimate in open-air cooking, a side of ribs for our lunch, but we all had fresh meat to carry with us into Norman, where we arrived at 7 p.m.

Brother Médard was especially grateful for what meat I had brought with me, for it had been a particularly hard winter to get meat, even rabbits. As I visited around the settlement during the following week I picked up rumours that caribou were in the area of Cleve Cinnamon's sawmill, some forty miles south on the Mackenzie. One thing led to another, and four local hunters eagerly joined me with their dog-teams for a caribou hunt in that area. It took a very short day to run up there with empty sleds and camp at the mill with Cleve and his crew who had killed caribou recently on the muskegs ten miles east across the river.

The following morning saw us crossing the frozen Mackenzie and then climbing a precipitous trail up a one-hundred-foot-high cutbank, and then on across country for an hour or so until we ran into the first fresh tracks. Then we tied our teams and proceeded on snowshoes, each in a different direction. It wasn't long before I spotted three bulls about a mile away in partly open country, walking slowly in my direction. I hid myself in a little island of spruce and waited nearly half an hour until they were so close I couldn't miss. Before leaving Bear Lake I had timed one of the natives out there while he skinned and butchered a young caribou – just over seven minutes. Now I kept track of my own time as I tackled these three bulls and it came to fifteen minutes each. There was room for improvement.

My trip back to the sawmill with my sled-load of meat was highlighted by our descent of that precipitous cutbank to the river. At the top of the bank I stopped and wound the heavy head rope around the load and under the sled, a manoeuvre called a roughlog. It afforded little breaking power, however, and it taxed all my strength to keep the sled from running over the dogs and breaking some of their legs.

Our return trip to Norman turned out to be something of a race. On the trip up two days before we had made fire on an island about half-way. Now one of the Fort Norman natives by the name of Ekokoolay, who was particularly proud of his team and often bragged of their speed, suggested that I go ahead and break trail to the fire spot and then he would take over from there. I agreed and took off in the lead, breaking trail in about four inches of snow that had fallen since we had come up. I got to the fire spot well ahead of my four companions, made a fire, boiled my tea and pulled out again just as they were coming up. Ekokoolay was yelling and waving at me to stop, but I paid no attention. He didn't even stop at the fire but swung right onto my trail determined to overtake me. When we passed close to some cutbanks he fired his rifle in an attempt to excite his dogs into thinking caribou were near, but even with this false encouragement he couldn't overtake me.

Far from having to encourage my dogs, I was worrying about them working so hard that they'd drop, especially the bitch Vicky. Once in a while when I'd stop for a rest, she would be panting so hard she looked like she would choke to death. I got into Norman before sundown, bells jingling and all seven tails waving triumphantly in the air, about four miles ahead of Ekokoolay and his comrades. He never again mentioned his dogs to me. For the first time I had a team of dogs I could be proud of. No longer would I be forced off the trail into deep snow to let faster teams pass or even get into camp at night after my companions were asleep, not to mention the charley horses that plagued me when I was forced to get off the sled and run for miles behind. On the other hand, having a good team did not make me any more popular with the natives; in fact, it seemed to rub them the wrong way, especially when I overtook them and they were forced off the trail to let me pass. Driving dogs was one of their specialties and for a newcomer to show them up took more humility than they could muster.

I made the return trip to Franklin alone in a day-and-a-half without getting out of the sled. When I arrived I was surprised to find the town practically empty. With the exception of the two whites and two old, crippled and blind couples, everyone had moved to the caribou muskegs eight miles south, where they were now living in fourteen tents.

After three more weeks devoted to the carpentry, I decided I needed a break and, driving over to the huge tent camp, moved in with the family of Arsene and Cecile Tetso. This gave me the opportunity of observing the people in intimate surroundings day and night, and my education in their way of living took a giant step forward.

The whole purpose of the tent camp was to be near the huge herd of caribou which had been feeding on the moss of this muskeg ever since our fall hunt. The men of the camp went out daily with their dog-teams, shot and butchered a few caribou and then returned to camp with their sled-load of meat. At this point the women took over to handle the meat and hides, most of which was temporarily thrown up on stages to keep it out of the reach of loose dogs, especially at night. With over 150 people crowded into tents, surrounded by 200 sled dogs, it was a lively scene.

As crowded as the tents were, there was always room for one more and during that first night in Arsene's tent we had to move over for a visitor from Fort Norman, Joe Dillon, a notorious rascal. He claimed that he had made the trip in thirteen hours, stopping only once to make fire, and this we could readily believe, because Joe's wicked, long-legged huskies were famous for their ability to cover ground in record time. The RCMP were aware of this, too; I happened to be visiting the barracks the winter before and watched the police entice Joe to part with five dogs by laying out 250 one-dollar bills on the table. He would never part with the huge bitch that produced these teams, however.

Joe was the darkest complexioned native I had seen and might have had some Negro blood in his veins. He told me of an incident when he was working as a guide on the Canol pipeline where the American Forces included a thousand black men whom their white counterparts often called "Midnight." Joe picked up the term and one day, when he greeted one of them, saying, "Hello there, Midnight," the black man, eyeing Joe's colour, replied, "You's about a quarter ta twelve youself!" Joe got a big kick out of it.

For a few years Joe was persona non grata at the Wells, accused of stealing equipment, but later he was re-hired to work at a salvage operation he had suggested. Joe had convinced the refinery manager at Imperial Oil that they were losing a lot of empty barrels off their dock during unloading operations. He offered to retrieve them for a dollar each. In order to do this work Joe installed himself and his wife Kapa in a tent a half-mile down river. It was soon apparent that far more drums were being lost than had been realized and Joe was busy from morning till night with his freighter canoe. Then one day the dock foreman happened to see an accomplice of Joe's "accidentally" kicking a barrel into the river and the scam was uncovered.

Another time at Fort Norman I had asked Joe if he knew of any old tent stove I could buy. The following day he brought me just what I needed and wouldn't accept a cent. I smelled a rat, but it was weeks before I heard a native talking about losing the stove from his tent across the river.

Joe threw his bedroll on the spruce boughs next to mine and snored peacefully that night as I recalled some of these incidents. True or not, the following day Joe proved himself to be quite a man in my eyes. We had decided to hunt together, harnessed up at first light and were off at breakneck speed in a crackling forty below. My team followed Joe's out of camp and all I could do was hold on to the handle bars as the small spruce raked our sleds and broke one of my mitt cords. Up ahead, there was Joe sitting nonchalantly inside his cariole facing backwards while, with bare hands, he proceeded to whittle a toothpick with his axe. Joe's performance could be compared to Gene Autrey's riding hell-bent-for-leather from a band of dangerous, mounted Apaches, arrows whistling all around him, while he sat backwards in the saddle rolling a cigarette. I was impressed.

In twenty minutes we entered the broad, open muskeg full of grazing caribou and Joe outlined his plan to drive a bunch of them right past me while I waited, concealed behind a clump of spruce. Joe carried out his drive perfectly, but when I raised my rifle to fire I couldn't pull the trigger and all the animals ran safely by me. Joe pulled up and we had a look at my gun. When I had broken the stock of this .270 earlier in the winter I had put an old stock on it without test-firing it. The trigger hole lacked about a quarter of an inch of clearance. It didn't take me long to make this adjustment with my jack-knife and we were successful in securing nine caribou with it before we returned to camp.

With our meat safely stowed up on Arsene's stage we retired to his tent for the night. And it was a night to remember: to my eyes it looked like something that might have happened in pre-historic times. We watched the children dig live warble fly larvae out of the fresh caribou hides and gobble them like jelly beans, while Arsene's ancient, toothless mother sat close to the candle cracking leg bones with the back of an old butcher knife to get at the marrow.

At the end of March I got an unexpected visitor in the person of Brother Henri Tesnière, flown in from Aklavik on orders from the bishop to help me finish the inside carpentry. Unfortunately he was about five months late and I had completed everything except the quarter-round moulding, which he finished in less than three days. Although he offered to spend the balance of the winter with me, he had instructions to proceed to Fort Smith to work on the construction of the new St. Anne's Hospital there as soon as my mission was completed, so I felt obliged to send him on. My aide-de-camp Naquerichile took him and his 300-pound tool box to Norman with my team.

Soon everyone moved back into the settlement to celebrate Easter. This time we not only had all the religious ceremonies connected with this great feast day, but I was able to hold the Ice Carnival the following day. With some difficulty I was able to persuade some of the younger men to run their dogs in a five-mile race out around the flags I had stuck in the snow of the bay, while the older men raced the clock to chip down to water with their ice chisels. Most of the afternoon, however, was occupied shooting at targets, a life-size caribou at two hundred yards for the men, using their .30-.30's, and a ptarmigan for the women, who shot with a .22. In the evening I awarded prizes to the winners. This was followed by a drum dance in the mission common room.

As the old log mission was now unoccupied, Joe Dillon asked to use it temporarily. I let him have it on condition that he didn't make any brew while he was in there. One day I could hear Joe's wife Kapa singing her drinking song, "You are my sunshine," so I made an excuse to go over there to look for something I had left in the attic. There I found a ten-gallon keg of simmering firewater. Joe feigned surprise and blamed it all on Kapa. Soon after, he returned to his home at Fort Norman and I got new tenants in the old mission, Arsene Tetso and his family.

Arsene needed a roof over his family's head because his little five-year-old boy John was sick. He had started getting headaches in the fall and would wake up at night crying. I kept a record of his pulse and temperature for a week and wired all the symptoms to the doctor in Aklavik. He replied that he suspected spinal meningitis and advised me to get the boy to Fort Norman for evacuation to hospital as soon as possible. When I discussed this with Arsene the first thing he did was to ask the boy if he wanted to go to the hospital. Of course, the boy said, "No!" This reply seemed to settle the matter for Arsene, but I was more insistent, trying to convince him that it was a matter of life or death. I offered to take the boy into Norman myself and to keep him with me until he left, but I could not get the father to agree. They left to spend the winter in the bush. When I camped with them at the big muskeg while caribou hunting, the boy seemed to be improving. I saw him out playing without a hat and running to the neighbour's tent bare-footed. After Easter, however, little John was worse again, and when they moved into the old mission house I was acutely aware of his suffering.

He began throwing up his food and was soon so weak that he lost all desire to play. His mother Cecile kept him in bed with no objections from him while I tempered my needle-and-penicillin visits by making sure I had some little gift with me which I let him search through my pockets to find. When he was more or less free from pain he would entertain me by playing a miniature drum his father had made him and singing one of the dance songs in imitation of the elders. Yet most days he would just lie there holding his little head and crying, *"Se kwi eya! Se kwi eya!"* – "My head hurts! My head hurts!" As the weeks dragged on and his condition deteriorated, his poor mother reflected his pain and tried in vain to alleviate it. Having already lost three of her six children, she was no stranger to sickness and death.

As the disease progressed and little John got worse, they took him from his wooden bed and placed him in the middle of the cabin floor, where I would invariably find him surrounded by visitors. Finally he began having fits or seizures that caused his muscles to twitch, while he ground his teeth and muttered incoherently. The good women of the village stayed by his side day and night holding his little hands and feet during seizures and putting a stick wrapped in caribou skin between his teeth so he wouldn't break them. I looked in vain in my *Merck Manual* for any medicine I could give him in addition to the penicillin, but could find none. Evidently tubercular meningitis was impossible to cure under these circumstances.

We did persevere in prayer, too, hoping for the miracle that never happened. I realized that his days were numbered, and yet when his time expired and the women ran to tell me, yelling, "Negille! Negille!" – "He's not breathing! He's not breathing!" – I felt a sudden pang of grief I hadn't felt with the other deaths we had experienced. I rushed to his side and felt for a pulse that was not there, but I could only watch helplessly as his mother kept rubbing his little limbs and calling him back through her tears. He was gone. Finally she raised her voice in that heart-rending chant of grief, the keening peculiar to her race, mournful and desolate. I think all of us standing by died a little that day with young John Tetso.

That afternoon Arsene came over with a notched length of spruce pole to indicate his son's length and together in silence we built a pine box. I suppose I could have told him that his son might still be alive if he had let me take him to the hospital the fall before, but what was the use now? The next day was a clear, warm Sunday in May. After the eleven o'clock mass we put the small casket on Arsene's sled and pulled it up to the cemetery. There on that peaceful knoll covered with caribou moss and sheltered by some huge pines we took turns digging down four feet into the soft sand. After I had blessed the grave and said the ritual prayers the box was lowered and the women, using tin plates as shovels, filled up the hole. Then Arsene and Cecile knelt by the grave's cross, praying, caressing that cross as if it were a part of their son. And above it, on a ten-foot pole, waved a small white flag which, I was informed, was put there to amuse the soul of the departed so that it would not leave the body until the day of judgement, when both would be reunited again and ascend to the Heavenly Father. All the graves had them and I thought it a rather nice custom dating back to pre-historic times and asserting this people's belief in an afterlife.

As I got closer to these people I became more aware that such old customs, superstitions – call them what you will – were still part of their lives. For example, I was on my way to Fort Norman by dogs the winter before, when one of the women came walking toward me with an armful of fish, suddenly dropped them, and ran back. I found out later that she had noticed the end sticks of a net set under the ice and it was taboo for her to cross any net. For a woman to break this taboo would doom that net from catching any more fish for its owner. This rule applied to nets set in open water in summertime too and, if those in a canoe could not avoid crossing a net, the women were first let off on the shore to walk until the net had been passed. In fact, almost all the taboos affected the women alone.

I had a bear skin on the floor at the door to my office and at first I didn't realize all the difficulty this was causing my female parishioners who, to get past it, had to shuffle along one side with their feet under the hide. As soon as I was made aware of this taboo, I moved it.

Pilot training in a WACO F-7, 1940.

The D.C.-3 that took me to Norman Wells, the northern terminus for Canadian Pacific
Airlines. It was December 1948, and the temperature was 44 degrees below zero (F).
I continued on to Fort Norman the next day with pilot Mike Zubko in his Waco biplane.

The Fort Norman Mission, built of logs, was an outpost since 1859.

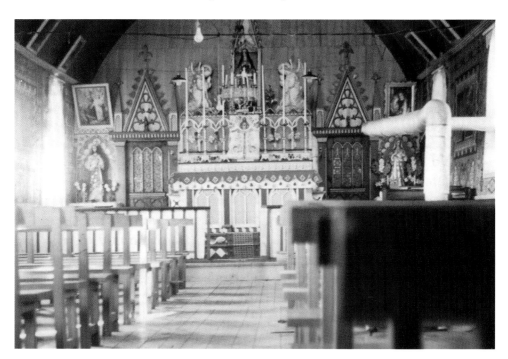

Inside St. Theresa Church. The paintings were done on the walls using powdered paint from France mixed with local fish oil. This church was torn down in 1962, but six of the windows and the two statues went into the Colville Lake church in 1964.

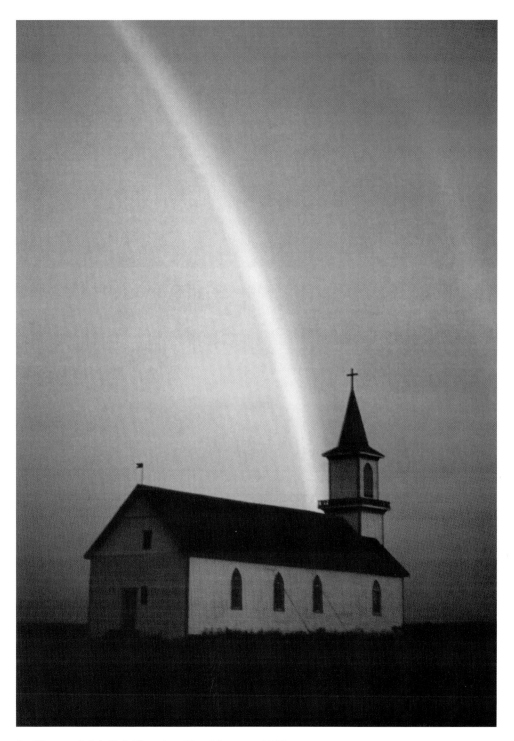

St. Theresa (of Avila) Church at Fort Norman, 1949.

Bringing in a load of firewood, 1949. As soon as I learned to drive dogs at Fort Norman I would spend most afternoons getting firewood or hunting ptarmigan.

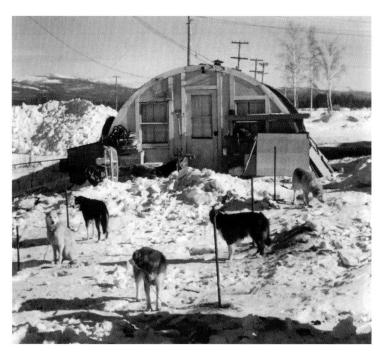

The Quonset hut chapel at Norman Wells, across from the RCAF mess hall, 1949.

Splitting a birch root at Fort Norman, 1949. To make the handles of a toboggan we use the natural bend of a birch root for strength.

At Canyon Creek. During 1949–50, I often travelled from Fort Norman to Norman Wells in this 22-foot freighter canoe, always stopping to visit the Tourangeaus here, 12 miles south (upstream) from the Wells.

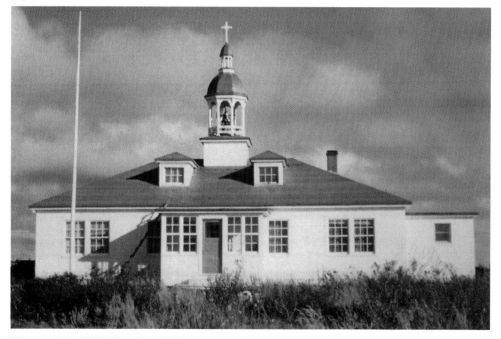

The completed Mission St. Thérèse at Fort Franklin, just before freeze-up, August 1950. The mission was boarded up in 1997.

During the first year at Fort Franklin only three aircraft visited me, including this De Havilland Beaver on skis. Teacher Roy Gravel stands to the left.

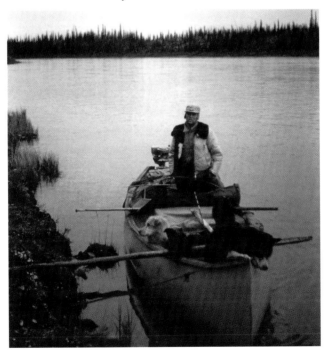

On Great Bear River headed for Fort Franklin, 1950. During the building of Mission St. Therese (Little Flower) at Fort Franklin that year, I made five round-trips to Fort Norman for supplies. On my last trip I brought up the Norman Mission's dog-team.

The Mission and church at Goldfields. We skidded both these buildings over to the new Uranium City on the ice. The church, right, later burned to the ground.

Baptizing two Chipewyan babies at Goldfields. These Chipewyan people came into Goldfields from Fond du Lac (100 miles east on Lake Athabaska) in the summer for casual work.

Philip Stenne and I working to get Mission St. Bernard closed in before freeze-up, Summer 1952.

Down by the shore of Lake Athabaska in front of Mission St. Bernard, painting a water-colour sketch. Local Cree natives watch, fascinated.

Completed Mission St. Bernard, 1953, with sled dogs and fish house.

At Johnson's trading post on the Slave River between Fort Chipewyan and Fort Smith.
I examine one of the blocks of frozen milk he sold.

Philip Stenne en route from Camsell Portage to Fort Smith, with Spider Island in the background.

Standing before the only painting I did during my four years at Camsell Portage.

In front of the old St. Anne's Hospital, Fort Smith, 1953. These Oblates are walking back to the adjacent Mission after a conference.

Mission "Our Lady of Seven Sorrows" at Fond du Lac, 1953. Fr. Charles Gamache, O.M.I., stands on the porch with his flock of Chipewyan natives.

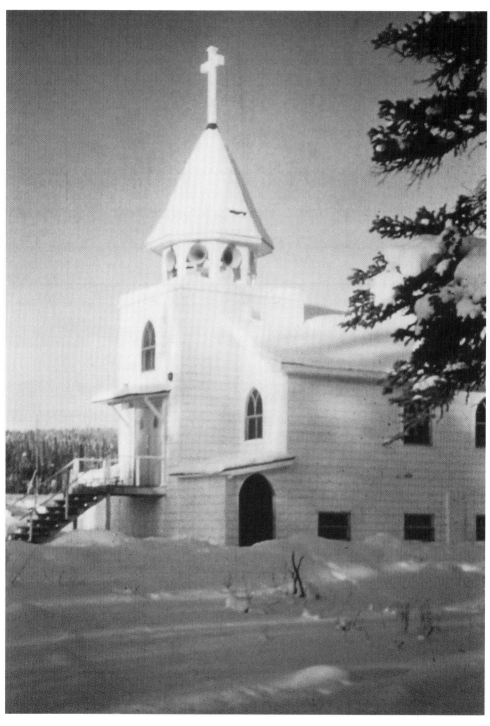

The completed Santa Barbara church at Uranium City, 1963, built by Burns & Dutton Contractors on the site of the burned-out church from Goldfields.

The *Sant'Anna* departed from Belle Rock near Fort Smith for the Arctic Coast twice every summer.

Bishop Breynat points to my future.

Re-canvassing the freighter canoe (a V-stern 22-foot Peterborough).

I was puzzled for a long time over the fact that young girls were tied to the centre pole of their tents just after they had learned to walk. I thought to myself that they were being restrained from running outside where they could be bitten by one of the sled dogs. I found out that the real reason for this was to keep them from inadvertently walking over a man's blanket or maybe putting on his cap, both strictly taboo for a girl.

One day Chief Francis Eya walked into the mission, as was his usual morning habit, and announced to me that a certain girl was having her first menstrual period. When I asked him what she would do to celebrate, he informed me that she would have to stay indoors for a month and that during this time she couldn't eat any choice food or sweets or she would be fond of a soft life all her years. Nor could she even look at a knife or she would be lazy. Just how any Hareskin woman could escape the drudgery of her race to a soft or lazy life seemed hard to imagine. Later, one of the women told me just how difficult her periods could make a woman's life. Besides having to inform the household and restrict her movement about, if they happened to be travelling she could not ride on the sled, nor even use the same trail. Instead she was obliged to break her own trail alongside! One can just imagine what this must have cost her if the snow was deep and she was forced to use snowshoes.

The women were also warned about leaving any stray hairs from their head lying about, under penalty of having to return after death to find every one of them. To avoid this they would stand by the fire when they combed their heads and put any loose hair directly into it. If the fire in the stove popped and hissed, as it often does when a pocket of sap burns, they must immediately feed the fire by throwing in a morsel of food: this was the evil spirit asking to be fed. There was a set formula to be said at the same time which meant: "Make me happy, fire, and give me a long life. Thank you."

Although these taboos made life so miserable for the women, it puzzled me that it was the older women especially who taught them to the young girls. When these girls asked me what I thought about them, I had to admit that I could see very little in them that contradicted Christianity and so they could observe them if they wished. Nonetheless, I had to add that I thought they could get to heaven just as easily by not keeping these taboos. Just keeping the ten commandments was work enough for any Christian. I could not help recalling the passage in Luke's Gospel in which Jesus addresses the penitent woman, saying, "Your faith has been your salvation. Now go in peace."

Not many of the taboos affected the men of the tribe and those that did caused little difficulty. On several occasions, however, I was asked to lend my rifle to shoot a wolf, as they believed that using their own for that purpose would jinx it for good. Being a white man, I was exempt from the effects of this taboo. Another admonition was never to strike a wounded caribou with a stick, though why anybody would resort to this means to dispatching the animal was not at all clear. If a hunter were out of shells, a blow to the animal's head with an axe, which everyone carried, would be far more effective.

Although there was at least one person living on Bear Lake who possessed a good deal of medicine power, called Inkon, I never heard of him actually performing any seances in exercise of this power. At Fort Norman I witnessed old David Yukon put on a performance the summer before. His patient, ironically named George Doctor, was suffering from torn ligaments in his shoulder and, although he had been to the nurse first, he didn't think he was healing fast enough. So he contracted David to work native medicine on him for the price of one tanned moose hide. Although David had a log cabin he preferred to practise his art in a tent where both doctor and patient sat cross-legged facing each other across the fire. David beat on a drum and chanted incantations for hours on end. One of the bystanders warned me not to walk behind David or he would automatically "eat your spirit," weakening his magic powers.

George submitted to the full treatment, paid the fee and was back at the nursing station the following day for more of the free white man's medicine. When I talked to him later, he confessed that he wasn't sure just what power, if any, David could conjure up, but when a person is in pain he will look for help from anyone. I got the same opinion from some of the youth at Franklin, who were sceptical of these old taboos, yet observed some of them just in case there was some truth in them. At least observing the minimum satisfied their more traditional parents and provided a fire escape if the dire predictions for those breaking the taboos proved true after all. This attitude reminded me of a grizzled old trapper I met at Fort Fitzgerald when I was coming into the North. Seeing my clerical garb, he was encouraged to regale me with his philosophy of life, which went something like this: "You only live once. Right, Father? So I whoop it up every time I get the chance. On the other hand, you never can tell, there might just be a hell after all, so I do a lot of praying too!"

After the death of little John Tetso, Arsene, following custom, moved his family out of the old mission cabin. They didn't seem to fear death itself as much as they feared the dead, the spirits surrounding the dead and the places where they died. I didn't mind using what little knowledge I had of medicine to help them, but those cases that ended in death – five during my first year there – were particularly frustrating and discouraging. When a few days later young Marie Naedzo came to me with a huge gash in her wrist and I was able to close it successfully with nine stitches, I felt I was accomplishing something. Soon after that Victor Beyonnie came with an axe cut in his ankle which I stitched up, but it festered later and I had to put him on penicillin shots to clear up the infection. The mission door was never locked, so if I were needed during the night for some medical emergency and I was asleep, the messenger would come right into my bedroom and hold a lit match in front of my eyes until I awakened. I learned later that this was standard procedure, because if a person is awakened too abruptly the spirit might not be able to rejoin the body in time and death would result.

About the middle of May the men of the village left town for the spring hunt of muskrat and beaver. Most took a thirteen-foot hunting canoe with them as well as some pack dogs, especially the older dogs, as they had outlived their usefulness and were making a one-way trip. Now that I had most of the essential inside work done, I turned to working out in the warm spring sun and built myself one of those hunting canoes, followed by a steel-shod runner-type sled the Eskimos call a *komatik* and the Bear Lakers call a *dechunkala,* literally "a ladder," because with its spaced wooden rungs across the top it resembles one.

When the wildfowl began flying north overhead I had little difficulty persuading the Hudson Bay manager Bob Williams to close up the store and accompany me on our own spring mini-hunt. I had new moose-hide moccasins for my team to protect them from the candling ice. With my new canoe on top of the komatik we headed northeast along the shore of the lake. With the surface snow melted down to a hard ice, the travelling was easy and the sun so hot we hardly needed parkas. Canada geese flew so low over us we actually shot some without getting off the sled. About twenty-five miles down the lake we set up our tent next to a small open lake, where we had ducks landing all night long and a midnight sun to shoot by.

Back at the mission three days later I built a few more chairs and put a new canvas on my twenty-two-foot freighter canoe. Open water was beginning to appear in the bay ice and the sight of ducks landing on it was too great a temptation to resist. One day I harnessed three dogs to the komatik and ran around on the ice near the settlement, shooting ducks in these spots of open water. I was using a lead dog named Taffy that I had bought from Victor Dolphus. When he saw a wounded duck flapping around on one of these open spots in the lake ice, he headed straight for it. I grabbed my shotgun and .22 and slid off the sled, just before it followed the dogs into the deep water. Taffy grabbed the wounded duck in his mouth, swam to the ice edge, and pulled himself out, followed by the other two dogs and the sled. They headed directly home. When I got there I found the duck sitting in my kitchen sink, still very much alive. My neighbour Beya had taken it from Taffy's mouth and put it safely inside the mission house. After that I quit hunting ducks by dog-team.

Toward the end of June, with no mail for months and old-age pensioners badly in need of their monthly sixty-five-dollar cheques, I decided to make the trip to Fort Norman. I had written the postal authorities requesting a monthly mail delivery by air, but was turned down because of our small population. Just as soon as there was enough open water along the shore I shoved off with a teenager named Onkie in my big freighter canoe powered by the faithful nine-horse Johnson. We got around the edge of the lake ice, but for the first ten miles down the Great Bear River I could not start the motor because the floating ice was so thick. Our arrival at Fort Norman coincided with the passage of the mission supply boat *Sant'Anna* heading down river and, because I had been suffering from toothaches, I decided to go at least as far as Norman Wells with her to seek the services of a dentist. Although the RCAF mapping contingent was still operating out of the Wells, they had no one capable of fixing teeth, but offered me a quick flight to Yellowknife on one of their Lancaster bombers. I not only got to ride on this historic plane, but when the crew heard that I had held a pilot's licence they let me handle the controls for a segment of the flight. My headphones were connected to the navigator on board and all I had to do was make the heading corrections he gave me.

While getting my teeth fixed in Yellowknife I resided at the log mission in the Old Town with the famous Father Alfred Gathy, a colourful character who sped around town on a motorcycle, his cassock flying in the wind. There were a lot of interesting people to visit around Yellowknife and it was a treat to be speaking my own language again. Henry Busse, the town's official photographer, showed me some of his interesting collection. Coming as I did from the Kodak City of Rochester, New York, it was only natural that I had carried a camera north with me and, although I didn't have it on this trip, I did have some of the thousand 35 mm slides I had taken while at Fort Franklin. One evening when I was showing them at the home of the mining engineer, Norm Byrne, he had as guest a young writer named Pierre Berton, to whom I sold a lot of photos later when he became Managing Editor of *Maclean's* magazine. One day Father

Gathy sent me by the mission canoe over to the Indian village on Vale Island to conduct services for the natives living there and the editor of the local newspaper, Ted Horton, sent his son with me to act as acolyte. Another day I took a walk up the dirt road two miles to the new townsite, where the only completed building was the new theatre. The new site of Yellowknife seemed to be out in the middle of nowhere and not nearly as picturesque as the original townsite along the blue waters of Yellowknife Bay. Fort Smith was still the unofficial capital of the Northwest Territories, but later Yellowknife would be officially designated.

After returning to Norman Wells I got a ride upstream to Fort Norman with Dolphus Norris in his roomy scow. From there I went on up the Great Bear River in my canoe, loaded with provisions. I hired a crew to go ten miles up along the north shore, and help me cut fifteen cords of green spruce, and raft them back to the settlement for next winter's fuel supply. With a team of growing huskies and eight hungry pups I had to visit my nets every day and make plans to get ahead on the dog food for the coming winter. So late in August I decided to move my fishing operation up along the north shore to a place known as Finger Bay. I invited my old friend Aunty Zole, another old crony, Natuzo, plus my steady worker, Naquerichile, to go with me.

Just before I set out, the Hudson Bay Company Beaver aircraft landed with a Mr. Scurfield, the District Manager, making the annual tour of his posts. He walked over to the mission with the mail he had picked up en route at Fort Norman and we chewed the fat for a few minutes. The war in Korea, he said, was threatening to close down so many of their northern stores that he was forced to raise the price of gas from $1.00 to $1.10 a gallon and other staples similarly. I took my unopened mail and ran down to the shore where my companions were patiently waiting in my canoe.

It was only after pitching tent thirty miles down the lake that I got a chance to open my mail. One letter that immediately caught my eye was postmarked Fort Smith and, as I suspected, it was from the bishop. What I didn't suspect was that it would terminate my life at Fort Franklin. It was a new obedience. I was being assigned to Goldfields, Saskatchewan! As I read on I learned the reason for this sudden transfer: a new mining town was soon to be built at a uranium discovery just north of Gold-fields. Because it would be populated mostly by English-speak-ing whites, the bishop needed an English-speaking priest there to start that mission.

In view of this turn of events I pulled up my nets the follow-ing day and headed back to Franklin. Two days later I received a message from Fort Norman via the HBC telegraph that the bishop was already winging his way north in his new plane with my replacement and would arrive in a few days. I packed my trunk and put the mission in A-1 shape, even baking a new batch of bread. Seeing that I still had time, I got busy building a badly needed dock. It was out fifty feet by the sixth of September when the bishop's Aeronca float plane appeared in the sky. Father Bill Leising, another American, was the one chosen to pilot it and he was now making his first flight north. For the first time, too, a float aircraft could taxi right in to shore and its passengers step off dry-shod onto terra firma.

I led the way on a tour of the new mission and premises, proud to show how much I and my people had accomplished during the past two years on less than eight thousand dollars. His Excellency seemed pleased with this latest in his chain of some forty-odd missions throughout the North. He predicted that my experience in carpentry work here would stand me in good stead as I started my next mission on Lake Athabaska.

The next morning the bishop presided at a Solemn High Mass and conferred the Sacrament of Confirmation on twenty-two young aspirants. It was a fitting climax and the ultimate use to which this new building could be put no matter how many years it would stand. I took advantage of the occasion to say a few words of farewell to my parishioners. If my halting Hareskin carried a note of sadness in it, it was genuine. In the future I would be working with many different peoples of the North, from Crees to Eskimos, but with none of them would I establish such a close bond as I had with the people of Fort Franklin.

After lunch Bill Leising flew the bishop back to Fort Norman and brought back my successor, Father Victor Philippe, with whom I had only a few minutes to share before my departure. Worst of all, the small cabin size of the Aeronca prevented me from taking my trunk or even one female dog with which to start up a new team. I showed Victor all the precious objects he was inheriting: not only the bright, snug mission, but the newly canvassed canoe at its new dock, seven fine sled-dogs plus the new litter of six brothers, the harnesses embroidered in silk, the two sleds and the large hunting canoe, three pairs of new snowshoes in the attic and three nets set in the lake. Nothing was lacking for the new incumbent. It was lucky for him, but wrenching for me to be so suddenly uprooted.

I finally got a chance to ride in the new aircraft that had been donated to the diocese, but it was a short trip. We took off at 2 p.m. and headed for Fort Norman, where I was to catch the *Sant'Anna* on her return trip up river. We were hardly half-way when the cylinder head temperature gauge shot up into the red, indicating trouble, and we were forced to put down on a small lake which was just where we needed it. We were stymied, however, in our efforts to locate the trouble, because the aircraft's set of Snap-On tools had been stolen off the dock at Fort Resolution the week before. Our only chance of getting help was through the aircraft's VHF radio, set to the Department of Transport's frequency, and we kept calling every half-hour. By supper time we had broken out the box of emergency rations; they were very sparse and mouldy. I took a walk around the lake with the .22, but couldn't even find a muskrat. The two of us squeezed into the Aeronca's cabin and tried to stretch out on its floor, passing the night in fitful sleep.

September 8th, the feast of the Birth of the Blessed Virgin Mary, a feast important to the Oblates, dawned foggy and wet with the temperature close to freezing. We resumed broadcasting blindly on the aircraft's radio, giving our position and predicament, rekindled the fire on shore and stood around it helplessly, trying to revive our spirits. Had we known it, we had reason to rejoice, because our message had been picked up by Royal Canadian Signalman Moe Lynn at Fort Wrigley, who had a reputation for picking up distress calls. At that moment help was on the way. A search and rescue C-47 aircraft had been searching for bush pilot Johnny Bourassa east of Great Bear Lake and refuelling at Norman Wells. They got our co-ordinates from Moe and were soon circling overhead, dropping three kegs of 80/87 Aviation gas, a wrench attached to a long streamer, and a note saying, "We will continue to orbit until you take off"! Apparently they figured that we were simply out of gas. What neither they nor we knew at the time was that we had a hole the size of a half-dollar through the head of No. 5 piston. The Aeronca wouldn't get airborne for another couple of days.

They soon left us, but it wasn't long before we heard the raucous sound of a Norseman aircraft approaching from the south. It turned out to be the Eldorado machine which was just finishing up their summer's work at Port Radium and ferrying men over to Bennett Field when they got word of our trouble from the RCAF Dakota. Our rescuers were pilot Don Ferris and engineer George Franks, who lent us his tools. When Bill Leising heard that they were on their way to the mine at Beaverlodge near Goldfields, he urged me to take advantage of this direct flight. Reluctantly abandoning my plans for a trip upriver and a chance to see new areas of the North, I agreed. I left on the Norseman, while Bill got a new piston up from Edmonton flown in by Pappy Hill. Ferris flew us back to the Great Bear River where he dropped off Franks. Then, because it was too late to cross Bear Lake, we decided to overnight at Franklin and landed in the small lake just west of the village.

As we walked through the village to the mission, the people thought that the bishop had changed his mind and sent me back. I felt like MacArthur returning to Corregidor with everyone running to greet me and following us right into the mission. It was difficult to explain to them all that had happened since 2 p.m. the previous afternoon and how I was now headed east instead of west. Anyway, I told them that I would conduct one last service the following morning, but it would have to be at 6 a.m., because we had a long flight ahead of us. The standing-room-only crowd that filled the chapel the next morning was the finest tribute I could have gotten from the people of Fort Franklin.

Our long walk through town and back to the aircraft provided a chance for further demonstrations of affection: little children breaking away from their parents and running after me, calling *"Yati"* – "Father," and wanting to be picked up for one last time and carried at least a few steps; Rosie Baton putting down her water pails, drying her hands on her apron before shaking hands; Cecile Tatti running to give me a farewell present, an embroidered tobacco pouch. Now I was glad the Aeronca had let us down, and doubly so, for now I had room to take my trunk, and one of the dogs. So I chose the pure white bitch Trinket. At least I had a living souvenir of two great years on the shores of Great Bear Lake.

10

GOLDFIELDS

Sunday, September 9th, 1951: a grey, dull, rainy day over Great Bear Lake, the weather perfectly in tune with my feelings as we taxied out and took off from Fort Franklin. I occupied the right front seat of the Norseman, with pilot Don Ferris at the controls to my left and Trinket crouched on the floor behind me, next to my trunk.

We headed east along the south shore of Keith Arm, flying over the legendary Gorabee Island, past Grizzly Bear Mountain, on across open water to Eldorado Mine on the east shore of the lake. We landed on Echo Bay and taxied up to the dock to refuel. There was no time to walk up to the cookhouse for coffee. In this kind of flying weather pilots tend to be in a particular hurry. Ferris was irritable and profane to boot. We filled both wing tanks and headed due south. The rain turned to snow, forcing us to fly just above the trees all the way to Yellowknife, where we again landed to refuel. Again, there was no time to visit. It was a race against the weather and the remaining daylight hours. I took Trinket out for a brief walk-around and we were again airborne across Great Slave Lake. Ferris noticed me praying my rosary and asked if I doubted his flying abilities. I didn't, but in flying weather like this a prayer for heavenly protection couldn't hurt.

At 6 p.m. we finally reached the north shore of Lake Athabaska. We could soon make out the huge headframe of the old Box Mine and, close to it, the town of Goldfields. I breathed a sigh of relief as we touched down on the protected bay in front of it and taxied to the town dock. The wooden buildings were scattered between huge rock outcrops and had those high, false fronts one associates with the western frontier. The few locals who sauntered down to the waterfront no doubt saw something unusual: out of the float plane came a young figure in black soutane leading a white sled-dog – obviously some sort of missionary. At least they weren't repelled by my clerical appearance, for a few of the boys took my luggage and led me to the RCMP barracks. Meanwhile the pilot took off to fly over to Eldorado's camp on Beaverlodge Lake a few miles north.

The local Mountie, Constable Bill Poole, received me cordially and walked me to the R.C. Mission, a clapboard church and rectory badly in need of paint, thoroughly abandoned and locked up tight. We had to break the padlock on the rectory door. Once in I was confronted by an empty barn of a place, two storeys high, practically empty of furniture and cooking utensils, draped in cobwebs with a very creaky floor. It was the exact opposite of the bright new mission I had left that morning at Fort Franklin. I sat down on my trunk and pulled out my pipe to ponder the situation. The constable dusted off a wooden bench and sat down gingerly, half expecting it to collapse under him as he remarked, "Understand there's been no one living here since Father Rivet was killed some ten years ago."

Father Rivet? My predecessor, killed? Right here? This was all news to me. Still, didn't it fit in with the general atmosphere of the place? I couldn't wait to hear the whole story and the young Mountie pieced it together as best he could from what the remaining old-timers had told him. The old missionary in his seventies had had a clique of enemies in Goldfields, men dead set against him. Some say that it was because he was instrumental in getting a couple of prostitutes run out of town. Whatever the reason, they hatched a grisly plan to get rid of him. One of their accomplices acted as a lookout upstairs, right above where we were sitting. He sat by the window, munching sandwiches, waiting for the priest to return on that ill-fated night. Then Father

Rivet completely disappeared from the community. Nobody had seen anything. Nobody knew anything.

Some six weeks later a group of Boy Scouts on a picnic three miles east of the town discovered his body at the foot of a cliff. There followed some sort of a frontier inquest and trial but it was mostly hush-hush. Names of some prominent men in town, including the doctor, were mentioned. It seemed as though a lot of people knew more than they were willing to tell. Father Rivet's superior, Bishop Breynat, never pressed the case. He simply closed up this mission and never even mentioned it in his published memoirs. This was the gist of what the constable told me that first night, but later in cleaning up the house I came across an interesting set of notes obviously written by someone following these events who had been doing some private investigating. This prompted him to ask the following questions:

Why were Botten and Hargreaves seen coming from the bush (in the direction where the body was later found) at four in the morning when they should have been coming off their eight p.m. to four a.m. shift at the Consolidated Mining and Smelting (Box) Mine?

Why was Cox, the manager of the local Bank of Montreal, seen running from the mission around midnight of that same night?

Why did Sam Hargreaves report to the policemen Ball and Lowe that the Father was missing at four in the morning?

Why were the scouts told by their director, Rev. Mr. Heather, on the day of their picnic, that if they looked in a certain section of the bush they would find something?

Why was the found body left wrapped in a piece of canvas on the point two days before an autopsy was performed by Dr. Brownridge?

Why would Police Inspector Desrosiers tell the two Catholics serving on the jury that he wanted a verdict "death by exposure" returned when the trial was held?

Why was a certain page torn from the Father's diary?

Why? Why? Why? Plenty of questions, but no answers. Had
I inherited an unsolved murder? Now, ten years later, would it
be advisable for me to raise the issue or even ask any questions?
I decided it would not. I also decided I wouldn't eat at the
haunted mission that night. So the constable and I walked downtown and had supper at Hap Cave's restaurant. Later I borrowed
a sleeping bag and a flashlight from the barracks and returned to
the darkened rectory. I did not sleep well that first night.

The following morning the blue waters of the bay sparkled
under a bright cobalt sky and my world looked rosier. I put on
my cassock and cross and walked down to Steve Yanik's hotel
and ordered breakfast, which was cheerfully served by a girl
known as Bubbles. Everyone seated around that counter seemed
friendly and eager to tell me about their town. I soon found out
that there were three restaurants, plus a bakery. There was also
the usual Hudson Bay Company store, plus two free-traders
with their own stores. McMurray Air Service ran a charter service out of the town, featuring four-place Stinsons. There was a
resident geologist and a mining recorder, a game officer and a
radio operator, a post office and a pool room that doubled as the
local theatre.

Although the town had been built on gold, I soon learned
that this mineral was passé, having been supplanted by uranium.
The radioactive mineral was the new topic of conversation and,
not only that, there was talk about moving Goldfields holus-
bolus over on the ice in winter ten miles to a new townsite to be
called Uranium City. With all this information under my hat and
a good breakfast under my belt, I lit my pipe and walked out.

Meeting two Chipewyan Indians outside, I tried out my
Hareskin language on them with discouraging results. It was
obvious that I would now be faced with learning a new dialect.
There were also some Crees in town whose language was absolutely foreign to me, but luckily they did speak some French.

Noticing some pots and pans in a window I wandered into
Alec MacIver's General Store and was pleasantly served by his
wife Del. When I walked out half-an-hour later I was laden down

with most of the vital items missing at the mission, like an axe, a gas lamp, a basin, pots and pans and some basic grub. I returned to my empty quarters and began a general cleanup. That afternoon, to get the dust out of my lungs, I went for a walk around the west end of the bay and came upon the one-room school house. I was invited in to meet the thirty-four children in attendance by their charming teacher, Miss Evelyn Lamontagne. Before I knew it I was at the blackboard drawing pictures of animals and cowboys or anything else my attentive audience requested, and the ice was broken.

As the days wore on I gradually met everyone in town including the average number of characters. One of the most unusual was a displaced Englishman named Gus Hawker, who operated one of the trading posts. He told me that his native wife deserted him in Fort McMurray and he was raising their six kids alone. Four of them he had named after months of the year; April, May, June and August. June was only thirteen at the time, but three years later when she turned sixteen, Gus married her! Just how he managed this legally I never heard. One year he made *Time Magazine* when he took a dozen beaver hides to Buckingham Palace and presented them to the Queen in the name of all Canadians. His store was an absolute mess, with everything thrown helter-skelter, the floor littered with mixed grub and hardware, and his money thrown in cardboard boxes. He claimed to be a member of my flock, but, like a lot of other nominal Catholics in town, I never saw him in church.

Another day I discovered a Mrs. Livingstone living alone in a house hidden among the rocks and trees. Her husband was a prospector and was seldom at home. To keep her company during his long absences she had acquired about two dozen cats which she kept inside, fearful of the sled-dogs roaming the town. She had opened a trap door into the attic and had a special ramp built so the cats could use the upper floor as their play area. I sat there drinking tea with her, her pets constantly going to and coming from the attic. Only the aromatic smoke from my pipe overcame the heavy scent of cat gas in the air and I marvelled that a person could live in such an atmosphere.

According to Gordon Carruthers, who ran the pool hall and sold beer on the side, Goldfields was an unusually thirsty town: it took a minimum of 700 cases of beer a month to quench that thirst. The effects of this addiction was particularly notable on Saturday nights. On one of these a group of inebriates got hold of the good constable and threw him in a mud hole. One midnight I answered a knock at the rectory door and a Mrs. Montgomery asked if I would accompany her to the church: her husband was on a drunk and in that condition he often felt religious. Sure enough, we did find him slumped over one of the benches. So if old John Barleycorn brought out the worst in some townsfolk, it brought out the best in others.

Constable Poole and Game Officer Chick Terry were making a trip over to the new Eldorado uranium mine site and invited me along. As we portaged the freighter canoe from Lake Athabaska some three hundred yards into Beaverlodge Lake we passed the cemetery and my eye fell upon the grave of Father Rivet. I said nothing to my companions. What was the awful secret that lay buried there with him? There was no answer to this question, but it disturbed and troubled me. My gloomy thoughts were soon chased from my mind by the bright, warm sun lighting up the colourful fall foliage. Chick picked off a half-dozen ducks with his twelve-gauge as we motored east into Beaverlodge Lake.

The Beaverlodge townsite was fronted by a long, sandy beach and the new homes were being constructed among the trees without disturbing them. Unlike the old townsite of Goldfields, there were no rocky outcroppings among dilapidated buildings. We pulled our boat up on the beach and walked up to the administration building. I was lucky to meet and have lunch in the "Blue Room" with some of the top men in the Eldorado hierarchy, including the President, Bill Bennett, the District Manager, Dr. E. B. (Gil) Gillanders, the Mine Manager, Robert Sexsmith, and the President of the Northern Transportation

Company, Frank Broderick. Also present at the table were a Mr. Merrit from the U.S. Atomic Energy Control Board and a Mr. Gooding from Saskatchewan Natural Resources. Our conversation centred on the building of the new townsite, to be called Uranium City, five miles west of the mine site. Following the meal I had a private meeting with Bennett and Gillanders about my role in serving the mine as chaplain and I was urged to begin at the earliest moment, possibly working out of the Goldfields mission as accommodations were at a premium at this stage of the Beaverlodge operation.

Back at Goldfields I continued to get acquainted. It was the rare walk through town when I didn't run into some inebriated character who didn't profess to be a good Catholic. I got into endless discussions on faith and morals and the meaning of life every time I took a meal at the hotel. Often I ate with the many native families who were drawn into town during the summer to take casual jobs.

Perhaps in their home settlements the natives were faithful to their religious obligations, but here on their "vacations," so to speak, they were slow to respond to the church bell. Nevertheless, I persevered in ringing for morning Mass and afternoon rosary. If success for a man of the cloth were to be judged solely by attendance at services, he could easily become discouraged. Yet we all know that God's work can be accomplished in mysterious ways, despite appearances. So, who knows, I argued to myself, maybe I'm having a good influence without realizing it.

An old pilot-friend from Norman Wells, Red Hammond, flew me and Trinket along the north shore of Lake Athabaska and landed us on the bay in front of the sprawling mission at Fort Chipewyan, where I was soon welcomed by its numerous staff. This mission, founded in the middle of the nineteenth century, was still in its golden years and growing, with a complement of 4 priests, 5 Brothers, 14 nuns and 150 children in its boarding school. I was absorbed into its vast structure without causing a ripple, just another figure in clerical garb. For me this was a relief after my conspicuous role at Goldfields.

I was conducted to the newly built rectory, a frame building, huge by northern standards, with a typical barn roof containing a beehive of rooms measuring a scant six by ten feet, one of which was assigned to me. That evening our religious superior treated the Oblate community to a "*Gaudeamus*," or celebration, of home-made wine and maple sugar in the recreation room in honour of my arrival. In my broken French I tried as best I could to express my appreciation.

If there was any doubt in my mind that I was back in a formal house of our congregation, it was dispelled the following morn-ing when the 4:50 wake-up bell echoed up the stairwell and stri-dently summoned us to morning prayer in the chapel at 5:15. There would be no more sleeping in until 7:30 as I had been doing the past two years at Franklin. Now my day was strictly regulated: no if's, and's or but's, just follow that bell. My recent freedom had made me forget how "caged in" the bell made me feel, but now I detected in my subconscious some empathy with Tennyson's lines, "Theirs not to make reply, Theirs not to reason why, Theirs but to do and die." Perhaps it was not that dramatic. Between that morning wake-up bell and the one at 8:45 p.m. call-ing us to night prayer, there were another dozen bells summon-ing us to a particular place for a certain activity. And there was plenty of activity besides the spiritual.

This mission, like all the others in the Mackenzie Vicariate, was practically self-supporting. It had a large farm under cultiva-tion and at one time got the prize for the best wheat in Alberta. It had an active fish camp on the lake fifty miles east, a wood camp fifteen miles to the west and of course a good team of horses. What particularly impressed me was their dog-team neatly caged in their individual corrals. They were huge animals, bred from stock in Tuktoyaktuk. Three were pure white. My Trinket was in heat, so I had a perfect mate for her.

The day after my arrival I was down in the potato field help-ing with this important yearly harvest. We were all there: Fathers, Brothers, Sisters, hired hands, even the school kids. It was a gala event and we made short work of the spuds. It was a good thing too, as a quick freeze-up on the 15th of October froze the ground as well as the lake. Many of the natives, having come by boat from their outlying trapping cabins, were still in town and now were caught. So they began building small log cabins just west of the mission and a veritable subdivision sprang up almost overnight. They called it "the United States"!

Old, abandoned buildings are fascinating to me and the old mission that had been abandoned when the Oblates moved into their new one and which had stood out in front since the last century proved especially interesting. It was full of the stuff with which one could start a museum. Most of the small rooms were furnished with handmade beds and chairs with seats woven from babiche. Many old steamer trunks were full of personal items from the past; old photos and even tintypes. On the top floor I discovered a stack of old muzzle-loading rifles. I emerged with simply one brass candle holder, but the superior, Father Mousseau, promised me I could take whatever I wanted and I decided I would certainly get those guns as soon as I had a permanent mission. When I returned the next year to get them, however, the entire building was gone and I was told the guns had been thrown into the dump and buried, along with everything else. Canadians in general seem to lack interest in preserving the past.

Fort Chipewyan is one of the oldest settlements in the North and consequently steeped in history. Alexander Mackenzie himself left here in 1789 to explore the great river named after him. Sir John Franklin and many other explorers followed in subsequent years. The population was about one thousand, half of Chipewyan extraction and half of Cree. Many of them were Métis. Almost all the early French-Canadian voyageurs passed through this Fort, along with a few Iroquois paddlers, and a few of them settled here. The French influence is evident in names like Marcel, Voyageur, Bourque, Vermillion, Lepine, Gibbot, Boucher, Poitras, Desjarlais and Tripe de Roche.

The Hudson Bay Company had always maintained a large establishment at this post and the principal origin of her recruits in the Orkney Islands or Scotland was also evident in names like Fraser, Flett, Wylie, McKay, Simpson and Stewart. Old Jack Wylie showed me the original contract on parchment that he had signed with the Bay when he was recruited in Scotland as a boy. He had signed on for two years for very few pounds sterling. His boys were now producing a fine example of the Chipewyan skiff, dynamiting out tree roots for the ribs of these boats so that they would have the natural curve.

The Chipewyan language had the reputation of being the mother tongue of the various Dene dialects spoken to the north of us, such as the Beaver, Yellowknife, Dog Rib, Slavey and Hare. Because I had a pretty good working knowledge of the latter, it was not too big a task to learn Chipewyan. I lost no time in solic- iting the aid of Father Picard as my instructor. We spent a couple of hours together daily and I started an English-Chipewyan grammar. Afternoons I spent walking around town and getting acquainted with the residents. It wasn't unusual to be invited to stay for supper, but when I did so I missed some of the exercises back at the mission. This didn't bother me too much, but evi- dently it did bother the superior. I soon received a letter from the bishop in Fort Smith informing me of this complaint which he had received by mail. His advice: continue visiting the people!

In late November Trinket presented me with eight pups, the start of a new dog-team, and I was elated. In early December the Barren Land caribou had reached the Brothers' fish camp east along the lake and they went there with the hired hands to lay in a fresh supply of meat for the hostel. The children preferred this to the buffalo meat supplied by the government from the Wood Buffalo Park downstream. I couldn't join the caribou hunt as I had been assigned to preach the three-day children's retreat. Fol- lowing this it was time to return to Goldfields for Christmas.

En route we flew over the small trapping settlement of Cam- sell Portage and I had the pilot land there so that I could meet the people. I found 102 of them, mostly Crees, a Hudson Bay store and a school in operation. In spite of the fact that ninety-eight of the residents were Catholic, a minister of the Northern

Evangelical Society of Meadow Lake and his family had moved in to convert the people. Although the mission at Chip had bought a log cabin in the village for possible use as an outpost, it had never been used and the people asked if I would come and stay with them for a while. I promised to return and then flew on to Goldfields. I would be back, and Camsell Portage was to become a large part of my life. I found one significant change at Holy Cross Mission at Goldfields in the person of Father Rudolph Perin, O.M.I., who had been transferred from Stoney Rapids to help me. It was comforting to have another human being to live with me in that spooky old house.

The new town of Uranium City was growing quickly and many buildings were being skidded over from Goldfields. Steve Yanik had his entire hotel moved over while Gus Hawker was operating out of a tent at the new town. Our plan was to jack up both church and rectory and get them moved as soon as possible. In the meantime I got Steve's brother Joe to let me use the new movie theatre in Uranium City for a Midnight Mass at Christmas. The Mounties agreed to stand at the door in their best scarlet uniforms to deter any drunks from going in. I ended up with a full house and the police said later they had prevented 150 from entering. From there I moved over to Eldorado's Beaverlodge Mine for New Year's. Since my last visit many families had moved into new homes, so it too was becoming an independent community worthy of my attention.

On the sixth of January I flew back to Camsell Portage and moved in with the family of Francis Powder, a patriarch of the community. His father, Paul Lepoudre, had moved to Camsell Portage from Plamondon, Alberta, raised twelve children and practically populated the settlement. It got its name, however, from Charles Camsell, who portaged north from this spot on one of his many geological expeditions. Later he sent me his book, *Son of the North*. During the twenties George McInnes established a fish cannery here and for a while the place was known as The Cannery. Fishing here was still excellent and most winters the Barren Land caribou migrated through the area. With the presence of the store and school it looked like a permanent community.

By living with one of the Powder families I quickly got acquainted with the whole village, but it was confusing, for sixty-five of the people all had the same last name. As they were mostly Cree-speaking, I started a dictionary of basic Cree words. Attendance at services was extremely good and I felt my presence was appreciated. They told me that a collection had been taken up around 1935 to build a proper mission, but nothing had been done. They showed me the old log cabin purchased by Father Picard as a possible mission house, but it looked terribly old and run down. I told the people that if they would help me I would immediately go out and cut enough logs for a proper building and if possible put it up the following summer.

All the able-bodied men went out with me the next day about a mile down the bay and began cutting logs. During the next ten days we cut down ninety good logs, flattening them on one side for ease in skidding. The temperature never rose above thirty-five below zero Fahrenheit and on one day it hit seventy-two below, but deep in the bush we hardly noticed it. In fact, it urged us to greater exertion. We not only cut and limbed them, but got them all skidded back into the centre of the village on an empty lot where a cabin had recently burnt down. It was an ideal location on the sand ridge some hundred and fifty feet from the lake edge. I heard from Dennis Murphy, the Bay Manager, that when the Pentecostal minister saw all our activity he sent a message to his headquarters suggesting a new assignment. Actually he was a fine fellow. I went to his cabin one evening and had supper with him, his wife and children. What puzzled me, however, was why he would be sent to evangelize a group that had already been completely baptized into another Christian faith when there were millions of pagans in the world who had yet to hear of Christ.

After a month at Camsell Portage I flew back to Goldfields and rejoined Father Perin, who was discouraged by all the drinking he found there. In fact, he had been asked to replace another priest at Fond du Lac, the next mission station east of us, during his vacation and he gladly accepted. I returned to my base at Fort Chip.

During my absence all of Trinket's pups had frozen to death outside and I was crestfallen. This discouragement was only temporary, however, as the Brothers promised to give me their splendid team for the winter. I resumed my daily classes in the Chipewyan language under the excellent tutelage of Father Picard and now included the Cree language as well, in which he was proficient. I was back in the classroom again, but I was an eager pupil. Our tight schedule was relaxed on Sunday afternoons, when a group of us would walk the three miles to the mission boat shack on a snye of the Slave River. I would pack my guitar and we would have some animated sing-songs around a red-hot, pot-bellied stove.

In early March I was sent over to the Brothers' wood camp on the Quatre-Fourches Channel in Wood Buffalo Park some fifteen miles west of the mission. Here all the wood needed to heat the various mission buildings at Chip were cut and decked by the water's edge for transport by barge in the summer. It was customary to have a chaplain there in case of accident and to conduct a morning Mass for the crew. Other than that I was on my own to help in any way I could. The first thing I did was to draw up detailed plans for the new log mission at Camsell Portage.

Our cook at the wood camp was the venerable Brother Louis Crenn, who had come to Fort Chipewyan in 1899 from Brittany in France. His obedience to this mission had never been changed nor had he ever taken a vacation. He had simply followed the exacting regimen with unwavering fidelity for over half a century. In addition to being a jack-of-all-trades, his abilities in several areas were outstanding. What impressed me most were his feats with his dog-team. The Mounties in Fort Resolution had told me how he carried one of the early bishops from Chip to Fort Fitzgerald with his dogsled in one day. He told me that he never carried a dog whip and never gave his dogs individual names, referring to them all simply as "chien." Surely he had a very unusual rapport with them, as all the old-timers in Chip attested. Now, at age seventy-three, his dog-driving days were over, but he was still a very useful member of the mission staff, acting as cook at the wood camp and on the mission tugboat and working long hours in his room at the mission repairing the shoes of nearly 200 people. For me he was a living link with a past, a past I would never see, but that seemed far more interesting and exciting than the present times. During the two weeks we were together at the wood camp I had a chance to listen undisturbed to many of his stories while the rest were out felling trees. What a book he could have written, but, like many knowledgeable northerners before and after him, he recorded none of his experiences.

At the end of March, Bert Burry, the owner of McMurray Air Service, flew me back to Goldfields in one of his Stinsons. I spent a week there and then went over to Eldorado, fourteen miles by ice road, in a bombardier or snowmobile. I was assigned an office in the staff house next to the clinic of Dr. Donald McMillan and we grew to be good friends. In view of the medical work I might be called upon to do at Camsell Portage, I was anxious to acquire more skill, especially in suturing wounds. In this the good doctor was most helpful, letting me do some sewing on his patients, under his direction. Unfortunately most of these wounds seemed to be to the scalp, probably the thickest skin to sew on the human anatomy. None of the patients objected, but they should have!

This staff house had some very educated and interesting men who knew a lot more than geology. Homer d'Aigle, for instance, had a great love for classical music and taught me to love the symphonies of Beethoven, especially the seventh, which he knew by heart. Another of the staff was Ben Allen, who had a room on the second floor which was dominated by a large record console he had flown in so that he could listen to his Mozart records. He considered all other classical composers inferior. When he got off work he retreated to his room, turned on Mozart and was immediately in a different world. People like Homer and Ben, who have such an appreciation for the finer things in life, are to be envied.

While I was at the mine this trip, Bill Bennett, President of Eldorado, landed in his private DC-3 en route to the Company's original mine site on Great Bear Lake near Port Radium. Frank Broderick was travelling with him and they invited me to join them. I first obtained permission to do so from the bishop in Fort Smith and from Father Gathy in Yellowknife, who regularly took care of this mine mission. Palm Sunday fell within the time of our trip, so I enlisted the help of Bill Bennett to read the long Gospel of the Passion and Frank Broderick to take up the collection. The day before the service I walked eight miles to Cameron Bay and invited a few families of Franklin Indians, who were spending the winter there, to join us for the Sunday Mass at the mine and they came by dog-team. Shortly after Gilbert LaBine had staked in this area in 1930, the town of Cameron Bay became the largest settlement in the Northwest Territories with over two thousand men and seven airlines operating out of it. Now it was a ghost-town, with the Indians occupying the abandoned Hudson Bay store and the Assay Office.

When I returned to Goldfields I found my companion Father Perin back from Fond du Lac. He was not, however, in good spirits, for the drinking in town greatly reduced attendance at services. This was especially noticeable for him after spending some time at Fond du Lac, where the mission chapel was full every day of the week and where the missionary was called upon every hour of the day to help in one way or another. In Goldfields the people were actually in greater spiritual need. For the man of the cloth pastoring was something like prospecting. If he looked he could dig up all kinds of work. If he waited for it to come to him, however, he could easily become discouraged.

I flew over to Camsell Portage for Easter where the situation was vastly different. Fifty-five of the adults presented themselves for the sacrament of penance on Holy Saturday evening and one hundred and ten attended the Mass held at the school on

Easter Sunday, including four girls and three boys who received their First Holy Communion. Afterwards I baptized two infants.

On this happy note I returned to Fort Chipewyan for the break-up. Pilot Bill Van Allen put me down safely on the rotting ice in front of the Fort. It was the last aircraft to land before open water. The next two months were to be my last at the big mission and I aimed to make the most of them. Using the well equipped workshop in the afternoons, I built a tabernacle for the Camsell mission as well as an octagonal belfry. I removed and packed a dozen windows from the old mission soon to be demolished. As soon as the lake ice melted the first barges down from Water-ways off-loaded the lumber I would need to build.

On the 18th of June we loaded the barge *The St. Eugene* with my materials and equipment, including my new steeple, a tent and stove, a twenty-foot freighter canoe and eight-horsepower Johnson outboard and, last of all, Trinket. With Brother Veillette at the helm and Brother Crenn in the galley, we headed east on a calm lake just newly freed of winter ice. We continued on through the night for eighteen hours, arriving in the protected harbour at Camsell Portage early in the morning. Leaving our barge there to be unloaded, we again nosed out into the lake and continued east to Goldfields. We rendezvoused there with Bishop Trocellier who landed shortly after our arrival. I put a large wood-burning cook stove and heater on board *The St. Eugene* for the new mission at Camsell and off-loaded my canoe and kicker. The Brothers returned to Camsell to get their barge which the natives had unloaded, and returned to Chip. Mean-while the bishop had a good look at the old church and rectory at Goldfields and discussed with Father Perin and me the wisdom of moving it over to the new townsite of Uranium City. We agreed that it should be done, as Goldfields was in its death throes and soon would be another northern ghost-town.

I now began the first of many solo trips on Lake Athabaska, going out with my canoe to the McInnes summer fish plant on Crackingstone Point. About 100 people were employed there, including many from Camsell Portage. Both lake trout and whitefish were netted nearby and brought into the plant, where they were filleted, packed in boxes and frozen for shipment south. Roy Schlader and Bill McPete were in charge of the operation and afforded me their gracious cooperation in conducting services for their workers. When I left there and continued west I stopped at the tent camp of Albert Zeemil and Walter Blair, who were prospecting for uranium for the legendary Gilbert LaBine. Labine is considered the "Father of Uranium" in Canada. Not long afterwards Albert hit a mine-size deposit of the precious ore a stone's throw from their tent and wired Gilbert in Toronto, "Have shot the elephant!" He was not exaggerating. It would become the Gunnar Mine with its own processing mill. About a year later I ran into Walter Blair in an old torn mackinaw helping to unload a barge on Beaverlodge Lake. I asked him how he had made out after staking Gunnar. "Gilbert gave me 50,000 shares," he told me. The stock was then worth over twenty dollars a share; he could have told me that he was a millionaire. His story was not typical, but the rush was definitely on and the country was crawling with prospectors and rapidly being staked.

I stopped at a few more prospecting camps on my way into Black Bay, where barge freight for both Uranium City and Eldorado Mine was being unloaded at a terminus called Bushell. I hitched a ride the eight miles into the boom town called "U-City" by the locals. I had been writing the CCF Government in Regina asking for a site in the new town for our buildings. I had tried to get the bishop to do this, thinking that his letters would carry more weight, but he had declined. At any rate, I had repeatedly been assured that definite parcels of land would be reserved for various denominations. One letter had been signed by Brokelbank himself, the top man in the ministry concerned with development at Uranium City. I had a piece of high ground above the townsite contour surveyed and drawn up by friends in the drafting office at Eldorado and submitted to Regina for consideration.

Now I went to see the Provincial Land Agent in town to see if the land had been set aside for us. I was dismayed to learn that, not only had no land been set aside for our purposes, but that it was practically all gone. The parcel I had originally chosen and had surveyed had been picked for the school site. This agent went around town with me showing what lots remained, but they could scarcely accommodate our two buildings from Goldfields even if they were butted up side by side. In desperation I finally took a piece of ground adjacent to the school site, most of which was down a ravine. My opinion of the CCF Government in Regina may be imagined as I continued on the remaining five miles to Eldorado. I was steaming!

The best I could do was to accept what was left of parcel "C" adjacent to the original lot I had chosen and now reserved for the school. In the following January I was back in Uranium City by dog-team and eating supper in Tom Embleton's tent cafe, when I happened to get seated at the counter next to a government land surveyor. His name was Alexander Stewart and it didn't take me long to explain to him all the troubles I had in trying to obtain a suitable piece of ground on which to locate our Goldfields buildings. He lent me a sympathetic ear and promised to look at our parcel "C" the next day – which he did, on snowshoes.

"How much land would you need along this boundary with the school to accommodate your church?" he asked me. I replied, "About a hundred feet would do it." Without hesitation he pulled up the steel pin marking the eastern border of our property and moved it over a hundred feet. Suddenly my problem had evaporated. And to secure it, when they moved the church and rectory over from Goldfields, I had them place each building at opposite ends of the parcel. To this day the church rests on that extra hundred feet of ground.

That Sunday at my Mass in the recreation room of the Eldorado staff house I informed the men that I would be away for the summer building a log mission for the natives at Camsell Portage, twenty-six air miles west. After the service a group of Irishmen came up to me offering to help, at least on weekends, if they could get there and back. This was unexpected and I promised to see if anything could be done.

The following day I went over to the new Nesbitt-LaBine Mine where shaft-sinking was in progress under the direction of Foss Irwin. Johnny Nesbitt was a well-known northern bush pilot who was in partnership with Gilbert LaBine on this new mine and he had a Beaver aircraft on nearby Martin Lake. Although Johnny was not of our religious persuasion he was anxious to help and readily agreed to take a volunteer crew back and forth to Camsell at no charge. (In later years Johnny published a book of his experiences entitled *Keep Your Nose on the Horizon*, but with characteristic modesty he neglected to mention this act of kindness.) I was elated when I went back to Eldorado to inform the volunteers. I also wrote to Father Perin at Goldfields asking him to help me with the construction work ahead.

The next day the skies were sunny and the lake calm as we pulled out of Black Bay, my canoe loaded with supplies. I rounded St. Joseph's Point and headed into Camsell Bay. I already felt pride in the thought that I was heading toward "my" mission. So what if it were nothing more than a pile of logs and lumber at this stage? In my mind's eye I could already see its steeple pointed to the sky. And it did officially bear the name of my patron saint, Mission Saint Bernard. Now it would take only a couple of months out of my young life to make it a reality.

11

Mission
Saint Bernard

On my return to Camsell Portage I first had to pitch my tent and get my trunk and bedroll under canvas in case it rained. After that I sorted and stacked my building material with the help of one of the local boys. Help was scarce: most of the able-bodied males were away at the fish camp or hired out staking claims in the area.

On July 1st, Dominion Day, Johnny Nesbitt made his first trip with an overload of volunteer workers – eight of them – led by Pat Hughes. Pat was a bricklayer by trade and in charge of a kiln at Eldorado where he made bricks and cinder blocks. Like most of his companions he had come over from Dublin, Ireland. The first job we tackled was taking the old log cabin apart and moving it, log by log, to the new site. This was the building bought by the Chip Mission but never used. The skies were bright and the sun so hot that most of the men stripped to the waist as they dragged these logs about two hundred yards. The bugs and mosquitoes were not nearly so bad here as they were around Great Bear Lake, where no one ever worked outside shirtless.

The next day after Mass in the school we laid out the perimeter of the new mission and positioned the sill logs on the sand. The main building measured twenty-four by thirty-two feet, including the front porch which ran the width of the building. A

wing running off this to contain the kitchen and workshop measured thirty-two by fourteen feet. By the time Johnny flew in early
Monday morning to pick up the men, the project was well under
way. And at the last minute I got an unexpected but welcome
surprise.

Philip Stenne had emigrated from France, a graduate of the
Sorbonne in his early twenties. His father was a sculptor of huge
equestrian statues. Philip had been working as a carpenter at the
Eldorado Mine, but the housing situation there in a huge Butler
building containing over 200 men was intolerable to him. I could
understand that. One evening I had visited the men in that building, mostly shaft-sinkers from Nova Scotia, and some of their
habits were downright dangerous. For example, they would
open a beer bottle by simply cracking off the top on the edge of a
table and when it was empty they threw it over the partition of
their cubicle to land and smash in one of their neighbours', spark-
ing some profane threats of retaliation. So Philip offered to stay
and spend the month of July helping me and I eagerly accepted.

Together we put in long hours under clear skies and the work
progressed. Father Perin came over and gave us a hand for two
weeks, then borrowed my canoe to go down to Fort Resolution
for that mission's centenary celebration. Young newlyweds from
Fort Chipewyan, Charley Flett and his bride, stopped by on their
honeymoon and worked with us for a couple of weeks. Nobody
could stand around watching us work for very long without having an axe put in his hands. During the month Trinket delivered
some good news when she dropped eleven pups. The bad news
was that nine of them were females.

Every weekend Johnny Nesbitt flew over faithfully with a
plane-load of helpers which not only doubled the work Philip
and I could do during the week, but also gave us a great morale
boost. On one trip he urged me to fly over to Crackingstone Point
with him and stake a few claims. I declined, arguing that if I took
any time off the building, the mission wouldn't be closed in
before cold weather. Later I realized that I had missed a golden

opportunity. Any claims staked at that point, especially after the Gunnar find, sold for thousands of dollars.

I had no reason to worry about finishing the job during that summer. I was far enough along to move into the new mission the 31st of August, my thirty-second birthday. When Pat Hughes came over the following day he put in front steps of cement, the finishing touch. The building was now completely closed in and I could work on the inside at my leisure during the winter. I now felt safe in leaving for a while to visit the miners.

At Eldorado I was still using my office in the staff house, but sleeping at the home of Hank and Colleen Bloy. To show my appreciation I got out my oil paints and did a painting of sled-dogs for them. I had been carrying my painting equipment ever since I arrived in the North, always telling myself that I would get back into it again, but there never seemed to be enough time. I had produced nothing in this line while at Franklin, although while I was there I had a visit from A. Y. Jackson, one of the famous Group of Seven. He was up at Port Radium at the invitation of Bill Bennett one summer painting scenes around Great Bear Lake and he encouraged me to get back to it. Later, at Beaverlodge, I started evening classes in painting for adults at the school, which sparked a lot of interest. I loved it, but I didn't seem able to get into it while occupied with mission work or on the move.

While at the mine this time I got another opportunity to visit the operation near Port Radium. A group of about forty Irishmen working there were most faithful in attending a very early morning Mass before going on shift. *The Radium Gilbert* was plying the lake regularly, crossing over to the mouth of the Great Bear River opposite Fort Franklin with bags of uranium concentrate and bringing back fuel oil. Captain Allen McInnes invited me to make a trip with him and I lost no time throwing my bag on board. Henry Christofferson, marine maintenance supervisor for the Northern Transportation Company, was on board too, and his humorous anecdotes all the way across provided a lot of fun.

It was a great thrill to see Mission St. Therese again, to go down the line and pet all my dogs and remember the long trips we had made together, to look around at all the familiar objects. My successor Father Victor Phillipe and his young assistant Father Felicien Labat were hard at work adding a closed porch to the chapel end of the building. Soon the natives were flocking to greet me with warm embraces reserved for their own kind, a special mark of affection. I thought I had pounded my last nail in this mission, but the next day Father Phillipe had me cut a new window into the outside wall of the sacristy. Mr. Gravel came to visit and I asked him if I could send him another cat. When I left I took one of the pair of snowshoes I had left in the attic.

The trip back across the lake in *The Radium Gilbert* was uneventful until we neared the east shore. We were proceeding in a dense fog at half-speed when suddenly a sheer granite cliff loomed up in front of us and Captain McInnes telegraphed for full-speed astern. His ship, although beautifully furnished, lacked any radar to aid navigation.

Back at Port Radium I heard about a group of some forty natives who were employed at a bush camp cutting spruce for underground timbers. Although many of the Bear Lakers had been trained to work underground and were good at it, they found this work too gruelling. So they ended up at Hunter Bay about forty miles north of the mine, cutting lagging timbers. Captain McInnes's brother captained a smaller, wooden barge named *The Radium Bear* and was making a trip to the natives' camp to take on a load of timbers, so I went with him.

I knew most of the people at this camp from Franklin, so I decided to spend a couple of days with them and then have them bring me back to the mine by canoe. Everything worked out as planned until we ran out of gas about half-way back. There were nine of us in a twenty-two-foot freighter canoe. We tore up the floor boards and made paddles out of them. We hadn't planned to camp out and the second day we were completely out of grub. The first day we expended all the shells in our only .30-.30, with the exception of one, vainly trying to shoot four otter. The remaining shell was used successfully the second day on a common loon. We immediately went ashore and built a fire. I was amazed how good that loon tasted. Finally we found an old fuel cache and got the kicker restarted.

Port Radium had no airstrip but used the old gravel strip at Sawmill Bay about thirty miles south and ferried passengers back and forth in *The Radium Bear.* In winter they landed the company DC-3 on the ice right in front of the mine. Over at Sawmill Bay there was a wrecked Dakota just off the runway with a large notice painted on it advising: "CAUTION, THIS COULD HAPPEN TO YOU!" I saw a similar wreck on the new strip at Beaverlodge after Alf Kaywood had flown me back south.

One dark, rainy night the following week the Eldorado DC-3 piloted by Jack Love circled overhead with a full load of men from Port Radium mine. They were unexpected: there were no lights on the new gravel strip still under construction. Two of us jumped in a pickup truck and went for the kerosene pots used to outline the strip in the dark. We found them all empty. While we were frantically trying to fill them the circling Dakota was burning the last of its fuel. As we put down the first three pots marking the end of the strip Pilot Love did touch down, but quickly got airborne again for another circuit. We had just put down the first light along the side of the runway when he came in again. This time he landed, but the plane was heading about fifteen degrees to the right of the runway and promptly hit a six-foot ridge of gravel. This severed the undercarriage and the plane slid some three hundred feet on its belly, stopping just short of a precipice. We rushed over to find that the props had sliced through the fuselage, rupturing the wing tanks. Gas was pouring out as the occupants scrambled for the exit in the pitch dark, lit only by the headlights on our truck. Fearing fire, we kept yelling, "Don't light a match!" "Don't light a match!" All twenty-one passengers got out unhurt. Among them I was surprised to see three of my Bear Lake Indians. This was their first plane ride and one of them said to me in the Hare language, "It must cost the white men a lot of money every time they land this flying boat."

After the engines were removed from this crippled bird Charlie Storm, the camp cook, bought it from the company for $300 and moved it just outside the mine gate. He fixed it up as a fast food diner and operated it successfully for several years. Later he moved it over to Uranium City, where he again altered it for use as living quarters and rented it out. Finally some men from the States bought it from him for $5,000 with the intention of rebuilding it. It may still be flying today.

Before returning to Camsell Portage I went over to Goldfields to visit my sometime companion missionary Father Perin to find out what he had done with my canoe and kicker. He told me he had left them over at Camsell while I was away and by way of compensation for keeping them so long had left a sled-dog there for me as well as a brass bell for the new belfry. Jack Walters took me and my considerable freight there in his large inboard motor boat. It was the 18th of October and shell ice was beginning to form along the shore. I now had ten dogs to feed; one brought by Father Perin, four I borrowed from Victor Augier, plus Trinket and four of her pups. It was late to start a fall fishery, but I borrowed four nets and set them. Then I took down an abandoned log building built in the early twenties by a Swede named Eric, and using the logs built a fish house down by the water's edge. I got about twenty-five days of net fishing before I was forced to pull out both the nets and the canoe when the bay froze completely on November 14th. As soon as the ice got thick enough the caribou came and we could see them crossing near the end of the bay. The first one I got had fallen through thin ice and I shot him in the water. Soon everyone who had not yet left the settlement for their traplines had plenty of meat.

The people were generous enough to keep me supplied with firewood so I could go ahead with the carpentry inside the new mission. I found myself doing the same kind of work I had been doing at Franklin twelve months earlier. Only this time I was a little more accomplished in building cabinets and furniture. I also built a wood sled as insurance against the day, fast coming, when my people would tire of bringing me wood. My supply of dog feed was rapidly being depleted and it was just a matter of days before I could no longer enjoy the luxury of staying home doing carpentry. Soon my time would be mostly taken up visiting nets and hooks set under the ice and hauling firewood.

In the meantime I rushed to build all the items necessary for Christmas, like the altar and benches. And it turned out to be a very holy and happy feast with the new mission absolutely filled to the walls for the Midnight Mass and not a drunk to mar the religious atmosphere. The once-a-year collection amounted to $55.79, with everyone donating. On Christmas afternoon we had Benediction of the Blessed Sacrament, followed that evening by a slide show. I had a generator from an American Sherman tank bought through war assets, and, although it produced a frightful din in the workshop, I was successful in showing about a thousand slides I had taken, mostly around Fort Franklin. I followed this with a bucket of ice cream which I had concocted with many secret ingredients and everyone declared it the best Christmas Camsell Portage had ever seen.

The New Year of 1953 was ushered in with some sporadic shooting around the village as the temperature dipped to twenty-four below zero. Philip Stenne was still in that Butler building at Eldorado Mine, but he had written me asking if he could team up with me and stay at the mission at Camsell. I agreed on condition that we converse only in French, because I was determined to gain more fluency in the language. So he quit his job and on January 2nd walked the thirty-five miles to Camsell. He arrived slightly frost-bitten but otherwise none the worse for the long hike in sub-zero weather. His arrival was an answer to prayer and I welcomed him with open arms. At the time I wasn't sure just how long he would stay, as I had no money with which to pay him. As it turned out, he stayed longer than I did and is still there today!

Philip adapted easily to bush life. It wasn't too many days before he could manage our new team of dogs himself as he took over the job of supplying us with firewood. I went with him to show him how we set a net under the ice, just as Brother Médard had shown me a short time before. We shot a few caribou and I showed him how we skinned and butchered them, keeping our hands in the warm blood so they wouldn't freeze. We lowered baited hooks through the ice in deep water for the big trout. It wasn't long before he could do all these things without my help.

About this time I was content to pass the rest of the winter peacefully at Camsell and completely forget about Goldfields or the mines or Uranium City. I received a telegram, however, from the Saskatchewan Government in Regina informing me that my request for Parcel C next to the school property in U-City had been granted and that I should sign the lease with the land agent there as soon as possible. Without hesitating, and in spite of the fifty-five-below-zero temperature, I left alone with the team the next day. Having no place to stay at U-City, I went right through to Eldorado's mine on Beaverlodge Lake, now safely frozen. I had a neat little shack there next to the staff house given to me by Lefty McLeod, one of Eldorado's pilots. With the cookhouse right next door I could count on Charlie Storm for scraps to feed my dogs indefinitely. The next day I drove the dogs back to U-City, where the town was booming. It was still practically a tent city, with the exception of the Saskatchewan Liquor Store which was solidly built of brick.

I lost no time in getting over to Goldfields where Father Perin was engaged in getting our two buildings jacked up, preparing them to be moved to U-City. I explained the situation carefully and the importance of putting the church on that top hundred feet of ground in order to hold it. In a month it was over there and placed exactly where we wanted it, while the old rectory occupied a site at the opposite end of the parcel. The following summer officials from Regina drew a line right through the middle of our property and ordered me to move the church back across that line! I expected this, but I held firm. We eventually won the fight and the church stayed put. No doubt about it, I was elated as I drove the dogs back to Camsell. That had been an important trip well worth the hardships involved.

In the meantime I had received a letter from Fort Smith setting out the date for the important annual retreat and a note saying that the bishop would fly to Camsell for an inspection of the new mission and take me back with him. Somehow those plans were changed and the plane trip cancelled with them. This gave me the idea of going by dogs and taking Philip with me to see the country. As we didn't yet have enough dogs for two teams we would have to double up on the same sled. It could be done and Philip was game. We packed and left on January 21st, following the north shore of the lake going west. Although we had no trail to follow, the lead dog Sandy did a good job cutting across bays from point to point. It was thirty below but calm, with a noticeable ice-haze hanging in the air. The sun was setting dead ahead of us about three in the afternoon, sending out rays in the form of a cross. It was an indescribably beautiful scene and it prompted me to stop the team and dig out my 35 mm camera. I walked out in a circle so as not to get my tracks in the picture and left Philip standing on the back of the sled silhouetted against the sun. That picture turned out to be the finest I ever took in the North and was reproduced thousands of times.

We made about thirty-five miles that day and pitched our tent on Morris Point. The following evening we got into the Brothers' fish camp at Fiddler Point. Luckily the cabin was heated and occupied by a group of hunters from the Chip mission who had just killed 100 caribou. An hour after our arrival the mission tractor arrived pulling a huge, empty freight sled called a sloop. There were about a dozen of us in that cabin and we slept warm.

The next morning the Brothers loaded all the frozen carcasses on their sled and lashed them down in preparation for the fifty-mile trip back to the mission. Philip decided to go with them and take one of our dogs which had played out. I continued with the seven dogs left and made it into Chip in seven hours. We had completed the first hundred and twenty-five miles and were about half-way between Camsell and Fort Smith, our destination. In spite of the fact that one dog died that night, it looked as if we could make it.

After resting up two days at Chip our dogs looked as though they were ready to tackle our final dash to Fort Smith. The route led us down the frozen Slave River. As there were a few trapping families living all along this route we anticipated finding our trail broken in the deep snow. In this fond hope we soon found we were mistaken. There was no trail at all. Whereas on Lake Athabaska we really didn't need a trail because the wind had blown the snow into a hard surface, here in the protected valley of the river it lay soft and deep. We had to take turns running ahead of the dogs on snowshoes. The first day we barely made twenty-five miles, were completely exhausted and we were showing signs of *mal de raquette*, that famous scourge of snowshoe travel that afflicts all the muscles from toes to hips. Fortunately we didn't have to make an open camp but moved into the cabin of Bill Moore at the mouth of the Peace River. After wading through that soft snow all day the poor dogs just dropped in their tracks and we had to drag them from their harnesses to chain them up for the night.

In the morning we were stiff and sore and the temperature looked even lower, but luckily we had no thermometer. There was nothing to do but get down on that river and continue breaking trail north, taking turns as we had done the day before. It definitely was colder, for ice formed on the bottom of the toboggan, making it pull like it was running on sand. Every few miles we had to stop, turn it over and scrape the ice off with an axe. About noon we came to the small cabin of an old Swedish trapper. We left the team down on the river and walked up the steep bank to the cabin. Once inside we were assailed by the pungent aroma of Sloan's Linament, which this old recluse must have been using by the case. It was so overpowering we couldn't really tell if we were drinking tea or not. The poor fellow was so starved for company he couldn't stop talking in his thick Scandinavian accent. He followed us back down to the river, jawing all the way. Even as we pulled away he was standing there waving his arms and shouting after us. One might diagnose this as incipient cabin fever.

We plodded on downriver through the deep snow. The exertion of running ahead on snowshoes so warmed us that in spite of the intense cold we were forced to remove our parkas. Our faces, however, were picking up patches of frostbite. By late afternoon we pulled into Johnson's Trading Post and stopped for tea. This post was unique: besides carrying the usual trade items, Johnson kept a bull and three cows. He froze the milk and sold it in solid blocks which were stacked up in the entranceway to his store. He had a thermometer hanging outside and it registered sixty-two below zero. We knew it was cold, but we didn't realize it was that low. This explained why our sled boards were icing up the way they did. When we queried him about the lack of any sign of a sled trail, he told us that they had had a lot of snow recently and everyone was waiting for someone else to break it. He predicted that there would now be plenty of traffic on our trail. As Tom Champaign's cabin was only another six miles down we decided to go at least that far before camping for the night. The river takes a big bend west at that point, so the blazed trail leaves the river and cuts straight across. Our lead dog had no trouble following it without benefit of a forerunner, though there were six inches of fresh snow on it. The warm light of a cabin window up ahead was a welcome sight as our harness bells echoed through the empty bush in the darkness.

Not having met Tom before, we weren't too sure if we would be invited to spend the night in his cabin with his wife and numerous children, so we left our dogs in their harness and followed him into the cabin. Tom did all the talking and never stopped. We shook hands with his wife, but the children mostly retreated under the bunk beds. It was evident that they weren't used to strangers. As usual, there was a kettle of hot tea on the stove, but Tom informed us that he would immediately send his eldest son over to the store to pick up a few things for our supper and he took off in the dark. We sat around smoking and drinking tea for three hours as Tom regaled us with his war stories. Finally the boy came in and put a tin of butter on the table. That was it! Why hadn't he said something? We had butter out in our sled. In fact we had plenty of caribou meat as well as bannock and beans and a lot of other grub that Tom evidently did not have.

It didn't take us long to bring in an armful which Tom's wife immediately began cooking. We unharnessed our dogs, brought in our bedrolls and were soon at the table with Tom stuffing ourselves. It is common practice in the North for the women and children to wait until the men have finished before eating. Evidently the smell of that good food overcame the shyness of the children as they crept closer and closer to our table. Their big eyes were riveted not on us but on the food. Philip and I became uneasy. Apparently they were practically starving. We weren't really finished when we excused ourselves and moved from the table to let those poor kids have a chance. Without a word they scrambled onto the benches and devoured everything in sight while Tom droned on about the moose he had been tracking and would probably shoot tomorrow. In the meantime "moose tracks alone make very thin soup," as the saying goes.

The following day was the same as the last two, more than sixty below and no trail. We pushed on doggedly mile after weary mile, staying as close to the banks as possible so as to avoid any overflow or thin ice in mid-stream. As we traded places breaking trail, we looked for the tell-tale white patches on each other's face indicating frostbite. You can easily freeze parts of your face without being aware of it. Later in the warmth of a cabin it feels like a burn and acts like one too, at first turning black, then blistering and peeling, leaving a very sensitive area of skin that can freeze even more readily the next time it is exposed. Finally that afternoon we reached the Wood Buffalo Park headquarters known as The Hay Camp. They had a well-organized abattoir there and were actually in the midst of their annual round-up and kill. There was plenty of room to throw our bedrolls and no shortage of buffalo meat for our weary dogs. Even if we had to pay for it, the going price of five cents a pound would have been cheap to the big commercial meat packers who were carting it away.

We still had forty-five miles to go to Fort Smith, but it was all over a recently plowed road. No more river travel. No more breaking trail on snowshoes. It took us just five hours to Fort Fitzgerald where we stopped for tea with Lawrence Yanik. He was the brother of both Steve and Joe, both of whom were prospering in Uranium City. He had built his log house here of huge logs that had drifted out of the Peace River. I had never seen four logs to a wall before. With only sixteen miles left to cross the portage road into Fort Smith we pushed on, anxious to get there in time for the opening ceremonies of the retreat. We missed it by forty-five minutes and stopped the team right in front of the chapel as the twenty-five Fathers and Brothers filed out to cross over to the mission residence. We must have presented quite a sight standing there by our sled, covered with frost, the steam rising from us, like two wraiths from ultima Thule. They all filed by without a word of greeting! The retreat had begun and they were all observing the rule of Grand Silence! *C'est la vie.*

Our return trip to Camsell Portage was remarkable only in that it was so easy compared to the trip out. This time, as Johnson had predicted, the trail up the Slave River to Chip had been kept open by the locals and we could ride instead of walk. The lake from Chip to Camsell was about the same, but the days were longer and warmer. We got in on the 26th of February, the very day I told the people I would return.

In our absence the teacherage had burned down, but the school was still in operation. After a few days, during which we set two nets and replenished our wood pile, I left alone with the dogs to visit the mines. At Uranium City I found the staking rush had accelerated and over at Goldfields I found that Father Perin had sat around the rectory as long as he could stand the inactivity and then went out and staked nine claims himself. When he confided to me that he had already been offered $500 apiece for these claims but was holding out for $1,000, the staking bug hit me too. On my way back to Camsell I picked up prospecting licences for both Philip and myself. We lost no time in going out and staking forty-two claims close to the settlement; not that we were aware of any uranium in the area, but we felt that we might just as well stake some land before it was completely gone. And we were aware of the fact that even "moose pasture" was selling. On my next sled trip to U-City I stood in line with all the other prospectors outside the mining recorder's tent and got our claims properly filed. We were now caught up in that frenzy that was sweeping the country.

At Camsell Portage we celebrated the great feast of the Lord's Resurrection with all the pomp and ceremony we could muster. The altar was beautifully decorated by the young women and everyone wore their finest. Following the late morning High Mass we were surprised to see three caribou bedded down out on the ice in front of the village. At 2:30 everyone returned to the mission for Benediction, at 5:30 for a common meal and at 7:30 for bingo. No doubt about it, the mission had become the centre of social activity in the settlement. On Easter Monday we had the first marriage, when Georgina Powder was joined to Herb Mercredi in Holy Matrimony, after which we all gathered on the front porch for a group photo. This event occasioned some alcoholic toasts around town which resulted in old Ira Allen getting a few ribs kicked in. I taped him up as best I could, then got a medevac to fly us over to Dr. McMillan, who examined him and pronounced my medical work A-1. He left my bandages just where I put them and Bert Barry flew us home again.

Philip and I had seen the country west of us, so it was time to familiarize ourselves with what lay to the east. I had heard a lot about the old mission at Fond du Lac and its resident missionary, Father Charlie Gamache, so we decided to visit him. As we would be travelling on the lake ice all the way, the proper sled to use would be the komatik, with its heavy wooden runners. So I built one sixteen feet long and shod it with steel runners. Traditionally the komatik is pulled by dogs harnessed in the "Nome hitch," that is, they pull in pairs, side by side, except for the leader. With webbing I made a set of nine Eskimo-type harnesses that have no collar, but do have individual whipple trees. In the meantime the mission at Chip sent me their six dogs, so we had two good teams.

With our best nine dogs in the new harness pulling a sled usually not seen on Lake Athabaska, Philip and I left Camsell on April 14th. Everything worked well and that night we made camp on Big Fowl Island east of Goldfields. The following day took us through the spring migration of caribou crossing our track going north to the Barrens. We shot and butchered four of them. With the sight and smell of so many caribou our dogs were incited to give their utmost all day long and we arrived at Fond du Lac early in the evening.

This northern post, more than any other, retained a flavour of the old times. Of course the 300-odd Chipewyan Indians here were all living in the log cabins they had built. Unlike any other settlement, however, they were still fencing in their yards with vertical poles similar to those I had seen in photos from the last century. Some had teepees or warehouses set up in their yards where they would tan hides. All had dog-teams.

The huge church stood by the edge of the lake and was mostly unheated in the winter. The mission building was separated from the church by the main road and contained a large chapel. Its yard was fenced in with a high, pole barrier. Once this gate was open we drove in with our team. With our load of fresh meat we got a warm reception from Father Gamache, a rotund figure in cassock, and from his wiry assistant, Brother Labonté. We unloaded our gear and were escorted to two cots upstairs.

In the kitchen that evening supper consisted of two staples on which these missionaries apparently lived most of the year. The first was a kind of stew made up of chunks of caribou and potatoes from their garden. The second was local raspberries. Both were preserved in mason jars and were delicious. Hundreds of similar jars were stored in the cellar. During the next five days we learned a lot: about living off the land, about the Chipewyans and about our host. He was a Canadian who had already spent a quarter of a century at this post. Like all our missionaries he was fluent in the local language. He was also an avid reader of world history and current affairs and well acquainted with the classics. Yet what particularly distinguished him was his inquisitive mind and willingness to test his ideas. This had led him into all sorts of experiments.

It was easy to guess that he had attempted to raise mink, as the pile of empty mink cages in the backyard attested. He had also tried foxes and marten. All these animals failed to reproduce, he told us, simply because of his location in the centre of the village surrounded by yapping sled-dogs. In an isolated location they could have been successful. He also had an idea that he could possibly improve on the type of sled-dog the natives were using. Toward this end he imported a pure-bred female St. Bernard and a pedigreed greyhound, the idea being that this combination might produce a fast dog that could withstand the cold. We looked at one product of this union chained out in the yard. With its pointed nose and long, woolly legs it resembled an orangutan. It was evident around the settlement that this particular experiment had been going on for years as nearly every dog in town had the long, pointed nose of the Greyhound, and even when we met these teams around Goldfields we knew immediately that they were from Fond du Lac.

Another ongoing experiment involved chickens, a good number of which kept themselves warm enough to survive the winter in an unheated hen house in the back yard. Unfortunately he had run out of proper chicken feed and had substituted dry fish. The birds, it seemed, were living well enough on this type of food, but their eggs tasted fishy. To encourage the production of larger eggs the Father made some plaster of Paris eggs of amazing sizes which he was placing in their nests to challenge them; the desk in his own room was covered with moulds. From time to time during the day he would slip out to the hen house and return with his cassock pockets filled with eggs which he would put in his sleeping bag on his bed. Just why he did this I never found out. Nor did I find out why the tea kettle was half-filled with egg shells.

Every summer Father Gamache would import two piglets on the first barge. They were kept in a log cabin out in the middle of the yard, fed any scraps the mission could spare and butchered each fall. One was always sold to the Hudson Bay manager and this paid for their initial cost. One summer when I was visiting I looked in the open window of the pig house and noticed that the two of them were standing in about six inches of water. When I notified the Father about this situation he replied that this was another experiment in making the meat more tender!

A very successful operation of this mission was its garden and we were shown how it took two years to make the proper soil by mixing moss into the sand. The potatoes this soil produced not only tasted great but they were especially suited for long winter storage. Another outstanding success of this Father and Brother teamwork was their smoked trout which I had seen for sale in MacIver's store in Goldfields.

The mission also housed the Post Office in one small room that seemed so crowded with unclaimed C.O.D. parcels that there was scarcely room to walk into it to get to the wicket. It looked to me like a place where mail could be lost for years without anyone ever noticing. Against the outside wall was a huge pile of beautifully tanned caribou hides for sale for $4 apiece. I bought several with which I later had a jacket made.

That first night Philip and I were comfortably in our cots upstairs ready for sleep when the two house cats started playing tag on the exposed rafters overhead. In the pitch dark one jumped down and hit me in the stomach. When I sat up the second one landed on my head. Apparently my bed had been their habitual landing site.

This mission at Fond du Lac had been established in 1853 and was currently just one year short of its centenary celebration. The people's long association with the church and its music was apparent when they sang at the daily services. What singing! I had never heard anything quite like it. Led by one of the male elders its sheer volume was astounding. I wished I could take a contingent of them to Camsell Portage to show the people there how a congregation could praise God in song. And apparently their pastor was satisfied that his flock was well schooled in their religion, because he never preached to them! He told me that after twenty-five years they had heard everything. And certainly they must have added to their knowledge of Christianity during their frequent visits to the mission common room where there were always a few visitors smoking pipes or chewing snuff and discussing local and world events with their knowledgeable pastor. I remember spending most of one day discussing with him Galileo's theory of a sun-oriented universe. No doubt about it, this visit to the Fond du Lac Mission was one of the high points of my first five years in the North and one I couldn't easily forget.

Our return trip took us through the continuing migration of the caribou, but the surface of the snow on the ice was beginning to melt and the temperature of the air was too warm for working dogs. We got our tent pitched again on Big Fowl Island just before we were hit by a spring blizzard of snow and rain that kept us pinned down all the following day. The storm blew itself out during the night and when we resumed our trip the third day the temperature was down below zero. Our komatik zipped along on its steel runners with little effort, even after we took on the meat of five caribou we killed. When we came to the large pressure ridge of ice off St. Joseph's Point we had to follow it for two miles toward shore in order to avoid the deepening water on either side of it. In spite of this detour we got back to Mission Saint Bernard in the early afternoon.

The following month saw us using our dogs almost daily to carry out our main tasks. Besides going to the nets, hunting caribou or hauling firewood, we went west twenty-five miles to stake another group of claims and made two more trips into U-City and area. By the 21st of May we had to leave the sled out on the rotting ice of the main lake as the bay in front of the settlement was now black and unsafe. When I totalled up our mileage for the winter I found that we had travelled 1,214 miles with the dogs, not counting all the short trips for wood and fish. It was time to hang up the harnesses for the summer.

12

THE EASIER LIFE

Spring came to Camsell Portage as usual on the wings of song, the song of all the birds that had left us for the winter and were now returning. As the sun rose higher day by day it melted the snow and released all the pungent aromas that had been dormant and imprisoned. The warm wind wafted the sweet scent of flowering lichens and pine. Even a blind man could have known that spring was in the air.

What a treat to sit out on my front porch watching the ice melt in the bay and feel the blessed heat. The dogs no longer had to curl up and hide their noses in their tails. They could stretch out full-length and rest their tired muscles, with no more travelling for a while. Too late for sleds, too early for boats; it was a time to relax, a time to be quiet and think. Which was what I was doing; thinking back over my first years in the North, comparing where I was now with where I had been over the past five years.

Already I had seen the four seasons come and go at Camsell Portage. The new mission was completed and in service. The natives' lives were enriched by it and they showed their appreciation by faithful attendance at services. We were isolated and yet close enough to get to most of the mines in a single day.

As there were far more people at the mines than there were at my home base I could say that I was ministering mostly among men working in a technically specialized world. Yet most of my time was spent with a people still living off the land and I shared part of that life, too. I could say that I had the best of both worlds. As at Fort Norman, I was still studying native languages, but I no longer had to answer to a dozen bells during my day. Without the bells I was freer, less constrained, but at the same time I had more personal initiative. More self-discipline was demanded for me to do on my own the things the bells had called me to do. After all, I was still living by the Rule Book of the Oblate Congregation to which I belonged. The Breviary, for example, still had to be said daily in its entirety, except when I was travelling. The Mass, too, was a daily event, but here the steeple bell called the faithful, not me. It was my job to be the faithful bell-ringer.

I could see more similarities than dissimilarities between my two years at Fort Franklin and my current circumstances. In both situations most of my time was consumed by the manual labour of building. Whether on Great Bear Lake or Lake Athabaska, I needed a dog-team to travel, so I had to keep nets in the water to feed them. All the missions were heating with wood, so I had to be continually cutting and hauling no matter where I was. So too with the hunting of caribou, our staple meat. At Franklin my people were concentrated in the one village, while here at Camsell Portage my flock was scattered, so that now I was obliged to do more travelling to reach them. The main difference between Franklin and Camsell was their geographical positions six hundred miles apart. Thus at Camsell the winters were not nearly as severe nor as long. Although I wasn't adverse to winter, still it was nice to feel the heat of spring in May instead of having to wait until July. No doubt about it, life was easier for me now than at any time before.

Eldorado had recently opened for staking all the land along the north shore of Lake Athabaska which they had reserved for two years while they had the first look at it. This was a Crown-owned company and the ore was militarily strategic material. The Crown had exercised its priority rights on that basis.

There was a rush to stake this land just as soon as it was declared open and among the first to do so was Pat Hughes and his Irish buddies. Their lack of knowledge in this field coupled with their evident zeal made them the butt of a lot of joking. I knew some of the boys working in Eldorado's map office where they kept copies of the charts used in all their airborne scintillometer work. These showed where they got the highest readings from ground radiation. Eldorado had already checked out these hot spots and found that most of them were caused by pegmatite, the uranium prospector's fool's gold. Anyway I had a copy of these maps made for me and I loaned them to the Irishmen along with my canoe or any other equipment they needed. They began to sell claims and stake others. Within a relatively short time they had quit their labour jobs at Eldorado and were into staking full-time. By the time the uranium boom had passed they had acquired considerable savings. When they announced that they intended to shift their scene of operations to Ireland they were again laughed at. Everyone knew that there was no prospecting for minerals in Ireland, but they persisted.

They got hold of the old Irish maps showing where the smithies were located near mineral deposits, probably iron ore. These became their original prospecting areas and, as luck would have it, they not only found iron, but lead and zinc and other more valuable minerals. The next thing people read in their mining newspapers was that Northgate, their company, was putting up a mill near Dublin to process this ore. And shortly after that a second mill. So the Irishmen who had been so generous with their time in helping to establish Mission Saint Bernard had been rewarded tenfold and their scoffers were left shaking their heads, silenced.

As soon as the lake was open in June I left by canoe for Uranium City and moved into the old rectory which had been skidded over from Goldfields during the winter. Father Perin had begun living in it but at the moment he was back around Goldfields looking for his skiff which had disappeared during break-up.

One afternoon I was upstairs putting up partitions to divide that area into rooms when I answered a knock at the door. I was dumbfounded to find my parents standing there, having just arrived from Rochester, New York. The telegrams they had sent ahead to inform me of this visit never reached me. As if this were not enough of a surprise for one day, in less than an hour after their arrival Bishop Trocellier walked in unannounced! He had landed at Camsell Portage in his new Norseman aircraft CF-GTM through the dense smoke of forest fires. His intention was to confer the Sacrament of Confirmation on the twenty candidates I had prepared there but he did not want to go ahead without me. Being unable to use his aircraft to get me, he had Philip bring him over to Uranium City in the canoe. We all went back to Camsell Portage the next day, a Sunday. The bishop confirmed the children with my parents acting as sponsors.

That afternoon after Benediction of the Blessed Sacrament, the smoke having cleared somewhat, I flew back to Uranium City with the bishop and his entourage and we spent the night at the rectory. This visit gave me the opportunity to show the bishop the new mission at Camsell Portage and the problems facing us at Uranium City. He agreed with me that the old frame church we had moved over from Goldfields was not going to meet our needs and gave his permission to make plans for a new one. At the same time he made it official that I was the Pastor of Uranium City with jurisdiction over Camsell Portage and the surrounding mines. The next day I went over to the Eldorado Mine and using one of their drafting rooms began drawing up plans for a new church. The bishop had flown on to visit the missions at Fond du Lac and Stoney Rapids and on his return two days later picked me up and flew me back to Camsell, where Philip had hosted my parents in my absence. I had a plan of a church to show the bishop and he approved it.

Dad wasn't too impressed with my hospitality. He had flown in on Saturday and here it was Wednesday and he had seen very little of me so far. I assured him that the past few days were very unusual and that I had a great spot picked out for a fishing trip the next day. Before we could get away the following day, however, a Beaver aircraft landed on floats bringing in Gordon Moore, a mining consultant who was sent by one of the big

uranium companies to look at the KAY group of claims we had
staked some thirty miles west of Camsell. He needed both Philip
and me to show him those claims, so the fishing trip with Dad
was suddenly off. Philip and I were flying west and Dad and
Mom were left alone in charge of Mission Saint Bernard.

My father was not at all comfortable being completely surrounded by Indians; he had read too much of the Oregon Trail.
Mother told me that on one occasion when the mission was full
of natives he had removed his hat to expose his bald head and
announced, "Look! Already scalped!" I didn't realize how
relieved he was when I returned two days later. As it turned out
we might just as well have stayed home. We ran around with
Gordon for two days with our Geiger counters but all the "hot"
rocks we picked up turned out to be pegmatite and we never did
sell those claims. My parents' second week proved to be less hectic and I did my best to make up for the lost first week by spending as much time with them as I could. It was a good thing I did,
for that was their first and last trip to the Canadian North.

In the meantime Uranium City was growing like Topsy as the
new inhabitants replaced their tents with more permanent frame
buildings. To pay for their new brick liquor store, the Saskatchewan Government barged in thirty-eight tons of beer and
assorted spirits. One enterprising young man named David
Good began editing a newspaper called *The Uranium Times.* He
also sold insurance on the side and I took out a $5,000 fire insur-
ance policy on our old church and sent the $35 premium to the
bishop. The bishop wrote back that none of his buildings in the
Vicariate were covered by insurance and that he confided their
safety to St. Joseph (his patron saint). So I let it expire.

Mines were springing up all over the area and I was having
some difficulty visiting them with my canoe and kicker. So I had
the Wylie boys of Fort Chipewyan send me one of their fine
twenty-two-foot skiffs and I bought a new fifteen-horsepower
Evinrude motor from Dana Spence. He had just opened a hardware store in Uranium City. The Wylies took pups in trade for

their boat and the sale of the old eight-horse Johnson and the canoe paid for the new motor.

I took the plans I had drawn for a new church to a local carpenter named Slim Demgard and he estimated that he could build it for about ten thousand. Shortly after that I was over at the new FAY shaft at Eldorado where Bill McKee, foreman for Burns and Dutton Contracting, was supervising the new headframe. I mentioned that I was working on the project of a new church for Uranium City and he asked to see my plans. He asked me to let his architect draw up a proper working blueprint at no charge, so I gladly agreed. A week later he showed me the completed plans and told me they could put it up for us for $36,000. The figure seemed astronomical to me and I told him the bishop would never approve such an outlay. Bill wasn't going to take my word as final and immediately asked where the bishop lived. Within an hour we were in a chartered aircraft flying to Fort Smith. The next thing I knew we were in the bishop's office with the blueprints spread over his desk and before the afternoon was out we were back at Beaverlodge with the bishop's signature on the contract. I was amazed, delighted and slightly awed by Bill's salesmanship. He even made two costly changes to the plans for me. One was the substitution of steel I-beams under the floor to avoid pillars in the church basement and the second was the installation of another gothic window in the front of the steeple.

About two weeks later, after the 11 a.m. Sunday Mass at the Uranium City church, I was walking along the shore of Martin Lake visiting some families living in tents when one of them casually remarked to me, "Too bad about your church burning down today!" This was the first I'd heard of it and by the time I got back it was just a pile of smoking ashes. Apparently it had started after one of my parishioners threw a cigarette into the moss following the service. As there was no fire brigade in town as yet, it simply burned itself out. I sent a telegram to the bishop saying, "St. Joseph let us down here today. STOP. The church completely destroyed by fire." On the following day, however,

Bill McKee had his bulldozer working in the hot ashes digging the new church basement.

As soon as the walls began to rise I realized that I needed a name for the church. About that time a Sister Mary Bernard, R.S.M., wrote me from Rochester reminding me that the patron saint of miners is Saint Barbara. Of course: what could be more appropriate? Subsequently I got a chance to fly to the original New World site of Mission Santa Barbara in California, still directed by the Franciscans. There I got the background of this saint of the early church. I decided to use the Spanish version of her name and got the bishop's approval.

Using the new skiff and kicker I zipped down fifteen miles to the end of Crackingstone Point to spend a few days at the new Gunnar Mine and also to visit the old McInnes Fish Plant a mile away. Roy Schlader at the plant always made me feel welcome and this time gave me a complete tour of the operation. They had one warehouse full of winter ice for cooling the fresh trout and whitefish and walk-in freezers to freeze the fillets once they were packed in attractive boxes which, if I remember correctly, carried the Birdseye label. Eating at their mess hall was an experience that reminded me of my scholastic days: the men ate in complete silence, although I don't think that this was a company rule. Most of the men were Icelanders who lived around Lake Winnipeg. Roy explained to me that originally their fishing boats were manned by natives from Lake Athabaska, but the arrangement proved unsatisfactory. Apparently the local boys often got wind-bound in the harbour at Goldfields, where liquor was readily available. Consequently much of the fish they brought in rotted in the nets. This was unfortunate. The natives, who knew the lake like the backs of their hands, were relegated to the status of deck hands, while the Icelanders captained the boats.

When the dishes were cleared from the mess hall I set up my equipment and used it for a chapel. On at least one occasion I conducted this service with wet feet. I was wearing moose-hide moccasins and the cement floor had been hosed down following the meal. It took time for the travelling missionary to learn to cope with his environment.

I made it my first priority to be at the new Mission Saint Bernard in Camsell Portage on August 20th to celebrate its annual feast day. And this year was special, for the saint had died on this day in 1153, exactly eight hundred years before. The forty souls remaining in town joined me in the offering of a High Mass of Thanksgiving in the morning, followed by Benediction of the Blessed Sacrament in the afternoon. Then we all crossed over the short portage behind the village to the sandy beach beyond, where we enjoyed a picnic together.

With the rectory now habitable at U-City and the new church rising rapidly, it became apparent that a priest would be needed there full-time. Father Perin had returned to the east end of Lake Athabaska to start a new log mission at Stoney Lake. The bishop realized that I didn't want to quit Camsell Portage, so he appointed one of the Oblates from the Eskimo country to fill this post, Father John L'Helgouach, who came down from Aklavik. He arrived aboard *The St. Eugene* from Fort Chip and I immediately joined him at U-City to familiarize him with the area. Once he knew his way around I was free to continue visiting the mines from Camsell Portage. This arrangement suited me fine. I never did feel comfortable in that old rectory.

Early in September I got another chance to visit Eldorado's mine at Port Radium. Not only that, but I was able to cross Great Bear Lake again on *The Radium Gilbert* and visit my old mission at Fort Franklin. There I offered a special Requiem Mass for all the people who had died from tuberculosis since I had left, and I dusted off my Hare language to venture a sermon. The local boys took me by canoe from there down the Great Bear River to Bennett Field from which point the Eldorado DC-3 picked me up and returned me to Beaverlodge. It was less wrenching to leave Franklin this time, what with a neat new mission to return to at Camsell Portage.

While I continued visiting the mines around Uranium City, Philip took Mike Powder up to Tazin Lake to stake twenty-one claims on David Island, which we named the DAV group. It had become the current rush area and we thought we might have shot our own "elephant." At least we had our iron in the fire.

What we actually had on our hands was about three dozen sled-dogs to feed, mostly pups. Harold Reed, Superintendent of Game from Regina, had visited and signified his willingness to pay twenty-five dollars each for as many pups as we could produce, so we were keeping five bitches. At the time this money looked like its own bonanza. Harold was using them to restock the trappers around Walliston Lake area whose strain of sled dogs had deteriorated. We saw that we would have to put up a substantial supply of fish for these dogs in the fall when the fish were running so that we could feed them later through the winter when the catch fell off. To do this we decided to establish a fishing camp about twenty-five miles west of Camsell.

We got away finally on the 15th of October. I borrowed an extra skiff, hired Mike and Archie Powder, and loaded the boats with our tent and gear, all our dogs and fifteen nets. Darkness caught us off Lobstick Island a little short of our destination. We probed around in the dark looking for a campsite for the night. We couldn't find one, and finally slept in the open. The following morning we decided on Spider Island as our base of operations and set up our tent. We were surprised to find the shore of this island littered with new dimension lumber that must have been lost off the deck of a barge during a storm. We gathered up a valuable pile of it and then put out three nets. We were torn between getting our fifteen nets out and salvaging as much of this lumber as we could before it got frozen to the rocks along the shore. The following day we did set the rest of our nets, besides picking up more lumber. We found our island covered with low bush cranberries which were attracting sharp-tailed grouse on their fall migration south. We succeeded in picking off six of them with the .22 for our supper.

On Saturday afternoon I loaded up my skiff with fish and returned to the mission at Camsell in order to conduct Sunday services. When I returned to Spider Island on Monday the boys had over 1,500 fish, mostly whitefish, the rest trout. Our principal antagonist was the weather, which was typically windy with rough seas and freezing temperatures. They were constantly pounding the ice out of their boat with axes so that it was beginning to leak. Late that evening I pulled out for home with another full load of fresh fish, but in the failing light and high seas I clipped the end of a reef and lost one blade of my prop. I stopped long enough to cut down the other two blades to reduce the vibration, but it was far from satisfactory. I limped into Camsell in the dark, thankful to have a safe harbour for the night, but I realized that I would be forced to go to Uranium City for a new prop.

The next day I was on the high seas of Lake Athabaska in one of the worst storms of the season. With gale-force winds streaking out of the southwest across a hundred miles of open water the surface of the lake was unfit for any kind of boat travel. Once I got out far enough from our protected bay and felt its full fury behind me I couldn't turn around to face it to beat my way back. I was committed. The next twenty miles was quite a ride. My speed was scary, just slightly faster than the huge waves themselves. I would gradually edge up their windward side, cut through the spray at the peak and then plunge down the lee side like a giant surf board. Going over the crests the prop was often out of the water despite the fact that this kicker had a long shaft. To lose directional control and broach in these conditions would have spelt disaster. I finally made it, nonetheless, thanks to a lot of praying and considerable luck. I was not unscathed, however: my nice new skiff had suffered a split bottom board and a broken rib. Once into Black Bay, Bob Heron told me that he had turned back in his large commercial fishing boat. It looked as if I were the only fool out on the lake that day.

After conducting service at the Eldorado Mine on Sunday, I was again out on an angry sea heading back on Monday. That same south-west wind was still blowing, though not as hard. Luckily so, as now I had to force myself directly into it. At least I had a new prop and the motor sounded normal. Still, when I gained the shelter of Camsell harbour I had split another bottom board and the boat was again leaking and covered with ice from the freezing spray. Nothing had been heard from my crew on Spider Island and I was anxious to get through to them with the supplies I was bringing from town.

I got back out into the lake late in the afternoon to face a new obstacle – blowing snow coming directly at me, reducing visibility to a few hundred feet. Twenty miles down the lake it got dark and my motor quit when the carburetor iced up. I was washed by the breakers pounding on a reef near Lobstick Point and had to jump into the water and beach the skiff as best I could. Using a flashlight I got the carburetor apart and thawed out without too much trouble, but getting that heavily iced skiff back through the surf where I could restart the motor was almost more than I could manage in the dark.

Under way again, I found my way to Spider Island where I tied up to our temporary dock at midnight. The boys were fast asleep in the tent, snug in their feather robes. They didn't even hear me come in. I was too tired to eat or even to make a fire, so I simply unrolled my own bag and crawled in. Lying there waiting for sleep to come as the tent creaked and groaned in the wind and the snow piled up against it and covered the ground, I began to wonder whether keeping sled-dogs was worth all the work involved. It seemed that there was really no alternative, for the age of the snowmobile had not yet arrived.

When we peered out our tent flap in the morning we saw six inches of snow covering the ground, shore ice frozen out thirty feet, a pea soup fog covering a flat sea with the temperature at zero Fahrenheit. The prospects for continuing our fall fishery were not good. Beaten by the weather? Yes, and we had started a couple of weeks too late. Besides that we had all come down with miserable colds. When we visited the nets we got only 250 fish, which indicated that the whitefish run was over. It was no use to prolong the agony. We decided to quit Spider Island. I had tried unsuccessfully to hire a large boat to come from Black Bay to get all our fish and lumber and bring them back to Camsell in one load, but no one wanted to risk the lake in the month of November. I decided to take a good load back immediately, leaving the three boys to pull all our nets and put the fish on a hastily erected stage which would protect them from wolves and other predators. They would return with me on the next trip.

Back at the mission dock, my skiff was rigid with ice. This time, however, instead of chipping it out, I simply sank the boat and left it under water overnight. In the morning it was wet but ice-free and I congratulated myself on discovering yet another way of coping with the environment. The next day the wind was up and the temperature still down, so I waited late in the day, hoping conditions would improve. They didn't, and I was forced to pull out and to battle again an angry head wind and freezing spray along thirty miles of open water. When I finally reached our camp in the dark I was completely covered in ice and stiff with cold. The thought of the warmth of the tent had helped keep my spirits up for the last hour, but I was robbed of this reward when I found the tent cold and empty: the boys had gone! I revived my circulation by spending an hour alone, trying to pull the heavy skiff up on the shore ice where it wouldn't freeze in overnight.

The next day the seas were running so high I couldn't risk leaving the island with a full load, so I busied myself around the camp cutting firewood, chipping ice off the skiff, all the while keeping one eye on the weather, anxious to leave. The other skiff was gone; it had been leaking so badly I had to conclude that the boys had used it only to reach the mainland and from there had walked back to the village. I spent another lonely night in the tent on Spider Island before the wind finally dropped and I could prepare to leave. Breaking shore ice, I got the skiff back into the water and loaded with all our nets, plus 500 fish. Now the boat was so heavy that it was resting on rocks below and I was forced to get into the water to lift it off. This was when I noticed that my sealskin mukluks were leaking; mice had chewed holes in them during the night. Ill fortune continued to plague me: I got under way and had completed half the distance home when I ran out of gas. Luckily I stopped within poling distance of an abandoned drill camp where I found some fuel. I got back to the mission at two in the afternoon and found Philip and the Powder boys had walked in during the night.

As the lake was unusually calm we quickly unloaded and Philip immediately set out to get another load of fish from Spider Island. He didn't show up by nightfall and I was worried, but he did walk in at midnight. The carburetor had again iced up and he was forced to abandon the heavily loaded skiff across the portage a mile away. When we brought it around into the bay the next morning the temperature registered fifteen above zero and the fresh fish had frozen into one solid block of ice. We had to sink the boat with rocks in order to melt the fish loose. As the ice now extended out seventy feet from shore we were forced to call it quits and haul the boat out for good.

Spider Island had taught us a few tough lessons for coping with the wind and waves in below-freezing temperatures in an open boat where one is practically immobile and exposed to bone-chilling winds. We suffered more from the cold under these circumstances than we ever did travelling in the dead of winter with dogs. We agreed that it was less painful picking fish from nets set under the ice in winter than removing them from the same nets from a boat pitching on the waves and covered with ice. Next year we would do it differently.

The colds we had contracted in that tent on Spider Island could have been pneumonia. Even after we were back in the warmth of the mission Philip was still suffering from his, and a curious side-effect was that his ankles began to swell up. As two of the boys were determined to make one last trip to Uranium City by boat before freeze-up, Philip jumped in with them and went over to see Dr. Don McMillan at Eldorado. They returned without him, carrying a note saying that the diagnosis looked like Bright's disease and that he was being flown to the General Hospital in Edmonton for observation and tests. It looked like we hadn't heard the last of Spider Island. The thought of losing my faithful companion to a prolonged sickness was enough to depress me. I had all the townspeople joining me in fervent prayer for his speedy recovery. What else could we do?

In mid-December I left our dogs in the care of Mike Powder and flew to Uranium City, then continued over to Eldorado by road. I decided that I would go up to the mine at Port Radium and stay there over Christmas and New Year's, something I had never done before. To get there I went in the opposite direction first, flying the Eldorado DC-3 to Edmonton where I could check up on Philip's condition. He was still suffering from a severe kidney infection, but was making progress. His doctor thought that he could soon be discharged. With this good news I left him in the General and boarded one of Eldorado's DC-3's for the long day's flight to Great Bear lake. I had gotten to know the pilots and they invited me up front to view the frozen panorama out the front windows. Just north of Hottah Lake we flew over a vast herd of caribou that were being harassed by ten wolves. They epitomized the wild North and its primitive law of the survival of the fittest just as we, safe above in our comfortable travelling quarters, represented the last word in civilization. It was interesting to speculate on which world would outlast the other.

As it was close to Christmas I found the mine personnel in a particularly festive mood. Everyone had a word of good cheer and welcomed my intention of staying with them over the holidays. As usual the contingent of Irishmen was conspicuous by their faithful presence at the early morning mass. For the Christmas Midnight Mass the rec hall was crowded with just about everyone living at the mine. Mine Manager Gil Gillanders was his usual hospitable self and had me comfortably bunked in the guest house along with the pilots. When I heard that there were still a few Indian families living over at the old Cameron Bay townsite I walked the six miles over there after Christmas to get all the news in Hareskin from Fort Franklin. They had moved into the assay office and were doing enough trapping and casual work around the mine to keep the proverbial wolf from the door. George Blondin brought me back to the mine with his dog-team, although I would really have preferred to stay with the Indians.

If Christmas had a religious aura about it that engendered an atmosphere of "Silent Night, Holy Night," New Year's was something entirely different. Parties were being held every night in various quarters and the pitch of these celebrations was building as the last days of the old year ran out. To add fuel to the fire the 300 men working there were given an extra ration of liquor on the last day of 1953 to help them celebrate.

Early that evening I was availing myself of the luxury of a shower when a hand appeared before my face with half a glass of rye in it and a voice yelled, "Here, Padre, you can add your own water!" Evidently the chaplain was expected to join in the general celebration. Later in the evening I was glad I wasn't down in one of the bunkhouses when two groups started a war with the high pressure fire hoses. Although there was a Mountie in camp for the holidays, he could do little to disarm the combatants alone as they drove each other from end to end of their building with their water cannons. As the water got deeper they tore the doors off their rooms to walk on. With an outside temperature of fifty below, these floors began to freeze and they were soon slipping and falling on ice. The upshot was that the entire bunkhouse had to be evacuated in the middle of the night – to another bunkhouse – where the celebrations continued till dawn.

On New Year's Day most of the camp had sobered up with the exception of a few who were suffering from delirium tremens – like Joe Leduc who was bunked in a room adjoining mine. He started pounding on my wall and yelling for me to come and help him. When I got over there Joe was wide-eyed with fear. "Help me get this highboy over against that window before that tidal wave hits!" he yelled. Not having had any experience with delirium tremens patients I thought perhaps the best way to calm him down was to go along with his fantasies no matter how bizarre, so the first thing I knew I was helping Joe move not only the highboy but the bed and all the furniture up against his window facing the lake. "Get down! Get down!" Joe yelled, "Here she comes!" And then, when he reopened his eyes he said,

"Lucky it missed us, but help me get that crocodile out of here!" Finally we got the crocodile back out the window and the furniture back in place and I eased myself out the door saying, "Let me know if any more tidal waves come along, Joe." Christmas at Port Radium proved to be anything but dull. Still I was glad I was only visiting and not a permanent chaplain at that mine.

We flew south past the Beaverlodge mine and landed at Edmonton where I hurried over to visit Philip, still in hospital. His physician told me he was going to be discharged, but he advised against his spending the rest of the winter at Camsell Portage. In view of this admonition Philip decided to return to France to visit his family and I turned over to him all the money I had to finance the trip.

When I finally landed back at Mission Saint Bernard, I found our meat and fish all gone and the dogs starving. Not only that, but King, a beautiful, pure white lead dog from the Chip mission kennel, was lame. I had left orders not to drive the dogs, but I was told that Eric Powder had been using them to haul wood for himself. We still had a good supply of fish on our stage at Spider Island, so I took off the following day with a long string of dogs, leaving King at home to recuperate.

It was late in the afternoon when I made my departure, but I wasn't worried as the moon was full and I planned on spending the night with Simon Bashaw, a Russian trapper. He had a cabin up Colin River, a stream on the mainland a couple of miles from Spider Island. I was near the mouth of this stream travelling in the moonlight about 9 p.m., when suddenly my world went dark! The earth's shadow covered the moon in a total eclipse.

Once off the wind-blown lake the snow was hip deep and I couldn't find a trail with my feet as I searched from bank to bank. I had left my snowshoes back at the mission, thinking I wouldn't need them. By the time I plowed my way to Simon's cabin I was wringing wet and there was nobody home. I took my dogs out of harness and chained them to Simon's unique dog posts which supported a circular, thatched roof, gazebo-like structure intended to shelter his dogs from the winter storms. Although individually chained they could all sleep together under this common roof. I then picked my grub packsack from my sled and entered the dark cabin. Finally I located the candle, lit it, kindled a fire in his stove and fried some caribou steaks.

Looking around at the unusual contents of that cabin reminded me of the nights Philip and I had spent in it with Simon on some of our dogsled trips. Simon rated high on my list of unforgettable characters. He said he was a White Russian and we had no reason to doubt him. When he first came into this country he had built himself such a small log cabin it looked almost like a doll house with just enough length for a bunk to accommodate his short stature and one tiny window with a single ten inch by twelve inch pane of glass. That building was still standing, although its sod roof was falling in. His present cabin was a normal size and featured strings of bells hung outside each window to scare bears away. On entering the cabin, the first thing one noticed was the floor covered with all types and sizes of empty tin cans. When I asked Simon about this, he replied that once, years ago, he was visited by another trapper who spent the night with him. Before retiring, this fellow had asked for a chamber pot so that he could answer the call of nature during the night without having to open the front door. Simon looked high and low but couldn't find one, but then and there vowed to himself that he would never again be caught short of such a basic item of hospitality. He had been saving his cans ever since. The floor was so cluttered with them, in fact, that he had formed pathways through them to get around the cabin.

Another odd item was the radio sitting by his bed. It was completely covered with wax that had dripped from a thousand candles placed on top of it to read by. Two holes were worn through this covering to get to the tuning knobs. Simon spent his long, lonely evenings reading geology books, of which he had a good library above the head of his bunk. He claimed to know where all the minerals in the area were hidden and told us his price was $200 per day to guide prospectors to them. This was a modest price to pay to locate a mine he assured us, but to date no one had engaged his services.

Simon had some interesting supernatural experiences, he confided to us late one night. I think he told these stories for my special benefit. All of the incidents occurred while he was travelling by dogs in winter and sleeping by an open fire. He said he didn't pray often, but when he did he always got an immediate response. He had to be careful. Late during World War II he had heard of his countryman Stalin and decided to pray. Immediately a beautiful figure clothed completely in white walked into the firelight and asked, "Simon, did you call me?" Without asking, Simon knew he was face-to-face with Christ. "Yes," replied Simon, "I've been reading about the terrible war in my homeland and I wanted to volunteer my services to go back and speak to Stalin about ending this conflict and bloodshed." According to Simon, Christ thanked him for his offer and promised that he would call on him if it became necessary, but he never did.

Another time when Simon was camped out for the night with his sled-dogs chained around him he was bothered by a pack of wolves that were circling his camp, just out of sight. The constant whimpering of his dogs was keeping him awake, so again, as a last resort, he prayed. Immediately a beautiful figure dressed entirely in green walked up to his fire to ask if he had called. Simon asked this time if it were Christ again, but the heavenly figure replied, "No, Simon, I'm the Archangel Michael. What can I do for you?" Simon explained how the pack of wolves was harassing him. Without another word the angel beckoned to his companions who were standing just out of the firelight and together they each took hold of a wolf by the scruff of the neck and led them all away. "That's the last time wolves annoyed me," concluded Simon. And then, bringing his face up close to mine he asked, "Are you thinking I'm crazy?" "Of course not, Simon," I replied as convincingly as I could under the circumstances, though I doubt that there was much conviction in my tone. When we hit the trail the next day we were convinced that Simon, if not crazy, was certainly bushed.

Recollections like these were passing through my mind as I stayed alone in Simon's cabin that evening after supper, pulling on my pipe and wondering where he'd gone and when he'd return. And then I thought I heard the distant bark of a dog and jumped to the conclusion that it was Simon returning. I walked out of the cabin into the full moonlight which lit up the surrounding forest almost like day. It was an incredibly beautiful midwinter evening, absolutely calm and still. I stood there listening for a repetition of the sound I had heard.

There it was again, more of a lonesome howl than a bark, but certainly made by a dog. Or a wolf? It was close, toward the lake, and not moving. There was a hard trail in the snow going in that same direction so I began following it slowly. Soon I saw another cabin about two hundred yards away, one I didn't know existed. There was a thin wisp of smoke coming out of a stove pipe. Who could be living that close to Simon? Or had Simon moved? Now I could see the source of the howling I had heard, three dogs chained out behind. I wanted to look through the window before I went any farther. Though the faint glow of a candle seemed to be reflecting from the inside, the glass was too frosted to see through. I tried the door, but it was evidently locked from the inside. An old and weak female voice asked in Chipewyan, "Who's there?" I replied, *"Yati"* – "the priest" – but she immediately rejoined with *"Ille, eketsele onte"* – "No, it's the devil!"

I wasn't going to stand outside all night arguing with her, so I threw enough weight against the door to break the file that had locked it from the inside. Well, there she was lying on the floor, a little, wizened old Chipewyan woman in her feather robe. Her head was propped up on several sacks of flour, sugar and rolled oats. To her right was a small camp stove and to her left a stack of split kindling and a few cakes of ice. After she saw me she calmed down and took me for whom I said I was.

I was able to get her story, mostly by asking questions. First of all, she was Simon's wife. Secondly, she had fallen through the thin ice of Colin River, got herself soaked, and as a result caught a cold that got worse and worse. Finally, she told Simon that the only thing to cure her would be the meat of a young caribou. So he had left to kill one, but had already been gone "two Sundays." A couple of days before, she had turned delirious and rolled against the hot stove, which burned her one leg so badly she could no longer walk on it. She showed me the burn, but I had no medicines with me and could only put some lard on it and wrap it up as best I could. She had some stick fish hanging off her stage, so I fed her dogs and she gave me enough to feed mine, too.

It was several months later that I heard from Simon about the strange circumstances of his wife living in a separate cabin. After their marriage at Fort Chipewyan nearly forty years before, they had lived together for "nearly two weeks." Then there was a disagreement over her cooking, so Simon fixed up his warehouse and she moved there. That had solved their problem; since then they had enjoyed a happy marriage. No children issued from it, but according to Simon they never had an argument and, although separated, were actually very close. "Some evenings I go over there to visit and some evenings she comes over here," said Simon. According to the Crees at Camsell I learned that they not only lived separately, but travelled the same way. In winter she followed his team with her own sled and dogs, and in summer he towed her small canoe behind his boat and motor.

The following morning I saw that the old woman was as comfortable as possible under the circumstances and tried to make her understand that although I had to leave I would send her help as soon as possible. I then harnessed up and drove the two or three miles out to Spider Island where I found that the drifting snow had built a natural ramp right up to our fish stage making it easily accessible to the foxes and wolves who had been helping themselves. I took only 150 fish because my dogs were still weak from their prolonged hunger while I was away and couldn't haul a full load. As it was, it took me six hours to get back to the mission.

I sent a telegram to the RCMP in Uranium City and they immediately dispatched a medevac plane for the old lady and flew her to the hospital. Another flight searched and found Simon camped on a lake about fifty miles north of his cabin. He was still waiting for caribou. His wife didn't live too many months following her ordeal and died in her cabin. When the Mounties came to investigate, Simon told them to give all her stuff to the mission at Chip. He didn't want to keep any of it. They were amazed to find under the loose floor boards at the back of her cabin many new items like guns, axes, bolts of cloth, and so on, things she had bought with her own fur money and hoarded. She had been an excellent hunter and trapper. The natives at Camsell said she drifted silently through the bush on snowshoes in winter, dressed all in white canvas clothing she had made. They were afraid of her. Simon, finding life alone too hard, later moved to Chip and Philip bought his cabin and trapline.

13

FOR EVERYTHING,
A SEASON

Living alone again, I had to be out driving a dog-team on a daily schedule, either cutting and hauling firewood to keep the mission warm, or bringing in fish to keep the huskies fuelled. Besides the regular trips to Spider Island, I was also visiting several nets set under the ice nearby. The fact that I had so many mature dogs, two full teams of six each, plus the corral full of pups in various stages of development, meant that we needed far more fish than our neighbours. And this particular winter with Philip gone I had to feed his non-working team as well. These sled-dogs required about five pounds of fish per night each, more if they were working or the temperature was extremely cold. I not only had to provide for them on a daily basis, but to stockpile ahead so a neighbour could feed them when I was away visiting the mines.

When I hitched up and left for Uranium City on January 26th it was forty-five below zero. King had had several weeks' rest to recuperate from his "sprain," so I put him in the lead position. He never let his traces slacken all the thirty miles to town although he began limping badly the last few miles. The next day I took him to see Dr. McMillan at the mine clinic and he X-rayed his front leg. The negative clearly showed that both bones had been broken. Neither of us could understand how he could have run

185

so far in that condition. It was an amazing testimony to sheer grit and determination that bolstered my already considerable admiration for these great animals.

Although we put his leg in a plaster cast, just like a human, he never regained full use of it and continued to limp even after it had fully knit. So I had to retire him from the team and presented him to Leon LaPrairie who kept him as a mascot for his mine on Beaverlodge Lake. The following year I was saddened to hear that King had been mistaken for a wolf and shot.

In the meantime, life was going ahead full-steam in the "Uranium Capital of the World" and in all the surrounding bush camps and nascent mines. The staking stampede was being compared to the Klondike fifty years before, as newcomers flocked in from all over the world. Although half the residents in town were still living in tents, houses were being skidded over from Goldfields in a steady stream and all kinds of frame buildings were going up even during the sub-zero months. Gus Hawker, still operating out of a tent, claimed he was doing up to $4,000 worth of business some days. The Eldorado Mine five miles away had become a small town in itself, with a population of 750. Brother Larocque was putting the final touches to the interior of Santa Barbara church with a beautiful spiral staircase to the choir loft. A second newspaper, *The Uranium Era*, was being published by Jock McMeekan who had quit Yellowknife for the new boom town.

In Prince Albert, five hundred miles south, the Saskatchewan Mines Branch of the government announced that dozens of prospectors had cashed in claims for amounts ranging from $10,000 to $1,000,000. I kept running into reporters from outside. Famous northern photographer Richard Harrington took pictures of me and my team and advised me to get a Rolleicord camera like the one he used. Soon afterwards, I was written up in the *Toronto Daily Star*, which mentioned that I had hung up a "For Sale" sign on over 100 uranium claims. The proceeds would help pay off a $50,000 debt on the new church in town.

Not long afterwards I received a telegram through the Saskatchewan Government Telegraph Office in town from some oil company in New York offering me $250,000 in cash, plus 300,000 shares of stock if I would turn over to them within ten days the twenty-seven claims Philip and I owned on David Island in Lake Tazin. This offer seemed too good to be true. I had just gotten over to Camsell Portage when it was relayed to me and I immediately harnessed up and went back to U-City singing all the way! I had just tied up my dogs outside the rectory at U-City and was inside thawing out when there came a knock at the door. A certain Mr. Watt claiming to represent a small prospecting company called Great West Uranium handed me a piece of paper and hastily departed. It was an official court order called a "Caveat" against our twenty-seven claims on David Island which we had registered as the DAV Group. The Latin word *caveat* means, literally, "let him beware" and pertains to anyone interested in the property, warning him not to proceed with any transaction until the party serving the notice is heard. In other words, Great West Uranium was claiming some unspecified interest in these claims for some reason they did not give. My high-flying spirits were shot down even before I could contact New York.

Now I needed someone I didn't think I would ever need: a lawyer. I needed him in a hurry, too, because I had never been the subject of any legal action and I had no idea of the consequences of a caveat. The only lawyer I had met in Uranium City was Edward Lussiere who had flown into town from Regina to organize a chapter of the Canadian Legion. I was glad at the time to let him use the basement of the new church to hold his meeting and he had told me afterwards that if I ever needed the services of a lawyer to contact him. Without delay I put the case completely in his hands. Soon he got word back to me that this caveat could not be lifted before it had gone before a judge of the Queen's Bench Court in Regina, and the earliest hearing we could get would be in nine months. One can imagine my thoughts as I stood on the back of my sled returning to Camsell.

I brightened considerably when I received a letter from one Albert Jacobs in Calgary who was also interested in claims we held. This time it involved the forty-two HAR Group of claims we had staked around Camsell Portage. A subsequent letter contained an airline ticket on Canadian Pacific's DC-3 and I soon found myself in Calgary. I was impressed with the apparent integrity of Jacobs and his group of business friends who owned and operated a company called Great Shield Uranium Mines Limited. Although they owned properties containing various minerals, they were anxious to acquire some uranium property before the bubble burst. Many companies were doing this to enhance their image and help sell stock. They were also interested in our DAV Group once we got the caveat lifted from it. The upshot of this meeting was that I flew home with 50,000 vendor's shares of stock in Great Shield Uranium. These could not be converted to cash as they were held in escrow (that is, held in trust by a third party for delivery only after fulfillment of the conditions specified).

In the meantime Philip had run out of money in Europe where he was touring by motorcycle, so I sent him $250. This money came from our sale of salvaged lumber on Spider Island. Any money I collected at the mines was going to Father L'Helgouach at Uranium City to help pay for the new church. The sale of a few uranium claims for cash at this time would have been welcome.

The day after our arrival in Regina we finally got to see our antagonists from Great West Uranium in a pre-trial discovery hearing. To our amazement their lawyer stated that his clients had made a mistake in filing the original caveat against us on the flimsy pretext that they had gotten the names of the Powder boys working with Philip mixed up with other Powders from Camsell Portage who had previously worked for them and who had signed a contract that they would not stake for anyone else for a period of three years. Would we settle out of court? Imagine waiting nine months to hear this and to have lost our $250,000 sale in the meantime. Our lawyer pointed out to them that we were not just fighting an unjust caveat, but suffered the consequent loss of sale.

Although we had already waited nine months, we still had to wait another week in Regina while the same judge heard another case. We sat in on it as it involved a conflict over staking claims in our area. The judge was constantly interrupting testimony to ask simple questions about the country and the fundamental rules for staking claims. Evidently he had never handled cases like these, but it seemed to me that he could have cut days off his hearing time if he had simply studied the rules for staking mineral claims. The defendant in this case was so certain of an outcome favourable to his case that he had gone ahead and spent thousands of dollars drilling on his disputed property. This judge, however, amazed us all by rendering a decision not only against the defendant, but contrary to Saskatchewan's own mining regulations. I had supper with this poor man following the verdict. He was a defeated man and a likely candidate for suicide. I had sat through the entire proceedings and felt strongly that it had not been a fair judgement. Besides that, I was beginning to have doubts about getting a just verdict for our own case.

When our case came up the next day it proved to be unique for this court, as neither our lawyer nor the judge himself had ever been involved in a caveat case involving mineral claims. When Great West Uranium's own lawyer admitted that they had made a mistake in their caveat the judge was forced to agree with him. In his brief, however, our lawyer had not only protested the false caveat, he had also claimed general damages of a modest $50,000 for the loss of a bona fide sale due to this caveat. At this point the judge knocked the ground out from under our case, declaring that our loss of the sale should have been termed "a particular" damage; if we wished to pursue this claim we would have to start proceedings for an entirely new action. In other words he dismissed our claim to a just compensation on the basis of one word. The only compensation we did realize was $1,600 to cover our travelling and hotel expenses. Our own lawyer, who represented a firm of nine law partners in Regina, was so disgusted with this verdict that he refused to charge anything for representing us.

As soon as the red-serge Mountie on duty in the courtroom dismissed us, I immediately walked over to the new Saskatchewan Mines Building where an old friend from Uranium City, Don Sheridan, was in charge. I told him the story of our caveat experience from beginning to end. As Saskatchewan mining regulations then stood, anyone could get a caveat injunction against any mining company or individual on the flimsiest of evidence or, as in our case, on a false accusation. Not only could such a property under caveat not be transferred or sold, the caveat effectively tied up all stock promotion work or other financing. Sheridan acknowledged the urgent need for new legislation to plug this loophole and several months later sent me a copy of the new ordinance respecting "false and vexatious" caveats such as the one we had just gotten lifted. There was now an automatic penalty attached to filing such a caveat of $25 per claim per day. If this law had been in effect nine months earlier Great West Uranium would have paid $675 per day or $182,250 for the nine months they had their caveat on our claims. As the five of us flew back to Uranium City we reflected on the low calibre of justice dispensed by the Court of Queen's Bench in Regina. One can easily imagine my reaction to an offer from this same company a few months later to act as their representative in our area.

In the end we fared little better in our association with Great Shield Uranium Mines. Philip got some money to do some trenching on our HAR Group of claims and mining engineer Gordon Moore did confirm that there was U308 present on this property, but for various reasons the company had difficulty selling enough stock to finance further work. Over time I was asked by Albert Jacobs to surrender to him my shares of vendor's stock until finally I was left with none and the company died. Chalk it all up to experience. From the outside it looked like an interesting game. We played it and lost.

More than know-how was involved in the staking and selling of uranium claims and in playing the market on the many stocks offered by the established mines in the area. Certainly Pat Hughes and his Hibernian cohorts had been blessed with the proverbial luck of the Irish. At Eldorado a group of executives had formed an investment club to pool their knowledge and funds in an effort to pick the right stocks. After the first year they found to their surprise that they had lost forty percent of their money. During the same time an illiterate immigrant hoistman at that mine had made a small fortune investing in similar stocks without the benefit of any professional advice. Simply luck.

Following the last heroic run of King to Eldorado I stayed around the area for two weeks, visiting various mines. Then I returned to Mission Saint Bernard and the simple life to wind down and regain my serenity and peace of mind. I cleaned out the rest of our fish from Spider Island, saw my wood pile grow again and joined the Crees on caribou hunts. I got the last of the cupboards built in the mission and found I could keep warm even overnight in this log cabin by stoking the cast iron heater with green birch just before retiring. The beautiful view out my front windows facing the bay more than compensated for the absence of electricity, running water and inside plumbing. I had these comforts at the mines, but was happier without them at Camsell Portage. They were nice, but not really necessary to happiness.

By the first part of April I was back visiting the mines and even flying up to visit the boys at Port Radium again. On Good Friday I left U-City by dogs and was back at Camsell before noon. The next day was Holy Saturday and in preparation for Easter a crew of women gave the mission a good house cleaning. In the midst of this activity a Beaver aircraft landed on skis in front of the village carrying four chief game wardens: Frank McCall from Northwest Territories, Harold Reed from Regina, Chick Terry from Stoney Rapids and Earl Shannon from U-City. The women retired to their homes and I rang the bell to summon the men to a trappers' meeting. When everyone was in and accounted for, Frank McCall took the floor to discuss the question of wolves.

He told us that in 1933 there had been fourteen white trappers working out of Fort Reliance who had been taking about 900 wolves per year. Last year, 1953, about 1,000 wolves were killed in N.W.T., without any bounty being paid, while during the same period 350 were killed by Saskatchewan trappers who were paid ten dollars per wolf. Eight trappers from Camsell Portage were trapping in the N.W.T. All four wardens present agreed that the bounty was simply another form of government subsidy and did not affect the number of wolves taken. Frank cited, as an example of politics interfering with game management, the recent election of Merv Hardy as the first Member of Parliament for the N.W.T. Keeping a promise he had made during his campaign, he immediately got the game laws changed, making the shooting of beaver legal, while five cases of transgression against the previous law were still pending in Fort Smith. The Game Department had had no say in the change in regulations. Various opinions were expressed back and forth regarding wolves and beavers while I took the minutes. After an afternoon of discussion it was finally resolved that the Camsell trappers would be allowed to take 13 beaver and 50 muskrat each during the upcoming spring hunt while the community as a whole would be allowed 6 permits for moose. Following the meeting I cooked up a caribou steak supper for the group and they took off.

Easter Sunday broke clear and ten above zero. My two bells, the first a half-hour before service and the second fifteen minutes before, saw the whole village crowding into the mission's common room. When the curtains were opened, revealing the altar at the far end, they were in church. We sang a High Mass to celebrate the Lord's Resurrection and the twenty-six children of school age outsang their elders. The first collection of the year (the second being at Christmas) amounted to $17.39. In the evening they returned to watch a slide show of local scenes and local people, which they loved.

While the airwaves those nights were filled with the hearings of the investigation by Senator Joe McCarthy, I much preferred to read about the North. I had a good library of Arctic books and practically confined all my reading to that subject, as I had done since high school days. The exploits of the early explorers particularly excited my imagination. In the back of my mind I entertained the thought that some day I would work along the Arctic Coast. I was perfectly happy on Lake Athabaska, but the Far North held a special challenge. Often when I would write the bishop I would end my report by reminding him that if ever he were in need of someone to fill an empty Arctic mission he had an eager volunteer in me.

Toward the end of April the warm rays of the sun had melted the drifts of snow on the main lake to a point where one could again use the sixteen-foot Eskimo komatik with its steel runners. I decided to make another trip to the far east end of Lake Athabaska and in Philip's place chose Archie Powder to accompany me. He went by the nickname "Curley" and had a special fondness for the Hank Williams tune "You Win Again," which he sang throughout our entire trip. Our first port of call was Gunnar Mine on the tip of Crackingstone Point where we stopped for lunch. Since my last visit there had been a few changes, one of which was a sign outside the mess hall which read, "This Mine Under the Atomic Energy Control Board – Authorized Personnel Only." In fact, we couldn't get into the mess hall without a proper ID card and by the time I had gotten one from the office the mess hall was closed. Curley and I drove the dogs across to the island and made a fire there.

Before camping that night on Big Fowl Island east of Goldfields we were lucky to have killed one caribou. The following day we pushed through to Fond du Lac in eight hours without stopping to make a fire. We passed a pleasant night at the mission with Father Gamache and Brother Labonté and then continued east down the centre of the narrowing lake. For the last ten miles into Stoney Rapids the shore of the lake is covered with giant arctic willows, which at the time of our passing were covered with thousands of migrating willow ptarmigan. I never saw so many congregated in one spot before, nor have I since. We passed by Stoney Village at 7:30 in the evening and then got on the portage trail to Black Lake and went for another hour before we hit the small settlement of Stoney Lake. Here I found my Goldfields companion, Father Rudolph Perin, busily engaged in building an addition to his log mission. As space was limited we decided to go on another few miles to the village of Black Lake where the old mission cabin was empty.

Curley and I spent an interesting week at Black Lake. Here we found the Chipewyan Indians to be very primitive, compared to others we had seen. For example, there was one cabin there that still had windows made of caribou skin, which had been used all over the North before the first glass was imported. Some were wearing parkas made of caribou hide and one girl wore a beautiful sable coat made entirely of marten skins. I took pictures of her. In fact I spent most of the week either walking about taking pictures or at the mission making sketches of various visitors. I now had a Bell and Howell 16 mm movie camera with plenty of Kodachrome film supplied by various friends in Rochester who worked for Eastman Kodak. The film I exposed then now holds a record of a way of life long since passed. These people were waiting for the spring migration of the caribou upon which they depended greatly, for government social assistance was still unknown in their country. As the snow was melting rapidly, most of the men of the village were busy attaching runners to the bottoms of their toboggans to protect the wood boards from the candling ice on which they would soon be running.

By the tenth of May I decided we had stayed as long as we could, given the deteriorating ice conditions we would meet before getting back to Camsell Portage. We left in a spring snow storm that turned to rain after we passed Stoney Rapids and completely soaked our winter parkas and moose-hide foot gear. Luckily we came upon a tent and pulled up in front of it. The occupant was a white trapper by the name of Fred Riddle who spent his winters out on the Barrens and was camped at this spot now to intercept some of the migrating caribou. He would put up the meat in mason jars for winter use.

During the afternoon a troop of these animals passed in front of the tent and we helped Fred shoot and butcher ten of them. In the evening around his camp stove this veteran of "the land of little sticks and silent places" regaled us with interesting stories of his life there. It was his custom to fly north to his remote log cabin with his dogs a month before the first snows came. He would spend this time gathering dry willows for his winter's fuel. One fall he encountered a huge Barren Lands grizzly rolling in fat just prior to hibernation. Fred shot him and got enough fat from his carcass to fill a forty-five-gallon barrel. At one time he had neighbours trapping out there who used to run into each other occasionally, but now he was all alone, the last of that breed.

We continued on our way the following morning in deteriorating ice conditions. In many places we detoured around black ice that was completely candled and ready to give way under any pressure from above. As usual, we dragged a forty-foot rope behind the sled which served many purposes. It was always securely tied when we were harnessing up in the morning lest the anxious dogs should give a lurch and the sled take off before we were ready. If we ran behind the sled to warm up on cold days we always held on to this rope in case we fell and could thereby drag the dogs to a stop. It served another purpose this day when we approached a patch of rotten ice going through the narrows at Pine Channel. When it looked inevitable that the sled would break through the ice, Curley and I jumped off holding this rope and circling to the side. The dogs fell through followed by the komatik just as we expected and they were able to scramble out again. If we hadn't been able to help them with that long rope, however, the dogs wouldn't have been able to pull our loaded sled up onto solid ice again. If we had not been alert we most certainly would have found ourselves floundering in very deep water.

Dog-driving, like piloting an aircraft, is not really very difficult to learn, but to do it successfully demands a certain amount of good judgement and common sense. Otherwise disaster can overtake one when least expected. It took us eight hours to get from Fred's tent to Fond du Lac, where the rain resumed just as we pulled into the mission yard. The following day was cooler, with the result that the candling ice was sharper on the dogs' feet and their pads were beginning to cut and bleed. This condition didn't seem to bother them, for they kept up a very brisk dog-trot all day, sometimes breaking into a run when we got close to a band of migrating caribou.

On day four of our trip home we entered St. Mary's Channel which cuts through the southern tip of Crackingstone Point. The ice in this area was particularly bad and we proceeded with caution past the deserted buildings of the McInnes summer fish plant and stopped on the island two miles farther on opposite Gunnar Mine. We pitched our tent here and prepared to spend the night. I had two objectives in mind. The first was to hold a service for the 150 men working at the mine under the capable direction of Manager Norm Grant. The second was to prevail upon Clementine Mercredi, whose family was camped nearby, to sew canvas shoes quickly for our nine dogs. As it turned out, I didn't get a one hundred percent turnout for the Mass I offered at Gunnar Mine, nor did Clementine finish enough shoes for all the dogs. Still, when we pushed on for the final leg of our journey the next day, at least the worst-cut feet were shod.

All across the thirty miles of open lake ice there was a constant ominous creaking under our sled and most of our dogs were limping. When we arrived at the entrance to Camsell Bay there was already a wide gap of open water between the ice and the shore and we had to look hard for a spot where we could get safely ashore. Once we were back on terra firma in the village, Curley's family rushed down to pump his hand like one returned from the dead. I unharnessed the dogs, feeling grateful for their splendid three-hundred-mile effort, and chained them to the line with the assurance that they could take it easy until the fall. It was the middle of May and we had been gone seventeen days. Time now to rest and loll under the warming sun of break-up.

It felt natural to slip back into the easy routine of life at the Camsell mission. I was hardly burning any wood now, so that was no longer a problem. Although the dogs were eating less than they did in winter I still had twenty to feed. With all our nets pulled out for break-up our only source of fish was the shallow water across the portage where the jackfish were numerous. A common method of catching them was to wade around in hip boots with a .22, and when one was spotted to approach as quietly as possible and then fire off the gun under water close to him. The concussion would generally stun him so that he would float to the surface long enough for us to grab him. If we delayed he would get his senses back and take off. I fed the dogs many a day after spending an hour or two at this pursuit. When more ice melted we could resume casting with a spoon hook.

Before the month was out there was enough open water in the bay for a float plane to land. It was a couple of local boys with a load of liquor from U-City. I had to wince as I watched it off-loaded, knowing what the consequences would be: a wild party followed by a fight, shouting, swearing, someone pounding on my door early in the morning to get a cut bandaged or sewn up, some women walking around the village the next day with black eyes. The Crees were unlike the Chipewyans or Hares: they held grudges for a long time; under the influence of liquor they often exploded in anger. Every time hard liquor came into the village I was apprehensive. For this reason I refused to drink with the natives and never bought any myself.

By the fifth of June there was enough open water to launch my skiff and go down to the far end of the bay a mile away and set a net. While down there I did some casting and caught a pike so large I had to go ashore and gradually drag him up on the beach. I didn't have any scales, but guessed he was over twenty-five pounds. It was the largest jackfish I ever caught. A week later the main lake was free enough of ice to permit me to return to Uranium City and the mines. The Mercredis, still camped near the McInnes fish camp, told me they could easily take care of my dogs there during the summer, when the fish plant had plenty of scraps for the taking. So I went back and brought them all over, relieved of that worry.

❋ ❋ ❋

The first winter I served as chaplain at Eldorado Mine I got my first exposure to Unionism. This was before the staff house was built and I was given an office off one of the bunkhouses. The office was separated by a thin partition and one could easily hear voices through it. I remember very vividly an organizer from the Mine, Mill and Smelters' Union talking to several of the workers in the bunkhouse about forming a union. He was evidently going about it by down-grading the present living conditions, telling the men that the slop they were eating was fit only for dogs, and that they should be sleeping in clean sheets and not sleeping bags. Many were Displaced Persons from Europe who had suffered through World War II and now thought they were in heaven. This organizer did his best to convince them that they were being short-changed by management. I was alarmed to hear this line of vitriolic dissension being sown among the men and began asking questions about this union. I found out that they had their headquarters in Sudbury, Ontario, and had been permanently barred from the Canadian Federation of Trade Unions. They were heavily infiltrated by Communists and used any means, fair or foul, to gain their ends.

When they started agitating at the Nesbitt-LaBine Mine the officials there attempted to thwart them by proposing to their men a company union. This move provoked the Mine-Mill organizers so much they began harrying and beating up some of the company men. Bernie Belec, for instance, could not leave the mine without a police escort. In the end Mine-Mill did get certification at this mine, but some of the votes were forged.

During the summer I was attracted to the Eldorado mess hall one night to attend a meeting called by one "Brother" Thibault, one of the Mine-Mill officials from Sudbury. I sat at the back and listened for two hours to this man calumniate the mine management people. It was vicious, untrue and calculated to drive a wedge between management and labour. It was "them" against "us," and of course Brother Thibault was one of "us." No member of the staff was there to defend management, but if I had not been in my position I would have loved to have stood and refuted some of his lies.

Shortly afterwards the mine had a visit from an official of the American Federation of Labor Union (A. F. of L.) in the person of Carl Berg. Here was a man devoid of deceit who took a good look around and observed just how well the men were being paid and treated and at his meeting told them that he was not about to promise pie in the sky if they joined his union, but that if they had a mind to unionize he would be glad to represent them. I was impressed with his sincerity, in marked contrast to the representatives of the other union.

By Saskatchewan law a mine could not really protect itself against unscrupulous labour unions. They are free to proselytize at will. As a Crown Company, however, Eldorado was exempt from this law and could have insulated its workers from the likes of the Mine-Mill Union, but it didn't. Perhaps it didn't want to encourage any unnecessary criticism from the press. Furthermore, its management at the time wouldn't believe that a union as corrupt as Mine-Mill could persuade its men to choose it as their bargaining agent. So they let it come to a vote without any hindrance and were amazed to see it ratified by a whopping eighty-seven percent!

By the time this happened Mine-Mill had gotten themselves certified as official bargaining agents for all the surrounding mines, with the exception of the Gunnar Mine. Its president and founder Gilbert LaBine wrote me and asked my help in preventing his mine from going "Communist" like the others in the area. He said he didn't care what union represented his men as long as it wasn't Mine-Mill. I immediately thought of Carl Berg and his A. F. of L. and wrote him in Edmonton. As a result he sent up two shop stewards who were signed on at Gunnar incognito to begin organizing the men. We had to be careful not to alarm the local

Mine-Mill officials who had not been able to get a foot in the door at Gunnar. One reason for this was its isolation: at the southern tip of Crackingstone Point, it had no road access from Uranium City. At the same time I began to conduct a series of talks and discussions on labour unions in general at the mine following my regular services. Of course I emphasized the importance and advantages of belonging to a union that was affiliated with the Canadian Congress of Labour. After two months the time looked right for a vote, so I wired Carl to fly up, signing my telegram "Mother"! I posted notices around Gunnar for an important meeting of the 220 hourly-rate workers at the mine, to be held Sunday, July 4th at 8 p.m. in the mess hall. Over 300 showed up.

The meeting came to order promptly and was chaired by Carl Berg who gave a brief synopsis of the labour movement in Canada in general. As soon as he mentioned his affiliation with the A. F. of L. we found that we had a contingent of the enemy in our midst. One rabid apostle of the Mine-Mill Union took the floor claiming to be one of many ex-seamen in the hall who were vehemently opposed to any American labour union in general and to the A. F. of L. in particular. He was backed up by a chorus of similar discontents who were yelling that there was no way that they would let their union dues go to an American organization, that this mine was not ready yet to vote on such a serious matter. Luckily the whole lot of them stormed out of the hall or it could have turned into a bloody brawl. They immediately started gathering signatures outside for certification of their union.

We still had a majority in the hall for certification for A. F. of L. if we could get them to sign up. It didn't look too promising. Carl looked worried. I felt weak in the knees. The moment of truth had arrived as Carl sent the voting cards out into the audience for signatures. The men brought them back one by one to the speakers at the table and they were counted. The results, fifty-one percent of the mine's total hourly-rate employees had elected the A. F. of L. Union as their official bargaining agent. It was as tight a victory as we could have won, but it was valid and completely above board. I felt greatly relieved. Carl felt vindicated. Gilbert was so happy with the outcome when he got the news that he sent me a cheque for $1,000 in appreciation for my part in the whole operation.

Two weeks later I was back in my office at Gunnar when I got an unexpected visit from another representative of the A. F. of L. Union. He was a tall gentleman with what sounded like a Russian accent. He said he had been sent out by Union headquarters to express their sincere thanks to me for helping them so effectively gain certification at this mine and with those words he ceremoniously handed me a cheque. I thanked him most sincerely saying how happy I had been personally with the outcome and looked forward to a happy and peaceful cooperation at the mine between management and labour. I couldn't wait for him to leave the room so I could look at the figure on his cheque. I must admit I was surprised when I read that it was made out for five dollars. Nonetheless, the experience was worth far more than that to me and it was a great satisfaction to see the good guys win for once.

I was in for another pleasant surprise when I got back to U-City. Philip arrived suddenly without any warning. He looked great and from what he said was completely cured of his Bright's disease. Never one to write, he had not sent back much news from France, but now he told me of his adventures. He spoke of his sculptor father who was working on another huge equestrian statue in marble, of his brother who ran an automobile plant, of his sister who had joined an order of nuns who pray especially for the souls in purgatory, and finally he got to himself. He had bought a motorcycle and toured a lot of Europe. What he was seeking primarily was a wife who would be willing and able to share his life at Camsell Portage. In this quest he had failed, so he was back to carry on helping me where he had left off eight months before. We lost no time getting down to the port at Black Bay, where our skiff with its motor was pulled up, waiting to take us back to Camsell Portage. Although there were only forty people spending the summer there, they welcomed Philip back as one of their own. His familiar presence back in Mission Saint Bernard made it far less lonely for me and gave me a morale boost too, not to mention the physical help his presence meant. I immediately took him out and showed him where our nets were set.

Once Philip was settled in again I took leave to visit my far-flung parish. First of all I crossed with the skiff to the McInnes fish camp at Crackingstone Point where I spent the night on one of their barges and said a 6:30 Mass in another. Then I crossed over to Gunnar Mine where the work force had swelled to 450 men during the erection of their mill. Gilbert LaBine himself happened to be visiting his mine and he explained to me that he was determined to have his own mill and process his own ore, rather than send it over to Eldorado's mill on Beaverlodge Lake as all the other mines in the area planned to do. He had a chip on his shoulder ever since Eldorado had taken over his operation on Great Bear Lake. For one thing, they had also taken his Northern Transportation system. They had promised to return it after the war, but they didn't.

Close by Gunnar on a small island there was a shrine to the Blessed Virgin set up in a tall pine tree, from which St. Mary's Channel got its name. Old-timer Father Riou told me that this shrine had been erected by Modest Ladoucer of Fond du Lac to fulfil a vow he had made to the Virgin following a safe crossing from St. Joseph's Point in a rowboat about 1890. Now I was told by one of the workers at the mine that the crew of one of the Northern Transportation barges, while unloading at Gunnar, had gone to this island for a picnic. One of the men found the shrine and had taken the statue of the Virgin from it and thrown it out into deep water in the channel. Others of the party were horrified at this callous act of vandalism and predicted bad luck for their boat. They hadn't long to wait. On their return trip to Waterways they encountered a bad storm near Bear Island toward the south shore of Lake Athabaska. The captain, in attempting to remove the barge they were pushing and put it on tow behind, had the misfortune of seeing the towing cable rake the deck of his boat, cutting all the superstructure, including his pilot house, clean off and sinking his boat. There were no survivors. When found, the barge was acting like a buoy still attached by its cable to the boat on the bottom of the lake. Subsequently I put another statue of Our Lady up in its niche, where I hope it remains to this day.

As these barges didn't go beyond Black Bay on Lake Athabaska, a new bell addressed to Father Perin's new mission at Stoney Lake was left there and I was asked to deliver it. This gave Philip and me a chance to travel to the east end of the lake for the first time by boat. At Fond du Lac we found Father Gamache building himself a new mission aided by his sidekick, Brother Labonté, and supervised by Brother Larocque, who had helped me establish the mission at Fort Franklin. When we stopped there for the night, I noticed a huge, thirty-foot skiff-shaped boat on the beach which I had not seen in the winter, possibly because it was drifted over with snow. It had been the brainchild, apparently, of a young missionary who had spent a year with Father Gamache and who abandoned it after its inboard engine failed to work. Father Gamache told me I could take it, so Philip and I tarried another day there filling in the hole in its bottom where the shaft had protruded and made it shipshape for launching.

When we got to Stoney Rapids with our heavy bronze cargo the following day we could find no way of transporting it overland the final five miles or so to Stoney Lake where the empty belfry waited. The locals told us that the rapids were too swift for a boat the size of ours to go up, but after hearing that some of the natives made it in their canoes I decided to give it a try. We made it up to Stoney Lake without touching a rock and were met by the missionary and some of his flock, who seemed quite amazed at our feat. Actually it was far easier than ascending the Great Bear River up to Great Bear Lake. We unloaded and sped back to Fond du Lac in three-and-a-half-hours. The next day we launched the giant skiff we dubbed *The Ark*, and, pulling it behind us, continued right down the middle of the lake. Luckily, it was flat calm and we got into Camsell at midnight, after running fourteen consecutive hours.

About the middle of August Philip took me in our skiff over to Black Bay and dropped me off so that I could visit the mines. He needed the boat to do some assessment work on our claims. I spent a week at the Eldorado Mine and then flew in their DC-3 up to their mine on Great Bear Lake. I was again able to cross over to Fort Franklin on *The Radium Gilbert* to spend a few days with my old parishioners. When I tried to converse with the natives I noticed I was losing my proficiency with the Hare language, but they were as warm and cordial as ever and asked if there was any way I could return and live with them again. I noticed some changes around the Fort, some new buildings going up. There were changes in the people too. One of the natives produced a camera and, for a change, took *my* picture. On the feast day of my patron, Saint Bernard, August 20th, Captain Allen McInnes took me back across the lake to continue my work at the mine. While there I again visited the natives living at Port Radium, six miles south of the mine. There, in the old Land Office building, I offered a Mass for them for the first time.

On my return flight south Alf Kaywood put the Eldorado Dakota down at Yellowknife to refuel and I decided to get off and visit Father Frank Ebner, one of the few American padres working in the Mackenzie Vicariate. While I was there for a few days he took me around to visit some of the interesting locals like John Anderson Thompson, a noted geologist, and Ernie Boffa, a bush pilot I had met at Port Radium. Ernie had the most northern books, outside the library, that I had seen in anyone's possession. I was impressed. Later he would have a book written about himself by another person I visited in Yellowknife, Flo Wyward. Father Ebner, who was working alone, took advantage of my presence to have me preside at a meeting of the parents of children attending St. Pat's School and to conduct a service for a group of Indian people a few miles south of town.

When I got back to Camsell Portage the geese were beginning to fly south, so it was time for our annual goose hunt in the Chip delta at the west end of the lake. We got away early enough on the 22nd of September, but had to buck a stiff head wind for eleven hours before we got into the lee of the islands at Fort Chipewyan. Because it was past supper time at the mission we stopped as we often did at the home of the Hudson Bay Company Manager, Allen Black. His wife, Phyllis, was a marvellous cook and perfectly willing to put a meal on the table for us at any hour.

After spending the night at the mission we crossed the lake to Moose Point and pitched our tent. Hap Cave, the former Goldfields cook, was already there with his wife, Slim, guiding for a party of hunters headed by Ship Shipley from Miles City, Montana. They were all great companions and didn't seem to mind our competition. In fact, we were not as effective against the higher flying birds, because they were using ten gauge shotguns with magnum shells that could bring down birds we wouldn't even fire at with our smaller bore shotguns. The snow geese had a habit of flying over this sandy point twice a day, early morning and late evening, and we had dug holes in the sand about a hundred feet apart in which to hide. The very first evening we waited as a flock came in across the calm lake directly toward us. They were right on the water and we anticipated that they would rise as they approached us, but evidently we were so well camouflaged they didn't see us and passed directly over us. They were so low we felt we could have touched them with our gun barrels. We were so taken by surprise that we failed to fire a shot!

As we sat there afterwards berating ourselves for being so stupid, Philip happened to touch the hair trigger of his sixteen-gauge double-barrel and it discharged directly over my head, a few pellets penetrating my wide-brimmed Borsalino hat. He was so shaken that he refused to use that gun again, and didn't, until months later back at our mission. One day I noticed a raven eating our fish on the stage down by our dogs and yelled for Philip to get his gun. He walked up behind me as I held the front door open a crack and – bang! – that temperamental gun discharged into the floor right behind my feet! That time we got rid of it for good. A third misfire might not have been so lucky. We did make a very successful hunt that fall, however, returning with thirty-five snow geese, four prairie chickens and one duck, some fancy eating for the Sundays of the coming winter.

On our way home we stopped at the Chi-Mac drilling camp which belonged to Mrs. Viola McMillan, President of the Prospectors' Association. The crew there had an interesting and unusual bear story to tell us. They had been throwing their garbage into a hole they dug about twenty-five feet out behind their framed cabin. A black bear began visiting this dump regularly at night and his rummaging through the tin cans woke up the whole crew. As they had no firearms, the cook decided to kill him with a concoction of honey mixed with broken glass. The bear ate all that was put out for him and kept coming back for more. When they ran out of honey and then jam, one of the drill crew came up with the brilliant idea of tying a bundle of dynamite sticks to the tree trunk right beside the trash hole with a fuse running into their bunkhouse. The next night when they saw the bear back at the dump they lit the fuse. As it burned toward him with its hissing sound he perked up and ran around in front of the cabin as if he had heard something approaching from the lake. Then it exploded with a deafening roar, knocking everything from the shelves of the cabin, breaking the back windows and lifting all the shingles from the roof on the dump side. The bear trotted back around to his feeding hole which was now a great, smoking crater. He took off, leaving the frustrated crew scrambling to cover the windows with sheets as the mosquitoes poured in.

When a person lives in the North his life is largely regulated by the seasons. In this sense he is living more in tune with nature than his city counterpart and, no doubt, it is a more natural kind of existence. The weather itself pushes him to do certain things, to undertake certain chores he might leave till later if it were a matter of his own initiative. There's a season for everything in the North and if the appropriate task is not completed in its proper time, its later completion can be infinitely more difficult, if not impossible. Our forced caveat hearing in Regina prevented us from beginning our yearly fall fishery until the 22nd of October, which we realized from our experience the year before on Spider Island was late. Anyway, on this date we loaded up dogs and nets and our recently acquired *Ark* and, towing it behind us, went east to Orbit Bay. This was on the west side of Black Bay, much closer to home than we had been the year before. Another benefit of this location was an old abandoned log cabin, which we quickly fixed up for our use. I certainly didn't want Philip to get another attack of Bright's disease by spending freeze-up in a tent. As it turned out we only got in two weeks of net fishing and had to content ourselves with 1,600 fish when we knew we needed over 5,000. Loading up *The Ark* with all our gear plus all our fish, we retreated to the protection of Camsell Bay and then set three nets near its entrance. By mid-November the temperature was down to zero Fahrenheit and Philip was using the dogs to bring in firewood.

While Philip took care of the outside work, I covered our workshop area with a smooth plywood floor over the old rough boards and then built a ping-pong table. This new indoor sport quickly attracted the youth of the village and the mission soon became the local sports arena.

The main topic around town, as always at that time of year, was caribou. When were they coming? Had anyone seen any tracks yet? Finally, on the last day of November, Alec Augier came in with a sled-load of meat from a lake north of our village and we all got a piece. Soon we were all heading in that direction with our teams and the hunt was on.

During this commotion our female sled-dogs were not sitting idle in their corrals. One after the other, Kapa and Princess presented us with new litters of pups. I had always wanted a team of pure white dogs and I did have a few, but now I had the pups to make a complete set. I built a new rock maple toboggan and covered it with a new moose-hide wrapper. This was a fancy job with handles made from the natural bent roots of a birch tree.

Ski-equipped planes began landing on the solid ice of our bay, even though there was still some open water on the main lake, so I flew over to the mines for a round of visits and then flew back again to Camsell Portage for Christmas. This year, in addition to our regular decorations, I put up an outside tree with coloured lights on it that we could illuminate with our small generator. And we had an unusual ceremony – a marriage – when Billy Shot was joined in Holy Matrimony to Regina Powder. Everyone predicted a successful union, for powder and shot always went well together! Following the special rubrics for Christmas I offered two Masses at midnight and then a plane picked me up the next afternoon after Benediction and I offered a third Mass that evening at Gunnar Mine. When I returned the following day we continued our celebrations with a community turkey dinner followed by a Christmas party for the children that evening. During this they consumed 200 ice cream cones and broke over 100 balloons, while their parents held a dance in our renovated workshop. By the time the last well-wishers had left for home, Philip and I fell into our bunks completely played out.

We were relaxing at the kitchen table drinking coffee the next day, glad that the big holiday was behind us and with little planned for the remaining five days of the year, when Budgie Larocque walked in and joined us. Budgie was a trapper we classified as "one tough cookie." He had been raised initially by the Yaniks at Fort Fitzgerald but soon gravitated east to the Barren Lands out from Fort Reliance where he fell in with the remnants of the now extinct band of Chipewyan Indians known as the Caribou-Eaters. This tribe was almost completely dependent upon the migrating Barren Land caribou and, when they didn't come, they were reduced to starvation. Budgie told us of one spring he kept alive by jigging a single ivory lure he made through a hole in the ice to attract a jackfish. And then, when the first caribou appeared, his group was out of ammunition. Budgie, however, was determined he would get one of the animals, so he launched himself in a tiny hunting canoe with no weapon aboard. Approaching a swimming buck from the rear, Budgie grasped its horns and pushed its head under water, trying to drown it. He could hold him down just so long and then the caribou bull would jerk its head up and get a breath of air. This went on for so long that Budgie was sorry he had tried it and yet he was afraid to let go, for fear that the enraged animal, once free, would gore and upset his frail craft. In the meantime a group of his friends were cheering him on from the shore, and his pride spurred him to expend every ounce of strength he could muster. The contest lasted nearly half an hour and Budgie did win, but he was so exhausted that he fell down in his canoe, unable to paddle himself ashore. He cautioned us never to try it.

This feat of raw courage and strength evidently made Budgie the object of a jealous contest between two women of the tribe, both of whom saw him as the perfect mate. They ended up wrestling for him and Madeleine won. She was presently living in his cabin at Camsell, the mother of his many young children and a very forceful character in her own right. One day in summer Philip and I watched a powerful little episode unfold in front of their cabin which clearly demonstrated Madeleine's power of persuasion. Budgie was in their canoe, about to start the outboard motor and take off again for Uranium City where liquor often attracted him. His better half was yelling a vehement veto to the trip with the words "Budgie, you no go!" He did not seem to be listening, though the rest of the village was. She ran right down into the water with the axe in one hand and with one overhead swing brought it down on the motor's flywheel in a crashing blow that disintegrated it. As Budgie calmly surveyed the damage, he said, "Well, I guess I won't go."

In the bars of Uranium City Budgie may have been nothing more than another "drunken Indian," but out in the bush in his own element he was the consummate expert. He showed me how he called spruce hens up so close they could be killed with a stick. Another trick of his that worked amazingly well was to shake a box of matches back and forth to imitate the sound of a beaver cutting down a tree. He'd do this near a lodge and the beaver, hearing this sound, would think it was a rival beaver cutting in his pond and swim right up to Budgie.

The toughest part of trapping out on the Barrens, according to Budgie, was thawing the white fox he caught in traps. During the day he would be picking them up frozen stiff and carrying them in his dogsled till evening when he slept in his tent. As wood was scarce and the tent was heated for a very short time, the foxes wouldn't have time to thaw out. Once skinned, their fur would be as light as feathers, but carrying them, carcass and all, would add too much weight to his sled. There was only one solution: to take the frozen foxes into his sleeping bag with him at night and let the heat of his body thaw them so that they could be skinned in the morning. I could just imagine the difficulty of keeping oneself warm out on the Barrens in an unheated tent at forty below, without being surrounded with frozen fox carcasses. With that kind of a life behind him, Budgie was finding life easy at Camsell and he often helped us. He even offered to help me extract teeth. He said he had extracted his own successfully using nothing but the sharp end of a file! I preferred to use my dental forceps.

On this occasion Budgie let us in on some information about rich uranium ground he had discovered a day's dogsled journey north of the settlement. You'd think that, by now, after all our bad luck with mineral claims, Philip and I would have been permanently cured of the staking bug. Yet apparently we weren't: for the next three days we were staking the twenty "fault" claims along with Budgie near the N.W.T. border. We got back home again just in time to celebrate New Year's.

As 1954 ticked its inexorable way into eternity I sat back and reviewed its history, some of which had been pleasant, some unpleasant, all of it important in the mosaic of my life in the North. I enjoyed the routine visits to the mines, including Port Radium, and my regular dogsled trips east and west, on which I went to the limits of our area. In both activities I was saved from monotony by the interesting people I encountered along the way. The year's unique encounter at court with the highest law in the province certainly proved disillusioning. The exposure to labour unions showed me how men could be manipulated and intimidated by dishonest elements with hidden agendas. Philip's sickness was sobering, bringing home to me forcibly just how precarious our health really is. As the events of the year passed through my mind on New Year's Eve, I could imagine myself spending another forty years at this mission, but I could not imagine any future experiences that would be much different from those of the past two-and-a-half. In my year-end letter to my superior, Bishop Trocellier, I reported as usual on the year's activities and then added two requests. First, my youngest brother, Thomas, was due to be ordained a priest in Washington, D.C., in June, and I asked if the usual ten-year wait for vacation could be shortened to seven in my case so that I could attend. Second, in view of the fact that both Mission Saint Bernard and Mission Santa Barbara were now well established, I again requested a transfer to work somewhere in the Far North. With this letter signed and sealed I was ready to meet the New Year and see what it held in store.

The mission was packed to the walls for the 10 o'clock High Mass with which we began the New Year, 1955. I delivered what I hoped was a convincing sermon on New Year's resolutions. Afterwards we all trooped over to Francis Powder's cabin to break our fast, then back to the mission for Benediction of the Blessed Sacrament at 2:30 p.m., and finally to the schoolhouse in the evening for a dance, to which I brought my guitar.

Three days later I left with my dog-team to visit the mines east of us, which wasn't at all unusual except for the fact that Philip accompanied me with his own team for the first time. Our four-day trip from mine to mine was a warm-up before we set out again for Fort Chipewyan, Fort Smith and the annual retreat. We left Camsell going west on the 9th of January. Now that we each had our own sled and dogs, the going was much easier than it had been two years before when we were both riding the same sled. It was an easy half-day's run to Simon Bashaw's cabin, where we stayed the first night. When we got to the Brothers' cabin on Fiddler Point the next evening, we were surprised to find it filled up with the same caribou-hunting Indians we had run into there two years previously. Only this time there were thirteen of them and we experienced some difficulty securing two bunks for ourselves. (It's no use to lock up a cabin that isolated because it is sure to be broken into if anyone is looking for shelter for the night.)

The next night, after an eight-hour run, we were well housed under the big roof of the mission at Chip. We tarried there the next day to give our dogs a little rest before tackling the trail, or lack of trail, on north to Fort Smith. We hadn't forgotten our days on snowshoes at sixty-two below zero on that frozen Slave River two years before.

Previously I mentioned the two Yanik brothers, Steve and Joe, who were occupied in Goldfields and Uranium City. A third was Lawrence, who had been working as a ranger for Wood Buffalo Park and who joined us at Chip to go north with us, driving his own team of dogs. I had lent one of my dogs to Philip at Chip, so was down to four, and two of them were the big white brothers of King, named Prince and Nanook. These four dogs proved superb on this run as they broke trail in eight inches of snow, and I scarcely got out of the sled all day. They were still breaking trail for the other two teams when we camped for the night at the 30th Base Line Cabin where Lawrence had cached buffalo meat. It snowed on us all the following day, but we kept right on going and reached Hay Camp at nine in the evening. There was a big crew of forty men there working at the annual buffalo roundup and slaughter. No problem to get dog feed or to find a warm cabin where one could throw his sleeping bag in that camp.

The next night we were at Fort Fitzgerald, where I camped with Father Napoleon Lafferty at the mission and Philip took a bunk with Lawrence over at the Yaniks' log home. The local pastor, Father Lafferty, born at Fort Rae, was one of only two native priests to be ordained in the Vicariate in over a hundred years. He told me that following his ordination by Bishop Breynat he had been asked to stay at Fitzgerald temporarily, pending his first official obedience. He had been there since 1923! I got the impression that his wait there in that house, now over a quarter of a century, was beginning to affect his mind. He made no effort to feed me, although I had been travelling all day without eating. Apparently he had given up on house-cleaning too some years before. It was one of those situations that badly needed some female help.

Philip and I continued on across the portage to Fort Smith the following day, where for the next eight days I attended our annual retreat. This yearly get-together of the Oblate Fathers and Brothers was calculated to give us a break from our home missions to follow a schedule of spiritual exercises which would renew our faith and commitment. Of prime importance to the success of this undertaking was the conference delivered twice each day by the designated Retreat Master. As these were invariably given in French, I was glad I had persevered in communicating with Philip only in this language. In addition to the religious aspects of the retreat, it was a happy time to meet and exchange experiences with other missionaries from all over our vast Vicariate.

Our return trip proved anything but a piece of cake. To begin with, the trail which we had broken in deep snow going down was now filled in again, as no one apparently had travelled on it. We were forced to take turns going ahead on snowshoes in spite of our light loads. We camped the first night with Tom Champaign's family and the next with Bill Moore's at the mouth of the Peace. Leaving Fort Chipewyan and heading east on the open Lake Athabaska we faced a head wind at thirty below for three solid days, about as tough as conditions can get for dogsled travel. We were completely played out when we came again into the shelter of the mission at Camsell, carrying with us the scars of frostbite. It was the last time I would make that trip.

While I was recuperating indoors the following week, I got out my oil paints and painted a burial scene from Fort Franklin as I remembered it. It turned out to be the only painting I left at Camsell Portage. A month later Gilbert LaBine's daughter Margaret flew in to pay us a visit and I took her out on a short caribou chase by dog-team. Some time later when I visited her home in Toronto I was surprised to see a very fine painting of the Camsell mission by A. Y. Jackson. Apparently he had flown in for an afternoon in summer when I was absent. I was sorry later that I had failed to paint the same scene myself.

The following month I relieved the pastor at Mission Santa Barbara, Father L'Helgouach, for ten days while he attended the second retreat at Fort Smith. While in Uranium City I visited Eldorado Mine as usual and other mines in the area. I spent three weeks at Eldorado and then a week at Gunnar Mine, so by the time I got back to Mission Saint Bernard, a month and a half had slipped by.

Among the pieces of mail that were waiting for me, once again, was one letter that was to alter the course of my life. It was from the Provincial Father, Jean-Louis Michel, O.M.I., who as Vicar of Missions for the Vicariate worked closely with the bishop. He informed me that I had been granted permission to attend my brother Thomas's ordination in June, following which I was to present myself at Fort Smith to receive a new obedience! Whoopee! This was the good news I had been waiting for. As much as I dreaded the inevitable pain of separation from all that I had built up again at Camsell Portage, the lure of the Far North was still so strong that I was willing to do violence to my emotions in order to follow it. Yet I was living under the vow of obedience and as such I could have been left indefinitely at this post, just as Father Lafferty had been left at Fort Fitzgerald. The thought that gives the Catholic missionary peace of mind in whatever situation he finds himself is that if he is doing what he is doing where he is doing it by order of his legitimate superiors, he is fulfilling the will of God. This thought is basic to his drive to spread the Good News and his consolation when things don't go as well as planned.

Realizing that my days at Mission Saint Bernard were now numbered, I was determined to make one last sled trip with Philip. So on the 14th of April, with nine of our dogs, we pulled out on the steel-shod komatik and headed east down the lake. Our first overnight stop was at Gunnar Mine, where I held a service the next morning. Then we continued on our way and that night pitched our tent on Beaver Island, near Oldman River. The following day we ran into migrating caribou, shot four, and carried the meat on to the mission at Fond du Lac.

Father Gamache and Brother Labonté were now living in the new building they had put up during the summer. Though it was an improvement over the old one, it lacked the atmosphere and charm that made the old one so appealing. We were given a room on the second floor next to a larger sitting room. This room was being used temporarily to house 250 chicks that had been flown in and which could not be left out in the cold. They were living in a large pen that covered most of the floor. Their chorus of peeps didn't bother us, but the dust they kicked up did, until we got our new window pried open and our door securely shut. We were forced to admit that we would have been more comfortable sleeping in our tent, but there was always some new adventure when we visited the Fond du Lac mission.

We didn't make Stoney Rapids in a single day, as we usually did. We got a late start, stopped to shoot another caribou and camped in the open at a beautiful natural campsite in Pine Channel. The next day we passed by Stoney and went on to Stoney Lake, where we expected to find Father Perin and his new assistant, Father Dauvet. They were camped in the bush, however, ten miles to the north. We went out and spent a night with them in their tent where they were busy cutting firewood. The story we got was that Father Perin had accepted a lot of volunteer labour to put up his new log mission at Stoney Lake on condition that he feed his workers, their families and dogs. In doing this he had run up a bill in the neighbourhood of $1,500 with the local Hudson Bay trading post and had contracted to cut them seventy-five cords of wood to pay it off. Leaving these two eager beavers to their work the following day, we proceeded on to the old, empty mission at Black Lake and moved in.

Our arrival there coincided with that time of year when the heat of the sun causes the snow to melt and drop, practically wiping out the sled trails. I offered a daily Mass at the mission and the main room was crowded. Each morning I took communion to a woman dying of TB in her tent. After three days we re-crossed the fifteen-mile portage road to Stoney Rapids. Here the teacher, Adeline Tomyn, was kind enough to make a set of canvas shoes for our dogs. It was a good thing we had them the next day, because the snow on the lake was melting, exposing the ice which was beginning to candle and get sharp. We pulled out at four in the morning to avoid the midday heat and took nine hours to get into Fond du Lac, with one stop for a tea fire. The next night we camped at the Nicholson Mine east of Goldfields, where I again said Mass for the men in the morning before continuing on to Gunnar. We over-nighted at Gunnar Mine and I held another service in the early morning before we set out to run the final leg of our trip into Camsell Portage. I hated to see the journey end, for I realized that this would be my last sled trip out of Mission Saint Bernard.

During the following two days I sadly packed my trunk with the books and clothing I could carry with me, all the while looking nostalgically at everything I would be forced to abandon. High on that list were my team of faithful dogs and the new toboggan I had recently made, with its fine moose-hide wrapper. The two boats were high and dry, waiting for open water, and the fish house held the motor, the nets and all our harness and gear. The mission itself was now completely equipped, including the workshop with all the tools a person would need. I took the .22 my father had bought me before I left home, my favourite hammer and axe, the brass candlestick from the old Chip mission and a few small personal items.

On the 7th of May everyone in the village attended a final Mass in the mission chapel. When all the goodbyes were said, Philip harnessed his team, I jumped in his sled and we took off for Uranium City. I had a lump in my throat as my mission in its picturesque setting slowly faded from sight and I recalled all the memories it held. Still, there was no turning back.

As for Philip Stenne, whom I left in charge on my departure, and who fell heir to the dogs and equipment and who continued to occupy the mission, his future was to be Camsell Portage. The following year he married one of the local girls, Mary Powder, and acquired Pierre Deneroo's cabin, where he proceeded to raise a family of a half-dozen fine children. He supported himself by trapping in winter out of Simon Bashaw's old cabin and in the summer by fishing commercially for the McInnes fish plant. He has managed to keep Mission Saint Bernard in repair for the visiting priests from Uranium City. He never made any fortune with our uranium claims, but his life has been satisfying and happy. What more can a man ask in this life?

14

DOWN TO
THE ARCTIC COAST

On the 21st of August, 1955, I arrived at Fort Smith, Northwest Territories, and immediately presented myself at the office of the jovial, pipe-smoking Bishop Joseph Trocellier, O.M.I. He was head of this thriving centre of the Western Arctic's Mackenzie Vicariate. I had come to receive my new obedience, or appointment, to another mission somewhere in the North.

I had just arrived back in the North from Hearthcliff, my home on the shore of Lake Ontario near Rochester, New York. Here I had spent the summer with my family, and especially my brother Thomas, who himself had received his official First Obedience to the Oblate Missions in Brazil in June. Thomas would be stationed farther south of Hearthcliff than I was north of it.

Since coming to the North in 1948, I had served at several northern communities, including Fort Norman, Norman Wells, Goldfields and Uranium City. I also had the privilege of founding Mission Saint Bernard at Camsell Portage, named for my patron saint, Mission St. Therese at Fort Franklin and Mission Santa Barbara. I had been perfectly happy on Lake Athabaska for the previous year or so, but I had entertained the thought that some day I would work in the *Far* North, along the Arctic Coast. Often when I wrote the bishop I would end my report by reminding him that if he ever needed someone to fill an empty Arctic mission he had an eager volunteer in me.

"His Excellency" told me in his thick French accent that I was headed for Aklavik, at the mouth of the Mackenzie River near the Arctic Coast. Not only was this good news, but I was also instructed to proceed north to my new posting aboard the mission supply boat the *Sant'Anna*, which was now due to dock after its first trip downriver. I would be able to visit each of the missions along the entire route. When I left the bishop's office I felt as if I were floating an inch off the ground.

Meanwhile I had five days to reacquaint myself with this interesting mission headquarters and its various personnel. As much as possible I absented myself from that insistent, raucous bell clanging in the mission stairwell and ran around the settlement taking pictures with my three cameras: a Rolleicord with black-and-white film, a 35mm for coloured slides, and a Bell and Howell DL-70 using 16mm Kodachrome movie film. Aided by friends at Eastman Kodak who supplied the film, I was becoming an avid shutter-bug.

In no time I found myself aboard the *Sant'Anna* as she slipped her moorings and slowly backed out into the Slave River. A crowd of mission personnel waved *bon voyage* from the shore. Among those going downriver with us were Brother Henri, in charge of the galley, and his own brother, Brother Médard, returning to Fort Norman, while up in the pilot house were those two veterans of the river, Brothers Dabrowski and Sareault. Scattered in tiny cabins in the boat and at both ends of the barge it was pushing were numerous nuns, Brothers and priests travelling to their respective posts.

When we reached the shore of Great Slave Lake the following noon, the barge we were pushing was unhitched and put behind on a tow line to better withstand rough seas. Sure enough, we did encounter them on our hour-and-a-half crossing to Fort Resolution. When I last visited this mission seven years before, my brother Justin was here serving his novitiate, training as a lay Brother. Now he was married and living in Carson City, Nevada.

Although we were only in this port for twenty-three hours, I had little time for sleep, what with preaching at the Sunday morning Mass, presiding at the afternoon Benediction service, playing guitar for the hospital patients, and running around the settlement taking pictures.

When we weighed anchor in the afternoon, the mission gas boat, *The Immaculata*, its decks crammed with nuns and children, escorted us a few miles out onto a flat, calm lake in farewell. I was accompanied by a single white dog, just as I was when I arrived in Goldfields four years earlier: I had acquired a pedigreed Samoyed bitch named Jasmine from Didi Woolgar in Yellowknife. I hoped this animal would provide the nucleus for a new team of sled-dogs in Aklavik. It was a striking scene: the white-coated Jasmine had the run of the flat barge roof, while the blood-red sun set across Great Slave Lake directly ahead of us.

By six the next morning we had entered the comparative safety of the Mackenzie River and by noon were tying up at Fort Providence. This fort was for many years the residence of the bishop of the whole Mackenzie Vicariate and still bore his name in its Indian title, *Yati-tewe Kwen*, "The Chief Father's Home." The Grey Nuns from Montreal had opened the first school in the Northwest Territories here in 1867, and it was still going strong. While the Brothers discharged the freight, Sister Elizabeth Kristoff took me on a tour of the mission buildings. The church itself, its clapboard exterior painted white, seemed huge and bore the name Notre Dame de la Providence – "Our Lady of Providence" – from which the settlement got its English name. Right beside it, still boarded up, stood the little log "cathedral" of the early bishops.

The mission proper was a huge log building which housed the Fathers and Brothers. All the floors were made of whipsawed spruce, and the door hinges of moosehide. This was a fascinating peek at the previous century, especially when we went up into the attic. There were enough fascinating old relics there to start a museum. I was particularly captivated by the many pairs of unused wooden shoes, resembling black oxfords, that hung from the roof. They had been made in France, Sister Kristoff told me. Later, when rubber boots were introduced by the traders, they so resembled those old black wooden shoes that the rubbers got the same name in Slavey: *dechinkke* – "wooden shoe."

We visited some of the boarding-school children who looked very neat and happy in their bright uniforms made by the nuns. Out behind the main buildings stood a long, straight pile of over 300 cords of four-foot firewood. As usual, it was spruce that had been cut and split while green the year before and stacked to dry. Behind this stood the rich acres of black soil under cultivation by the Brothers, whose Belgian horses now replaced the oxen used formerly. This whole mission set-up was a joy to behold and proof that dedicated souls could produce miracles with little more than willing hands and a lot of faith.

The next day, as we were edging our way out into the deep, swift current of the Mackenzie, Brother Henri told me a strange tale of a time some fifty years previous when, during break-up, the ice jammed above Fort Providence so tightly that for two days the riverbed was dry enough that people could cross it on foot! Down river a few miles, the shallow, weedy river, a summer haven for wildfowl, widens into Mills Lake. It was spectacularly beautiful the evening we crossed. The sun setting ahead of us through crimson clouds was perfectly reflected in the calm waters, a sight which drew all hands on deck, and to join in evening prayer.

Later that evening we stopped at the homestead of F.J. Browning to deliver his freight and pick up lumber and potatoes. Browning was a true pioneer and one of only six men to have homesteaded in the Territories. He had broken about twenty acres of bush and, besides keeping horses and cows, cultivated a thriving garden. In winter he cut logs and, with the help of his many sons, operated a small sawmill. That evening, sitting in his comfortable cabin, he told us that it wasn't the cost of land here that kept others from coming into the country and homesteading as he had, because the Government of Canada sold land for only six dollars an acre. The hitch was that a person had first to get the land surveyed at his own expense, and bringing a surveyor into the country was very expensive. Browning also lamented that, since 1939, a white man like himself could no longer get a trapping licence. About the only thing he could do legally was cut timber. He felt that there was definite discrimination against whites in the N.W.T. A few years later he was killed operating his caterpillar tractor at his sawmill.

The mighty Mackenzie was so rough the next day when we arrived at Fort Simpson that we couldn't tie up at the town dock. Instead we anchored in the lee of the island three miles down stream and ferried into town with the jolly boat. I celebrated my thirty-fifth birthday by visiting the wards full of TB patients from Fort Franklin. In the evening, when the wind fell, the *Sant'Anna* was moved to Fort Simpson and the cargo was unloaded, including my trunk. In the meantime, the Brother captain had decided to return to Fort Smith: this was the end of the line for the mission supply boat for this season.

I moved into the spacious mission and began inquiring about transportation to Aklavik. It turned out that I had four days to explore this interesting island community at Fort Simpson. The thing that most impressed me was the size of the mission farm. If the farms at Fort Smith and Fort Providence were impressive, this one was doubly so. Besides the horses, cattle and chickens, the fields of potatoes and other vegetables, this mission was raising enough grain to warrant a threshing machine. I was there at the proper time to see it in operation and to photograph it. And what a monstrous Rube Goldberg contraption it was, with all its belts and pulleys flying in every direction and shaking as if it would self-destruct, with a cacophony of sound that prevented voice communication within a hundred feet. Taking Jasmine with me, I walked to the north end of the island to look at the flourishing government experimental farm. This farm demonstrated just how many varieties of vegetables one could grow successfully that far north. During the evenings I could be found either in the mission or at the hospital, showing slides of other parts of the North.

The *Sant'Anna* boarded the school children going to the residential school at Fort Providence and took off south, leaving me to find some way to continue in the opposite direction. As luck would have it, the Shell Oil Company had a Beaver aircraft going north with room for me, my trunk and Jasmine, so I jumped aboard and was whisked down to Fort Norman. There I found the same old log mission that had become my first home in the North, unchanged except for the personnel. Father Grias was now in charge, with Brother Claeys his assistant. During my two days there I was reminded several times just how low the various doors had been cut. Then, completely unannounced, the mission Norseman made a surprise landing on floats, with Father Bill Leising at the controls, Brother Slim Beauchemin the engineer, and Dr. Jack Melling the passenger. They had come over to pick me up for a week's retreat at Fort Franklin. Father Jean Drouart, O.M.I., who was visiting the Vicariate from the Oblate General House in Rome, would conduct the retreat. Before we left to fly back to Great Bear Lake we dug up two bags' worth of potatoes for the mission there.

Being able to spend a week at my old Mission St. Therese at Fort Franklin was an unexpected bonus to my trip downriver to Aklavik. I had gone to the community on Great Bear Lake in 1950 to build a mission and saw it officially named after the French St. Thérèse the same year. My successor, Father Victor Philippe, was still in charge; his assistant, Father Felicien Labat, was quickly picking up the Hare language. Although most of my day was spent attending conferences and discussions under the capable and inspiring direction of Father Drouart, I did manage to get around the settlement in the off-hours to visit all the natives. The whites, however, had completely changed, as usual. There was a new Bay manager and a new teacher; a Mr. Bill Bowerman had replaced Mr. Gravel.

Bill the teacher had more practical ideas for improving the community, like building seventeen new privies. He had twenty-three new cook stoves on order from the government, one for every cabin in town, plus new Yukon chimneys to go with them.

His plans included bringing in a D-2 caterpillar tractor and a portable sawmill with an eye to constructing new three-bedroom bungalows for every family in town. When he got a shipment of .303 Lee-Enfield rifles from the Canadian Armed Forces, Bill immediately organized a company of Canadian Rangers. Others in the settlement described to me how the schoolteacher turned sergeant-major on Saturday mornings and had his company of rangers line up along the shore in front of the school. On his command they discharged a volley of lethal lead out across Bear Lake to repel an imagined Russian invasion. Everyone was impressed. Bill didn't stay long enough to see all his projects realized, but he planted the seeds of change that were to spell the end of the old log-cabin village I had known.

September 8th, the birthday of the Blessed Virgin, saw me at the altar presiding in the marriage of Alice Tanniton to Pierre Ferdinand. It was a joyful ceremony, and was followed by the traditional feast and drum dance. I didn't join in the dance, but I did take pictures of it in the cabin of Suze Tu Cho. Visiting aircraft were still few and far between at Fort Franklin, but the next day our conference was interrupted by the arrival of a Cessna 180 on floats. It was the bush pilot Ernie Boffa out of Yellowknife, scouting the route for a proposed new road from Mills Lake to Coppermine. He had just stopped in to say hello. We were glad to have the interruption for a tea break and to swap news. We were prepared to take to the air ourselves the next day, but a Morse code message from Fort Norman advised that the Mackenzie River was running a heavy sea. This would make landing dangerous, so we sat tight for another night at Franklin. On the morrow we got safely into Fort Norman, where we loaded seventeen 100-pound bags of potatoes onto the Oblate aircraft bearing the letters GTM, threw my trunk and Jasmine in on top of them, and took off downriver. We were definitely overloaded: by the time we reached Bear Rock, three miles downstream, we had managed to gain only fifty feet of elevation. Yet, as we were on floats, with the river under us all the way, we felt perfectly confident. We had a nice flight past Norman Wells and the Ramparts and landed on the river out in front of Fort Good Hope. As the plane nosed into shore I jumped off the float with a rope and tied up so we could unload. Just as soon as we did GTM headed back up river to Fort Smith, while I and the cargo awaited furtherance to Aklavik. The mission boat *Immaculata II*, which was already on her way from downriver, would carry us there.

I was welcomed to the ninety-year-old Mission of Our Lady of Good Hope by a veteran who had himself already passed forty years at this post, Father Alexis Robin, still going strong as he went into his eightieth year. He was working on his yearly harvest of potatoes, carrots and cabbage assisted by Brother Roger Mahé. Father Robin told me that he was proud of the fact that, through his yearly sale of vegetables to the residential school at Aklavik, he was completely self-supporting. He was also quick to complain to me that he wasn't getting any help from his assistant, Father René Fumoleau, in his harvest, as the latter was preoccupied with putting the ancient church on a cement foundation, aided by Brother Henri Tesnière. I could easily understand the old missionary's concern. Taking the long view, however, the work of putting the old church on a firm foundation and preserving it was really more important. This log structure was begun in 1865, twenty-one years before Father Robin was born; now it was the masterpiece of all the churches along the Mackenzie, old or new. Although its exterior is not particularly noteworthy, its interior is a marvel of intricate fretwork and colourful paintings. It is particularly impressive when one realizes that all the wood was whipsawed from local black spruce logs and the paint made from powdered pigment sent from France and mixed with local fish oil. If one had the chance to see but one item of interest along the whole length of the vast Mackenzie River, it would have to be this church.

Across from the church stood the old mission residence which possessed a charm of its own and in which I was given a bunk. Here I rested much of the following day, as I had acquired a cold on Bear Lake. I confined my activities to reading the *Codex Historicus*, the official diary kept in each of our missions, and which is continued religiously by whichever missionary is in charge. Some entries are merely commentaries on the weather or dry statistics, while others recount with graphic detail incidents of high drama. To read these priceless books today is an education in the lives and hardships of a bygone era. Many of the books in the second-storey library of this mission were bound in caribou skin. In the refectory was an interesting mural painted right on the surface of the handmade boards that lined the walls.

While I didn't feel great, the second day I got outside to help old Father Robin with his harvest. He had a half-dozen older Indian women helping him, whom he paid in carrots. The following evening I had just finished showing slides to all the community in the school, when the *Immaculata* pulled in from Aklavik. It had taken them three days to push 320 miles against the current. On board was Father Antoine Binamé, my new superior, and Brother Petrin, captain of the boat which was pushing a hundred-foot barge. They had come, as they did every year at this time, to pick up the yearly harvest of spuds from this mission. We had a wet, muddy, miserable job the next day loading 300 sacks of potatoes on the barge in the rain. We shoved off after supper, but only got a few miles downstream before darkness forced us to tie up for the night.

In spite of the fog and the rain, we continued on our way the next morning at 4:00. Brother Petrin was in the pilot house above while Father Binamé was in the engine room below, so the only logical place for me was in the galley, acting as cook. I spent most of the day cleaning up in there because, by temperament and training, I find it difficult to work in a place that's out of order or dirty, or, in this case, both. The only time we stopped during the day was when Brother Petrin shot a goose, which was quickly plucked and put in the pot for supper. Brother was part native and never lost an opportunity to bag game. The noise of the engine, where Father Binamé kept constant vigil during operating hours, precluded conversation. Still, in the evening, after we had tied up for the night and shut down the motor, I was regaled with stories of the country into which we were coming. It was all very interesting and instructive, but I did notice that the majority of the tales ended in tragedy.

Although we were operating as any other of the many boats and barges on the river, there was one difference befitting religious men. We started our day with Mass offered in the covered barge in order to consecrate our work to a higher cause. After all, we weren't being paid to do what we were doing, so it was important to keep reminding ourselves of our religious commitment and to leave the recompense to the Almighty.

We arrived at Arctic Red River at noon on Saturday and decided to lay over into Sunday. Father Gilbert Levesque and Brother Rosaire Girouard were happy to entertain us and to have some new faces to present to their congregation for the Sunday morning High Mass and sermon. An ex-Grey Nun by the name of Margaret Poirier was the local school teacher and she cooked us a splendid lunch before we left Sunday afternoon. During our twenty-four-hour stop the rain stopped too. The skies cleared, revealing the majestic, snow-covered Richardson Mountains to the west as we descended the Peel Channel. We were soon into the vast delta of the Mackenzie River, with its myriad lakes and channels that to the newcomer can become a baffling maze. Nearing home we didn't tie up at dark, but continued on, reaching Aklavik at midnight. As my eyes wandered over the sleeping town, I wondered to myself what adventures lay in store for me here. It was now too late to unload our cargo, so we simply tied up and slept aboard to await the new day.

Compared with many up stream, Aklavik was a new settlement, having been started only in 1915. It attracted Eskimos from the Arctic Coast as well as some Loucheux Indians from around Fort McPherson. They came mainly to trade their furs, yet gradually more and more of them were putting up temporary or quasi-permanent log cabins. The government, too, was expanding various offices in town to serve the Western Arctic. The Navy had a small contingent stationed here on a rotating basis. But the Catholic and Anglican missions dominated the town, as both were operating hospitals and boarding schools as well as their churches.

The centre of the settlement and the hub of its downtown activity was Stan Peffer's café and trading post which featured various extracts and shaving lotions at its "candy" counter. Down the road a few doors Bill Strong operated the North Star Café, which featured a barber shop. Across the dirt road from Peffer's stood the large, two-storey detachment of the RCMP. Several small cabins were strung out in their backyard compound, while their husky-dog corral was fenced in close to the riverbank.

The Hudson Bay Company post fronted on the water at the west end of town and nearby was the small log-cabin trading post of Knut Lang. Knut operated it whenever he was in town, but most often he ran his home-base trading post about thirty miles up stream. Karl Gardlund, a local veteran, had formed the posse in pursuit of the "Mad Trapper," Albert Johnson, in the early thirties. Now he operated the 250 kW generator that supplied the town's electricity. Mrs. Dolphus Norris ran the town's rooming house and Mike Zubko operated the local airline, Aklavik Flying Service, with a Cessna 170.

The town had grown up at a horseshoe bend of the Peel Channel where two other channels ran into it, the Poliak and the Hudson Bay. There were two cabins and tents on each of these tributaries across from the main settlement, including the trading post of Slim Semmler. All these establishments formed the heart of Aklavik in 1955, a bustling little community of about 750 northerners of mixed descent, thrown together by circumstances in the centre of the vast Mackenzie delta. The whole set-up looked very interesting to me and I was anxious to settle in with them.

Meeting the staff of the Roman Catholic mission and getting Jasmine and my trunk off the *Immaculata* occupied my first day in town. Father Binamé who had been travelling from Fort Good Hope with me was the superior of the whole organization, while I was to be his assistant in charge of finances and supplies. I would be replacing temporarily Father Max Ruyant who was in

France on vacation. We had two assistants, Brothers Petrin and
Delisle, so the four of us occupied the mission itself. Over in the
convent there were fifteen Grey Nuns of Montreal and I was
immediately pleased that I had persevered in improving my
French at Camsell Portage. I was taken through the hospital
wards to meet the forty-five patients, most of whom suffered
from TB, and to the hostel to see its 160 children from settlements
all over the Western Arctic. This group of 230 souls was actually
larger than most Arctic settlements and comprised a close-knit
little community within Aklavik proper.

Again I found myself locked into the typical schedule of the
larger mission establishments along the Mackenzie River. The
rising bell sounded at 5:30 a.m., followed by morning prayer and
Mass. We ate our meals over in the hospital refectory: breakfast
at 7:00, lunch at 11:20. If one wanted to get enough sleep, one had
to avoid late evening visits and be in bed by 10:00.

I had arrived just before the natives returned to their winter
trapping grounds before freeze-up. It was immediately evident
that these people took their trapping life seriously. Many of them
had their own schooners and barges pulled up in front of the settlement and were living on board. It was nice to see them dressed
in their own style of clothing, especially the Eskimos with their
large wolf and wolverine parka ruffs and sealskin mukluks.
Those of Indian extraction, mainly Loucheux, depended mostly
on muskrats inhabiting the delta proper for their fur income,
while the Eskimos trapped out on the Arctic Coast and caught
mainly white fox. Wherever they based their operations they all
seemed to be getting enough fur to live comfortably; government
assistance was rare. I found a sixteen-foot canoe at the mission
and, while the water remained open, I tried to get away from the
office daily to paddle around and visit these people and if possible to take a meal with them to sample their style of food. Luckily
I carried a camera with me and recorded a way of life that has
since vanished.

My job as bursar involved a lot of paper work, making out
government reports on the running of the hostel and hospital. It

also included the more physical job of keeping the main kitchen staff supplied with the food needed to prepare meals. Most of the food came downriver annually from Fort Smith in the barge pushed by the *Sant'Anna* and was stored in one large warehouse. Two freezer rooms dug twenty-five feet into the permafrost held fish and meat. The Brothers operated a fish camp on the Mackenzie River about thirty miles to the east which provided thousands of whitefish. The meat came from the reindeer station off to the east of the delta a hundred miles away. I used a D-2 caterpillar tractor and a stone boat to move these supplies to the kitchen.

Although I was called to run to the warehouse for some item of food needed almost every day, the main re-supply day came once every two weeks. Sister Rachel Deschaines, the chief cook, would give me a list like this one, which I actually filled at that time.

14 bags (100 lbs) flour		1 case each: dried prunes, figs, pears
3 bags " beans		1 case each: corn flakes,
2 bags " rolled oats		rice krispies,
2 bags " sugar		puffed wheat
1 bag " rice		1 case: wieners
1 bag " brown sugar		1 case: corned beef
1 bag " barley		1 case: pork & beans
1 case: boiled dinner		1 case: coffee
1 case: Spork		1 case: tea
1 case: spiced ham		1 case: salmon
1 case: margarine		1 case: cocoa
1 case: bologna sausage		2 pails: peanut butter
1 case: garlic sausage		1 case: jam
6 barrels: Klim milk powder		1 case: corn syrup
1 case: condensed milk		1 case: macaroni
2 cases: pilot biscuit		1 case: vermicelli
1 case: soda biscuit		1 case: molasses
1 case: oatmeal biscuits		1 case: butter
2 fifty-lb pails lard		1 doz. electric light bulbs
		25, 40, 60, 100 watts
1 fifty-lb pail shortening		1 case: soda, baking
1 case: baking powder		1 case: sardines

In between times I made an inventory of the warehouse and found that we had enough cocoa to last into the 1990s and enough peanut butter to last into the next century. Needless to say, I began doubling up on these orders. I also found in a heated stock room in the basement of the hospital an oversupply of sauerkraut and pickles. I was told by Mother Superior that nobody liked the sauerkraut and the pickles were being kept for the big feasts.

The mission operated its own 7 kW Wakashaw generators, but everyone was careful using the electric lights. When the days got shorter and darker I noticed that the kitchen staff were working by two 60-watt bulbs which dimly lit their large room. I found a three-tube fluorescent light in one of the warehouses and installed it for them right over their huge wood-burning stove. Several days later when I walked into the kitchen the crew was again working under those two 60-watt bulbs. When I asked Sister Deschaines why she wasn't using the new light I installed, she replied, "When we light the new light it is so bright that we don't get any light from the old bulbs!" I was completely stumped by her logic.

The annual run of herring in the Peel Channel came just prior to freeze-up. Just about every family in town had a net set right out in front of our place and some got as many as a thousand a day. We used the herring mainly to feed our mission team of huskies. Our people, however, preferred whitefish, so the Brothers had built a large log cabin near the main branch of the Mackenzie River. They moved there with a couple of hired men when they could still travel by boat, and froze in there as they caught a year's supply of fish. After they left, Father Binamé caught a bad cold and moved into a bed in the hospital, leaving me alone in the thirteen-room mission. When the *Immaculata* and barge got back from the fish camp I hired Fred Norris to skid the Brothers' log cabin out for the winter with his D-8 cat.

Later in the fall, when we had a foot of ice to support our D-2 cat and the sloop it pulled on runners, the Brothers hauled all their fish back to the mission and stacked them in the permafrost fish pit. Then they shifted operations to their wood camp thirty miles up the Peel Channel. To heat all our buildings – which involved a dozen separate fires – required over 300 cords of wood. This wood was cut green in the winter in four-foot lengths and piled along the riverbank close to the wood camp. After the ice went out in the summer the boat and barge were again put into service. With the help of the senior boys the wood was stacked on the barge and brought down to the mission dock. The quickest way to unload it was to use a chain of people who would stand still and pass each stick on to the next person in line. Every able hand was pressed into service for this annual job, which became a kind of holiday.

As this huge stack of firewood extended for hundreds of feet along the road in front of the hospital and school it presented a temptation to certain townsfolk who ran short of wood during the winter. This resulted in some tell-tale gaps in the pile, which did not sit well with Brother Delisle, so he drilled a hole into some of the logs and put in a small charge of black powder. It wasn't long before we got word of a certain stove blowing up in the neighbourhood. The pilfering suddenly stopped.

To get away once in a while from institutional living in the hostel, we put up two large log cabins a half-mile north of the mission, one for the boys and another for the girls. Any kind of excuse was used to gather at one of these cabins for supper or a day's outing – to which I usually got an invitation if I brought my guitar. Adjacent to the boys' shack was an area set aside as their registered trapline which was especially popular in the spring during the muskrat season. One morning I found myself over in the office of the local game management officer renewing both the stumpage permit for the wood camp and the licence for the boys' trapping area. I had no trouble renewing the wood-cutting permit, but ran into a lot of opposition to the registered trapping area. We at the mission felt that it was best for our native students to keep in touch with their roots while away from home. The trapping was all part of their education and most likely a prelude to their life's work after they left us. The game officer disagreed with me and argued that our boys could do all the trapping they wanted to do while at home, but while at school they should stick to their books. I finally got their permit renewed, but it wasn't easy.

Slowly I was getting myself oriented to Aklavik and especially to our little corner of it. My main job was down in my front
office, where I was trying to keep current on all our financial
dealings. I had started in that department at a disadvantage,
because Father Max Ruyant had left before I arrived and I had no
one to show me the ropes. Besides, I didn't like office work and
was poor in mathematics. If I didn't understand all the forms, at
least I had them all in good order. Among the books was a heavy
ledger listing local accounts receivable and it contained the
names of 131 men who owed us more than $13,000. Most of it
was for pipe fittings and plumbing supplies. It seems that six
years previously Father Bill Leising had bought from Crown
Assets the abandoned Loran station at Kitigazuit down below
the reindeer station. Among the prizes that accrued to the mission at that time were tons of pipes and fittings, so many in fact
that a special warehouse was built to hold them. As Aklavik had
no hardware store this warehouse behind the mission became a
mecca for anyone trying to do any plumbing. Although the
prices were mostly by guess and ridiculously low, few seemed
inclined to pay for them.

These debts were a kind of millstone around our necks, preventing many of these debtors from even visiting the missionaries for fear we might remind them of their debt. I talked the situation over with Father Binamé and we decided to send out a bill
to each of the 131, take what they paid, then burn that ledger and
forget it. We agreed that in the future we would sell for cash or,
if the person were needy, give him the material *gratis*. We collected less than $300 and then turned over a new leaf. I learned a
valuable lesson from this incident that stood me in good stead in
the years ahead at other missions. The missionary simply cannot
afford to alienate people by selling or lending them things they
are not going to pay for or return. For some reason, people in the
North especially resent being reminded that they owe something. And where there's resentment there's no chance of conver-
sion.

If my work at the mission were not enough to keep me occupied, there were other community-oriented jobs begging to be filled by volunteers. One was the boy scouts, always in need of supervision and training – and one particularly difficult to get help with. And so I soon found myself the "Akela," or pack leader, of twenty-four cubs. Another was the community broadcasting station CHAK, "The Friendly Voice of the Arctic, 1490 on your radio dial." A small shack next to the police barracks served as the studio, but volunteer broadcasters were needed to keep the station on the air daily. The good women of the settlement interrupted their household chores to spell each other off during the afternoon period, and following a town meeting the evening broadcasts were assigned as follows: Sunday – the Royal Canadian Navy; Monday – The Royal Canadian Mounted Police; Tuesday – The Roman Catholic Mission; Wednesday – The Anglican Mission; Thursday – Government Personnel; Friday – The Natives; and Saturday – The School.

It wasn't long before I was delegated to the Tuesday night spot and seated before the mike with a turntable and a stack of cowboy records and instructions to keep something on the air from 7:00 till sign-off time at 11:00. With no ambitions in this direction, I nevertheless found myself a once-a-week radio personality, if only as a lowly disc jockey. Those four uninterrupted hours of records plus a little local news soon got monotonous, so I invited Stan Peffer to come across the street and let me interview him live on my program. This was an instant hit with my listeners, so from then on I had a guest, generally an old-timer, as a regular feature of my Tuesday night broadcasts.

By the end of October the channel was covered with eight inches of ice, just right for cutting ice, which everyone needed for drinking water. We had a grandstand seat overlooking this scene as the various organizations in town staked out their section of ice and began cutting with huge ice saws and then hauling it out with ice tongs. And you could see a friendly rivalry going on between the Navy, the police, the signal corps and others to see whose pile of blocks grew fastest. We weren't in the race, as we had rigged up a pump and hose that sucked fresh water directly into a huge cement cistern in the hospital basement. On the other hand we had no reason to boast, because our line often froze up in mid-winter and we had a devil of a job defrosting it.

With the presence of a military contingent based in Aklavik, November 11th, Remembrance Day, took on a more important role as a public holiday. Everyone in full uniform, including the Mounties, the Navy, the Army Signal Corps and the scouts, marched solemnly into the Federal Day School where the town assembled. I was honoured to be chosen to deliver a short address on the occasion, following which we all reassembled outside to a hastily erected cenotaph where each group laid a wreath in memory of our war dead. I was particularly proud of my cub group marching in new scarlet parkas with white fox trim and white mukluks. A brisk wind blowing at thirty-below whisked everyone along at a smart pace and we were back home in time for 11:30 lunch.

By mid-November, pilot Stu Hill brought in the CPA Norseman from Norman Wells with the first load of mail since before freeze-up. At the same time the new government liquor store opened in the court house. On one of the last barges of the summer 400 cases of hard liquor, plus beer, worth $32,000 was off-loaded at Aklavik. Now those with valid permits could slake their thirst on bottled liquor without the trouble of sending cash to the Norman Wells outlet and paying air freight. The locals showed their appreciation for this new arrangement by purchasing $1,400 worth the first hour. Government people predicted that the novelty would soon wear off, but in fact it never did. Like Topsy, it just kept growing. The local guardians of law and order experienced a sharp increase in crime.

Not all the results were bad, however. Sales of extracts and shaving lotions plummeted as did the production of home brew. Friends of Joe Vitch no longer gathered around his mysterious barrel of secret ingredients to dip their cups. On one of those occasions Joe had discovered his drowned cat in the barrel. With pained dignity Joe pulled out the cat by its head and with his other hand squeezed the juice back into the barrel. His drinking buddies sat transfixed by this demonstration of economy.

Back at the mission my duties ranged from cleaning out a cluttered attic to pumping out a leaking basement. Next door to this building stood the old log mission built by Bishop Trocellier in the first years of the settlement. Once Father Binamé was back on his feet he decided to fix up this old building and move into it with six of his senior scouts. He had me over there wiring it for electricity and was soon moved in. To occupy his boys during their leisure hours he decided to have them paint six large five-foot panels to go into the church at Fort Good Hope. When this historic church was built a hundred years before, those early missionaries had left six spaces along the side walls between the windows vacant, pending the arrival of some competent artist. Now at last they were to be filled by the scouts of Aklavik. At the same time I had initiated an art class in a hostel classroom one night a week. But when I began offering some suggestions to the scouts on their ambitious project, Father Binamé didn't appreciate my help and told me to back off. Later in the year, when he found me in my room at the mission working on a painting for the same church, he was surprised and said I was the first American he had met who said he could do something and could actually do it. Either he was prejudiced or had encountered some poor examples of my former countrymen. At any rate, the art work went ahead and the empty panels in the old church were finally filled. The scouts certainly did their best, but I felt that neither they nor I possessed the talent to put the final touches to that historic church. Yet how many centuries could it wait for someone with adequate talent to show up?

The only printed news of our town appeared in a column entitled "Aklavik News" in the *News of the North* printed every two weeks in Yellowknife. Evidently it was supplied by someone over on the Anglican side of town, because it seldom mentioned anything that happened in our area. I wrote to Ted Horton, Editor of *News of the North,* and offered to send in regular contributions at no charge to balance the picture he was getting, but got no response. In rearranging the junk in our attic I had come across an old Gestetner duplicator and an idea began to grow in my mind. Would it be feasible to print some sort of local newspaper? In my visits around town I began asking the various organizations if they would be able to supply me with news on a regular basis. Everyone seemed to be enthusiastic and some indicated that they would be willing to place ads. On the strength of the reaction I got, I mailed an order to Edmonton for paper and stencils. Meanwhile I kept my ears open for newsworthy bits of information. Ellen Binder, whose husband worked as a Special Constable for the RCMP, promised to do the same.

The culmination of this idea appeared in print form on the 19th of November when I ran off the first 225 copies of *The Aklavik Journal*. It contained eight pages of barely legible print and was priced at ten cents a copy. Among the titles were: "Gale Hits the Coast," "Aklavik Gets Liquor," "Death on the DEW Line," and "300,000 Caribou Missing." Ads were placed by all the traders, plus the North Star Inn Barber Shop, The Aklavik Power & Service Company, Aklavik Flying Service and The Canadian Legion. Irish Coulter put an ad in the "personals" column that read, "If the person who removed my house from the end of the runway puts it back like they found it nothing will be done." My cubs were eager to peddle this newspaper after school for a commission of five cents a copy and by nightfall we were sold out. Because of popular demand I had to run off an additional hundred copies.

Encouraged by the success of the first issue, I immediately began gathering material for the December issue and printed 350 copies just before Christmas. This time I was more familiar with inking the Gestetner and the print was more readable and the pages were increased to ten. Lead items included a forced landing by Stu Hill, an Eskimo murder near Perry River and a new gold-strike on the Firth River. Subscriptions by mail were beginning to come in and included some influential people like Ed Ogle, the Canadian editor of *Time* magazine; Mr. George Drew, leader of the opposition in Parliament; the Northern Research

Library; and various other government offices. Peter Freuchen, famous Arctic explorer, wrote me from Denmark to say that he was translating the *Journal* into Danish. A Northern Affairs representative from Ottawa told me his staff spent a couple of days on each issue to check out the information printed.

In a community supported mainly through trapping, what could be of more interest to readers than the current prices of furs? To omit them would be comparable to a Prairie newspaper not printing the price of grain, yet it took me a few issues to realize my omission. Once I started printing them, however, I got an immediate objection from the Hudson Bay Company, which threatened to cancel their ad if I persisted. I did persist and, in order to forestall any more criticism of this policy, I furthermore refused to accept any more advertising except for personal items. As I was now printing 500 copies at twenty-five cents a copy, I could afford to do this, for all I wanted to do was cover my printing costs. In the end I printed a total of eighteen issues of the *Aklavik Journal* over three years; I would have continued if I had remained in the area. It was a lot of fun – a real education in journalism – and I made some valuable contacts that have endured over the years. In 1996 I decided to reprint all of those *Aklavik Journal* newspapers in book form. The 2,000 copies printed have sold well and I soon will have sold out. I am mailing out copies for $25 each.

In the meantime the Brothers had finished their fall fishery and returned to the mission by dog-team. They went back to the fish camp with the caterpillar tractor and freight sled and began hauling in the 7,000 whitefish they had caught. When they had completed this job they set out for the reindeer station to bring back the 250 carcasses I had ordered. Unfortunately they could only get 130, since a big portion of the reindeer herd had run away with the wild caribou. This was bad news indeed, for it meant that during the coming year all our people would be faced with far more fish meals than the usual one-a-day at noon.

With so many activities occupying my time, the days flew by and I hardly noticed the complete disappearance of the sun.

Every day we got a little more snow; driven by the northwest storm winds, it drifted over all the fences in town and hardened to the consistency of cement. There was no need to follow the streets any more: one could simply walk directly to one's destination.

Then, suddenly, it was Christmas. And if the joy at this season is enhanced by the presence of children, we were rich indeed. Of course there were all the religious aspects of the celebration of Christ's birth, including Midnight Mass, but on top of that we organized all sorts of diversions for the kids. There were parties with gifts for all, banquets and games and trips out to the bush cabins. I went over to Peffer's Hotel and borrowed a 16mm movie that I knew would be a special treat for the kids, as it featured Gene Autrey. With my tape recorder I got each child to record a message to his or her family, which I aired over radio CHAK.

When activities calmed down at the mission I finally got my chance to get away and visit the many native families around town who had come in for the feast. They initiated me in the eating of frozen beluga whale, a dish called *muktuk*. One of their favourites, whale dipped in seal oil, was called *uksuk*. It reminded me of Oka cheese in a way, but it had the consistency of a Goodyear tire. It took strong jaws and teeth to masticate it.

The new liquor outlet in operation ensured that this Christmas would be wilder than those that had preceded it, and this expectation prompted a citizens' meeting at the Day School. All sorts of suggestions were put forward aimed at controlling the drinking that was going on. Some suggested rationing, while others advocated that liquor permits be curtailed or that the local JPs put more offenders on the dreaded "Interdict List." Since the opening of the government liquor store, the weekly court sessions had become standing-room-only sessions which, as a reporter for the *Aklavik Journal*, I regularly attended. On the day following the public meeting I was again in court where a Navy officer acted as judge and one of the ten local RCMP as the crown prosecutor. Fifteen natives pleaded guilty to being intoxicated in a public place and paid fines ranging from ten to twenty dollars. When the Territorial Council met the following month, our representative, Frank Carmichael, succeeded in getting a law passed that limited permit-holders to two twenty-six-ounce bottles of liquor a week. The effect was negligible.

Although some memories of my last mission, Saint Bernard at Camsell Portage, were beginning to fade after six months, that didn't apply to my recollection of the team of fine white huskies I had had to leave behind. All my hopes for a future team were now dependent on my little white Samoyed bitch, Jasmine. When she came in heat about this time I borrowed a large white male named Dynamite from the RCMP and put them together. In sixty-four days I would know if I had a new team or not.

❊ ❊ ❊

The number one topic of conversation in Aklavik during the winter of 1955–56 was the government proposal that they move the town to a new site over on the east side of the delta. The reason given for the move was that Aklavik was gradually sinking into the river silt it was built on. Many residents disputed this assessment, among them the Roman Catholic mission personnel. When the Canada Research Council visited us, I showed them down into the 200-foot-long basement under the hostel and hospital. The Brothers who built it were knowledgeable enough about permafrost conditions to build their cement forms on a cushion of brush and sawdust to act as a buffer when the ground surrounding it froze and expanded. The heat of the buildings in summer warmed the ground surrounding this basement; the permafrost melted; so that you actually had a cement ship floating in a foot of melt-water. The experts were amazed that after ten years this biggest cement cellar in town had survived without a crack.

As strong as this evidence was that Aklavik would not in fact sink out of sight in a sea of mud, the government apparently had made up its mind about the move. They had hired a company of professional engineers called FENCO to examine the area for an alternate site and they came up with six, three on the mainland west of the delta and three on the east side. The government preferred the third site on the east side, so it became known temporarily as "East-Three," or "E-3" for short.

The majority of the residents in Aklavik didn't want to move anywhere, but if they had to move, they preferred for many reasons to move off the delta to the west. First, the E-3 site was in the reindeer preserve in which hunting was prohibited. The caribou rarely migrated into that area anyway, but the Porcupine herd appeared yearly in the hills west of Aklavik. Trapping, too, was better on the west side of the delta. Besides, if a road ever connected Aklavik to the outside world it would come in from the west via the Yukon. The Federal Government offered many inducements to get the people of Aklavik to accept their plan. For example, the residents could pick a lot of their choice at the new townsite at no cost. If they chose to abandon their old house in Aklavik and build a new one at East-Three, they would be compensated what it would cost to build a similar one at the new location, less depreciation, plus fifteen percent for "disturbance."

In order to forestall a riot over this forced move, two senior government officials came down from Ottawa to hold a public meeting. Brooking every argument brought forward by the locals, Northern Affairs Minister Jean Lesage and his Deputy Minister, Frank Cunningham, announced their iron-clad time table: 1956, pick your lot; 1957, get piling driven on it to support your home; 1958, build your new home; 1959, move your old home over from Aklavik; 1960, deadline for moving all government buildings.

Already underway was the clearing of a forty-mile winter road over to the new site at a cost of $5,000. Adolph Kosiak, a local trapper, was in charge of the crew who were paid eight dollars a day and all they could eat. The story had already hit southern newspapers and one report read: "A 20th Century community has started to rise in desolate wastes above the Arctic Circle some 1,500 miles northwest of Edmonton." When fears were

"Woman Threading Needle" This is Thérèse Codzi of Colville Lake.

"Arctic Reflections"

"Ahson" The word means *grandmother* in Hareskin. Her name was Verona Pascal. One of my tasks as the local medic was to remove and clean her glass eye weekly. She died at Colville in 1980.

"Evening chores"

"Margaret's huskies" Oil on canvas. 24" x 30"

"Breaking trail" Oil on canvas. 16" x 20"

The first church at E-3.

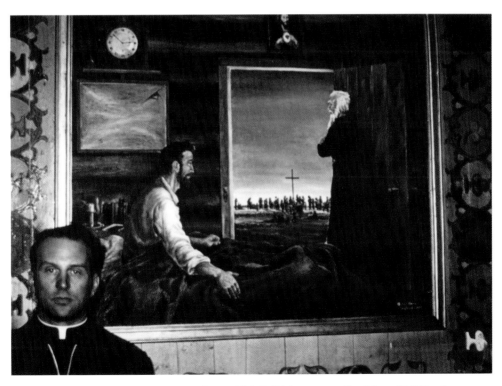

The painting of the death of Fr. Grollier, which I did in my small cabin at E-3 for the Fort Good Hope church.

The Old Mission at Fort McMurray.

The Nuns enjoying their new cabin.

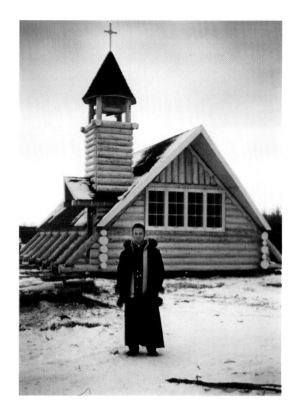

November 11, 1961. The church after 25 working days.

On the Slave River with my five Aquinas volunteers.

Beginning the new foundation at Colville Lake.

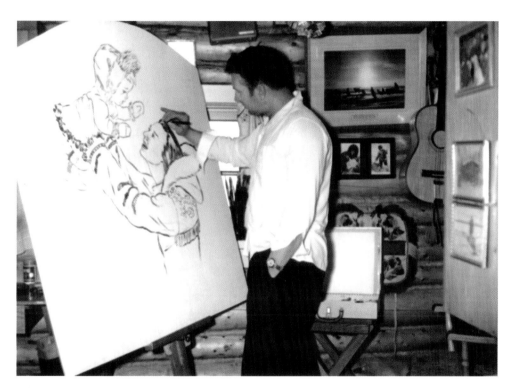

With the Mission built, I turn to art.

"Arctic Whaler" Oil on canvas. 24" x 30"

Our Lady of the Snows church completed.

"Our Lady of the Snows" Oil on canvas. 7 x 8 feet.

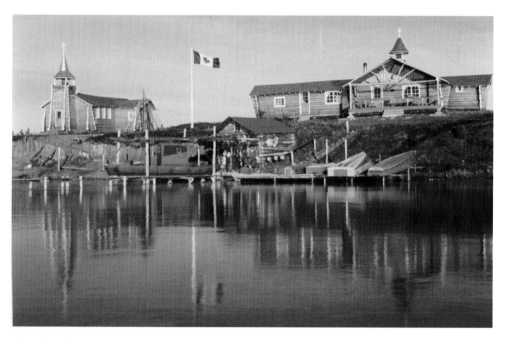

The church and Mission reflected in the new ice at freeze-up.

Our wedding, July 19, 1971.

expressed that the new Aklavik would be an artificial government town without benefit of industry or even trapping (which
would mean that the residents, once the construction phase was
ended, would either be working for the government or living on
relief) the reply from Lesage was, "Nonsense," seconded by Cunningham. Lesage added prophetically, "You people will be moving out of this mud hole and into the twentieth century! We'll
bulldoze what's left of this shack town into the river!" At this
point Cunningham got emotional and confessed that this new
townsite was the dream and consummation of his professional
career. A few years later he died in Florida.

I got caught up in this debate in two ways. For one, I had to
gather all the facts for my newspaper. For another, I was elected
the secretary of the newly formed Town Planning Committee.
On top of that, it was more or less taken for granted that I would
be the one to move over to the new townsite to establish the new
mission when the time came. After going through the turmoil
and headaches of getting a mission established in Uranium City
a few years before, the idea of doing it all over again did not
appeal to me. But I wasn't the one to make that decision. In any
case, the possibility made me keep a close eye on developments.

❈ ❈ ❈

The New Year didn't really dawn, for the sun was too far
south below the horizon to cast any warm glow. We were living
under a constantly revolving pale moon, accompanied by the
stars and the aurora borealis. That northwest wind never seemed
to stop, always blowing the snow into higher and harder drifts.
The cutbank in front of our buildings was drifted so high that the
kids used it for sliding. Most of the New Year celebrating was
done indoors.

I made it a point, however, to get out and walk around to visit
as many families as I could and wish them a Happy New Year.
As I walked through the dark snow porch to the cabin of an
Eskimo name Jake Ipana, I heard a snarl and felt a stabbing pain

in my right thigh. It was the family sled-dog, a bitch chained near her litter of new pups; she had reacted instinctively to the intrusion of a stranger. My greetings to Jake were a little less than enthusiastic as I sat by his barrel stove and wondered just how bad my wound was. On the spur of the moment I said, "Having your bitch bite me like this on the first day of the New Year means bad luck for you, Jake."

That visit terminated my walk around town and I limped back to our hospital, where Dr. Black administered two cc's of penicillin. This was the first time I had taken this drug and my reaction quickly showed that I was allergic to it. I swelled up in fifteen minutes and felt as if I had a bad case of hives. Only a follow-up shot of adrenalin gradually reduced the swelling and itching, which was more painful than the original bite. A few months later, when Jake dropped dead of a heart attack, his widow came to see me and accused me of being a medicine man who had cast an evil spell on her husband! I regretted making that remark.

On the 11th of January we greeted the return of the sun after its two-month absence. It barely showed itself on the southern horizon, slid along for a few miles and then disappeared again, but it was a harbinger of the light and warmth to come: it raised our spirits. Along with the return of the sun came our missionaries from all over the Western Arctic for their annual retreat. Some of the conferences may have put us to sleep, but the late-night bull sessions often kept us from bed till midnight. Then the mission was quiet for a short five hours. At 5:30 that inexorable wake-up bell would sound again.

All our missionaries prided themselves on their fluid mastery of the native language of the particular group with which they worked. While at Forts Norman and Franklin, I had gained a working knowledge of the Hare Indian language. While I was in the Lake Athabaska area it had not been too difficult to pick up some Chipewyan. At the same time I was working on a Cree grammar, which was entirely different. These languages, however, were of no use around Aklavik so I decided to start learning

Eskimo. With the help of Father Maurice Métayer from Cambridge Bay I began a new grammar. When he left to return to his mission I continued with the help of an Eskimo TB patient. The first phrase he taught me was *kraloktoami*, "I'm hungry," certainly a very practical sentence to memorize.

With everyone burning wood for heat and cooking and the natives lighting their cabins with gasoline or kerosene lamps, it was inevitable that there would be fires. One evening in the dark of supper time we were drawn to the windows by the wailing of the town's fire siren. Across the Peel River on the Poliak Channel we could see Nels Hvatum's cabin on fire. We grabbed our parkas and joined the crowd rushing across the ice. Dr. Black passed us in the Navy's Bombardier (a tracked vehicle that could hold about a dozen people) while the volunteer fire brigade stuck one end of its hose into the town's heated pump shack in mid-river. There really wasn't much we could do to help except keep out of the way. Slowly we got the story of what had happened. Nels himself had gone with his dog-team to get a load of firewood. His seventeen-year-old son Herschel went outside the cabin to get lamp gas in a jerrycan. On his way back he accidentally hit the door jamb with the can. It slipped from his hand and spilled its volatile contents over the floor. He dropped to the floor and started to mop up the fuel with his moosehide mittens, at the same time calling to his mother in the back room to bring a blanket to absorb the fuel. There wasn't time. Fumes from the gas were sucked into the stove in the middle of the floor and they ignited with a mighty whoosh! Noel Firth, who lives right across their channel, told us that he saw six feet of fire shoot out the Hvatum chimney.

The pressure of the expanding gas sealed the single door so that Herschel couldn't pull it open immediately. When he finally succeeded, all his clothes were on fire. He rolled himself in the snow to extinguish them and then rushed back into the burning cabin to rescue his sister Lillian, aged three. Meanwhile his mother got out through a small window in the bedroom, but she was also on fire and her legs were badly burned. Six-year-old

Harold was found on a burning bed and lived only a short time after he was taken out. His one-year-old brother Hans burned to death on a cot.

As sad as this tragedy was, our deep feelings of sympathy were doubled when we learned that nine years before, almost to the day, this family had suffered a similar fire in the same place that destroyed their cabin and two other boys. It's at times like this that a family needs strong faith to overcome depression. One can just imagine the thoughts that raced through the head of the father of this family when he returned to find that, once again, he had lost his home and two sons to fire. Talk about trials that test a man's soul! As we trudged home across the frozen channel discussing these events, our own troubles seemed insignificant.

We were now into the coldest time of the winter and saw the temperature gradually slip down to sixty below zero. I don't know if the temperature was responsible, but everyone seemed to have a sore throat, a cold or the flu. Many blamed it on the lack of sunshine, fresh fruit and vegetables. If I was in our hospital when the doctor made his rounds, I would accompany him in hopes of picking up some information that might be useful to me at some future time. I had him write an article on treating burns for the *Aklavik Journal* and interviewed him on my regular Tuesday night radio program. Another Tuesday I interviewed old-timers like Charlie Stewart, who had been a guide for the RCMP when they lost Corporal Dempster and two of his companions on the patrol from Dawson City to Fort MacPherson in 1905. Another night I had one-eyed Tommy Clark on and he enthralled us with his story of a $50,000 fur robbery, which took place during the time he traded for the Hudson Bay Company.

❄ ❄ ❄

The classic story for Aklavik was told by Karl Gardlund the night I interviewed him on CHAK. It involved Albert Johnson, the famous "Mad Trapper" of Rat River. Many and various versions of this story have appeared in print, but that night we were getting it from an eye-witness. Karl told how Johnson first came into the country in 1931, floating down the Peel River to Fort McPherson on a raft. That fall he settled up the Rat River where he built himself a log cabin. This river was on the route taken by many of the Stampeders of 1898 who came down the Mackenzie River from Edmonton and then crossed over the divide into the Yukon.

After freeze-up, when Johnson started trapping, he would run into traps set by the Loucheux Indians out of Fort McPherson. He would spring these and hang them up as a warning that they were set too close to his area. This irked the natives and they reported it to the Mounties. Right after Christmas, a patrol left Arctic Red River by dog-team to mush the seventy-odd miles to Johnson's cabin. Breaking trail on that trip was an Indian by the name of Joe Bernard whom I interviewed later and who gave me the wool leggings he wore on that trip. The intent of the police on this trip was to check on Johnson's trapping licence. Johnson, however, wouldn't let them in, so they were forced to go on to Aklavik and report to the inspector. They returned to Johnson's cabin in greater strength: two Mounties, plus two special constables, and a search warrant.

One of the constables walked up to Johnson's cabin alone and knocked on the door. Johnson's response was a shot from a .30-.30 rifle that tore through his chest an inch from his heart. His three companions had to rush him back to Aklavik to save his life. This turn of events had the whole town buzzing. Nothing like it had ever happened before. When a posse of seven armed men pulled out on January 4th with forty-two sled-dogs, Karl Gardlund was with them. They laid siege to Johnson's cabin and for eighteen straight hours they pumped hundreds of rounds of .30-.30 slugs into it and even blew off part of his roof with dynamite. Later they found that he was able to survive this barrage because he had dug the floor down a couple of feet below ground level when he built the cabin. Johnson wasn't simply crouching low during the shooting, however: at one point during the night

Karl had a flashlight shot out of his hand. The posse finally ran out of ammo and returned to Aklavik.

Two days later a posse of twenty men was formed and Karl and a constable of the RCMP left ahead of them to break trail. When these two arrived at the cabin they found it deserted. Snowshoe tracks headed west toward the divide. It took the posse twenty days to catch up to Johnson. When they did, he was hidden among fallen trees and large boulders in a creek bed. Gardlund got one clear shot at him and thought he had fatally hit him, but after a two-hour wait, when they began closing in, Johnson suddenly sprang to life again and shot one of the Mounties dead. When this news reached Aklavik an even bigger posse was recruited and a wireless message sent out to Edmonton for an aircraft.

Meanwhile, the not-so-mad trapper had slipped out of his barricade and disappeared into the polar night. No sign of blood was found at his campsite to indicate that Karl had wounded him. Now the foothills of the Richardson Mountains were crawling with pursuers. Bush pilot Wop May joined them in his low-wing Bellanca. They picked up Johnson's trails going in every direction: apparently Johnson even put his snowshoes on backwards to make his pursuers think that he was going in the opposite direction. Another posse was formed at Old Crow in the Yukon and started in by dogs from the west. Then, suddenly, blowing snow completely obliterated Johnson's trail. When it was picked up again, three days later, he was ninety miles to the west. He had crossed the 5,000-foot divide. The aircraft was out ahead scouting and the posse followed.

By this time Albert Johnson had frozen both his hands and his feet and his weight had dropped from 170 to 145. He didn't dare kindle a fire for fear that smoke would betray his whereabouts, nor was he able to kill a caribou, because the echoing sound of the rifle would carry miles in that sub-zero temperature. He came up behind a herd of caribou and walked in their steps a good many miles to obliterate his own tracks.

On February 17th the posse was following a fresh trail on the snow-covered Eagle River in Yukon Territory when they got their first sight of their prey. A 300-yard shot from Johnson's .30-.30 felled an army Signal Corps man who was in the lead. The fugitive then scrambled toward the river's bank, but it was too steep to climb and it had no trees for protection. When Gardlund crossed the river to try to get behind Johnson, Johnson turned and tried to dash across to the opposite bank of the river where there were a few trees. He never made it: he was hit fatally in mid-river.

Thus ended the epic manhunt for the Mad Trapper of Rat River, as the story was told to me and my CHAK audience by my guest, Karl Gardlund. This story was of interest all across Canada, but especially in Aklavik where the people knew the country as well as all the characters involved. Now Johnson's body lay in an isolated grave on the main street near the police barracks, his initials "A. J." cut in the stump of a dead tree above it.

❊ ❊ ❊

Not all my radio guests had such a tragic story to tell. The following week I interviewed an Eskimo named Donald Greenland, who was very outspoken and humorous. He told of a meeting held the year before by the natives of Aklavik who were discussing whether or not the white man should be allowed to remain in the area. Donald reported that he introduced a winning argument for allowing the white men to remain when he stood and said, "Have you people ever thought who we'd steal gas from if the whites were all gone?" On another occasion Donald was selling fresh fish at the end of Aklavik's main street next to the river. After selling one to Gallagher Arey for fifty cents, Shorty Wilson bought one and Donald asked one dollar for it. Shorty complained saying, "But you only charged Gallagher fifty cents for his!" "I know," replied Donald, "that was a special price for Gallagher 'cause I stole the fish from his net."

Jasmine dropped her litter of pups on schedule the 22nd of February, but they were a disappointment: only three males, and they were not white as I had hoped. Still, they would form the nucleus of my new team. Meanwhile I was using the fine, big, black-and-white team that was kept by the mission. Once in a while I would drive them out twenty-five miles to the Brothers' wood camp to give them some exercise and to keep my hand in the skill of dog driving. When the RCMP had an auction of the trapping gear of the late Pat Keevik, I bought his old basket sled and Nome-style dog harness for seventeen dollars. I wasn't quite sure what I would do with that type of sled, but I had lots of fun rebuilding it. And I was actually teaching Eskimos to build igloos! That is, I would get my twenty-four cub scouts down on the riverbank in front of the mission and with a few butcher knives attempt to cut out suitable snow blocks and build them into a reasonable facsimile of a snow house. We had a lot of fun together and who knows, maybe a few of them learned enough of the technique that it would serve them in later life if they were forced to spend a cold night out on the Barrens.

The scouts didn't have any funding, so they had to devise ways of raising money for themselves. By now I had a good collection of slides from all over the North, so I decided to put on a benefit show for my pack. They sold tickets all over town for a dollar each and we packed the Federal Day School one evening and realized a $195 profit. On top of this windfall my little pack got some unexpected publicity when the Governor General, Vincent Massey, paid an official visit at the end of March. On Easter Sunday afternoon the Mounties brought this distinguished visitor out to the boys' shack by dog team. The press were not far behind and filmed my cubs as they put on an outside demonstration for the Governor General. He was so impressed he shook hands and talked briefly with each of the boys.

Just prior to this historic event I got a chance to fly down to Tuktoyaktuk with the school inspector, Gordon Devitt. I hadn't seen the settlement for six years and never in its winter garb. Pat Carey, veteran bush pilot from Fort Smith and an old friend of mine, flew us down in his Beaver on skis. En route we got a good look at those odd conical hills the Eskimos call pingos. So now I could fill another gap in my slide collection. Although the Eskimos at Tuk were no longer living in igloos, we noticed that some living in tents had snow or ice blocks completely surrounding them and those in cabins had built snow porches to break the constant wind. There were some small igloos that served as privies. While Gordon Devitt went to the school I went over to the mission to spend the night with Father Franche. He was occupied with an ambitious boat-building project which employed a half-dozen local natives. They had a heated thirty-foot building they had been working in all winter. Besides a twenty-six-foot whale boat nearing completion in the shed, there were a dozen smaller round bottom "Jolly boats" out in the snow, ready to be sold come summer. I watched, fascinated, as they steamed and bent oak ribs. The whole operation looked very professional to me. Of course I'm prejudiced in that I love working in wood and I love wooden boats. And there was a beauty, frozen in the harbour, called the *Fort Hearne*, the Hudson Bay Company's huge wooden-hulled vessel used to supply their posts along the Arctic Coast. They kept a man on board all winter, whose duty it was to keep cutting the ice all around her so that no damaging ice pressure would build up. Unfortunately, this fine old ship was to be dealt a death blow by the ice of Coronation Gulf a few years later and today she lies at the bottom of Bernard Harbour north of Coppermine.

Another interesting old marine veteran up on the beach at Tuk at that time was the mission supply schooner *Our Lady of Lourdes*. This forty-ton wooden boat had been brought up from San Francisco by Captain Ted Pederson on the deck of his ship *Patterson* and off-loaded at Herschel Island. Of the many schooners Pederson brought up to the Beaufort Sea and traded to the Eskimos, this was the largest. He told me he nearly lost it in the unloading process. I photographed it nostalgically, all the time wishing I could have gone on one of its many exciting voyages along the coast supplying our remote mission stations.

On our return we flew over Kitigazuit and the 600-foot Loran tower which now lay stretched out and broken on the tundra. Fearing that it might prove dangerous to aircraft flying between Tuk and Aklavik, the Navy had blown it down with dynamite. This was one item from "Kitty" that the mission didn't pick up along with the rest of the station it bought.

As the months rolled by, each punctuated by another issue of the *Aklavik Journal*, I was becoming aware that I was not just gathering local news for our townsfolk, but that it was having some impact on people far to the south. In the April issue, under the "News Roundup" column, I had mentioned that a Weems Alaska Airways C-46 had landed on the ice at Aklavik with five tons of meat for Bill Strong's North Star Café. I happened to mention that the freight rate on this charter was fourteen cents per pound compared to sixty cents per pound if it had been brought up from Edmonton via our scheduled carrier, Canadian Pacific Airlines. Including the three cents-per-pound import duty, we were able to get Seattle choice carcass beef for sixty-three cents per pound, while the inferior reindeer carcasses were costing us sixty-two cents per pound at the reindeer station. This item was picked up by the *Edmonton Journal* and spread right across Canada. The result of this bad publicity for CPA sparked them to fly their Supervisor of Sales and Traffic into Aklavik in mid-May in one of their DC-3s. He held a public meeting at the school in an attempt to stop us from chartering out of Alaska. But his prices were not competitive and his trip was in vain. He appealed to our patriotism, but it wouldn't cover forty-six cents a pound on freight.

Almost all the incidents I have described here have little to do with my real purpose for being there – the spiritual good of the people. One must remember that these took place while I was engaged with daily Mass, community prayers, the hearing of confessions and the visiting of the sick. These routine duties rarely varied and seem not to merit special attention in these pages, but they occupied a significant portion of each day. It wasn't till March that I was called upon to perform a marriage, when I joined in holy wedlock Peter Thrasher and Mary Green-land. I can't remember ever baptizing anyone in Aklavik.

On the 4th of April, Father Max Ruyant arrived back from his holidays in France and resumed his proper position as bursar. This made a big change in my life, as I was relieved of all the front office accounts and a job that was necessarily demanding and incessant. I moved my personal effects upstairs to my bedroom and heaved a sigh of relief. Now that I was no longer needed on a day-to-day basis I immediately began planning a solo dogsled trip around the delta, a chance to stretch my legs, see more of the country and breathe some fresh air.

A week later I was on the trail heading east across the delta behind the mission's fine team of black-and-white huskies. I wasn't exactly alone: Paschal Baptiste, a fine Loucheux trapper, was heading in the same direction and we teamed up. But the skies were now bright and the days long and warm under a rising sun. We stopped briefly at Henry John's cabin for tea, then continued on to Benoit's cabin on the banks of the Mackenzie River to rest the night. The next morning I continued on up river alone, as Paschal's trail had forked off to the left. The dogs were running well on a hard trail. The skies were clear and the wind behind us. I never felt better just being alive and out in God's wonderland. At 3:30 in the afternoon I pulled into the camp of Emil Larson, a Swede, and one of the dwindling number of white trappers in the country. Over a great feed of boiled beaver Emil told me story after story of his interesting life as a trapper. In fact he proved such a good story-teller that my brief stopover consumed three hours before I was again back on the trail. The sun began to set and the shadows of tall spruce lengthened across the snow-covered Mackenzie. My eyes were dazzled by the absolute beauty of this land of silent places and my mind was still occupied with thoughts of the life of a man like Larson. It certainly had its compensations.

The lights of the village of Arctic Red River, high on the bluff above the river, could be seen for miles before I finally reached there at 11 p.m. Father Levesque and Brother Girouard had heard via their mission short-wave radio that I was on my way, so they and a dozen of their Loucheux flock had been on the look-out for me and had spotted me an hour before I reached them. They helped me chain up my six dogs and I gave each dog a good whitefish as a reward for a good day's run. In the mission I was given supper as we exchanged news and talked shop. It was late in the night when I finally crawled into my sleeping bag on a cot in the refectory.

The following day the two Oblates at Arctic Red River hitched up their teams and joined me in crossing the portage to Fort McPherson. We made very slow progress: the trail was com-pletely blown in and the dogs had to plow through a foot of soft snow. We stopped twice to make tea-fires. It was eleven at night when we arrived at the Fort and aroused Father Jean Colas from a sound sleep. This determined missionary had spent nine years there in a settlement that was at least ninety percent Anglican. His own flock could not have numbered more than a dozen. Many in our own church thought that he was wasting his time on so few, but evidently Jean didn't see it that way. And who can say with certainty that he wasn't right? The merit for the work we were doing for the Lord was not necessarily dependent upon the size of our flocks.

During the next three days we three visitors pitched in and helped Father Colas cut five cords of firewood which he pro-ceeded to pull out of the bush and back to his mission with an entirely new contraption. It was called a motor toboggan and it was the first one in the country, a harbinger of a new era in sled travel. When it got stuck repeatedly in the soft snow we were not too favourably impressed with its usefulness. Once its throttle got stuck at full speed and it lost its driver when it climbed a pile of wood. This performance left us very doubtful about its future, nor were we at all tempted to trade our faithful dogs for such a mechanical marvel.

On Saturday night we finished our wood haul and on Sun-day morning at ten I was honoured with the role of celebrant at the community Mass. The community turned out to be just one woman, but we went ahead with the full ceremony, at which I preached just as if I were at Aklavik before a crowd of 200. Later in the day I got the opportunity to visit some interesting local characters. One was Bob Douglas, whom I had known at Norman Wells and who was now filling the position of local game warden. He showed me something unusual in a team of six wolves he was using in place of sled-dogs. Bob had adopted this litter just after they were born, so they hardly ever knew the wild. But they were far from ideal for this domestic role. Their feet were larger than dogs' feet, so they got sore on the hard-packed trails. They are also slightly knock-kneed and their chests are not broad like a husky's. According to Bob, they started out strong but didn't seem to harbour their strength for the long haul, and they ran better at night than in daylight. Though they had received good treatment at the hands of their master, they were hard to catch if they got loose. All in all, this team bore out the wise words of many old trappers I had talked with over the years, who told me that a quarter-wolf is as much wolf as a sled-dog could stand.

Another interesting local was Mike Krutko, who ran a trading post in opposition to the Hudson Bay Company. Mike also maintained an outpost store in Old Crow over the divide in the Yukon Territory, which he serviced with his Stinson aircraft. He had had a lot of hair-raising flights, including a few crack-ups. Like most of the other white traders in the country, he had a native wife and raised a large family of Métis children.

Early Monday morning I pulled out of Fort McPherson, heading back to Aklavik with a local native named Isaac Kunnize. Fifteen miles down the frozen Peel River we stopped for tea at the tent camp of Bill Smith. When his wife first spotted me she took me for the police and dove back into the tent yelling, "Holy Smoke!" But I soon calmed her fears. We did drink tea, but they had no sugar and in fact very little of any grub. I got to thinking of this as we continued on north and when we met a team heading back toward the Fort I gave the driver all my bannock and sugar plus three pounds of tallow to drop off at the Smith tent.

After that my conscience let me continue in peace. At noon we arrived at a group of cabins at the mouth of the Peel occupied by a family with the hybrid name of Bonnetplume. We took lunch there and continued on till 6 p.m. when we arrived at the camp of Tommy Clark, who was operating a trading post for Stan Peffer. Tommy was a middle-aged Métis bachelor who had lost one eye. Later when I had tied up my dogs and moved into his cabin he told me the accident had happened when a willow struck his eye when he was driving his dogs. He was a surprisingly good cook and made splendid bread. The natives swarmed through his home at all hours and seemed perfectly at home. He certainly kept me enthralled far into the night with his fascinating stories. At last I succumbed to drowsiness and fell into my sleeping bag on the floor behind the kitchen stove to sleep just as well as I would have on a spring mattress.

Tommy saw me off the next morning with a parting gift of a new tea pail and a handful of White Owl cigars. My mushing companion turned out to be trapper George Roberts, who was heading his dogs in the same direction. At noon we rested our dogs while we ate lunch at the tent camp of Louie Chum. There were ten kids running in and out of the tent here, not all Louie's. Three at least he was keeping for Rosalie Harris, who was in the hospital with TB. Louie's older boys were helping him trap about thirty muskrats a day and at about a dollar apiece for the pelts he wasn't making too much and maybe would have been short of food if the carcasses weren't as edible as they were. We sure enjoyed a frying pan full of that meat for our lunch. Taking a few pictures and picking up their mail, George and I continued on fifteen miles to the next camp – that of William Snowshoe, who was also in hospital with TB. After a meal of moose-meat with his wife and family, I took a little snooze stretched out on the neat spruce bough floor of their tent while George filed their Swede saw blade.

We made one more tea stop that day, at the tent of Charlie Stewart, another old-timer who had been one of the Mad Trapper's posse. By 6 p.m. Tuesday George and I arrived at the imposing trading post of Knut Lang. Knut was a big man in more ways than one. Standing six-foot-four in his moccasins, he had worked his way down to Aklavik in 1928 by cutting firewood for the Mackenzie River steamers. Later he became an influential member of the elected N.W.T. Council. His home base here on the west bank of the Peel Channel in the shadow of Red Mountain was a picturesque set-up. His main cabin was large by bachelor standards and had one of the best libraries of northern books in the country. Right out behind was another cabin used as a bunkhouse by trappers who came to trade their furs. On the door, in large painted letters, was inscribed NEVERCLOSE HOTEL!

The aptness of this title became clearer as the night wore on and dog-teams continued to come and go. Out behind this roadhouse were a half-dozen assorted warehouses in a neat row, some up off the ground on posts like a Yukon cache. A raw bearhide was nailed to one wall. Certainly Knut Lang's was the epitome of the fur-trading post in the Far North. We had just finished a good supper when an Indian named Johnny Semple came in and Knut cooked another supper for him. After we had talked till midnight, Knut whittled shavings to start his fire in the morning and we all rolled up in our eiderdowns. Three hours later another native pulled in from Aklavik, used Knut's shavings to build a fire and make himself tea, and in general wrecked what could have been a good night's sleep. Apparently, to be a successful trader one had to be very accommodating to one's clientele.

The following morning, after a fine breakfast of buckwheat flapjacks, George and I harnessed up for the last twenty-five miles into Aklavik. We arrived at 11:30, just in time for lunch at the mission. After that I fell on my bed and slept all afternoon.

April gave way to May as the sun climbed higher in the sky and the kids started playing outside without their parkas. I was able to devote more hours of my day to painting the first of two panels for the Fort Good Hope church. I answered the front door bell one sunny afternoon to find six Mounties pulled up in front with a stone boat pulled by a tractor. Without any explanation, they inquired where our meat house was and proceeded to load their sled with frozen reindeer carcasses. They made several trips over to their reefer at the barracks before we got a phone call through to the commanding officer asking for an explanation. We found out that they thought they were confiscating illegal caribou meat.

It was illegal to serve any "wild" meat in a boarding school or hospital at that time. As we were able to get only half the number of legal reindeer carcasses we needed, I had begun buying the odd illegal caribou carcass from local hunters. One of them happened to get picked up on a drunk charge and when asked where he got the money to buy the booze confessed he had sold meat to the mission. It is difficult to distinguish frozen caribou meat from reindeer, the main difference being that the reindeer seem to acquire more fat and their meat looks marbled with white streaks. The Mounties were obliged to haul all the reindeer carcasses back to our underground permafrost pit. But with the help of their Special Constable, Otto Binder, they were finally able to distinguish some caribou meat in our possession and we were duly charged with contravening the N.W.T. Game Act. The penalty imposed by the law could be a fine or imprisonment or both! As Father Ruyant was now the official buyer for the mission, the charge was laid against him, while I had actually bought most of the illegal meat. At any rate I accompanied him over to the barracks to face the music. He pleaded guilty and was let off with a hundred-dollar fine. Normally such illegal meat was distributed between the Anglican and Catholic hospitals, but in this case they were faced with a dilemma. We never did find out what happened to our meat.

With the Federal Government solidly behind the building of a new Aklavik over on the East-Three site, our arguments against it had very little effect. Whether we moved or not, it was going to be built. As soon as this decision was definite, the bishop designated me chaplain to the project with the understanding that, as it went ahead, I would assume the role as its first permanent missionary. It was Saturday, the 12th of May, when Mike Zubko flew me over to assess the situation and we landed on skis on the ice of the East Branch of the Mackenzie. As there was open water running along near the shore we were taken off the ice in a freighter canoe. Curt Merrill, the project manager, greeted me and took me for a short drive in his pick-up to the end of the existing gravel road. The snow was melted off the ground, and the gently rising moss-covered ground, with a sprinkling of white birch on it, gave a park-like appearance. It was not at all unpleasant, I had to admit. I visited several native families camped near the riverbank, including Peter and Tommy Thrasher. Then I was taken to meet Charlie Walrath, who had two dozen Department of Public Works carpenters working for him to construct the first of many small frame buildings. These were called "512's," because that was the number of square feet of floor space in each. That night I threw my bedroll on the floor of Charlie's office shack and slept there.

The next morning, a Sunday, I said Mass and preached to a crowd of twenty-five in the mess hall. This was the first religious service to be conducted in the new townsite, so it was rather an historic occasion. After lunch, armed with the most recent survey map of the townsite, I walked up into the bush and located the lot designated for our mission. It seemed far too small and a long way from the riverbank. I determined immediately to get it enlarged and moved closer to the water. But in the meantime I would need some kind of small shack to use as a base of operations.

I got back to the cookhouse at 5 p.m., just as the waitresses Rosa McCloud and Ellen Martin were ringing the steel triangle and announcing supper. It turned out to be turkey which had been found, along with 500 pounds of jettisoned meat, near Kitigazuit, apparently left by a DEW Line caterpillar tractor train. ("DEW" stands for Distant Early Warning, a series of radar sites which stretched from the Aleutians in the west to Greenland in the east, and which was built by the U.S. Government as a joint U.S. – Canadian defence project.) Mike picked me up at 9:30 that evening with his Cessna 170 and flew me back home. The flight across the delta toward the setting sun was particularly beautiful that evening, with the magnificent, snowy Richardson Mountains forming a purple background ahead. The rays of the setting sun illuminated Aklavik sitting peacefully in its loop of the Peel Channel. I wondered to myself if it would survive the onslaught of East-Three. Was it doomed to become a ghost-town?

15

Moving into East-Three

The midday sun is so warm in Aklavik in the middle of May that the hard-packed winter snow trails will no longer support one's weight. Walking is very difficult. It is the time of year to switch from winter's mukluks to spring's boots – or get your feet wet. People drive their dog-teams at night so that the trails will support them. Aklavik's principal cash crop comes from the sale of muskrat pelts and at this time of year there is open water appearing around a thousand small lakes in the delta in which these animals swim at night. Most people move out to their "rat camps" to take advantage of this time when they can easily shoot the rats, instead of the more laborious work of trapping them. It is also the best time of the year to enjoy living out on the land, because it is warm, but the mosquitoes have not yet made their appearance.

This spring exodus from the town didn't really affect us at the mission. The hospital patients couldn't move from their beds and the school children couldn't leave their desks, with the exception of the bigger boys who did go out after school. But our schedule of early morning devotions and three meals a day went on with monotonous regularity, broken now and then by feast days. I occupied my time with painting, typing stencils for the *Aklavik Journal*, taping interviews for my CHAK broadcasts and attending meetings of the New Town Planning Committee. After supper I visited all our patients and I was often invited out to either the boys' or the girls' shacks to play guitar and encourage a sing-song.

With the beginning of June, some out-of-the-ordinary things began to happen. First the ice on the Peel Channel began moving out, although it had moved just far enough two days earlier to win Mike Kosiak the $134 ice sweepstakes. The Brothers got excited, anticipating an early boat season, and they were racing around with their truck and cat. In the confusion, one of them backed over Jasmine, putting her in an early grave. I was feeling that loss keenly, until Inspector Bill Fraser of the RCMP gave me back one of Jasmine's white female pups so I could continue the strain. Bill was a strong believer in the use of dog-teams to build character and resourcefulness in new Mountie recruits to the North. It was somewhat akin to the Navy maintaining square-rigged sailing ships to give their new members a basic feel for the high seas. Mainly through Bill's efforts the force now had an active dog kennel and breeding station for Siberian huskies on Herschel Island. He gave me two of these dogs to try out in harness.

❊ ❊ ❊

About a dozen native girls, some Eskimo, some Indian, were employed by the Sisters to help in the kitchen and laundry and to act as ward aids in the hospital. Their main off-duty recreation seemed to be flirting with the young Navy boys in town and their hangout was Peffer's Hotel coffee shop. A recent innovation there was a juke box and the favourite record was "I Walk the Line" by Johnny Cash. At first I didn't understand why the native girls would try to attract these white boys who were only serving a hitch in the North and would soon be back outside. Going by the record, those in the past who had married such boys and moved south to civilization were now back in the North, alone or with a couple of kids. Still, this didn't seem to deter them.

It wasn't until I got talking with Otto Binder's wife Ellen that I began to understand the girls' point of view. Ellen was born of Lapp parents who had originally driven the reindeer over from Alaska some thirty years before. She explained that the basic motive that attracted the native girls toward white men was one of self-preservation. Most of these girls had seen how their mothers were treated by their native husbands who, in general, held them in low esteem and when drinking would often beat them. On the other hand they never saw any white women with black eyes. They got the idea that they would be safer with a white husband. Another motive was the fact that the girls saw in the whites better providers for themselves and their children. It was certainly true that the early white traders and trappers in the country who had taken native wives had lived successful lives. John Firth, the Hudson Bay Company trader at Fort McPherson, was a well-known example of that. And so the goal of a native gal was to have blue-eyed babies someday. They did not realize that this was a genetic impossibility for them.

Sister Bourgeois was in charge of these girls and when they got in late at night she often had trouble rousing them to their duties on time the next morning. One day she happened to mention to me that Mary Rose, a Hareskin from Fort Good Hope, was still in bed complaining of pains in her stomach. From her reputation I doubted this girl was simply feigning sickness and suggested very strongly that the doctor check her over at once. This Dr. Black did, and diagnosed her trouble as acute appendicitis. It was immediately agreed that he would operate at midnight when the patients were asleep and the hospital quiet. Furthermore, knowing that I would soon be living over at E-3, where there were no medical personnel, he invited me to be present at the operation, with the hope that I would learn to cope with such an emergency should it arise over there.

At midnight we scrubbed up and donned our white coats, caps and masks. Dr. Hagen, who was just out of medical school in Scotland, would perform his first appendectomy while Dr. Black would supervise. I would act as the anaesthetist, keeping a rag soaked with chloroform under the patient's nose and a tongue depressor in her mouth so that she wouldn't swallow her tongue. Several medical Sisters would supply the instruments as needed. The initial incision was tackled with so much zeal that the young doctor sliced into Mary Rose's bladder. "No big problem," commented Dr. Black, encouragingly, "this often happens to the best of us." Once the bladder was sutured, the operation continued, but the initial incision had to be enlarged. Groping around for the appendix, Dr. Hagen came up with a lump which proved to be an ovarian cyst! This was an unexpected bonus and was promptly removed. Still searching for the appendix, the young physician began removing some of the intestines, but again the incision proved too small and he enlarged it. I was having no trouble keeping Mary Rose completely unaware of all that was going on and she made no effort to swallow her tongue. More of her intestines were removed in an effort to locate the offending appendix, which had all but disappeared. The incision was enlarged a fourth time and with most of her intestines removed what was left of her ruptured appendix was lying at the bottom of the peritoneum. Dr. Black examined it with the aid of a flashlight, but was unable to get any of it out. Sulfa powder was sprinkled in the cavity, a drain inserted, the intestines replaced and Dr. Hagen sutured his incision.

The operation had ended, but it had taken exactly four hours. I felt on the verge of collapse myself, when Dr. Black turned to me and said, "I hope you got that, Father Brown?" I can't remember what I answered, but I know that I was thinking to myself, "I hope I don't have to tackle the removal of an appendix over at E-3." As for our patient, though she was a sick girl for a few days, she was soon back at her job as a ward aide and later, when married, produced many healthy children. Little episodes like this certainly helped to relieve the tedium of life in the big mission station.

❉ ❉ ❉

As soon as the ice had cleared out of the Peel, the Brothers launched their boat and barge and I joined them on the first trip upstream to get a load of the firewood they had cut during the winter. The forty-five cords we brought back on the barge were unloaded and stacked in our front yard in an hour-and-a-half. But it took another seven trips to bring down a year's supply. On June 8th, Stu Hill landed on floats from Norman Wells with our first mail following break-up. Right behind him came the yearly migration of cliff swallows that loved to build their mud nests under the eaves of our buildings, much to the annoyance of Brother Delisle. On the 17th, Streeper's "Banana Boat" had again beaten the fleet down the Mackenzie River and Alec Greenland won the $500 pool for the first boat. Trying to think up some excuse for spending more time outdoors in the balmy weather, I decided to build my own shack for E-3. I brought in two sturdy skids and laid out a floor on them, nine feet by seventeen feet. I made sure it was well insulated with fibreglass and found some very nice siding to finish it off.

Before that glorious month of June expired, our mission supply boat the *Sant'Anna* arrived from Fort Smith, loaded to the gunwales with freight for us and other missions along the Arctic coast. On board as usual were many priests, Brothers and Sisters we hadn't seen for years, so the boat's arrival signalled a grand reunion. A few bottles of our sacramental wine were sacrificed for non-sacramental purposes. Brother Médard was on board in charge of the galley and we resumed the chess games we had enjoyed while we were together at Fort Norman. As usual, he won. It was a particularly busy time for me as I was hurrying to finish my little shack and at the same time to get the June issue of the *Aklavik Journal* printed before we ran into July. The trappers hadn't returned to town, so news was scarce. I filled the entire front page with a map of the new townsite at E-3 and got the newspaper out on the streets on the last day of the month.

With the ending of the school year, most of our hostel students returned to their families for the summer and the school-yard became suddenly and strangely silent. On the hospital

floors, too, I noticed a few empty beds as some patients con-
quered their TB and were discharged. Soon it became my turn to
leave Aklavik, as the population at the new townsite was growing by leaps and bounds. With my little shack completed, I
packed my trunk, dragged it inside and the Brothers skidded the
shack down onto the *Immaculata*'s Canol barge. We backed out
into the Peel at 9 p.m. We travelled all night under the midnight
sun. This enabled Brother Petrin to thread his way some seventy-
odd miles across the delta, a passage which involved twenty-one
critical points where a pilot must know whether to turn left or
right without benefit of markers. By 10:00 the following morning
we were nosed into the bank at E-3. Jim Biggs skidded my shack
off the barge with his D-8 caterpillar and parked it between some
white birch, fifty feet up from the riverbank. Curt Merrill was on
hand to welcome me and the Brothers stayed overnight to see
that I got my little building properly levelled.

It didn't take me long to get myself comfortably organized in
my new surroundings. Slim Semmler was already trading out of
a tent and he sold me a small oil stove and a chemical toilet,
which I promptly installed. One of the electricians gave me 200
feet of wire and I got permission from the Department of Public
Works to connect up to their cookhouse. I now had electricity
and connected a radio, but all that I could get on it was the U.S.
Armed Forces station in Los Angeles and Moscow Mollie, who
was amazingly well informed on activities around the new DEW
Line sites. Just how much secrecy actually protected these new
military installations was questionable. When L.A.C.O. Hunt
assumed the position of Administrator at Aklavik about this time
he had a map on his office wall with all the sites well marked. A
visiting member of the Armed Forces was horrified when he saw
it and had it removed immediately. But Moscow Mollie evidently knew where they were and who came or left each site
daily. As soon as I was comfortably installed in my shack I began
visiting around.

The new town had already swelled to 200 people, most of
them Eskimos who were camped in tents pitched in the willows

along the riverbank. In dry weather this site wasn't bad, but after some rain this ground turned to a greasy, slippery clay that was the worst campsite imaginable. A high percentage of the kids were infected with impetigo, for which Dr. Black sent me a supply of gentian violet. I was suddenly launched on my new medical career. My afternoon routine became a walk among all the tents carrying my black medical bag. There were now 130 DPW employees eating at the mess hall and, thanks to Charlie Walrath, I was invited to join them, thus eliminating any need to worry about cooking for myself. This was the luckiest break of all. They were also showing 16mm films there Saturday evenings. In order for workers to be on time for the 7 a.m. breakfast I was scheduling a daily morning Mass at 6:15, and there were always a few in attendance. Some may have spent the night sleeping on my floor, as there were people coming in daily by boat from up river looking for work and my shack was handy.

East-Three not only attracted native workers from as far south as Fort Franklin, it also attracted many government specialists. I got acquainted with two of them who were studying permafrost conditions. One day Curt Merrill got a radio message for them with a request from their office in Ottawa to count the driftwood along the Arctic Coast between the mouth of the Mackenzie River and Herschel Island. They invited me to join them for a look at a corner of the Arctic I had not yet seen. The weather was perfect as we flew west in our float plane along the ocean shore, counting huge pockets of driftwood in acres. It was easy to understand how the early whalers wintering at Herschel Island were able to gather a winter's supply of firewood from the nearby beaches. As we were carrying the mail for the anthropologist Dr. Richard MacNeish and his party working near the Firth River, we landed on a small lake and walked over to the site. Five years earlier, in 1950, I had written this scientist at the National Museum in Ottawa about a cave on an island in Keith Arm of Great Bear Lake and he had come up to investigate it. That expedition had proven unproductive, but now he was back digging up the bones of some prehistoric buffalo and stone spear points belonging to their hunters, gathering evidence to prove a theory that the natives of the Canadian North had once migrated along this route from the west. This visit out in the middle of nowhere was the highlight of a day I'll never forget.

My day in the air was followed by a day on the water in a freighter canoe. Hyacinthe Andre, the Chief of the Loucheux at Arctic Red River, came and took me up river thirty-two miles to visit a small fishing camp at a place called Big Rock. There were only three permanent log cabins on this east branch of the Mackenzie River, so with the summer population swollen to forty, most were living in tents. The attraction to this particular place was the excellent whitefish netting in several local eddies. Most of the fishermen came from Arctic Red River, but Charlie Masuzumi was a Hare Indian who had brought his family clear down from Fort Good Hope. He was in the employ of the RCMP there as a special constable in charge of their dog-teams and was busy laying up a supply of dry fish for winter dog food.

If Big Rock had a mayor, it would have been Fabien Coyen who, with his large family, lived there year round. He had my bedroll and chapel kit moved from the chief's canoe to his cabin and communicated with me in French. Both he and his wife were admirable graduates of the mission school at Fort Providence. Their little cabin was as neat as a pin and all was kept in order in the surrounding yard as well. Each sled-dog had its own little log cabin, plus a water pail anchored to a stick so it wouldn't accidentally upset it. Their sleds, snowshoes and other winter gear were up out of the way on top of their warehouse and their stage was absolutely loaded with hanging and drying split fish under which a smoky fire was kept smouldering to discourage the flies. Fabien's wife put in long hours at her outside filleting table, gutting and splitting the whitefish her husband brought up from his net, but still she couldn't keep up with the volume, so Fabien was putting a good portion of his catch in a pit dug into the sand. As he explained it to me, the trick was to seal the opening so that no flies could get to the fish. The roof of this pit was supported with a layer of logs. An empty fifty-pound Klim can, sticking out of the sand at the top, served as a fly-proof entrance. Although it was cool down there, the fish did not actually freeze, nor did they need to be frozen to be preserved. They kept piling up there all summer and their weight squeezed the water out of them. After freeze-up the pit could be opened and the fish transferred to the stage. This fish kept limber even in the coldest weather because only the natural oil remained. It smelled to high heaven and was not meant for human consumption, but the dogs loved it and it made great bait for traps.

The next morning at nine the whole camp of forty-odd souls crowded into Fabien's cabin, where I offered a Mass for their intentions and delivered a homily on the miraculous draught of fishes. It was an appropriate setting in which to meditate on this passage of the Gospel. After a good lunch of boiled duck and bannock, Fabien brought me back to E-3 in his canoe. There were several tents set right in front of my shack and in one lived Victor and Bertha Allen. As soon as I landed, Bertha had me look at her sick boy. When I found his temperature was over 104 degrees, I had Curt send a message to Aklavik and Mike Zubko flew over and took him out. I didn't feel all that great myself, for I had been suffering from a nagging toothache for the past week. On the other hand, the nearest dentist was at Yellowknife, some 600 miles south and it was not easy to get there. I decided to tough it out, especially after talking with Cliff Hagen, a local cat skinner. Dr. Black had attempted to get four of his rotten teeth out and broke them all off in the process.

It was the end of July when the New Town Planning Committee sent a plane over from Aklavik to get me to attend an important meeting in my capacity as secretary. Actually, I was happy to take advantage of the free flight, because it was time to put out another issue of the *Aklavik Journal*. When I got there, I found the mission in high turmoil in anticipation of the visit of the French ambassador to Canada, on top of the annual visit of the bishop in company with the Provincial of the Oblates. In spite of this, I succeeded in printing 525 copies of the *Journal*, of which the scouts sold locally 200 copies. Two hundred more were mailed out to subscribers, and the rest I took back to sell at E-3.

Bishop Trocellier had not yet seen the new townsite, so I had the honour of accompanying him there in the *Immaculata* and giving him a tour. Satisfied that things were going according to plan, he next decided to continue north to Tuk and invited me along. Father Alexis Robin, veteran of forty years at Fort Good Hope, was on board, as well as Brother Michel Dabrowski, acting captain. The bishop had taken over the galley, so we had an interesting crew.

By the second day we ran out of the delta and onto the ocean. Here we encountered three Eskimo schooners off Whitefish Station: the *Northstar*, the *Fox* and the *Only Way*. We were comfortably into Tuk harbour and tied safely at the mission dock before dark. Fathers Franche and Le Meur greeted us there. We began to realize just how lucky we were to encounter calm seas in traversing the open ocean when the weather turned bad: snow, driven by gale-force winds, lashed the coast for the next six days. We learned later just how far inland this storm penetrated when we heard that it even froze the potatoes at Fort Good Hope. We were kept warm in the mission, but the Eskimos living in tents presented an entirely different picture. Though it was still early August, they were forced to wear their parkas. The bishop cancelled his plan to fly east to rendezvous with Father Leonce Dehurtevent at Cape Parry: ice around Letty Harbour prevented the Father getting north by boat from Paulatuk. When we finally headed the *Immaculata* south after the storm I had on board two good Eskimo sled-dogs, both females, which augured well for another good dog-team. We stopped briefly at E-3 and then continued on south to Big Rock, where I left the party.

The following day a speedboat pulled into the camp and a reporter named Alan Philipps introduced himself. He had been sent from Toronto by Pierre Berton, the editor of *Maclean's* magazine, to get a story on me. We went back to E-3 and spent the next four days in my shack, talking and looking at my slides. This long interview produced a lead article in the January 5th issue of their magazine under the title, "The Chequered Career of an Arctic Priest," which paid me enough to buy a boat and kicker of my own from Eddy McLeod. Although I wasn't too pleased with the slant of the article, I was very happy to have water transportation.

❊ ❊ ❊

Despite minimal accommodations at E-3, the government decided to hold the eleventh session of the North West Territorial Council there in late August. The Commissioner of the Territories, Gordon Robertson, said in his opening remarks: "The very fact that the Council has come to East-Three, the new site of Aklavik, at such an early stage in its creation shows its eagerness, as the legislative body of the Territories, to visit this region. It is a particularly happy circumstance that we should be meeting in this embryo town, for the decision of the Government of Canada to build a new Aklavik in this place to become the educational, administrative and welfare centre not only of the delta but of the Western Arctic and the lower Mackenzie River Valley was one of far-reaching significance." That decision met far less than complete acceptance: a large majority living at Aklavik were opposed to it. Just a few weeks prior to this statement, the Honourable T. A. Crerar said in Parliament : "I remain quite unconvinced of the need of spending several million dollars to move 600 to 700 people from their present location in Aklavik to some point forty miles distant."

In spite of the opposition, the project was going ahead full steam. To bestow official recognition on the new site, the Territorial Council chose it for its annual meeting They didn't even have any suitable building for their deliberations, so they held them in a large, empty garage. I found myself among the handful of residents who attended; the rest either couldn't get time off or simply weren't interested. The principal topic on the agenda was the question of liquor. The consensus of opinion was that the government had made a mistake in opening the liquor store in Aklavik the previous October. Since then the residents had invested a total of $54,100 in bottled spirits, resulting in the tripling of convictions for the misuse of liquor. On stock at present were 12,015 bottles of over-proof rum. Council members Carmichael, Goodall, Porrit, Parker, Drury, Audette, Cunningham, Boucher and Nicholson debated the question hour after hour for the next two days, while I took notes for the *Journal* and even sketched their portraits for my publication. Arguments raged back and forth ranging from a complete ban on liquor to its wide-open sale. Commissioner Nicholson of the RCMP, an appointed member of the Council, drew on his prior knowledge of the way similar problems had been handled with the Plains Indians and sagely advised the Council to adopt a middle-of-the-road course and "open the tap gradually." Unfortunately his advice was not heeded.

The discussions finally resulted in the Council legislating a ration of two bottles of hard liquor and one case of beer per permit-holder per week, plus a recommendation to the federal government that the Indian Act be amended to permit all treaty Indians free access to liquor permits and finally that the Aklavik liquor store be moved over to E-3.

I was getting a reputation for having some claim to knowledge of the North for, following the Council sessions, some of its members asked me to give them a show of some of the 8,000 slides I had taken to date. I was pleased to comply and kept them entertained for two hours. Somehow word of my picture collection got back to the National Museum of Man in Ottawa, for I got a letter from them asking if I would consider donating my slides so that they would be available to all the people of Canada. I was flattered, but I wasn't willing at that time to part with this record of my travels.

❊ ❊ ❊

With a new town like E-3, every significant event became an historic first, like the marriage I performed there at the end of that summer, uniting John Pascal with Rosie Pokiak. It was not only the first marriage at the new site, it was unusual in that it joined an Indian with an Eskimo, traditional enemies. Just a few years back such a union would have been all but impossible. But this one was apparently well accepted by both families and proved successful and happy. Hundreds of others followed in succeeding years, but I would not have traded the honour of witnessing the first for all the rest.

On the last day of August I celebrated my thirty-sixth birthday with thirteen well-wishers crowded into my small shack. After several toasts and the consumption of an appropriate cake, I ended up entertaining the gang with a show of slides of the area and later we joined in song as I strummed my guitar. It was a rich time; when everyone had left and I lay in my bunk waiting for sleep, I counted my blessings. During the past eight years I had seen a lot of the North, and had had many interesting experiences in the process. Although the pastoral work was often lacking, there was always the manual work, the travelling and a host of other activities that always seemed to engage me. If it was a lonely life as a celibate – and it often was – still, people of all faiths were friendly and hospitable. They seemed to understand the problems I faced and were sympathetic. For myself, I had to forge ahead using the talents God gave me to try to make each day count, letting the chips fall where they may. East-Three may not have been my idea of an ideal posting – far from it – but I was sent to found a new mission, just as I had been sent to Fort Franklin, Camsell Portage and Uranium City. I would do the best I could under the circumstances; if it wasn't good enough, others would follow to make it better. And now to sleep, to awake tomorrow and see what my thirty-seventh year had in store for me.

Although I could type out the stencils for the *Journal* at E-3, I had to go over to Aklavik to use the old Gestetner in order to print it. That's what I was doing the first week in September. While there, I got word from E-3 that the "512" church had been built, so I was anxious to get back to inaugurate it the coming Sunday. One thing after another delayed me the Saturday before, as I rushed to get my new speedboat gassed and loaded. At the last minute, the Sisters asked me to deliver two young Eskimo girls to the Tingmiak family at E-3. After I shoved off, I was delayed another hour with gear trouble. It was 7:30 before I actually began to travel. It was 9 p.m. and dark when I hit the main branch of the Mackenzie. I was a novice at finding my way across the seventy-odd miles of delta separating the old from the new town.

I realized that if I made one mistake at any of the twenty-one critical junctions on the route, I could easily get lost. When I asked Father Binamé why some route signs hadn't been put up, he replied that newcomers should learn the route the way the old-timers had, by trial and error. I was carrying a map, but with no flashlight I had to stop and light a match to read it. I kept getting stuck on sandbars and had to reduce speed. The girls soon fell asleep in the bow as I probed my way along the narrow channels, all the time regretting the fact that I hadn't left earlier. It was nearly midnight when we finally arrived at E-3 and I took the girls up to the garage, where the usual Saturday night dance was held, and delivered them to their parents. Somebody told me that the radio operator was looking for me. When I found him, it turned out that he had had an enquiry from Aklavik asking if I had arrived. Apparently two fellows over there had a hundred-dollar bet that I wouldn't make it that night.

The next day, Sunday, I had an overflow congregation in the new church. Although it lacked almost all the usual ecclesiastical furnishings, it was a lot more devotional than the garage we had been using. It was isolated, away back in the bush, but it had been put on the lot assigned to us, and from the plan I realized that someday it would be right in the centre of town. The collection amounted to just twenty-two dollars; I was glad I didn't have to depend on it for all my expenses. Still, nothing can beat a church to pep up the morale of a pastor who has been working without one.

From the window in my shack facing the river I could see a constantly changing parade of boats, coming and going. Natives in large freight canoes arrived daily from places as far away as Great Bear Lake. Others from around the delta arrived in power barges, self-contained house boats which I often visited to play cards or eat. Still others, like Harry Harrison, came in schooners towing logs to be sold as piling. I was in an ideal position to watch all this activity. Now I had my own little sixteen-foot, cedar-planked speedboat, with its powerful thirty-horse Evinrude motor pulled up on the bank, constantly tempting me to go places. My boat was completely open to the wind and rain; with the weather growing colder, I realized that I should build a cabin on it, which I proceeded to do. Then I had to rig up remote controls so that I could operate it from up front behind the windshield. When I was finished, I had a speedy boat with some of the comforts of the larger cabin outfits. I was ready to keep travelling on the water till the ice forced me off for the winter. I made several more trips over to Aklavik and up to Big Rock, and then an Eskimo lad named John Dillon joined me for a trip to the north end of the delta for fall geese. We stopped at the tent camp of John Kivek, local Eskimo chief, for a tea break and he informed me that the E-3 site had had a name for years: *Kegeaktuk* – place of the beaver – and he urged me to get the white men to adopt it as official. I did suggest it in the next issue of the *Journal* but later Ottawa chose a new name, *Inuvik*, meaning "The place of man." When we returned a week later, we found that the ground had frozen solid and Twin Lakes, adjacent to town, had frozen over. Winter was closing in fast.

I had no more than gotten into my shack when a couple of Loucheux Indians from Arctic Red River came in to announce that Ernest Kendo had been shot and killed by Amos Niditchie while hunting moose at Point Separation. This sort of thing was not unusual. Joe Gully had told me about killing his hunting partner on a moose hunt nearby a few years back. The danger comes when the hunters split up and one of them is mistaken for the moose. When Amos first shot at Ernest he missed him. If Ernest had only dropped down until Amos could get close enough to identify him, he would have saved his life. Instead, he started running. The second shot opened the artery in his right thigh. Possibly a tourniquet could have stopped the flow of blood. Amos, however, was blinded by grief and cradled his fallen partner in his arms until he died a half-hour later from loss of blood. I was asked to break the news to his widow and children: not a pleasant task. Over in the morgue shack in Aklavik the police later showed me Ernest's body. I was struck by the fact that he looked like a youth, perfectly trim, without a wrinkle or grey hair, and no mark of injury except for that one small hole in his upper right leg. Yet he was sixty-two years old.

Joe Bernard, who had been the RCMP special constable on the Albert Johnson chase, lived in a cabin at Big Rock and was now brought in with a broken ankle. I decided to take him over to the Aklavik hospital. As the Brothers were already installed in their fishing cabin on our route across the Delta, we stopped there for lunch. Boy, that cabin felt good after bucking rough seas and a snow storm and we were tempted to stay overnight, but the lateness of the season goaded us to keep moving before we got frozen in some place. I had been making the trip on ten gallons of gas, but this time it wasn't enough and we ran out about five miles short. After paddling for two hours at a painfully slow speed we came to Billy Day's empty cabin and called it quits. All we had in the way of grub was one dry fish and two hardtacks and neither of us were carrying our sleeping bags. It was a rough night and we had the fire going early the next morning when we heard a kicker coming. It turned out to be John Joseph, but he couldn't spare a drop of gas. We resumed paddling and at eleven o'clock Harry Harrison approached in his schooner *Golden Hind* and lent us three gallons of gas, enough to see us finally into Aklavik.

After an eventful trip, I found that a crust of new ice had formed on the Peel overnight. Stu Hill had to land his Norseman up stream to avoid it when he brought in the last load of mail and passengers from Norman Wells before the freeze-up. That skin of ice on the water warned me not to tarry in Aklavik, so I quickly gathered up the grub and equipment the Brothers had ordered for their fish camp, plus three dogs I had borrowed from Fred Norris and an old sled I had found around the mission. When Joe Bernard and I pushed out into the channel after lunch we had a good load on board. After breaking thin ice for the first 200 yards, we had clear sailing from there on.

At the fish camp, the Brothers told me that, as the weather was not below freezing during the days, some of their whitefish might spoil before they could get them over to Aklavik. They asked if I could make one more trip for them. I reluctantly agreed and pushed on to E-3, where Joe and I arrived at 7:30, just before dark. The next noon I was back alone at the fish camp. I loaded 900 pounds of fresh fish and continued on at a greatly reduced speed toward Aklavik. I stopped at Albert Oliver's cabin at the mouth of the Napoyak Channel to pick up his daughter who was supposed to be attending school. Albert turned out to be so drunk he fell headlong into the mud trying to walk down to the shore. When I got into his cabin I found his wife sick in bed and the daughter so upset and crying over the prospect of going to school that I didn't press the issue and left without her. Albert's wife didn't speak any English. If Albert had been sober, perhaps he could have told me just how sick his wife really was; two days later she was dead.

Father Max Ruyant helped me unload the fish, which he expected would tide them over until they could get a herring net under the new ice in front of the mission. The hostel was again full-up for winter and the kids were already skating on the mission pond. Overnight the ice froze again on all the water visible from the mission and I began to think that I had tempted the fates just once too often: I might now be caught in Aklavik for freeze-up. Luckily, during the next night two boats arrived from the south, breaking all the ice: Fred Norris in his *Barbara Jean* and Earl Harcourt in his NTCL boat *The Saline*. I got away at ten in the morning, carrying the mail, plus many parcels for E-3 as well as for the reindeer station. I had scarcely covered the first mile when I ran into re-frozen ice. Before I was clear of it I had badly damaged the cedar planking of my boat, though as yet it was not leaking water. I stopped at Dan McLeod's camp and found everyone well, then went on to the Benoit cabin on the Mackenzie, where Adeline was sick in bed and living on straight fish. I left over a hundred pounds of caribou meat and grub and promised I would try to return with medicine. At Miles Dillon's camp all was okay, except that Miles was out of tobacco. I made one more stop to see how the Harrison sisters were making out before pulling into the Brothers' camp to spend the night.

The next day was Sunday and I had to get away early in order to be back at E-3 in time to conduct the 11 a.m. Mass in the new church. Overnight it snowed and the East Branch of the Mackenzie in front of the new town was running thin ice when I peered out my front window. I still wanted to make one more run as far as the Brothers' camp to deliver a radio battery and pick up the three sled-dogs I had left there. Tom Lynch, the DPW cook, joined me after lunch and we left practically empty. On the first cross-channel turning west we quickly ran into solid ice and had to turn back and try the second channel, but again ran into ice and this time it cut through the planking at the water line and water poured in. We immediately turned around and with both of us in the stern to raise the hole above the water, we had just enough gas left to get back to E-3. That afternoon I temporarily patched the hole with hot tar and hoped that a big wind might break up the new ice. It didn't: on October 10th the river was frozen solid and I had to pull my boat out for the season. I regretted not being able to get back to Adeline with medicine and I didn't like having to leave my dogs at the fish camp, but I had no alternative. Summer was over.

Although activity had ground to a halt on the water, it quickened on land at the new townsite. The Hudson Bay Company was putting up a new store right behind my shack, while Slim Semmler had moved over from Aklavik and was doing a land-office business from a large tent. Mrs Shamahorn, the teacher, however, was swamped with forty-six pupils the day school opened. She was forced to split them into morning classes for the first-graders, with the others attending in the afternoons. A new company calling itself Aklavik Constructors had won the airport contract, plus the nine-mile connecting road. They had put Henning Jensen in charge of the wagon drills that were blasting out dolomite for rock-fill. All the newly created jobs were keeping many erstwhile trappers from returning to the bush. In fact there were about 200 of them, mostly Eskimo, living in tents pitched among the willows along the riverbank in front of the town.

When a flu epidemic swept through town, those hardest hit seemed to be the natives living in tents. I found myself completely occupied running around with my little black bag, administering two-cc shots of penicillin to those with high temperatures. I was called across the river to look at Mary Ruth Aviugana, age thirteen, who besides running a temperature of 104 was vomiting and complaining of pains in her lower abdomen. Suddenly I had visions of trying to perform my first appendectomy. At the same time, in another tent on that side of the river Maggie Joe was in her eighth month of pregnancy and was convinced that it would result in a breach presentation. Bertha Allen delivered a baby girl in her tent right in front of my shack; I tied the umbilical cord with net twine – no problem. But Emma Dick's eleven-month-old son Lawrence was sick, and I kept poring over my Merck's Manual looking for a solution. She told me he kept vomiting and all I had to give her was Kaopectate, which didn't seem to help much.

Meanwhile, I sent a message over to Mike Zubko to fly over from Aklavik and pick up Maggie and Mary Ruth. He said that he would, just as soon as we had seven inches of ice on Shell Lake, so I was running up there with my three-dog team every day, measuring the ice. Finally we had seven inches. I gave him the go-ahead by wireless. I got my two patients up there and built a fire by the shore to await his arrival. Maggie was carrying a small cardboard suitcase and asked me if I could guess what she had in it. I gave up. She opened it to reveal a solid block of *muktuk* (whale meat), cut exactly to fit. She said she needed it to fortify her for her upcoming delivery.

The day after they left, I was visiting my patients in the Eskimo tents along the riverbank; Lawrence seemed to be improving so much that Emma gave me back my Kaopectate. An hour later Curt Merrill drove me up to the airport site, where

Aklavik Constructors had their camp, called East-Four by the locals. The carpenter-foreman had suffered some pain resembling a heart attack. I gave him two cc's of Demerol. We left him resting comfortably and bounced back to my place in Curt's pick-up over a partially built roadbed. As soon as I got there, I was met by someone in the dark, saying that Emma Dick's baby was dead! Grabbing a flashlight from my shack, I hurried over to their tent and found Lawrence, still warm, in a cardboard box up on the stage. My efforts at artificial respiration produced no result, so I asked the Dick family for permission to send the body over to Aklavik for an autopsy. Months later I was advised that the cause of death was a strangulated hernia.

The two patients I had evacuated were soon back to normal. Mary Ruth didn't have appendicitis, and Maggie Joe's baby was born normally. I was faulting myself for not having evacuated Lawrence, but Dr. Black advised me that they had had two similar cases recently in Aklavik and both had died. Practising medicine certainly carried with it serious responsibilities, but, with the training and equipment I had, it was not easy to arrive at a correct diagnosis. They say a doctor's mistakes are in the ground, but a priest's are in hell! One of my fervent prayers was that no soul confided to my care would be lost. Certainly after nine years of training in the seminary I felt far more confident treating spiritual problems than I did treating physical ones.

Toward the end of October I began thinking of getting over to Aklavik to run off another issue of the *Aklavik Journal*. With ten inches of ice, it was now safe to run the Bombardier around on the frozen channels, so Curt Merrill took me, my three dogs and sled over to the Brothers' fish camp. Here I planned to pick up the three dogs I had left and continue on under my own power. When we got there I found that I had only two dogs left: Brother Delisle had shot my lead-dog when he got loose and they couldn't catch him. This was a real disappointment to me. Moreover, I had to walk ahead of my five dogs on snowshoes, as I had no other leader. After six miles I arrived at Billy Thrasher's cabin. Luckily he let me borrow three dogs, including a leader.

It was nearly dark when I pulled into Bill Storr's camp. Bill worked as captain of the police schooner *Aklavik* during the summer. The long winters he spent in his comfortable trapping cabin with his wife, Elvira. I never learned to appreciate beer, but Bill persuaded me to sample his, which he bottled himself and kept cool in a cellar dug under his cabin floor. I sat there listening to his interesting tales of the North till I couldn't keep my eyes open and crawled into a bunk. When I awoke in the morning, Bill was already up ahead of me, enjoying his first beer of the day. I passed, and started my day with a breakfast of rolled oats. My trip that day into Aklavik was uneventful, except for the last fifteen miles when I came upon old Simon and his wife heading in the same direction by dog-teamfrom their camp on the Napoyak. These two were dressed in the old traditional caribou skin parkas and pants, and she was tattooed. I wondered to myself just how long it would be before such a scene would disappear completely from the North.

At Aklavik the next ten days were spent composing and printing another 500 copies of the *Journal*, attending another Remembrance Day ceremony, preaching at the Sunday High Mass, and getting reacquainted with the kids at the hostel and the patients at the hospital. When time permitted, I harnessed up my dogs and took a short run to train Brandy, my new leader. Finally, on November 12th, I packed my sled and headed back across the delta, accompanied by Harry Harrison driving his own team. It was almost dark at 7 p.m. when we arrived at Gallagher Arey's cabin and I decided to camp with him. Gallagher was a special friend of mine. We had spent hours together drinking coffee at Peffer's Hotel while he recounted interesting details of his colourful life along the Arctic Coast. In 1910 he had discovered gold up the Okpilak River west of Barter Island. Camping overnight with men like Gallagher was not just a question of getting out of the elements for a warm night's rest; it was an opportunity to learn the North's history from men who had made it. Brandy was working better in the lead every day and the following day he led my team into E-3 by noon.

I now considered my little shack at E-3 home; I was always happy to get back to it after a trip. My new dog-team had replaced the boat as a means of transportation. Unlike the boat, however, they required attention every day, even if they weren't working. For one thing, they had to be fed; to do this, I needed to get a net in the water somewhere. People told me that there were hardly any fish in the East Branch flowing past the new townsite, though many of us had taken losch on hooks, jigging under the new ice. I drove my team up river two miles to the tent camp of Bella Adams, and her son Bobby helped me set my net in an eddy close by. I didn't catch many fish, but I did get enough to feed my six dogs. For the balance of the winter I would go up there every second day I was in town. A typical catch might include white-fish, jackfish, northern pike and connie (enconnu), as well as losch (ling cod). Some dogs wouldn't eat the losch, but their large, fat livers were considered a great delicacy by the natives.

After the hassle of keeping ahead with firewood for the previous four years at Camsell Portage, one luxury I was now enjoying immensely was my little Coleman oil stove. It burnt only about a gallon-and-a-half every twenty-four hours and gave off plenty of heat. I had a permanent altar built against the partition of my shack, at which I conducted a daily 6 a.m. Mass for the workers. On Sundays I used the new church building, which I heated with a large oil stove I lit on Saturdays. Although the flu had all but run its course, there was hardly a day when I wasn't called on to give someone a shot of penicillin. I was glad to be helpful in this way, but, unfortunately, in one instance it produced an adverse reaction. Cliff Hagen had a tentful of friendly children on the shore of Twin Lakes, but when they saw me poke their little sister Marilyn with that ugly needle and heard her cries, they all hid the next time they saw me coming. For a man of the cloth, this is not a response he wants to cultivate, but I could hardly avoid it.

Though I would have liked to have stayed all winter in my shack at E-3, Father Ruyant was alone at the big mission at Akla-vik and I got a letter from the bishop advising me to give him a hand. So, following a brief ten-day visit to E-3, I found myself behind my dogs again on the trail west. I had in mind to spend the night with Miles Dillon on the main branch of the Mackenzie, for I had never visited him. Actually it got dark before I found his cabin: as I was on the lookout for a light, I went three miles past the cabin before I realized that I had missed it. I had to turn the dogs around.

When I got there, I realized why they were sitting in the dark. They had no light of any kind, not even candles. I soon learned that this family was completely out of many items we consider essentials in the bush. They were practically out of grub and were living on pit fish. This has got to be the next thing to outright starvation, because the smell alone is enough to turn one's stomach. Miles was keeping his son John's children and they were a great help in tying up my dogs and carrying the contents of my sled into the cabin. Luckily, I had some candles; we soon could see each other. Miles' wife cooked up some of my grub. While I was eating, the dogs started barking. Miles' wife ran out and came back with a snowshoe rabbit that had been caught in one of their snares. The kids were ecstatic as they passed the rabbit around, examining it, playing with it and, I suppose, drooling over the prospect of eating it. Mrs. Dillon soon grabbed it from them and, with a few deft strokes of her "ulu," skinned, gutted and plunked it into a kettle of boiling water on the wood stove. I was glad to share what grub I was carrying, for I expected to be in Aklavik the next day. After everyone had eaten, I asked Miles' wife if she would sew up a tear in my mukluks. She replied that she would if she had a needle, but she didn't. I've run into many families in the North whom I consider down on their luck and even destitute, but none were so hard up as the family of Miles Dillon.

❄ ❄ ❄

At Aklavik that weekend I learned that many caribou had moved into an area in the high country forty miles west of Aklavik; hunters were finding it easy to get a sled-load of meat. On

the east side of the delta there was no possibility of getting caribou, so this was my only chance. Monday morning I was on the
trail up the Peel Channel with Charlie, one of Billy Thrasher's
boys, eager to join the hunt. After ten miles we left the river and
cut across gently rising muskeg for another ten miles, until we
came to a lake. Here we made a fire and boiled up a copper pot
of tea. We also gathering up all the dry wood we could find, for
we were on the edge of timber country: when we wanted to make
our next fire, we would have to use wood we were carrying with
us.

Now the trail started to rise, gently at first and then more
steeply. We ran into Eddie McLeod, who was coming down with
a huge sled-load of fresh meat. He told us that it would be no
problem to fill our own sleds. I had never before encountered a
trail that was all uphill for twenty-five miles, and when we
finally topped the ridge at 5 p.m. it was dark. Following the trail
a couple more miles led us into a gully that covered Martin
Creek. There in a clump of willows was the hunters' camp, five
tents pitched around a huge pile of fresh meat and a hundred-
odd sled-dogs chained to the willows. As soon as Charlie and I
had my nine-by-seven-foot tent pitched, we had a stream of
hunters asking to throw their sleeping bags in our tent because
the others were too crowded. We ended up with nine of us
squeezed into my tent for the night, a night punctuated by the
fighting of loose dogs over the meat and the continual yelling of
"*Tekarluk!*" by the Eskimos. I presumed it meant "Quiet!"
Nobody got up to stop the fights.

It was dark and still below zero at eight the next morning
when we harnessed up. Joe Bourke, Buck Semmler and Roger
Allen joined Charlie and me with their teams as we headed up
the frozen creek bed over the first range of the Richardson Mountains. Every few miles we would stop and, on snowshoes, climb
up the banks surrounding us to have a look. Finally, Joe and Buck
sighted a herd of caribou a mile away, so we tied our dogs to the
willows and proceeded on snowshoes, carrying our rifles and
skinning knives. As we walked toward the herd, a warm wind

blowing from the west soon brought the temperature up above the freezing mark. After we had made our kill and finished butchering, our moosehide mukluks were wet through. By the time we got our teams up there and loaded the meat, we were wet to our thighs. On our return to camp, the creek we followed was running water! I had never before experienced these Chinook winds that could produce such a sudden change in temperature. It was as if a month during break-up was compressed into two hours.

That afternoon, passing through a rock defile that was glistening with running melt-water, I noticed a yellow stain that reminded me of similar signs of uranium I had seen on the north shore of Lake Athabaska. I stopped my team, climbed up with my axe and broke off a few chunks which I later sent out to Consolidated Mining and Smelting Company in Trail, B.C. The results of their assay showed that my rock contained 1.05 percent of U308, the first time uranium ore had been found in the Aklavik area.

When we got back to camp, we were surprised to find all our tents blown flat and all the snow melted off the ground around them. We spent the night drying out and feasting. The following morning we pulled out for town with our sleds loaded. At first the going was slow because the snow was wet and the ground bare in spots. Roger Allen broke both of his wheel-dog traces at one spot where the trail rose over a cutbank. But the lower we got, the cooler it got, and the easier the sleds slid over the downhill trail as we struggled to keep our heavy toboggans from overturning. It was 5 p.m. when we sledded down into timber again and made fire. The temperature was back to well below zero, so we had clear sailing back to town that evening.

While the Brothers were out at their wood camp during most of the winter, the Fathers took care of keeping the fires going at home. There were a total of nine cast iron heaters of various sizes situated in the mission, the hospital, the hostel, the powerhouse, the laundry and the school. We each took a month's turn doing this essential work and, during that time, occupied a small room

in the cellar of the hostel. We had to be readily available in case
it got cool during the night. My turn for this job began the 15th of
December. That effectively put an end to any more extended
dogsled trips, and certainly overnight trips. Some fires were
banked at midnight, others restarted at 4 a.m., so it was all but
impossible to get a good night's sleep during that month. The
hardest part was to get out of a warm bed at 4 a.m. and face a stiff
wind at forty-below across the 300 yards of open yard to the
school, called the Kost House, and there to fumble with stiff fingers to kindle fires in two large wood stoves. Many a frosty
morning I wished I were back in the easy comfort of my shack at
E-3, but I wasn't my own boss: I had chosen to live under the vow
of obedience.

The New Year, 1957, was ushered in with the usual fusillade
of rifles at midnight, just as I was walking over to the Kost House
to bank the fires. It was a clear, cold night, with a brilliant ribbon
of northern lights streaming overhead, toward which the lead
being fired sporadically from around Aklavik seemed to rattle
and squeak. All our lights had long been extinguished. I seemed
to be the only person awake, except for the night nurse, Sister
Bourgeois. After the usual religious services on New Year's Day,
I tape-recorded messages from our patients and boarders for
broadcast over CHAK. This chore done, I decided to repeat what
I had done the same day a year earlier, that is, to walk around
town wishing people a Happy New Year.

It was time to put together the January issue of the *Aklavik
Journal*. My nightly coffee breaks over at Peffer's Hotel helped me
keep current with what was going on around town. If I missed
something, Ellen Binder would usually bring it to my attention. I
got in the habit of carrying a small notebook and making entries
as soon as I heard something interesting. Among the items I
picked up for the "News Roundup" column that month were:
Fred Norris had harvested a record crop of ice from Peel Channel
– 600 tons!; Freddy Carmichael got his flying licence and was ferrying a Stinson aircraft to Aklavik; The Hudson Bay Company
had run out of malt at its Tuktoyaktuk store; Irish Coulter

walked thirty miles into town December 20th in order to be the first to get his liquor on the last day the government liquor store was open before Christmas; old Jonas Alaska lost his sled and equipment on the DEW Line when his dog-team ran away from him in a snowstorm; Billy Jacobson shot a wolverine in the abandoned Roman Catholic Mission at Stanton; Charlie Gruben shot thirty times at three polar bears at close range, but wounded only one, claiming his barrel was twisted.

These were run-of-the-mill items, but with every issue there always seemed to be at least one real tragedy. This month was no different. In the ice of the Peel Channel, right in front of the town, a water-hole was kept open all winter in case of fire. A plywood shack closed it in and an oil stove heated it. Many of the towns-people who didn't harvest ice in the fall hauled their water in buckets from this hole. Consequently, the sides of the hole built up with ice to form a large ice funnel. When the government fuel man went into this shack one morning to refuel the stove he was startled to see two moccasin-clad feet just below the surface of the water. Apparently fourteen-year-old Isaac Selamio had tried to drink from the hole the night before and slipped. With no dip-per, he had to lie on his stomach to get his mouth down to water level. If that wasn't difficult enough, the stunt of pulling himself back up was. With nothing to grab onto and the weight of his own body pulling him down, young Isaac could not prevent himself from sliding down until his head was under water and his arms pinned to his sides.

Different organizations in town asked me to print their news or public information items. For example, the post office had me print letter rates in the December issue in time for Christmas mail. Unsealed cards would require two cents postage, while local sealed mail would need four cents. For other than local mail, which included Aklavik and E-3, the postage for first class was five cents. The RCMP had me insert a "WANTED" notice for a certain Anthony Gregson, who had previously been in the Aklavik region prospecting, and had recently quit work at a mine near Yellowknife and had Max Ward fly him to Hay River.

On the same flight the mine was shipping two gold bars worth $50,000. One weighed seventy-two pounds and the other fifty-two. Gregson had difficulty lifting his heavy packsack off the Beaver aircraft, but wouldn't let Max help; he had substituted two lead bars for the gold, and was now one of Canada's six most wanted men.

I put in a paragraph about "someone" discovering uranium west of Aklavik and got some secret visitors who wanted to invest in promoting the find. While discouraging them, I became aware that there are people who are willing to risk hard-earned funds in wildcat mining ventures. At the same time, the *Maclean's* article on me had appeared across Canada and I got a letter in the weekly mail from Dodd-Mead & Company, asking if I would be interested in writing a book for them. As flattering as the invitation was, I realized that I couldn't possibly find the time to devote to such a project.

As soon as the *Journal* was printed and distributed and I had finished my month's shift as fireman-stoker, I harnessed up and left for E-3. After an absence of two months I found some changes in the town. My old friend and town boss Curt Merrill had been replaced by Tom Taylor, but of more importance to me was the arrival on December 10th of a bona fide nurse in the person of Miss Shirley Mason. Her presence, I hoped, would relieve me of a job that absorbed most of my time when I was there. The assembly-line construction of more "512" cabins was going ahead full-steam, as was the crew driving piles, on which the heavier buildings would be built. The blasting and crushing of rock for the roads continued and the actual construction of the airport was about to commence. The new Hudson Bay store was in full operation right behind my shack and new workers from surrounding settlements continued to swell the population. One of the first things I did was to go up to the first bend in the river and check my net. Peter Thrasher went with me to help me chop through three feet of ice. We found only nine fish in the nets, as most of the floats and rocks were gone.

I could spend only a week at E-3 because the annual retreat was coming up at Aklavik and I had to attend. The trip across the delta by dogs could be done easily in a day if the trail was good, but when it got snowed-in the picture changed completely. It had snowed heavily during the week I was at E-3 and no traffic had followed me, so most of the trail was invisible. At every lake I had to put on my snowshoes and walk ahead of the dogs. By 4 p.m. it was again snowing and blowing and getting dark when I pulled into Louie Kaglik's camp and stopped for tea. Although they urged me to quit there and camp with them, I was anxious to get at least half-way across the delta and planned on camping with the Kalineks.

About 7 p.m. I was following a small channel where the snow was particularly deep. I was going ahead on snowshoes, but my dogs were unable to follow me. After breaking trail for a hundred yards I had to go back and help the dogs by pushing behind the sled. It was not only slow going, but my dogs were beginning to play out. These huskies can pull their weight steadily for ten hours on a hard trail. Once they are in soft snow where there is no firm footing, however, they must jump, and their stamina is quickly sapped. I hated to quit, because I was only a few miles from the Mackenzie River and the Kalinek cabins, but I had no choice. I went up into the tall spruce, cut down dead trees and, after clearing a spot of ground with my snowshoes, laid out my fire place and lit it. Then I called my dogs up off the river, unharnessed and chained them for the night. Luckily, I had enough dry fish with me for dog-feed, but I got a scare when I lost my axe in the deep snow and it took me half an hour to find it. Clearing the snow on the windward side of my fire, I laid out a thick bed of spruce boughs and threw my sleeping bag on it. Once I had eaten and gotten into my bedroll I slept for ten hours in spite of the wind. Although my fire went out during the night, the falling snow completely covered me and formed a layer of insulation.

After breakfast the next morning I re-harnessed my dogs and continued where I had left off the night before, going ahead to break trail and then helping the dogs by pushing behind my sled.

When it got light enough I could see that there was overflow water beneath the snow, keeping the dogs' feet wet. They were soon panting and I was wet with perspiration. I never encountered tougher travelling conditions either before or after this trip. It was four hours before we finally got to the Kalinek cabin, although we had actually travelled little more than two miles. Though it was only noon, we were so played out that I decided to call it a day and camp. On the following day, once we had crossed the frozen Mackenzie, we found less snow covering the old trail and made it into Aklavik in seven hours.

The next week was completely devoted to spiritual matters as all the Fathers and Brothers of the Western Arctic gathered for their annual retreat. Our days were tightly scheduled to ensure a maximum amount of time in chapel, either participating in religious exercises or listening to lectures delivered by the retreat master. Late in the evenings we found time to get together, renew acquaintances and find out what was happening at other mission stations. These reunions were important to esprit de corps, for most of us worked alone the greater part of the year. Though in the ordinary course of my work I seldom used the French I had acquired living with my friend Philip Stenne at Camsell Portage, here it suddenly became of paramount importance: all the conferences were in French, as were most of the conversations among the French-speaking Oblates. I was the solitary Anglophone; without the French language I would have been lost.

※ ※ ※

The first club to be formed at E-3 was the Home and School Association; I was happy to become a charter member. At one of our weekly meetings in the one-room schoolhouse I presented the idea of putting on an ice carnival around Easter time. The reaction I got from the other members was less than enthusiastic, especially after I estimated that it would take all $700 of the Association's savings to promote it. I must have been persuasive, however, because I finally got a majority to agree, on condition that I take charge of the whole show. I certainly had talked myself into one big undertaking. First I had to go over to Aklavik to print 200 raffle tickets to be sold by the four young women we had chosen to run for the title of Carnival Queen. Then I made a life-size target of a caribou for the men's shooting event and another of a ptarmigan for the women. Next I needed fifty flags to mark the dogsled course. I needed a large building in which to hold the evening dance following the crowning of the Queen and was successful in getting the loan of the thirty-two-foot-by-one-hundred-foot new and still empty liquor warehouse. To prepare it I painted a giant mural to cover one end, under which I built a temporary stage.

I don't know when I got the idea of building a large igloo out on the ice of the channel for the ice cream and hot dog booth, but I thought it was a gem! Yet I didn't realize then that the snow out there was packed so hard that it couldn't be cut with a regular snow knife, and carpenter's wood saws had to be used to cut the blocks. I was successful in rounding up a crew of Eskimos who volunteered their evenings for three nights. In that time they put up a picture-perfect igloo that was twenty-five feet in diameter and twelve feet to the ceiling. It provided the eye-catching centrepiece for our carnival. Lee Post, acting government head of the reindeer station, promised to send down a pair of reindeer harnessed to a *komatik* to give the kids rides. This was a steel-shod runner-type sled that the Eskimos call a *komatik* and the Bear Laker Indians call a *dechunkala*, literally "a ladder," because with its spaced wooden rungs across the top it resembles one.

The great day, April 23rd, arrived with perfect weather, sunny skies and the temperature around zero. Mike Zubko and his pilots were busy all morning flying in visitors from Aklavik, while Bruno Weiderman had a huge load in his Bombardier. Many others came in by dog-team. The team of reindeer trotted up the middle of the river in gay holiday harness, driven by two proud herders and loaded with a huge bale of moss for their supper. The shooting events started at 1 p.m. as scheduled, supervised by the young Mountie who had just recently been assigned to E-3. Unfortunately I had to relieve him of this duty in a hurry when he arrested a pair of drunks and had to lock them up in his cabin. The shooting competition was followed by the ice-chopping and tea-boiling contests and then the two-mile snowshoe race. I was running around like a chicken with its head cut off, making sure that each event was properly run and the winners correctly recorded. I was trying all the while to get movie and still pictures of everything happening, so I was loaded down with cameras.

The dogsled races proved the high point of the afternoon, with separate races for the children, the women and finally, the men. When you consider that there were eight teams of dogs in the first race, twelve in the second and eighteen in the third, all harnessed and started two minutes apart, you can better understand the excitement that filled the air. After Isaac Simon won the hundred dollar first prize and Big Jim got the watch, a huge two-inch hawser was hauled out on the ice for the tug-of-war between the men of E-3 and those working for Aklavik Constructors, the airport crew they called the East-Four bunch. George Harry captained the E-3 team to victory in the best two-out-of-three pulls. A lively broomball game concluded the afternoon's outdoor activities. While Buster Kailak and Silas Kangegana drove their weary reindeer downstream a couple of miles to tether them for the night, I stopped in the igloo to find out how Agnes Semmler had made out. She reported that her crew had sold 700 hot dogs, 800 ice cream cones and eleven pails of hot coffee.

That evening we all gathered in our parkas in the unheated liquor warehouse for the dance. But before that began I assisted the Queen, Florence Hagen, in picking the winning raffle ticket and awarding fifty dollars to Ellen Gordon, in pinning blue ribbons on all the afternoon's winners, and in cutting the Queen's giant cake. Once the fiddlers got under way and the square dances started, nobody complained about the lack of heat. Never before had a warehouse had such a slam-bang housewarming, but the new floor held up to the hundreds of pounding feet and when the party broke up in the early hours of the morning everyone said it was a great Easter Carnival. Best of all, when I reported to the Home and School Association at our next meeting I was not only able to pay back their $700 investment, but turned in an additional $600 in profit.

❄ ❄ ❄

The bishop wrote, saying that he was thinking of dismantling the vacant missions at Stanton and Paulatuk and moving them out to the DEW Line post at Cape Parry called Pin Main. He asked me to go down and check out the advisability of this move. If it looked practical, I was to go over to Tuk and see if the mission schooner *Our Lady of Lourdes* could be used to do the moving. We were into May when I drove my team north along the East Branch of the Mackenzie toward the Arctic Coast. The temperature was up around zero, but there was such a violent wind blowing from the east that the ice had been blown clear of snow most of the way. Therefore the dogs often slipped and fell and the toboggan swung around at right angles to the team. When I reached the reindeer station I spent the night with Marie and Finlay McInnes.

I still had sixty miles to go to reach Wallace Lucas' reindeer camp on Husky Lakes. The route was up over the Barrens, with no trail and few landmarks. The following morning I started anyway, in spite of much warmer temperatures and light falling snow. After a couple of miles in soft snow with no trail, however, I realized that I would never make it, and turned back. It took me six-and-a-half hours to return to E-3 in wet snow all the way. Three days later the cloudy weather changed to blue skies; the sun was so hot in the afternoon that the roof of the igloo collapsed. I picked up the mail for the reindeer station and pulled out at 8 p.m., when the sun was low and the trail north frozen. In two-and-a-half hours I stopped for tea at Chief John Kivek's tent on the Oniak Channel. An hour later I again pulled into the reindeer station and camped with the McInnes couple.

The next day the weather was as bad as it could get for sled travel, with skies overcast, temperature forty-six degrees in light rain. I whiled away the morning by visiting the school, an old army Quonset hut where nine pupils, children of the herders, were being taught by Mrs. Peters. I kept them amused for an hour by drawing animals on their blackboard. After lunch the weather hadn't changed much, but as it was getting late in the season, I decided to give it a try anyway. I harnessed up and started the long climb to the height of land behind the station. When we finally topped the ridge, the dogs had their tongues hanging out and I was stripped to my wool underwear. I took a compass bearing, taking into account that the variation here was about forty-eight degrees east of true north. Even if we lost the old trail completely, I was confident that we could strike across country and hit Husky Lakes. Although I could not see a tree or a hill or any other notable feature of the terrain, there were trail-markers, blocks of snow cut by some previous traveller and stood on edge about a mile apart. In the present whiteout conditions, however, they were hard to spot. Intermittent hail pelted us as we slogged along in the wet snow, stopping to rest every mile or so. It was comforting to see many ptarmigan which had turned to their dark summer plumage from their head to their wings. As I was only carrying one night's feed for the dogs, I thought that these birds would be a good source of feed and it wouldn't be difficult to shoot a good number of them with my .22.

By 7 p.m. we came on a small lake where I found a cache of firewood, so I stopped and boiled tea. I figured that we had made about ten miles so far. I looked at the little thermometer I carried in an aluminium tube tied to the handlebars; it registered thirty-eight degrees Fahrenheit. Just as we started on again, I noticed a beautiful silver fox coming along on our trail behind us, but he was wary and kept his distance. Though we had no sunlight, still at this time of year the night has no darkness either, so there was no reason to camp. At midnight we finally reached the edge of Husky Lakes and a small clump of spruce trees where I was able to kindle our second tea-fire. The temperature was now twenty-eight degrees, so I changed my wet mukluks and pulled out my parka. Then I changed the dogs around into different harness so they wouldn't get chafed, and put in a different leader. We were ready for our final dash, but it turned out to be anticlimactic, for the trail across the frozen water was very visible and, better yet, it was now frozen. I arrived at the herd camp of Wallace Lucas at four in the morning. Billy Kikuak got up to make tea for me while I unharnessed my dogs and brought my sleeping bag and gear into the tent. Although I was dead tired, I was above all gratefully happy to have traversed that long trail over the barrens safely.

The wind flapping the canvas tent wall woke me at 1:00 the next afternoon. Edgar Kutukut was playing checkers with Billy and said he had his dogs in harness and had been waiting for me to wake up before leaving for Tuk. I rolled up my bag and ate a hurried breakfast as I was glad to have someone to travel with in this featureless land. Before we left I got out my cameras and took pictures of the four tents pitched there and the reindeer tethered out behind like dogs. I was sorry I had to rush on, as this was a very interesting camp, so different from any I had seen before. As we got under way, a cold wind blew directly in our faces and I had to put on my wolverine mitts and hold them to my face to keep it from freezing.

After a run of three hours we came upon Eskimos. They had chopped holes through seven feet of salt ice and then cut snow blocks to build wind shelters, behind which they sat jigging for trout through the ice, patiently jerking home-made ivory lures in the water below. It looked to me like a mighty cold way to catch fish, but these people, sitting for hours like that on blocks of snow, evidently thought nothing of it. Mona Felix, Edgar's daughter, took us to her tent a half-mile away and made tea for us on her primus stove. As we headed north it kept getting colder with every mile we travelled. Finally the trail turned left and climbed up off Husky Lakes and onto the tundra. At ten in the evening we came up to two families who were heading for the jigging camp and who had stopped their teams to make tea behind a canvas windbreak. We had been going five hours without a break, so were glad to join them. I grabbed some pilot biscuit and canned meat from my sled and Edgar and I squeezed in behind their tarp, which the wind threatened to tear away any minute.

Winnie Dick had her first-born down inside her *artiggi* and it was crying, perhaps from the cold, but she herself was far from warm. I noticed that she couldn't hold her hand steady enough to strike a match. It was hard to believe that I had been stripped to my undershirt while travelling the day before. Following a very brief snack we pushed on again into the wind and never stopped until we reached Tuk at one in the morning. I woke up Father Robert LeMeur at the mission and he fried me one egg. The other egg was rotten, but I was more interested in a warm bunk anyway.

During lunch the next day Father Franche pulled in from Blow River. He had the first Bombardier in the area, the tracked vehicle that could carry a dozen people, was completely closed in, and could go just about anywhere in the North. The few Eskimo words which have been adopted into the English language include igloo, kayak, mukluk, poke and *pingo*, and the conversation got around to the last. *Pingo* is an Eskimo word for a peculiar ice formation of which there were many in the Tuk area. We were soon being driven over in the Bombardier to inspect one up close. From what I could discover, these huge frost boils that rise a couple of hundred feet in the air are formed when shallow lakes dry up. Then water seepage and permafrost go to work and build up inside the old lake bed and keep expanding in the only direction they can go: straight up. When the pingo gets old, its top cracks open, exposing the ice core which the sun slowly melts. As this action proceeds over the centuries, the soil covering the pingo piles up around the perimeter and the end result is a water-filled crater with a high rim.

Tuktuktiaktuk or Tuktoyaktuk, commonly referred to simply as Tuk, was only a couple of miles from one of the DEW Line posts. At night the giant plastic dome covering one of their radar installations was lit up, making it look like an over-sized igloo. The DEW Line was to go into service officially in July that year, so at this time it was practically completed. As my orders from Bishop Trocellier were to check out Cape Parry, I was now looking for a ride over there, 200 miles east. Father Franche was a chaplain for the Line and quickly arranged for me to get on one of the DC-3s that were continually hauling men and supplies between the sites.

Cape Parry was called Site #8, or Pin Main, and when the initial construction work attracted all the Eskimos from the Paulatuk area, two missionaries there, Fathers Leonce Dehurtevent and André Vermaut, soon followed. They had travelled the ninety miles along the east shore of Darnley Bay with their small tractor, hauling a caboose on skids. Now I found them two miles from the radar site, living in a very drafty fourteen-foot-by-sixteen-foot shack. During the next three days I shared their meals, which consisted mainly of frozen potatoes and wieners which they had scrounged from the camp dump. The Eskimos were camped around them in makeshift shacks built from discarded lumber and plywood. At this stage of development and especially because it was still winter, most of the temporary labour jobs had terminated and the few Eskimos who were still on the payroll were supporting their non-working relatives. The situation was not good and the prospects for any future permanent settlement here for the natives did not look promising. I discussed all these factors with the two Fathers and they agreed that it would be a mistake to dismantle the missions at Paulatuk and Stanton and move them here. But we didn't just sit around their oil stove for three days jawing, for there was pressing work to be done. They had found enough discarded material at the dump to build a ceiling in their shack and insulate it with fibreglass, so I pitched in. While I was with them we finished the work and immediately noticed a rise in room temperature.

I got a chance to see how the other half lived when we went over on Sunday to the DEW module to conduct a service at 4 p.m. in the reading room. As the visiting missionary, I had the honour of both saying the Mass and delivering the sermon. The tour of the camp which followed ended in an elegant dining room,

where we ate a six-course dinner along with the U.S. Navy Officers on the base, followed by a movie out of Hollywood. We
watched "Forever Darling," with Lucille Ball and Desi Arnaz, sitting in deep easy chairs in the lounge. The cumulative effect of all
this luxury was just slightly over-powering. The background
hum of motors and soft music, the soft, indirect lighting, the feel
of deep carpets underfoot, the smell of civilized food – all these
conspired to create an atmosphere absolutely alien to its Arctic
setting. Stepping out of that fantasy world into the northern
night with its chilly blast and drifting snow was the ultimate in
contrasts. The shack which was called the mission, with its bare
walls, frozen floor and monotonous meals of potatoes and wieners, did little to cushion the contrast between it and the DEW
Line station two miles away. Coming as I did from the United
States, this visit reminded me as nothing else could of just how
much I had given up in coming into the Arctic.

Although the building of the DEW Line across the Canadian
Arctic did provide some temporary jobs, for many of the native
Eskimos its total effect was more disruptive than beneficial. Bert
Boxer had visited me at E-3 earlier and explained how the government was sending him around the Arctic communities to
recruit candidates for courses on welding and operating heavy
equipment, courses being taught at Leduc, Alberta. He was convinced that the men he chose from each community were also the
best trappers in those communities. In giving these men up, these
groups lost those who were the most successful in earning a living from traditional pursuits, hunting and trapping. During the
few years that they were absent from their communities, they
lost many of their sled-dogs and much of their trapping gear,
both indispensable to life on the land. Besides that, they acquired
a taste for the very best food from the south and they found it
difficult to resume eating their traditional foods. These foods,
though probably better for them, lacked the variety and appetiz-
ing preparation of the meals they had been served on the DEW
Line. The end result was not healthy from the standpoint of eco-
nomics or morale. In an extreme case, like that at Cape Parry

where I was visiting, you had an entire community uprooted and left stranded in degrading circumstances.

As I discussed this situation with the two missionaries at Cape Parry, I could see some similarities with what was in progress at E-3. There, the need for piling on which to build the town and for temporary labourers had attracted, and was still attracting, men – some with families – from all the nearby settlements. The question was whether they would return to their homes once the construction phase had ended or would stay on in makeshift housing and become a generation of welfare bums. In trying to allocate the available temporary jobs to as many communities as possible, the government was unwittingly disturbing the tranquillity of those communities and alienating some of the best workers from them. These men would find it difficult to return to the life they had left. I could see that it might have been better to let those living in the vicinity be naturally attracted to the jobs, so that they could return home more easily afterwards. Taking an even longer-range view, it might have proven better for the natives involved if as many jobs as possible were filled by complete strangers to the North. This view would not have been politically agreeable at the time, for it was argued that work on these projects should first benefit the people of the North, and never mind the long term consequences.

In my report to the bishop I advised him that it could be a mistake to dismantle and move the mission from Paulatuk. As it turned out, all the Eskimos who were then living at Cape Parry eventually moved back to Paulatuk and all built new houses there. The last I heard, there was only one who gained permanent employment at Pin Main as a heavy equipment operator.

When I landed back at Tuk it was still zero, with blowing snow, and a measles epidemic in progress. Many were sick in bed and, having little knowledge of this disease, feared that it was fatal. I just hoped that I wouldn't carry it back with me, although I wasn't worried for myself: I had been through it in my childhood. I prepared for my return dogsled trip by pulling my toboggan into the boat-building workshop and attaching steel runners to the bottom. This would protect it against bare ice or bare ground. It was the middle of May and four in the afternoon when I finally got under way to retrace my route overland to Husky Lakes. Twelve miles out I caught up with Steve and Suzie Kikuak who were going my way. At first I didn't realize that they had three kids bedded down in their Banksland-type sled. They were on their way over to Husky Lakes to join the many who traditionally leave Tuk at this time of year to jig for trout. I lent Steve one of my six dogs, because he had a big load and his high runners dug deep in the loose snow and slowed him down. We had made twenty-five miles when we came to the first camp of fishermen and decided to pitch our tent and call it a day. As though to alert us to the fact that spring was on the way, three swans flew over, heading north.

The sky was clear, the sun bright, when I continued on south alone the next day. Eventually I found my old trail leading up off Husky Lakes and across the Barrens to the Mackenzie. I made fire again in the same little stand of gnarled spruce by the lake-shore and then rolled up in my blanket for a short siesta. It was about 7 p.m. when we resumed our march up onto the Barren-lands. The weather was perfect for the crossing: clear, with no wind and the temperature around zero. The only sound to break the absolute silence was the jingle of our harness bells and the raucous call of the male ptarmigan, which sounds something like "dry bread." They were pairing off prior to mating and could be seen every hundred yards. The sun swung low across the north-west horizon, casting long, purple shadows and lighting up those snow-block trail-markers like beacons. It was difficult to judge just how far ahead they were, for there was no contrast to give a sense of distance. Several times I would have sworn I was looking at a tent set by the trail up ahead, only to have it shrink down to two feet as we approached. Now I could understand better those stories I had read about Arctic hunters who thought they were stalking a musk-ox, only to find it was really a fox or a raven. Around midnight I descended the long hill that ended at the reindeer station and spent the night again with the McInnes family.

With a bright sun beating down out of a clear sky and no wind, the following day was really too warm for the dogs to work. When I looked out at the river and saw how much open water there was along the edges of the ice, however, I became anxious to cover that last thirty miles home. Once underway, the toboggan slid along easily on its new steel runners and I sat in the sled and let the dogs trot along at an easy pace. At John Kivek's camp we found his dogs tied out on ice which was separated from the shore by a hundred feet of open water. Although he sent one of his sons out in a canoe to get me for tea, I had no place to tie my team out on the ice. I feared that they would follow me in the water, swamping my sled and everything in it, so I declined and kept going. It took us six hours to get to E-3. When we arrived, I found I was again separated from shore by deep, open water. I finally located a partial ice bridge and urged my leader to try it. Although he had to swim to make it, I was able to keep the toboggan upright and the load dry, though my legs got wet. It didn't matter. It was the last dogsled trip of the season and we were safely home.

16

AROUND AND ABOUT THE MACKENZIE DELTA

The Arctic is a land of violent contrasts. This applies especially to the weather and the seasons. Spring and fall are not the gradual transition periods experienced in southern Canada. One day you could be boating in open water, and the next day that same water would be covered with ice. The day after my return from my sled trip to the Arctic Coast, I was sitting out on the front step of my little shack in my shirt-sleeves, smoking my pipe and soaking up the hot sun while my dogs stretched out and enjoyed the first day of their summer vacation. The only sounds in the air were the buzzing of the first flies and the tinkling of candled ice as it fell in the widening strip of water along each shore of the river. The huge snowbanks that had accumulated since September were finally melting under a sun that circled the sky day and night. It hardly seemed possible that less than a week ago I was battling against a head wind at ten below zero, covering my face with the backs of my wolverine mitts to avoid frostbite. In another three days all the snow was gone from our side of the channel and we were surrounded by bare ground. It had been winter last week. Now it was summer!

Following the success of our ice carnival I proposed to the Home and School Association at one of our weekly meetings that we could raise additional funds by running an ice break-up pool. Again I got their approval, provided I organize and run it. This involved, first of all, the printing of 5,000 tickets on my Gestetner and their distribution to all the surrounding settlements. Then I had to fix a post in the ice in the middle of the river and run a wire from it to my shack. Here I connected it to the cord of my electric clock. I was only home a week after my dogsled trip when the ice moved enough to pull the cord from its socket and stop the clock, indicating the winning time for the pool. This guessing-game created a lot of speculation, sold many tickets at twenty-five cents each and earned our Association over $300 .

The call of the wild that spring was the insistent honking of White Wavey geese as they winged their way north to their summer nesting sites. Victor Allen, who lived in a tent in front of my shack, and I both watched these huge V's of birds increase day by day. We could only restrain ourselves up to a point. After all, it was against the Migratory Bird Convention Act to shoot geese or ducks in the spring. At last we could restrain ourselves no longer, however, so with Jim MacDonald we dragged a twenty-foot canoe across the ice of the portage separating us from a large lake to the west of the settlement. Once over there, it didn't take us long to find an ideal pond of open water, surrounded by tall grasses. We cut small spruce and constructed makeshift blinds and then used the first birds we got for decoys. What a feast we had that night around an open fire, eating those plump, grain-fed birds from the South. Nor could we quit until we had used up all our shells, so we spent the night over there.

When we returned to E-3, word spread quickly that we had had a successful hunt and our friends soon relieved us of the surplus birds we had brought home. This didn't bother us, because the weather was now too warm to keep them anyway. A few days later the game warden flew over from Aklavik and paid me an unexpected visit. At first I thought it was merely a social call, but after chewing the fat for half-an-hour the officer asked if he might "look around." Of course, I said, "Go right ahead," but was totally surprised when he walked over to my portable chapel kit and opened it! Right there I demanded to know what he was looking for. He replied, "Illegal birds," and added that he had received a report that I had been killing wildfowl out of season. I readily admitted that I had recently taken some birds, but if I had kept any I certainly wouldn't have put them in my heated shack and above all not in my chapel kit. Unable to find any evidence, this zealous guardian of the game laws was unable to press a charge against me and departed just a little disgruntled. Victor and I agreed that civilization was quickly catching up with the new Aklavik.

Nor was E-3 what you might call a peaceful little settlement. Like similar boom towns that preceded it in the North, it had its element of male workers who, freed from the restraints of home life, enjoyed whooping it up, especially on weekends. They were encouraged by the fact that, as yet, the town had no jail. Furthermore, a Mountie was not permanently stationed there, but only sent over from time to time from the Aklavik detachment. Most Saturday nights saw a dance organized in some empty warehouse in the townsite, but as soon as a suitable building had been erected by Aklavik Constructors, nine miles south at the airport site, a special house-warming invitation went out. Although the dance out there got started late, it was terminated early by the camp boss, Henning Jensen, when a number of fights broke out, spurred by the consumption of over-proof rum. His men then proceeded to commandeer his pick-up trucks to return the guests to the townsite. None of the trucks returned! On Sunday they were found, most of them in the ditch, and one was completely wrecked. Henning paid me a visit at three in the afternoon to describe the whole fiasco. Unfortunately, the main offenders turned out to be natives. In the contract his company had signed with the federal government, there was a clause to the effect that they would hire as many natives as possible. Jensen had enthusiastically carried this out: he had already hired and fired, at least once, every able-bodied Eskimo and Indian in the area. He ended up downright discouraged with this work force.

His story was no revelation to me, for I had heard the same tale at Port Radium, Uranium City and other places. In most cases it was not the employer's fault, because he was usually under the gun to complete a job within a specified time-limit and could not afford the leisure of overlooking absenteeism or any misconduct that slowed down the work. On the other hand, the native attitude to being punctual, to missing days, or to borrowing equipment had been formed in bush camps. There, all this behaviour was normal and the idea of discipline was extremely vague. Almost all these natives had come right off the land where they had been their own boss, so it was extremely hard for them to appreciate Jensen's position. Just how long it would take them to change their attitude was anyone's guess, but Jensen couldn't afford to wait and see. He fired them all and the next day brought in the first of many DC-3-loads of workers from Edmonton.

The annual spring break-up continued swiftly. With the rapid melting of the winter's snows, the creeks were pouring their torrents of melt-water into the river. Soon the river had lifted what was left of its winter cover of ice fifteen feet above normal. Some of the Eskimos camped on low ground along the bank found themselves completely surrounded by water. Boats that had been hauled up high and dry in the fall were again floating. We watched fascinated as the ice began to move downstream with the current, followed by miles of broken ice and uprooted trees, jammed from bank to bank. I hauled my cedar-planked speedboat up next to my shack and proceeded to replace the boards the ice had cut the previous fall.

I was occupied, too, with more artistic work. The painting I had done in Aklavik for the Fort Good Hope church had been delivered and hung and I was working on a second one depicting the death of Father Grollier, founder of the mission. He had died at Good Hope of a respiratory problem at the early age of thirty-eight. I pictured him on his deathbed with his companion missionary Father Seguin standing by, and both looking out the open door of their log cabin as a huge cross was erected by the natives on the riverbank. Earlier in the winter I had made sketches, using as a model Jim Pierrot, a Good Hope native being treated for TB in our Aklavik hospital. I added a heavy black beard which I presumed Father Grollier must have worn, like all the French missionaries of that time. I presumed wrong, however. Father Robin later told me that this particular missionary hated beards and always kept himself clean-shaven. Further, I should take my paints to the church at Fort Good Hope some day and remove the founder's beard.

As the river was clear of ice and drift logs in the first week of June, I launched my boat. The first few trips were local duck-hunting excursions with various native friends like Nap Cardinal, Tommy Ross and Pierre Benoit. At the end of that week the official harbinger of summer made its first trip to the new community. I refer, of course, to the famous "Banana Boat," Streeper's boat and barge from Fort Nelson, B.C. It didn't actually carry bananas, but it did have oranges and apples and a good variety of vegetables. It did a land-office business tied up to the new town dock, which just recently had been two feet under water. Right behind him came Dick Bullock, towing a raft of a hundred logs for pilings which he had cut up stream at Tree River. The next day I walked over to the river bank to greet Johnny Desroshier as he tied up Stan Peffer's boat and barge. He had the complete store and trade stock from their Axel River post, which they proceeded to erect as the third store in the new town. With the advent of open water, people were arriving day and night from all over the country.

One of the new arrivals was Eddie Cook, his wife, Mary, and their six children. I had met Eddie first in his hometown of Fort Good Hope. I later ran into him at Fort Chipewyan, where he was filling the post of Assistant Indian Agent under Jack Stewart. As Hareskins they didn't really feel at home among the Chipewyans and Crees there, and prevailed upon me to write a letter on their behalf, requesting that they be stationed among their own people. The request was granted: they were posted to Aklavik under Agent Al Cottrell. The opening of the new Aklavik called for the establishment of a new agency, and Eddie was named the official agent, the first time, as far as I know, that a native of the country got such an appointment.

I wasn't surprised, because I realized that Eddie was a college grad fluent in both English and French as well as his native Hare-skin dialect. At one time he had studied for the priesthood in Edmonton. So Eddie and family moved into one of the new "512's" at E-3 and they were surely proud and happy when I first visited them. During the summer, however, their neat little home became a mecca for friends and relatives from their hometown up river. Hardly a night passed that there weren't at least a few visitors sleeping on their living-room floor. This inevitably led to drinking parties, with the result that Eddie found it increasingly difficult to get to his office in the morning. Complaints got back to his superior in Aklavik and he was warned. But if there is one thing that is hard, if not impossible, for a Dene person, it is to refuse hospitality to one of his own people. The upshot was that Eddie's career as Indian Agent was short-lived. The next time I ran into him, he was back in Fort Good Hope with a shovel in his hand, working for the town on the roads. He was the best edu-cated person his tribe had produced! There should be a moral here and I guess it would be that it takes more than mere educa-tion to be successful in the white man's world. High on the list would be discipline and the realization that pleasure or even hos-pitality can't be allowed to interfere with business.

❄ ❄ ❄

Two things happened together on the 17th of June to change the out-of-doors completely. First the temperature rose to a record seventy-five degrees under a brilliant sun. As a result, the willows and birches burst into leaf, changing the colour of our world from brown to green. Unfortunately the heat also acti-vated the mosquitoes which had lain dormant all winter. The poor dogs began digging holes in the ground to get away from them. I built a screen door for my shack and bought some bug repellent from Slim Semmler. No doubt about it, the mosquitoes are the real scourge of the North, but without them we'd probably be overrun with tourists. We enjoyed just two days of this balmy weather when we were hit by a snowstorm that for the next three days turned our world white again. The dogs looked happy and probably thought summer was over.

Our town was buzzing over the disappearance of the Aklavik Constructors' foreman Henning Jensen. When he ran out of dynamite for his wagon drills he decided to go over to Aklavik and get a supply. Taking the company's thirty-ton powered barge, with an engineer to run it and a native to guide, they had no trouble crossing the delta. The trouble started after he put two tons of the explosives aboard and was ready to leave. His native guide got drunk and failed to show. For Henning, this situation was typical of the bad luck he had had hiring natives, but, as his crew at E-3 badly needed his cargo, he decided to shove off without the guide. He completely disappeared into the myriad channels of the vast Mackenzie delta.

No one had seen him for a week, when his boss from Calgary, Vince Dunn, showed up at my shack one day. He was justifiably riled up over the disappearance of his foreman, especially in view of the highly explosive cargo he was carrying, plus the fact that his multi-million-dollar airport project had ground to a halt. Someone had told him that I had been crossing the delta to Aklavik regularly and knew the route, so he asked if I could be talked into doing a search if he rented a plane.

That afternoon I was airborne in Mike Zubko's float plane carrying my delta map and my powerful Bausch and Lomb 7 x 50 binoculars. I asked Mike to climb up to 5,000 feet and from that altitude, on a cloud-free day, I could see most of the delta. It didn't take fifteen minutes to spot the missing barge on the Oniak Channel and we landed next to it. Poor Jensen was fit to be tied. In spite of being hopelessly lost, he had managed to keep going every day with the help of a couple of barrels of fuel he had luckily found. But his boat was leaking so badly that he and the engineer had to unload the two tons of dynamite every night before sleeping and then reload them every morning. He said that with every heavy case he carried, he thought of that drunken guide!

At any rate, I showed him where he was on my map and left it with him, his route to E-3 clearly marked. Vince Dunn was elated when we landed and gave him the good news. Later he rewarded me by sending in a nice twelve-gauge Ithaca shotgun as a token of thanks from Aklavik Constructors.

One windy, wet evening a few days later, two of Pascal's boys came in from their cabin on the Enik Channel forty miles south to announce that their brother Denis, along with the two sons of Pierre Tazzi, Richard and Joseph, had drowned. Apparently, this triple tragedy occurred at midnight near their camp, when the three teenage boys, just back from the mission boarding school in Aklavik, had taken off in their father's eighteen-foot canoe, powered by a two-and-a-half horsepower kicker. The next morning the overturned canoe was found within sight of the cabin down river, but there was no sign of the boys. I decided to go back with them right away and help in the search, or at least console the parents.

After leaving a message to be sent to the RCMP and mixing twenty gallons of gas, we three set out in the rain and reached their cabin at 1:30 in the morning. After a short night's sleep, I offered a requiem Mass for the deceased in Pascal's cabin. The police arrived from Aklavik in their boat at 10 a.m. They were equipped with drags that consisted of ten-foot lengths of pipe with large hooks attached a foot apart. We spent most of the day dragging the area where the capsized canoe was found. The water throughout the delta is so full of sediment that you can't see more than a foot in it. Several times we snagged sunken logs and thought we were pulling up one of the bodies, but no such luck. Late in the day the police gave up and returned to Aklavik, while I returned to E-3 with Pierre Tazzi. He was so broken up over the loss of his two sons that he wanted to get away from the scene completely.

If I sometimes felt that there were too few hours in the day to do all that needed to be done, I was absolutely sure of it after Bishop Trocellier's two-hour visit. He landed in his bright red Norseman float plane the following day and tied up to the bank right in front of my shack. We proceeded to discuss the move to the new townsite, a move he was reluctant to make, but for which he had no alternative. I borrowed a pick-up truck and drove him up to see E-3's first church. Though it stood out in the middle of nowhere, it had been filled to capacity the Sunday before. The bishop readily agreed that we would soon need a larger one and told me to start working on its plan. While I was at it, I was to design a rectory to go with it. On top of this, as a preliminary, he wanted me to put up a thirty-by-seventy-foot warehouse this summer to house building material. He promised to send the Brothers down with two barge-loads of lumber from their mill near Fort Smith as soon as possible. With a final order to pick out a cemetery site my superior boarded his aircraft and took off into the summer sky. I was left standing on the dock with enough commissions to make my head spin.

It was a week before I could get back to the grief-stricken Pascal camp where none of the three missing bodies had turned up. The following day, however, when I was out helping them remove fish from one of their nets, we found we had caught more than fish. Up from the murky depths came the bloated body of the boy Denis. A fisherman might visit his nets all the years of his life with joyful anticipation, but the day he catches one of his own sons is a dark one indeed. It fell to me to bring the body back to E-3 and it took me all day in the rain. Till that time I had not been aware of the over-powering stench of a decaying body, but I had all day to meditate on this fact of life and death. My only defence was a series of cigars I smoked en route.

❄ ❄ ❄

I arrived back at the Pascal cabin again shortly afterwards. While waiting for the other two bodies to surface I was told of an interesting couple living farther up in the delta in an inaccessible side channel. These were the white trapper Tom Throne and his native wife Philamene. Tom had originated in Texas and was fifty-two when he began courting George Adam's daughter, who had just turned fourteen. Their camps were twenty miles apart, and when Philamene heard Tom's kicker coming on a courtship visit she hid herself. That bearded old white man with the strange drawl scared her out of her wits. The courtship continued for two years, during which time Tom drew a glowing picture of the benefits to George if he would consent to the marriage of his daughter. Among other things, he told him, he had a lot of money back in Texas which could greatly benefit George in his declining years. Furthermore, he intended to take his daughter on a grand shopping spree in the world outside and show her sights she never dreamed of. To the girl herself Tom promised blue-eyed children, the dream of every native maiden. Finally, when Philamene reached the legal age of sixteen, her father consented and Tom took her to Aklavik in his canoe for the ceremony.

The Adam family are all Catholic, but Tom, never having been baptized, was strictly speaking a pagan and as such could not be married in the church, a condition his bride's family insisted upon. There was a way open for Tom to change his status and that was to join the church of his future in-laws and become a Christian. He lost no time in informing the Father in charge of his intentions and an intense course of instructions began immediately. No one around the mission at Aklavik had ever seen a more fervent and regular candidate for baptism than Tom Throne during the next two weeks. He attended every religious ceremony and if he was not in church or in the Father's office he was out on the riverbank studying the catechism. The great day soon arrived and Tom received two sacraments of the church, baptism followed by his marriage to Philamene. A suitable banquet and dance followed and the community all wished the newlyweds a long, happy married life together. Then they got into Tom's freighter canoe and headed back to his cabin on the other side of the delta on their honeymoon.

Philamene's dark premonitions were soon realized; she had been pushed into one of the wily old trapper's traps. The honeymoon was short-lived. Far from seeing the outside world, she was not even allowed to visit her mother twenty miles downstream. Tom enforced strict obedience with a stout stick, which Philamene began to feel too often across her young back. Visitors were unwelcome to the Throne cabin. Even the winter dogsled patrol of the Mounties was locked out. They never had any children and Tom never entered a church again. This was the situation twenty-one years later when I came on the scene. As soon as I heard this story, I wanted to visit them and see if I couldn't change the situation, though, frankly, I had no definite plan.

Pascal went with me in my boat as guide and moral support on my first visit to the Throne cabin. He admitted he knew very little about the couple. In fact he had never visited their cabin, although they were practically neighbours. He feared he wouldn't be welcome and perhaps he was right: few, if any, were. When we pulled up to Tom Throne's dock that calm summer evening we found a typical low, sod-roofed cabin on the bank of a narrow channel. There was a log warehouse a few yards from the main cabin, plus a stage hanging with freshly split fish and numerous dogs chained out in back.

Tom, now in his eighties, didn't lock his door against us as I feared he might, but came down to the dock and shook my hand. He was evidently shrunken from his former robust height and had cut off his beard. He was friendly and entertaining and it was difficult to believe that this was the man I had been hearing about. In spite of his age he was not at all feeble and continued to trap and to drive his seven powerful huskies into Arctic Red River monthly to pick up his social security cheque. Philamene peeked out of the window as we walked up to the cabin and after taking our hands busied herself making tea at their wood stove. We followed Tom into the cabin and sat at his table up against the window facing the river.

I was surprised to find him so talkative as he told us the story of his early years in Texas, where he worked as a cowboy and carried a six-shooter. He described all his wanderings that finally ended in the Mackenzie delta and his present life as a trapper. Although he knew I was a representative of the church, he never once mentioned religion. In speaking of his wife, whom he referred to as "the little girl," he said casually, "Of course, I told her we'd never have any children."

If Tom lacked a friendly rapport with his fellow humans, he was the opposite with wildlife, instilling an unusual trust and confidence in them. To demonstrate this as we sat at table, he called a red squirrel by name. It immediately entered a hole in the window screen and ate out of his hand, followed by a whiskey jack. No one we knew had ever done this before. Later, outside the cabin, he had a flock of gulls swooping down to take bits of bannock from his hand.

Over at Aklavik hostel there were at least a dozen orphan children we had to keep during the summer vacation as they had no family to return to. I was always on the lookout for families who would take them and receive a daily stipend of fifty cents per child. It now occurred to me that this couple, who had never known the laughter of a child in their cabin, could profit by such an arrangement. I promptly broached the idea to Tom and told him that I could get him either an Indian or Eskimo boy or a girl from age seven to fifteen. As we talked the idea over he began to warm to it. Finally, when he agreed to the proposal, I followed it up with another idea that would give Philamene her first vacation away from the old man in twenty-one years. I suggested that his wife might accompany me back to E-3 to receive and accompany the child they would adopt for the summer. To this Tom immediately objected, saying that she was needed there to feed their thirteen dogs. I countered by arguing that such a chore should be an easy one for an old-timer like himself, who must have fed his dogs many a day on the trail. Finally he said, "Well, it's up to the little girl herself."

When I turned to put the question to Philamene she was already digging in a trunk, taking out a new dress and a bonnet that looked like the one my mother used to wear when she dusted the house. In two shakes she was dressed and down on the dock ahead of us. She was ready to leave before Tom changed his mind. We did get away promptly, leaving Tom standing alone on his dock, looking for all the world like a lost soul.

The plan was first to drop off Pascal at his cabin, which I did, and then to leave Philamene at her mother's camp. Her mother was gone, however, so I took Philamene right on through to E-3. During this trip I got the whole story of life with Tom Throne, and, the more I heard, the more I congratulated myself on organizing this break for her. Her eyes lit up with wonder as we approached the imposing buildings of the new Aklavik and when we located her mother in one of the tents along the riverbank the two couldn't seem to let go of each other. It took me a week finally to get the twelve-year-old Eskimo boy, Paul Ipillum, over from Aklavik. Philamene had been away from home much longer than I had estimated to her husband and we approached the return trip with some fear and trepidation. Still, we had the new boy with us to placate the irascible old Tom.

It was midnight when the three of us pulled up at Tom's dock and, though the dogs were barking, the old man did not appear. We feared that he was inside the cabin in a murderous mood. When we got up to the door Philamene suddenly ran around to the back of the cabin. I thought that she found the door locked and had gone to get a hidden key, but when she failed to return I walked to the other end of the cabin and found her chinking the logs with more moss! Apparently the door was not locked, but she lacked the courage to go in and face her husband. Finally I got her to follow in behind me and Paul.

We found Tom hunched over his radio, his ear pressed to the speaker as his batteries were weak and that was why he didn't hear our arrival. Before he had a chance to complain of our delay I pushed Paul forward to shake his hand and Tom's eyes lit up. The crisis was over and Philamene, with relief, began building a fire in the stove. While we were eating our late supper of fried potatoes and boiled rhubarb old Tom was in a good mood as he regaled me with stories of his youth in Texas with a special emphasis on his ability to handle a pistol. I left them a happy threesome that night, not a little pleased over the outcome of the whole affair.

In late August when I got back to pick up Paul for school I found him dressed in new clothes sewn for him with loving care by Philamene. Tom had taken him on a successful moose hunt, taught him how to fish with a net and had made a neat bow with arrows for hunting around their camp. In two short months the old man had taken to the boy as I had hoped he would. "I think we'll try to adopt him legally," Tom told me, "I can't live forever and he could have my trapline and all this equipment." Paul jumped into my boat and we headed west across the delta to Aklavik and another winter of school.

❄ ❄ ❄

Before the season for hunting beluga whales ended, I was determined to get down to the coast and see just how they were taken. So, late in July, Joe Kaglik and I shoved off in my speed-boat and headed north. We stopped for lunch at the reindeer sta-tion and at Tununik to mix more gas. Soon we were at the old abandoned Hudson Bay warehouse at the mouth of the White-fish Channel. We made a fire here and cooked two birds we had shot, but what made this particular stop memorable were the mosquitoes. I had never encountered them so numerous and per-sistent. Though we were well doped with repellent, they contin-ually flew into our eyes, ears and mouth and completely covered our clothing in a solid, moving mass, not unlike photos you see of beekeepers covered with bees at a hive.

While the birds were cooking, I took a short walk around a nearby Eskimo graveyard that was littered with loose skulls. There were no crosses or headstones of any kind and the bodies apparently had been simply laid out on the tundra and covered with some drift logs or stones. Their earthly possessions had been placed near the corpses. The ribs of a decayed kayak or the runners of a *komatik* or even spears or bows and arrows marked the men's graves. Those of the women could be identified by such items as their *ulus* or a stone lamp or beads. On one of more recent vintage I noted a rusting portable sewing machine. Evi-dently the wolves had dislodged the heads and rolled them about. Joe mentioned to me that such graveyards are invariably inhabited by colonies of Richardson's ground squirrels, called *"siksiks,"* and their burrowing does much to obliterate the graves as they throw up a lot of dirt. Because most of the bodies had been laid out fully clothed, mainly in caribou skins and pants, and were pressed to the permafrost, they were remarkably well preserved. It was an intriguing look at a way of life that had now passed. I was amazed to find sled runners that were shod with whale bone, using some sort of ivory peg for nails. There were copper kettles and ivory combs and turquoise beads lying around half-buried, enough to fill a small museum. I hated to leave, but those pesky mosquitoes drove us back to our fire.

After supper we went on about four miles to the Eskimo whaling camp known as Whitefish Station. The channel widens here just before emptying into the Arctic Ocean and it forms a neat little sheltered harbour. Tied up in it were four schooners and two motor barges. Up on the high ground on either side about twenty tents were pitched. We pulled up alongside the schooner *Only Way* and were welcomed aboard by its owner, Tom Kalinek, his son, Elias, and his wife, Madeleine. Tom said his boat had been named by its previous owner, a white trapper, who felt it was the "only way" to travel along the Arctic Coast. We were invited to carry our sleeping bags on board and were soon sitting in the galley, eating a huge beluga heart that tasted like beef. We were also served *muktuk*, the white outer skin of the beluga, which had a nice nutty flavour but was so tough I couldn't chew it. Its consistency resembled nothing less than a Goodyear, white-walled tire!

The whole camp was in a festive mood. The weather was balmy under a midnight sun, especially appreciated after a long, cold winter. Eskimos were attracted here from all over the Mackenzie delta and along the coast. Many hadn't seen each other since they met here last year. The next morning I said Mass aboard Billy Thrasher's scow *Normandie*. Billy got his name, Thrasher, from the New Bedford whaling schooner he was born on at Herschel Island. His father hailed from Portugal. I got a second breakfast of sourdough pancakes that morning when I visited the tent of Alec Stefansson, the Métis son of the explorer Vilhjalmur Stefansson.

Later I joined the men all congregated on a hill behind the camp watching for whales. I had my own Bausch and Lomb binoculars with me as usual and the others shared several old brass telescopes which had been brought into the country along with their schooners by the famous Captain Ted Pederson. Although 1936 was the last year the captain made a trading trip into the Western Arctic, many of the worthwhile items he had traded for white fox were still being used. After sitting up there swapping stories for a couple of hours, someone spotted the tell-tale spray of a blowing whale and we all rushed down the hill and made for the schooners. I helped Tom Kalinek weigh the *Only Way*'s anchor and we chugged out of the narrow opening of the harbour into the open sea. Tom's son, Elias, working in the engine room, opened the old motor full-throttle.

We were out from shore four miles before we actually spotted the pod of belugas and another mile or two before we got in their wake. The water there is only about two fathoms deep and too silty to see into it, but the whales leave a distinct trail of eddies on the surface which can be followed if it isn't too rough. Tom was soon following this wake and closing the distance between us and the belugas. Archie Headpoint was on deck attaching the head to a harpoon and readying the lines and floats. As soon as we were within range, he and Elias positioned themselves at the bow with their rifles at the ready.

Every thirty seconds or so the belugas would surface in unison to blow and inhale. The trick was to get off an accurate shot during the two or three seconds their backs were above water. I stood next to Tom at the helm. He explained to me that it was important not to hit the whale in the head and kill it instantly, because then it would sink and it would be hard to locate it. If it was hit along the backbone, however, it would thrash around in the water long enough for the men to hit it on the surface with the harpoon.

The first whale struck was killed instantly and it sank out of sight. Nonetheless, it was retrieved with the *niksik,* a sharp, three-pronged grappling iron that was heaved out on a long line and then pulled back to the boat. As soon as this whale was pulled up to the gunwale his lower jaw was cut with a knife so a rope could be passed through for towing. We soon had this whale in tow and went on to get a second. This one was properly wounded and then hit with a harpoon. The harpoon immediately detached from its throwing handle, but it was securely tied to a long line, attached in turn to a ten-gallon keg float. With two belugas in tow, Tom called it a day and hoisted a flag to the top of the forward mast to indicate to those on shore that the boat had made a kill and was returning. Perhaps it also indicated to the women on shore that they should sharpen their *ulus* and get ready for work.

Although the white whales couldn't have been more stream-lined, their 1,000-pound bulk slowed down our speed back to port considerably, but it was a joyful return trip for both captain and crew. Once inside the lagoon of the Whitefish River, all hands, including the women and children, got together on a heavy rope attached to the whale's tail. Pulling in unison, they managed to beach the animal in shallow water, though they lacked the strength to skid it up high and dry. After the final tug the men's work was finished and the women took over, wading into the shallow water with their moon-faced knives to strip the carcasses of that outer six inches of white *muktuk.*

This fatty layer came off in sections, like floating mattresses. These sections were hauled ashore and draped over a huge drift log, hide-side down. The women fleshed these hides, removing all the fat, then staked the thin hide out on the tundra to dry. Later it would be cut up for dog harness and any other traces or lines needed. Other sections of *muktuk* were cut into small pieces. These were draped over drying racks, under which fires were kept burning to repel flies. Some of it was melted in large pots into clear oil simmering over hot fires. This provided the staple *uksuk,* or seasoning oil, that was generally on the table no matter what was being eaten. The huge six-foot-long stomachs of these whales were blown up and tied to dry inflated. I learned that they were often used to store cranberries. With all four schooners bringing in whales every day and all the women swarming over them and processing the *muktuk*, the scene along the beach front resembled something between an abattoir and a rendering plant. It certainly presented all kinds of camera opportunities and I took full advantage of it, using both my Rolleicord and my Bell and Howell 16mm.

When I saw a teenage boy go out with a freighter canoe and bag a beluga, I decided to do the same thing with my speedboat. So, the next day, my companion Joe, along with another Eskimo, joined me for a solo hunt. We soon got on the track of a whale. I turned the motor controls over to one of them, while the second handled the rifle and I my movie camera mounted on a tripod. Our rifleman wounded a beluga. As we bore down on it, my camera grinding away, our pilot, unfamiliar with the controls, turned the throttle the wrong way. Instead of stopping over the wounded animal, we shot ahead full-speed just as it raised its tail out of the water to dive. We hit the tail hard enough to shear the motor pin and knock me to the floor of the boat with my equipment on top of me. Luckily the boat was undamaged, but by the time we had replaced the pin the whale had disappeared. In spite of the goof, the film turned out fine. Later I was able to sell a copy of all the footage I took at Whitefish Station to KOMO-TV in Seattle for their program *Adventure Northwest*.

❋ ❋ ❋

Back at E-3 again, I could see the landscape change from week to week as the big bulldozers continued to tear up the muskeg and build new roads. The pile-driving crew kept steaming in a forest of logs upon which all the major buildings would rise. This activity seemed to accelerate as the nights began to get dark again. The shorter days reminded them that most of this work would stop after freeze-up. The days of my week would build toward Sunday when, as with any man of the cloth, I performed my major services for the community – a morning Mass in our chapel building, followed by a second late in the afternoon out at the airport site.

Unfortunately, a good portion of the flock were unable to get on their feet to attend either service. The reason for this was a little schooner that appeared at the dock each Saturday evening: this was the weekly delivery of liquor from the government liquor store in Aklavik to the new townsite. The owner of the boat, Fred (Jake) Jacobson, trader and trapper, had an interesting history, quite compatible with the job he now held. Jake was originally from Russia, where he started his business life with a schooner under sail in the Bering Straits region, trading alcohol for ivory and furs. He said he was successful at this trade only when he could ply the Cossacks with his home-made vodka and keep them off his back, for his trade was strictly illegal. One day, under a heavy fog, he steered his schooner across the straits and landed on the Alaskan shore. Slowly he worked his way up around Point Barrow and on east to Herschel Island, where he was in Canadian waters. The RCMP detachment there acted as customs officers and Jake got the proper clearance to continue east to trap white fox. He eventually married a Mackenzie delta Eskimo, spent most of his life trapping and trading between Tuk and Coppermine, and raised many children. His services as "Ice Captain" for the RCMP patrol boat *St. Roch* were sought yearly by Captain Henry Larsen.

With this background it was not surprising that Jake was chosen to shepherd the weekly cargo of spirits over to the new townsite. I can still see the line-up of thirsty workers down at his schooner with permits in hand every Saturday evening. Although this allotment was merely a trickle from a huge stockpile, it was enough to fuel all-night parties that consigned Sundays to recuperating. In the end the whole liquor store was moved over to E-3.

We were already into August and it was time to publish the summer edition of the *Aklavik Journal*. As it turned out, this eighteenth edition was to be the last. I spent the next three days on the second floor of the mission in Aklavik typing stencils and then cranking out 500 copies on the faithful old Gestetner. The main item of news was the political race to replace Frank Carmichael on the Territorial Council. Knut Lang, Stan Mackie, Thomas Njootli and George White were running, but veteran trader-trapper Knut Lang won, hands down, at the August 19th polls.

In the meantime the Brothers had brought down 50,000 feet of dimension lumber from their sawmill at Fort Smith and off-loaded it at Aklavik. They were to take it across to the new town-site with the smaller *Immaculata* and barge. Brother Delisle and I went ahead in my speed-boat to prepare the mud sills on which this lumber would be piled. When the *Immaculata* arrived at E-3 two days later, we were surprised to see eight of the Grey Nuns aboard, plus thirty of the hostel kids. It had turned out to be a picnic, but not for me and the Brothers: we had to move that pile of lumber using that ancient ten-wheel army truck. With roughly five tons of lumber on her back, she protested mightily, sputtering, coughing and backfiring all the way up the hill from the river. She had a cracked block and kept pouring water out of the exhaust. We poured in coffee grounds, pepper and molasses and every other home remedy we could think of to plug that leak, to no avail. Yet she didn't quit outright and we got all the lumber off the barge and stockpiled on the new mission lot. The last thing I did was to drive her onto our barge and wish her God-speed back to Aklavik. The picnic over, the good Sisters left with their charges and fifty pounds of dried fish I was sending over to the patients. I stayed behind to finish my second painting for the Good Hope Church. After I had signed it three days later, I too crossed the delta to Aklavik in order to gather up tools with which to build the warehouse at E-3. As soon as I got in my old room at the mission I found my mail on the desk. It included a letter which would be decisive for all my plans.

It was notice from Jean-Louis Michel, O.M.I., the provincial in Fort Smith that I had been chosen from the Mackenzie area to attend a six-month mission seminar in Rome, beginning in November. This was a yearly event and I had submitted my name several years earlier with little hope of being chosen. I was elated at this opportunity of seeing Europe as well as the Eternal City, but it also meant that I would be gone all winter. Another missionary was bound to replace me at E-3. The more I thought about it, the more I began to realize that my tour of duty in this area of the North was rapidly coming to a close. Every day became precious. I had promised the hospital Sisters that I would take them berry-picking, so I delayed no longer: my little boat was full as we motored up the Peel Channel twenty miles to spend a glorious day under Red Mountain.

Back across the delta again at the end of August, I celebrated my thirty-seventh birthday in my little shack. I knew it would be my last there. I was faced again with the task of packing my trunk and disposing of my dog-team. I made a deal with a veteran trapper named Mike O'Donnell who paid me $125 for the white bitch Princess, which Philip had sent down from Camsell Portage. There was one condition: if I returned, I could have one litter of her pups with which to start a new team. The rest of the dogs I sold for $25 apiece, a real bargain price, but I was forced to get rid of them as soon as I pulled out my net. I was getting proficient at packing my trunk, putting back into it just about the same things I had packed at Camsell, mostly books. With my dogs gone and my trunk in the boat, I said a last few good-byes, locked the cabin and shoved off. Going down the East Branch eight miles, I picked up two of Gus Tardiff's boys for school. It was a cold, rainy day, perfectly matching my mood. Joe Gully waved me in at his camp to pick up three letters and incidentally to borrow four gallons of gas from me. The three of us continued on in the rain without incident until I hit a submerged log near Jake Peffer's camp on Schooner Channel and sheared a pin. Once this was replaced, we had made scarcely 500 yards when the motor stopped again and I spent the next hour in the rain trying to figure out my trouble. I finally gave up and put the little auxiliary two-and-a-half horse-power motor on the transom. We continued on at a snail's pace. Later I found out that I had broken the crankshaft key on the big Evinrude. A few miles down the Aklavik River we were over-taken by Hans Hanson in the barge *King's Highway* and he towed us on to Aklavik. Here I cut our boat loose in the middle of the channel opposite the town. I intended to go the last few hundred yards to the mission using our small motor, but, to cap a day plagued with bad luck, I broke the starting rope on the first pull and we were left drifting in the middle of the river as darkness set in. We put the single paddle to work with no noticeable progress for a half-hour. Finally we were rescued by two Eskimo girls paddling their canoe, who towed us ashore. It was 10 p.m. and dark as I finally completed the last of my many crossings of the Mackenzie delta between E-3 and Aklavik.

Father Max Ruyant soon informed me that my replacement had already been named. He was Father Jules Adam, recently recuperated from a bout with tuberculosis. He had left that afternoon on Fred Norris's boat, the *Barbara Jean,* to visit me at E-3, but had passed me while I was being towed by Hans Hanson. He returned to Aklavik the following day and we spent a good deal of time together talking of the work to be done at the new townsite, work that would now fall on his shoulders. That evening I attended a farewell party arranged by Sister Kristoff at which we ate ice cream and listened to records.

September 12th dawned foggy and wet, definitely not good flying weather, but I left anyway in the Canadian Pacific Airlines float-equipped Norseman. The pilot followed the Aklavik River south out of the delta at tree-top level. At Norman Wells we transferred to the "Mainliner," a DC-3 that plied the route between that point and Edmonton. It dropped me off at Fort Smith that evening. Now I found myself back in the old mission there (the one with that clamorous bell in the stairwell that called us, night and day, to all our activities!). I was greeted by the man who orchestrated my life, Bishop Joseph Trocellier.

The following morning I had coffee with Gordon Robertson, the Commissioner of the Northwest Territories; his Director, Curt Merrill, who had been in charge of the initial phase of E-3; and Merv Hardy, the first Member of Parliament from our Territory. Topics of conversation ranged from the surprise victory of the Conservative Party in Ottawa, the resignation of Louis St. Laurent from the Liberal leadership, the new road to Hay River, liquor rights for the natives, the new Roman Catholic hostel being built at Fort Smith and, of course, the current situation at E-3. I came away from this meeting with some important concessions, including the transfer of our warehouse site from down near the dock to up next to the future hostel area, a change in our church lot line and the approval of the site I had chosen for a cemetery. I flew on to Edmonton the next day with the feeling that, though I was never enthusiastic for E-3 or its location, and I could never return to it, at least I had had a hand in its beginning.

❈ ❈ ❈

I was now able to spend a six-week furlough with my folks back home at Hearthcliff on the south shore of Lake Ontario. My priest-brother Thomas had sustained a torn Achilles tendon and was home too. While confined to a wheelchair to convalesce, he was teaching in Fallon High School in Buffalo. We managed to see each other often, but he soon mended and returned south to his mission assignment in Brazil. Late in October I joined two other Oblate delegates, Father Bill McSweeney from the U.S. and Father Don Canon from the Yukon, and together we boarded the *Constitution* at New York City for our voyage to Italy. En route we were able to go ashore and do some sightseeing in North Africa, Spain and France. Finally we were deposited safely at Naples to clear customs and continue on by train to Rome.

Once inside the huge Oblate General House we were assigned rooms and immediately joined the daily regimen of the seventy or more Oblates who lived there and directed the far-flung works of the Oblates of Mary Immaculate. The next six months saw us following a daily schedule of lectures given by various experts in their field, as well as attending the regular spiritual exercises of this religious community. We were twenty-one missionary priests from all over the world and, besides enjoying the opportunity of a lifetime to study in the Eternal City, we each had interesting background experiences to share. Various committees were formed and I was assigned to organize a weekly bus excursion to some significant landmarks.

Thus the winter passed in the Eternal City, the time divided between classes in mission theology and visits to historical sites. When the six months were up, we dispersed to our various mission fields all over the world. Father Don Canon and I teamed up and bought an aged Hillman Minx for forty-eight Canadian dollars and proceeded to tour Europe. We drove south to Naples, then east to the Adriatic, visited the famous stigmatist Padre Pio en route, spent a weekend in Venice and watched the future Pope John XXIII as he presided at Holy Thursday ceremonies in his Cathedral of St. Mark. By Easter we had passed through Milan and were in the Italian Alps trying to drive through to Switzerland, but the road was blocked with snow and we were forced to turn south again to the Mediterranean, visiting Monaco and its famous casino.

In spite of repeated flat tires and all kinds of motor problems, we rolled into Paris and immediately stalled under the Arc de Triomphe. We had to be pushed out of the circle of traffic by a friendly taxi driver. When we got to the Oblate house, we spent the weekend removing the cylinder head, putting in a new gasket and a generous amount of sealant to plug various leaks in the cooling system. With these minor repairs we were able to reach Brussels safely and see some of the World's Fair which was then in progress. Our final run was down to the seaport of Ostend, where we boarded a ferry for Dover, England. Oddly enough, we could not restart our Minx when we landed and the stevedores were obliged to push us off the boat and into British Customs. We were promptly informed that we had no proof that the purchase tax on our machine had ever been paid and $159 was now due if we wished to proceed to London. Our precious vehicle was placed in the customs garage, where we bid it a fond adieu, and proceeded to London by rail. After over 4,000 miles the Hillman had repaid us well for its purchase price and we had no regrets as we boarded the S.S. *United States* at Southampton for New York.

When I had arrived in Paris, I had received a telegram telling me that my father had died, so now I returned to Hearthcliff to find my widowed mother living alone. The bishop allowed me to spend the next two months with her, most of which time I spent under her aging house, tunnelling, jacking it up and placing it on cement piers to keep it from falling down completely. It was hot, dirty work, but it kept me from brooding over the loss our family had suffered and made me think I was doing something useful to help my mother. In June, Bishop Trocellier wrote asking me to stop off in Fort McMurray en route back to Fort Smith and temporarily replace the pastor there while he took a brief holiday. So I left home again in July and flew west to Reno where I spent a couple of days with my brother Justin and his family. Then I continued on to Edmonton, and north 235 miles to Fort McMurray.

17

THE SOUTH
OF THE NORTH

Fort McMurray was known in the early days as the "Fort of the Forks" because it was built at the junction of the Athabaska and Clearwater Rivers. These rivers had provided the early voyageurs with alternative water routes from the south which connected to the mighty Mackenzie River flowing into the Arctic Ocean. About 1920 a narrow-gauge railroad spur called the Northern Alberta Railroad – or NAR to the locals – was run up from Edmonton. It ended three miles short of the Fort, and the community that grew up around this terminus became the town of Waterways. Most of the North's freight came in by rail and was transferred to barges. This seasonal work occupied a good segment of the local population of 1,200. Both the Northern Transportation Company Limited and the Hudson Bay Company maintained warehouse facilities here as well as pull-out yards for their vessels.

The local population was a mixture of whites and Cree Indians, resulting in a high proportion of Métis. Some of them ran traplines in winter, but fur was not particularly plentiful. Moose were, however, but they were protected by the heavy bush country they occupied. A salt mine had been in operation for a number of years, but had closed down. There was a unique belt of tar sands paralleling the river for a hundred miles in this area.

This was recognized as a potential bonanza for oil if it could be successfully extracted. Up to 1958 efforts in this regard had largely failed, but they had not ceased. Some optimistic business-men kept buying up land in the area, hoping for an eventual boom.

The mission, now fifty years old, occupied seven acres in the heart of Fort McMurray and there was another small church over in Waterways. The mission was comprised of the mission house itself, with a Father and three Brothers, a twenty-five bed hospi-tal staffed by fourteen Grey Nuns, a school with six teachers, and the church proper next to the mission. Most of the land around these buildings, however, was empty.

When I got off the Canadian Pacific Airlines DC-3 at McMur-ray's airport on July 12th, I was met by the Pastor, Father Joseph Turcotte, O.M.I. He proceeded to drive me the five miles into town in a rather beat-up old panel truck which he promptly ran off the road and into a ditch. While we waited for someone to pull us back onto the road, he began reviewing for me his past ten years as head of this mission. His duties had included the positions of Administrator of the hospital, Secretary-Treasurer of the school board, and Chaplain of the Mid-Canada DEW Line station of Stoney Mountain, thirty miles to the south, as well as spiritual director or member of various religious or secular organizations. It sounded like too much for any single individ-ual; I secretly rejoiced that I was just passing through and not permanently replacing him.

This happy feeling soon evaporated when we got to the mis-sion and Father Turcotte handed me a letter from our Provincial: it contained a formal obedience to this mission. I was stunned. Of all the missions in our vast Vicariate, this one in the southern-most corner of our spiritual empire would have been the very last I would have chosen to work in. Yet there it was, in black and white, from my religious superior to whom I had bound myself by a vow of obedience. There was no turning back. I would just have to accept it and do the best I could in hopes it would not last too long. Although I tried not to let it show, deep down I was devastated.

The next day, Sunday, I got my baptism by fire when I preached at three different Masses; two at Fort McMurray and one at the military post at Stoney Mountain, to which I was taken by helicopter. On top of that, Bishop Trocellier landed out of nowhere in his Beaver aircraft, piloted by Father Bill Leising. This gave me the opportunity to sound him out on just why he had assigned me here and how long he expected me to be detained. Evidently trying to console me, he told me he was appointing me Regional Superior of other mission stations north and south of Fort McMurray. Consequently, I would have the opportunity of doing a lot of travelling. As most of the missionary priests in charge of these missions were much older than me in both age and experience, I doubted my official visits would be met with any enthusiasm. The next day the bishop flew north, while my predecessor, Father Turcotte, flew south.

This left me with the three French Brothers. I couldn't imagine three companions less sympathetic to the outlook of a brash, young, American missionary. The first was Brother Philip Latreille, whose many years in northern missions had left him partly crippled and missing an index finger. The second was Brother René Guérin, whose brand of Québecois French I had a particular difficulty in interpreting. The third was old Brother Vincent Cadoret, who was troubled with scruples and spoke to no one.

For meals we crossed over to a dingy basement dining room under the hospital, where the large table came up to our chests and we ate all the courses out of our soup bowls. The meals, especially for an American, did absolutely nothing to compensate for other privations. On top of the culture shock I felt in this strange place, nature itself seemed to conspire against me, as the humid temperature stood around a hundred degrees Fahrenheit for the first weeks and the air was choked with the smoke of forest fires burning all around us.

The various duties inherent in my new position quickly established my daily routine. With the three Brothers I rose at 5:30 a.m. Fifteen minutes later we assembled in the mission chapel for the customary morning prayers and meditation. At 6:30 we trooped across to the Sisters' chapel where I offered the morning Mass, followed by the distribution of Holy Communion to the hospital patients in their beds. On some mornings I carried Communion to sick parishioners about town, using our little red panel truck. After a breakfast of toast and coffee, I had my daily official priestly prayers, called the Office, to recite in private. I usually did so while walking up and down in the backyard. This duty done, I went to the mission's business office to spend the balance of the morning writing cheques or answering correspondence.

We four reassembled in our own little chapel at 11:15 for our customary Oblate prayers and then walked over to the hospital basement for lunch at 11:30. After lunch I looked for some kind of manual labour that would give me exercise outdoors. I found it immediately in a huge pile of gravel that needed to be spread over our roads. Ordinarily I would have relished this job, but, in the heat and smoke we were experiencing, I got worked up into a sweat. To cool down I grabbed my bathing trunks and drove down to the river for a swim. At 5 p.m. we were back in chapel for a half-hour of prayers preceding supper. Following that, I was more or less free until night prayers at 9 p.m., but I soon found out that my presence was required most evenings at 7 p.m. for various meetings, like the men's club, the Catholic Women's League, the scouts, the school board, the hospital staff meeting, the town council, and so forth. Never in my previous ten years in the North had I been committed to such a full daily schedule. I wondered to myself how long I could cope with it.

The following week I found a valid excuse to get away for a two-day break when I was asked to visit the small community of Fort McKay, forty miles down river. Father Raymond Danto came into town from his post at Chipewyan Prairie to replace me while I was away. Fort McKay had a resident priest in the person of Father Georges Bégin, but he was back in Quebec for the summer on vacation. A Shell Oil Beaver aircraft on floats dropped me off there and I picked up the key to the mission from the school teacher, Miss Margaret Poirier. The first thing I did was to get the thirty-two-volt generator going and start recharging the batteries. Then I cleaned the mice nests out of the vestment drawers and swept out the cobwebs. With the mission house more or less in order, I walked around the village with some of the children, visiting every log cabin and tent informing the natives that, when I rang the bell that evening, it would be for rosary and confessions. The chapel was filled that evening and I ended up hearing some forty-five confessions, some of them in the Chipewyan dialect. Following these religious duties I walked over to the Hudson Bay Company residence and had an interesting visit with the resident manager, Jim Figney. I walked back to the mission at midnight; the settlement had gone to sleep and the only sound to be heard was the howling of a solitary sled-dog. The full moon reflecting off the roofs looked like frost. I tried to remember when I had last been in the midst of such utter tranquillity – perhaps at Aklavik. Following the well-attended Mass the next morning, the teacher treated me to a fine breakfast. Then the Bay manager took me out to a passing barge, the *Radium Miner*, skippered by Billy Bird. I arrived back at Fort McMurray at 8 p.m. after a fine day on the Athabaska River.

Following this visit to one of my outpost stations I got the opportunity to see another the following Sunday when I was flown by chopper to Stoney Mountain to conduct the regular Sunday service there. One of the officers drove me west eleven miles on a gravel road to visit the town of Anzac, built along the NAR tracks. Father Turcotte had bought a log cabin there recently which had been owned and occupied by a retired member of the RCMP by the name of John Waring. I found this picturesque cabin nestled below a stand of huge spruce. It had been locked and left undisturbed since its sole occupant had died suddenly of a heart attack the previous September. It was as neat as a pin and furnished with many carefully crafted, homemade household items that indicated a man who had the time and talent to equip his home with the various items he needed to live comfortably in the bush. It was evident, too, that he was an amateur artist. One of the items I picked up and kept was a maulstick made from a riding crop which he no doubt had been issued in the force when he attended their riding school in Regina. A small log warehouse contained a complete set of tools. Later, when I began visiting Anzac regularly, this cabin became my overnight headquarters while I ministered to the seventy-five Cree and Chipewyan Indians living in the community.

My twin roles as Chaplain and Administrator of St. Gabriel's Hospital put me in daily contact with our two doctors, our many Sisters who operated it, and the twenty-odd patients who regularly occupied its beds. I not only made myself available for any spiritual help I could give these patients, but I was anxious to pick up any medical knowledge I could with an eye to the future when I would again find myself in some isolated northern community in charge of their medical as well as spiritual welfare. I got a good firsthand lesson in delivery when a fifteen-year-old girl from Anzac gave birth in our operating room. Dr. McDonald was the physician-in-charge, while I stood at his side in white coat and mask and Sisters Bourgeois and Coté supplied the various instruments as they were called for. The poor girl was in pain and literally pinned down, with her arms buckled in straps at her sides and her legs tied in stirrups. Her bare stomach was grotesquely distended, with blue veins indicating the strain it was under.

The doctor put white pant legs on her and then disinfected her perineum, which had previously been shaved by the Sisters. The doctor ordered 1 cc of the drug pituitin, which he told me would strengthen the muscle action of her womb, and had the two Sisters on either side of her pushing down on her abdomen. They placed a mask saturated with some kind of anaesthetic over her face at the peak of each contraction. The doctor kept up a steady patter of encouraging words, until finally we could see a little of the baby's hair emerging. This happened after he had punctured the amniotic sac and let the fluid run out. This surprised me, as I had heard about the difficulty of a "dry birth." As this young mother was evidently having difficulty expelling the head of her first child, the doctor took his scissors and cut into the right side of the extended labia majora. The girl let out a scream.

Dr. McDonald explained to me that this procedure is called episiotomy and is done to prevent a tear occurring back toward the rectum. It wasn't long after this incision that the head of the newborn appeared completely, face down. The next contraction turned it on its side and then it slipped out easily in a rush of blood and fluid. Next the doctor took a large syringe and sucked out some fluid from its mouth so that it could breathe freely. He cautioned me not to cut the umbilical cord until the pulse coursing through it became feeble. Three minutes later he tied this cord securely with stout twine on the outside and a clamp an inch or so toward the mother's body. Then he cut between the two points. A child is not officially born, he said, until the umbilical cord is severed.

Now that the newborn baby was safely in the capable hands of the Sisters, the doctor proceeded to sew up the cut he had made with four quick stitches, but he did not tie them. The patient had first to expel the placenta. He helped her do this by pulling on the cord while pushing above the womb with his other hand. After fifteen minutes it was out. He examined it carefully to make sure that no part of it had remained in the womb. Then he tied the four stitches he had put in and explained that, if he had tied them immediately, the expulsion of the placenta could have torn them out. He felt her womb and had me feel it too. It was hard; that was a good sign, he said. He took her pulse and said that it was nearly back to normal. So she was untied and led back to bed. The baby was a girl weighing eight pounds, two ounces. I left, completely exhausted, though I hadn't done a bit of work. I did come away from that delivery room, however, with a lasting respect for all mothers for the pain they endure to produce new life. And many of the lessons I learned that day were to stand me in good stead when in later years I presided at other deliveries alone.

✻ ✻ ✻

As the summer wore on, the heat gradually dissipated and one heavy rain put out most of the forest fires. We played host to a steady stream of missionaries, both male and female, travelling north and south through McMurray. Some of them were real characters. Father Danto, for example, rode a bicycle while dressed in a Prince Albert swallow-tailed coat over a pair of heavy lumberman's pants; his feet were in moccasins, his head in a beret, and his luxurious beard was flowing in the breeze. Even Philip Stenne came in from Camsell Portage with his wife, Mary, and spent a few days. He brought me one of my white sled-dogs; I had in mind to build up a new team and I had asked that one of my females be sent down from Aklavik as well. When I talked about having a dog-team at McMurray people told me that I would have a tough time feeding them, because there were no fish in the rivers. Undaunted, I went over to the McInnes Fish Company dock at Waterways, where my old friend Bill McPete gave me one of their old nets. I repaired a decrepit skiff I found in the mission yard. Taking Brother Vincent with me, I set the net in the water off the island at the junction of the Clearwater and Athabaska Rivers. The next day we found all kinds of debris in it, but only seven whitefish, so we pulled it out and reset it in the first eddy we could find up the Athabaska. On our next visit we realized that we had hit the jackpot: our gill net was full of white-fish. It continued that way till freeze-up. I built a smokehouse and soon found myself selling smoked fish to the Indians! Not one had a net in the water and everyone seemed surprised to learn that all these fish had been going right by their door without them knowing it. I took over 3,000 fish that fall. When the bitch arrived from Aklavik aboard CPA, I had no worries about feeding a new team of sled-dogs.

Any one of the several jobs I was doing could have kept me busy. One of the most demanding was that of secretary-treasurer of St. John's School. There were 210 children enrolled, with eight teachers, three of whom were Grey Nuns. Our budget of $21,000 per year just couldn't cover our expenses, so we were constantly strapped for funds and devising ways of raising more money. We maintained three teacherages; when the teachers came back for school in early September with a car, they prevailed upon the school board to put up a garage for them. I ended up pouring the cement foundation. Then I had to represent our board at a three-day meeting of the Alberta School Trustees Association in Edmonton. Next I had to agree to teach catechism daily to the senior classes. While I was in Edmonton I visited government offices to request a grant to cover art supplies for a dozen students. When this grant came through, I bought easels and paints and began teaching art to a dozen students who showed talent in this field. I didn't have time to do any painting on my own, though I would have liked to, but this class forced me to keep my hand in it at least one afternoon a week.

We had been using the old wooden wall-mounted telephones that you crank. They were connected around town, but not beyond. The Alberta Government Telephone Company installed the modern dial phones at this time and we were suddenly connected to the outside world. I could telephone my mother on Lake Ontario and even my younger brother Thomas at his mission in Brazil. To celebrate this historic event, a banquet was given at the Waterways Community Hall and I was invited to say the grace before meals. It was mid-November and the temperature was down around zero, so the wood-burning barrel heater was red hot. My place at the head of the long table was the closest to the fire, so my backside got scorched and I had to excuse myself early.

I was telling the Brothers that Waterways was one hot spot, when we heard the volunteer fire department roaring in that direction. We learned later that their theatre, as well as the home of a Mrs. Laboucan next door, burned to the ground.

A telegram on the 27th of November announced the sudden death of Bishop Joseph Trocellier, our spiritual head. I was on hand a few days later for his funeral in Fort Smith, carrying my 16mm camera to record this solemn occasion. As he was lowered into the earth, the outside temperature hovered at thirty-five below zero. This man of God had been directly responsible for all my movements during the past decade and I had always found him a sympathetic and caring spiritual father. His passing marked the end of an era in the Mackenzie Vicariate and I, for one, would sincerely miss him. Although the occasion itself was sad, it had a happy side-effect in bringing together twenty-six of us missionaries, many of whom hadn't seen each other for years. I managed to detour on my return to Fort McMurray, spending nights at Fort Chipewyan, Camsell Portage and Uranium City. I also dropped in at the abattoir at Claire Lake, where the wardens had just dispatched 270 Wood Park buffalo. After an absence of ten days I arrived back at my mission to find my desk piled high with mail.

It was now mid-December and time to get my 500 Christmas cards out. Several seniors from school helped by addressing envelopes, while Brother Guérin and I took the stake truck out of town to find a suitable tree to erect in front of the church. With the aid of a winch we were able to bring back a thirty-five-foot spruce that must have weighed close to a ton. It wasn't easy, but when we finally got it up and illuminated with forty blue lights, we felt our efforts were well worth it. We had anticipated such a large crowd for the Christmas Midnight Mass that we held it in the school auditorium. We were not disappointed, as over 300 attended. It was nearly four in the morning before we finished and I had all the nuns over to the mission for hot buttered rum! The following evening I drove all the Brothers to the local cinema to see the movie *The Man Who Made a Bargain with God*, starring Walter Brennan. The next day I took both the Sisters and Brothers downriver five miles on the ice road using the panel truck. We proceeded to make a huge fire of driftwood and have a winter picnic. I capped my year's activities on December 30th by presenting a slide show to the public in the school auditorium. I entitled it "The Arctic in Colour."

We began the New Year, 1959, at midnight in the Sisters' chapel with a special Mass for our religious community, asking God's blessing on the year just beginning. Later that day I walked about town, trying to visit as many families as I could to wish them a Happy New Year. What a year it soon became, weather-wise, with snow, high winds and sub-zero temperatures! On the 5th the thermometer stood at fifty-below. The snow in the school yard was so deep and hard that I proceeded to build the kids a genuine igloo, something they had never seen before in McMurray. Once it was up it became a real curiosity and a great play-house until it melted months later.

It hadn't taken me long after arriving in McMurray to realize that too many of the parents had little time to devote to their children; that is, they didn't make time, being preoccupied with their own amusements, especially in the local beer hall. As a result, too many of their children, especially the boys, were left on their own and were getting into trouble. I felt that the boy scout movement might help in this situation, so in November I revived the defunct Fort McMurray boy scout troop. I got two of the teachers and two laymen to agree to help and we soon had twenty-eight senior scouts and thirty-eight cubs registered. This led to regular indoor meetings in the school auditorium, but also to winter camp outs. In spite of the cold I started taking twenty-four scouts at a time out ten or fifteen miles on the back roads on Friday afternoons using our big flat deck truck. We'd pitch a large tent for the night and come back to town the next day. Sometimes I got one of the male teachers to go with us, but, if one wasn't available, I would take them myself.

Two of the younger, more adventurous Sisters prevailed on me to give them driving lessons. I had no trouble in getting them licensed, but they ran into a snag with their own Provincial, who balked at giving them permission to use those licences. (They should have cleared this with her before approaching me.) They had received a small English car from one of our parishioners and eventually did get permission to use it. This greatly reduced my own driving around town. Though I often had some difficulty in expressing myself in French, the nuns had me over in their chapel once a week, giving them a conference in their language, and this was another new experience for me.

❄ ❄ ❄

The parameters of my activities were constantly expanding, but most of my activities themselves were fairly predictable. Then, once in a while, the unusual would come along, affording a welcome relief. An example of this was a phone call I got one morning from the sales manager of the Sealy Posturepedic Mattress Company in Toronto. He asked if I would cooperate in an advertising stunt they wanted to film for television, involving the delivery of one of their mattresses by dog-team. He wanted to know if I knew of some worthy family living out of town, to whom they could deliver a new mattress by dog-team. I couldn't actually think of a family, but I knew a half-breed trapper by the name of Joe who was up in years, lived with his girlfriend, and trapped from a log cabin about five miles west, past Horse Creek. He would fill the bill, declared the sales manager. Now, did I have a dog-team? Not yet, I had to admit, but I could hire one. So the stage was set for one of the most entertaining, if dubious, little schemes I ever participated in.

About a month later the sales manager appeared with two photographers. We picked up a local trapper with his sled and four dogs and loaded everything on the mission truck. I drove them to Waterways, where they filmed a huge, king-size mattress, with the name Sealy painted across it in huge letters, as it was lowered from a freight train into the waiting dogsled. With the film rolling, the driver snapped his whip and his huge load moved ahead a hundred feet and stopped. We loaded the truck again with everything, including the gift mattress, and drove out of town to Joe's cabin.

Luckily he was home. I stopped 200 yards short of our destination so that the mattress could again be loaded in the dogsled and the movie cameras positioned for the final delivery scene.

That accomplished, the sales-manager-turned-director met Joe and companion and instructed them to break up their home-made wooden bed and throw the pieces out the cabin door. This done, the driver pushed the new mattress through the door and had Joe help him screw four legs into it. "Now, Joe," said the director, "you and your wife jump up and down on the side of the new bed and smile." The two of them did this like real pros, while the cameras rolled – no need for a retake; it was all "in the can" the first time.

To this point, it all looked to me like a grand but simple gesture of largesse on the part of the mattress company, but then the sales manager pulled out a letter scribbled roughly in pencil and asked Joe to sign it. I might not have been allowed to see just what was written on that paper, had Joe not refused to sign it until I had checked it out. What I read went something like this: "Dear Sir, I am a poor trapper living with my wife out in the wilds of Northern Canada. We don't enjoy many pleasures in life, but I have always dreamed of sleeping on a king-size Sealy Posturepedic Mattress and wonder if you could deliver one up here by dog-team? We would be eternally grateful." Signed, "Joe."

This letter had most likely been written at a sales convention in Chicago and was completely phoney. In any case, I got a gift sleeping bag out of it for my cooperation, the dog-driver got twenty dollars, and Joe got the mattress, so I guess everyone was happy.

❆ ❆ ❆

The month of March came in like a lion in the person of the travelling missionary, Father J. A. Clermont of the Redemptorist Order. I had heard of his success in preaching "missions" at Yellowknife and Uranium City, so I invited him to preach one in McMurray. We had a schedule printed well ahead of time: first a week for the women, and then a week for the men. The turnout morning and evening at the church was truly unusual. The abil-

ity of this man to rouse and motivate a congregation was remarkable. I stood in the rear, listening with some envy to his delivery
and observing the effect it was having on my parishioners. After
his sermon, "The Last Judgement," one evening, a woman hurried up to me asking, "Where's the confessional?" I had local carpenter Mike Ponte make a twelve-foot cross from solid oak; at the
end of the two-week mission we marked this historic event by
raising it in front of the church.

Little by little, I was acquiring the means to become more
mobile both summer and winter. Linda, the bitch sent down
from Aklavik, gave birth to a litter of pups, so I looked forward
again to having a dog-team. Northern Transportation Co. Ltd.,
which damaged a nice twenty-two-foot Peterborough canoe destined for the Mounties in Spence Bay, sold it to me for $355. I
repaired the bow and soon had it in A-1 shape, ready for the
water. I was also making myself a new pair of snowshoes. Work
permitting, I sometimes got away to the bush to hunt spruce
grouse or rabbits.

Once, when the snow had started melting, I came across the
tracks of a black bear just out of hibernation. I mentioned this to
Swan Pederson, an old trapper, and he told me of an encounter
with such a bear that almost killed him. He was on his trapline
down river, driving his dog-team with his Chipewyan wife in the
cariole, when he came across a bear just out of hibernation. The
bear circled them menacingly, so Swan started shooting at it with
his .30-.30. He emptied his gun without hitting it. The bear
charged, backing Swan against a tree. It raked his face with one
paw, breaking his jaw and knocking him to the ground. Swan
was yelling to his wife for help, but she fainted right in the sled.
Luckily, the bear didn't take advantage of his blinded victim; it
could have killed him right there. As it was, it left him with a
badly disfigured face.

George Sanderson was another local trapper who survived a
run-in with a black bear. George had lost a leg when he was mistaken for a deer in the bush and was shot by another hunter. Now
he had a wooden leg, to which he had ingeniously fitted a special

snowshoe so he could continue trapping in winter. One spring day he was walking on an old logging road, a half-mile west of the settlement, when he came upon a black bear which he wounded. When he was out of shells the bear charged him. George broke his rifle barrel over its head, just as it hit him and broke his wooden leg. George limped back to town very slowly on his shattered stump and I went out with our truck and picked up a dead bear. George was another lucky trapper.

May 8th is the yearly feast day chosen for the Superior of the Mission of Fort McMurray, so I was feted that evening at a special play put on by the children on the school stage. It turned out to be the story of my life, from the marriage of my parents to my ordination, presented in a series of vignettes and all in authentic costumes! The good Sisters who researched this bit of history and so skilfully coached the children deserved a lot of credit. I sat there transfixed, as my own life unfolded before my astonished eyes. At its conclusion I was presented with a gift of $200. The least I could do in my thank-you speech was to declare a school holiday. Surprises like this went a long way to easing the pain I still felt on not returning to the North.

I always wanted to be a catskinner and Hector Demers lent me a TD-9 to practise with. I started by moving some buildings around. These included a small shack which I spotted at the snye, an offshoot of the Clearwater River. I decided to use it as my boathouse. Then I levelled the lawn in front of the convent so that we could plant grass on it.

On the day I had arrived in Fort McMurray, Father Turcotte planted the seed for an ambitious project that would require these heavy machines. He had driven me on a tour of the town and pointed out the Old Mission that had been built in 1911, but was long since abandoned. In fact, the land on which it now stood didn't belong to us, so he sold the mission building for ten dollars for firewood. I immediately recognized its historical importance and subsequently tried to buy it back, even offering the new owner far more than he had paid for it. He refused every offer, however, because he anticipated that it would greatly increase the value of his property if ever a bridge were built at this spot to span the Athabaska River. My plan to recover and renovate the Old Mission was delayed a year until I found another building of equal size and value and could move it to his property in exchange.

I borrowed Hector's TD-9 one day, clattered out of town on the Abasand Road, and skidded back two fifty-foot spruce trees. From these I built the huge skid I would need. Brother Guérin and René Theriault strengthened the old building with lumber and jacked it up. I got the Northern Transportation Company Limited (NTCL) to donate two International TD-18 cats for the actual move and on the 5th of June we got it under way. We progressed down McMurray's dirt main street, Franklin Avenue, successfully passing under some intervening wires. We reached an impasse, however, when we got to the Mackenzie Hotel. I knew that the peak of the old mission roof was twenty-four feet above the road surface and that the telephone wires blocking our way were only eighteen feet above it. I had asked the Alberta Government Telephone Company in Edmonton if they would send up a crew to lift them until we passed. When they had quoted me $1,000 a day, however, I had realized that I would have to think of another solution.

My plan was to stop in front of the hotel and go in and ask the owner, Mr. Jack Wagner, for permission to dig down six feet in his parking lot next to his building. When I got there, I found out that he was indisposed and asleep, so I gave the order to my two cat-skinners to dig a hundred-foot-long trench, which they did in no time. The green skids I had made bent alarmingly under the huge load of the Old Mission as it was pulled down into that six-foot trench. Still, they held: we got in and out of our ditch and past the telephone lines. I had the men fill in our hole immediately, before Jack woke up and saw it. Then we continued on to the lot that I had designated behind our church. The whole move was accomplished successfully in less than two hours. I congratulated my crew and had our picture taken in front of the rescued old log building. The hardest part of our project had been completed.

Just as soon as the ice went out in early June, I got my new freighter canoe in the water, powered by a new, twenty-horse-power Scott outboard motor. We got word that we had a new bishop in the person of the Most Reverend Paul Piché, O.M.I. He was consecrated in his hometown of Gravelbourg, Saskatchewan, and would be officially installed the following week at our headquarters in Fort Smith as the Bishop of the Mackenzie Vicariate. We could have flown down, but Brother Philip and I decided that this would be a great trip in the canoe and give us a splendid opportunity to see the country in between. The first day on the Athabaska River we got three-quarters of the way down to Lake Athabaska.

We camped there with Andrew Dahl, an old trapper. He told us about a trip he had made to Edmonton after staying in the bush for forty years. I asked him if he had noticed many changes in Edmonton. He replied, "The main thing, all the horses were gone!" Andrew had attached a peeled spruce branch to the front of his cabin to act as accurate barometer. It would bend with changes in atmospheric pressure, giving one a good idea of the approaching weather. Unfortunately, Brother and I didn't get a good first night's sleep on this trip. For one thing, there were no spare bunks, so we had to sleep on the cabin floor. For another, Andrew's three sled-dogs ran loose at night and tangled with a porcupine, which drove them so mad that they jumped right through the window above our heads, showering us with glass.

Before reaching Lake Athabaska, we stopped at the McInnes Fish Camp, where Philip Stenne was employed netting pickerel and his wife, Mary, was working in the cookhouse. We got a good meal under our belts before crossing the west end of the lake; the seas there were running high before an east wind. We were soaking wet when we landed at the mission dock at Fort Chipewyan and just in time to help celebrate Brother Louis Crenn's sixtieth anniversary at this mission. The remarkable thing about his tenure at this post was that he had never returned to his native France and had never even taken a vacation during those sixty years. The next day Brother Philip and I had an easy run down the Slave River to Fort Fitzgerald, where we were met by his two biological brothers, Henri and Médard. They took us over the sixteen-mile portage to Fort Smith in the mission truck and we joined the crowd of fellow missionaries gathered to meet and welcome the new bishop.

Accommodations being scarce, I was billeted in the morgue. Fortunately it was otherwise empty. As soon as I got my gear in this small frame cabin, I took my 16mm movie camera and walked over to St. Joseph's Cathedral, which they were still building. It was huge, considering the size of the town it would serve, and built mainly of poured concrete. There were all kinds of events taking place during the next few days, including a Solemn High Mass with sermons, confirmations, a banquet and the annual departure of the mission supply boat *Sant'Anna* for the Arctic missions. While Brother Philip returned by aircraft, I went back alone with the canoe.

As I made my way upstream, following the eddies along the banks to avoid the fast water, I was surprised to see so many mallard ducks sitting along the banks, all of them drakes. By the time I stopped at Bill Moore's cabin at the mouth of the Peace River I had bagged six. Bill himself was away for the summer, working at a sawmill, and his family was in dire straits. His wife explained that the children had adopted a bear cub that spring. It became such a family pet it slept inside the cabin with them. One day, when they were away picking berries, the bear got into their kitchen cabinet and either ate or wrecked all their grub. So, naturally, I gave them my ducks. As I came into Fort Chipewyan that evening I noticed I was being followed by the local Game Warden, Bob McArthur, in a speedboat. As I pulled into the mission dock, he pulled up alongside and asked if he could check my boat. Noticing the feathers stuck to the motor, (I had been plucking the ducks as I went), he asked me if I had any birds and I told him no. I had given them all to the Moore family. He told me I was lucky, because they were out of season: if he had found just one, he would have had to impound my boat and fine me $300! Charity pays.

The next day I turned east along the north shore of Lake Athabaska and that evening I was back inside my old Mission St. Bernard at Camsell Portage. Hardly anyone had visited it during the past four years since I had left and it was showing alarming deterioration. After the care I had given it during the previous four years, I now decided to spend a week here and make it ship-shape. Most of the Cree inhabitants were away for the summer at fish camps, but enough remained to help me with the work. Because the sand which had been banked around the building for warmth held moisture, the lower logs were starting to rot. I had the boys shovel it away, while the men helped me to replace four broken windows. One day I took the canoe over to Gunnar Mine at Crackingstone Point, thirty miles east, where the manager, Foss Irwin, supplied me with paint, boiled linseed oil and various other items I needed for repairs. We re-tarred the roof where it was leaking, refitted doors that were stuck, re-varnished all the logs and re-painted the white trim, while the women cleaned the mice out of the drawers and washed the bedding. When I left on the 1st of July the mission was looking almost as good as it did when I left in 1955.

At one time there was a priest resident in the rectory next to St. Peter's Church in Waterways, three miles from Fort McMurray. When I arrived, the rectory had been rented to a family and the church boarded up. We sent the school bus there every Sunday to bring the faithful over to McMurray for Mass. I decided to re-open this church and sent a crew of carpenters over there to jack it up and put it on a cement foundation. They were followed by the Sisters, who did a thorough cleaning. On July 5th I officially re-opened St. Peter's by celebrating a 9 a.m. Sunday Mass there. About the same time I was able to purchase from Crown Assets Disposal Corporation a surplus building situated up at the military base on Stoney Mountain. I skidded it down the fourteen miles to Anzac, where I had leased a lot in the centre of the village. We sent a crew of carpenters over by truck to put it on a good foundation and convert it to a church. Subsequently I opened it under the title of Saint Claire. I also obtained for my scouts from the Crown Assets Disposal Corporation four tents measuring twelve by eighteen feet.

I was having so much success bidding on surplus material in the area with Crown Assets that I decided to put in a bid on sixteen general purpose buildings at Stoney Mountain. They measured sixteen feet by eighty-four feet each. They were bolted together in four-foot by eight-foot sections, making their removal easy. Before I tendered my bid I conferred with two local businessmen, Hector Demers and Alec McIver, who were also interested in them. They agreed not to bid against me, if I would resell them half at the same price I paid. I was successful in getting all sixteen for about $150 each, a real gift. This material enabled me to put up many buildings that we needed, like a carpentry shop, a garage, an extension to the hospital laundry, and an apartment for the girls working at the hospital. In the same deal I got two walk-in freezers for the hospital at $250 each.

The sight of the mission's seven acres of unoccupied land all around it growing nothing but weeds got me searching for some constructive use for it. When I found an old potato digger out behind the garage my mind was made up. With the help of the Brothers I planted the whole thing in potatoes. This summer was not as hot as the previous one, so we didn't need any artificial irrigation for our fields of green. Brother Philip on his rubber-tired tractor kept the potatoes weeded and hilled. Early in September I hired two dozen men to help with the harvest: not to dig them, because we had the digger, but to scrape the mud off them and put them in hundred-pound bags. When we finished, we had a harvest of 500 bags. Now began the job of selling them, for we had far more than we could use, despite the fact that we were feeding over fifty people daily. I was asking four dollars a bag, but learned that the big commercial farmers to the south were selling theirs for only three. Moreover, theirs were washed and graded for size, operations for which we were not equipped. I ended up selling about half of them. We built bins in the cellar of the mission for the rest, but the following spring we had to consign most of these to the dump. That ended my experiment with potatoes.

The following year I put all the fields into alfalfa. I needed this crop because I now kept a horse. On one of my trips to Fort McKay I had noticed a colt with the horses that the natives let run loose around the settlement; when the owner told me I could have it for fifteen dollars, I bought it on the spot. The colt put up some resistance while I tied its legs securely and put it into my canoe. Some pessimistic bystanders predicted that I wouldn't get it back to McMurray without wrecking my fragile craft, but, thank God, I did. We named him "Tonka" and he became a great hit with the scouts.

There was no end to the visitors that kept coming into Fort McMurray and some of them were bona fide VIP's, like my old friend Frank Broderick, head of the Northern Transportation Company, and another old friend from Aklavik, Inspector Bill Fraser of the RCMP. Fraser brought with him the Commissioner of the Force, Carnac-Rivet, whose book I had read. Then there was the constant stream of Oblate missionaries, like Fathers Pat Mercredi and Napoleon Lafferty, the two native priests in the Vicariate. Last, but not least, I had the pleasure of hosting both my mother and my brother Justin, with his wife and two girls. As usual, I delegated the regular religious ceremonies to the visiting clergy so that I could get away with my brother and family for a two-night camping trip up the Clearwater River. We put up a typical Indian teepee and spent two glorious evenings by the fire in front of it, singing to the music of the guitar.

Following this outing, Justin had to return to his gas station in Reno, Nevada, but Mother stayed on for a month. I had to leave her for a couple of nights when I flew down to Uranium City to buy a second school bus. When our school opened, I had succeeded in hiring six new teachers and I resumed teaching religion to grades seven, eight and nine. The new bus arrived on a Northern Transportation Company barge, along with a fine white lead-dog from Philip. The work of putting the old mission on a firm cement foundation was completed. I hired a bricklayer to put up a chimney while I built a steeple on its roof. Father Bill Leising flew our new bishop in for his first official visit. On Sunday he preached at a High Mass and later confirmed forty youngsters. I took a good opportunity to talk with him privately in the evening about my wish to return to the northern missions and he promised to replace me here just as soon as he located someone suitable. The next day I took him down to Fort McKay in the canoe, where he had a further twelve confirmations. Once he was gone, I made plans to get away for a week to hunt geese around the Athabaska delta at the lake. We were into the late fall now, so, to protect myself from the weather in that open canoe, I built a deck and windshield up forward with a proper steering wheel and controls.

Philip came from Camsell Portage in the skiff and met me on the Athabaska River near Reed's Store. We camped a night there and then continued on down into the delta, towing his boat and shooting ducks as we went. At Moose Point on the south shore of Lake Athabaska we again set up camp, built two blinds and spent the week alternately talking and shooting geese. What a change of pace from my ordinary routine at McMurray and how I wished I could return to Camsell Portage. Finally, however, we broke camp and headed in opposite directions. I was thankful for the windshield as I headed up river through rain that turned to snow.

Back at the mission at McMurray I resumed my hectic schedule: going from my office desk where I might have been making out payroll cheques, then running out to the nets, hurrying back for a baptism, and then attending another meeting. There was no end to it. The Mounties phoned me in the evening and asked me to accompany them to Waterways and to bring my camera and flash. We went to the McDonald home, where we found the body of fifteen-year-old Josephine lying on the floor in a pool of blood. Her parents had gone out to a drinking party and left their daughter home with a younger brother. We learned later that these two began playing a game of cowboys and Indians using the father's loaded guns, she with a .22 and he with a .30-.30. The boy accidentally discharged his gun, hitting his sister in the lower jaw. We found her teeth scattered all over the room. She had quickly bled to death, while the boy bolted out the door and headed for the bush, where he hid for two days. I took the photos the police wanted and we brought her body back to our morgue. This was just another in a series of violent deaths around town. Josephine had been one of our students.

Armand Phaneuf had been a faithful janitor at our school for years. A quiet, conscientious man, his life could have been serene except for the fact that he had several teenage daughters who were involved in the love affairs common to their age. One of them had a son by a boy from Lac La Biche and the town police brought him to my office, telling me that either he marry the girl or he would face a jail term. I talked to both of them and they appeared quite willing to marry, nor were there any church impediments, so I witnessed their marriage in a private ceremony. Shortly afterwards Armand moved his family to the small hamlet of Anzac, thirty miles south, where he hoped life would be simple and quiet. The new son-in-law drank heavily, however; his young wife was worried about the reckless way he handled their son when he was drunk, so they split up and the girl joined her family in Anzac. At 3 a.m. one Sunday morning the boy showed up drunk at their locked cabin door, demanding to see his son. They wouldn't open up. The boy wouldn't go away. Armand, thinking to scare him off, poked a .22 rifle out a window and shot in his general direction. The bullet hit the boy in the heart. He staggered back into the bush fifty feet from the house, dropped to his knees and set a partially consumed bottle of beer in front of him in the snow. Passers-by that night heard him groaning, but, thinking he was merely drunk, they didn't go near him. In the morning he was found dead and frozen. Armand was kept in the McMurray jail overnight for questioning, but later released and no charges were laid. The father of the boy came up from Lac La Biche for the funeral and told me he harboured no ill feelings against the killer. Yet I couldn't help thinking that I might have saved the boy's life if I had refused to marry him.

One of the most satisfying things I did in the New Year, 1960, was to resume driving my own team of dogs. I had only four that were big enough for harness, but they could pull me around in the new sled I had made. With their help I was soon getting out into moose country. It wasn't long before I bagged one and used the team to pull the meat out of the bush. Now when I walked around town, visiting the natives, I could carry with me a chunk of meat to make my visits more palatable! Once I had the dogs working, I tried to steal time every afternoon to take them even for a short run.

One of my regular stops was at the trapping cabin of Dmitri Salin across the Athabaska River. Although "Dim" had a fine wife and children living in town, he preferred to tough it out alone, living with his team of horses a mile away across the river in his small log cabin. He had a colourful past in Russia and hated to give in to the insipid demands of civilization. In spite of his solitary ways and humble abode I enjoyed my visits to him and learned to like his home-made caviar and fresh lemon in my tea. He was a superb cook. He taught me how to make excellent bannock and how important bay leaves are in the cooking of white fish. He also proved conclusively to me the superiority of meat over fish in raising a dog. I gave him one of my pups, which he fed on the carcasses of squirrels he had snared, while I fed the others of the litter on fish. His turned out to be six inches taller and much heavier.

The Richfield Oil Corporation was developing a tar sands extraction plant at Mildred Lake below Fort McKay and we saw all kinds of heavy equipment going north down the main drag in front of the mission while the ground was still frozen. Once they got across the ice of the Athabaska River, they had to cross right by Dim's cabin, through his registered trapping area. Seeing an opportunity to extract a modest price for this trespass, Dim levied a small toll on each vehicle. At first they thought it was a joke, but when Dim started stopping trucks and cats with a loaded rifle, the oil company was forced to capitulate. An independent trapper was successful in taking on a huge corporation and the townsfolk of Fort McMurray applauded.

Closer to home I was waging my own war against an aging and inefficient kitchen under the hospital and against a church whose walls were ominously out of line and whose roof was sagging. I had my crew knock down a couple of walls in the kitchen, completely remodel it, and install good fluorescent lighting. On top of that, I got the Grey Nuns to bring in an excellent cook in the person of Sister Claire Hamelin. That finished, I had them build a huge scaffold in the church, bring the side walls back into line, and put in a new ceiling. While they were in there, I had them rebuild the altar, the altar rail, the side altars and the cupboards and vestment cases in the sacristy. When we were finished, the interior looked like a new church.

During this period we did not neglect the complete renovation of the Old Mission which we had moved. I had found only one window sash left in it, but from that pattern I was able to get an Edmonton sash and door company to manufacture a complete set of new windows. We tore off the old shingles and put down a good roof of cedar shakes. We scraped all the old paint off the interior and varnished it, put down an old-style pegged floor, built new stairs to the second floor and built an altar, which we separated from the main room with folding doors. When Ash Wednesday rolled around in March, it was ready for a religious service and over seventy attended. Only the very old-timers could remember when it had been last used as a church, but they loved its atmosphere. I continued conducting services here all during Lent while the main church was under repairs.

I never seemed to run out of ideas for new buildings and improvements. It seemed to me that our devoted Sisters would appreciate having a log cabin in a secluded area in the heavy timber on our property near the grotto. I drew up a preliminary plan, gave Bill Malcolm a contract to cut fifty good logs for two dollars apiece, and this project was under way. I had to fly to Edmonton to interview prospective teachers at the University of Alberta for the coming year. While there, I saw an orthopaedic surgeon about my back: I had injured it in the spring and the pain had not gone away. He gave me instructions on exercises to strengthen my back and pills to kill the pain. I bought a saddle and tack for our growing colt Tonka and visited the Hayward Lumber Yard to pick out some nice wood with which to finish the interior of the church.

Although the ice started moving on the Athabaska River on the 18th of April, it was three weeks later that I attempted to reset my net there. Even then I had to give up, for there was still too much small ice coming down. Since I was the first of the locals with a boat in the water, the Mounties asked me if I would take them down river forty miles near Bitumont, where trapper John McDonald had reported seeing a body washed up on the shore. We found it without any difficulty and the police proceeded to pour quicklime on it before putting it in a canvas bag. Our trip back up river through floating ice and drift logs became a little hectic when we ran out of daylight. Sheer luck prevented us from damaging the canoe or shearing a pin on the kicker, and we made it. The body was sent out to Edmonton for autopsy and the results were interesting. It was that of an adult male and had evidently been in the water all winter. In his one clenched fist they found the index finger of another person! The Mounties concluded that two men had fallen into the river up around Athabaska Landing and drowned, either clutching each other for support or in mortal combat. When the bodies began to disintegrate one was left with the other's finger. As far as I know they never found out who they were or where they came from.

In early June I was invited to attend the consecration of the newly built St. Joseph's Cathedral at Fort Smith. So I took one of the Canadian Air Force boys from the Stoney Mountain Mid-Canada Line and went down to Fort Chipewyan in the canoe, now powered with a forty-three-horsepower Scott motor. There we joined the mission crew of the St. Eugene diesel tug and went on down the Slave River to Fort Smith. I put all the ceremonies here on 16mm colour film. Back at Chip we two continued on with my canoe to Camsell Portage, where I found twenty people and the mission in good order. No one had used it since the previous summer when I was there. Besides holding the regular religious ceremonies daily, I went up the lake with Philip Stenne, shot some geese, and put on a big supper for all the inhabitants at the mission. As I was there for ten days, I decided to visit my old friend Father Gamache at Fond du Lac, stopping en route at Gunnar Mine where my mail had been forwarded. Luckily Gilbert LaBine and his two daughters, Lillian and Helen, happened to be visiting their uranium mine with its adjacent refinery; I got to take them all out fishing for lake trout. The mine manager, Foss Irwin, noticing that I smoked a pipe, gave me a Brigham made in Toronto. From then on I never smoked any other brand. The Air Force man, Jacques, and I took every opportunity on this trip to get some good photos. At Fond du Lac I used my Rolleicord and a flash to take one of an old Chipewyan woman in a tent smoking her pipe. It became, for me, a classic.

Back at Gunnar Mine my travelling companion left me and flew back to McMurray while I went on alone with my canoe. I came close to disaster once on my way up the Athabaska River. As darkness descended one evening and a fine rain enveloped the river in haze, I looked for a place to spend the night. Spotting an empty barge tied up to the willows, I decided to tie on to it. Then I slid under my bow decking and into my sleeping bag, anticipating an undisturbed sleep. I was just about asleep when I heard the sound of a heavy marine diesel rounding the bend downriver. In less time than it takes to tell the story, I was out of my blanket and on my feet, looking into the glare of a powerful searchlight mounted on a huge black hulk. I lost no time untying my headline and starting my kicker in my underwear. While I was crossing the river, the boat slammed into the rear of the barge, intending to push it on upriver. I retied my canoe to the willows on the opposite bank, slightly shaken by the near miss and wondering if their crew had even noticed me.

The grotto put up by my predecessor in memory of the Blessed Virgin's appearance to St. Bernadette in Lourdes was a fine gesture, but so far up the side of the hill beyond the mission that few ever visited it. The statue itself was about five feet tall and a beautiful work of art. I decided to put it in a more conspicuous setting, next to the mission and facing the main road. To this end I designed a cement dish about twelve feet in diameter and two feet high, with a projecting pedestal rising up another six feet, on which the statue would be fixed. I had water pipes embedded in the concrete to provide fountains of water spraying up at the foot of the statue, and electrical outlets to provide nighttime illumination. The end result was far better than I had anticipated. The nuns were so pleased that they kept it decorated with flowers. It was a pleasure to see them out there gathered around it in prayer.

I had another brainstorm which I ran by the bishop on his next visit to McMurray. I learned that I could get an old, unused barge from the Northern Transportation Company for nothing. If it were sunk in the ground behind the Old Mission and filled with water, it would make a great swimming pool for the kids. The Bishop, however, vetoed the idea, so I never found out how it might have worked out. On one of my canoe trips up the Clearwater River, I got as far as the Christina Indian Reserve, where I noticed a nice three-year-old mare. I soon made a deal with Ralph Cree to have her delivered to McMurray for fifty dollars. Once we had her equipped with saddle and bridle, we had two fine riding horses for the scouts. Constable Ed Kokoska taught them how to ride correctly. I also set up one of the big tents off a sandy shore up the Clearwater and ferried the boys back and forth to it all summer. I also built a kind of surfboard which I towed behind my boat; we had a lot of fun seeing who could stay on it the longest. Between the scouts, the nets and the Sisters' weekly picnics, the big canoe got constant use that summer.

As soon as the carpentry was finished in the Old Mission, we shifted our efforts to beautifying the land surrounding it. To this end we brought in a lot of dirt fill and a good layer of black loam for a lawn, which we soon seeded. Then we transplanted a couple of dozen eight-foot spruce trees and put up a rail fence around the edge of the yard. Hans de Vroom built a neat sundial on a cement pedestal in the middle of a cement walkway leading to the front entrance; it bore the optimistic words: *Nisi Horas Serenas* – Nothing but serene hours! The transformation of this old log building from its previous dilapidation to its present beautiful state was a small miracle.

My original intention was to use the Old Mission for religious purposes only, but, once the church renovations were complete, we really didn't need it. The teenagers in my catechism class at that time were complaining about the lack of any place for them in town to hold teen dances, so I decided to convert it to their use. With this end in view I persuaded a group of French-Canadians living in The Prairie (halfway to Waterways) to form a seven-man orchestra. I temporarily removed the altar and upstairs built a long counter, plus tables and chairs, to make it into a coffee shop. We started holding Friday night dances in November and the teachers were on deck to sell food and drink at the snack bar. All of those who worked at this effort donated their time. The dances ran from eight until midnight and for the first four months they were well attended. Then the kids started showing up only after they had attended the town show hall – about 11 p.m. As a result they started pressing me to extend the closing time, but I couldn't expect our volunteers to stay any longer than they did and had to refuse. After six months the novelty of these dances had worn off. Joe Gauthier and Leo Gaudet complained that their musical companions didn't think it worth their time to put in four hours for so few kids. I agreed. We converted the Old Mission back to what it was originally intended for: a chapel.

18

AN A-FRAME CHURCH FOR NAHANNI BUTTE

The New Year, 1961, dawned clear and cool at forty below zero over Fort McMurray as we joined in the usual ceremonies and turkey dinners and wished each other the best of the season. I presided over a Mass at Waterways and flew up as well to Stoney Mountain by helicopter. On the following day the workers were back on the job and on the 4th the kids were back in school. I had to fly down to Fort Chipewyan to preach the children's retreat for three days while a couple of passing missionaries filled in for me at McMurray.

My third year at this post was beginning to look like the previous two, when my back got so bad that I suddenly found myself in bed in the Grey Nuns' hospital in Edmonton. Dr. Moreau had the reputation of being the best orthopaedic surgeon in Western Canada, so I couldn't have been in better hands. After the usual X-rays, however, he had me on total bed rest and aspirins. The phone next to me might have provided a chance to forget my health problems, except that the calls I got from McMurray were bad news, like the casual mention that our cesspool was plugged up and none of the toilets were functioning. I lay there for two weeks looking at the ceiling; there was no lessening of the pain in my back from the pinched nerve.

And then the good Lord took pity on me and sent a liberating angel in the person of Hans de Vroom, the same parishioner who had made the sundial for the Old Mission. He told me he had a similar problem that was cured in five minutes by a chiropractor named Dr. Herb Taylor. Dr. Taylor's office in the Tegler Building was only five minutes away. I had been brainwashed against chiropractors by my medical uncle, but this was a dire predicament and I might be excused for grasping at any lifesaver thrown my way. On the spur of the moment I sprang from my bed and got into my street clothes; in a matter of minutes the two of us were in a taxi heading for Dr. Taylor's office. He lived up to my friend's lavish praise. Positioning me on my side on a table, he gave a forceful push to my hip bone and the pain vanished. I could hardly believe it! This instant cure was worth a great deal to me, yet he wouldn't accept a cent. We went back to the hospital where I picked up my suitcase, left the cumbersome metal back brace made for me and simply walked out. I've never been in a hospital since, and I'm glad I didn't consent to a fusion of my vertebrae while I was there.

I immediately took a taxi over to Charles Camsell Hospital to visit the northern patients in the TB wards. Within the hour I went from being a patient myself to being a visitor to other patients. That evening I had supper with Mr. and Mrs. Louis Ringette, from whom I bought a used four-wheel-drive International panel truck. Hans and I decided to drive it back to McMurray on the winter road, so we bought 1,000 pounds of cement to carry in the back for added traction. It took us two days and at one point it looked as if we might not make it. I lost the first and second gears and was proceeding in third, when we came down a steep hill and into a two-foot-deep flooded creek. Not having the low gears, we hit the water at full speed. We barely had enough momentum to carry us through, but we made it. We regretted our choice of ballast when we finally got home, because we were both covered in cement dust.

The ice went out peacefully on the Athabaska River the 1st of May and the fears of those who predicted another flood on the lower side of town proved groundless. A few weeks later it was time to put up one of the big tents up the Clearwater River. The boat-load of scouts in my freighter canoe were enjoying a sunny day. As I picked my way up river trying to avoid rocks, we came across a lynx swimming. Most of the boys had never seen one of these large cats in the wild; I circled him several times so that they could have a good look. Suddenly the cat decided to take a closer look at us. He hopped up on the bow of the boat as the scouts scrambled over the thwarts and back around me in the stern. I had to cut the motor and drive the lynx back overboard with a paddle. This little brush with wildlife was just what was needed to make it another memorable scout outing.

I was used to travelling by aircraft and helicopter, by truck, dog-team and boats, but I had never ridden the rails on one of those small motor-driven handcars, called "speeders," used by the railway workmen. The RCMP were engaged in taking a federal census and Constable Gatafoni invited me to join him for a run south on the Northern Alberta Railway. It was a great ride on that little open-air platform as we zipped along the rail bed, stopping to count the people at Anzac, Cheechum, Linton, and finally stopping for the night at Chard. We had supper with the trader Stepanovich there while he informed me of a charge he had put against our local missionary, Father Raymond Danto, who occupied the mission on the Chipewyan Prairie Indian Reserve a few miles east. It involved trading with the Indians without a licence. When the case later came to trial the judge gave the missionary a choice between paying a twenty-five-dollar fine or spending a day in jail. He refused to pay the fine and was quite ready to spend a day behind bars when one of the natives stepped forward and paid his fine for him.

I went over and spent the night at the mission, which appeared to be a model of disorder. Although I was technically the local superior of Father Danto, my chances of getting him to clean up his mess were next to nil. I didn't try. Instead, I spent a sleepless night swatting mosquitoes and listening to the mice scurry about my cot. The next day the constable put on his red serge uniform, paid the annual five dollars treaty money and made his count of the population. We caught the weekly NAR "Muskrat Express" train back to Waterways that evening.

❄ ❄ ❄

Besides Fort McMurray's small contingent of Mounties, the town employed a policeman by the name of Roger Henriet, whose duty it was to enforce the town bylaws. In addition to three teacherages and the new building which housed staff girls from the hospital, the mission also rented out the old rectory in Waterways, as well as two small homes directly behind our property. In one of them lived Maureen Moore, who worked at the hospital. She seemed a quiet girl who lived alone and had no dependants. One morning Roger asked me to accompany him to the hospital with my camera to take pictures of an assault case. It turned out to be Maureen. I could scarcely recognize her. She had been badly beaten about the face, her eyes black and blue, cuts and bruises everywhere. I couldn't imagine anyone venting such rage on a female who was practically defenceless. She made a statement: she had been visited the night before by a transient name Frenchie Morneau who, following a few bottles of beer, had turned on her without provocation. Roger next interviewed Frenchie and then came back to my office. According to Frenchie, Maureen had robbed him of seventy dollars. Though I believed Maureen's story, I took my duplicate key and we both went over to view the scene of the crime and to look for the money, allegedly stolen. Our little home was a complete mess and the blood on the walls and even the ceiling testified to the ferocity of the attack. Roger proceeded with a very thorough search for the missing money. To my great astonishment he found all seventy dollars of it stuck in a can of baking powder!

I had to attend the subsequent trial at Waterways, where Frenchie was ordered to pay me twenty-five dollars to clean up the mess he had made in Maureen's house and was then released. This did not strike me as a just sentence. Frenchie's savage attack was out of all proportion to the theft involved. He could have killed her, yet the judge allowed him to get away with a very small penalty. He was a transient and I never saw him again, but I am sure in a different court at a later date he would have had to serve time. My sympathies were with Maureen and this little episode made me realize just what a woman will suffer for a little money and, after so much pain, how convincingly she will lie to protect so little gain. I also gained a new respect for our town cop.

❊ ❊ ❊

About this time Mother flew up from Rochester to spend a month with me, was given a suitable room by the nuns in their convent and was treated like a queen. I was especially pleased that she was to be present for the fiftieth anniversary of the founding of the Old Mission on the 6th of July. I spared no effort to make this a day for the whole town to remember: I had commemorative badges printed, we made a twenty-foot banner to be draped across the front entrance, and Sister Hamelin made a huge cake in the shape of the mission, perfect in every detail. The mission's Beaver aircraft, CF-OMI, landed on floats the day before, bringing not only the bishop and our Provincial, but the Superior General of the Oblates, Rev. Leo Deschatelets, who came all the way from Rome for the occasion. We all participated in a commemorative High Mass in the Old Mission chapel downstairs in the morning and then, at noon, gathered upstairs at one long table for the banquet. The weather was great. Everything we had planned went off without a hitch and everyone agreed that this fiftieth anniversary had been suitably celebrated.

The dust from this event had barely settled when we officially opened the Sisters' new retreat cabin, Chateau Gai. With its cedar-shake roof, large enclosed front porch and fireplace made of huge field stones, it presented a perfect picture in its forest setting. The good Sisters were delighted. I had a permanent bronze tablet made for the front entrance, dedicating the building to the Grey Nuns in recognition of their devoted work for the community. All our religious community gathered there for a rare buffet supper and Mother was with us again to join in the celebration.

The next day I chartered the Cessna float plane belonging to local bush pilot Milt McDougall to fly us over to Portage La Loche for a visit. Father Bertrand Mathieu, the missionary in charge there, had visited us during the winter with his fine dog-team. He certainly took good care of them, as I could see on this visit. He had their chains hooked onto long overhead wires leading from their houses down into the lake so that they could get fresh water or even take a swim any time they wanted. There were a dozen Grey Nuns at this mission and they gave us a tour of their facilities during a perfect afternoon. Although we weren't far apart, this was the only time I got to see this typical Indian community during my time at Fort McMurray.

Mid-July was the time for the annual parish picnic. To prepare a proper place for it, Clare Peden used his D-8 cat to clear the bush down at the snye. We set up two of the large tents for the refreshments and game material and the whole town gathered there on a splendid Sunday afternoon. The usual games, like the three-legged race and the egg-throwing contest, ran through the afternoon to conclude with a spectacular water skiing exhibition by Cyril Barlow, the local Pacific Western Airlines agent. We had been practising together, with me pulling him behind my canoe. Though our practice runs had gone without incident, this time, in front of the huge audience, everything went wrong. First of all, on his first wide turn he miscalculated the arc of his swing and aborted, coming up under a huge floating log. The crowd cheered! Under way again, the plan was to finish the demonstration by having him release his hold on the tow rope right in front of the spectators and glide right up to the beach under his own momentum. He held on a few seconds too long, however, and hit the shore with so much speed that he rolled across the sand and gravel in a tangle of arms, legs and skis. He got a standing ovation from all present and was rushed to one of the tents for first aid.

We took a break for supper and returned at 8:00 that evening to resume our fun with the giant tug-of-war, the men against the women. I had provided a heavy, new, one-inch manila rope for this event, but hadn't counted on the number of participants. On the first pull they broke it in two! While the adults were having their fun – like the women feeding beer to the men from nippled bottles – the kids were taking turns riding Tonka and digging in a sawdust pile for silver change. When it started getting dark at 10:00 we began the aerial fireworks. One happened to fall on an old derelict barge, setting it afire and providing light for a sing-along that lasted longer than I stayed. It was another great day in the life of the parish.

I noted in the previous chapter that Fort McMurray had orig-inally been called Fort of the Forks because of its position at the junction of two rivers. Somehow over the years the name Fort McMurray was reduced to McMurray, but at one of the town meetings I attended, the Anglican Pastor, Mr. Dunster, intro-duced a motion that the "Fort" be restored to the title. The vote was unanimous: from that time on it would again be known offi-cially as "Fort McMurray."

Riding the horses into the bush country just west of town became even more interesting when we discovered just how many black bears there were over there. So we started packing rifles and one evening I made the mistake of getting off Princess to chase two cubs up a tree when I heard their mother crashing through the bush toward me. There I was, off my horse, without my rifle and threatening the safety of a sow's cubs, one of the most dangerous situations one can encounter in the Canadian wilds. I could have ended up like Swan Pederson did. Luckily, however, I got mounted and out of there before being charged. I promised myself never to leave the safety of my horse on another bear hunt.

As fall approached and the birds were on the wing I started running up the Clearwater River to shoot ducks. On the first trip I ran across a moose swimming the river and shot him with the shotgun at arm's length from the canoe. I then tied a rope to his rack and towed him down river five miles to Napesis Cree's camp where I tied him to his dock. He said it was a great pleasure having a white man deliver so much meat to his doorstep. Two weeks later I got a second one off a cutbank using the .270 rifle and delivered it also to Napesis. After paying a fifty-dollar fine the winter before for possessing illegal moose-meat I decided not to bring any more to town.

Later in September Brother Philip joined me on another canoe trip down to Lake Athabaska for geese. I combined business with pleasure by stopping at various camps and holding services for the isolated people. I always carried a Mass kit in the canoe. When we arrived at the big mission at Fort Chipewyan we were carrying thirty-nine ducks shot along our way. The Grey Nuns took them all for their boarding students. We went on to Camsell Portage to spend a week there at Mission Saint Bernard; while there we jacked up and levelled the log building in a few places where it had sagged. We also held another banquet for the Cree people there and seventy-one attended. That evening we lit a few aerial rockets I had saved from the McMurray parish picnic. We had such a great week there it was difficult to leave and return up river to the endless grind I was committed to, but duty is duty. So we wished the little community *au revoir* and pointed the canoe west. We got about forty miles when a rising sea forced us to camp at Morris Point early in the evening.

With the binoculars I spotted one moose feeding in the willows in the bay to the east and another to the west. Just for fun, I made the traditional bark megaphone and started calling, imitating a bull moose in rut. The huge bull to the west answered me and immediately started toward us. Brother Philip was intrigued with the effectiveness of this imitation call which, for all his experience in the North, he had never seen demonstrated before. As the moose got closer darkness fell and we had to depend on our ears to judge his progress, but it wasn't difficult as he clattered along the rocky shore and splashed through shallow water, stopping now and then to answer my call. With each hundred yard's progress Brother Philip got more nervous and finally told me, in

French, that if I persisted that enraged bull would charge right into our camp and bust up our canoe and tent! I finally relented and fired the rifle in his direction, ending the charge, but it was a powerful demonstration of the call of the wild.

The next day we made only about fifty miles against a very stiff west wind and again pitched our tent at the mouth of Fishing River. On the following day it calmed enough so that we could cross Lake Athabaska to the south shore. Here we found Hap Cave camped at Moose Point, guiding some American goose-hunters. The geese were scarce so we didn't tarry, but continued west and up into the Athabaska River. Near Reed's trading post, ripping right along at full speed in a back eddy, I hit a low, dry sandbar and drove my canoe up fifty feet from the water! We had to empty it completely before we could slide it back. Finally we got to within two miles of our destination when the forty-three-horsepower Scott quit completely and we got a tow by a Northern Transportation Company barge into the Fort.

As usual, there was a good pile of mail awaiting me after a week's absence. Among the letters was one from Bishop Piché, asking me if I would fly down to Nahanni Butte and put up a log church there for that community. I lost no time in packing my tool box and flying, two days later, to Edmonton to catch the connecting flight to Fort Simpson. Stopping briefly at Hay River, I was appalled to see five-foot drifts of snow and surmised that it might now be too late in the fall to begin any outside construction. It was the 10th of October. At Fort Simpson I was met by Father Henri Posset who had phoned to Fort Nelson for a plane to come and pick me up for the flight into the Butte. After waiting in vain for two days, we got news that my pilot, Don Yaeger, had killed himself in his plane at Fort Nelson. He had made a wager in the bar there that he could fly under the local bridge.

When I heard that the trader at Nahanni Butte, Dick Turner, had a small Piper Super-Cub, I phoned him and asked if he could come and get me, as there was no plane available at Simpson. We flew back up the Liard River and, seeing me with my 16mm movie camera in hand, Dick flew just off the water so that I could get some spectacular shots. Seeing those vertical limestone cliffs on either side of us and realizing that on wheels we wouldn't stand a chance if the engine failed, I motioned to him to gain some altitude. My pictures weren't *that* important. We landed safely on the small dirt strip at the Butte and the legendary Gus Kraus met us and took me to his cabin to meet his wife, Mary.

About a hundred Slavey Indians lived in this settlement at the junction of the South Nahanni and Liard Rivers, supporting themselves by hunting and trapping. Dick ran a neat little trading post on an island in front of the village where he also had his private landing strip. Father Pierre Mary, stationed at Fort Liard, visited this community as an outpost mission. He had actually collected all the logs and materials with which to put up a church some three years back, but had failed to do any construction. He did have a small log cabin here into which I moved the next day, but I continued to eat with the Kraus family nearby. Although there was some snow on the ground here, the weather was mild and I decided to go ahead with my instructions to build a church. First I measured and counted the logs piled there; only then did I begin to draw my plan. I had seen a very nice A-frame log church at Squaw Valley when visiting my brother Justin at Reno, Nevada, and thought to myself that this would be interesting to build here. Taking into consideration the length of the logs I had at hand, I decided on a floor plan measuring twenty by forty feet. It seemed to me that, to put up this type of building, I would first have to erect eight triangular log spans that would support the roof as well as the floor. This would enable me to finish the roof first in case real winter weather caught up to us.

Visiting around the village the second day, I met two off-work white guides by the names of John Brucker and George Bayer. I hired them as well as five Indians. I arrived on Thursday and by Saturday I had my crew peeling and tarring the foundation sills. Ten days later we had the roof completely shingled just before a foot of snow fell on us. Then we got a warm Chinook wind from the west that completely melted it again. I managed to keep one day ahead of my crew with the plans. The shape of this church was so completely different from anything these workers had ever seen before that they had to be directed every step of the way. Even Gus thought that the whole idea of an A-frame log building was a little crazy.

❊ ❊ ❊

Every evening after supper Gus kept me enthralled with stories of his experiences. I found them so interesting I kept notes. Gus was born in Chicago of German immigrants about 1897 and came north into the Peace River country with a brother in 1924. Instead of farming he began trapping and moving north toward Great Slave Lake, where he traded for a spell at Hay River, N.W.T. He then moved farther north and met and married his Slavey wife, Mary, at Fort Liard. He eventually worked his way up the South Nahanni River trapping in winter and prospecting in summer.

As an all-round bushman and jack-of-all-trades, Gus couldn't be beat. He was a good carpenter and could put up a fine log cabin, but he was also a first-class boat-builder. And he was one of the few men alive who can whipsaw boards out of raw logs with which to build a skiff, or floor a cabin. In the art of trapping even the Indians could learn from him. He developed a bait so powerful, animals were attracted to it for miles around. Even if he was out of steel traps he could make equally effective deadfalls. He could even construct a cage trap from green polls that would hold a grizzly bear alive. Generally speaking, tanning hides is the work of women, but even his wife admits that he could tan a moose hide better than she can. He is the only person I have met in the North who knew how to make the old-style teepee tent; that is, knew how to cut and sew hides to cover it, how to construct the smoke vent, and what kind of wood to burn in it to avoid sparks.

Not long after I met him Gus moved to the five acres he had leased from the federal government at the hot springs up river. There he built a large log cabin, a log warehouse and two storage stages ten feet off the ground. The mineral springs there flow out of the ground at ninety-seven degrees Fahrenheit. Gus dammed up a pool at its source where he would bathe all winter. He claimed that the sulphur in the water causes skin to peel off, but the new skin beneath is as smooth as a baby's. The heat from this spring so warmed the ground around it that he really needed no fire in his cabin except for cooking. His garden there was extremely lush, but he was unable to store potatoes in a basement he had dug under the cabin because the ground heat kept them sprouting. Many birds, including some ducks, stayed around this spot all winter. Gus held this property for years, hoping someone with money would come along and develop it as a health spa, but they never came and the government decided to make the whole area into a national park. Prime Minister Pierre Trudeau came to visit Gus and offered to move him anywhere he wanted, plus give him a lump-sum payment of $6,000. He was persuaded to relocate to Little Doctor Lake about fifty miles east toward Fort Simpson, where he built yet another log home.

For twenty-three years after our meeting, I continued to talk with Gus every night at 10:00, first using the mission frequency, and later the single side band Forestry frequency. Even in later years, when I was 300 miles northeast of him in Colville Lake, we still felt like neighbours. I never tired of listening to Gus' wry comments on life in the Northwest Territories.

❋ ❋ ❋

We worked steadily on the construction of the new church at the Butte in weather ranging from ten below zero to fifty above in wind, sleet and snow, putting in some eleven-hour days. The result after twenty-five working days was that I was able to celebrate the first Mass in the new church on November 12th and the whole population of Nahanni Butte attended. The next day I put in order and covered all the unused material and contacted Fort Simpson asking them to send a plane for me. Father Henri Posset flew in with the pick-up aircraft to see for himself if I had actually finished the job after being there exactly one month. Afterwards

Colville Lake, April 1975. Charles, Prince of Wales, visits Margaret and me.

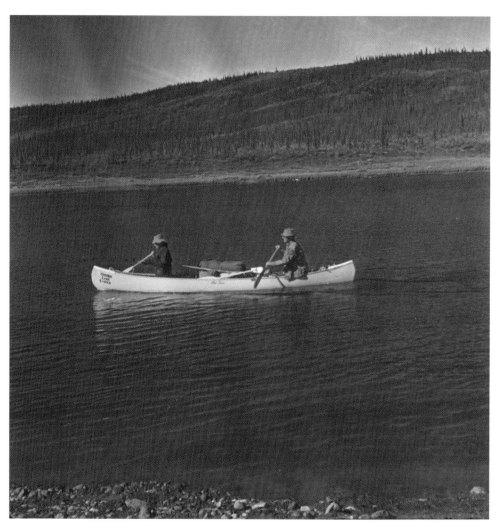

Anderson River, 1976. Margaret and I are paddling from Colville Lake to the Arctic Coast: 27 days en route.

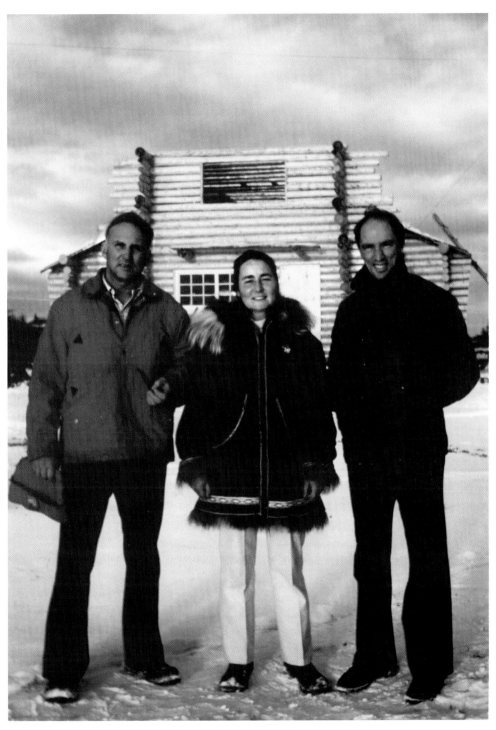

Colville Lake, 1980. Prime Minister Pierre Trudeau visits Margaret and me. The new Museum and Gallery is in the background.

Margaret and the pups.

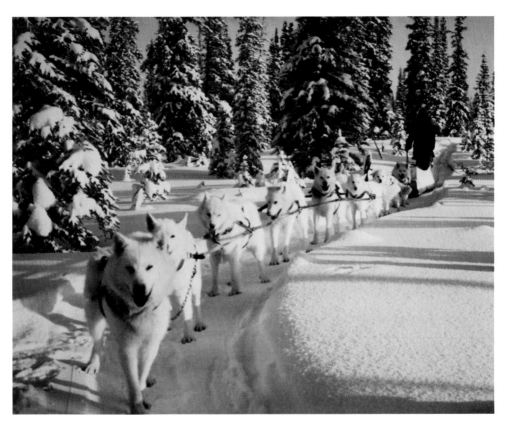

Colville Lake, 1995. Margaret driving her team in the bush.

Colville Lake, 1990. Margaret out picking fall cranberries with her faithful dog team (to warn against bears).

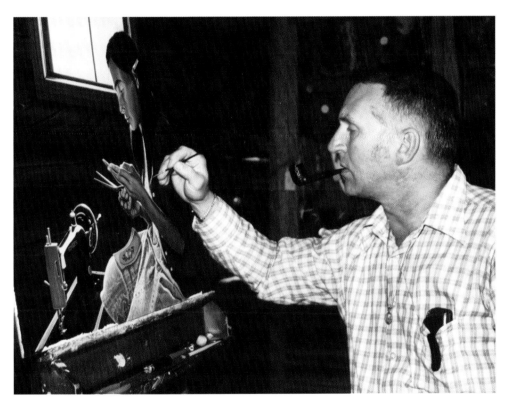

Painting "Woman with Sewing Machine" in the Mission at Colville Lake.

"Woman with Sewing Machine" Oil on masonite. 22" x 26". This native woman at Fort Franklin is making a set of "uppers" for a pair of slippers.

"Midnight Mass"

"Born to Lose" Oil on canvas. 20" x 24", 1982. A commentary on spousal assault in the North. Note husband with club and cup of home brew in the background.

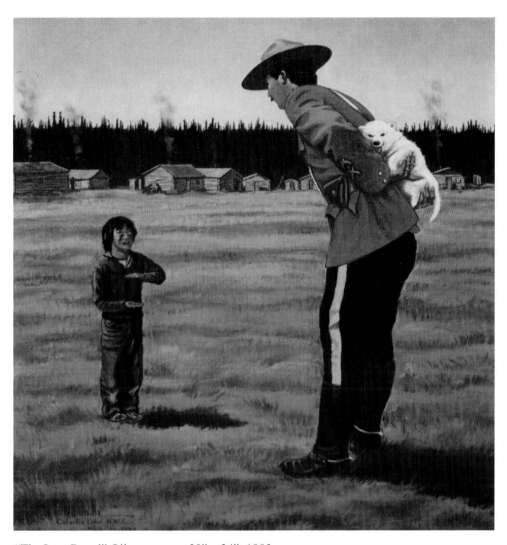

"The Lost Patrol" Oil on canvas. 20" x 24", 1983.

"Under the Parhelion" Oil on canvas. 24" x 30", 1989.

"Heading for the Hills" Oil on canvas. 36" x 48"

"Margaret at Her Net"

Out for a load of firewood.

A young Hare Indian, dressed in a hareskin parka, holds a snowshoe rabbit.

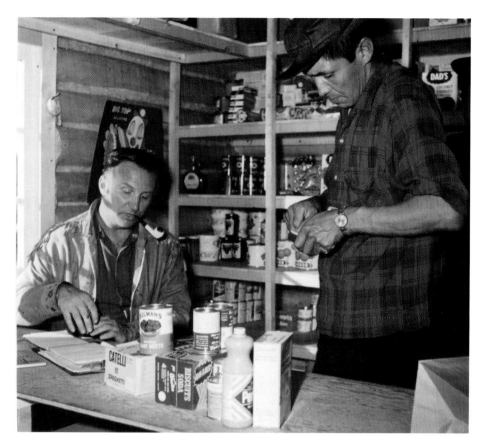

Playing the role of storekeeper.

Finishing the 29-foot work boat the *Loon*.

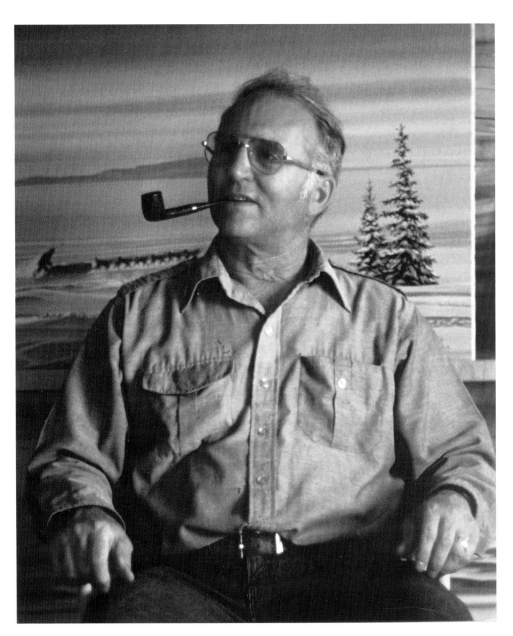

Seated in front of one of my paintings.

I sent the bishop my list of expenses which were $1,585.10 for labour and $1,924.30 for material, for a total cost of $3,509.40. He was so favourably impressed with my work that he asked me if I would be willing to go into the remote area of Colville Lake, N.W.T., the following summer and repeat it. Of course, I readily accepted and returned to Fort McMurray light-hearted, knowing that this would be my last winter there.

That winter turned out to be a tough one, not only because of the daily workload, but because I seemed to catch one cold after another and even got strep throat. This happened when one of our nurses swabbed my throat with a solution of glycerine and iodine that was outdated and doubly potent. I ended up mute in bed for a solid week. Our school was bursting at the seams with an enrolment that had jumped from 196 last year to 217 this. I had to advertise for another teacher. The mayor came to see me about one of our doctors, who was reputed to be preparing people for various operations, including teeth extractions, and then demanding his fee right there or he wouldn't proceed. Some reported that he even cut cards with some patients to wager a double-or-nothing fee for his services! The outcome was that I had to put in another ad, this time for a doctor, in the *Canadian Medical Journal*.

My work crew of carpenters, mechanics and bus drivers was basically dependable, but I had to be ready to shift them around or hire substitutes from day to day if for any reason they failed to show up. Thank God for the Sisters and the Brothers whom I could rely on to do their work. We put in a completely new septic field for the hospital and then had to replace all the galvanized plumbing in the building with copper pipes. In studying the Alberta government's rules on operating hospitals, I found a few items that helped explain why we were still so far in debt. For example, the Catholic Women's League worked hard with bake sales and other projects to raise $2,500 with which to buy a crou-pette for the pediatric ward when we were not using the $5,000 yearly grant available for such purposes. I hired a new hospital secretary out of Edmonton and changed our auditors. We had not been following the proper procedures in sending out three consecutive bills to ex-patients and then claiming seventy-five percent of these unpaid bills from the government, another reason we kept ending each year in the red.

As Christmas approached we again went out to the bush and came back with an even bigger spruce to light up the churchyard, but this time the McMurray Power Company helped us raise it with their boom truck. We celebrated the great feast itself with all the pomp we could muster. The Mounties attended in their colourful red serge.

Sister Lapointe had the school choir there singing like the Vatican choir and the new church interior looked beautiful. Later in the morning I held a service in our church at Waterways. Then the Mounties drove me to Anzac along with some of the Sisters for Mass at our new church there and later up to Stoney Mountain for a final service at their pleasing little chapel. It was one long Christmas day, but when I returned to the mission at McMurray I was not that played out that I could not accept a box of Christmas cigars from Mr. Walter Hill, the local pharmacist.

Ever since I had taken over as Pastor of St. John the Baptist Parish in 1958, I had composed a weekly parish bulletin which Sister Lapointe printed on her Gestetner and distributed after each Mass. It contained the weekly Mass schedule, a report on the collections, the Legion of Decency ratings for the movies to be shown the next week at our local cinema, the admissions to hospital, and announcements for the various parish organizations. As our town had no local newspaper, and to insure that parishioners read the bulletin, I put in a long paragraph of local news, rather like a mini *Aklavik Journal*. In the bulletin of February 4th, 1962, for example, I had highlights from the previous week's town council meeting: items like the $10,000 owed the town in back taxes by MacInnes Fish Products, termination of the thirty-dollars-per-month contract for the local dog-catcher for lack of funds, and a letter of complaint from a resident stating that too many riders were using the town police panel truck. Then I had a synopsis of ten cases tried in the Waterways court room the previous Wednesday by Magistrate Franchuk. Most were in violation of the Alberta Liquor Control Act and many of those appearing were interdicted. As it was also an offence to give a drink to those who were on this list I published their names. Many parishioners told me they not only read my Sunday bulletins, but kept them for future reference.

Letters postmarked "Fort Smith" were always opened first and with some trepidation. Two arrived about mid-April. The first, containing some bad news, came from our Provincial: he told me to get rid of both the dogs and the horses! Someone must have reported to him that I was spending too much time away from my desk. (We had already shot one dog when we got word that the Provincial who had written the letter had been moved to the Hudson Bay Vicariate.) The second letter, from the bishop, contained the good news. He confirmed that I would definitely be going north this summer to start a new mission at Colville Lake and he was lavish in his praise for what I had accomplished at Fort McMurray and for having stuck with a tough assignment for four years.

Once I had that letter in hand, I started making plans to move on. I decided to use the same plan for the log mission I had built at Camsell Portage ten years before. I wrote to Charlie Masuzumi, an old friend I got to know in Aklavik, now living at Colville Lake, giving him a list of logs I would need for the new mission. I ordered a chain-saw from Edmonton and had my chief carpenter, Borge Jensen, start building some strong-boxes in which to ship my gear north by barge. Before departing I wanted to leave at least one finished oil painting behind as evidence of my passing, so now I got to work on a dogsled scene I had begun a year ago. On April 22nd, the day the ice went out on the Athabaska River, Constable Ed Kokoska and I took a final ride on the two scout horses. The good Sisters gave me a farewell supper up at the log cabin I had built them and presented me with a few practical gifts for use in my new home. The bishop had approved my request to pay a visit to my mother before tackling my new assignment. After that my plan was to return to McMurray and go north by canoe, taking my dog-team with me. It just happened that there were no visiting clergy to replace me and without one I couldn't leave. So for two days I spent some anxious moments on the telephone trying to contact Father Pat Mercredi at either Calgary or Edmonton. When I finally reached him, he promised to be on the Pacific Western DC-3 on April 28th. I was relieved to see him get off that plane so I could get on it and fly south.

19

COLVILLE LAKE

While visiting my mother in Rochester, New York, I had an invitation to address the students at the Aquinas Institute, a boys' school with nearly 1,000 students. After telling them that I was about to return to the Arctic to build a log mission, I had about fifty volunteers. I interviewed them all and picked out five from the graduating seniors whom I thought had the best qualifications: Barry Haefele, Bob Haughout, Brian Martin, Frank McDermott and Frank Wratni. They accompanied me when I flew back to Fort McMurray in early July. There we spent a few days getting all our gear together for the trip north. I bought another, smaller, freighter canoe to carry my dog-team.

When we shoved off from the town dock on July 12th the six of us were in the twenty-two-foot canoe. Piled high with all our baggage and towing six dogs in the smaller canoe behind, it was powered by the forty-three horsepower Scott outboard. All went well as we followed the Athabaska River down into Lake Athabaska. Here we put up our tent on the shore in front of the mission at Fort Chipewyan. Then we entered the Slave River to continue down to Fort Fitzgerald where the Brothers met us with a truck. They took us over the sixteen-mile portage to Fort Smith. We spent four days there visiting the bishop and his large religious community. While there, I decided to go on with only two of the boys and send the other three ahead by air to lighten our load crossing Great Slave Lake.

I continued on with Frank Wratni and Brian and the dogs in
tow. We stopped at Fort Resolution for gas and then we struck
out west for Hay River without delay, as the lake was calm. A
strong wind, however, came up and we were forced to camp on
Dead Man's Island after making only twenty miles. The next day
it was still too rough to continue. Not knowing how many days
we might still be wind-bound, we killed and ate a porcupine to
save what grub we were carrying. After three nights there the
seas calmed and we succeeded in getting into the protected
mouth of the Hay River. Here we camped at the Indian mission
with Father Le Coat. After the weekend there we made a successful crossing of the west end of Great Slave Lake and entered the
mighty Mackenzie River. It carried us easily down to Fort Providence. Since Bishop Grandin had founded this settlement in
1861 and made it his headquarters it was known by the Indians
as *Yati tewe kon*, or "The Bishop's House". He was joined by the
first contingent of Grey Nuns in 1867 who came to open the first
school. They had been there ever since. We were warmly welcomed into this big mission, spent the night with them and had
a chance to see the fruits of a century of work: the huge church
and mission, the large hostel, the farm, the stock and so forth.
Father Robin demonstrated their technique of binding books and
Father Lusson took us up into the attic to see some fifty kerosene
lamps with which all their buildings were once lit. I took four of
them with us for light at Colville Lake. The following day we
continued on our way downstream and stopped at the sawmill
of F. J. Browning.

We stopped at Fort Simpson to take on fuel and to give a few
outgoing letters to Father Henri Posset. Then we continued,
camping along the shore whenever darkness overtook us. We
stopped long enough at Fort Wrigley to visit the unmanned mission there, then went on to Fort Norman where we took a three-
day rest. This was my first posting in 1948 and it held a lot of
good memories for me. I knew all the Hare Indians there. I was
pleased to preside at the Sunday High Mass in the old church
while the Pastor, Father Felicien Labat, directed the singing. On
Monday we ran the remaining fifty-three miles of river effort-

lessly to Norman Wells. We could easily have gone on to Fort
Good Hope, which is closer to Colville Lake, but as there was no
water route into it and no aircraft stationed there, we stopped
where we were. We made arrangements with a bush pilot to fly
us the last 124 miles.

Crammed into the PWA Beaver float plane were the three of
us, the seven dogs (I had picked one up at Fort Smith), one of the
fourteen-by-eighteen-foot tents and all the gear and grub we
could persuade the pilot to let us take. This included one precious item, a ten-pound bronze plaque inscribed with the words
"OUR LADY OF THE SNOWS MISSION – 1962." My job was to
build the mission that would carry this sign. As we flew over
lakes and spruce forests in a cloudless sky the pilot harangued
me about the "stupidity" of going into such a God-forsaken place
as Colville Lake to build a mission. His unsolicited remarks,
throwing cold water on my project, might have been prompted
by animosity toward the Church or a view of Colville Lake as a
hostile environment. Whatever was behind them, they weren't
going to dampen my enthusiasm. He was the first, but not the
last, to try to discourage me. I refused to be discouraged.

When we arrived we found about two-dozen Hare Indians
living in tents. They helped us get our dogs ashore and chained
up. Then, as soon as we emptied the plane, the pilot took off
again with a promise to return for me in two hours. I was anxious
about the canoe we had left in the water at the Wells with my
trunks still sitting in it. We needed above all to locate a suitable
site for the new mission so my two companions could work on it
during my absence. I ran up on a hill with a shovel, testing the
soil, and then along the shore trying to determine the depth of the
water. In less than an hour I had decided on a spot that looked
suitable, though it was covered in shoulder-high Arctic willows.

We cleared a space with axes and then set up our tent. The
pilot failed to return so I borrowed a sleeping bag from one of the
natives and spent my first night at Colville in the tent with my
two volunteers. He didn't show up the next day either and we
had no way of finding out what had happened to him. The

natives put down a nice spruce-bough floor in our tent and brought us an old stove and some firewood, plus fish, caribou ribs and blueberries. We set to work with all the available males in the camp building a seventy-five-foot dock out into the lake with green logs. We had no nails so we used rope instead. The next day the dock was suddenly in use when the float plane returned. To our amazement, out jumped the three volunteers we had left behind at Fort Smith. I got into the plane and was flown to Fort Good Hope. I found our canoe had been safely towed by my friend Otto Binder piloting the RCMP schooner.

I was surprised to receive a rather frosty welcome to the mission there by its Pastor, Father Aloyse Brettar. Fr. Brettar told me that he had not been informed of my mandate to put up the new mission at Colville Lake. He considered Colville Lake to be part of his parish, even though it was ninety air-miles to the north-east. There wasn't much I could do to smooth his ruffled feathers: we both got our orders from the same bishop and it was up to him to announce his plans. At any rate the bishop himself was due to land there in his own plane on the Feast of the Assumption, August 15th. At that time he would have me flown back to Colville. In the intervening five days I busied myself unloading my freighter canoe and storing it safely, receiving my freight off the barge *Radium Charles*, and taking apart all the old church benches so I could use the planks for the new construction.

On the 15th, as promised, Bill Leising flew me back to Colville Lake in his Beaver float plane. He also carried nearly 2,000 pounds of materials, including my Mass kit. That evening in the big tent I offered my first Mass on the new site surrounded by my five helpers and all the natives living there. It was an historic moment. Two days later the Beaver made four more trips hauling in building material from Fort Good Hope. In the meantime, at the going rate of a dollar an hour, I hired all the available men in the camp who began bringing gravel by boat from an island a half-mile away. I would use this to make cement footings for the new mission.

Colville Lake was given its name in 1857 by the Hudson Bay Company manager in Good Hope, Roderick MacFarlane, who had crossed it on his return from a reconnaissance trip down the Anderson River. He named it after one of the London Governors of the Company. This Englishman spelled his name "Colvile," but somehow during the years its spelling got changed. In 1863, when Father Petitot visited the lake by dog-team, he found the chief living in a small village of seven log cabins on the river flowing in from Aubrey Lake. Now only the cemetery of this settlement remained. Later, toward the turn of the century, most of the inhabitants of the region were camped around the north end of Colville Lake where the ruins of three log cabins and a cemetery were still visible.

When the DEW Line was under construction in 1955, Canadian Pacific Airlines built a frame house at that site. They installed a diesel generator and hired a man named Ole Pederson to stay there for two years to keep a non-directional beacon in operation. It was a navigational aid to planes ferrying material between Norman Wells and Pin Main at Cape Parry on the Arctic Coast. When we had gone through Fort Smith, I visited Ole and his wife, Gertrude. They showed me their photos taken at that isolated spot and I noted some of the huge trout taken there. Father Robin, who worked out of Good Hope for forty years, told me that he estimated there may have been around 200 Indians living in the Colville Lake region at one time. Most of them now congregated at Lac des Bois, twenty miles farther east. Most of the whites living in Good Hope in those days were French-speaking and they referred to those natives living out around Colville Lake as the *gens au large*. In English this was corrupted to "The Lodge People." Father Petitot, in the monograph preceding his monumental dictionary of the *Peau de Lievre* or Hareskin Indian language, further defines this segment of the tribe occupying the Colville area as the *Nne la gottine* – "The End of the Earth People," because they occupied those lands farthest north, near the Eskimos.

At one time upwards of 200 natives belonging to this End of the Earth group lived in this area. Through the years, however, starvation and disease had decimated their ranks. MacFarlane had opened his trading post at Fort Anderson in 1861, but an epidemic of scarlet fever in 1865 forced its closure the following year. Early in the twentieth century tuberculosis accounted for the deaths of many in the area. Their graves may be found on most of the larger lakes. At one point along the shore of Colville Lake I found five graves; an old-timer told me that they had starved to death. Though the lake was full of fish, they had been fishing with very short gill nets made of willow bark that tended to break in cold weather.

In earlier times the men would walk into Fort Good Hope from the Colville area, using pack dogs to help carry their winter fur. They left behind the women and children to await their return with trade goods. When Treaty 11 was signed in 1921, however, the government started giving every man, woman and child five dollars in cash, plus nets and ammunition. This was an inducement for the whole family to go into the Fort together in summer.

Gradually the Colville area natives got into the habit of commuting back and forth once a year, with the exception of the single family of Antoine Codzi. He was known locally as Saklay. He alone, with his wife and children, had remained around Colville Lake even during the summer. Others had hunted and trapped with him in winter, but during the open water season they had left to visit Fort Good Hope. Now his family was the last of the End of the Earth People alive in the area. When I sent word in to Charlie Masuzumi that I would be in to build a mission at Colville Lake this summer, several other families stayed put. Late in the summer, when word got into Good Hope that I was actually in the process of building something permanent, a group of thirty-five former Colville-Lakers walked out to the Lake with their dogs.

On the day I claim as my special feast day, that of St. Bernard on the 20th of August, we had a surprise visit from the RCMP

Otter aircraft on floats out of Inuvik. They brought with them the mail from the post office in Fort Good Hope and vaccinated all sixty-six sled-dogs against rabies. The next day Bob Engle landed in his single Otter aircraft – the entire fleet of his charter aircraft company entitled North West Territorial Airways. He had obtained a contract from the bishop to ferry in all our lumber that had been off-loaded at Fort Good Hope. On this trip, however, he was loaded with 100/130 AV gas; his floats were so low in the water that he ran aground twenty feet beyond the end of our new dock. Fortunately the lake bottom was sandy. We had a tough job getting the forty-five-gallon barrels ashore and made plans to cut more green logs and extend the dock as soon as possible.

After we had cut down all the willows, we found that the ground was covered with a carpet of moss about ten inches thick. Below it the ground was frozen in permafrost. To make a quick Frigidaire, we simply lifted up a section of moss with a shovel and put our meat beneath it. Without disturbing this moss cover – so as not to melt the permafrost below – we poured twenty-one blocks of concrete on small gravel pads. On top of these we put the large foundation logs of the mission. If I had known better, I would have used pads of tamarack logs; the cement drew the heat of the summer sun and had a tendency to sink. The first building we finished was the privy. To dig the hole we had to chip the frozen ground with axes. By the 24th of the month the wind shifted to the north-west, the temperature dropped and a cold rain set in, marking the end of summer. At least the bother-some black flies disappeared as we worked to level the floor joists. The waves on the lake, however, threatened to destroy the dock. One of my volunteer workers got blood poisoning and I administered two cc's of penicillin. On the 29th a PWA Otter landed from Inuvik to pick up the children for the school hostel there. Three went with them.

To celebrate my forty-second birthday, on the last day of the month, the Good Lord sent us four inches of fresh snow, fol-lowed by gale force winds. These blew our tent down and forced us to move it back from the bank of the lake. Most of my workers also quit the job to rescue their own tents. The day had started badly when we slept in and went to work without any breakfast. I told Frank McDermott to stay behind and build a fire in our wood stove. The next thing we saw was Mac running down the bank and diving into the lake! He told us later that when he had trouble getting the fire going he had poured some gas on the embers. He was blowing on them when they exploded, taking off his glasses as well as his eyebrows and catching his hair on fire. He had certainly not followed the safety procedures he had learned in scouts. The day ended, however, on an optimistic note: two beautiful rainbows spanned the south-eastern sky and the local girls brought in a surprise birthday cake.

Yet the snow stayed, the ground froze and we were suddenly into winter. In our construction we had reached the level of the plate logs on the top of the mission walls. We had actually run short of logs, though we had a crew out in the bush cutting fresh trees continually. As a result I was forced to notch-in the ceiling rafters less than seven feet above the floor, a foot shorter than I had anticipated. With men working on slippery, snow covered logs, there were bound to be accidents and I had to put stitches in the leg of Frank Codzi and then apply for workmen's compensation for him. At the same time our cook Sarah Kochon took a kind of epileptic fit. I had to give her a shot of Demerol to calm her down while four men tried to hold her steady.

On one of the Otter's freight trips we received the eighteen-foot freighter canoe tied to one float. We immediately used it to set a gill net for fish to feed the dogs. We didn't set it in deep enough water, however, and the first storm filled it with moss. We had to pull it out, clean it and then reset it. The seven dogs ate more than the five of us did.

Most evenings, weather permitting, there was a native game called *ayati* being played in the centre of the village. They used a ball, slightly smaller than a regular baseball, made of caribou hide filled with moss. The object of the game was to keep the ball away from the opposite sex, so it was men against women. There were no age limits and no boundaries. Getting the ball away from the opposing team involved a lot of wrestling and tickling and everyone seemed to have a great time. Later, when I marked out a diamond and taught them the American game of baseball they found the rules too complicated and restraining. It never really caught on.

One day the PWA Beaver aircraft landed from Norman Wells with a young oriental woman by the name of Hiroki Sue. She told us that she came from Tokyo but was taking a course in anthropology at Bryn Mawr College in Pennsylvania. She had come to study the Hare Indians, so she moved into a tent with Mary Barnaby. In the following days she filled her notebooks with all the information she could gather. A month-and-a-half later, when she was absent from her tent, two of the girls who had attended school began reading her notes, especially those in which she had recorded their dreams. When this information got around, everyone suddenly clammed up on her. Though she intended to spend the winter with the tribe, she had to give up on her research and fly back to the States.

Five of the men working on the mission were also in the process of building themselves log cabins so that they could move out of their tents when the winter came. Three very old sod-roofed cabins were still standing and one was temporarily occupied by Pierre Blancho, but they were soon torn down for firewood. Charlie Masuzumi put up a cabin to serve as a small trading post and was acting as an agent for free-trader Bill McNeely in Fort Good Hope. I bought out all the canned food he had in stock the first week.

As usual in the fall, the water in the lake kept dropping. As it did, we were forced to extend our dock so that the float planes could reach it. Finally the dock got to be 200 feet long and we quit. We were also building a fish house on the shore of the lake fifty feet below the mission and putting up three forty-five-foot antenna poles. These would carry the wires for a Marconi HF radio. Bill Leising, the mission pilot, brought in the radio along with an Onan generator. Now we had communication out of Colville Lake and began a regular "sched," or scheduled exchange with our central mission at Fort Smith every evening at seven. It was apparent that I could not keep all five of my Rochester volunteers all winter, so we decided that Frank Wratni and Brian Martin would stay with me while the others would go out on the mission Beaver and help out at other missions for the winter.

The daylight hours were diminishing, but we now had the generator and could rig up lights so that we could work after it got dark. I built an octagonal steeple on the ground and on the 20th of September we raised it into place, along with the bell I had brought. After that we could proceed to shingle the roof and did not have to worry so much about rain and snow. At the same time the bitch Duchess dropped six nice pups in a hole she had dug in the bank.

By the end of September Bob Engle had finished making seventeen trips for us with his Otter and had me sign a bill for just over $3,000. Later I found out from our main office in Fort Smith that he had added $1,600 above my signature for ferrying charges. He had agreed not to charge these as he was working in our area anyway. It was a clever deception on his part. Though I complained, Bishop Piché decided not to contest it and it was paid in full.

As the days grew shorter and the temperature fell, I was anxious to get all the outside work completed. The natives would soon leave the village for their winter traplines and I would be reduced to my two volunteers from Rochester. We watched the Kochon family pack up and leave: it was an interesting scene. Though they had one team of dogs in harness pulling a loaded sled, most of the dogs were also saddled with packs. One dog had a pup tied securely on top of its load. The mother of the family had a huge packsack on her back and on top of it was a four-year-old boy sitting triumphantly like a maharajah on top of his elephant. At the last minute she grabbed another pup and staggered off on the trail to Lake Belot. Finally all the packed dogs were untied from their posts and the family disappeared with them into the bush as the blowing snow drove us back to the shelter of our cabins.

Besides getting the mission walls up and the building closed in, I was not neglecting our own dog-team. Soon it would be our only means of transportation. We brought in several boat-loads of small logs, built a corral next to the fish house at the water's edge and moved Duchess and her pups from the hole in the bank in which they had been born. We went to our nets every day too, and were getting an average of fifty trout and whitefish. Most of these we skewered on sticks and put up on a fish stage to freeze for winter dog feed.

One calm day I decided to take a break and cross the bay on a moose hunt. Several natives went with me. When we reached a ridge overlooking a large muskeg I began calling with an appropriate megaphone. After a few minutes I seemed to be getting some sort of reply, but it didn't sound like a bull moose and the sound came from behind us. It turned out to be a pine marten, his head stuck out of a woodpecker's hole in a dead tree. The natives quickly dispatched it. One of the men shot a swan on our trip back, but we didn't get any moose.

As I was notching-in the last of the porch logs one afternoon, a float plane landed and taxied to our dock. Out stepped a middle-aged man who introduced himself as Robert Schneider, a Pentecostal minister. He informed me that he intended to winter in the settlement and preach the Gospel to the natives. I informed him that I also intended to spend the winter taking care of the spiritual needs of the fifty-odd natives here, and I asked him if having the two of us men of the cloth here wasn't a case of overkill. He countered by informing me that he got his marching orders directly from on high. This I doubted, as all the Colville-Lakers had been baptized Catholic long ago. But this zealot was not to be discouraged: he put up his small tent and lived in it all winter, much to my amazement. I told him that he was wasting his time in this village among the already converted and that there were millions of pagans in many parts of the world just waiting for the Word of God. He admitted it was true, but again countered that he simply couldn't change his field of work until God Himself gave the order. In fact, ministers of his church were now moving into all the Catholic native settlements up and down the Mackenzie River.

On the 20th of October we rushed to get our last two gill nets pulled from the lake as ice began forming all across the bay in front of the settlement. We were now content to wait until thick ice before resetting them. We already had over 1,000 fish hanging from the stage for dog feed. As soon as my companions Brian and Frank had nailed plywood under the floor joists to hold fibreglass insulation I began laying the plywood sheets on top to form the permanent floor. I began with the north end of the building which would be the workshop area. As soon as I had that room's floor down, I installed the workbench with the hundred-year-old wagon vice I had picked up from the mission cellar in Fort Good Hope.

Our second bitch, Cora, came in heat at this time. To make sure that she was bred by a good male, I had to move Princess out of her new corral and put Cora in there. I made a mistake, however, in leaving Princess' five pups in there with Cora, for during the first night she killed all of them. They were thirty-three days old, all males, and had promise of becoming a good team. From that incident I learned how vulnerable pups can be to a strange bitch.

The big day was October 27th: we moved out of the tent and into the new mission. What a relief it was to get out of the wind and flapping canvas and into a warm and quiet building. But there were some drawbacks, chief of which was the increased demand for firewood. We now found ourselves borrowing logs off the dock. This practice escalated until we had completely burned up our dock – but we weren't going to need it for eight months anyway. We soon had enough snow that we could use our dogs in harness to start a daily haul of wood from the nearby bush.

At the same time the five one-room cabins around the settlement were nearing completion and each moving-in seemed to call for a housewarming in the form of a home-brew party. Most of the natives were experiencing the first solid roof over their heads. The transition certainly called for a celebration, but unfortunately each party seemed to end in a fight. Often I was called during the night to sew someone up. More dangerous yet, it seemed to me, were those who left the village for their traplines while intoxicated. One could only hope that their dogs would automatically stop for them if they fell off the sled.

Our work prevented the three of us from going out hunting as often as we would have liked. We heard all kinds of rumours of game in the neighbourhood, but were prevented from checking them out. We depended instead upon the charity of our neighbours. One morning we got a gift of game from an unusual hunter. We were sitting at the breakfast table, looking out over the frozen lake, when we saw a raven flying above a duck heading south. All of a sudden the raven dove and struck the duck, which fell to the ice. I immediately sent one of the boys out and he came back with the duck. We ate it for supper. I wouldn't have believed that a raven was swift enough to overtake a duck, let alone knock it out of the sky, but we had seen it happen.

When the lake ice got strong enough I took my two boys out and showed them how to set two gill nets. This is easy to do when the ice is thin, but very difficult when it gets thick. Then when we got enough snow on the ground to use the dogsled, I took them up into the bush and showed them how to find dry spruce for firewood. Teaching them how to drive the dogs was the most difficult challenge, and they never did master it. One reason for this was that they made pets of the dogs, always running out to them with tidbits from the kitchen, petting and wrestling with them. Then, when they put them in harness, the dogs wanted to play instead of work and they had trouble making them go. As soon as the boys learned the ropes, I let them go out to the nets and for firewood on their own. That way, I could go ahead partitioning the inside of the mission and building the bunks and furniture. After the workshop room was finished, the first thing I built in it was the kitchen cabinet.

About the only hunting I did that fall was for ptarmigan. These could be seen every day in the surrounding willows. In fact, that was why the native name for this place was *Kapami tue*, or "Ptarmigan Net Lake." They used to drape their old fish nets on the willows to catch these birds. We did the same, but I got most of them with the .22. A dozen wasn't an unusual bag for a half-hour's work. My two companions bet me that they could get fifty in a single day if they had no other work, so I made them a proposition that, if they did it, I would cut out their workload in half. They left highly confident the next morning after breakfast, each armed with a .22. They didn't return until 2:30 in the afternoon with a total of nineteen. They didn't want to hear the word "ptarmigan" again.

As the fall wore on it became more and more evident that the two recruits I was keeping for the winter were having trouble coping with their assigned tasks – tending the nets to keep the dogs fed and getting enough wood to heat our home. The net job, which would have occupied two native boys their age about two hours, occupied them all day. Every trip seemed to occasion some mishap, like losing one of the net lines, or stepping into the hole or losing one of the dogs. On the wood haul they invariably used the first wood they cut to build a huge fire to warm themselves, when in fact cutting firewood deep in the bush quickly warms one up no matter what the temperature of the air. They would return to the mission so beat that they often fell asleep on the floor next to our heater before I had cooked supper for them. I figured it would have been easier to train a native boy their age to live out in civilization than to get these two fellows adjusted to a boy's chores at Colville Lake. Then when the sun set for the last time in mid-November and the days got darker, so did their spirits. It began to look as if they wouldn't persevere all winter.

We had been reduced to a half-dozen people around the settlement all fall, but then, just before Christmas, we saw dogteams coming in from all directions. We watched fascinated as they dug through the snow and cleared spots to pitch their tents behind the mission. I got the new altar made and the chapel room separated by folding doors just in time for the Midnight Mass. Everyone in town crowded in and there were over fifty. The following days saw us all together again at least twice a day, once in the morning for Mass and then again in the evening for games or slide shows. The latter ended in a feast of cake and my home-made ice cream. The Christmas collection amounted to forty-five dollars, a gesture of good will given out of their own poverty to mine.

As the year drew to a close I could take comfort in the fact that I had been successful in carrying out my orders and had another mission built and practically finished. I was living in the kind of North I loved, doing the kind of missionary work I seemed best fitted for, so my spirits were suddenly soaring after the previous four years stuck at Fort McMurray. Bringing five young high school graduates up here with me as volunteer labour had not proved successful, but it had been an interesting experiment nonetheless. I was surprised at how difficult it had been for them to adjust and to pick up the skills of northern living. I had never experienced this difficulty myself and I had come from the same environment.

The two boys had been itching to go with our dog-team on a caribou hunt, but the nearest reported caribou were down on Aubrey Lake at least twenty miles away. I knew they weren't ready for such a trip, as they had failed to master the trick of driving our team. Finally one day I suggested to Frank that he make a trial run to visit Martin's tent eight miles to the east. Just for insurance I sent with him a native, Alfred, with his own team. When he returned that night there was no longer any talk of taking the dogs on a long caribou hunt. It had taken him hours to get to Martin's as the dogs kept running off the lake trail into the bush or lying down on the trail to rest. In order to get back he was forced to tie our leader to the back of Alfred's sled. That did it! The boys condemned my team as the very worst in the area. In fact, they flatly refused to drive them any longer, even to bring in the firewood. So for the balance of the winter they cut the wood and I drove the team out to bring it back. They were amazed at how well the dogs suddenly behaved and what a huge load they could pull.

We were now into the new year, 1963, and following the feast of Epiphany on January 6th I urged the people to get back out on their traplines to continue earning a living the only way they could. The season for fine fur like marten only lasted from the first of November until the end of February and I always regretted that the Christmas and New Year's holidays happened to come right in the middle of this period. It would not have been too costly an interruption if they came into the settlement for a week, but once they were all together again it was difficult for them to leave town and go their separate ways. This year we saw eleven dog-teams leave for the bush only on the 19th of January. Once they had left, peace and quiet pervaded. I could continue with my carpentry with fewer interruptions.

My two companions began bringing up the ice we had cut in the fall for our drinking water. We found that it was far easier to carry our water frozen in blocks than liquid in pails. It was piled up outside our back door and brought into the kitchen to melt in two ten gallon barrels next to the cook stove. This was about the last work they did at Colville Lake. They had already confessed to me that they found life here just too difficult. It was a combination of work they really didn't like and had trouble mastering, the cumulative depression they felt during the long, dark winter days and the lack of any diversions. I agreed with them: I could see that their attitude had changed as the months wore on. The initial enthusiasm they once enjoyed had completely disappeared. They were willing to go on, however, until such time as an aircraft appeared which could fly them out. This happened on the 17th of February. The CPA Otter CF-IKK landed out front on skis, carrying trade goods for the trading post along with some mail for us. My companions, dressed in the new parkas I had given them for Christmas and carrying a bundle of furs I gave them as a parting gift, apologized for leaving me alone as they said goodbye and walked to the aircraft.

Just as our little town fell silent when the Indians left for their traplines, so now with the two teenagers gone a new silence fell on the mission. This was not a new experience for me, however, and being alone had its compensations. I no longer had to cook for three or suffer from endless rock-and-roll music turned up a few decibels too high. As soon as they were out of sight, the trader's wife LaLouise came and washed all the dirty dishes. Now I could start with a clean slate. In the days following I never really did the dishes myself. I would just let them pile up until she or another of the local women happened by and were willing to lend a hand.

The next day I cleaned out the boys' room and was surprised to find so many boxes of candy and cookies stashed under their bunks, parcels they had continually received from home. They never left for the woodlot or net without their pockets full of this junk food. I decided to turn their room into my clinic, so I built medicine cabinets covering the wall and left the double bunks there, plus a small table under the window.

From the day I arrived at Colville Lake I had carried my 16mm camera plus another that took 35mm slides. Recently I had received a small projector so that I could show these films. Nothing proved more popular with my congregation than these scenes – they were the stars. I continued taking these moving pictures so long as my friends back in Rochester kept sending me the film from Eastman Kodak.

About a week later Luke stayed behind after the morning Mass. During our breakfast together he suggested I go north with him and a group of local hunters to look for caribou. The idea appealed to me: I had been working inside the new mission ever since freeze-up and I needed a break. Monday morning saw six of us driving our dog-teams north across Colville Lake. What a change of pace that following week was to be for me. Every day I was either on the back of my sled or walking on snowshoes; every night we were gathered around an open fire to cook meat, swap stories and then sleep under the stars. We all shot enough caribou to fill our sleds so it was a successful hunt. I even managed to get some interesting photographs of a typical northern bush safari in mid-winter.

During my week's absence I had let the mission freeze up, but little was damaged except a couple of bottles of lime juice and I had little use for them anyway. The wine froze, of course, but I had left the bottles half full on their sides, so no damage was done. It takes about a day to warm up a log building, however, as the walls themselves seem to absorb a lot of heat. So you keep your parka on for the first few hours. I had two wood stoves. The big 750-pound cook stove in the kitchen had been too large to get in through a door, so I had set it on the ground in the kitchen area and then built the mission around it. The cast iron heater was connected to the same flue, and sat in the common room. When the outside temperature was far below zero I needed them both going, but when my cooking was done I let the fire in the kitchen stove die out and kept only the heater going during the night.

The best local wood for starting and quick heat, I soon learned, was that of black spruce which had been killed by a forest fire but left standing. The Hare called this wood *gollerey.* To keep a fire all night, however, I needed green tamarack. There was a knack to banking the fire so that it would hold for eight hours: you needed just enough hot coals to ignite a single dry log which would act as the wick for the surrounding green tamarack. If you did it right, you would find a bed of red hot coals in the morning and the mission would be warm enough for the 8:30 Mass. Until I learned to do this perfectly I often woke up to find even the water in my basin had turned to ice.

When this happened I delayed ringing the steeple bell until the mission had warmed up. Most of my parishioners didn't bother to keep white man's time but depended on the bell, so one hour more or less mattered little to them. Though there were very few natives living in town at this time of year, some were constantly coming in by dog-team to trade at the store or to have me attend to some medical problem, repair a rifle or send a message on the mission radio. They usually spent the night in the village, attended the saying of the rosary in the evening with me and then Mass the next morning before they left for their tent camps again. So I never lacked for at least a few to attend these religious gatherings. They were also faithful in seeking regularly the sacraments of confession and communion. Although they were not perfect, I slowly began to realize that they formed about as good a group of native Catholics as one could find in the Far North.

After the boys left, the only major carpentry job remaining for me was the building of the altar and the vestment case in the sacristy. It wasn't too pressing, so I could work at it whenever I had the outside work under control. In order to keep my dogs well fed, however, I found that I had to set two more nets under the ice as the catch diminished during the winter. I was able to feed the young pups on ptarmigan I shot nearby and they were a far more natural food for a dog than fish. Although we fed the dogs on caribou when out on the trail, it was too valuable to use at home, and against the Game Act to boot. To thrive on fish, the dogs needed the entire fish – head, guts and all – and it was amazing to me that they seldom got a bone stuck in their throats. The only drawback was that they picked up worms from this raw fish, and these had to be cleaned out of them from time to time. To do this, the natives sometimes used gunpowder or the chopped hair of moose. When the game warden at Fort McPherson, Frank Bailey, flew in to visit he brought me a good quantity of worm pills which I was to sell to the people at five cents apiece. They were soon gone.

The people realized that I wasn't using my dogs every day and so they were continually borrowing one or two. This was fine with me, because it relieved the pressure on my short supply of fish, but I had to stop when an epidemic of distemper began to kill the dogs. I alerted the Mounties and they flew in with a good supply of distemper serum to administer to all the dogs. This dread disease soon died out completely.

As the winter wore on, we were constantly finding new uses for the mission. Besides providing a home for the resident missionary and a separate chapel for religious services, the mission now had a clinic room to keep a good supply of medicine, an office which contained the transceiver radio to provide communication to the outside world, and an unofficial post office to handle incoming and outgoing mail. On the 8th of April it became a Canadian government polling station as thirty-nine locals voted for a new Member of Parliament to represent them in Ottawa. Merv Hardy, the first to be elected from the Northwest Territories, had died suddenly. Now we had his widow, Tibbie, running against Gene Rhéaume who had been born in Fort Norman where his father had been Hudson Bay manager. To acquaint himself with his prospective constituency Gene accompanied Bob Engle on some of his summer freight hauls with the Otter aircraft. He was no stranger to us and we were not surprised to learn later that he had won the election.

This election day coincided with the return of the mission Beaver aircraft, now on skis, bringing, besides supplies and mail, Barry Haefele, one of my five Rochester volunteers. Since leaving Colville in September he had been helping out at our Inuvik mission. He accompanied me the next day as I drove six dogs out onto the lake ice to look at two nets. Just before I rang the bell for rosary that evening I bragged a little about how well the people attended services. Nobody showed up. Fifteen minutes later I rang the second bell and still nobody came. This would have been very unusual for any time of the year, but now we were into Holy Week preceding Easter. I suspected that there must be a brew party in progress in one of the five log cabins in the settlement, but didn't know which. Then I got an idea.

I had ordered some fireworks from Edmonton, including some aerial bombs to be used for the bishop's first visit. I got a couple of them out of the warehouse. Barry and I proceeded to stick one of the launching canisters in a snowbank behind the mission, insert a bomb about the size of a pound of butter, and light the fuse. It arced up over the village and exploded a hundred feet overhead with a report that had all the dogs in town howling. A dozen people staggered out of Louie's cabin, pointing at the white cloud floating overhead.

Louie himself made his way to his outhouse. When he was comfortably inside, I sent off the second bomb with a lower trajectory that detonated fifty feet over Louie's privy. The results were a sight to behold. The members of the drinking party again rushed out to gaze at the tell-tale white cloud as someone muttered, "The A bomb!" Louie himself rushed from his outhouse to his stage, where he grabbed his .30-.30 rifle and began pumping shots at the little white cloud. Then everyone ran to the mission to tell me about it. Barry and I tried to keep straight faces as we suggested to them that they might as well stay for the rosary. Although I preferred calling the faithful to prayers with the traditional bell, in this case it took gunpowder to attract their attention.

Up to this point I had had no time to do any artistic work, but when I got the furniture placed in the new chapel I realized that what it lacked was a suitable painting on the wall behind the altar. This gave me the excuse I needed, so I cut a piece of plywood about four feet by five feet and designed a Madonna holding the Christ Child aloft, both of them dressed in traditional Dene parkas. So that my work would be out of the way for daily services, I had to make room for my easel in the office. I began working on this painting as time allowed.

Barry proved an agreeable companion both for the outside work as well as at the chess board in the evenings, but when an aircraft came in two weeks later he felt he should continue on his way, so I had to let him go.

Remembering the fun produced by the ice carnival I had organized in Inuvik eight years before, I decided to try one this year at Colville Lake and scheduled it for the Sunday following Easter. In order to make the events more interesting I had solicited prizes from various companies who donated guns, binoculars, knives and money. The day itself was clear and warm. We got the events under way after we had all participated in the regular Sunday services at 4 p.m. The first competition involved the men shooting their high-powered rifles at a mock caribou target I had made and set up on the lake ice at 200 yards. Then the

women used .22s to shoot at a ptarmigan target. This was followed by an ice-chiselling contest – two teams competing to hit
water. Then came the snowshoe run for both men and women,
followed by dogsled races. We held a party at the mission that
evening, during which we watched movies, ate ice cream and
cake and awarded the prizes. It looked as if it could become an
annual event.

The advent of May saw the snow melting, the ptarmigan
growing their dark summer plumage and the first geese flying
north high overhead. We should all have been in a happy mood
after the long, cold winter, but with the heat came an epidemic of
flu that put nearly all of us in bed with high fevers. I made the
rounds of the cabins and tents twice a day, taking temperatures
and dispensing Tri-Sulf until I was confined to my own bed.
After a week we were all recovering except Therese Codzi,
whose temperature hovered around 104. I talked to Dr. Joe
Cramer at Inuvik and he sent a helicopter from Fort Simpson to
take her out on May 11th. Two days before, I helped Mary Barnaby give birth to Stella and I tied her umbilical cord with net
twine. So within two days I had participated in my first delivery
at Colville Lake and our first medevac. Both turned out fine.

Now that I had the mission built, I began thinking of the possibility of putting up a proper church next to it. I corresponded
with the bishop on the idea and he approved, so the next step
was to draw up a plan and then consider how I would get in
enough logs for a building this large. Rather than bringing them
all in by dog-team, it occurred to me that it might be possible to
cut them around the perimeter of the lake and tow them in during open water. This got me thinking of a boat big enough to do
the job. It would include a cabin in which I could cook for a crew
while we were working away from the village. I came up with a
plan for a V-bottomed boat twenty-nine feet long by six feet wide
and immediately began fabricating the ribs in my new workshop. By the end of May I was laying the keel out in the side yard
and the natives reacted to its size as if I had started building
another ark.

The end of May was notable for two events, one sad and the other joyful. The sad one was the radio announcement of the sudden death of our beloved Pontiff, John XXIII. On a happier note, I succeeded in finishing my painting of Our Lady of the Snows for the mission chapel. After varnishing it I had it mounted in its proper place. A few days later we got our first rain of the season and the dark sky over the melting ice formed a picture that was both beautiful and eerie. I couldn't help setting up my easel on the front porch and capturing this unusual scene in oil paint. In just an hour and forty-five minutes I had captured on canvas and preserved one of those spectacular wild moods of nature we so often saw from our front windows.

The first plane of summer landed in a narrow strip of open water on the 9th of June. It was Bill Levine who owned the Edmonton Fur Auction Company and who auctioned off all our fur. With him was Bill McNeely who operated as a free-trader and who paid Charlie Masuzumi to take care of his small outpost store at Colville. They were doubly welcome when they produced three sacks of mail. Levine encouraged the local trappers when he predicted high prices for furs for the next five years. We all shared in a duck supper at Charlie's cabin but the pilot would not dare stay over-night, as the ice could move in and cover what open water there was.

I also had to keep one eye on the wind and the shifting of the ice, because I had a net set off the end of my dock to feed the dogs and I didn't want to lose it. I had to pull it out temporarily when the ice came right up to the dock. And then my dogs had to wait patiently until I could reset it: I had no reserve dog food. The day the ice cleared out of our bay I set three nets out near the island and from then on I had more than enough fish.

By the middle of June the natives had all the beaver and muskrats they wanted and returned to our new settlement. It was interesting to watch them arrive with their dogs running loose around them, each carrying a pack on its back loaded with all their camp gear plus their dried fur. The only items the dogs couldn't manage were the hunting canoes which the younger men carried on their shoulders. I would be out in the side yard working on the boat when one of these brigades arrived, and I couldn't resist fetching my camera to record the scene.

On the 20th of the month I had the one visitor I wanted most to see the new mission – Bishop Paul Piché. He came in his Beaver on floats, CF-OMI, carrying the first Grey Nun to see Colville Lake, Sister Marie Lemire. Two of them spent the night, while the pilot, Father Leising, and his helper, Brother Eugene Morin, flew to Norman Wells to pick up some freight for me. How happy I was to have the bishop bless the new foundation and to officiate at Mass in the newly built chapel. Having him stay overnight gave me time to discuss the future with him. I realized that, with a population of only fifty people here, I could not hope to stay indefinitely, but I liked the place so much I was anxious to find excuses for extending my stay. Towards that end I pushed the idea of building a proper church. Luckily the bishop shared my view, reaffirming what he had written to me earlier, or I might have been faced with a new assignment and a change of address. When my superior saw what I had accomplished in less than a year, he realized that I had not been sitting on my hands. Perhaps his approval of my church was a kind of reward for the effort and enthusiasm I had shown for this whole resettlement project.

After I had shown him my plans we walked out back to look at the site I proposed, but it didn't meet with the bishop's approval. He told me to build it near the lake, just north of the mission, so that was that. My reason for picking the site I had was that the ground there was solid gravel with no permafrost. The next afternoon the mission aircraft returned from Norman Wells with a surprise: another of my five volunteers, Bob Haughout, was now returning to see how the finished mission looked. So when my ecclesiastical guests departed I was happy to have more permanent company staying.

Among the variety of freight the Beaver brought back from Norman Wells were several boxes of 16mm film I had ordered from Calgary. They were mostly cowboy epics with a few "Tarzan" films and "The Three Stooges." So that night we used the mission's common room as a theatre for the first time and an enthusiastic audience of twenty-six paid a dollar apiece to defray the cost of renting and returning these shows. From that evening on, movies at the mission at least once a week became an integral part of the social life in the community.

Bob joined me the next day in building a fish pit. This was a hole in the brow of the hill above the lake about six feet by five feet and six feet deep. The ground there had no moss and was exposed to the full heat of the sun, so we encountered no perma-frost until we were nearly at the bottom. Then we laid a log floor and notched-in log walls so that we ended up with a completely underground log house. In the roof I set a wooden box form with a tight lid attached by hinges and a hasp so that it could be locked. Then we covered the roof with sod and dirt so that it was absolutely fly-proof. Over the summer we would regularly throw fresh whole fish into this pit and keep it tightly closed to prevent flies from getting in and introducing maggots. I would open it in the winter by removing half the logs from its roof. Then we would pitch the fish out onto the snow with a long-handled hook. The water would be completely drained from them so that even in sub-zero temperatures they would remain supple. Though their smell would be overpowering, the dogs would love them.

The following week we began an excavation of a different order through the back wall of the fish house. Here the ground was protected from the sun and permanently frozen, so we had to work with axes and ice chisels. We cut a passage two-and-a-half feet wide by four feet high straight into the bank and cribbed it with plywood and boards every two feet so it couldn't cave in on us as we worked. Once we got this project under way, I hired Charlie and Pierre Codzi to replace us so that I could go ahead with the boat. After they got twenty feet into the bank, they exca-vated a room six feet square, where the temperature remained about twenty degrees Fahrenheit all through the summer. I put up two insulated doors in the passage and began using it to store fish and meat for human consumption. The work was slowed, however, by the abrasiveness of the frozen sand that they had to chip through, as it quickly dulled their tools. Half their time was spent resharpening with files until I got a powered carborundum wheel.

After the day's work, Bob and I would go out to our three nets in the eighteen-foot freighter canoe. We were getting around fifty fish a day. One evening on the way back we tried fishing with rod and reel and caught trout as fast as we could throw the daredevil spoons out. By the time we got back to our dock, the bottom of the canoe was covered with fish. There was no doubt that Colville Lake was blessed with an abundance of fish and my dogs were putting on more fat than they really needed. I sunk a series of stout poles in the bank near the water and strung a hundred feet of chain between them. To this I tethered my team. They were securely tied, yet still could take a drink whenever they were thirsty.

Unfortunately the native dogs were not so lucky. They were tied mostly to insecure willows and sometimes by a short eighteen-inch trap chain. Because they were seldom given water, we were constantly bothered by loose dogs during the night. After giving everyone a warning, I stood it as long as I could and then one night I shot one of the offenders. It just happened to be one of the chief's dogs. He immediately pulled up stakes and moved his tent across the bay where his dogs could run loose and not bother anyone. Actually, as the summer wore on, more and more people moved across the bay, a mile-and-a-half away, put up their tents and built extensive drying racks for fish. It got to the point that I had to hold Sunday services over there.

Before July was out, I finally finished the new cabin-cruiser, which I christened *"Quimpay,"* the Hareskin word for the arctic loon. Unfortunately my companion Bob cut deeply into his left thumb with a hand saw just prior to finishing the job. Though I put four stitches in it, there was at least one severed sinew and he would need more sophisticated surgery later. To give the *Quimpay* a good shakedown cruise, Bob and I were joined by seven of the natives on a camping and hunting trip to the extreme north end of the lake, twenty-five miles away. We stopped en route at an island with a gull rookery, where the locals picked up a supply of fresh eggs. Following this we were lucky in shooting two geese. During the five days we camped down there, I got to taste wild swan for the first time. I even shot a bear from the canoe, but only wounded him in a tangle of low willows. We made the mistake of trying to locate and finish him off on foot. He could have mauled one of us, but luckily this time we found and killed him before he got to us. I promised myself I would never get myself in a similar situation again. I had forgotten the similar promise I had made in Fort McMurray!

Another thing I learned on this trip was that a swan can swim far underwater. The next lake north, into which Colville Lake empties, is connected by three miles of mostly fast water and a few minor rapids. Two of the teenage natives wanted to go with me, but when we got to the head of the first rapids they indicated in no uncertain words that they would prefer to walk down and let me run the rapids alone. This I did and found them to be completely safe. But I also found out that this attitude to white water is fairly common among most northern natives and may stem from the fact that most of them cannot swim. The inability to swim has nothing to do, however, with a fear of climbing ladders, which is also a common phobia among them. Anyway, I picked up my hunting companions at the foot of the rapids and we continued down into the next lake, called *Ketaniahtue*. There we shot a few ducks and ran into a few moulting swans who escaped by diving under water. We chased one with the canoe. Finally, after twenty minutes, Olawee was successful in hitting it with a paddle when it came up for air. A full-grown swan can dive deep and cover an amazing distance swimming underwater before surfacing.

Our stay at the north end of the lake was interrupted when a boat came up with the news that a twelve-year-old boy had cut his eye and I was needed to attend him. Apparently he had built himself a toy helicopter out of some bent tin and was launching it off a stick with a length of string to get it spinning. It had spun right into his left eye and cut deep into the cornea. There was nothing I could do but call for a medevac plane. When he got to hospital they had to remove his eye. At the same time, Bob's thumb was still bothering him, so he decided to fly out to see a specialist who spliced his severed tendons together again. He never returned to Colville Lake.

Now it was time to put the *Quimpay* to work bringing in the logs for next year's church. To do this I hired eight men and moved them down the lake ten miles to a tent camp. There they cut logs and piled them on the shore while I tied them end-to-end with short ropes and towed them back to the mission. This work went on for weeks. When they had cut all the big trees in one area I would move them to another, or we would move along slowly with the *Quimpay* while they cut and floated logs out to me. We needed only the biggest trees, as this building was to be huge by local standards. After we had nearly 300 good logs back home, we skidded them up the twenty-foot bank and onto the church site one by one, using about ten men and a stout rope. Before the onslaught of winter I got all the cement footings poured and we were ready to build the following summer.

While this log harvest was going on, two men were constantly at work, chipping steadily into the permafrost to build my underground freezer. I had no time to fish with rod and reel, but the gill-net fishing was a daily chore. It increased toward fall, as more fish entered shallow water. Every evening at 7:00 I tried to be in the mission so that I could report to Fort Smith on my Marconi transceiver, get the news, and send out any messages from the community. Of course, I couldn't neglect my religious duties, so I rang the bell and called the people to attend daily Mass. On the first anniversary of my arrival, August 15th, the feast of the Assumption, I was pleased to officiate at the first marriage in Colville. Frank Codzi wed Mary Charney in the mission chapel, and this was followed by the traditional feast and drum dance.

Although I had initially learned to speak the Hare language fourteen years earlier at Fort Norman, I was now working to improve my facility with it. Charlie and his wife LaLouise were a constant help in correcting the sermons I wrote. When our work was done, they would often join me in a game of cribbage. Sometimes, when I had closed the chapel doors after the evening Mass, a crowd would gather on the common room floor to engage in a game of high-low poker, while I entertained the children with my guitar. In this way the new mission was also filling the role of community clubhouse.

With the dramatic increase in population, the store was needing more and more trade goods. To facilitate this restocking, Bill McNeely engaged the services of an ex-Royal Canadian Signalman by the name of Pat Kelly. Pat purchased a Cessna 180 on floats and began flying in goods from Fort Good Hope, including the mail. He often tied up at my dock and spent the night with me. In return for taking him out fishing in the *Quimpay*, he once flew me down to Aubrey Lake, where I shot a young moose. According to custom, I took a little meat for myself and then distributed the rest among all the inhabitants. One evening Pat left his plane at the dock and joined us for an evening movie. When the film was over it was pitch dark. I encouraged him not to leave the plane where it was, as a wind could come up during the night. He felt that it was perfectly safe, but he woke me at four o'clock to help him move it. We did so, but it was already too late, as the pounding against the dock had opened a crack in the side of one float. As a result he had to fly south to get it repaired. He never returned.

Toward the end of August, CF-OMI returned suddenly out of the sky, bearing more freight and the government nurse from Fort Good Hope, Cecilia Walsh. She brought a supply of medicine and gave everyone an anti-polio cocktail. All the people drank it, though they had never even heard of polio. Two days later, when they had left, I was celebrating my forty-third birthday when the RCMP Otter landed, bearing their Chief Superintendent from Ottawa, C. B. MacDonell. He had heard of my satellite foundation at Colville Lake from members of G Division at

Inuvik and stopped by to see how we were doing. I took him out in the *Quimpay* so he could catch a lake trout.

New log cabins were continually going up around our settlement and I was often called upon to help cut and place the rafters or to cut-in and hang doors and windows. For one thing, I had the only chain-saw in town. For another, no one locally knew how to use a steel square to mark roof rafters for the proper roof angle. On top of that, I had a table saw in the workshop and could make window and door frames. The consequence was that I was far busier as a carpenter than as a missionary. On the other hand, isn't helping part of being a missionary?

As the days shortened and the air cooled the trout moved slowly into shallower water closer to our village. To take advantage of this I began adding to the nets I had set until I had six in all, mostly set out toward Duka Island, two miles to the north. I had built a hatch on the bow of the *Quimpay* so that two men could stand in it, run the net over the deck in front of them, and pick out the fish as it went by. When the bow got too heavy, we would switch to the open stern of the boat behind the cabin. The daily catch kept increasing from 300 to 400, then 500 fish, mostly trout, and averaging five pounds each. On the 5th of October, when the temperature was six degrees below freezing and ice covered our boat, we took a record 575 fish, which could have weighed 2,875 pounds. Our work was only half-finished when we got back to the dock; all these fish had to be put on sticks and then lifted up onto a high stage I had built in front of the fish house by the water's edge. A "stick" of fish was ten fish skewered on a sharp willow. But the heavier trout went only 1 or 2 to a stick. Whitefish were kept separate. When the lake started freezing over I was forced to pull out all the nets, but by then I had 3,775 fish on the stage with another 675 in the fish pit, so I was in far better shape for dog feed than I had been the previous fall. On the other hand, I had a lot more dogs, for, besides my working team of seven, Cora had recently borne ten pups.

In spite of the many trips Pat Kelly had made with his float plane bringing in foodstuffs, by early October the store was completely out of flour, sugar, lard, soap and other essentials. I began mentioning this shortage over the air on my nightly "scheds." The word got through to the Indian Agent, who promised to send in a relief plane. When it finally arrived on the 19th of October our bay was completely frozen over, so he landed our supplies four miles down the shore and we got it with dog-teams.

Although the shortage of these items had caused us all some discomfort, I experienced a lot more from a broken tooth that gave me constant pain. And although I had been regularly extracting the teeth of the natives, somehow I couldn't get up enough courage to extract my own. By putting iodine on it constantly I succeeded in killing the nerve.

The view I got from my kitchen window of the change of seasons was dramatic as I watched the sun dip below the horizon a little farther to the south each evening. As it receded, the mercury in my thermometer steadily dropped. This drop in temperature caused the surface of the lake to turn to ice, and the ice was soon covered with snow. The Indians left, family by family, with canoes at first and then with dog-teams, until only Charlie the storekeeper, his wife, one son, the Pentecostal minister and myself remained. So our population was reduced to five, but I still rang the bell daily and called them to join me for Mass and the rosary.

I had just gotten out to the nets with my dog-team one morning when I heard the motor of an aircraft and immediately turned around and returned to the mission. I was not disappointed when I received four bags of mail, the first we had received since freeze-up. I also got two visitors in the persons of Dora Lafferty and Simone Kochon, natives of Good Hope and Colville Lake, who occupied the boys' bunks for a few nights until they could get transportation out to their families' tents. These girls more than paid for their room and board by cooking and cleaning for me and I was glad to give them temporary shelter. One evening as I returned in the dark from the bush with a sled-load of firewood, I had the unusual pleasure of finding the mission warm and lighted and a good supper ready for me, and

I couldn't help thinking how comfortable my life could be if I had a wife. It was wishful thinking I knew, but how natural the thought.

Wolves do occasionally kill and eat a tethered sled-dog during the night, but more often they are after a bitch in heat. At any rate, one of our trappers over on Aubrey Lake got a letter through to the game warden, Frank Bailey, at Fort McPherson saying that wolves were bothering his camp, so Frank flew in with some quarters of caribou meat laced with strychnine which he placed in the surrounding area. He and his pilot spent the night with me and I took advantage of the chance to sell and ship four of my pups. I always enjoyed having visitors and tried to treat them the same way I would want to be treated if our roles were reversed. Meals and a bunk for the night were taken for granted, with nothing asked in return, but some travellers did think ahead and brought some fresh foodstuffs which I greatly appreciated.

My fellow member of the cloth, the Pentecostal minister, persevered in his tent at the other end of the settlement and I seldom saw him. One day he suddenly appeared, dragging one foot that was well wrapped in blood-soaked towels. As he told me about an accident with his axe I got his foot up on the kitchen table and proceeded to close the gash with nine stitches. When I finished he seemed very grateful and offered me three dollars with the quotation from Scripture, "A labourer is worthy of his hire." I of course refused it, quoting Christ's words about a reward in heaven for anyone giving even a cup of cold water in his name. So it was a theological stand-off.

I had heard about the Anglican "Rat Sunday" in Aklavik, a Sunday in spring when the congregation put a muskrat skin in the collection instead of money. I thought it a good idea to adopt in this area where the principal fur is pine marten. So, as the people began arriving by dog-team for Christmas and coming to the mission to pay their respects, I started suggesting that an appropriate gift would be one marten pelt, which was selling at the trading post on average for seven dollars. The idea met with an enthusiastic response. Following the Midnight Mass there was a sizeable bundle of twenty-four marten pelts hanging from the ceiling next to the chapel. I later sent them to the bishop, who had them sold at auction. This once-a-year donation to their church, though largely symbolic, was a big morale-booster for the missionary.

As we prepared for my second Christmas at Colville I got other help in the form of four sled-loads of firewood and eight young men to cut it up. One of them also brought me a small tree to trim in the mission's common room. The girls, far from being outdone, donated a lot of their time cleaning and decorating the mission and its chapel, which looked lovely for the Midnight Mass.

Boxing Day turned out to be far from joyful. For one thing, someone had opened the trap door in the common room ceiling to cool the room and I didn't notice it when they left, so I awoke to find the water in my wash basin frozen solid. The crowd that left after the movie were far from calling the celebrations quits and proceeded to spend the rest of the night drinking home brew. The result was that I had to patch up one poor reveller who had been hit with the stock of a rifle. While I was engaged in this work of mercy, Charlie Masuzumi, the trader, walked in and handed me the keys to the trading post, saying he had quit! I had to report this to the owner, Bill McNeely, in Fort Good Hope that evening over the radio. He lost no time flying out to take personal charge. He bunked at the mission for the first few nights, hoping for a reconciliation with his clerk. When that failed, however, he had no alternative but to stay on and run his outpost store himself. He bunked with me until he got Charlie moved out of his cabin.

Finally we were down to the last day of the year. I planned on making it a day of quiet reflection while I wrote my sermon, but it was not to be. Before I had even finished my breakfast, I had the Pentecostal minister's foot on the kitchen table while I removed his stitches. As soon as he left, two men carried in Paul's wife, Monique, with a similar gash in one foot that required five stitches, so again my kitchen table became my operating table. In this case, however, there were complications when Monique fainted at the sight of her own blood and I had some difficulty reviving her. She had been in the day before to have one of her molars extracted and the strain of a repeat visit so soon was more than her system could take. The day was almost over before I got to my desk to write my sermon.

As the old year, 1963, ended, I rang the bell in the mission steeple calling everyone for another Midnight Mass that would begin the New Year. In my brief sermon I reviewed the progress that had been made during the past twelve months, with special praise for the hard work they had done harvesting over 300 large logs destined for our new church. I predicted that in a year's time we would be celebrating the New Year, 1965, in that new building. I congratulated those who had put up their own new log homes and urged them to get more of their families and friends to move out from Fort Good Hope and join us. In just eighteen months the changes we had made together were impressive. If we could maintain this momentum, I promised we would soon have built a thriving new community.

20

A Time to Build

The New Year came in quietly and proved to be a natural continuation of the old. The free-trader, Billy, continued to occupy one of the bunks in my clinic room when he wasn't over at his store. His partner in the aircraft, Pat Kelly, obtained the services of a new pilot, Duncan Grant, to ferry in freight for the store from Fort Good Hope. Landing on skis in front of the village, he started bringing in 1,300 pounds of freight with each trip and I was using my team to haul all this stuff up to the store.

Early in the new year we five priests in the Hare district held a week's meeting at Fort Norman. During the previous summer the old mission and church there had been torn down. A new, larger building served both capacities, and included a half-dozen rooms to accommodate just such regional conferences. Our days were spent discussing common problems like the prevalence of alcohol and ways in which we could help our natives both spiritually and materially. We talked of the feasibility of introducing AA meetings and initiating co-ops. We were generally free in the evenings, so I took advantage of this to visit all my old friends around the Fort. These visits were disheartening, for I stumbled into many drunken parties. I came away convinced that this town had gone downhill significantly since I had left it fourteen years before. The missionary in charge, Father Felicien Labat, agreed with me that the trend would continue until it hit rock bottom. Then, perhaps, the people would realize their sad state and begin to climb back up. It presented a real challenge for us men of the cloth.

Back at Colville Lake I could thank God that alcohol had not yet become that addictive among my parishioners. Still, we were not completely free from it. The people at Fort Norman were more apt to drink hard liquor from the government liquor store at Norman Wells, while those at Colville substituted home-brew. I soon found out that they could make brew from just about anything as long as they had yeast and sugar. Such store items as navy beans, raisins, currants, rolled oats, canned fruit and even catsup were often added to the pot. Although it could be manufactured practically overnight, its alcohol content was probably only about five percent. When ten gallons were made at a time, however, the cumulative effect could be enough to produce drunks. It wouldn't have been so bad if we were dealing with solitary drinkers, but the Dene people love to socialize with their neighbours, and that includes drinking. The consequence is that, if anyone makes a pot of brew, he wants everyone to taste it. So in a small community like ours, even one good-sized pot affected everyone. Even those who didn't drink – a very small minority – were adversely affected by the hounding they got for not joining in. By the attendance at religious services I learned whether or not a brew-party was in progress.

The idea of the missionary travelling around in winter with his trusty dog-team to hold religious services in the various native tents might sound romantic, but it was far from painless. On Ash Wednesday I was visiting the tent of Saklay on *Saluetue*, about twenty-five miles north of the mission, after a hard day breaking trail for my dogs. I should have slept like a log except for the fact that Saklay's mother-in-law Verona had a continuous series of nightmares and kept waking us with her screams. And to add to that, she kept yelling to her son Seesa from 6 a.m. to 8, to get up and make a fire, as she was cold. After two nights of her I was glad to move on to the next camp, hoping for a better night's rest. I did it in spite of the fact that I was sandwiched between eight other sleepers, but when I went to leave I discov-

ered their loose pups had badly chewed my harness during the
night. I got back to the mission just at dark and noticed that the
thermometer read forty below Fahrenheit. It took a few hours to
get the chill out of my cabin.

I was returning with a load of wood when an aircraft flew
over and I recognized the identification, CF-OMI, on the wing –
the mission Beaver. It was my fellow American priest, Bill Leising, bringing with him our Provincial, Rev. Lucien Casterman,
and Brother "Slim" Beauchemin as engineer. We had a good
lunch and then I showed them some recent 16mm colour movies
I had taken around Colville. This led to the subject of the use of
film to promote the missions. Due to medical difficulties, Bill was
not flying during the winter, but intended to use the time to put
together film for the office of the Propagation of the Faith. When
he heard how much original footage I had accumulated, he
started putting pressure on me to lend him this potential
bonanza. We were talking about a large wooden box I had that
contained around 25,000 feet of unspliced 16mm Kodachrome
film weighing about 150 pounds. At first I adamantly resisted his
arguments that this rare documentary footage should be put into
his hands for cutting, splicing and eventual screening. I would
lose all control over it and would be left without even a duplicate
copy. We argued the matter most of the afternoon. In the end he
won. With the help of Brother Beauchemin, he carried the film
box down to the aircraft and took off with it.

Later that fall I got letters from Bill in Edmonton, where he
had set up an office and studio with the intention of working on
my film and others he had taken. In one letter he invited me to
join him to form a working team, with me in the field taking more
footage and himself processing the film and working it up into
finished programs that could be used to advertise the work of the
missionaries in the North. He bolstered this idea with the opinion that I was wasting my time and talents in such a small backwater as Colville Lake! Frankly, I didn't like the idea at all, but
sent his letter to the bishop for his comments. He agreed with me
and told me to forget it, which I promptly did. Correspondence

from Bill suddenly ceased. The next thing I heard was that he had left Edmonton and was working to set up a TV station for the Oblates down in Belleville, Illinois, where the Oblates have a shrine they also call Our Lady of the Snows. My letter asking what had happened to my precious film went unanswered. I began to worry.

It wasn't until late the following winter that I was able to get down as far as Fort Smith for our annual retreat and then on to Edmonton with some fellow Oblates. The large rectory of the French Parish of St. Joachim in Edmonton served as a hotel for all the transient Oblates out of the North. I learned that Bill Leising had stayed there before returning to the States, so I got the rector to help me search for the missing film. We finally found it in a broom closet under the church! So much for lending things to good friends, or believing them when they vow: "I promise to return them to you personally."

Canadian Pacific Airlines kept a Beaver and a single Otter based at Norman Wells; these were the two aircraft we saw most often. I had had all the lumber for the building of the church brought down the Mackenzie River by barge the previous summer and was bringing it out little by little every chance I got, mostly by splitting charters with those coming our way. Their pilot named Keniston, the one who had originally flown me in and had scoffed at the idea of building a mission at Colville, had been flying in this lumber and told me he had taken it all except for some sixteen-foot planks that he couldn't get in the aircraft. Did I want them cut in half or a foot taken off one end? I told him I had a letter from his main office advising that a sixteen-foot plank would fit the single Otter, but if he couldn't get them in to cut off a foot rather than cut them in half. He landed out in front on skis early in May with my lumber, which I was surprised to find uncut. He confessed to having found that it did fit after all. But the few planks he brought could have been put in on my last trip without any trouble – and here the mission was being charged for another charter. He said that this was all that remained of my lumber at Norman Wells. So I gave him a small box of outgoing mail containing about thirty letters, including all our barge orders for the summer. I didn't find out until September that more of my lumber had turned up on the Wells strip when the snow melted, so on September 12th I sent pilot Ray Douglas out of Inuvik over there with his Otter to get it. Besides the missing lumber he handed me another surprise – the same box of mail I had sent out with Keniston in May! It had been found accidentally in a warehouse at the Wells, soaking wet and now too late for the barge season. Such irresponsibility was not characteristic of your regular northern bush pilot, most of whom you could depend upon.

On the 7th of May, Ascension Thursday, we got the worst snowstorm of the winter. It left three-foot snow drifts and buried all our trails. While I was waiting for the snow to stop falling I had an unexpected visit from the game warden, Frank Bailey, along with Constable John Hayes from Fort Good Hope, who brought the mail. They overnighted with me and the following day the pilot, Blaine Wells of Connolly-Dawson Airways, flew Frank north to check the poison bait he had planted on an earlier visit. He brought me the carcasses of two large, near-white wolves. The following week saw the temperature above freezing every day and the snow melting rapidly. I busied myself skinning the wolves and stretching the pelts, breaking a new trail to my woodlot and pulling my two gill nets from under the ice. Though only the trader and his wife were habitually in town to attend my religious services, I continued to conduct them daily.

I continued to paint and was beginning to wonder if I would ever get away on my sled trip north as we saw flocks of swans flying north and ducks landing in the slough behind the village. The ice had already moved on the Mackenzie River at Fort Good Hope and there were eight inches of melt water under the snow covering Colville Lake. Generally this water lies on top of the ice for three days. Then, as the ice gradually candles, it runs down and leaves the ice dry on top. It was the 25th of May before this happened, fourteen days after my last attempt to travel, but it looked as if I had to go now or forget the trip for this year.

I had built a ten-foot Eskimo-type komatik with steel runners, which I now used to cross the lake ice. On top I put my regular bush toboggan. The sun was just setting at 11 p.m. when I got out on the lake with my team to begin my trip north. The air was clear with the temperature at ten above zero Fahrenheit as we picked our way across fifteen miles of open lake, trying to avoid the snow drifts and plot a course across the darker patches where the snow cover was thin. I had three of the younger pups in harness for their first long trip: Starbuck, Nevada and Spook. They were working well, though the soft pads of their feet were soon showing signs of blood. At 1:30 in the morning the sun rose again and at 3:30 we reached the shore at the mouth of the Bekadu River and made camp. I unharnessed the dogs and chained them to trees while I rolled into my sleeping bag before the fire.

It was noon when I again awoke and rekindled the fire. As I sat by my fire heating a copper kettle of snow for tea, I listened on my small transistor radio as a news broadcaster described increased tension in Vietnam. This seemed a world away from my tranquil setting. It was again cooling off before I put the dogs back in harness and resumed my trek north at seven that evening. The runners of my komatik were sinking about three inches into the melting snow, so the dogs had to work to keep us moving at a dog trot. About every half hour I stopped to let them rest and to check the younger dogs' feet, which concerned me greatly. Before midnight I spotted smoke from a tent camp. When I pulled in there, I found Echale and his family. There were nine at home, with three of the men gone hunting beaver and muskrats. After I had tied up my dogs and moved into the main tent, they fed me a supper of fresh beaver meat. I had learned to like it, and it was a welcome change from the caribou I had been eating all winter. After we had said the rosary together at midnight we all wrapped ourselves in our blankets and went to sleep.

The hunters had returned and were cooking for themselves on the portable wood stove by the time we got up at 10 a.m.

Those of us who had spent the night sleeping now joined the hunters for breakfast. When we had finished, they took our places on the spruce-floored tent to spend the day asleep. During the spring hunt the work was divided into two shifts: those who hunted by night and those who did the camp work by day. After we had eaten, Echale harnessed a few dogs and went off to visit his net, while his wife, Veronique, began skinning and stretching beaver. The daughters, Sarah and Simone, brought in some dry wood which was cut up for the fire with a Swede saw by the old grandfather Saiten. Then I gave the girls a piece of canvas tarp and had them cut it up and make moccasins for all my dogs to protect their feet from the sharpening ice. Late in the afternoon I built a makeshift altar at the back of the tent. I heard five confessions and then said Mass there at eight in the evening. Echale wanted to send his boy Byadi with me as a guide through the tricky three-mile portage around the fast water up ahead. Byadi, however, did not get back from a hunt when it was time again for me to pack up and get on the trail at 11 p.m., so I left alone.

For the first five miles the going was good, as I proceeded alone with my toboggan over the freezing snow and bare patches of ice. I skirted many large, open holes of water in which the ducks had landed. The pups would have gone directly at them, had not the older dogs up ahead kept to the trail. When I came to the three-mile portage through the bush, however, I found the trail bare of snow, with a foot or more of running water in the gullies. Soon my caribou overpants were wet above my mukluks. After midnight I was into the feast of Corpus Christi, the day I had promised Saklay I would be at his camp on the next lake north to offer a Mass with his group. There was still a chance that I might make it when the trail turned left along the edge of a raging, spring-flooded river. I was on a sheet of sheer ice that followed the bank and tipped toward the open water, so I stopped the team and walked ahead holding the lead dog's harness. I hadn't reckoned with the three young dogs who were just ahead of the sled. They were attracted to the edge of the ice by all the waterfowl swimming about. Before I knew it, they got so close behind my back that the sled plunged over the lip and into the river. I had no alternative but to jump in myself and keep the sled upright, before it pulled the whole team into the water.

Out of the corner of my eye I saw the five-gallon Klim can containing my precious camera and film float downstream. I was struggling with the sled in water up to my chest with the wheel dog dangling off the ice in his harness and looking for a place where I might get the sled up over that four foot wall of concave ice. There was a broken spot about 200 feet upstream and I managed to get the lead dog to work his way slowly along that slippery footing until I finally reached my exit point. But with the contents of the sled now soaked it had gained a couple of hundred pounds in weight. It was all I could do, aided by the dogs, to skid the toboggan up out of the water and back onto the ice. I just sat down by the sled, while my heart pounded, and surveyed my dreary situation. There I was, in the middle of nowhere, at one in the morning on the 28th of May, with the temperature at zero, sitting completely soaked on the ice next to my soggy sled-load of gear.

But I didn't sit there long: my wet clothes were freezing to the ice. As soon as I had caught my breath, I drove the dogs off the ice and up into the bush. To lighten the load, I had thrown up onto the ice everything I could get from the sled, but the axe was still in it. I lost no time in chopping up some dry wood. Luckily I had a waterproof vial of matches in my breast pocket. With these I quickly kindled a fire. Then I gathered up the packsacks I had thrown up on the ice and dumped their contents out on spruce boughs around the fire to dry out. I had taken off my parka when we started over the rough portage trail and had put it on top of the load. Now it was gone somewhere downriver.

What a night I spent around that miserable fire and walking all over the hillside in wet feet looking for dry wood to keep it going. By morning I finally had a set of clothing dried out. I immediately decided to push on. This time I put in the sled only the barest necessities: a tea pail and a little grub, the rifle, the axe and the tarp. My sleeping bag, Mass kit, binoculars, Rolleicord and spare clothing I left behind as useless. I put only three dogs in harness, too, so that I could control them. The other four and the three young dogs I let run loose. So we followed that ice ledge cautiously for two miles until we came to the next lake, Ketani-ahtue. There I could see the sealed can which contained my film and the Bell and Howell movie camera, floating among a flock of swans! I spent some time cutting two long green poles which I tied end-to-end and used to coax the can over to the edge of the ice. Next I caught and re-harnessed the four loose dogs. Then we could continue under full dog-power.

After eight miles down the middle of this lake I went through the narrows in its centre which give it its native name. Then we turned west into a bay, where Saklay told me I'd find his camp. I found it deserted, however – not a soul around – and the tracks leading out showed that the group had gone north over the lake ice. I had come so far that I was not about to give up at this point and go back, so I continued down the middle of the lake. As the sun rose higher in a cloudless sky, the ice continued to candle. Its sharp surface cut through the dogs' new moccasins and they were leaving a trail of bloody tracks. I didn't like the prospect of their going entirely lame from their sore feet, so after an hour I stopped them. They immediately fell to the ice and began to gnaw at it to slake their thirst, while I fired off my .30-.30 in the hope that somebody ahead was close enough to hear it.

After two long minutes I heard an answering shot off to the northeast. Thank God, because I really was beginning to entertain thoughts of turning around. I continued on toward the last shot with assurance that they were not far up ahead. After a few more miles I fired again. This time I got a much closer answering shot that even the dogs noticed and understood. Another three miles and we could see the tent camp on the shore ahead. Soon we were off the ice and among friends. Saklay, the chief, welcomed me along with his brothers Debieh, Alphonse and Jige and their respective families. First they fed my dogs and then I borrowed a blanket and promptly fell asleep. I now knew what it meant to be dog-tired.

Yes, I had made it for the feast of Corpus Christi, but with no Mass kit I was unable to celebrate it as I had planned. No matter, we said the rosary together after I woke up. Then I was again given a good supper of fresh beaver meat. Some dark patches of ice indicated that it was getting weak and in danger of breaking under strain. Saklay didn't want me to proceed alone. By midnight I was again on the back of my sled heading south down the middle of Ketaniahtue with a young buck named Olawee, his team leading the way. We had gone about an hour when we spotted a black bear on our trail up ahead. Olawee actually hit it with one of three shots he fired from his sled, but the bear ran ashore and we didn't pursue it. When we reached the south end of this lake we took to the bush portage trail instead of following the ice along the riverbank as I had. It was rough going, however, as we made our way over fallen logs, through knee-deep streams, running behind our sleds. Finally we stopped opposite the point I figured I had left my gear the night before, tied our dogs and walked a half mile down to the river. We found my campsite and loaded ourselves with 150 pounds each of wet gear and took three hours to get back to the sleds. It was five in the morning when we finally got into Echale's camp. After a snack of cold beaver meat we wrapped ourselves in wet blankets and slept till afternoon. Late that evening after rosary I again loaded my toboggan onto the komatik, now badly torn from its bush passage. Luckily I had left my radio at this camp, or it would have been wrecked by the waters of the Ross River. I continued on alone across the frozen surface of Colville Lake. Although all the dogs' feet were now cut and bleeding, we got back to the mission at four in the morning.

That was the final dogsled trip of the winter and I was glad it was over. Not only were the dogs left lame with sore feet, but I had strained my left knee somewhere on the trip and was also limping for a few days. But suddenly it was spring, with the annual good news – ducks – and the bad news – mosquitoes. My good Bausch and Lomb binoculars had water trapped in them. I tried every way I could think of to get them open, even making a couple of special tools, but in the end I had to give up and mail them back to the Rochester company to fix. With nobody around town but the trader, his wife and the Pentecostal minister, I had few interruptions and got right to work putting a new canvas on the eighteen-foot freighter canoe. When the ice melted out to the end of the dock, I filled up all my water barrels using an ancient yoke and two pails. I also began a new oil painting of Eskimos on their barge in the Mackenzie delta. Ever since I had been living at Fort Franklin I had begun notes on the Dene people. Now I began typing these notes out, with the idea of eventually getting them into print. So in the evenings, when the light was poor for painting, I could be found in the office at my Royal portable, typing.

Spring in the Arctic is something beautiful to see, especially if you've just lived through the long, cold winter. First of all, there's the unaccustomed long sunlight hours and the heat generated by so much sun. Just to be able to go out of doors without bundling up makes one feel suddenly liberated from the constraints of the cold. Then there's a sudden influx of wildfowl, when all one has seen for eight months were ravens and ptarmigan. As soon as there were a few yards of open water in front of the mission, they used the surface as though on a landing strip: pairs of widgeons, teal, old squaws, pintails and various species of mergansers and loons. The air above this water was suddenly patrolled by Arctic terns hunting for minnows. At the same time, smaller land birds like robins, swallows and sparrows were flying about, looking for nest sites and filling the air with their own special music. Every day we watched flocks of swans and geese winging their way north and sometimes a pair of bald eagles. I built a blind over in the slough behind our village and shot a few ducks with my twelve gauge until I found I could get just as many from my workshop door with the .22, and with less effort.

After mid-June the natives started returning from their spring hunt using pack dogs to transport their camp gear and furs. Unfortunately we had heard that the Hudson Bay Company at Fort Good Hope was paying a top price of only nine dollars for beaver pelts and fifty-five cents for muskrats. This made our local free-trader, Bill, hesitate to buy any fur until he had received word on the current market from his backer, Bill Levine of Edmonton Fur Auction.

On the 7th of July I was suddenly inundated with important visitors off-loaded at the end of my dock from a Wardair Otter aircraft. They included the annual treaty party consisting of the Indian Agent, Al Cottrell; his assistant, Danny Norris; plus Corporal John Hayes dressed in the traditional Mountie's red serge. Dr. Joe Cramer was also with them, bringing in a portable X-ray machine, plus a nurse and technicians. These last proceeded to set up in the mission's common room, while the treaty was paid on my front porch, followed by a meeting with all the natives. Although we had a local chief in the person of Saklay the people were officially part of the Fort Good Hope band where all of the decisions affecting them were made. Now they asked for a local native to be placed on the Good Hope Tribal Council. In a show of hands, veteran Saklay was re-elected chief and he immediately asked that he be paid twenty-five dollars annually as the other chiefs were, instead of the five dollars he had been getting as a sub-chief. He also asked for the traditional blue serge suit worn by chiefs.

The Indian Agent promised to send in lumber with which to build more cabins, plus cartridges and nets, and asked me to take charge of these items. Up to now I had been helping the people build their homes with no thought of remuneration, but now the government agent told me I was to be paid two dollars and forty cents per hour for my work, and an additional eighty-seven cents an hour for gas when I had to use my chain-saw. Finally a contract was worked out to sell a minimum of 3,000 pounds of trout at thirty cents per pound to be shipped by any passing free charter to Good Hope for distribution as relief. I guess this idea originated in Good Hope, where up to now only buffalo meat was distributed every Friday to the needy. The business ended, all the visitors went out on the lake to fish.

Following the excitement of this official annual visit I got down to the start of the new church by beginning to pour cement for its thirty-two footings. It took a day to mix the cement down by the lake and fill six of the twenty-eight- by twenty-eight-inch plywood boxes I had made as forms. Over the mission radio hook-up I learned that Father Felicien Labat at Fort Norman was tearing down that beautiful old church there, so I asked him to send me six of the hand-made gothic windows, plus two statues. If I couldn't save that historic building, at least I could incorporate some if it into our new church.

Talk about a job that covers a variety of duties! That of the missionary can't be beat, especially if he is a bachelor. One day, and a fairly typical one, I was supervising the mixing and pouring of concrete while monitoring a batch of baking bread, when Chief Beargrease interrupted to ask me to referee a domestic fight going on in the village. I found Efficially beating up his crippled wife Mary while engaging in a brew party. Actually the fight was all one way, which is usual when husband and wife are involved, but I was especially disturbed because I had married the couple less than a year before. In fact, I got so wrought up over the unwarranted beating Mary had been given that I'm afraid I threatened her bullying husband with a like beating if I ever caught him repeating such a performance. When I got back to the mission, my bread was burning and my cement crew were sitting around waiting for further orders. Then Simone brought me her two-day old boy asking me to dress his umbilical cord. In spite of such interruptions, I had all the cement footings for the new church poured by mid-July and could now begin the log construction.

As the news spread around the North that Colville Lake had a mission and that a church was being built, people came to the conclusion that there must now be people settling there permanently. And they were right. This prompted the visit of various government people like the flying doctor from Inuvik. In general they rushed through their official duties so that I could take them out fishing. They were happy that this generally included their pilot, for then he would not add waiting time to their bill. These visitors were seldom if ever disappointed in their catch and generally took most of it back with them.

We were in the process of laying the first tier of twenty logs on the church foundation when I threw my back out while cutting with the chain-saw. It was that old slipped disk I had injured back in Fort McMurray returning to plague me. For the next couple of days I walked in a Groucho Marx kind of crouch. I was still in this condition a couple of days later when I happened to notice from a window that Efficially was drunk again. So I hobbled over to his tent and dumped out his brew pot. When I went on to his father's cabin I didn't notice that he was following me with a loaded .30-.30, bent on ending my career then and there. Before he could carry out his execution plan, however, some of his relatives disarmed him. From this incident I learned that trying to keep the peace in a small community could be hazardous to one's health. Still, my intentions were good and my fears for Mary were well-founded: we found out a few years later that one of Efficially's drunken beatings proved fatal to her. Actually, I had not taken it upon myself to spill brew pots, but had been encouraged to do so by Corporal Hayes in Fort Good Hope. He thought that this would reduce the risk of serious trouble in a small village that had no police protection and no lock-up.

We were only on the second tier of logs on the church walls when I noticed that we were short of the larger size. We had to temporarily shut down the project and take a crew of eight men fifteen miles down the lake and set them up in a logging camp. Two days later I returned with the *Quimpay* and put thirty-two big logs in tow back to the mission. When I got there I found Cessna CF-HID tied to our dock. Pilot Eustace Bowhay had brought in a load of trade goods for the store and he and his companion camped with me. The next day I took the two of them five miles down the shore to the Packsack River, where they caught twenty-one grayling.

Sundays were days of rest and of attending Mass in the morning at 11:00 and Benediction in the afternoon at 2:00, after which all the kids in town piled into the *Quimpay* and I took them out to Duka, an island two miles off shore. There we had great times gathering eggs in season or picking berries and fishing. It got to be a Sunday tradition in summer that went on year after year. When we returned in the evening I presented a slide show in the common room. And that's how my day of rest went.

On the following day I returned to my logging crew at the mouth of the Bekadu River where we put fifty-seven logs in tow and picked up the six men who had been working there. It took us seven hours to return. It was late when I got back to the mission, and I had three medical cases waiting for me. The next day a Beaver aircraft landed from Inuvik with dentist Dr. Chymura and his assistant Raymond Chow who carried up their portable drill and equipment. They moved into the mission for a week's stay.

The following day another Beaver on floats brought six American fishermen from Grand Rapids, Michigan. They were on a raft trip down the Mackenzie River and took this side trip in order to catch trout, of which the big silty river has none. As I had no more spare beds in the mission these men had to throw their sleeping bags on the common room floor for the three nights they were there. But they were so impressed with the fish they caught that they promised to return for a week the next summer if I would put up a log cabin to accommodate them. This suggestion put the idea of a fishing lodge in my head, an idea that would soon become Colville Lake Lodge. When their aircraft came back to pick them up it brought me six old handmade gothic windows from the log church at Fort Norman which Father Labat was dismantling. With all these visitors I was side-tracked from my work on the church and had to depend on my crew to notch logs as the walls slowly rose.

The American fishermen had just gotten away when a Connolly-Dawson Cessna 185 piloted by Blaine Wells landed from Inuvik with Dr. Rooks. Dr. Rooks was in charge of the Inuvik hospital and as such directed my own medical practice. He also happened to like fishing and got to be a frequent visitor. We would conduct a clinic together and then go out on the lake. He had just left when they brought in a young boy with a nasty cut in his knee that required six stitches to close.

The rash of visitors finally subsided and I could devote myself full-time to the church project. I noticed that, when I was not on the job, very few logs went up during an eight-hour work day, but with me helping, my eight workers notched-in forty logs in one day. That represented two complete tiers. When we got up fourteen logs, I put on the final, or plate, log. Then I built scaffolding to hold us as we put up the roof rafters. The work was proceeding on schedule and I had every hope of getting it completely closed in before winter came.

Then came the big feast of summer, the Feast of the Assumption, August 15th. The mission was full for the morning's High Mass, at which thirty-five received communion. The girls plucked a bag of ptarmigan I had kept from winter for a grand picnic. After Benediction, fifteen of the kids joined me on the *Quimpay* as we crossed the end of the lake and built a big fire. One of the boys tried to help me by carrying my two cameras off the boat, but unfortunately he fell in and soaked them. On our return we had a second mishap: we hit a reef and had to go ashore to hammer out the propeller before we could continue back to the settlement. When we returned at 8:30 in the evening we found the whole town torn by drinking and fighting. I felt sorry for the children who had to return to those parents. The chief and I spent the rest of the evening patrolling around trying, with poor results, to keep the people in their own tents or cabins. Louie threw his son Edward out of his cabin, sleeping bag and all, but as Edward tried to leave by canoe someone stole his paddle, so he moved into the mission with me. Then, using a stick of kindling, I broke up a fight in Louie's cabin between his brother Martin and Olawee. When I walked Martin to his cabin I found the door locked, so I broke it with an axe (which I later had to repair), but I finally got him washed up and into bed. Then I discovered his wife Angele dead drunk in their tiny log warehouse. I carried her into the cabin and threw her in bed with Martin. The evening's revelries ended when I sewed a few stitches in the head of another combatant and sent him home so that Edward and I could get some sleep. I was glad August 15th came but once a year.

We had been plagued by mosquitoes all summer, but now the black flies arrived to torment us as we worked to fit in the church's roof rafters. Having no repellent, we tied kerchiefs around our heads, but black flies are ingenious in finding their way up under a person's pants. And they leave a welt that can itch for days.

Someone sent me a volleyball, so I put up two poles, stretched an old fish net between them, and taught the young people the game. We lacked the means of marking the outside lines, so the rules were modified to a point where it became a game between two sides of any number of players who lost the point only when the ball hit the ground on their side. Next I laid out a baseball diamond and introduced this popular American sport with a soft ball and a stick that more or less resembled the traditional bat. The rules proved a little too complicated, however, so it turned out to be a game between the batter and the rest of the players. If he could hit the ball and get to first base and back home, he won, and that was it. For sheer exuberance and total participation, however, my new sports couldn't beat the traditional game of *ayati*.

As we neared the end of August we could feel fall in the air and see frost on the willows in the mornings. Wencho had ten pups and I set more nets to make a fall harvest of dogfeed. I also took a crew of men out along the shore with me in the *Quimpay* to get a few cords of firewood. And often I'd get back so late and tired I lacked the ambition to cook supper and simply fell into my bunk. The flu was going around and I frequently made the rounds of the cabins dispensing medicine. I even took one patient into my clinic room for a few days of isolation.

Just when the nets were beginning to produce a lot of fish I lost the use of the forty-three-horsepower Scott outboard. A connecting rod went through the block and I was reduced to using my little three-horsepower Seagull. Pilot Alan Loutit landed one day in his Otter aircraft to pick up our single student for school at Grollier Hall in Inuvik. I spent my forty-fourth birthday at the end of August making window frames for three new cabins that were going up in the village and omitted any celebration. We had had enough lately. Now into September we got frost during the night and the willows turned yellow as we sheeted in the church roof with plywood. I was also building an octagonal steeple down on the ground and sheeting it with some aluminium shingles I had gotten from the mission at Fort Franklin.

September 15th turned out to be a red-letter day: we got the new steeple up on the roof and secured. Now the new building looked like a proper church. Meanwhile, the natives not working on the church were putting up their own log cabins and I was helping them with the more difficult aspects, like cutting in the windows and hanging their doors. We were all being rushed by the weather and the prospect of imminent snowstorms.

Then Constable John Hayes, our nearest member of the RCMP stationed at Fort Good Hope, flew in with the Force's own Otter to do the yearly vaccination of the dogs for rabies. He also held a meeting and told the people that in his absence he had authorized me to keep the peace and to either dump any brew pots I found or keep them as evidence until he came out on patrol. This honorary duty at first seemed to me to be an effective way of curbing drunkenness, but in time I found it was hopeless and generated ill feeling which interfered with my missionary role, so I finally gave it up. He also brought in the parts necessary to repair my big Scott outboard and I soon had it running again.

When the free-trader Billy McNeely decided to move his store to Colville Lake from Fort Good Hope I gave him all the encouragement and help I could. I even had him stay with me at the mission until such time as he had his place built. More important than the tools and equipment I loaned him to build his store was my support and encouragement, urging the natives to deal with him rather than taking their furs to the Hudson Bay Company store in Fort Good Hope. The only return I looked for was his exemplary attendance at Mass on Sundays, an obligation already incumbent on him as a Catholic.

After a year, however, he stopped attending Mass. I called on him to enquire if there was some reason for his absence. As his pastor I was concerned for him, but I was also concerned for the effect his absence would have on my little community of relatively new Christians. He was honest with me, admitting that he had joined the Catholic Church out of convenience at the time of his wedding to a Catholic native woman at Arctic Red River. His candid thoughts on the matter surprised and saddened me. I tried but failed to resolve his religious doubts. Our isolation from the outside world made the loss of his support seem to me like a betrayal and as a result our former happy friendship suffered and never really recovered.

Late in September I got a visit from our Father Provincial, Lucien Casterman, O.M.I. He brought Brother Roger Mahé, O.M.I., age fifty-one, who had been assigned to the mission at Fort Good Hope but was experiencing difficulty living with the resident missionary, Aloyse Brettar. Casterman suggested that I keep him with me for the winter and I readily agreed. I never did like living alone. I soon found out, however, that this new companion was a liability as well as an asset. I was anxious to get the new church completely closed in so that I could work in it during the winter. I saw Brother Mahé as a good man to take over the fall fishery, freeing me to devote all my time to the church.

To introduce him to this work and acquaint him with the twenty-nine-foot *Quimpay* and its forty-three-horsepower Scott outboard, I took him out to run our six gill nets. First I had to suit him in hip boots, rubber pants and jacket, but he refused the rubber gloves, saying he had handled nets before at Arctic Red River and never wore gloves. Out at the nets we were both standing in the bow hatch, pulling the nets over the bow as we took out the fish and threw them into the hold. After an hour he complained that his hands were so cold and stiff that they wouldn't work. The temperature was a few degrees above freezing and I had to complete the work alone. When we got back his hands, showed signs of frostbite and he couldn't work with them for several days.

About a week later, when he had recuperated, I sent him out again with a native. In restarting the motor out there he had not reduced the r.p.m. when shifting into gear and had sheared the pin. Instead of replacing the pin or throwing the anchor, he let the boat drift right past the village to the south shore, across the bay, where I met them in the canoe and replaced the broken pin. A week later he was again out at the nets with Martin Oudzi and failed to return at dark. On the nightly radio "sched" with Fort Smith I reported him missing. The next day it was so rough on the lake that we couldn't go out looking for him with the canoe. I had visions of them with a fire on board. If they had had motor trouble, they still had the three-horsepower Seagull as a backup. With the native Martin on board, the idea of their being lost out there seemed an impossibility.

At any rate, he limped into the mission at 4:30 that afternoon, still wearing his hip boots and rubber clothing, and told me an incredible story of getting lost the day before. After looking at all our nets and loading some 1,500 pounds of fish aboard, they circled the lake all night until at 4 a.m. they drove the boat up on a rocky shoal and abandoned ship! They were about fifteen miles north and had been walking twelve hours! Martin claimed that he had told Brother Mahé the way to get home, but that he wouldn't listen to him. One of them had inadvertently pulled out the wire connecting the lights to the battery, so they had neither searchlight nor cabin lights, nor could they find the matches to light the galley primus stove. Three days later, when the storm subsided and I got to the *Quimpay* in the canoe, I found six inches of water in the cabin and an inch of ice. John Baptiste and I threw enough fish from the hold to get it floating again and found no damage to the hull at all, which surprised me. We had no trouble getting the boat back to the village, but this incident shook my faith in Brother's ability to cope with our way of life at Colville Lake.

With over 2,000 fish in the pit and nearly 1,000 hung on the stage, I decided to terminate our fall fishery and pulled out the *Quimpay* for the season. When I tried to get out the last three nets with our eighteen-foot canoe, however, I nearly ended my career then and there. I was a half-mile out off the point, alone and standing in the bow of the boat, trying to haul in an anchor line. It suddenly snapped, and I fell backwards over a thwart. I was in hip boots and heavy rain gear. If I had gone overboard I would have had an all-but-impossible chance of reaching shore and nobody would have noticed till it was all over. I had to abandon the last three nets to the oncoming freeze-up and get back to the mission with at least my own life intact. This incident made me realize how dangerous life could be on this lake.

As October drew to a frigid close, Brother, I, and as many local natives as had not already left for their winter traplines were busy on several fronts. Foremost was the rush to get the windows and doors in the new church so work could continue inside during the cold months. Another crew had all the wall logs up on the new fishing lodge which was built, using all the small and crooked logs rejected from the church. I had to harness the dogs for the first time to go deep into the bush to find two good twenty-six-foot plate logs to support the roof rafters. At the same time Brother Mahé, with the help of two natives, was working underground to deepen our ice house.

As soon as I realized there was enough ice on the lake to set nets under it Brother and I lost no time in getting out there and setting three nets. It is important to net fish as early in the fall as possible because, as the winter goes on, the catch slowly drops off and the work of opening holes through the thickening ice to empty the nets gets more difficult.

At this time in the fall, there generally isn't enough snow to make the trail smooth for toboggans. The second half of our trail to the nets wound its way over a quarter mile of muskeg dotted with niggerheads that were very bumpy and hard as rocks. I would drive six dogs from the back of the sled while Brother Mahé sat in the cariole, but he complained about the rough ride out every second day and suggested that we take two sleds, each driving three dogs. On our first trip he was up ahead of me, when he fell off his sled. I was following so closely and going so fast that my dogs and sled ran right over him. He might have emerged unscathed, except that I was standing on my pointed iron brake in an effort to stop and it caught and twisted his knee. He was so badly injured that for the next two weeks he could barely walk. Poor Brother, he was finding life at Colville Lake even more difficult than any of his other postings.

As we worked our way into November, the sun's arc got lower and lower until it finally disappeared altogether. Life took on a predictable routine for us. Brother slept in one of the double bunks in the clinic room while I slept in the single bunk in my office. We got up together about seven, built a wood fire and rang the bell at 7:30 for the 8 a.m. Mass while we observed our congregation's morning prayers and half-hour of meditation. After a simple breakfast of toast and coffee we pursued our regular work, which for me at present was to go over and start a fire in the church before continuing work on the interior. For Brother it was to continue work on the underground permafrost freezer. We got together for a lunch of caribou soup and bread and then went back to work. For some reason the work of cooking supper, our main meal of the day, fell on my shoulders, but Brother did the dishes while I fulfilled my daily obligation of reading Divine Office, which took about an hour. Brothers were exempt from this obligation. Most evenings we spent playing cribbage with the trader or any of the trappers who happened to be in town. I always started the generator and went on the air for the nightly "sched" with the other missions. This was both a priority and a ritual I wouldn't miss if I was home. We rarely got into our bunks before midnight and often past 1 a.m. The result of this schedule was that I never seemed to get enough sleep. I had to drag myself out of my bunk most mornings, feeling more like a crippled old man than a vigorous young missionary.

Christmas came and went as it had the previous year, with the usual religious ceremonies and children's gifts and games that included contests such as eating a long string, transferring lifesavers on toothpicks held in one's teeth, whistling after eating a mouthful of dry crackers, driving nails, lighting candles, transferring oranges held under one's chin, and musical chairs. After supper I showed two western movies and then set off fireworks.

There wasn't a drunk to be seen and my feast turned out a total success.

On the day after Christmas a Connolly-Dawson Cessna 185 on skis landed out in front with nurse Cecilia Walsh from Fort Good Hope. She brought with her a portable X-ray machine. We immediately set this up in the common room because she expected to be picked up in a day or two and wanted to complete her work as soon as possible. By supper time we had taken X-rays of everybody in the village and had the equipment all packed again for immediate shipment. Having a woman in the mission and the only spare bunk in the Brother's room presented a predicament. I suggested that the Brother move up to the top bunk and let Cecilia sleep in the lower. She refused and insisted on curling up in her sleeping bag in the middle of the common room floor.

We played bridge till midnight and all three of us were asleep at 2 a.m., when the local hypochondriac, Byadi, burst in the front door with a flashlight, yelling at the nurse. She yelled at me to interpret for her and I relayed the message that Byadi said his heart had stopped! She yelled back to tell him to turn off his flashlight and she would get out of her sleeping bag. When she checked his pulse he was fine, so she advised him to go home and quit worrying about his heart.

That interruption in the middle of the night, however, caused Cecilia to oversleep in the morning. Consequently, when people started coming in for the 8:00 Mass she was dead to the world in her bag in the middle of the floor. She hadn't even heard the bells, so Brother and I grabbed hold of her bag, slid her into the clinic room and closed the door. When she finally emerged after breakfast she claimed she hadn't heard or felt a thing!

The temperature was now reading fifty below zero, Fahrenheit. After she was packed and ready to leave when her plane appeared, Cecilia spent the rest of the day knitting, with her feet stuck in the open door of our kitchen oven. We played bridge again that night until after midnight, but still she refused to use the empty bunk in the clinic room, but again bedded down in her sleeping bag in the middle of the common room floor. I had my dogs chained right outside the back of the mission and, if any trouble erupted during the night, their barking would waken me instantly. I kept the twelve-gauge shotgun loaded in my bedroom for use on dogs running loose. We were all finally asleep when, at about 3 a.m., my barking dogs awakened me. I lost no time getting out of the bunk and into my bathrobe and slippers. I grabbed the shotgun as I left my room. I was not carrying a flashlight, but thought I knew where Cecilia was lying in the middle of the floor. I was mistaken, however, for I tripped over her feet and went sprawling on the floor with the gun in hand. Luckily it didn't discharge.

Cecilia was out of her bag in record time and at my side expecting to find me hurt. I wasn't. The dogfight outside ceased, however, as soon as they heard all the ruckus inside, so I limped back to my bunk to try to regain sleep. Evidently Cecilia also had trouble returning to sleep because we had to repeat the same ritual the following morning as before, sliding her, bag and all, into the clinic room and carrying on with Mass.

The visiting nurse again spent her day with her feet in our oven as the temperature was now down to sixty below and our floor was very cold. I tried in vain to find out over our mission radio what had happened to her aircraft, so she was faced with another night with us. Yet this time, during our late night game of bridge, we persuaded her to use the bottom bunk while Brother moved up into the top one. We congratulated her on her decision and promised her that she would at last get a good night's uninterrupted sleep.

All was quiet in the mission until about 4 a.m. when I was awakened by a terrible crash coming from the clinic room. I rushed in there to find the nurse on the floor cradling Brother's head in her lap. He was unconscious, his teeth gone and his eyes rolled back in his head. Cecilia sent me for water which we threw in his face. Gradually he regained consciousness. When he could talk he mumbled something about getting up to answer a call of nature but having forgotten that he was on the top bunk. He stepped out into mid-air and fell to the floor on his back.

We couldn't find any broken bones and considered him lucky. We all lost some sleep, but this time we didn't have to move the nurse to clear the common room floor for morning Mass. She caught up on her sleep as we went to work, but later commented that her first impressions of this place being so quiet were quite wrong. As it turned out, she spent New Year's with us and it was nine days before she was picked up. So, though her first three nights were hectic, the following six passed serenely.

Cecilia was picked up by an Otter aircraft on January 4th. Then, the following day, her supervisor, Merle Pottinger, landed from Inuvik looking for her. Her supervisor ended up flying on to Fort Good Hope to see her! It was a waste of air charter flights due to faulty communication – at the taxpayers' expense. For the next couple of weeks the temperature stayed down near sixty below, so cold that I could not heat the church enough to continue my work laying the floor. I shifted to our mission workshop, where I began building the first of many birch chairs.

In spite of this very cold weather, the game warden, Len Colosimo, had Freddy Carmichael fly him in from Fort McPherson. The purpose of the trip was to kill more wolves. To do this Len brought with him another half-dozen hind quarters of caribou impregnated with strychnine. I flew out with Freddy to make these deadly sets on neighbouring lakes. At each stop we had to chisel down to water so that we could freeze-in each poisoned quarter. My reward for helping was to reap the harvest of animals killed in the following months. I got five white Arctic wolves from one set, none of which was more than forty feet from the bait. This poison, however, also killed wolverines, foxes and ravens. The game department soon abandoned this form of extermination. The wolves, in fact, were not unusually numerous and were not a nuisance, but someone in the Department of Game Management decided that their numbers should be reduced.

The sun reappeared on our horizon on January 10th. About this time Al Cottrell, the Indian Agent, flew in from Inuvik with Tom Butters who worked for Northern Affairs and Natural Resources. We spent an evening discussing ways and means of building up our new settlement. Butters, however, told me he planned on leaving the government and starting a newspaper similar to my defunct *Aklavik Journal,* which he subsequently did.

My dogs were generally well-behaved and obedient in harness, but I never liked being dependent upon just one leader in case something happened to him. So now I was breaking in a new leader, my largest white husky named Samson, who must have weighed 125 pounds. He could break a new trail in deep snow where the other leader would need me to go ahead of the team on snowshoes. One day I was out about three miles with a load of logs on the sled, heading for home, when I stopped to check a trap set for marten. I was too far from the sled to grab the trailing head rope when he suddenly started without me and continued on home at a fast dog trot. I followed on foot. Luckily we were not out on a long trip: a leader who will start up without the command can be dangerous.

To add a little zest to our nightly cribbage games with the trader, we started playing for five cents a peg. Both the Brother and I had over a hundred dollars cash from the sale of fish to the oil camps, so we were not using any mission funds if we lost. Brother proved to be a poor loser, however, and late one evening, after he had lost and Bill had returned home, I was talking to him about not taking the game so seriously. He was standing with his back to the wood heater in the common room when he suddenly fainted right in front of me and fell like a sack of potatoes to the floor. I ran into the kitchen for a dipper of water. This quickly revived him, but the incident had me worried. A few days later, out in the bush getting wood, he froze the stump of a finger he had chopped off some years before while splitting firewood. A series of such incidents convinced me that, sooner or later, something really serious could happen to him. I would feel responsible. So when we flew down to Fort Smith in March for the annual retreat he stayed there in the big mission.

It wasn't unusual to see two aircraft on skis land and park on the frozen lake in front of the mission on the same day, but to see four at once, as we did on April 7th, was a record. Among those who came were the new Indian Agent, the fisheries officer, the administrator from Inuvik, the supervisor of education, a visiting Oblate, a dentist, two patients returning from hospital and a load of groceries for the trading post.

As interesting as they all were, one stood out above the rest: he was Dr. Dowler, the dentist. I assisted him from a Cessna 180 and was surprised to see him well bundled up in an old-time buffalo coat, the kind the Mounties once wore. When I got him inside the mission, I offered to hang up this coat for him, but he refused, saying that he couldn't work without it on. Opening it, he showed me why. The lining held all the tools of his trade in an array of small pockets and clasps. He explained that he was truly a travelling dentist. Declining coffee, he asked immediately where he was to work. I showed him into my clinic room and lit the gas lamp.

A goodly crowd of natives had been attracted by all the visitors and were sitting around our common room. Dr. Dowler explained to me that he was in a rush and therefore would do extractions only and to bring in my first patient. I knew that Luke Tinatchie had been troubled recently by rotten teeth, so I presented him as the first victim. Luke didn't even get time to remove his cap. The doctor took a look into his mouth with the aid of a flashlight and, quickly assessing the problem, took a syringe already filled with novocaine from his coat lining and pumped it into Luke's front gums. He then began gently slapping his mouth, while humming a cheerful tune. In less than ten minutes he had four teeth out.

Luke stumbled from the clinic room. As he passed across the common room, he held his mouth with one hand and held up four fingers of the other. The signal was immediately understood by those waiting and they quickly filed out the front door behind him. Dr. Dowler was calling out, "Next!" but there was no next in sight. I persuaded him to join us for coffee in the kitchen. While we were sitting there, in came Chief Beargrease to find out what was happening. He had just gotten in the front door, when the dentist took him by the arm, escorted him into the clinic room and proceeded to look into his mouth. Now I had been aware that the chief had been suffering for years from pyorrhoea and all his lower front teeth were loose, but he wouldn't let me touch them. Without needing any anaesthetic, Dr. Dowler removed one in a jiffy and would have gone on to take out all the loose ones, but Beargrease jumped from the chair and came storming out to the kitchen, yelling at me in Hareskin that he had come in the mission not to see the dentist, but to find out what was going on.

This little white man had removed one of his teeth without his consent and he wanted it put back where it was in his mouth or he would report him to the Indian Agent. All the dentist could do was retrieve it from the waste basket and present it to him in a Kleenex. Dr. Dowler resumed drinking his coffee, shaking his head at the strange attitude of our Indians.

Not long afterwards, the old patriarch of the tribe, Saiten, appeared at the door. Again the dentist escorted him into the clinic and looked in his mouth. "This old fellow doesn't have any teeth at all!" he called out to me in the kitchen. I replied that I knew that, but he had heard that the white men were so smart that they could make artificial teeth to replace those lost. Even this situation didn't faze our travelling dentist: he produced the material needed to make an impression of Saiten's gums. The weather turned bad and the dentist was forced to spend the night with us, but the extra time wasn't lost. Using my workshop, he proceeded to cast the impression he had made in plaster of Paris. The contents of that buffalo coat never ceased to amaze us.

Two months later, I received in the mail a set of upper dentures for old Saiten. They fitted all right, but he complained that when he used them he bit into his lower gums. He asked me to write the dentist and ask him to send the lower set. Dr. Dowler wrote to me saying that these dentures were very expensive and the department didn't want to invest in a lower set until Saiten learned to use the uppers. As a result Saiten never did use them to eat, but kept them in a rag in his shirt pocket. The only time I saw him put them in was when someone was about to take his picture. When he died, we buried him with those unused uppers in his shirt pocket.

The next day I had more time to discuss the possibility of a school for our settlement with Harold Darkes, Superintendent of Education. He informed me that a small hostel was to be built at Fort Good Hope to accommodate students from Colville Lake. I realized that a day school at Colville without a hostel could be detrimental to the trapping, because the women would be required to stay in town to take care of their kids. Without the women out on the traplines, the men's work would more than double. Consequently, they would not go as far or stay as long. The result would be far fewer furs, their only source of income. So we concluded that the best arrangement for the immediate future would be to send our children to the Fort Good Hope school and hostel.

With so many aircraft suddenly available, it was no surprise that a group of our natives chartered one of them on a shopping trip to the Fort. Unfortunately, besides groceries, they managed to buy a case of hard liquor from someone. This, plus several barrels of home-brew, began to take effect after all the visitors had departed. People were staggering or crawling from cabin to tent, with fights erupting all over town. The chief and I walked around most of the night, trying as best we could to get people to stay in their own places. Alfred Masuzumi was a teenager who had not participated in the drinking, but had been beaten up by two of the older men. They threatened to finish the job the following night. He ran to me, seeking asylum, so I kept him in the mission overnight. The next day I persuaded him to return to his cabin on the promise that the chief and I would keep up the night patrol and prevent his two antagonists from getting at him. We were with him at his cabin the next night when his two enemies showed up and attempted to enter. In the melee that ensued in the dark, blows were struck and the night air rent with howls of pain, but the two intruders never got inside the door. I took one of them back with me and put four stitches in his head, at the same time delivering a stern lecture. Alfred, thoroughly shaken, again slept at the mission.

When the dust settled, Corporal Hayes flew in with a Justice of the Peace. Court was held in our common room and various small fines were levied against those who had been making home-brew or injuring people in fights. There were complaints against me for acting as a Mountie, but Corporal Hayes backed me up, saying he had asked me to act in that capacity in his absence as the village was completely helpless against drunks. Nonetheless, then and there I decided to quit my peace-keeping efforts and confine my work strictly to the mission. I went even further than that at the Mass the next day, when I announced that, from now on, I would no longer handle the medicine, give movie shows, deliver messages over the radio, act as the post office or help with the building of new cabins. This announcement must have had a sobering effect on my little congregation because on Holy Saturday I had three hours of confessions and everyone appeared sober for the Midnight Mass for Easter. During the following week I had a full house for services, which gradually renewed my enthusiasm and I relented on all the help I had threatened to cut off.

We were into warm weather the first of May before I finally got the six gothic windows from Fort Norman set into the church walls. I now had a crew inside, helping me with the finishing work, trimming the log ends, staining and putting stars up on the ceiling. Two other natives resumed work on the fishing lodge, cutting the last of the wall logs. After they had finished, Charlie Masuzumi and I moved over to that project to put up the roof and build six bunks inside.

As the month progressed and the sun climbed higher in our sky, we began to see the snow melt and run down onto the lake ice. Soon we were seeing caribou crossing our bay, heading northeast, and this attracted local hunters with their dog-teams to chase and, they hoped, knock down a few. I already had a few chunks of meat stashed down in my new icehouse, so I didn't bother to go out. Yet when the ducks began to land in a narrow stretch of open water in front of the mission, I rarely missed a chance to get my supper. I must admit, however, that my carpentry interfered with my cooking: I often put a bird in the oven and then came in at supper time to find it cooked to a crisp. Either that, or the fire went out and I had to cool my heels until my supper was cooked. Such were the woes of bachelor life in the far North.

We were into June, and the sun never left our sky. It simply made a shallow dip along the northern horizon and one could work all night if one had the energy. On the 24th we had enough open water to land a float plane. The PWA Beaver took advantage of this to bring in my very first party of fishermen from Norman Wells. They were Walter Phelan from Cheyenne, Wyoming, with his son Bernard and his nephew Paul. We had completed the new six-bunk lodge just ahead of their arrival and they were very pleased to move into it. It was a great improvement over sleeping on the mission's common room floor, as our previous fishermen had done. The next day I took them out fishing despite all the ice surrounding our bay. They hooked a lot of trout, including one that weighed fifteen pounds. The next week, the ice cleared out of almost the whole lake, so I took my three guests down to the north end for Arctic grayling and northern pike.

As the summer of '65 wore on, I found myself engaged in all the usual pursuits. Besides operating a mission with the regular daily religious services, I was busy trying to put the finishing touches on the new church: building an altar and pouring cement for a large set of front steps, among other things. Jeannie Branson flew some guests over from her lodge on Great Bear Lake and, noticing that I had no bell in my new church, promised to look for one for me when she got back outside.

21

THE COMMODORE

The Northwest Territories, along with the Yukon and the Provinces, was invited to participate in a mammoth Centennial Voyageur Canoe Race during the centennial year of Canada's Confederation, 1967. The race would start in the Rocky Mountains and end at Montreal. Before the event itself, two years of training would be necessary for the crews. I listened for over a month to an appeal broadcast over the Canadian Broadcasting Corporation's northern radio network for a commodore to head up our training team. Among the qualifications listed were: a valid driver's licence, previous experience in canoeing, ability to work with natives, and so on. The position didn't appeal to me, but evidently Jacques Van Pelt, head of our Territorial Recreation Department, thought I'd be the man for the job and got permission from the bishop to use me for a month! I got the message at the last minute and, before I knew what I was getting into, found myself on a plane to Fort Smith.

At that time, Fort Smith was still the unofficial capital of the Northwest Territories and all government offices were there. Once there, I was introduced to my crew: seven Eskimos from around Aklavik and six Dog-ribs from Fort Rae, including the fifty-eight-year-old son of their chief. The Centennial Committee there gave me a preliminary briefing, $750, and wished me *bon voyage*. The next day we were in Edmonton, waiting for a night flight to Toronto. Some of these boys had never been on an aircraft and some couldn't even speak English. It was nearly midnight when we got on board Trans Canada Airlines' prop-driven airliner heading east. The stewardess gave us each a small blanket when we got airborne and asked if there was anything else she could do for us. Ed Lafferty was the interpreter for the Dogribs and he piped up in a voice that could be heard half-way down the aisle, "This guy here wants to know, where is shithouse?" "Oh, you must mean the washroom," replied the stewardess, pointing out the facility, and then on the side to me, "Your boys have such quaint expressions."

At Toronto I couldn't get a flight to North Bay, so we all trouped down to the Canadian National Railway (CNR) station and boarded the train. A conductor showed us to fourteen seats in their last car and told me to keep my Indians together, and, if they wanted to smoke, to wait till the train stopped and then go outside. This struck me as strange, as we had passed through a smoking car up ahead. We obeyed him anyway during our six-hour trip to North Bay. It proved rough, mostly because we had slept little the previous night on the plane. We finally arrived in a pouring rainstorm and I took my ragged troupe to Vernon Gray's Motel to get some sleep. I looked in vain for our camp gear, which was supposed to have been delivered, and then attended a commodores' meeting. On the following day, a huge army truck arrived from Ottawa with our camp gear, which it discharged on the motel's front lawn. I could hardly believe my eyes as I saw what our government had supplied us with for the month's paddling ahead. Where the other crews were outfitted with the latest in lightweight, mountaineering-type gear, ours looked like residue from World War I. The army tents were huge and heavy and the poles alone would be a load for one of our canoes. And then off came a case of toilet paper, a case of soap chips and several large plastic garbage cans for portaging!

That afternoon we all participated in a 1,000-meter rowing sprint for the benefit of the press which was to accompany us every mile of our trip. One of my two twenty-four foot canoes came in second, so I was pleased. To end the race, however, the boats had to be pulled up high and dry. To do this all my boys got their moccasins wet, so that evening at an official reception and supper one solicitous member of the Women's Aide noticed my boys in stocking feet. She immediately took up a collection and presented all our crew with new moccasins the next morning. Actually, all our boys had spare moccasins with them. Later I noticed them doing a brisk trade in moccasins at one of our campsites.

That evening I called my thirteen stalwarts to a final meeting at the motel. I told them to get a good night's sleep, as all canoes would pull out the next day and cross Lake Nipissing. One of the crew captains asked if they could walk across the road for a coffee before they went to bed. Foolishly I gave them permission, with the proviso that they all be in bed by midnight. I had Jack Elanik, captain of the Eskimo canoe, bunking with me and he didn't show up until 4:30 in the morning. He told me a tale of their night's escapades that raised my blood pressure several degrees. He said that they started talking at the coffee shop about being deprived of the benefits of civilization for the next few weeks, so they decided to get some taxis and see the town. The taxi drivers took them to a house full of beautiful girls who also gave them drinks. It was one wonderful night!

The next morning I was at a meeting at the government pier when I got a phone call from Mr. Gray, the proprietor of the motel. "I've got one of your Eskimo boys here in my office," he began, "he is quite intoxicated and there are several Indians outside who are trying to get in. He says they are going to kill him. Should I phone the police?" I told him to hold on and I would be there in minutes. The boy was Selamio from Aklavik. He had brought back a bottle of gin the previous night and apparently drank it alone. The Dog-ribs outside said they were only trying to get him back to his room before he caused any trouble.

At twelve noon all the canoes got away while the commodores were taken in a large Ontario Provincial Police launch. I carried my binoculars and noticed that Selamio was drinking a lot of lake water. The press was on board interviewing us and one of them asked me how my native boys were being treated by the world outside. I remembered the incident about smoking on the CNR train and mentioned it. This item made the Associated Press wire service and I was hounded about it for the duration of the trip. The train officials insisted that there must have been some misunderstanding, but I stuck to my original story.

It took over four hours to cross Lake Nipissing and I was let off to check on my boys' first campsite. I was horrified to see that they were preparing to pitch tent right in the midst of a luxurious patch of poison ivy, which of course they didn't recognize as it is unknown in the North. I had purchased one complete casting pole and reel for each canoe. As we picked out an alternate site for the tent, Sam Selamio came up to me and asked if he could borrow the Dog-rib's pole. I said No, use your own boat's rig, but he replied that he had lost it on the first cast! This seemed preposterous, but when he took me to the huge rock overlooking deep water to explain how it had slipped out of his hand into the deep, I had to believe him. But he didn't get the other boat's outfit.

Once the boys were safely camped for the night, I again crossed over with the police boat to North Bay where I spent the next two days shipping most of the army gear back to Ottawa and replacing it with lightweight tents (no poles) and gear, including new canvas packsacks I had manufactured on the spot. In a rental car I drove west to the French River that drains Lake Nipissing into Georgian Bay and rejoined my crews.

Bad luck seemed to be following them as they had a nasty hole punctured in one canoe by a rock. Worse than that was the report I got on Sam Selamio, who apparently was doing his best to aggravate the other crew. As I had seven men for the Eskimo canoe where they could only accommodate six, I immediately drove Sam to Toronto and put him on a plane for Edmonton. The next time I ran into him was several years later. I was on a tour of the new correctional facility in Yellowknife when, whom do I see in the kitchen but Sam, peeling potatoes. "What are you doing here Sam?" I asked. "Learning to be a cook," he replied.

The longest day's run of the trip was to be from the mouth of the French River, south on Georgian Bay to Honey Harbour. We obtained the services of the Coast Guard's large cruiser, which was to run ahead of all the canoes so no one strayed off course. I told my boys to follow the big steel boat. And they did. In fact when all the other canoes turned in at Honey Harbour and the Coast Guard turned out to the open lake, my boys continued to follow them! They were ten miles out into Georgian Bay before I could stop them and turn them around. All the canoe teams had paddled over sixty miles that day, but those two from the North-west Territories must have done over eighty. That evening when we finally got our two tents pitched at Honey Harbour my boys noticed that the crew from the Yukon, six men who worked year round as forest rangers, were all enjoying a beer around their fire. They asked why they couldn't do the same. My experience to date with them made me hesitate before I started supplying them with any kind of intoxicating beverage.

The next day we entered the Trent Canal that would take us across Ontario to Kingston on the St. Lawrence River. One of the first towns we arrived at was Orillia, where we were met by the mayor, Mrs. Post, and literally thousands of well-wishers. We were directed to pitch our tents on the beautifully manicured lawn of Couchiching Park surrounded by the crowds and the CBC television crews. We could hardly drive a peg without someone offering to help and, because I had the only native crew, we were the centre of attention. I don't know how many fathers came up to me with questions such as, "Pardon me, but is that a real Eskimo? Would he mind if my son shook his hand? He'll remember it all his life."

We couldn't see any firewood, but soon a truck appeared out of nowhere and dumped a huge pile of birch dowels. That evening we were invited by the town to a beautiful buffet supper at the Legion Hall. As usual a free bar was set up and I instructed my boys to limit themselves to two drinks. I might as well have saved my breath: once they got near that bar they couldn't leave. When I finally got them over to the food table, they were so drunk they could not carry a plate of food to their table without spilling most of it on the floor, a performance highly amusing to the other crews.

On several occasions I paddled in one of the canoes, but mostly I drove on into a nearby town to purchase grub, which might include a side of beef for a barbecue. Most of my boys preferred fish for breakfast rather than bacon and eggs, but I had trouble getting fresh fish. Nor could I buy a gill net and I wished that I had brought one with us. We spent the weekend in Peterborough, during which Ernie Dillon, one of the Eskimo crew, disappeared completely. No one had seen him and no one had any idea where he had gone. I put an appeal on the local radio station and wasted a lot of time visiting the local jails. Just before we shoved off on Monday morning he sauntered back to the group with a story of having been taken to some summer cottage by a couple of young women. This commodore's job was beginning to get on my nerves and yet with the press hounding us so closely I had to keep up a cheerful front. Reporters from all over kept meeting me at every stop to get more information on the CNR story.

When we finally reached Kingston we were directed to pitch our tents on the beautiful front lawn of their yacht club. As we were setting up camp, a reporter with a tape recorder interviewed me and I was warm with my praise for the beautiful site the city had provided for our camp. After I had exhausted all my thankful words of praise for the city fathers, the reporter thanked me, switched off his recorder, and asked if I minded if he hung around a little to watch us put up our camp. I had no objections and now that the interview was over I could go about the work at hand. The lowest branches on those huge oaks were up about thirty feet off the ground and the reporter asked me how we were going to reach them. "Well, we'll just have to look for some smaller trees to cut for poles," I replied. "What about firewood?" he continued and I said, "Well I guess I'll send a few boys down along the lakeshore to look for driftwood." "Does this stiff wind off the lake bother you?" he asked. Finally I broke down and admitted that this was not a good campsite. In fact, it was one of the worst we had encountered on the whole trip from North Bay. I guess this was the kind of confrontational attitude he was looking for, because this was the only part of the conversation aired the next day on the local radio. All my pleasant, complimentary remarks had been deleted. I learned never to trust a reporter again.

The following morning all the canoes were pulling out to paddle the last few miles to Gananoque for the annual North American Canoe Races to be covered by the CBS Wide World of Sport. All, that is, but the two canoes from the N.W.T. I had a strike on my hands: my men were saying that they were told that they would be finished when they reached the St. Lawrence River; now they were there, and they wanted to go home. Besides, they wanted the seven dollars per day they had been promised. It took all my persuasive powers to get them back into those two canoes for the last short paddle. I finally did it by promising to go to a bank and draw out all their back pay in cash and pay them at Gananoque when they arrived. They got there at noon. I paid them off as promised after they pitched their tents for the last time.

The town was in a festive mood, crowded with visitors to watch their annual big event. The CBS TV crew held a quick meeting with us commodores, asking us to stage a quick, final sprint, with all our boats appearing across the nation in their weekly "Wide World of Sports" show. A special large cup would be presented to the winning crew. I went back with this news to my crews with some misgivings. They asked what they'd do with the cup if they won it? I replied, "You will proudly carry it back home and put it on your mantle." They asked, "What's a mantle?" They wouldn't budge. I ended up recruiting six of the commodores, including myself, to paddle one of our canoes while my voyageurs cheered us madly from the bleachers on shore.

After the weekend we were all invited to Ottawa and put up at the beautiful Chateau Laurier Hotel. We had a private visit

with Prime Minister Lester B. Pearson himself in his office. Afterwards Ben Sivertz, the Commissioner of the Northwest Territories, and his Deputy, Stuart M. Hodgson, hosted us to a banquet
where the press had a last chance to photograph us. I took advantage of all the good feelings expressed by the various members of
the government to get the ear of Mr. Hodgson and impress upon
him how desperately we needed an airport at Colville Lake. Two
days later I got my crew safely back into the N.W.T. and turned
them over to the Centennial Voyageur Committee in Fort Smith.
I experienced a feeling of relief I had never experienced before.
Would I take the job again next summer? Never! I had learned
once and for all just how difficult it was to shepherd a group of
natives down into "civilization." None of the crew that had been
hand-picked for me continued on to compete in the final big race
in 1967.

※ ※ ※

During my month in Ontario, summer had slipped by
Colville Lake, and when I returned in early September I found
snow already on the ground. A couple of days later three fishermen flew in from Wisconsin and moved into the new lodge cabin
for a week. An Otter landed, too, to pick up the kids for school
and to bring in the new nurse, Florence Emmott. She moved into
the clinic room for a few days. In a brief time I had seven gill nets
set and the rush was on to put in a good supply of dog feed for
the winter before the lake froze over. Some days we would take
300 or 400 trout and whitefish, but most days the lake was so
rough we couldn't visit the nets.

Old, abandoned cabins hold a special fascination for me. I
had heard of a group of four of them at a place called Soka, about
fifty miles north of us, that had been abandoned for nearly forty
years. When Perry Linton was in one day with his Helio-Courier
aircraft I chartered him up there and took Debieh with us, as he
had been raised there. His father had operated a small trading
post there for the Hudson Bay Company and he showed us the
long flag pole lying on the ground that had once flown their flag.

Because these old log cabins were built on a dry esker they were well preserved. I noticed a broken armchair that looked a lot like the one I had recently made. Among the old rifles lying around, I picked up a nickel-barrelled .30-.30, and also found one of the old Hudson Bay copper kettles which had been manufactured in England. Debieh brought the old settlement alive with his descriptions of how things looked when he lived there as a boy. The North is dotted with such abandoned cabins, as people continue to move into the populated centres. My Colville Lake resettlement project was the only exception to this trend.

We had to break thin ice out to the nets on October 2nd, so I pulled them all out. My count was 350 fish hanging from the stage on sticks and 2,900 put down in the fish pit, enough to feed my dogs well into the winter. At that late date, pilot Willie Lazarus began fifteen trips with his single Otter to haul in building material for Indian Affairs. Most days he had to break ice with his pontoons to get in to the dock. At the same time, well-known northern pilot Smokey Hornby flew his Beaver in from Yellowknife with Gene Rhéaume and his campaign manager, Bryan Pearson. Rhéaume was campaigning for the seat of the single Member of Parliament for the N.W.T. I was appointed Deputy Returning Officer for the federal election on the 8th of November. For this event a ballot box had been dropped to me by parachute, because the aircraft carrying it was on wheels. As an American citizen, I was ineligible to act in this capacity, but apparently no one asked. Using the mission as the polling station, three people cast votes. Most were already out trapping. A Liberal, Bud Orange, was elected our Member and I figured that it had cost the government about $700 per vote at Colville Lake!

By the end of November it was time to quit the village and visit some of my people camped out on the land north of us. So I harnessed up six dogs and for the next ten days carried my portable Mass kit from tent to tent, conducting services just as if I were in church. It was certainly a change of pace, but no holiday. The days were short and I did a lot of travelling by moonlight over strange or non-existent trails. I was often cold or worried that I might be headed in the wrong direction. Sleeping on the ground in sub-zero temperatures and eating native-style at ground level was anything but a vacation. Yet it was all part of missionary life and I did not question it. Nonetheless, the night I returned to the mission it felt good to get out of my clothes and into pyjamas and to sleep in a bed again.

In mid-December, Corporal John Hayes made his first dog-sled patrol, accompanied by Special Constable George Codzi. They were driving two teams of Siberian huskies totalling thirteen dogs, which they tied up along my bank while the two of them occupied the bunks in the clinic room for the next five nights. After a day to rest up, the corporal accompanied me out to my net, where we got 172 fish. But our real passion was for chess, to which we devoted a lot of time. We were well matched and could have played day in and day out without losing our enthusiam for the game. I could well imagine how two people such as we could play right through the long winter months without noticing the darkness outside.

These two visitors were scarcely out of sight when a Cessna 180 on skis landed to deliver the travelling eye-doctor, Elizabeth Cass, along with her 250 pounds of gear and equipment. She moved into the clinic room and I put up a table and eye chart for her in the common room. Here she kept busy for the next three days, examining the people's eyes. Apparently the room temperature in the mission was a little below her comfort level, because she never took off her mink coat.

I was busy in the workshop doing some cabinet work to finish the church, building items such as the vesting cabinet and the new tabernacle, when Dr. Cass came in one afternoon to tell me that one of the men she was trying to examine kept flirting with her! "Unless you can get that Romeo to desist I won't be able to go on," she told me. She indicated to me that the culprit was Debieh, in his sixties. I concluded that her complaints were only imaginary, though she might have been close to that age herself. Maybe it was wishful thinking. Debieh had been married to Ethloleh for over forty years and was known locally as "the crazy captain," although he was far from crazy. A brother of Saklay, the chief, he was a fine example of the old-timers who had spent their lives in the bush. A quiet, industrious and honest individual who seldom drank, he was the opposite of the partying type. That he could have done anything to prompt Dr. Cass's accusation in front of a room full of people was simply beyond belief.

When I tried to stop her from lighting a gas lamp on my new kitchen table, she talked me into believing that she was more competent in bush living then she really was. "I've lit these things a thousand times," she assured me, and proceeded to touch a match to a lamp over-primed. She not only burnt the lamp, but the burning gas left an ugly ring in the table itself. "Just rub it with a little vinegar and it will disappear," she assured me, but it didn't. I had to glue a new layer of plywood onto the table after she left. When Tommy Gordon flew back to pick her up, I came down to the plane to help her load up. When she was finally ready to depart, I assisted her up into the right front seat. She had one leg up, but then got such a cramp that we had to bring her back up into the mission to straighten out that one leg before we could try again. Doctor Cass's visit was certainly a memorable one.

On a second trip that day the Cessna 180 brought me a surprise visit from one of my Oblate brothers, Father Aloyse Brettar, Pastor of the Fort Good Hope Mission. Although he could have been a great help to me in starting this new mission, he was still hurting over the fact that he had not been its builder and had lost his best parishioners, or so he said. As a result, his mood swung from grudging cooperation to outright hostility and I never knew what to expect next. For example, I often asked him to put the mail on a flight coming our way, but more often than not he told me he was too busy. The next day, while I baked a batch of bread, we aired our difficulties. As a result, Aloyse stated that he now understood the situation and henceforth would be behind me a hundred percent. When he left that afternoon I gave him a gunny sack of fish as a good will offering and he assured me that his visit was prompted by "sheer divine inspiration." I saw him off with a prayer that his present cooperative mood would persevere.

Now we were into Christmas week and every day brought back the families who had been out on the land trapping. The sound of their dog bells echoed clear in the sub-zero air. The momentum of the upcoming feast was gradually building, as I rushed to prepare the new church for its first service. I had finished the benches, the sanctuary chairs, the credence table and was frantically trying to put in wiring as two of the boys brought in a large Christmas tree and two of the girls were sewing the curtains. I kept a fire going in there every day so we could work, but had to appeal to my parishioners for sled-loads of firewood to feed a voracious large barrel heater.

The hours of my days seemed to grow shorter and, before I knew it, we had run out of Advent and it was midnight, Christmas night. The angels must have looked down with approval as our rustic log church came alive for the first time to celebrate Christ's birth with a Christ-Mass. My two altar boys flanked me in the sanctuary as I intoned the Preface of the Mass and the congregation took up the ancient Gregorian Chant in Latin. A lot of toil and sweat had been expended to produce this day. To prevent me from too much pride in my accomplishments, however, the Good Lord allowed a cloud to temporarily darken the horizon: three drunks noisily interfered with the singing from the back of the church. I had to halt the service until they had left. One came back in and forcibly pushed his wife and children out too. Once they were gone, we could return to "Silent Night, Holy Night" and the peaceful celebration of the three Masses of that special night.

When the ceremonies were over, we all gathered in the mission's common room to wish each other "Merry Christmas!" I lit the gas lamp and turned off the generator that had powered the church lights. The girls helped me serve a lunch, while the drunks were celebrating their own version of "peace on earth" in another part of the village. It wasn't perfect, but it was the best Christmas Colville Lake had seen to date.

With the temperature at forty-eight below zero, we carried on the next evening with a party at the mission around its decorated tree. Underneath were presents for all the children. Then I showed a home movie I had taken of the people during the previous two-and-a-half years, called by them a "Dene Show," and always their favourite. We had something special at the mission every evening right up to New Year's Eve, when we again heated the church and reassembled at midnight to begin 1966 with a Mass. This time there were no interruptions. Then over we went to the mission for cake, ice cream and cigars, after which I passed out new calendars. Following this, everyone crowded out onto the front porch, in spite of the fifty below weather, to watch some impressive aerial rockets. As their brilliance faded and their echoes died away, I bid everyone a good night and retired to my bunk to sleep the sleep of the completely exhausted.

Planes kept landing with various visitors. Often I had overnight guests. Following the trapping season, at the end of February, the natives again moved back into town and the Mounties came out to inoculate our 200 sled-dogs against rabies. About this time I was officially appointed the dog officer, with instructions to shoot any loose dogs. It wasn't a job I was particularly fond of, but someone had to do it. Then Easter came and went. Our sun got hot again and melted all the snow. Our lake turned from white to green. It was glorious summer.

The first of July saw the end of the ice and the first of our summer fishing lodge guests, three men from Amherstberg, Ontario. On the following day I guided them out ten miles in the *Quimpay* to Folendu, an Arctic tern rookery on a small island. We looked for nests and dodged a hundred diving terns for half-an-hour. Then I decided to try a cast for trout off a rocky point of this island. I was surprised to get a strike on my first cast and even more surprised when I reeled it in to find I had snagged a duck! Apparently it had been swimming underwater and my hook just caught it on the skin of its back. It was a one-in-a-million occurrence. I told Bill Schwimmer to use his camera to record it, but he refused, saying, "No one will believe how you did it and they'll accuse us of cruelty in catching the duck and then hooking it with your lure." So I never had any proof for this strangest of all fish stories.

Before these fishermen left, three more arrived – Mormon bishops from California who wouldn't drink tea or coffee. Following them, I had Larry Chateauvert, head of the government's new tourist bureau from Fort Smith, bringing in two sports writers from the States. They were so impressed with the size of the trout they caught the following days that one of them, Ed Park, wrote an article. It was published in *Sports Afield*, and in consequence many more fishermen came up the following years. I soon discovered that such first-person, published accounts were worth far more than any advertising.

In August, Bob Tucker, an old flying buddy from Rochester, flew in with a friend from Kodak and another from Xerox. For the first few days my guide, Charlie, took them out fishing local waters. Then I decided to give them a little more adventure and took them myself in the cabin-cruiser twenty-five miles down to the north end of the lake. Here I pitched a tent for overnighting. One of the boys got a nineteen-pound trout and we started back home the next day, stopping at various creeks to catch pike. The wind started to blow from the north and we stayed in one of these protected creek mouths until it was nearly dark, hoping the wind would drop. It didn't. We had a decision to make: either spend the night there, or try to get home the last fifteen miles in a very heavy sea in the dark. As they were expecting a pick-up plane the next day, they decided to push on, so we again headed out onto the lake.

We had the eighteen-foot freighter canoe in tow and its line soon parted, setting it adrift. In the failing light and monstrous seas, one of the fishermen tried unsuccessfully to catch it off the bow with a boat hook. I ran over the canoe, cutting a nasty gash in its side with our propeller. We finally caught it alongside and pulled it up over the stern. Now it was completely dark as we proceeded south toward the village, with only the stars to guide us. The breaking waves were soon coming over the transom, flooding the boat. My three fishermen were kept busy bailing with pails, as I hung grimly to the wheel in the cabin, but at one point it came loose in my hands. Once under way, we had to see the trip through to the end: there was no protective harbour along this stretch of the lake. It was one in the morning when we finally reached the safety of our dock and could breathe a sigh of relief. My fishermen spent most of the night warming and drying themselves around the wood heater in their cabin. The next day, however, their pick-up plane got in so late that they missed their connecting flight south out of Norman Wells and had to spend an extra three days there.

When I saw them the following year in Rochester, one of them was wearing a conspicuous silver cross around his neck. When I asked him when he had started wearing it, he said, "Right after we got home that night on Colville Lake." My friend Bob recounted his experiences in the South Pacific, flying from a carrier during the Second World War. He had been shot down by the Japanese and had to use his revolver to shoot himself free from his tangled parachute. Then he spent nine hours in shark-infested waters before being rescued by a P.T. boat. Yet he concluded by saying, "During that ordeal I had never been as scared as I was that night on Colville Lake."

Except for a suitable bell for its steeple and a painting I had planned for the wall behind the main altar, the new church was now complete. To prepare for this painting, I finally located in Montreal a piece of canvas seven by eight feet which I glued to a plywood backing and mounted on the wall. I made sketches of one of the local girls holding a child. They would be my Lady of the Snows. Then I went up on the hill behind the settlement and made a sketch of all our log buildings. Now I proceeded to outline a composite picture on my primed canvas. It was going to be a slow job and I wanted to get it right the first time. I wouldn't get a second chance. It was hardly under way, when our bishop landed unexpectedly one day with the Apostolic Delegate to Canada, Archbishop Sergio Pignedoli. He had come to bless our church officially. For Colville Lake it was an historic day, which, as usual, happened without any planning or forewarning. Of course, a High Mass was offered in the newly blessed church, during which I led the congregation's singing and entered the sanctuary to present the bishop with the Christmas donations. These amounted to $190. As long as this church stands it will probably never see another Archbishop. Archbishop Pignedoli was later to be named a Cardinal and was considered *papabile* (stood a good chance of being elected) at the time of the Papal election at which Pope Paul VI was chosen.

We were beginning to get snow flurries on the 8th of September when a Grumman Goose landed with Fred C. Mannix and a party from Calgary which included his son Ronald, his physician Dr. William Boyar and the noted wildlife author Andy Russell. They lost no time getting out on the lake fishing and by supper time had taken fifty lake trout. On the following day my guide took them to the north shore of the lake where, in shallow water, they saw some giant trout which refused to take any bait they threw at them and Ronny, in his excitement, fell overboard! In the meantime their pilot flew me to Fort Good Hope to pick up my mail and on to Norman Wells, where I collected a few hundred pounds of barge freight. A snow storm the next day prevented any boats from going out, but Fred Mannix had his shotgun and a lab retriever with him and used the bad fishing weather to walk around our surrounding tundra and bag six ptarmigan. Unfortunately our native cook chose this day to get drunk so she couldn't prepare them for our supper and I was pressed into service to cook us caribou steaks.

22

A Bell for a Church in a Hospitable Place

For the fifth year I made preparations for freeze-in at Colville Lake. When I first arrived, I had thought the bishop would allow me to stay until the construction phase was over and then move me on, as he had done so many times before. But the years were slipping by, and the subject had not come up. With every month, my living conditions got better as I gradually built things to make life easier. I now had a good warm mission house in which to live, a built-in chapel for daily religious services, and a church in which to accommodate the larger crowds for the big feast days of the year. I now had a good team of seven working dogs, a boat, a fish pit and plenty of nets to provide them with the food they needed. Month by month, too, I was acquiring all the little items that make life in the North, if not easy, at least tolerable.

When the temperature fell below zero, I opened the fish pit, hooked the fish out onto the snow to freeze, and then stacked them up on the stage near the dog line. By that time I had set two nets under the new ice to be left there all winter. Indian Affairs and Northern Development sent down Tom Yate and Don Waleski from Inuvik to make a survey of our airport site. More precisely, these two engineers proceeded to test the soil of the site

457

just above the village which I had chosen as the best location for an airport.

One day I was out on my trapline with the dogs, when a plane landed on the lake, bringing Stu Hodgson, Deputy Commissioner of the N.W.T., along with the Administrator from Inuvik, Sid Hancock, and Lyall Trimble, our Member of the Territorial Council. They walked into the mission kitchen, stoked the wood fire and sat there waiting four hours for me. Of course I hadn't received any message they were coming. Stu brought a bottle of rum, anticipating I would immediately open it, but, after I thanked him, I told him I would keep it for some important visitor, and put it away. He often told this story later and, now that I look back on it, I realize those visitors were about as important as I would get during the year. Anyway, we had a good caribou steak supper, followed by a meeting of all the people and finally some Dene movies.

All my parishioners returned from the bush for Christmas, which we celebrated suitably in a most sober atmosphere for a change. Then came New Year's, and suddenly we had to change our calendars to 1967. We were only a week into the New Year, when an Otter aircraft landed from Norman Wells with two cases of hard liquor ordered by the free-trader McNeely. The effect was immediate and devastating. I didn't get a taste of the liquor, but I did get my fill of the consequences. Charlie Masuzumi came to ask my help in clearing his cabin of drunken and unwelcome visitors. Fights had erupted all over the village, while some were on their hands and knees trying to empty their stomachs on the snow. I had to take a few of them back to the mission for first aid and then walk around, trying to get people to stay in their own cabins or tents. It was midnight before I gave up and climbed into my own bed with a new awareness of just how tragic and disruptive the white man's powerful liquor can be in a native settlement.

These drinking sprees also generated some work for the RCMP. Charges were laid against Charlie Barnaby and John Baptiste Gully, but when police got their Otter CF-MPW to fly them in with a justice of the peace, the two culprits had left town on a hunt. So I was picked up as a guide and, thinking they were at a bush camp on Aubrey Lake, we flew there. They had left, however. So we took off again, followed their sled track north, and spotted them on another lake walking on snowshoes after a herd of caribou. We landed on skis right next to them, took them on board, and flew back to our settlement at Colville Lake. The trial was held promptly at the mission and both were found guilty and fined twenty-two dollars and fourteen dollars respectively. They were then flown back to where they had been picked up and allowed to continue their hunt. The result was a new awareness of the long arm of the law in our village. We may not have had any law enforcement officers stationed nearby, but that didn't mean they couldn't materialize suddenly.

We were now into Canada's centennial year of Confederation and I was getting letters from the government, suggesting various ways of celebrating this occasion. It had been a long time since I had used my snow knife to build an igloo, but, as the snow had recently been blown to the right consistency, I decided to make one down on the lake. When it was finished I made a sign for it which read "Colville Lake Centennial Post Office"! Actually, we didn't have a post office: I handled the mail from the mission office. Another idea I got was to put up an old-time moss teepee. To this end, I had one of the boys bring in a supply of long poles and we erected it after the snow had melted.

Late in April when the snow was beginning to melt, we saw something unusual coming across the ice of our bay. It was two caterpillar tractors, a D-7 and a D-4, pulling sleds and caboose, and driven by Karl Mueller and Wayne McNeill. They had come across country from Norman Wells to begin work on our airport. If they hadn't been so late, they might have done the job that summer, but, after clearing the snow from an area 2,700 feet by 200 feet, they returned to Fort Smith. Karl didn't get back to continue the work until the 9th of July, by which time the strip area had melted so deeply that it was all but impossible to work on it. The cat continually got stuck. Finally, after repeatedly pulling one stuck cat out with the other for a week, Karl gave up and returned to Smith. With all the protective moss scraped from the permafrost the twenty-four-hour summer sun soon turned the whole strip area to a quagmire.

During the previous winter, Karl had chartered Wardair to fly their Bristol aircraft in from Yellowknife to Norman Wells, from which they would ferry fuel for his cats. Their chief pilot, Don Braun, had tested the thickness of our ice and found sixty inches, far more than the thirty-six inches required to bring in a payload of 11,500 pounds, or twenty-eight barrels of diesel fuel. Besides, all the snow had melted on the lake, so the ice was as smooth as a runway for their wheeled plane. They proceeded to make four trips to Norman Wells for fuel. Don had been the first pilot to land at the North Pole using this same aircraft.

The Bristol crew was still working, when a new Cessna 206 landed from Fort Smith with Forestry Officer Pete Ferguson and his pilot Gordon Pachell, who brought in a load of firefighting equipment for our community. They carried, as well, an appointment for me from the Commissioner, making me an official Forestry Officer. Pete had never been to our community before and remarked how quiet it was. I fed the Bristol crew at one in the morning, and it was two before Pete, Gordon and I hit the sack. We had just dozed off, when Julia Turo rushed in the front door and demanded that I go to her tent to talk to her husband Gully, who was drunk and threatening to beat her up. As it was late and no damage had been done, I urged her to move in with friends for the night. I put her out and locked our doors. She was back pounding at the doors for the next four hours, but I wouldn't answer. When we got up in the morning, we found she had broken our front door window, cut her hand, and had left her blood on all of our three outside doors. Pete revised his first impression of this being a quiet, peaceful settlement.

Pete had to visit the settlement of Paulatuk, 170 miles north of us on the Arctic Coast. He invited me to accompany him, so we took off after a good breakfast. When we had passed the tree line I spotted a herd of muskox and, as I was carrying my 16mm camera, I asked Gordon to make a pass so that I could photograph them. He turned his aircraft 180 degrees and descended as we looked ahead for the muskox. Up ahead we spotted what looked like a flock of geese coming toward us. Since it was the 18th of May, this was possible. As we got closer, however, we could see we were actually looking at a line of willows growing along the top of an esker. We were flying under them! Gordon pulled up just in time to skim over that hill of gravel. A cold sweat broke out on all of us: we had come as close as possible to flying right into the ground in the partial whiteout. If those willows hadn't been growing there, we would have been demolished. When we spotted the muskox again, Gordon decided to land on his skis and let me approach them on foot, which I did, and got some impressive close-up footage. As soon as we landed safely at Paulatuk I felt like kissing the ground, so happy was I to be on terra firma again.

We went over to the mission to visit Father Leonce Dehurtevent and found him in his usual happy, optimistic mood, although he was living poorer than his Eskimos. An old friend of mine, Joe Thrasher, took me over to see their new Co-op store and I bought a sealskin for ten dollars, while Pete, a gun collector, bought a couple of old rifles from the Eskimo people who were all living in tents. We took a quick supper of fried caribou and bannock at the mission and flew south.

The next day I was busy in my workshop, building a small motor-boat for the outpost, when a Piper Champion landed out in front. It was the Fort Franklin teacher, Claire Barnabé, flown in by Don Stickney. Don had been working over at Ford Bay on Great Bear Lake, halfway to Fort Franklin, using a D-4 to make a runway. He told me that a group of businessmen from Ponoka, Alberta, had gotten together to start a new sport fishing lodge. They needed a landing strip before they could start flying in their building material. Don got to be a regular visitor on weekends and I enjoyed his company, especially our cribbage games. Claire, a former nun, was also an interesting guest. In the following years she went on to become a well-known northerner in a variety of government jobs.

As soon as I got the boat out of the workshop and painted, I was free to go ahead, full-speed, on my warehouse. It was to go up forty feet behind the mission and replace the large, now rotting tent I had been using ever since 1962. I laid out the mud sills for the new building, which gave me a floor space of about twenty-four feet by twelve feet, to be divided into two rooms. There would be a low attic in which to store lumber. This project, so badly needed, kept me and a couple of men occupied for the next few weeks. As soon as the weather got warm, I resumed holding services in the church where I also continued to work on my large painting of Our Lady of the Snows. One evening we all walked up to our little cemetery on the hill behind the village, where I set up a temporary altar and offered a Mass for the dozen whose bodies were buried there. As I stood there, I wondered to myself if my own body would lay there among them one day.

By the end of July we had finished the new warehouse behind the mission. I fixed up half of it as a store, stocked with groceries for my workers. I had a lot of items not carried by the local trader and it was convenient for my men to pick up a few items when they quit work at 5 p.m. The old trading post in the centre of the village was now owned by Philip Codzi. Its sixteen by thirty-six feet made it too large for his use, so he sold it to me for $150 and some sled boards. I fixed it up as a show-hall with a counter at the front end, which I stocked with candy, pop and cigarettes. Now every Saturday night we gathered at the show-hall to watch Tarzan or the cowboys fighting Indians.

My two-year experience operating a fishing lodge convinced me that I couldn't go on feeding these guests in my own kitchen, so I planned two new log buildings near the six-bunk lodge. They would consist of a kitchen with an adjacent chef's quarters and a dining room connected to the kitchen by a short corridor. During the sledding season I had a number of people skidding in logs for this project. Now we were levelling the floor before notching-in the wall logs. These buildings would have been enough to keep me well occupied for the summer, but then I got an unexpected visit from the government administrator from Inuvik, George Thompson. He persuaded me to take on more work. I signed a contract to put up a small log cabin for old Granny Verona Paschal for $1,100, and a larger, three-room cabin for Alfred Saiten for $2,200, plus a contract to clear the brush on the approach to the runway, an area of 300 by 400 feet. Suddenly I had so many projects going simultaneously that I found it difficult to find enough workers for all of them.

We were engaged in this work when George Clark flew in from Inuvik with Forestry Officer Wilf Taylor. He made out cheques for the people who had helped me fight our recent forest fire, but he also took a picture of my dogs tied along the bank which later appeared on the cover of the *Alaska Magazine.*

The next week a Twin Beechcraft pulled into my dock with a young fellow named Robert Ruzicka, who introduced himself as the new dentist. As we moved his portable drill and gear up to the mission, I noticed he was carrying a guitar. It wasn't long before we found out that he could play it and sing as well. Although I didn't play it as often as I would have liked, I also had a guitar hanging on the wall. In between patients for the following week, we two could be heard jamming it up together. I had recently done a palette knife painting of an Eskimo that Bob wanted to buy, but I didn't want to sell. When he offered me his harmony Sovereign guitar, however, in exchange for it, I couldn't resist. In later years Bob broke into TV with his musical talent and composed such famous northern songs as Muktuk Annie. As a dentist, too, he was a worthy successor to Dr. Dowler.

With the arrival of the August 15th Feast of the Assumption, I marked the completion of five years at Colville Lake. It hardly seemed possible – the time had gone by so fast. I celebrated a Mass of Thanksgiving in the church at 10:30 that morning which everyone attended and at which forty-five received Holy Communion. We all got together again at 4:30 in the afternoon for the beautiful ceremony of Benediction of the Blessed Sacrament. I took a census and found that we now numbered eighty souls, a dramatic increase that assured our future survival as an independent community.

Once it got too cool to continue on my large painting of Our Lady of the Snows in the unheated church, I shifted my artistic efforts to the heated mission house. Here I worked in oil on plywood to paint various northern scenes. This work was a welcome change from the carpentry that had occupied me all summer. Now, however, we had snow, so I could resume driving my dog-team, which I did either to visit the nets, to haul firewood or to set out traps for marten.

Every few weeks I had to spend a day in the kitchen baking a batch of bread, pies and cakes. In the winter it was easy to keep this stuff frozen out in the warehouse and to bring it in as it was needed. If all that I needed for breakfast was toast and coffee, and for lunch, soup and a sandwich, supper demanded more preparation. I often found myself coming back to the mission late, tired, and dirty, and having to start cooking my supper. About this time I read an article by the noted theologian at Notre Dame University, the Reverend John A. O'Brien, suggesting that the obligation of celibacy imposed on the Catholic clergy was not all that necessary. The idea struck a sympathetic chord in me and prompted me to write him a letter. I outlined my situation and suggested that isolated foreign missionaries like myself could perhaps do a better job if we had more of a home life with the help of a wife. He published my letter in a leading Catholic periodical. Consequently, I got a lot of sympathetic mail. Yet I secretly hoped my bishop wouldn't read it, or he would surely transfer me immediately! As far as I know, he didn't read it. But that idea planted a seed in my mind that would grow with time.

In February I joined the other Oblates of the North and flew to Fort Smith for our annual retreat. Following this week of conferences and prayer I flew to Yellowknife, where Frank McCall, head of the N.W.T. Game Branch, invited me to accompany him on a flight into the Arctic coastal area. Another game officer, Terry Lines, joined us. The purpose of the trip was to inform the

Eskimos of a quota soon to be placed on the killing of polar bear. Needless to say, we did not expect that our message would be met with any enthusiasm; a lot of diplomacy would be needed by the messengers. On our first night out, we camped at Echo Bay Mine at Port Radium, where the manager, John Sigarlik, made us welcome. He even arranged for me to conduct a service in the cookhouse.

The following day, we flew north to Coppermine, where my companions held a meeting of the hunters. I visited my old friend Father Ovila Lapointe and slept at the mission. Next, we flew on north to Holman Island where I found a bunk at the vacant mission. Our missionary, Father Henri Tardy, was away on tour, promoting the new form of native art he had introduced, limited edition stone prints, or lithographs. I had met him the week before in Edmonton, where he was escorting a venerable, tattooed Eskimo grandmother, Kalvak, who was becoming a celebrated artist. He told me then how it all had evolved. He had a steady stream of visitors to his mission, many of whom told stories of olden times, of a way of life that had all but passed and the remarkable feats of the fabled shamans. He encouraged them to draw some of these memories on paper. From these drawings came the idea of making the best of them permanent. He had to go south into civilization himself to learn the process so that he could teach his people. Once he was back with the tools needed, they began cutting these images into local soapstone, inking them, and then running off thirty or forty prints. Then the stone images were destroyed, insuring their limited number. These works immediately received an enthusiastic reception: a successful new native art form was launched. They had also started a sewing co-op that was being ably run by Sister Monique Piché, O.M.M.I., who provided me with my first sealskin parka, a lifetime souvenir. At the same time I bought a dozen of Kalvak's lithographs for thirty-five dollars apiece, which I proceeded to send to friends as gifts. Later they became very valuable, but I failed to keep one for myself.

While in Holman I had time to visit the legendary Billy Joss, an old-time Hudson Bay Company manager, who had seen many of the Arctic explorers and talked familiarly of men I had only read about in books. A driving storm kept us for an extra night. When we finally got airborne for Cambridge Bay, I was sitting behind our pilot, Clem Bekar, when I noticed a lot of fuel spraying from the fuel fill cap on the port wing. When I called his attention to this, we were about twenty minutes into the flight. He immediately turned 180 degrees and returned to Holman. During the previous night's storm, we learned, the tank vent had become blocked with driving snow. With a little altitude, pressure was created in the gas tank which forced fuel out the fill cap. Once we had cleaned out the air vent with a pipe cleaner, we got airborne again and had no more problems. Prior to taking off, however, we had to replace twenty missing gallons.

At Cambridge Bay I put up for the night with the Administrator, Alex Gordon, and his wife, Rosalind. I enjoyed comparing experiences of our northern living and learning how effectively he coped with an influx of Eskimos who had formerly been out living on the land. By cutting welfare payments in half he had a lot of people back on the land again. This move, though unpopular, automatically did away with a lot of problems that had been plaguing their settlement.

The next day we flew on to Spence Bay, where I met the Oblate, Joseph Le Verge, living in his two-storey stone mission. He had an outpost mission about sixty miles north-east at Thom Bay and a few loyal families of Eskimos living on the land there, but the government absolutely refused to give them any aid. Government policy was that they should all move into Spence Bay, which they finally did. Again I realized how fortunate I was to be going ahead with the satellite community of Colville Lake in the face of the current trend. I admired Father Le Verge's French-style bread, so he gave me his secret recipe. (We were two typical bachelors on the fringes of civilization discussing ways of improving our cuisine!)

Abe Ookpit, an Eskimo himself, was the acting administrator in Spence and he was dispensing free fuel oil to his people. They were not only using it to heat their new, pre-fab plywood homes, but also using it in their Coleman lamps. This produced a low-watt orange glow, reminiscent of the seal-oil lamps with which these people had lit their igloos. Another factor in the high consumption of fuel oil in this community, I learned from Abe, was the fact that the fuel man was paid by the gallon of fuel he pumped.

After two nights in Spence Bay, we flew on to Pelly Bay, where I met Father Andrew Goussaert. He was one of the most dynamic Oblates I had met to date. He had started a Co-op that had succeeded in getting the contract to put up their own new homes. Granted, they were all identical little boxes arranged in neat rows, like every Arctic community we had seen, but here, at least, they had put them up themselves. They had an interesting Co-op store stocked with all kinds of native crafts, among which I found their miniature ivory carvings to be outstanding. I noticed one carving of an Arctic fox that had a full set of actual teeth taken from some species of local mouse! They fitted perfectly.

I was given a tour of the old stone mission, now abandoned, and was intrigued to see in it an ingenious oil stove that used seal blubber. It was a home-made contraption with a hopper above in which were put chunks of fat. These melted and ran down a copper tube into the fire pot. And then there was the predecessor to this mission building, put up by Fathers Henry and Vandevelde, a little square, stone, one-room building about ten feet by twelve feet. It had a liner of sewn sealskin to protect one from the cold stone walls.

When we flew back to Cambridge Bay again, I met my old friend Commissioner Stu Hodgson, who had chartered a DC-4 and was taking fifty prospective businessmen on a tour of the Arctic. He hoped to interest them in extending their businesses into this country. It did not take him long to persuade me to jump ship and join his group, as they continued on even farther north.

The following night I was with them in Resolute Bay at the DEW Line station. Here they put on an elaborate ceremony to mark their crossing of the Arctic Circle. The following day we were driven down to the nearby Eskimo settlement. I met the famous Idlout, with whom Doug Wilkinson had spent a year while he was gathering the material for his book, *The Land of the Long Day*. Following this interesting stop, we went on to Hall Beach. Father Louis Fournier put me up at his mission here and we talked by candlelight long into the night about missionary life on the coast of Hudson Bay. On the following night I was in another mission, this time at Baker Lake. My host was Father Joseph Choque. As usual, the locals put on a grand feed for all of us, followed by a traditional Eskimo drum dance, so different from those I was accustomed to among the Dene people.

Finally we got to Churchill, where I met Bishop Marc Lacroix. Brother Jacques Volant gave me a tour of the Oblates' excellent museum there. That night we attended a farewell banquet at the Aurora Club. During this event we were all presented with gold cufflinks featuring the N.W.T.'s polar bear motif. I had to bid farewell to many new-found friends, some of whom later visited me at Colville Lake and others with whom I kept up a correspondence for years. I was anxious to get my film developed when we got back to Yellowknife, but I found that I hadn't taken any pictures at all! The 35mm camera I had borrowed from one of the Oblates in Yellowknife malfunctioned: the films never turned on their spindles. What I regretted most was not getting all the pictures I had taken of the Gary Lake Eskimos. They were still waiting for housing in Baker Lake and continued to live in their igloos. That scene could never be repeated.

It was mid-March when I got back to my own little mission and could resume living the life I was used to. Everything was as I had left it, and all my dogs were alive and well. In my Sunday sermon, I told my congregation about the interesting natives who lived north and east of us, but I think they were more interested in the cowboy movie I showed that evening. It took me several days to open all the mail that had come in while I was gone, including a few deposits for the fishing lodge. My back was again giving me some pain, but, in spite of it, I drove the dogs out for a load of firewood.

Then, one day, a Beaver on skis landed and changed all my plans for the next two weeks. It was John Foster, a CBC program host from Toronto, who had come to make two half-hour films for his weekly show, *This Land of Ours*. With him were cameramen Norman Allen and Rod Graham, and sound man Bill McClelland. They brought Trudy Hodgson from Inuvik as cook and I put them up in the six-man lodge. John was so impressed with our log buildings that he told me that, even if they had built it expressly as a set for the film, they couldn't have improved on it! He wanted to make one film of me, to be entitled *The Man From the End of the Earth*, and another of the people, entitled *The People From the End of the Earth*.

He had me doing most of the things I ordinarily did, like conducting a service in church, driving the dogs for wood, pulling a tooth in the clinic room, painting, baking bread, showing a movie, talking over the transmitter, playing guitar for the kids, visiting a hunt camp and even reading in bed by the gas lamp, which I did every night before I went to sleep. This time, however, with the floodlight and sound boom, it was slightly different and perhaps not all that natural. Making a movie in your own home certainly means giving up your privacy, but I guess the final outcome was worth it.

Except for the fact that they were shooting in black and white, they did finally come up with an interesting picture of life at Colville Lake, my life and the lives of the Indians living here. From the mail I got following its airing, it must have been shown all across Canada. Too bad I didn't get paid for acting myself! But they remain the most popular movies that can be shown here, simply because we recognize all the participants.

Although I had been running into a lot of understandable opposition from our local free-trader, I had persisted in pushing Commissioner Stu Hodgson to let us organize a co-operative. Finally he sent down a representative of the Department of Economic Development from Inuvik with all the papers needed. On the 24th of April we got the necessary signatures at my kitchen table. It really didn't seem all that significant to the people at the time, but subsequent events proved just how important it really was to the life of our community.

When all the ice had finally melted in Colville Lake, late in June, we were into another season for the fishing lodge. This year I had something new to offer our guests with the completion of the new log dining-room cabin, connected to the new kitchen and chef's quarters. I had the kitchen completely equipped with propane range, Frigidaire and tile floor, and the dining room with a set of ten oak captain's chairs and a beautiful set of French china. The finishing touch to this elegant set-up was a bona fide chef whom I located in Inuvik. Alberto Ricci had been in charge of Grollier Hall kitchen staff at the residential school in Inuvik during the school year.

Among the many visitors I got that summer, the one I appreciated most had to be my youngest brother, Thomas, an Oblate priest working in Brazil. He was back in Rochester on a sabbatical, visiting Mother, and he persuaded several friends, including one who owned an aircraft, to fly him up into the Arctic to visit me. Our week together included concelebrating Mass daily for the people, as well as getting out on the lake to catch trout. While he was here, a fire broke out at the south end of the runway, where we had been burning brush. Pushed by a forty-mile-per-hour wind, it quickly spread. If it weren't for the two caterpillar tractors still left up there after work on the runway, I doubt we could have arrested it with hand pumps and shovels. With one of the guests on one cat, however, and me on the other, we finally succeeded in bringing it under control after a long day. I hadn't been on a cat since Fort McMurray, but hadn't lost the touch. Nonetheless, it was a new experience to be running one through smoke and flames, while keeping a wary eye out for the kids running around with buckets of water.

When this group of visitors left another group came in for a great week: Bill McLallen, who ran the Capilano Timber Company in Vancouver and a group of his friends. One of them, however, a banker by the name of Lew Shea, ordered me to call a plane for him in mid-week – he had an opportunity to buy six banks. I felt sorry for a fellow who was so wrapped up in his work that he couldn't take a week off to relax, and I wasn't too surprised to learn that he died of a heart attack less than six months later.

The plane that came to take Bill and his party out brought in a group of officials of the Teamsters' Union from Milwaukee. They had heard from friends who had been in earlier in the summer that I was in need of a more powerful outboard to push the twenty-nine-foot cabin-cruiser. To rectify this problem these gentlemen brought with them a new seventy-five-horsepower Chrysler motor. It looked huge alongside the forty-three-horsepower Scott I had been using, and weighed over 200 pounds. It was a spontaneous gift that forever made me partial to the Union that had provided it. It occasioned, however, a bizarre legal incident the next winter. The RCMP came out by ski-doo on patrol at forty below zero to inform me that they had orders to seize this motor and put it in their cabin until it had been cleared by Customs! The Teamsters maintained that they had declared it to the customs officer as a gift when they had been inspected in their private plane in Winnipeg. It had passed duty-free. But they were perfectly willing to pay duty if such were warranted. I had considerable difficulty persuading the Mountie that there was no point in removing it from the boat in mid-winter, so he left it. By the following summer I had heard no word from Canadian Customs so I went ahead and used the motor. Finally, after three years, I got official clearance from Customs that I could go ahead and use it. No duty had been levied.

The summer of 1968 was proving by far to be the busiest one to date, and rather historic too. Float aircraft continued to tie up to the mission dock carrying lodge guests or government personnel, but on the 30th of August, for the first time, an aircraft landed on wheels on our newly completed airstrip. It was a Cessna 180, piloted by Malcolm McAllister, the first of thousands to follow.

In spite of the steady stream of visitors, I continued to supervise the building of the two log cabins commissioned by the Department of Economic Development for the native elders. I kept a tent pitched at the north end of Colville Lake in the summers to provide an alternate base for fishermen wishing to try the waters in that area twenty-five miles from the main lodge. It proved so popular that I then decided to put up a permanent log cabin there. To get it started, I took a crew of men down there in the *Quimpay*. In two days we had levelled a site on a high, sandy point on which to begin construction of a fourteen-by-sixteen-foot cabin. We also dug a privy hole and built a dock. I left the men down there to continue the work and reluctantly returned to the mission, where I had so many other projects in progress. I kept shuttling back and forth with supplies and material every chance I got. Finally I spent a week with them to finish the cabin on the 21st of September. We returned in the *Quimpay* with the five workers, their tent and gear, a moose they had shot and two cords of firewood for the mission.

We got back in the dark, so it wasn't until the next day that I discovered that the church and warehouse had been vandalized in my absence. The damage had been done by a group of young children led by a nine-year-old who had moved into the community from Fort Good Hope. He had led them into the church, where he had put on my vestments, lit all the candles and proceeded to conduct his version of a religious service, opening the tabernacle, distributing communion – and incidentally losing that precious key. As an encore he tried his hand as an artist. I was nearing the finishing stages of my large oil of the Madonna and all my paints and brushes were at hand in the sacristy. He painted over my work as far up as he could reach! Not content with this demonstration of his talents, he led his docile crew into the large, unlocked warehouse out behind the mission. The ground floor was separated from the store room by a locked door. Luckily he was unable to get this door open, though he broke the door knob with a sixteen-pound sledge hammer. Frustrated, he went up the stairs to the attic. Here I had stored several thousands of my 35mm colour slides to prevent them from being destroyed if ever I had a fire in the mission. The slides themselves apparently did not interest him, but the metal boxes in which they were stored did, so he dumped them all out and left with their containers. Seeing these precious slides dumped all over the floor made me see red, but what can one do with a juvenile culprit of nine years?

I did complain to his parents, who blamed it on the other kids and helped me to clean up the mess, but they failed to mete out any punishment on their errant son. Following that incident, I was careful to lock the mission and warehouse when I was absent for any length of time. Still, I've never locked the church; I just pray that it will never again be vandalized.

The ice house in the bank below the mission was proving very helpful in keeping caribou meat all through the summer. At first I put the meat in layers of snow in a bin, but later discovered that if I glazed the meat with ice in sub-zero weather it kept much better. We now had a four-foot passageway, just above lake level, dug straight into the bank for thirty-five feet, with a room seven feet square at its end. The plan was to continue digging down in this room until we were twenty feet down and below lake level, but it was a slow process: we were chipping a very abrasive frozen sand with axes and ice chisels and carrying the dirt out in five-gallon buckets. The temperature down there remained at twenty-two degrees above zero Fahrenheit, winter and summer.

I was letting some of the natives put fish in there, until one of them left the doors open and we suffered a sudden thaw. So I petitioned the government to finance the building of a community ice house. Funds were subsequently allotted for the project through the government administrator in Fort Good Hope, but he decided to bypass me completely and let the local natives handle it on their own. The native project manager was soon borrowing a half-dozen axes I was keeping for the Department of Forestry for firefighting. When I saw where he started digging the pit, I told him that he had chosen the wrong site, a place where the spring run-off would flood it. But my advice was evidently unwelcome. After a couple of weeks, when the ten-by-twelve-foot hole was down eight feet, it began filling with water, so the project manager came to me to borrow Forestry's Wajax pump. He assured me that he had gotten permission, so I let him take it. They pumped out the hole and then lined it with two-by-twelve-inch planks that had been brought in during the winter by cat train. When I next visited the site they had built a staircase down into the room and a roof covering it. They had thrown all the dirt they had excavated up on the ground surrounding the hole, however; I could see that this formed a funnel that would direct all the snow melting off the roof to run down into the hole. I pointed this out to the foreman, but apparently he couldn't appreciate the problem. When I finally got the axes back they had not been resharpened as promised and the water pump had pumped so much sandy water its vanes were ground down to the point that it would no longer pump.

When I reported this to Wilf Taylor, the Forestry man in Inuvik, he told me that Forestry had not authorized the loan. The following spring, when the snow melted, the new community ice house filled completely with water, and that fall it froze solid and has remained that way ever since. No one was ever able to put any fish or meat in it. It was too bad that all that work, money and material were wasted on a project that, with a little direction, could have been a real benefit to the community. The attitude of the local government administrator was that the natives were learning by trial and error, and this was partly true. Yet when I made my first set of snowshoes at Fort Norman, I welcomed all the advice I could get from those who had the knowledge and experience. As a result, my first efforts met with success. When one is spending taxpayers' money, every effort should be made to see that it will not be wasted.

The last and largest party of fishermen flew in from Minnesota on September 4th in two rented Piper Comanchies. There were ten of them, nine men and one woman. During the following week they caught a lot of trout, but that one woman completely out-fished the men. She consistently caught all the trophy-sized trout, which ran around thirty pounds each, and no one could figure out how she did it. They spent their last day here filleting fish and filling some large plastic bags. Before they took off from the airport, I gave one of the pilots all our outgoing mail, about two dozen letters, including an envelope going to the bank with their $1,100 cheque. He stuffed the packet into his shirt promising to leave it with the fuel man in Norman Wells when they made their first stop for gas.

Three months later the bank had not received this deposit. I wrote these people in Minnesota, but got no answer. It was six months before I finally got to a telephone and talked to the pilot. He told me that they had forgotten to mail my letters in Canada and had carried them on into the States, but that one of them was expecting to drive into Canada soon and mail them! Of course, I told him to put U.S. stamps on them and mail them immediately. Another few months passed before I had the opportunity to phone them again. This time they told me that the fellow carrying my mail back into Canada was involved in a wreck, and that the State Police had seized the letters! I told him to send me a certified cheque without further delay. He promised to do so, but it never showed up. I began to realize I was getting the runaround, so I wrote my cousin Mark Brown, a lawyer in Albany, and asked him to pursue the case. Through his efforts I finally got a certified cheque in the mail. Nothing more was heard from these people for six years, until one day I got a packet of letters from an aircraft rental agency in Minneapolis. They said that they had found this mail in the lining of an aircraft seat when they were reupholstering the interior! A few years later I got a letter from this same party enquiring about returning to our lodge. I didn't reply.

The story of how I capped my new log church with a Methodist bell in the summer of 1968 deserves a special place in this narrative. I give the lion's share of the credit to Jean Branson. The summer of the year before, when she noticed my new church lacked a bell, she took it upon herself to locate one – which she did, south of the border in Iowa. She was promoting her fishing lodge on TV in Des Moines and mentioned her search. She got a reply from a Methodist deacon, who told her he knew of a big bell hanging in an unused Methodist church in rural Indianola. Jean, with her usual flair and determination, got that 1,000-pound bell flown up to the strip on Sawmill Bay below her lodge on Great Bear Lake. From there she had it transferred to her Norseman and flown to my dock.

Now the fun began, because we had to get it unloaded with no mechanical equipment to help us. We proceeded by opening both side doors of the aircraft and pushing a stout, twenty-foot pole through, attaching the bell to its centre. Now, with six men on the dock end of the pole and another six on the opposite end in a boat, we all lifted. But as we lifted it up the first foot, the plane came up with it! By persisting, however, we gradually won the battle, easing it slowly out onto the dock and finally up under the belfry of the church. From there I later winched it up along two long poles into the steeple, using a chain hoist Karl Mueller lent me. A few weeks later, when I had it properly installed, Jean returned, bringing Luther Williams, who had found it; John Porath, the Pastor of the Methodist church in Des Moines; Eleanor Farnham from a Cleveland newspaper; and John Schmidt from the Calgary Herald. They all got a chance to ring the bell and listen to its commanding peeling as it reverberated through our quiet village, setting the sled-dogs howling. Jean got some well-deserved publicity from this charitable project and a lot of newspaper readers across the continent heard of Colville Lake and its little log church.

23

WINGS TO FLY

With the departure of our problematic guests from Minnesota we called the fishing lodge season over. Alberto put on one final banquet for all the locals who had helped us during the summer and then returned to his job as head cook for Grollier Hall. I reluctantly resumed cooking for myself at the mission, a hit-and-miss affair at best. All through September we watched the sun setting farther and farther to the south across the bay, drawing the heat with it, and the chill of the coming winter slowly crept in upon us. As the air chilled, the trout and whitefish returned to shallower water and my nets were full. Soon I counted over 2,500 in the fish pit, plus many on sticks on the stage.

In early October I celebrated the first marriage in four years, when Johnny Blancho and Madeleine Codzi decided to tie the knot. It was not surprising to learn that the bride's parents were dead set against this union: Hare mothers hated to lose their daughters because they carried the lion's share of household chores. In this case Madeleine was the only daughter among three unmarried sons. On the other hand, I felt that this girl had every right to a life of her own and I had to respect that. I was surprised at the length to which these parents carried their obvious displeasure when they pulled up stakes and moved their tent a mile across the bay until after the ceremony. Then, following the marriage, they promptly moved back and carried on as if

477

nothing had happened. Johnny and Madeleine's union would produce a half-dozen children.

Our little settlement suffered from an imbalance of the sexes. While we had a dozen boys of marriageable age, we had only three girls. Furthermore, many of these young people were related. Most of our population consisted of old-timers: their average age was over fifty. In contrast, the average age in Fort Franklin was around eighteen, and in the Territories as a whole, twenty-one.

The weather was now so cool I had to burn precious firewood in the church to heat it in order to continue on my large painting of Our Lady of the Snows. Although it was a labour of love, I had been working on it now for over three years and looked forward to seeing it completed. In a final burst of energy – which burnt up all the wood cut for the church – I finally signed it on the 13th of October. Since then, visitors have often asked me how the locals like it. I have to admit that not one of them has ever expressed an opinion. Visitors, on the other hand, like it. I myself have to be content with it, because it's the best that I can do.

Without any official authorization I had been acting as Postmaster, accumulating the outgoing mail, selling stamps if necessary, and seeing that incoming mail got safely to its proper destination. I used the mission radio to arrange for mail to be brought in on any planes or even sleds coming in our direction out of Fort Good Hope. Our incoming mail was generally very light and the local bush pilots were very cooperative in picking it up for us. When the first ski-equipped 180 landed on the lake ice early in November it had been weeks since we had received any mail. I learned that postage had gone up from five to six cents. Once the intervening rivers were safely frozen between Colville Lake and Good Hope, the winter sled trail was soon seeing heavy travel and most of our outgoing mail was going by dogsled. I had a rubber stamp made to add interest to my Christmas cards. It read, "This mail carried 100 miles by dogsled to post office." Some letters stamped this way found their way to Europe. I soon got a lot of mail from philatelists in West Germany, Belgium and

Switzerland, asking for the postmark on their letters. I guess we were one of the last places in the Arctic still using dogs to carry mail.

One night we saw a brilliant phenomenon around a full moon. The parhelion, also known as "sun dogs," is a luminous halo around the sun caused by the sun's rays reflecting off ice crystals in the atmosphere. It is peculiar to Arctic regions, and we were used to seeing it around the sun on the horizon. Often there were bright spots, like satellite suns, at the nine and three o'clock positions. This parhelion encircled the moon. About the same time we heard on the radio that three Apollo astronauts had circled the moon in their spacecraft.

During the summer I had gotten some small birch trees from Good Hope and now I was busy building six chairs and caning them with babiche. One day we were surprised to see a DC-3 land on the strip, by far the biggest aircraft to visit the settlement. The pilot, Joe Langlois from Whitehorse, said they had no trouble landing on our 2700-foot strip. Among other things, he had brought my 22-foot freighter canoe, the one I had used to come down from Fort McMurray six years before and which I had been forced to leave at Fort Good Hope.

Our visitors sometimes arrived in unusual vehicles. The game warden, for example, drove out with the truck-size, tracked vehicle called a Bombardier. He brought some hunters with him from Good Hope. They shot a dozen caribou and then took the meat back home. We were beginning to see new "motor toboggans" too. The Mounties had gotten rid of their dogs and came out on patrol on two of these ski-doos.

The New Year, 1969, was ushered in under dark skies at thirty-six below zero and the inhabitants of Colville Lake dragged themselves from their warm beds about noon. Most of them, those sober and on their feet, managed to attend the Benediction of the Blessed Sacrament at the mission at 2:30 p.m. I had planned a party of games to follow, but so many were missing that I had to cancel it. However, later in the evening a drum dance got under way. It didn't require the participants to be sober, so it was a roaring good time.

When the days got brighter in February and the sun's rays again lit up the common room, I got my easel down out of the attic and resumed painting. I had sold one oil painting for $150 to one of the Mountie's friends and this encouraged me. In fact, I enjoyed painting so much that I think I would have continued even if I didn't sell any. If there were not so many more pressing obligations, I would have liked to devote more of my time to it.

The 25th of March proved to be a milestone for me: I was at last sworn in as a bone fide Canadian citizen. I had applied for citizenship five years earlier, after Commissioner Stu Hodgson informed me that I was acting as a Returning Officer illegally. As I had no intention of ever leaving Canada or the North, it was a perfectly logical thing to do. Oddly enough, the authorities had no record of my crossing the border into Canada in 1948, so I had to live a further five years as a landed immigrant. When these five years were up, the RCMP Officer in command of the Inuvik detachment flew down and presented me with my official Citizenship Certificate, signed by Judy LaMarsh, Secretary of State. Although I was no longer a foreigner, I really didn't feel different.

Cutting and splicing 16mm movie film can be a very tedious and time-consuming task. I had an awful pile of short, hundred-foot lengths that had to be put together before I could show them. As I mentioned before, friends in Rochester kept sending me film which I used and then sent to a film processor in Washington, D.C. He was developing and duplicating it for me at no cost. The people were very anxious to see these scenes, which were mostly of themselves either building the mission and church or out on their traplines. I spent many hours trying to splice these scenes in chronological order. When I finally filled up a 1,600-foot reel, they proved to be the most popular film I could show.

❄ ❄ ❄

Charlie Masuzumi was my age, the son of a Hare mother and a Japanese father. He had organized the cutting of logs for me the winter before I arrived at Colville Lake. He then became my most competent worker as we began our buildings. He also proved to be a competent and congenial guide for our summer fishermen. Without a doubt, Charlie was my most valuable friend at Colville Lake. I showed my appreciation by helping him put up a nice log house and by building him a kitchen cabinet just like mine.

Then, after Charlie and I had worked together for seven years, a teacher from Norman Wells named Maurice Kenny happened to visit our community and met Charlie. He told him that a bright fellow like him was wasting his time and talent at a backwater like Colville Lake. Maurice, besides teaching at the Wells, was acting as a government administrator and building a large log hotel. He told Charlie that he had an important job for him and promised him a new frame house that included electricity and a telephone. When Charlie came to me with this offer I threw cold water on it, pointing out, among other things, that he would be close to a government liquor store and probably would not resist the temptation. Finally Charlie succumbed to the offer and was flown to the Wells, along with his wife, three sons, an adopted daughter and thirteen sled-dogs.

When I got to visit Charlie over a year later, I found that my dire predictions had become reality. While at Colville he had been our official interpreter and leader of our community, here he was working as a janitor for the Department of Transport, at the low end of the social scale in Norman Wells. Moreover, both he and his family got into heavy drinking at the Wells. His own boys started fighting him and the welfare people took his daughter away from them. His home became a mecca for friends visiting from Fort Good Hope. He had to remove his telephone. While at Colville, he had been able to save enough money to put up his own home, without any government help, and he was the only one to do so. At the Wells, however, he said he couldn't save any money, despite his steady job, and he was watching his family disintegrate before his eyes. In short, he confessed that he had made one horrendous mistake; he was moving back to Colville. Before he could put this plan into action, however, he was killed. One night, after too many drinks at a dance, he fell under the wheels of a pickup truck. I had only one consolation: Maurice Kenny had not recruited more of my people to join his Utopia at Norman Wells. Otherwise, we could have been reduced to a handful of old-timers.

❅ ❅ ❅

As predictably as the sun rose and set every twenty-four hours, the cold of winter gradually gave way to the warmth of spring. April and May are wonderful months in the Arctic, with a bright sun reflecting off the snow nearly around the clock. My life followed its normal pattern of work indoors and out, shooting a few caribou on the lake or a few ptarmigan around the mission, signing a few paintings, installing a plywood lining in the ice house and keeping up my correspondence with many friends.

A group of visitors arrived by Okanagan Helicopter CF-OKR early in June. The leader was Fred Hamilton, a geologist whose brother Alvin was a national political figure. With him was Matt Fjarnison. Both worked for Texaco Canada and had an exploratory drill site at Ennak Lake, about seventy-five miles north of us. They hadn't hit oil yet, but they were optimistic. I fed them, gave them a tour of our buildings, and we chewed the fat for three hours. Before they left to return to their bush camp, I sold Fred a copy of the book *Irish of the Arctic*, the life of a Brother Kearney who had worked at the mission at Fort Good Hope for fifty-seven years. Fred opened his wallet and handed me a twenty-dollar bill saying, "Keep the change." Then he added, "See these hundreds? Not much chance to spend money here in the Arctic." As they were leaving I gave them the outgoing mail. It included a lot of cheques en route to the bank, plus a lot of valuable negatives I was sending out for a brochure for the lodge. As usual, I told them to have a safe flight and Fred commented that their pilot Hugh Hughes had had thousands of air miles on that particular type of Bell helicopter.

The next day, the three of them again took off from their Ennak Lake camp, bound for Norman Wells. They vanished without a trace. Three days later, Freddy Carmichael stopped by in his Piper en route from Coppermine to Inuvik and bought twenty gallons of AV gas from me. He said that everyone was out looking for the missing helicopter and he indicated on the map a spot where he had seen some smoke three days earlier. Two days later we got a visit from a Royal Canadian Air Force rescue team of seven men flying in a C-47. I showed the search master, Major Syd Burrows, the spot indicated on my map by Freddy, but he said they had to follow routine and fly a regular grid pattern. If they followed up every rumour reported to them, he said, they would be flying all over the map. Another RCAF search C-47 landed on our strip near midnight and took coffee at the mission while we discussed the missing OKR. Again I showed the search master the spot on the map where Freddy had seen the smoke, but they didn't seem impressed with the clue.

The official search went on for about nine days and was then abandoned. Friends of Fred Hamilton out of Calgary, however, continued looking in their private plane. Three days later, they were successful in finding what was left of OKR. It had crashed and burned in the bush about thirty miles south of Ennak Lake. The accident was due to a malfunction of the main rotor shaft. This was the very spot indicated to me at the beginning of the search by Freddy Carmichael. The police flew in there from Inuvik with their Otter float plane, MPW, and found a sorry mess. The helicopter had burned on impact and they estimated that the remains of the three bodies together weighed less than seventy pounds. Only one could be identified, because his wallet was intact, and that was Fred Hamilton. All my mail had burned up.

In order to get the remains out of the bush and down to a nearby lake where they could be taken back by the police Otter, another Okanagan helicopter, CF-OKV was dispatched from Fort Good Hope. Pilot Dan Hayes and engineer Carl Eden were in the area fighting summer forest fires. In fact, the smoke was so thick when they took off that they followed a compass heading towards the crash site. They never arrived! Now we had another search under way, but this time with a curious twist. The missing chopper carried a portable transmitter which used the standard Forestry frequency of 4270; we could talk to them. As a Forestry Officer myself, I also had one of their transceivers. The missing men told me that they had run out of gas and had landed safely on the west side of Aubrey Lake, which emptied into Colville from the northwest.

Two days later Sandy McKenzie flew in from the Wells in a Cessna 206 on floats. He took me down to the west side of Aubrey Lake, where I proceeded to set up the radio on a hill. I talked to pilot Hayes, but he said that he had not heard us land, so he couldn't be on this lake. I asked him if he had landed anywhere before he had run out of gas. He told me that they had landed to put twenty gallons of gas in their tank and had seen there an old log cabin and a green boat. This ruled out my outpost cabin, which was new, and the boat beside it which, like all my boats, was painted orange. So we flew on to Lakes Maunoir, Estabrook, Stopover and Horton, landing, setting up the radio and speaking to the lost men at each place. They had neither seen nor heard us. We returned to the mission at three in the morning.

The next day the RCMP flew down from Inuvik in the single-engine Otter MPW. I set up my Forestry radio in the backyard and let them talk to the downed helicopter. They insisted that they had followed a stream into Aubrey Lake and were definitely on a big body of water. Still, we had investigated every lake in our area. The only place we hadn't looked was Great Bear Lake, some eighty miles to the south and in the opposite direction from Ennak lake, but the police decided to look down there anyway. And that's where they found them, two very embarrassed flyers. Later we found their two empty ten gallon kegs under some willows at the outpost. So they had landed there to gas up and then continued on east to the Anderson River where they turned south. When they hit Great Bear Lake they turned east and ran out of gas about thirty miles along its north shore, about 140 air miles southeast of Ennak Lake. Flying in the Arctic can be confusing to a stranger and especially if the terrain is hazy in smoke. The saga of OKR and OKV had made flying history in our area.

❋ ❋ ❋

I had hoped to get Alberto Ricci back again as the lodge chef, but he had made other plans for the summer. He suggested as a substitute a young native girl named Clara Philips, who had recently qualified as the first native chef from the N.W.T. She flew down from Inuvik and brought with her as assistant another native girl, Margaret Steen, who had been raised on the Arctic Coast north of Colville Lake. These girls moved into the twin bunks in the chef's room off the kitchen and suddenly my cooking chores were ended. They not only fed me, but also any transients passing through.

Their main job was to feed our lodge guests, who began arriving early in July. We soon had four guests living with us, including one from Baton Rouge who kept asking when we were going to serve them trout. I had built a kitchen cabinet and a front window for the outpost cabin and decided to go down there in the *Quimpay* and take the four fishermen with me. Our trip across the lake passed without incident. The four guests lost no time in getting out fishing, while I tackled the carpentry work. We had reached the outpost just ahead of a storm, however, which gathered strength as it came down from the north. Soon we were buffeted by a driving rain which came through the fibreglass chinking between the logs. The storm increased the following day. What grub we had brought with us was soon gone and we had to be content with straight fish. In fact for the next three days we lived exclusively on fish. My guest from Baton Rouge remarked, "I remember asking to eat fish at the main lodge, but this is too much of a good thing!"

One day he put on hip boots and rain gear and took off on a walk in the bush with my .30-.30 to look for moose. When he got back, he said he had seen nothing but a very large grey dog which had followed him. When I told him that there were no loose sled-dogs in this area and that it had to be an Arctic wolf, he took no more walks. Once I finished the construction at this outpost cabin, we stocked it with a month's grub.

Though we had all kinds of drinking parties going on continuously, and resulting fights, it was very rare that anyone laid a charge against anyone else. So we seldom saw a Justice of the Peace. But when I got back from the outpost, Judge William Morrow flew in with an official court party and they held a session in the mission to change someone's name and to formalize an adoption. Of course, I took them all fishing. The judge enjoyed his stay so much that he told me he wished we had more work for him!

Now that summer was in full swing I was again using my show-hall cabin to give weekly movies. The cowboy shows were always popular and so was the snack bar. I had to bring my portable generator over there in the wheelbarrow, stand just inside the door where I could collect the dollar admission fee, and at the same time run the projector. If an aircraft happened to land during the show, I would announce an intermission so that I could check on who had arrived. Once in a while we'd have a drunk fall off one of the benches, but this was no interruption. A couple of his friends could drag him home after the show.

❄ ❄ ❄

Lac des Bois, some twenty miles to the east, is a lake about the size of Colville. It has some unique features. For example, one can find there, along a mile of its shore below a cutbank, rocks of various sizes that are perfectly round. These rocks are striated and often split into flat sheets when they fall, or are hit with an axe. Oddly enough one can find all kinds of fossils embedded in these rocks. A mile south of this spot there is an acre of land adjacent to the lake that is covered with hard tar. The natives told me about using this tar in the old days to patch their birchbark canoes. Geologists scouting in our area had also noted it and soon a company from Calgary called V. Zay Smith & Company moved in there with a helicopter and drilling crew. They pitched the various tents of their camp right on top of the surface tar which looked like an ideal flat area. But they had no protection from a violent three-day rain storm that struck out of the north-west a week later and flooded them out. Their crew chief Keith Braid flew over in their chopper and made arrangements with me to take over the lodge buildings at the modest fee of fifteen dollars per night per man, so they struck their tent camp.

Anticipating that they would be drilling in frozen ground they bought a special hard rock drill from Eastern Canada that would pump down a special ice melting fluid. But they ran into a lot of trouble with this drill because the drill tip kept spinning off in the hole. They thought that the thread ran in the wrong direction so they called in the inventor, Vaughan Thompson, from Ontario. He explained that he had purposely threaded the tip that way to avoid it getting so tightened they couldn't get it off. He also demonstrated how a coat of rosin would cure their trouble.

When they started bringing up core they ran into another problem. As soon as they laid the tar sand core out in their core boxes it melted and ran out like heavy oil. Now they needed refrigeration, which they had not anticipated. The helicopter they had chartered from Associated Helicopters in Edmonton was one of the older models with the main rotor made of wood. In spite of its age the pilot, Bruce Carr, and the engineer, Doug Palmer, took particular pride in keeping it in tip-top shape and I couldn't help but notice the long hours they lavished on it eve-nings as it sat out behind my warehouse. They kept it polished and gleaming. Their routine was to ferry the drill crew over to Lac des Bois in the morning and then return at noon to get their lunches. On September 6th they failed to come at noon for the lunches so when Stan Edkins landed in his Cessna 180, CF SPY, at 8 in the evening I sent him over to the rig site to see if they had trouble. They did have trouble. Serious trouble. At 10:08 that morning their chopper was in the process of moving some drill rods in a sling when a piece of polyethylene was sucked up through the main rotor and wrapped itself around the tail rotor shearing it off. As soon as this happened the tail boom started to rotate and Bruce couldn't set the machine down as there was a worker beneath him attaching the sling. He had no choice but to tilt to one side and as soon as he did the main rotor struck the ground, shattering, followed by the destruction of the canopy. Luckily no one was injured, but the beautiful bird was broken beyond repair and Edkins brought back a very sad and dejected crew. In fact that ended the project completely. V. Zay Smith & Company moved back to Calgary and the Lac des Bois tar seep reverted to nature. The incident taught me just how expensive and frustrating exploration for oil in the N.W.T. could be.

In the meantime Imperial Oil had leased my outpost cabin for three weeks to base an exploration crew there with an Okanagan helicopter. I asked them if they would be needing my boats and motors there, but the field supervisor replied that they would have no time for fishing. However, when I went down there to check on them several days later they were all out fishing! And they were again out fishing when I returned a week later. One of the geologists explained to me that the chopper pilot from England was an avid fisherman and if the weather was marginal he wouldn't fly, so they all went fishing. During the three weeks they were down there they encountered an unusual number of bad flying days.

❄ ❄ ❄

Colville Lake free-trader Bill McNeely died of a heart attack in a dental chair in Edmonton in the fall of 1968. Ever since that time, his sons had been trying to keep his store open, but they were running into problems buying stock since their credit rating was near zero. So they were often away in Fort Good Hope, the store locked up. I kept my own little canteen operating out of the warehouse for the convenience of my workers, but was reluctant to enlarge it. I was pressuring the Commissioner, Stu Hodgson, for funds to get a Co-op store opened, but money was scarce. In the meantime, without my asking for it, he sent me an official trading licence with instructions to bring in enough necessities to keep the people from moving back to Fort Good Hope. I didn't increase the size of my store room, but I did stock more grub than I had been carrying for my workers.

One Sunday morning in September, before the usual eleven o'clock Mass, the Northward Otter landed from Norman Wells with Troy and Jean Mannix. I had heard of Troy, as he had been managing the main hotel in the Wells for the past year. He said they had flown over for a few days' fishing and wanted to rent a boat. When he saw my 16-foot aluminum Princecraft convertible with its electric start 33 h.p. Evinrude motor, he said it was almost the same as he had at the Wells and he was so used to running it he declined the guide I wanted to send with him. So they took off alone. When they hadn't returned by supper time I got worried and went out in the Loon to look for them. I landed on Duka Island two miles north and from a hill, using my binoculars, could spot the white canvas top of my boat. They were another four miles northwest, and when I got there the waves were crashing on such a rocky beach that I had to throw the anchor and walk ashore with chest waders. My nice Princecraft was in a sorry state on the rocky shore, with waves breaking over its transom, the battery and tool box under water, and the floor rug floating. Troy had salvaged only their picnic basket and bottle of wine and told me a sad tale of having sheared a pin on the point just after they had set out from our village. Because the kicker shaft was long he could not replace it. He never thought of unclamping it and bringing it into the boat to work on. Anyway, driven by a brisk southeast wind they had drifted four hours until they were blown up on shore. I proceeded to take the motor off the Princecraft, bail it out and tie it to the Loon. I packed Jean out to the boat and then took Troy, being careful to avoid both the large hunting knife and the pistol he had hanging from his belt. We pulled anchor and towed the Princecraft a mile to a protected spot where I left it and continued home, arriving in the dark.

At supper in the lodge dining room, Troy was most effusive in his praise of my timely rescue and promised to reward me handsomely. The next morning he called in an aircraft to return home to the Wells and asked to settle his bill. When I told him he owed me $135 he asked if in lieu of money could he send me some gas? I agreed to that. After he left I went and picked up my boat, which had been dented along the keel, and the outboard, which had a broken clamp. He never did send any gas. When I got to Norman Wells the following winter I went to the Mackenzie Valley Hotel looking for him, but he was long gone. I talked with Georgie Laycock, the owner, who had hired him in the first place and she asked what he owed me. When I told her she replied, "You're lucky. He owes me over $10,000 and he's wanted in three provinces for cheque writing." She gave me his wife Jean's address in Edmonton, so when I got out there I phoned and her story went something like this: "Troy and I were never married. In fact, that's not even his real name. And if I knew where he was I think I'd kill him!" And that was the sad end of the trail that began on such a sunny Sunday morning. Luckily I didn't get many guests of this calibre or I'd soon have been out of the fishing lodge business.

❋ ❋ ❋

My chef, Clara Philips, left in mid-August when V. Zay Smith & Company took over the lodge kitchen. Her companion, Margaret Steen, however, stayed on to the end of the month before returning to her job as supervisor of the junior girls at Grollier Hall hostel in Inuvik. When she left, I really felt the loss. I began to realize that the bachelor life at Colville Lake was not really my ideal. She had filled a void that was becoming more and more apparent to me.

Walter Luchensky worked in the area of co-operatives and tourism for the Department of Economic Development in Inuvik, and over five years made many trips into Colville. He became a good friend. One day he picked me up in his chartered aircraft and flew me to Fort Franklin, where we staked out ground for a future native tourist lodge. We then flew back to Inuvik, where he had me working for several days in their drafting office drawing plans for the log buildings needed for this project. Nothing ever came of it, but I later drew plans for a large log Co-op store for Fort Franklin, and this did get built. Because Colville Lake settlement was being built exclusively of logs, I became recognized as something of an expert in this field. When I got back home, I found old Alfred Saiten had died, and his body was lying in the church. His was the first of many burials I was destined to preside over at Colville.

The next day a Wardair Twin Otter landed and out jumped the Commissioner with sixteen senior government officials from Yellowknife. Over lunch at the lodge dining room, Stu advised me that he was negotiating with the British government to have the Queen visit the N.W.T. next summer. If he succeeded, he intended to have her stay overnight at Colville Lake. In view of a possible royal visit, he suggested that I dig a new privy hole behind the lodge cabin. Unfortunately his plans didn't work out, but a few years later he was successful in bringing in Charles, the Prince of Wales. The reason the Commissioner steered such dignitaries as Pierre Trudeau into Colville Lake was to show them how the old North looked when all the settlements had log buildings. So we were getting notoriety because we were behind the times!

In September the sun sets directly across the bay in front of the mission. As it moves south it crosses the range connecting to our one mountain, "Bedzeaiyu." Progressively its arc moves lower in the sky and the days shorten, heralding the approach of winter and sunless days. This sight always spurred me to finish work on the open water before freeze-up. I hired a crew and, using the *Quimpay*, cut and hauled in spruce logs. With these I built up the bank to prevent further erosion. We also cut and hauled squares of moss with which to seal off the open areas below the mission's log sills. This would help conserve heat in winter. This was a yearly chore, because the moss had to be removed in summer in order to air the foundation logs; otherwise they would rot.

The idea of actually locating myself in a more remote area for trapping appealed to me, so I decided to build a winter tent camp at the end of Ketaniahtue, the next lake to the north. To prepare for this outing, I took one of the men and the supplies in the *Quimpay* as far as the outpost. Here we transferred to the eighteen-foot freighter canoe to descend the rapids connecting Colville Lake and Ketaniahtue. It was the first of October and the first ice was forming in back-water areas, so it was a cool trip in the open canoe. We got to my campsite without incident, however, and proceeded to build a stage on which I could cache my tent, stove, traps and dry grub. To make it safe from wolverines, I built this stage ten feet off the ground on two standing spruce trees. Its calculated overhang would prevent a wolverine from climbing up and actually getting into the cache. Back at the outpost, twenty miles to the south, we cut thirty spruce trees which we made into a raft and proceeded to tow home across the lake. With this drag on the boat, the ordinary two-hour trip lengthened to six, but at least we had beaten the ice.

I showed one last movie in the show-hall Saturday evening. It was simply becoming too much work because, besides having to haul the generator 200 yards, I had to build a fire to heat the building. I decided it would be the last show of the summer. Besides, there were only two dozen people left in the village as they slowly returned to the bush for winter trapping. In a few more days our population was reduced to ten.

Now was the time to get as many fish as possible for the dogs before we were forced to pull out the nets. The trout were still in shallow water chasing whitefish and my nets were full day after day. It was cold work out there in an open boat, and worse if the wind was blowing and the waves freezing as they sprayed on board. Finally, on the 18th of October I had to break thin ice all the way to the nets, so I pulled the last of them out and then winched the *Quimpay* out for the winter. In a couple of days we could walk out on the new ice. With the freeze-up, the ptarmigan came in off the Barrens in their new white winter plumage and I managed to shoot five immediately, a nice change of diet.

With the nets in, the boats out of the water and all but six of my parishioners gone, I could relax and do some of the things I had neglected all summer – like painting. Now I managed to spend a few hours at my easel every day, to bring the Codex Historicus* up to date and to write correspondents I had neglected. With the death of free-trader Bill McNeely and the closing of his trading post, people depended on me to get in enough food to keep them going. They expected me to buy their fur so that they in turn could buy the necessities of life. Before the end of October I was buying the first beaver and muskrat. Soon the marten and long-haired fur would be prime. My work in my little store out in the warehouse increased. The trick was to pay enough for the fur to keep the trappers satisfied, but not more than they could bring at auction outside. What made it risky was the way the price of fur fluctuated from month to month.

On October 30th, Brother Josset reported from Aklavik that Margaret's father, Paul Steen, was found frozen to death at Tuk. He had been living in his small schooner pulled up on the shore for winter. Apparently he was outside near his dog-team, cutting up firewood, when he was felled by a heart attack. He wasn't found for two days. He was seventy-five. He died as he had lived, a tough man for a harsh environment. Now I had to compose a fitting letter of condolence to Margaret.

As the snow deepened and the fur got prime, I was anxious to get away to my trapping area about forty-five miles to the north. First, however, I had to wait for the visit from Inuvik of Walter Luchensky. I was working with him to put our Co-op in business as a trading post, but when he finally flew in on November 6th he had bad news for me. His department was not prepared to go ahead with funding to stock our store. So I had to be resigned to continue filling in as a pseudo-trader, at least when I was in town. Nonetheless, I wasn't prepared to forgo my planned trip north. Forty-five minutes after they took off I was harnessed up and away on the trail north, though it was late in

---

* The *Codex Historicus* is a written record of significant events in the life of the mission.

the afternoon. I only got ten miles out when darkness descended, but I found the tent of one of our trapping families and spent the night with them. In the morning I was joined by Seesa and we continued on together to my outpost cabin at the end of the lake. Here I found an unexpected setback. I looked at the stage on which I had left 300 fish hanging for dogfeed and found that the ravens had eaten practically all of them. They accomplished this by standing above the fish, which were hanging from willow sticks eight feet off the ground; by pecking through their heads, they loosened the fish so that they fell to the ground. Here the ravens could easily consume them. I learned from this mishap that one must cover the fish sticks with thick spruce boughs in order to protect them from ravens. We were heading out without a meal for the dogs, and without a necessary supply for dogsled travel.

The next day we continued north over a very rough portage trail of five miles that left me with two broken harnesses. Seesa found he had lost his rifle, which must have fallen out of his toboggan. When we finally got to my tent spot, our first priority was to set a net in hopes of getting fish for the dogs. To do this, however, we needed rocks to tie along its lower edge to keep it perpendicular in the water. The snow covered all available rocks. We solved the problem by felling some large spruce out into the shallow stream from which we were successful in locating rocks of the proper size under water. We took our net out after it had been set only two hours, but we had caught only three whitefish, not nearly enough for thirteen dogs. Seesa suddenly decided to backtrack to look for his rifle and let me worry about dogfeed. I could hardly blame him.

So now I was alone, just me and my seven sled-dogs. It had been so long, I couldn't remember the last time I had lived alone in a tent in winter, with the temperature at forty below zero. I had to find a supply of dry wood and cut it up for the small tin tent stove and then cover the tent floor with spruce boughs to keep myself off the frozen ground. The net hole was too far out, so I chopped a water hole just below the tent. Just cooking a meal proved a challenge, so I did it only once a day. All of these chores are routinely done by the women of the native trappers – a distinct advantage for them.

As soon as I had my tent operating satisfactorily, I could turn my attention to the business of trapping. To do this I had to cut a line that the dogs pulling my sled could follow. I was following an esker and had to use the chain-saw to remove some fallen trees. Every mile demanded a lot of sweat, so that, in spite of the bitter cold, I found myself taking my parka off and working in a heavy woollen shirt. I let my beard grow, but found that after a week it would collect frost, increasing the danger that the skin beneath would freeze. Since it was too difficult to shave in the tent, however, I let it grow anyway. The stream to the north just past my tent flowed so fast it remained ice-free. It gave off so much steam in that temperature that a perpetual fog hung over it. One day I followed it, setting traps for mink, and thought I saw an otter, but it turned out to be a duck. I couldn't imagine a duck remaining behind to fight this cold when all its kind were now far to the south enjoying the sun. I admired its stamina and welcomed its company. In a way we were two of a kind.

Now, late in November, our sun was set for the year and the short days were merely a glow in the southern sky. I had to return to the tent about four in the afternoon, which gave me a long evening alone. Luckily I had a small radio with me and listened to the Canadian Broadcasting Corporation's station in Inuvik. Apollo 12 had just landed on the moon and I shared in the celebration of their triumph, though the dogs must have been puzzled when they heard cheering coming from the tent. I felt like I was all alone on the moon myself, but the isolation was conducive to reading and reflection. I think I needed it after so many days crowded with work and distractions back at the mission. It had been seven years of endless activity and I knew that I needed a break. I realized that my bishop couldn't afford to keep me indefinitely at Colville Lake to serve fifty people, most of whom were living in the bush most of the year. Still, I couldn't picture myself going on to start another mission at my age. I had used up most of the enthusiasm that had propelled me over the past thirty years in building seven new missions.

The very idea of continuing to live the bachelor life was becoming more insupportable. When at age twenty-six I had taken the vow of celibacy I really didn't know what it would eventually entail. Then I was surrounded by fellow scholastics and supported by all the active comradeship of a bustling college community. To dedicate myself to an unwed life looked perfectly normal and easy. Now I was having second thoughts. I wrote to Margaret and admitted that I missed her. It was the truth, although I hated to admit it to myself. Just what I could do about it was another matter.

Finally, after a month, I decided that I had had enough of the solitary trapper's life and struck my tent, putting it up on the stage along with the traps and other gear. I mushed south toward the mission, spending a couple of nights along the way with several native families and offering Mass for them on makeshift altars. More than ever, I appreciated their warm tents and hot meals that entailed no work on my part. They had women who did all this routine housework. When I finally got back home, I built a big fire, washed, cut off my beard and, feeling like a king in my own bunk, slept for twelve solid hours. By the next evening the generator was warm enough to start and I resumed my nightly mission network "sched." There was all kinds of news: another Oblate had taken over my old job as pastor at Fort McMurray; Brother Crépeau had died at Fort Resolution; Bev Woznia had crashed in his Cessna in the mountains west of Inuvik and froze his feet walking out; the game warden Dave Lepp was coming out from Fort Good Hope in his Bombardier. One of the natives sold me his marten furs and bought supplies. I was back in the swing of it again.

Not one, but two Bombardiers came in the next day with, among other things, 150 pounds of mail and nine men on a caribou hunt, two of whom stayed with me. The next day my bitch Wencho had seven pups, but unfortunately only two of them were white; I had hoped to raise an all-white team. Two boys helped me open up my fish pit and hook out 1,500 trout and whitefish, which we threw up on the stage for the dogs. At least I didn't have to worry about dog food for a while. I turned my attention to answering mail and stole a couple of hours daily, when the light was best, to do a little painting at my easel by the front window. Soon, however, the light was too poor to continue. I put my paints away until the New Year.

In order to establish a line of all-white sled-dogs, I ordered a pure white malamute bitch from a kennel in Burns Lake, British Columbia. It was eventually delivered by pilot Stan Edkins. He had recently moved into the area at Fort Franklin and I was to see a lot of him in the following years. I even tried to talk him into running our trading post, but he decided to stick with flying.

As Christmas approached the pace accelerated, with dog-teams of natives arriving every day for the holidays. Trading was brisk. I had soon bought over a hundred marten for an average of fifteen dollars apiece and was worried about losing my shirt on them when they sold at auction in Vancouver. I was also having trouble keeping my little one-room store stocked with the basic food items and took advantage of every plane, Bombardier and sled coming into Colville to bring something, if possible. To arrange this took up a lot of my time in the evenings on the mission transceiver. I didn't have much to sell my parishioners, but at least I had enough to keep them from leaving the community altogether and returning to Fort Good Hope, as some had threatened to do.

A week after Christmas, a Wardair Twin Otter from Yellow-knife landed, piloted by Darryl Brown and Bill Monaghan, and carrying Commissioner Stu Hodgson, his assistant Jake Ootes and several VIPs. The Commissioner presented me with a bottle of Beefeater gin and borrowed a 35mm slide of my dog-team which I had taken on Lake Athabaska in 1953. He would put this photo on the dust jacket of his annual report to the federal Minister of Northern Affairs. I was happy to see one of my photos used on such a prestigious book. Before leaving on his official visit of Northern communities, he also bought two of my paintings, a powerful stimulus to my budding painting career.

The beginning of 1970 and a new decade saw me and the thirty-six souls present in the village gathered in church for Mass. In my sermon I told the people it was unlikely they would see me here to begin the following year, 1971, as I really felt this New Year would see me moving on to new fields. Following the religious service, everyone moved to the mission for the traditional tea and well-wishes, but this time I thought it was appropriate to serve wine, as it would be the last time. As a result, the traditional feud between the Codzi and Kochon clans flared up in a heated argument. The party broke up in a storm of hot words flying in both directions. Our 'Happy New Year' had begun on a sour note, so I locked the front door and went to bed.

As the new year progressed, my days were full of the ordinary activities shared by most missionaries in the North. I begrudged the time I needed to cook my own meals every day. Once a month I would spend the whole day in the kitchen baking bread, plus a few pies and cakes. I made some huge pots of soup of caribou meat with barley, and potatoes and carrots if I had them. It would last a week, so all I had to do was heat it up. Supper was caribou meat in some form and potatoes. I neither gained nor lost weight, so I must have been eating what I needed. Still, my cooking was very monotonous and I took advantage of any female visitors to have them take over the kitchen duties.

The job of cutting and splicing 16mm film into an interesting and logical sequence occupied a few days and then I turned my attention to about ten thousand 35mm slides. I had to go through them in order to pick out some shots that would illustrate a brochure I was going to have printed for the fishing lodge. At the same time, I needed a couple for ads I was placing in the *Explorers' Journal* and *Outdoor Life*. While I was at it, I also made up a twenty-three-minute film about fishing at Colville Lake for promotional use. It was a good time to be working inside, for the temperature outside was forty below. To raise my room temperature and cut down on draughts I nailed strips of moosehide to the bottoms of all the outside doors. My film work was completed just as the sun returned on January 18th, and I quickly got my paints out again. Meanwhile the natives were finding it difficult to get back to the bush and their traplines. There seemed to be a succession of birthdays to celebrate with brew parties.

It was late in January and I hadn't yet seen any Christmas cards when Reindeer Air Services' 185, CF-XLU, was flown in by Cece Hanson on the 26th. He was bringing Walter Luchensky again. After I had cooked supper for them, I spent half the night opening mail. One letter from the bishop got my undivided attention: in it he suggested that I solve the problem of the trading post by forming a company and then getting an aircraft with which to keep it stocked! I was doubly surprised by his idea, because I was expecting him to say that he felt it necessary to move me on to a new mission. Certainly the idea of flying again now appealed to me because, in my fiftieth year, I was finding it more and more difficult to drive dogs. Yet the idea of being saddled with the running of a permanent store wasn't at all agreeable. Luchensky went on to Fort Franklin to check on their Co-op store there and then returned to spend another night with me. We talked long about the feasibility of introducing a similar store at Colville Lake.

Early in February the RCMP Otter landed with Corporal Bob Anderson from the Fort Good Hope Detachment. He brought with him Game Warden John Stephen and two nurses, Margot Hogan and Kay Thomas, but, most important, he remembered to bring the mail. They all returned the same day, with the exception of Stephen, who said he planned to stay a week. In fact he talked me into letting him take my dog-team for a week's trip around the bush camps. He had never driven dogs before, so I insisted that he hire a local native and his team to go with him. His preparations for the trip were impressive. First he rubbed himself all over with a special liquid heat, then strapped batteries to his legs for his electric socks and lit the wicks in his mitt warmers. Finally he covered his face with a special balaclava with only two holes for his eyes. As they were loading up, the young warden showed me a nifty, little, pressurized Swedish primer stove for making tea on the trail. When they pulled out of the yard I wished them a bon voyage and returned to my work.

When they returned a week later in twenty-five below weather I got a sad story that simply confirmed my first anxieties. Stephen's face was badly frost-bitten in spite of, or maybe because of, his balaclava: with it on, no one would notice a patch of white frostbite forming. When he pulled off his mitts he showed me the rabbit fur he had used to replace his special heated hand-warmers once they had gone cold. And in his mukluks he now had caribou hair, because his leg batteries had gone dead soon after he left here. "And what about the primer stove?" I asked. "No good," he replied. "It doesn't throw enough heat to warm up by, so we built fires when we stopped for tea." Well, live and learn. Nonetheless, I had to admire the young warden for getting out on the trail in sub-zero weather and learning to travel by dogs by doing it.

My urgent letters to the Commissioner for financial help in getting our Co-operative stocked and operating finally paid off when I got a government cheque for $9,000 to start the ball rolling. I immediately made out a requisition for groceries to a wholesaler in Edmonton and looked about for a suitable store manager. I finally decided on a native from Fort Good Hope named George Barnaby. He flew out with his wife Florence and their small kids and moved into the store. As soon as the groceries were flown in, the Kapami Co-op was in business. I named it after the native name for Colville Lake: *Kapa*, meaning ptarmigan, and *mi*, meaning net. I immediately shut down my own little store.

❊ ❊ ❊

Of greater concern to me was what I was going to do about my own life. My feelings about it were building to a crisis point: I had to make some difficult and far-reaching decisions. One of the factors that was influencing my thinking was a government report on Herschel Island by Ralph C. Currie. As I read, I became enthusiastic over the possibilities that this small, uninhabited island off the Yukon coast held. I could picture a viable Co-op starting up there with a few Eskimo families from Aklavik. If I had an aircraft, I could take them there myself. According to Currie, Pauline Cove teemed with Arctic char at certain times of the year and the Mounties had once kept many of their sled-dogs there, so they could be easily fed. Many seals were also killed around the shore. I could picture taking a payload of char and seal to Aklavik with my aircraft and then bringing back a load of groceries and other supplies. Offshore in winter polar bears roamed the sea ice and in summer the beluga passed this area. What an opportunity for a small schooner to attract tourists to participate in the hunts! The Firth River, a popular mecca for gold-seekers, empties into the ocean nearby. Maybe we could get a small jet boat to take people up river to pan for gold!

The more I studied the area, the more enthusiastic I became. The Mounties had abandoned their two buildings on the island and I began writing to see if I could buy or lease them. I also sent letters to Jim Smith, the Commissioner of the Yukon; the federal Minister of Public Works; the Federal Electric Corporation which operated the DEW Line; the Department of Indian Affairs and Northern Development; the Crown Assets Disposal Corporation; and the Inuvik Research Laboratory, among others. I contacted my old friend L.A.C.O. Hunt, now working for the federal government in Ottawa, who used his influence in the nation's capital to try to get my proposed project off the ground.

While this was going on I started burning some bridges behind me. I sold my dog-team to Piet Van Loon in Fort McPherson and my sled to Seesa. I wrote to my old mining friend of Uranium City days, Pat Hughes, about getting an aircraft and he replied quickly that he had a good bush plane and floats for me. I began studying the material necessary for writing the exam that I would need to pass to get a Canadian flying licence. Margaret wrote from Inuvik that she was on the N.W.T. cross-country ski team and was to compete in both Montreal and Fairbanks.

In September I had written to Bishop Paul Piché before he left for his Ad Limina visit (a visit a bishop makes to Rome every five years to see the Pope and present a report on his diocese). I asked him to sound out the possibility of an isolated missionary like me taking a wife and still continuing his missionary activity. I told him that, if the Vatican would allow it, I would agree to stay on at Colville Lake. Now in March, with the prospect of starting a new community at Herschel Island, I again wrote, but this time I formally requested to have my vow of celibacy lifted and to be "laicized," or returned to the lay state. I also assured him that if my request were not granted, I would not attempt to marry nor would I quit my missionary post. Once I had made this decision, it was up to the Church to act. I had only to wait.

In the meantime life was going ahead at Colville Lake. A large TD-14 cat was driven across country from Fort Good Hope and immediately began forming a 5,000-foot strip on the ice so that we could land a DC-4 with a year's supply of groceries for the Co-op. I devoted any spare time I could find to painting and turned out an oil painting of the *George Askew*, the last stern-wheeler to work the Western Arctic. I used a slide I had taken of it in 1950 on Great Bear River and traded the painting to Bruce Hunter of the Northern Transportation Company of their Edmonton office for $75 worth of free freighting. I received a cheque from the Edmonton Fur Auction for a bag of fur I had sent three months earlier and the average for marten (sold by them as Canadian sable) was $19.91, just slightly above what I had paid for them. But I had paid $280 for ten mink which sold for $228.25. So I lost on that one.

With my dogs gone, I had to start buying firewood at twenty-five dollars a cord. Dr. Mary Hapgood, M.D., flew in from Inuvik with an ophthalmologist, Dr. David Reynolds, who tested my eyes and advised me that I now needed reading glasses. My volunteer work for the Department of Health continued; hardly a day passed that I didn't have patients coming to see me for first aid or to pull an aching tooth. Stan Edkins flew in and out from Fort Franklin regularly with his Cessna 180, hauling people and freight and often staying overnight with me. Thanks to him, we were getting mail out of the post office at Fort Good Hope quite frequently. A Cessna 185-XLU landed one day from Inuvik carrying the first of many oil drillers to start work in our area. It carried men from Sherwood Drilling Western Limited of Kirkland Lake, Ontario. They had a contract to drill a hole for Mobil Oil on the northwest edge of Colville Lake. A week later pilot Leon LaPrairie flew the same plane back with men from Heath and Sherwood Drilling, plus Colin Dobbin from Pacific Western Airlines to test the thickness of our ice for their DC-4. A few days later we saw the Wardair Twin Otter CF-WAH land with veteran Arctic pilot Rocky Parsons. He was bringing in men from Canada Engineering Surveys to work for Mobil Oil. This was followed by a helicopter from Calgary. Finally, on April 10th, the big bird appeared in the sky and we all watched, fascinated, as PWA's DC-4 landed out on our new ice strip and proceeded to unload 18,000 pounds of groceries for the Co-op. He then flew over to Norman Wells and returned with forty steel barrels of fuel before returning to Yellowknife.

Anticipating that I would need to fly south in order to get the aircraft, I had petitioned our Provincial and got his permission to take a short leave of absence. So when Walter Luchensky stopped in on April 13th en route to Inuvik, I jumped in with him. The next day I found myself the only candidate writing the Department of Transport's three-hour pilot examination monitored by one of the Mounties. I passed it with little trouble and flew south to Edmonton where I joined the Edmonton Flying Club. An instructor there gave me two hours of dual instruction in a Cessna 150 at the municipal airport and then had me practise three hours of solo touch-and-go landings. I hadn't handled the controls of an aircraft alone since 1941, but found that, like riding a bicycle, once one learns the fundamentals, one never forgets. The next day I picked up my Canadian private pilot's licence and flew on to Toronto where I found my Cessna 180, CF-SLA, at the Island Airport. The floats that Pat Hughes had offered me for it, however, were still in Dublin, Ireland, so I had a couple of days to wait while he managed to get them flown over to the Royal

Canadian Air Force base at Trenton, just outside Toronto. It cost me just thirty-five dollars to get them trucked into town. Once they were put on my aircraft I was able to fly across Lake Ontario to Rochester and land at Irondequoit Bay a few miles from our home on the lakeshore.

During the following month I took instructions from veteran pilot Gordon Stoppelbein in order to obtain my float endorsement. Having had this background, I felt confident enough in my ability to handle the machine on floats that I decided to take my mother, her sister and a niece on a trip down the St. Lawrence River to visit the shrine of Our Lady at Cap de la Madeleine. We left in high good spirits and had just recited the rosary, asking the protection of the Virgin Mary on our trip, when I ran into a rainstorm thirty miles up along Lake Ontario's shore. It became so black I decided to turn around. We were only about 200 feet off the water, and in turning we lost altitude, striking the lake under full power, which felt like a crash-landing. Luckily, after I had pulled the power and floated to a stop, nothing seemed to be broken. So I taxied into the shelter of Sodus Bay and waited out the storm. Needless to say, we returned to Rochester thankful to be alive. It was a close call.

A friend of our family by the name of Mike Herbert had just returned from Vietnam and expressed an interest in returning to the North with me, so we teamed up and flew north together. Flying along the north shore of Lake Superior we ran into heavy rain and reduced visibility, so we landed at a small town named Nipigon, at the mouth of the Nipigon River. Although it was marked on my charts as a seaplane base, we taxied around in the pouring rain looking in vain for a docking space. I finally had to run it up on the shore a half-mile downstream. The next day the weather was fine and we pumped the floats as usual prior to departure. We couldn't get the water out of two compartments, however. Reaching inside this float I could feel an open cut near the keel. A passer-by suggested that we stuff rags in the tear and then wedge the rags in with a sawed-off axe handle. For want of a better idea we did it, but under full power I was unable to get the plane up on the step for takeoff. We were forced to abort and head for shore. We were sinking fast.

In fact, I managed only to get the nose of the floats onto the steep bank. The tail was so far under water that we were in danger of losing the aircraft which was heavily loaded with full gas tanks. We jumped out and threw our weight on the front of the floats, looking at each other in desperation, not knowing how we could save it. Just then a native American from California with a mini-bus full of his family stopped by and asked if we needed any help. He proved to be our salvation. We threw a rope to him and he pulled us ahead with his Volkswagen. We moved only a yard, but this was enough to tip the aircraft forward and prevent it from sliding back into deep water. Now we emptied the plane of our considerable freight and pumped most of the gas out of the wings. I went back to the Catholic rectory where I had spent the night and phoned ahead to Port Arthur to an aircraft marine shop, asking them to clear a ramp so that I could be hauled out of the water as soon as I landed. The local priest took Mike and our gear in his car.

I succeeded in getting the injured 180 into the air alone. When I landed at Port Arthur I got it quickly out of the water, too. It took two repairmen three days to replace a rib and patch the tear that ran into two of the float's eight compartments. Apparently I had taxied over some piece of hidden junk in the water at Nipigon that cut like a knife. We never felt a thing. The rest of the flight was ideal: with clear skies we could fly above 5,000 feet and easily read our maps. In two-and-a-half days we landed on Colville Lake, safe and sound.

It was July, and time to get the fishing lodge into operation. I left Mike painting boats while I flew on to Inuvik to pick up our cook, Margaret, who brought her sister Agnes as helper. The next day Fred P. Mannix (the son of Fred C. Mannix) flew in from Calgary with a party of eight for three days of fishing. During this time anthropologist Donald W. Clark flew in from the National Museum of Man in Ottawa to search for traces of prehistoric Dene people. He amazed us by promptly finding some ancient stone tools up at the airport site. I engaged one of the local boys to accompany him in a twenty-foot freighter canoe clear down the Anderson River to the Arctic Coast. His most significant finds were right behind my outpost cabin.

It was a great feeling to have an aircraft tied to the dock, ready to take me anywhere I needed to go at the drop of a hat. With Herschel Island still on my mind I was anxious to get over there and see it firsthand. I flew down to Inuvik and picked up Father Max Ruyant, who was running Grollier Hall, and Walter Luchensky. We were soon landing on the sheltered waters of Pauling Cove. I found the old RCMP staff house occupied by a group under Dr. Fred Roots, head of the Polar Continental Shelf Project, and from talking to them it looked as if they were antici-pating using this building for some time to come. What we didn't expect to find, however, were two very large steel Butler build-ings belonging to Northern Affairs. They had been forgotten, it seemed, for Walter said that they were not on his inventory! In them was a good supply of heavy ropes and seal or beluga nets. They could be gotten quite easily, Walter advised, if I did go ahead with a Co-operative at this site. We also visited the whal-ers' graves which had been dug around the beginning of this cen-tury. Herschel Island had then been a mecca for U.S. whalers who spent the winter in the Arctic. If I came away with one last-ing impression, however, it was the ferocity of the mosquitoes that harried us unmercifully, in spite of the breeze, from the moment we left the plane until we got back in and slammed the doors against them.

Back at Colville, the number of visitors was escalating, with planes coming and going every day, not counting my own. Some were the usual government people, some were oil people, but a lot were coming to fish. An old friend from my goose-hunting days on Lake Athabaska, R. D. "Ship" Shipley, flew in from Miles City, Montana, to catch a few trout. He brought with him a pilot hood for practising flying on instruments of which I had little experience, but wanted badly to learn. We flew down to Paulatuk together and I got some valuable time flying my SLA in simulated whiteout conditions. It was reassuring to learn that I could pilot my aircraft safely even if I lost sight of the ground and the horizon. Father Leonce received us warmly in his mission on the Arctic Coast along with nearly a hundred Eskimos who had moved back from Cape Parry. Father Franche had come over from Tuk to help them put up the first frame houses and everyone was determined to stay put this time.

My old friends Bill Schwimmer from Detroit and Stan Dupont from Amherstberg, Ontario, came in. This was their fifth visit; they not only kept coming back year after year, but on their first visit actually brought their own boats, motors and fishing equipment, which they conveniently left behind. They had already fished Colville Lake from end to end and wanted to try something new, so I put up a tent for them on Aubrey Lake which drains into Colville from the northwest. They needed an extra boat over there, so I volunteered to fly their sixteen-foot aluminium boat over on one of SLA's floats. It proved to be an experiment I wouldn't repeat, because its wide transom created so much drag that I had to use full opposition rudder to fly in a straight line. I had the guides return it by water.

When the weather turned sour and the lodge guests couldn't get out fishing, I felt an obligation to keep them occupied so they wouldn't get bored. My 16mm films of life in the winter time were popular, and so were two trunks of artefacts I kept up in the mission attic. Some even wanted to see the sled-dogs work in harness, so to oblige them I would harness up and drive a few yards on the bare ground. Another demonstration that proved popular was the dog whip. I would have a guest hold out a rolled newspaper, and then cut it cleanly with the crack of a whip.

Bishop Piché sent word over our mission radio from Fort Norman where he was visiting Father Labat that he would like to be flown in to Fort Franklin, so I flew over there and lifted him into my old mission on Great Bear Lake. I left him there and started back to Colville, but ran into bad weather half way. So I spent a pleasant night at Trophy Lodge with the manager, Jack Wilder. A couple of days later I brought the bishop to Colville,

where I had my first opportunity to talk over my reasons for asking for a dispensation from my religious vows. After a long discussion he agreed with me and promised to speed up my appli-
cation to Rome.

In the meantime I had an unusual visit from Dr. Gordon Butler, head of the federal Department of Health. He arrived in
Weldy Phipps' famous Otter, WWP (Whisky, Whisky, Papa),
based in Resolute, piloted by Jack Austin and carrying a full load
of people from the Northern Health and Welfare Departments.
At Dr. Butler's request, I had drawn plans for a log nursing station for our community which we now went over carefully. He
took them back with him to Ottawa for approval. I estimated that
I could build it for them for $7,000.

The bishop spent three days with me before I flew him down
to Paulatuk on the Arctic Coast to make his yearly visit. Once
there I met Dick Hargrave who was flying around the North
looking for sites for National Parks. He was interested in Pierce
Point, some ninety miles farther north, so I flew him down there.
On the way back I landed at the mouth of the Brock River, where
Margaret had been raised. Nothing now remained of their ramshackle cabin on the bank of the lagoon. The sand there was only
about four feet above the level of the ocean and a westerly storm
must have washed it entirely away. Luckily Margaret's family
were no longer living in it. The next day I flew the bishop on to
Inuvik, along with Dick, who stayed on with me right back to
Colville.

❊ ❊ ❊

Once home again I felt confident enough to seal my engage-
ment with Margaret by giving her a diamond ring. I now felt
committed to her for the rest of my life. It had been a big decision,
but now my mind was at rest.

The story of Margaret's family background reads like an Arctic version of Robinson Crusoe. Her father, Paul Steen, had come
from a family of poor homesteaders in Texas. Leaving home at

age eighteen, he shipped out of San Diego on a four-masted schooner in 1912. They were wrecked by the ice near Point Barrow, Alaska, and forced to abandon ship. Paul got work there as a roustabout doing odd jobs, including floor whaling and hunting polar bear.

The next year he continued east along the Arctic Coast in a small schooner into Canadian waters and at age twenty-one was trapping white fox at Keats Point. During that winter, alone in a tent, he had no fresh food except for fox carcasses which he soaked in brine overnight, so he contracted scurvy.

A few years later Paul fell in love with sixteen-year-old Bessie, daughter of trapper Jake Jacobson, at Inman River. The story of their courtship is told by Captain Henry Larsen in his book *The Big Ship*, in the chapter entitled "Eskimo Love and Drama." They were married at Coppermine and returned to trap at Inman River.

Their first child was due the following winter, so Paul and Bessie hitched up their separate dog-teams and mushed 300 miles west to Aklavik. The trip took them a month and the baby arrived the very next day.

Always looking for a better trapping area, Paul next moved his family thirty miles up the Anderson River, but found game there scarce. He wrote that this move was a mistake and all but finished his young family. They survived the winter living on cranberries and muskrats. When the river ice broke in the spring, it took their schooner *Rob Roy* with it. They had one dog left when they floated down to the Arctic Coast again the following summer in their rowboat.

Paul built his family a small cabin of drift logs near the mouth of the Anderson River and here Margaret was born on February 12, 1945. Later they moved to the mouth of the Brock River on the east side of Darnley Bay and built a ramshackle cabin of driftwood and canvas. As his family increased he kept adding to this house. He found a seam of coal two miles inland and, using black powder, blasted some loose and brought it home by dog-team for their fuel.

The Steen family lived forty miles from their nearest neighbours at Paulatuk, so they rarely had visitors. Paul and Bessie had fourteen children, most of them born in this crowded cabin. Their only income came from the pelts of the Arctic fox whose numbers increased or decreased in yearly cycles. The family was often reduced to near starvation. There was no family allowance or social assistance in those years to aid a family in distress.

During the long, severe winters the snow would drift level with their roof peak, so Paul cut a window in the roof to let in some light. When he was expected to return from his long trapline, Bessie would hang their solitary kerosene lantern outside on a pole so he wouldn't miss the cabin entirely.

In the summer the children walked the beach in their bare feet, collecting driftwood or setting traps to catch ground squirrels for them to eat. Their yearly outing occurred at Christmas, when the entire family mushed into Paulatuk and camped on the common room floor of the mission. Margaret remembers getting just one toy in her childhood, a little tin pig. She was thirteen when she was finally picked up by the schooner *Our Lady of Lourdes* and taken to the hostel in Aklavik for her education.

She never returned to Brock River, but following her schooling went to work at Grollier Hall in Inuvik as supervisor of the junior girls. Her exemplary life there made the Grey Nuns think she might be a candidate for their Order. This was the girl with whom I was in love and whom I had engaged to marry, a woman half my age who experienced more hardship than had I or any of the natives living at Colville Lake.

After twenty-two years counselling married couples, I realized that when a person falls in love they can be blinded to obvious defects in their intended partners, defects that could later surface and wreck their union. For a time they become captive to their emotions. There is an element of risk involved. As a priest and celibate for so many years, I felt a special need to proceed with prudence and caution lest my emotions sway my judgment.

I found Margaret quiet and undemonstrative, no doubt the result of her isolated upbringing. But her character and temperament appealed to me. She is a rare example of a true daughter of the North, one inured to hardship and isolation. This observation has proven to have been well founded. In fact, I underestimated her.

❄ ❄ ❄

On one trip to Fort Good Hope for supplies, I picked up Brother Jean Boucher who was eager to see what I had built at Colville Lake. He was a Brother skilled in carpentry and he spent a week with us, mainly working in our shop with the table saw. One of the things he made was a cross to be erected on the grave of Father Frapsauce. This priest had died in 1920 on Great Bear Lake, when he went through the ice with his dog-team. I flew the Brother over there and we searched for the old mission and the grave, but we couldn't find it. We took advantage of the fact that we were now on the east side of Great Bear Lake, some 200 miles from Colville, to visit the various fishing lodges that were operating in that area. Finally we landed back at Fort Franklin to spend the night. The next day, Sunday, I celebrated the High Mass there before leaving Brother Boucher with Father Victor Phillipe and flying back to Colville, still carrying the cross. I wanted to be home to celebrate my fiftieth birthday on the following day, August 31st, 1970. It was a significant milestone for me.

Now Margaret and I started talking marriage and where we would live once I had been relieved of my missionary duties. We decided that the outpost site where I had a lease on six acres would be a good location, in case we were forced to vacate the mission itself. The cabin I had built down there, however, would be far too small, so I decided to build a second, larger one. To get this project under way in early September I took several men there to clear willows from the point. Others cut and hauled building logs, plus 200 poles to support the roof moss. While this preliminary work went ahead, I built a door with a window in it and put glass in the large picture-window frame that Brother Boucher had made for me. This was no small job, for the glass I had on hand had to be cut into forty-eight smaller panes, which Margaret proceeded to putty to seal the double glass. It took us most of a week. We were short of lumber, so I tore down my show-hall and salvaged the shiplap from the roof and floor.

On the 9th of September we loaded up the *Quimpay* with a ton of material we would need to build this cabin, including the shiplap boards, nails, window and door, insulation and a cast iron stove. I tied the aircraft to its new dock with double ropes and Margaret and I crossed the twenty-five miles of mostly open water to the outpost in two-and-a-half hours. Luckily for us the lake was calm. The weather for the next week was anything but calm, with strong northeast winds carrying rain and then snow to make building anything with logs outside miserable. Despite this handicap, we made good progress. Before dark the day we arrived, I had the mud sills set on flat rocks and the floor joists above them level and spiked down. I also had half this area sheeted with shiplap. Five men living in a tent just behind formed my crew and the work went smoothly. I picked out the logs and cut them to length, while Seesa and his brother Philly peeled them with my big Swedish knives. When they were clean of bark, we put them up on the wall and I marked in pencil where they were to be notched. The men then did this with axes. Finally we put a pad of fibreglass down where the logs joined and drove twelve-inch spikes through them.

The ground was now covered with snow and one morning we found the tracks of a black bear which had circled the cabin we were sleeping in. We were getting a lot of trout off the dock, casting in the evening, so I hung one off our stage. Beneath it I set a No. 4 Victor trap, attached to a long dog chain. I figured that, if the bear stepped in it during the night, I would hear the chain rattling, as it was only twenty-five feet below our cabin. I left the

.30-.30 loaded out on the porch so I could get a quick shot at him: I knew that he would kick a trap that size off his foot in no time.

We were in our bunks around midnight that night when I heard the chains rattling and sprung out of bed. Before I could get my jeans on, however, I heard the bear tear through the porch screen and land with a thud on the porch. I pulled back the curtain and there he was, standing up and looking at me eye to eye through the window. He was right next to my rifle. Luckily, I had the twelve-gauge shotgun loaded and sitting against the cabin wall, just inside the door. With one motion I opened the door with my left hand, grabbed up the shotgun with the right, and fired into the bear's chest from a distance of only three feet.

Even birdshot at that close range acts like a solid slug and is deadly. The bear plunged through the screening mortally wounded and rolled down the hill. There I shot him once more with the .30-.30 for good measure. It all happened so quickly I didn't have time to feel any fear. Still, I did know that this bear did not act normally: he should have high-tailed it for the bush once he had kicked the trap off his toes. Instead, he came up the hill to enter a cabin where he knew humans were living. Was his motive to seek revenge for a sore toe? If I didn't have a gun inside the cabin, would his next move have been to crash through the window? We will never know.

Louie skinned the bear for me and we all ate it. A few months later someone suggested that I submit a story of the incident to the magazine *Outdoor Life* for their monthly feature, "This Happened to Me," so I did and five years later it was printed. Their staff artist didn't quite capture the sequence accurately, but basically it was correct and I got a cheque for fifty dollars.

I said that the weather was bad when we were down there building this cabin, but I really didn't know how bad it was until we heard from Inuvik over our transistor radio that it was the worst storm since 1944. Many boats and even aircraft had been wrecked. I worried whether I had tied my own aircraft securely enough to ride out this storm. As soon as the lake calmed enough, I took Margaret and a couple of the men's wives back to the village, where I found my aircraft undamaged. John Baptiste and I flew back to the outpost to finish the work. In spite of the snowstorms, we were successful in getting the roof covered with moss, the logs chinked from the outside with fibreglass and the door and window in place. On the 24th, less than two weeks after we had begun, we had the cabin essentially completed and decided to call it quits. We swept the snow off the wings of SLA, but couldn't pump out the floats because the pump-out cocks were frozen in ice. I took three of my workers and flew back across the lake, but when I landed the rudders were frozen solid, so I had to cut the motor and wait for a boat to tow us into the dock.

During my absence a final guest had landed at the lodge. He was Jim Ryan from Albany, New York, who told me that I had met him thirteen years before in Rochester and had invited him up. I couldn't remember that, but he moved into the lodge and stayed a month. He was too late for fishing, but he kept himself busy shooting ducks and helping me pull out the boats and other chores. Then an Aztec aircraft piloted by Herb Bachor landed on the strip. Herb was accompanied by the administrator of the Inuvik General Hospital, David Gardner. He brought a contract for me to sign for the building of the nursing station. I objected to such a building project at this time of the year, but he insisted that their funds for the job would be cut off at the end of March, so it had to go up now or never. I signed under protest.

The Co-op was running out of groceries, so I managed to charter Reindeer Air Services' DC-3 out of Inuvik to bring in a 7,000-pound order. Now we had enough to supply our trappers before they left for the bush. Another DC-3 owned by Transair out of Prince Albert, Saskatchewan, landed at this time from Norman Wells with fuel for the oil companies. In their load was a new OMC Snowcruiser being sent to me by the Rotary Club of Milwaukee. I had given this group a talk in the spring when I was south on vacation, visiting my cousins the Doyles in Chicago. It represented my transition from dogs to snowmobiles and proved a faithful iron workhorse.

The bad weather never ceased and I began to worry about getting the aircraft changed over from floats to wheels. I had arranged with Fred Carmichael to have this done by his engineer in Inuvik. Carldon Aviation in Toronto, where I picked up the aircraft, was to ship the wheels ahead by barge. By September 29th our bay started freezing over and I could delay no longer. I got away at three in the afternoon, after knocking ice off the floats and taxiing through thin ice for a mile before getting airborne. When I landed two hours later in the east branch of the Mackenzie River at Inuvik, it too was already running ice. Mine was the last float plane out of the water. I had made it in the nick of time.

On the 8th of October I flew home on wheels, stopping at Fort Good Hope en route to get the mail. I found Margaret had moved into the mission clinic room, while Jim stayed in the six-bunk lodge. The next morning I chopped the twenty-nine-foot *Quimpay* out of seven inches of ice and got it pulled up for the winter. In the afternoon I began setting the mud sills in place for the new nursing station, just a hundred feet south of the mission. I could have built it anywhere, for there were no surveyed lots in our town. Mobil Oil was still drilling a hole on the north shore of Colville Lake fifteen miles away. They had a DC-3 landing supplies regularly on our strip and a helicopter ferrying these supplies over to their rig site.

By mid-October the ground was covered with over ten inches of fresh snow. We slowly and carefully laid about two-and-a-half rungs of logs per day. That represented over fifty logs, because it took twenty-two of them to go completely around the thirty-by-twenty-six-foot building, and then there were those that had to be notched into the outside logs for the inside room walls. A week later we had reached the top or plate logs, but the temperature was now down to zero and it didn't look as if we were going to be able to put any roofing on. After we had covered the rafters with plywood, however, the weather took an odd turn and warmed up to thirty-four degrees, the warmest it had been since early September. I hurriedly hired extra men. We got the roof finished in two days and the whole job done by the 7th of November, a total of twenty-four working days.

I thought to myself often during those 9 a.m. to 6 p.m. work days how much more difficult they would have been if I had to cook for myself at the same time. With Margaret in the mission kitchen life had suddenly become a pure joy. I couldn't wait to make it a permanent situation. In fact, I was so optimistic I persuaded her not to return to her old job as supervisor of girls at Grollier Hall in view of the fact that I expected to get permission to marry in the very near future.

Once the nursing station was built, I could afford time to continue painting during the midday hours when it was light enough. Those days, however, didn't last too long. The Bluenose Lake caribou generally hit Colville Lake en masse in late October, but this year they didn't show up until November. When they did, I went out and took eight, enough to last us for the year. Without my dogs I didn't need to set a net under ice or worry about dog food. The new motor toboggan was working fine and Margaret and I would often go for firewood and especially for tamarack to hold the fire at night. I set some No. 4 traps where I butchered the caribou and got one large grey wolf by a toe. Apparently I got to the trap right after he was caught, because once his toe had frozen it would have broken off and freed him.

With the dogs I had often gone through overflow without suffering too much trouble, although I would have to turn the sled over and scrape the ice off with my axe. But now I learned just how difficult it could be when one is driving a 500-pound Snowcruiser. On a trail across our bay in front of the settlement, which I had been using every day, Margaret and I suddenly found ourselves mired in a foot of slush. We both got wet feet and I sent Margaret home. I continued to run backwards and forwards in an effort to get up on solid snow again. I had to detach the empty sled I was hauling, but it still took me over half-an-hour to get out and I was wet up to my knees in sub-zero temperature. Apparently the ice had cracked open under the trail during the night, allowing the water to flood the surface and thoroughly saturate the snow. There was no discoloration of the snow to warn one. I have found that this happens only in the late fall and not after mid-winter. Overflow is a dreaded word in the North.

When it got too dark to continue painting in late November, I began to type this manuscript which I planned on some day publishing under the title *Arctic Journal*. The mechanics of typing were tedious and a lot harder than painting, but I persevered through the years at a snail's pace. Twenty years later I was still working at it.

On the 23rd of December the town came alive with the return of the natives from the bush. I banked the church with snow in preparation for re-heating, which I did the following day. As usual, we all gathered in church for the traditional Midnight Mass. Thankfully, my congregation had remained sober, so there were no interruptions. The following day the mission was permeated with the delicious aroma of roasting turkey as Margaret presided in the kitchen. On the last day of the year a Reindeer Air Service Cessna 185, piloted by Max Weib, brought out a new nurse, Maggie McInnes, for a clinic. Although she had to bunk with Margaret in the mission's clinic room, I was able to show her through the new nursing station which would soon be in operation when we got it furnished inside. As the New Year broke, I fired my last two aerial rockets off the front porch. With them I saluted a milestone in my life in the year just ended.

24

THE MESSAGE FROM ROME

The New Year, 1971, dawned a sunless thirty below as I filled the cast-iron heater with dry spruce and opened all the draughts. A haze of ice-crystal fog hung over the lake as far as one could see, a typical mid-winter day on Colville Lake. I celebrated Mass in the mission chapel at 11:30 and our common room was crowded. Lit by a pair of gas lamps, the room wasn't exactly bright, but we made up for it with our own warm exchange of New Year's greetings.

That evening we were joined by store manager George Barnaby and his wife, Florence, and we played four-handed pinochle. When our guests were gone home I looked out at a new moon and wondered to myself what this new year would bring. The important decisions I had made the previous year would shape the rest of my life and I couldn't be sure they were the right ones. Only time would tell.

Three days later, the Cessna NLN from Inuvik landed on skis out in front, bringing a new dentist, Dr. Darryl Hunter, who proceeded to set up his portable drill in the mission's common room. For the next five days we tried, with poor results, to entice the people to come in and have their teeth checked. He spent a lot of his time standing around waiting for patients who didn't realize just how much they needed his services. If they hadn't suffered recently from toothache, they saw no need to expose themselves to the pain of the drill. For my part, I was anxious that they got

519

their cavities filled; otherwise, in the months ahead, they would be calling on me to extract teeth that could now be saved. Their attitude reminded me of the trouble I had experienced in Fort Franklin in trying to get tubercular patients to submit to an X-ray. Of course, there was no fee for this service, but that didn't seem to make any difference.

At this time I decided to use the big wooden box of photographic equipment sent me by Bill Schwimmer from Detroit, who owned two camera shops there. I lacked a dark room, so I converted the workshop by blocking off all its three windows. With neither electricity nor running water, however, printing film is not an easy process. In spite of these drawbacks, I went ahead and, during the next month, used up all the packs of photographic paper he had sent me. Then I put the enlarger and the chemicals and equipment all back in the attic and never brought them down again.

As the month of January wore on, our sun returned, but the higher it rose, the lower the temperature dropped, until it hit sixty-below. Seesa came in off his trapline and asked if I had any work for him; there were few marten moving about in that temperature. On the 26th a young pilot, Jerry Toews, flew in from Fort Franklin with the game warden, Ted Boodle. Now that he had two aircraft, Stan Edkins had hired Jerry and both of them were kept busy. When Jerry was sitting across from me eating his lunch, I remarked on the cuts showing on one of his wrists. He said that they were caused by spinning the prop by hand on his 180, CF-EPP, whose battery was very weak. Not only that, but his vacuum pump had failed and therefore he was flying without a few crucial instruments, like his artificial horizon, his turn-and-bank indicator, and his gyro-compass.

The loss of these instruments came back to haunt him a week later. He was flying from Franklin to pick up a tent and equipment for natives there who had left them on the shore of Lake Belot, just south of Colville. Unfortunately, he had invited his girl friend, the nurse Pat Smith, to come along for the ride. As he was flying over the fifteen miles of ice covering the Smith Arm of

Great Bear Lake in whiteout conditions, he lost his horizon completely. Without realizing what was happening, he flew right down onto the lake ice, completely disintegrating the plane and killing them both instantly. The lesson was not lost on me.

We not only had an unusually large number of Barren Land caribou wintering in our area this year, but unusually deep snow was forcing them to look for moss along the edge of Colville Lake where the wind reduced the drifts. Almost any day we could see a large herd of them across our bay a mile west, digging for food. One game warden flew around and estimated a total of around 5,000 animals. This news soon got about to the settlements in the area and we were inundated with native hunters from Fort Franklin and Fort Norman. Mobil Oil had a good winter road from Fort Good Hope to its drill site on the north-west corner of the lake. This enabled trucks to drive in from all those settlements for the first time in history.

Commissioner Hodgson responded to a request by Noel Kakfwi of Good Hope to fund a community hunt out of that settlement. Consequently, eight young native hunters drove out by dog-team with Noel as their leader. Although some of these young bucks had never shot a caribou before in their lives, each was given two boxes of shells for their .30-.30 rifles, a total of 320 shells, and turned loose on the herd. The local game wardens, John Stephen and apprentice Richard Binder, who should have supervised the hunt, had been completely bypassed, but were here to gather up the lower jaws of the animals for analysis in Yellowknife. They were out on the killing ground when the young hunters opened fire.

They told me that night that they were soon in fear for their lives, as stray bullets whizzed over their heads. They had to dive into the craters dug in the snow by the caribou to keep out of the line of fire. There was no question of looking for caribou jaw bones as long as the shooting continued. When the smoke cleared, the boys started the work of skinning and butchering their kill. Some of them had apparently forgotten their hunting knives and attacked the carcasses with axes! Noel reported a kill of only thirty caribou that first day, but John and Richard said they saw a lot of wounded animals limping off into the bush. Unfazed, Noel went down to the Co-op store and bought his young hunters another two boxes of shells each and sent them out the next day to continue the slaughter. It occurred to me that the sensible way to conduct such a hunt would be to have just one sharpshooter kill those animals needed with a single shot to the head, thereby spoiling none of the meat. Like the game officers, however, I was only a silent spectator.

For the next couple of weeks Colville Lake was the scene of the biggest caribou hunt in its history, as hunters from all over the area chased the herds around its shores and shot them by the hundreds. The game officers estimated upwards of 1,000 slaughtered. One big flat-top trailer-truck from Fort Franklin hauled back over a hundred carcasses. The following summer some carcasses appeared floating in the lake. Everyone at Colville was glad to see the hunters finally leave – especially the caribou.

A lot of this activity took place on the ice right out in front of the mission and was clearly visible from the large window of our common room by which I sat to paint. They were a distraction. On the other hand, at least one scene turned out to be the inspiration for a painting when some caribou were skidded in close to the village at night and skinned by the light of the ski-doos. I sketched the scene right from my easel.

One night in early March we could see the lights of a cat train in the hills across the bay to the west, but didn't really know who was coming until an aircraft landed on skis the next day. It was a strange looking plane, called a Porter Polaris, and belonged to Arctic Air of Fort Simpson. It brought in managers for Northern Geophysical and Bain Brothers Construction. Over lunch they told me that they had been contracted to cut seismic lines down around the outpost and, on the way, to plow out our airstrip and make another one 5,000 feet long on the lake ice twenty miles north. The next day their machines rumbled across the ice of our bay – two cats, a D-6 followed by a D-7 pulling cabooses, followed by two fuel trucks. We were amazed to learn that these trucks had been driven all the way from Calgary, Alberta. Working around the clock, they plowed out both the landing strips on land and on ice in three days. Then they continued north.

With the airport snow removed, I was now able to get my own Cessna back in operation, after having been snowed in for five months. By this time I had purchased a set of hydraulic skis for it, but I would have to fly to Inuvik to have them installed by an aircraft engineer. Margaret joined me the following day as I flew the 220 miles to Inuvik. There I put SLA into Freddy Carmichael's new hangar, where Dennis Hansen went to work installing the skis. The work took nearly a week, but Father Max Ruyant housed and fed us in great style at Grollier Hall and Margaret got the chance to gather up some of her belongings.

Once back at Colville on skis, I could park the Cessna on the lake ice just below the mission. Yet with the temperature still twenty-five below zero, it was not just a case of turning off the engine and walking away. First I had to drain the oil out of the crankcase while it was still warm and take it and the battery up to the mission. Next I would put the nose cover on, a canvas tent that reached to the ground, and then the wing covers. Finally I had to pump the hydraulic skis off the snow so they wouldn't stick. When it was time to fly again the whole process was repeated in reverse, but first I had to put the gas blow pot under the nose tent and watch it carefully for an hour until the prop was loose. Then I had to bring down the battery and the oil which had been heating on the kitchen stove. After they were put in, I started the engine and ran it until the cylinder heat gauge was in the green. Then I shut it down and put the nose tent back on, to let the heat dissipate through the engine compartment and warm the instruments. After fifteen minutes the wheels could be pumped up on the skis again, and I was ready for takeoff. With all this work, a flight to Fort Good Hope simply to pick up the mail took the better part of a day.

When I was in Inuvik I talked to Slim Semmler about selling him Colville Lake whitefish for his trading post there and also to Tony Finto about selling him caribou meat for the restaurant he ran in the Eskimo Inn. The following week I brought them the first load of country food. After that I always managed to take a payload any time I flew back to Inuvik. With the cost of AV gas so high, I had to plan ahead to make every flight pay for itself. I received an invitation from John Sigarlik Jr., Manager of Echo Bay Mine at Port Radium, to deliver a talk there at their bonspiel curling banquet. So I took three of the local natives who wanted to visit relatives at Fort Franklin and dropped them off there en route to the east side of Great Bear Lake. This gave me the opportunity to concelebrate a Mass in my old mission with the present Pastor, Father Jean Denis, and to renew acquaintance with my old parishioners. It had been sixteen years since I had visited the mine as chaplain for Eldorado Mining at Beaverlodge and this bonspiel attracted a lot of old friends.

After the middle of April the temperature soared and the snow began to melt, forcing us to move all the meat we had been keeping in a warehouse down into the permafrost ice house. About the same time a regional meeting was called for the Oblate missionaries at Inuvik and I flew down there, carrying a load of meat and fish as usual. The next day I took Father Franche and Brother Dabrowski with me to fly to Paulatuk to pick up Father Leonce so he could attend the meeting. Two things on the return flight made it memorable. First, as I passed the Smoking Hills west of Langton Bay, my magnetic compass started going around in circles and I began going off course. Later I learned that there is a huge iron ore deposit in the area that makes all compasses for miles around unreliable. Second, when Father Leonce had finished eating a candy bar, he opened the door on his side to throw out the wrapper and then couldn't get it closed again. For the rest of the 260-mile flight he had to hold the door handle as tight as he could, while the below-zero wind whistled in to cool the two passengers in the back seat.

While attending the meeting at Inuvik I got a chance to talk to the Oblate Provincial about my decision to ask Rome for a release from my vows. After we had discussed the pros and cons for over an hour, he surprised me by agreeing with my decision and undertook to press my request for an "indult" with Rome.

I went shopping at the Hudson Bay store and flew back to Colville with a planeload of the kind of fresh stuff we couldn't stock at our store. A week later we got 21,000 pounds of groceries and hardware flown in to our ice strip from Yellowknife by a North West Territorial DC-6, our yearly re-supply. It was amazing to see a plane that big parked right out in front of our Co-op and everyone pitching in with their sleds to get all the freight up into the warehouse.

With the advent of the longer days and clear skies of May, the North becomes a warm, friendly place again. One day I flew in to Fort Good Hope, picked up the game officer John Stephen, and then flew on another hundred miles west into the mountains to visit Sven Johansson and his wife Norma. He was living in a log cabin he had built on the upper Red River. He used it for trapping in the winter and for guiding big-game hunters in the fall. He brought in all his building material with his Super Cub, so nothing could be longer than four feet! It was the first log cabin I had seen completely wrapped with pink fibreglass and looking like a big birthday cake. Still, apparently it had been warm during the winter and the two of them looked fit. I had to land on a frozen lake a mile above the cabin and wade down through snowdrifts to their house. While we were there, some low clouds moved in quickly, obscuring everything, so Sven had to lead us out through the passes with his plane. It was not the kind of country I would enjoy flying in regularly, as he did.

A few days later I had to do some work with fibreglass myself to complete the insulation of the new cabin we had built in the fall at the outpost. There were two native families camped down there who gave me a hand. We were surprised to see a herd of about 200 caribou being chased all around my cabins by a loose sled-dog. They would come rushing by in one direction and ten minutes later be running back with their tongues hanging out. I think that if I had had a rifle with me I would have shot that dog, but the Indians seemed to get a big kick out of the spectacle.

Before coming North I had been influenced by books such as *Mid Snow and Ice* by Duchaussois, *The Friendly Arctic* by Stefansson, and *Silent Places* by Stewart Edward White. Once I had been established at Colville Lake, I kept searching for books that were relevant to the area. They were few. Only Petitot, in his book *Autour de Grand Lac d'Ours*, wrote of visiting people of Colville Lake in 1863. George Douglas wrote the splendid book *Lands Forlorn*, telling of his winter around the mouth of the Dease River some 200 miles east of us. I was genuinely interested in the history of the North and the more I learned, the more interesting it became.

As spring wore on, my nearest Oblate confrere, Father Aloyse Brettar in Fort Good Hope, developed some health problems that required him to be moved to Edmonton. He was replaced by a Grey Nun, Sister Blanche Matte, with whom I was continuing a nightly radio discussion in French via the mission Marconi transceiver. On the evening of May 14th she informed me that Bishop Piché was in Inuvik and wanted to see me. I knew immediately what it was about and flew down there the next day. He told me that he had received the indult from Rome, dated the 2nd of April, and that it would be effective as soon as he put it in my hands. Before he did that, he told me that there was still time to change my mind; if I had any last minute misgivings he would like to assign me to Cambridge Bay where he needed a new mission built. I told him truthfully that I had no hesitation whatsoever about accepting the indult, so he finally handed it to me and I was automatically "reduced" to the lay state.

That didn't mean that I was no longer a priest, because the sacrament of holy orders, like baptism, is permanent and cannot be erased even by Rome. I still retained, too, my certificate as a registered clergyman for the Northwest Territories. In return for receiving the cancellation of my three religious vows of poverty, chastity and obedience, and for the permission to marry, however, I had to agree to certain conditions. One was to refrain from the celebration of Mass. Another was not to hear confessions, except in the case of someone in danger of death. The bishop turned over to me all the buildings I had built, with the exception of the church and mission. He was quite willing, however, that I go on living in the mission and taking care of it and the church so that I could be host to any visiting clergy. I would be allowed to conduct a service in church without the Mass, but could say a Mass if hosts needed to be consecrated for communion. Discussing the terms of my laicization took over two hours. When we finished, the first thing I did was go across the street and buy a marriage licence. I requested the bishop to come to Colville and conduct our marriage ceremony himself, to which he agreed, but he could not make the trip immediately. Father Donald Kroetch, who was now stationed in Inuvik, volunteered to marry us right away, but I preferred to wait and have it done by the bishop so that there would be no doubt in the minds of the people that it had full ecclesiastical approval.

My flight back to Colville was a happy one, with the good news I was carrying to Margaret and the relief I felt after the positive response from Rome. I had waited a lot longer than I had anticipated, but now the waiting was over: we could go ahead and plan our future. I had gotten nowhere with my plans for founding a Co-op at Herschel Island, so now I had to abandon it. This might have been a real disappointment if I had been forced to move from Colville. All we had to do now was be patient a little longer and wait for the day when Margaret could wear her wedding ring.

So life resumed its normal pace at Colville Lake. Margaret and I flew down to Paulatuk, 170 miles north. I landed first on skis on the small lake behind the settlement, but found that the townspeople had vacated, as was their custom in late May. When the snow began to melt around town, exposing all the winter's garbage, they would move into tents about a mile east and return only after one of their men used their bulldozer to push all the offending honey bags and other debris down the bank into the ocean. So we flew over to their camp and landed on wheels among the tents for a visit and a feed of fresh goose.

On the 2nd of June two things descended on us from the air. The first was a Cessna 185 on skis, piloted by John Thorenson and carrying the Inuvik Hospital carpenter, Jim Birch. Jim had come to install all the cupboards in the new nursing station. The second was the annual arrival of a million bloodthirsty mosquitoes – which put an end to my sitting out on the front porch after supper to smoke my pipe. The next day, pilot Keith Nordstrom flew in with a Dornier, bringing the administrator of the Inuvik hospital and the supervisor of nurses to check how well I had built their new log nursing station. A few days later pilot Klaus Krey flew the Reindeer Air Service Twin Beech in from Inuvik with the annual X-ray party, headed by Iseault Gunning, R.N. They still had to use my front room because the new nursing station was not finished.

In between my own flights around the country I began building a twenty-foot flat-bottomed boat to be used at the outpost for running the fast water down river to catch Arctic grayling. I put it together on the front porch, the only available flat surface. Once I had it completed, I built a large kitchen cabinet for the new outpost lodge. I got the *Quimpay* repainted and launched and when the ice disappeared on the lake on the twentieth of June, we loaded up and crossed the lake to finish the work we had begun there the previous fall. During the next three days we got the log ends trimmed, the Yukon chimney installed, the front porch railing logs in place, the logs varnished and the floor and boats painted. We also enjoyed some succulent trout we caught off the dock. It would have been good to spend more time down at the outpost, but we were expecting fishing guests at the main lodge and had to return.

Before leaving for Inuvik to get the floats reattached to SLA, I got Margaret moved back into the chef's quarters in the lodge kitchen so that we were again prepared to feed our guests. I spent five nights down in Inuvik as a guest of Father Ruyant, who put me up regally in the No. 2 suite of Grollier Hall. Since my last visit to Inuvik, the Pastor, Father Adam, had announced from the pulpit of the igloo church that I was to be married. So everyone knew, including a couple of women who kept phoning late at night to caution me about making any hasty decisions on my choice of a wife! I appreciated their concern, but my mind had long been made up on that point.

Stan Dupont from Amherstberg, Ontario, had written that he would be making his sixth annual fishing trip to the lodge, along with his grandson. He asked me to be at Norman Wells to pick him up on July 16th. With heavy rains and a very low ceiling, it was not a day I would have chosen to fly, but I had given my word and felt I had to go. I had to detour around by Fort Good Hope and then follow the river at tree-top level. The visibility at times was reduced to a few hundred feet. The carburetor needed engine heat to run properly, and more than once I thought of turning back, but the thought of Stan waiting there for me and counting on me spurred me on. Finally I was able to land at D.O.T. Lake five miles south of the Norman Wells airstrip. Before landing I had contacted the tower and asked them to notify the Pacific Western agent that I had arrived to pick up passenger Dupont.

I waited in the plane for forty-five minutes in the driving rain before a pickup truck arrived to give me a lift to the terminal. There the agent told me that he had never gotten my message from the air radio office upstairs. Passenger Dupont had gotten back on their jet for Inuvik after a local bush pilot told him that no small aircraft were able to fly today. The agent mentioned casually that Bishop Piché had gotten off the same 737 jet and went into town. When I tracked the bishop down, he told me he was on his way to Fort Good Hope to visit the mission there. Then he would go to Colville for my wedding. I ended up flying back down the Mackenzie River with the bishop, depositing him safely at Fort Good Hope. I borrowed the parish station wagon and brought six kegs of heating oil and the mail down to the town dock so I wouldn't be going back empty. I was within sight of Colville Lake when my engine started sputtering and my gas gauges were showing empty. I had not gassed up at Norman Wells because of the heavy rain. Now I regretted it. In a silent glide I just made it to the lake and landed on the water with a dead stick, just across from the village a mile-and-a-half to the west. Margaret was on the lookout for me and soon came out with a boat to tow me in. If this had happened two weeks before, when I was hauling fuel with the aircraft on wheels, I would have demolished the plane completely landing in the bush. I always carried my rosary in the plane and felt that the Blessed Mother was looking out for me.

The next day the skies were a little clearer as I flew down to Inuvik to pick up Stan and his grandson and finally get them into Colville Lake and settled in the lodge. The next day was a Sunday. I rang the bell for the eleven o'clock service as usual and between the rosary and communion read the Gospel and followed it with a sermon in which I told of the imminent visit of the bishop and my marriage to Margaret.

At last the fateful day arrived, Monday, July 19th. As it was arranged, I flew into Fort Good Hope in the morning and brought back Bishop Paul Piché. We had sunny skies. My log church was packed to the walls as the Nuptial High Mass began at eight that evening. Margaret, in a pretty yellow dress and veil, and I in a navy blue blazer, sat side by side up in front, flanked by the bridesmaid and the best man. In his sermon the bishop explained this precedent-setting ceremony in which he was about to marry one of his missionary priests in the very church the missionary had built. His words were simultaneously translated into the Hare language by George Codzi Senior. Although there had been ten other priests of the bishop's Vicariate who had left of their own volition, none of them had been married by the bishop and none of them had remained in the North, let alone at their post. So mine was a unique case. Finally the rings were blessed and exchanged and we were officially declared man and wife.

Outside, after the ceremony, no rice was thrown at us, for this custom was unheard of here. Nonetheless, all the people shook our hands and wished us well. One of the visitors took our picture on the church steps. We then accompanied the bishop over to the lodge dining room, where we signed the books and were toasted to a long, happy married life. I had left the aircraft ready at the end of the dock, so now Margaret and I got on board and flew off to the outpost for a one-night honeymoon.

25

MARRIED LIFE

My life at Colville Lake after our marriage was simply a happier continuation of what it had been before. Although I had been relieved of most of my priestly duties, I was still officiating at Sunday services in church. I would always be a priest, but I was no longer acting in that capacity. It was something akin to a medical doctor who has had his licence to practise lifted. I no longer felt responsible for the moral conduct of the community. I felt liberated.

On the day following our marriage, I flew the bishop to Fort Franklin and things returned to normal. During the summer I was occupied taking care of visiting fishermen. One day each week I flew to Fort Good Hope to pick up the community mail. After more than thirty-five years, the mission is still acting as the unofficial post office for the community. Some years later, after corresponding with our member of parliament and the Canada Post Corporation, I finally succeeded in getting them to sign a contract with North Wright Air to bring in our mail on their weekly flight out of Norman Wells. I no longer had to fly during the winter.

Our marriage prompted some restructuring of the mission's interior. I tore out the bunk I had been using in my office for the past ten years, moved the wall separating it from the clinic room three feet, and built a queen-size bunk for Margaret and me. Then I dismantled the mission chapel and built three bunks in that room for visitors. Next door to the church I built a four-bunk cabin with a sod roof that could be heated in winter. All this work involved a lot of cabinet-making in the workshop as well.

In spite of my preoccupation with carpentry, I felt an urge to take a break and live out on the land for a spell. Both Margaret and I held general hunting licences, so following freeze-up we decided to move out to the bush and use them. We went down to the north end of the lake twenty-five miles and moved into our outpost cabin. From there I set out marten traps farther north, while Margaret put out rabbit snares. I shot some caribou within sight of our cabin and then set traps where I had butchered them and soon caught five fox.

We could have happily spent the winter down there, except for the fact that my presence was needed back at the village. Besides keeping the community medicine and acting as the medic, I had the only means of communication in case of an emergency. Then there was my work as secretary for the Co-op, agent for the airline, and acting Postmaster. I was far from being divorced from the day-to-day operation of our growing community. As much as I might want to, in conscience I really couldn't absent myself for too long. So we returned.

Margaret is a woman who has never once complained about using an outdoor privy in the coldest weather. Although we were used to an outside privy, most of our visitors were not, and this occasioned some amusing incidents. In January, with the temperature at fifty-four degrees below zero Fahrenheit, Dr. Dan Dimitroff flew in from Inuvik with a nurse to conduct a clinic. When she asked to use the "powder room," I advised her to take the flashlight with her because it was dark in there. She declined, saying she didn't think she needed it, so I let her go. A few minutes later we heard a scream. I told the doctor he had better check on his nurse. He returned to report that she had not noticed that the hinged seat had been left open. When she sat down she went right through. She caught herself by her elbows before she disappeared completely, but she was still unable to lift herself up. With the help of the doctor she got out of her predicament and, back in the kitchen, admitted that she should have taken my advice. To this point we hadn't realized just how dangerous our outhouse could be. Perhaps I was learning too, as a married man, always to leave the seat down!

❋ ❋ ❋

Geophysical Services Incorporated from Houston, Texas, were drilling an exploratory well for oil about fifty miles north of us and I flew up there to visit them. When they told me that they where looking for a spot to park their equipment for the summer, I suggested they use the edge of our new runway. My motive was to get their D-7 cats working to drag our strip and fill in some potholes that had developed. At the end of April we watched their long procession of heavy sleds come across the lake and park along the airstrip above the village.

As is usually the case, the men operating and living in this camp were well disposed toward the natives and were eager to help in any way they could. Their cookhouse was open twenty-four hours a day and the locals took advantage of free coffee and snacks, until the day that the camp cook found all the sugar stolen. He had also been saving all his potato peelings for one of our people, until someone informed him that they were not being used for dog food, but were going into a home-brew pot!

One day two very cold little girls came into the mission to report that their mother had not come home for two days. I finally located her in one of the company trailers on the air strip. I was beginning to have second thoughts about the proximity of this camp so close to our village.

In May, two of the company's trailers were torn apart with the help of our locals and the pieces thrown into a huge pit to be buried according to government regulations. Before this material got covered up, however, two of our natives carried pieces of this bright silver and orange aluminium siding down to our village and covered their warehouses with them. They stood out like sore thumbs. On his next visit the commissioner immediately noticed them and had his environmental agent in Yellowknife notify GSI to reclaim their material and bury it. This caused a lot of grumbling. I got some flak from people who assumed that I had lodged the complaint, but I had not. It was apparent from this incident that it was going to be difficult to preserve the rustic beauty of our village entirely made of logs.

Though I was successful in getting a $5,000 grant from the government for upgrading our airstrip, the few men left over- hauling their cats in the summer were so anxious to get out that they didn't use half of the money. When they finally left with their equipment the next winter, I was glad to see them go, regretting that I had ever suggested they park near us in the first place. Hindsight is always 20-20!

❄ ❄ ❄

Every year the muskox seem to be edging in closer to Colville Lake from the barren lands to the east. In some places in the Arc- tic they are becoming so numerous that they are taking over vast areas once populated only by the caribou. At one time muskox were completely protected from hunters, but now more and more tags are being issued by the Department of Renewable Resources to try to keep them in check. Our settlement was issued two tags one year and, when none of the natives shot any, I decided to take one of them with me and fly out about seventy miles to the Barren Lands on the last day of the open season.

It was easy to spot two of them and land nearby on skis. The actual shooting of the large bull was like shooting a domestic cow in a field. This animal has only one natural enemy, the Arctic wolf, so it is merely curious when approached by a human. I can't see where there is any incentive here for sports hunters to pursue them. As we were skinning and butchering him, the cow would not leave and we had to shoo her away, a pitiful exhibition of loyalty in the wild. We returned with a heavy load of head, hide and meat which I distributed to the people. The meat, however, was so tough that we had to grind it up into burgers before we could eat it. I have no desire ever to shoot another muskox.

❊ ❊ ❊

For his 1969 annual report to the Minister of Northern Affairs, Commissioner Stuart Hodgson borrowed one of my photos of a dog-team to illustrate its dust jacket. When the Explorers Hotel opened in Yellowknife in 1974, I happened to be there with the Commissioner and a local lawyer, David Searle. In the hotel's gift shop I noticed some thirty-six-inch prints for sale which were identical to my photo. To add insult to injury, they had printed below the image the warning, "All rights reserved." When I pointed this out to Stu he immediately said, "They can't do that. It's a copyright infringement and David here will handle it for you."

Apparently this was the first case of a copyright infringement to appear in the Northwest Territories and David had to go to his counterparts in Ottawa to learn how to handle it. The upshot was that it took two years before we settled out of court with the culprit for $200 plus ten percent of future sales. But by this time the lawyer's fee had escalated to over $1,100.

The following year I went down to Calgary to collect my ten percent royalty from this enterprising merchant. He proudly showed me six Vietnamese boat people he had working in a warehouse. They formed an assembly line, busily gluing copies of my photo to fancy plywood panels which they were covering with a thick coat of clear, acrylic resin. I was told that they were being sold up and down the Alaska Highway for seventy-five dollars each. Then, however, I was informed that my photo only cost one dollar to print, so my share of the finished product came to exactly ten cents! At this point I was in no mood to hire another lawyer to dispute it. When we saw this same photo on cups and

dishes at the Toronto airport later, I simply smiled. I had had
enough of copyright infringements.

❄ ❄ ❄

Commissioner Hodgson liked to show off Colville Lake as a
picturesque log village that resembled the old North that was
rapidly passing into history. At one time he told me he was sending the Queen of England for a visit and even had me dig a new
privy for her use. She never came, but in April, 1975, her son
Charles, the Prince of Wales, came in her stead. The security
involved in this visit was impressive. One Sunday preceding the
visit I had twenty-one members of the RCMP in our common
room going over the security details. When the day arrived we
had a Department of Transport fire-fighter in an asbestos suit
positioned on the runway with several fire extinguishers in hand
as two plane-loads of the press landed first. A barrier of crowd
control rope had been strung up around the airport exit area,
hardly necessary for the two dozen natives who walked up there
any more than was the medical doctor standing by in our nursing
station.

I gave the Prince a walking tour of my buildings including
the underground, permafrost ice house. In the church he didn't
seem to notice my painting of Our Lady of the Snows, but was
fascinated by the muskox hide rug on the floor. Out in front of
the mission the chief of Fort Good Hope tried to get him to sign
a petition to Ottawa to stop all development in the area until the
land claims had been renegotiated. The Prince later told me that
as a matter of policy and to avoid being embroiled in contro-
versy, no member of a royal party signs any local petitions on
their official tours.

Next we went out a mile on the frozen lake by dog-team to
show the Prince how gill nets are operated under ice. After taking two dozen fish the Prince insisted on trying his hand at driving one of our four teams on our return to the village. Although
he fell off once he didn't seem to mind it. Four of the Mounties

armed with telescopic rifles escorted us at a respectful distance on ski-doos, but luckily their services were not needed. Back at the mission he posed with Margaret and me for a photo we used on our next Christmas card. When he asked me if there was anything he could do for me when back in London I asked him to send me the addresses of old book stores there dealing in Canadiana and from that list I subsequently got a dozen good books on the North to add to my collection. A few years later he was sent one of my paintings as a wedding present from the Government of the Northwest Territories on the occasion of his marriage to Diana Spencer. So maybe a sample of my art now hangs in Buckingham Palace. The Prince of Wales signed our guest book simply as "Charles." He impressed me as a very well informed guest who asked many intelligent questions.

❅ ❅ ❅

The idea of canoeing from Colville Lake down to the Arctic Ocean had been in the back of my mind for years. Now, with Margaret, I had the perfect companion for the trip. I ordered a good seventeen-foot vinyl-foam canoe from the Old Town Canoe Company in Maine, closed down the lodge since we could find no one to run it for us, and shoved off the following June just as soon as the ice on the lake permitted. For the next twenty-seven days we paddled over 500 miles of lakes and connecting streams until we finally reached the Anderson River. The route was easy to follow. Good campsites were abundant and the four portages totalled less than half a mile. We caught trout or grayling every day and I got one fat caribou so we didn't need most of the freeze-dried grub we were carrying. We were constantly fascinated by the game we saw, including a huge grizzly bear that approached our tent one night, wolves that paced us along the banks like curious dogs, and miles of moulting geese.

We rested on Sundays. Then I got my sketch pad and watercolour paints out and braved the mosquitoes to record the landscape in scenes I later used for oil paintings. Margaret carried her 8mm camera and produced a remarkably good film of our trip.

In fact, I later carried it with me to Brazil where my brother Tom and I showed it in many schools. He supplied a Portuguese commentary. When we reached the Arctic coast we were met by Canada Wildlife biologist Tom Barry, who had been branding geese there for years. We were flown back home by old friend Bill Cook in his vintage Grumman Widgeon. Bill had often visited us from Bellevue, Washington. We returned, tanned and lean, with a new appreciation for the great country in which we live.

Both Margaret and I had lost our fathers, but our mothers were still alive. That fall we flew our Cessna down to Calgary and left it there for an engine change while we flew on to Rochester to spend Christmas with my mother. The following summer one of Margaret's nine brothers brought her mother to Colville Lake to spend a week with us.

The then Minister of Northern Affairs (and later, Prime Minister), Jean Chrétien, had hired Judge Thomas Berger to hold hearings in the communities adjacent to the Mackenzie River corridor in order to ascertain what effects a future oil pipeline might have on the people and the environment. Although Colville Lake was ninety air miles east of this river, for some reason we got included in this survey. So later that summer a DC-3 landed on our airstrip with members of the press and a lawyer in charge from British Columbia. He borrowed a projector from me as well as benches in order to show our people just what had been said to the judge in other northern communities.

The hearing itself got under way the following day when the judge himself arrived, but it was evident very quickly that, with the press in attendance, the natives were going to use this opportunity to air grievances that had nothing to do with the pipeline. The fact that their statements were similar to what he had heard before prompted Berger to conclude that the natives of the Northwest Territories were of one mind in their opposition to the building of a pipeline. In fact they had been well coached in advance on what to say. Finally, the judge's recommendations led to a ten-year delay of this project so that more natives could be prepared for higher paying jobs. Chrétien was not pleased with the outcome of the hearings and I heard many people express the opinion that nothing to date had done more to drive a wedge between whites and natives.

❋ ❋ ❋

While in Calgary, I visited George Payne who ran the Gainsborough Gallery. He told me that I could continue painting at Colville until I died and nobody would ever know of my art. The way to get ahead in this field, he advised me, was to get a minimum of thirty-five paintings together and hold a show at his gallery. I took his advice and had my first show in November of 1979. Thirty-two of my thirty-five paintings sold in the first hour – unprecedented for an unknown artist.

Next year, my second show at this gallery provoked even more intense interest. Each painting in the show had a perforated price tag affixed, which was to be torn off and presented at the counter by the intended purchaser. When the front doors of the Gainsborough were thrown open at one o'clock that Sunday, a horde of people who had lined up on the sidewalk rushed in. One woman headed directly for the painting "The Daily Woodhaul" and reached for its tag. Another woman rushed up behind her and sent her flying! Before the melee had been quelled by the manager, the frame of another painting had been smashed, a decorative baseboard torn from the wall and the first woman lay sprawled on the floor with a cut to her knee. The dispute over who had actually gotten the price tag off first ended in a court case. Twenty-eight of my paintings were sold in the first ten minutes. At my show the following year a security guard was hired.

The success I was meeting in the sale of original paintings prompted a friend to suggest that I have some limited edition prints made. I took samples of the first two off the press into the headquarters of the Arctic Federated Co-ops in Yellowknife.

They liked them so much that they subsequently bought out all these first two editions for their retail outlets called "Northern Images." This was an encouraging beginning for the two dozen other editions that were to follow. Thanks to this God-given talent in art, Margaret and I could quit worrying about how we were going to support ourselves.

❄ ❄ ❄

Now into our tenth year of marriage we were finding ourselves very compatible and our life together happy. Besides my painting, the medical work at the nursing station and the work as agent for Nahanni Air Line kept me busy. I delivered some babies and buried some elders. The community had built a recreation cabin, a $21,000 fiasco which was never used. I was asked to draw up plans for a replacement. I designed a hexagonal log building which was built in 1988 and immediately put into use temporarily as our first school. Don Payne arrived as the first teacher. Two years later a much bigger log school was built as well as a teacherage.

Although I had abandoned my dog-team when I got the aircraft, Margaret decided she wanted a team, so we gathered up some of my original dogs around the village and soon they were producing some fine pure white pups. It was our habit to spend a week at the outpost every year in late May when the first wildfowl arrived. When we returned on the ice in the spring of 1987 I drove the ski-doo back while Margaret followed with ten dogs in harness. About half way across the lake she stopped to change the positions of several dogs. A bird happened to swoop down in front of her leader, who lunged ahead, along with the four dogs behind him. Margaret's left leg was caught in the harness as the sled shot forward, and this broke her tibia bone and tore the ligaments under her knee cap. She managed to fall into her sled and the dogs pulled her home.

I had rushed on ahead to receive the doctor who, as luck would have it, happened to be flying in from Inuvik for a clinic.

When he looked at Margaret's leg he strongly advised her to return with him to Inuvik for X-rays. But, as usual, she made light of her injury, saying it was merely a muscle strain. A week later she was forced to fly out for the X-rays and subsequently underwent three operations in Edmonton. The leg healed, but she never got the therapy she needed to return that leg to normal. Driving huskies can be risky, and a team of ten is doubly so.

❄ ❄ ❄

The following July a tragic drama unfolded on a lake fifty miles north of us at precisely the spot where I had landed without power in my Cessna six years before. A young French couple had been writing me from France during the winter, asking if I knew of a spot where they could build a cabin and spend the winter studying the caribou. I suggested that they use one of our outpost cabins. When they arrived in the country they came in via the Dempster Highway through the Yukon and had a bush pilot drop them off at Taketue Lake. When their incoming mail accumulated and pilots dropped off some 200 pounds of grub for them, I decided to fly down there and deliver it.

When I flew over their lake I found that a forest fire had burned right up to the east shore where they had been camped for a month. I searched the entire shore, but could find no sign of life. So I returned to notify the RCMP in Fort Good Hope. They flew in the next day in a helicopter. While they were out searching, Lydia walked in and told me in French her sorry tale. She said that when she and Jacques saw the fire approaching their camp they were seized with fear and realized they would have to get out before it was too late. They first dug a pit in the ground and buried their most precious items, including cameras and film. Then they loaded their small thirteen-foot canoe with half of their gear and paddled west across the lake, which is about a mile and a half wide at that point.

They managed to get across safely with the first load on a flat calm lake, but were not so lucky on their second trip. The canoe

was swamped in the middle of the lake and turned over, emptying its contents. The two paddlers were in the water, holding on
desperately across the keel. They managed for nearly half an
hour, until Jacques succumbed to hypothermia, released his grip
and sank out of sight. She said that when he went down, she was
so desperate she wanted to go down with him. One can just
imagine her thoughts as she clutched the overturned canoe, now
alone, to face her own precarious situation. Luckily, she was in
excellent physical condition, for she had been a physical fitness
instructor in France. As a woman, too, she had more insulating
fat to slow the paralysing effects of that cold water. Finally she
made up her mind to try to swim to shore – and made it!

If she had had a mind to, Lydia could have survived right
there on the western shore of that lake, using the tent, axe, sleeping bag, gill net and dried food they had ferried across on their
first trip. Instead, after that first sleepless night, she decided to
walk to Colville Lake. Taking some macaroni, rice, the nylon
cover of the sleeping bag and a map, she started walking south
the following day. The bugs proved so bothersome she altered
her schedule and walked at night, sleeping during the day,
although at that time of year it is light around the clock. At one
point she encountered a black bear that had her shaking with
fright because she had nothing with which to protect herself.

After five weary nights trudging through spongy muskeg
country she came to a large lake that she thought was Colville.
She was so elated she ate the last of her rice. She was mistaken,
however, and had to backtrack. She walked two more nights on
an empty stomach. Finally she reached a small cabin on the west
shore of Colville Lake, found a little grub in it and rested her blis-
tered feet a couple of days. It was here that one of our locals spotted her from his speedboat and brought her in the last ten miles.

The next day the police returned to Taketue Lake with their
helicopter. They found the body of Jacques floating along the
shore. It was flown to Edmonton for an autopsy at the request of
the French consul there and Lydia took his ashes back to France
for burial. This tragedy struck me as doubly sad because it could

easily have been avoided. If they had simply paddled south along the lakeshore in shallow water they would have been out of the fire zone in three miles. If they had notified the RCMP, as they should have, where they were setting up camp, the many fire patrol aircraft flying in the area over the past month would have checked on them. The north country can easily take advantage of the uninitiated and its frigid waters are a lethal trap.

❄ ❄ ❄

The fifteenth of August that summer of 1987 marked the completion of the twenty-five years I had spent at Colville Lake. I aimed to celebrate the silver anniversary of Our Lady of the Snows Mission in style. I had a commemorative booklet printed with pictures of the construction of the mission in 1962, as well as banners, caps and buttons. I mailed out invitations and friends flew in under a clear blue sky from all directions. The commissioner of the RCMP flew in from Yellowknife and used the occasion to present a special bravery award to their corporal from Fort Norman. The Commissioner of the Northwest Territories, John Parker, presented me with a special plaque.

A ribbon was cut to open my museum officially. All the visitors crowded in to look at the artefacts on the first floor and the paintings and library on the second. The church was overflowing when the bishop began his Mass at 4:00 in the afternoon. Following the ceremony, Margaret and her crew fed 140 people from tents set up in the side yard on tables built especially for the occasion. Some musicians from Tuk then played square dance music in the recreation hall until the fire marshall from Inuvik set off a display of aerial rockets at 10:30 p.m. As the smoke cleared, everyone agreed that it had been one whale of a day.

My mother died in 1986 and left me our old homestead Hearthcliff on the shore of Lake Ontario. As I had no intention of ever living there again, I sold it and used the money to buy a better Cessna 180, this time an amphibian. When Pope John Paul II visited Fort Simpson that September of 1987, I flew down to

Fort Smith and picked up Bishop Denis Croteau, along with one of the Brothers, and flew them to the event.

It was bound to happen sooner or later that we would get electricity in our settlement. A preliminary assessment had been made by the N.W.T. Power Corporation, but when the government administrator wrote me from Inuvik, he stated that the estimated cost of $375,000 to locate a generator here for sixty-five people was simply far too expensive. Yet, despite the cost, not one but three generators were brought in by cat train two years later. By 1991, all our cabins had electricity at a cost of over a million! After lighting gas lamps for twenty-nine years, it seemed strange to simply turn on a switch.

Although most of our fuel was being flown in at a transportation cost of about $3.80 a gallon, the few cat trains we got in winter seemed to be loaded mostly with building material for new houses. They were supplied by the N.W.T. Housing Corporation and given to the natives at no cost if they occupied them for at least five years. Unfortunately they turned out to be frame houses, so we immediately lost our uniqueness as the only all log community in the Territories. The plans of these new houses, with all the lumber pre-cut in Hay River, bore little resemblance to the needs of people living above the Arctic Circle. For one thing, they made no provisions for a workshop where ski-doos could be heated or repaired in winter. Secondly, the extravagant high ceilings and seven-foot doors showed no concern for the difficulty entailed in heating them. The windowpanes were large and difficult to replace. I could go on, but you get the picture.

Next the government put up a twelve-foot satellite dish so that everyone could get live TV. Visitors comment on all the modern improvements they see around town and presume that these automatically raise the standard of living. What they don't realize is that Colville Lake was an experiment to attract only those who wanted to get back to the land, to preserve their cultural heritage and throw off the shackles of government handouts. If one sits comfortably in a new house equipped with an electric stove, a deep-freeze, an electric washing machine and dryer, electric lights and TV, one will hardly be drawn to move out into a tent and to trap for a living in winter. When this resettlement project began, and for the first twenty-five years, all the people lived in the bush during the trapping season and made their living off the fur they caught. As modern improvements increased, time spent in the bush trapping decreased. As this prime source of income dropped, social assistance increased, and so did crime.

❊ ❊ ❊

The dream of visiting the Eastern Arctic with my own plane often crossed my mind. It took a visit from my brother Tom in 1994, however, to make this dream a reality. In early August we took off together from Colville Lake and flew to Coppermine. The fact that I was now equipped with wheels as well as floats meant that I could land on runways and avoid the corrosive effects of salt water. Over the succeeding days we continued east, stopping at Cambridge Bay, Gjoa Haven, Pelly Bay and Repulse Bay, staying each night in a comfortable but empty mission. The Catholic clergy were becoming almost as scarce as dodo birds – not extinct – yet certainly thinning out.

With the use of the new GPS (Global Positioning System), flying from one Eskimo settlement to the next was a piece of cake. But there was one hazard we couldn't avoid, and that was the miles of ocean surface covered with broken chunks of ice. These chunks weren't big enough to land on with wheels, and neither was there enough open water between them to use our floats. If we had a loss of power in one of those areas, we would have added one more statistic to the list of aircraft lost in the high Arctic.

We followed the western shore of Hudson Bay south and stopped overnight at Chesterfield Inlet. Here was the original mission that was put up by Bishop Arsene Turquetil, O.M.I., who had ordained both Thomas and myself. That building was still standing in 1998. After spending a night at Rankin Inlet, we continued south to Churchill where we spent two nights with genial Bishop Reynald Rouleau, O.M.I. His beautiful museum of Eskimo artefacts is a tribute to the Oblates who collected them through the years.

From there we turned west, crossed over 400 miles of tundra, and landed at Stoney Rapids, Saskatchewan. After gassing up we flew on to Mission St. Bernard at Camsell Portage on the north shore of Lake Athabaska, the mission I had built in 1952. My old companion Philip Stenne was still there to welcome us and help us carry our bed rolls up to the mission. Thomas had received many letters from me during the four years I had lived here, but had never seen the place. We concelebrated a Mass together the next day, a Sunday, for the fifty or so Cree natives who still lived there, and then continued on to the west end of the lake to visit the old mission at Fort Chipewyan.

After leaving Hay River and crossing Great Slave Lake we began following the mighty Mackenzie River north. Around Wrigley the visibility was reduced to a quarter of a mile by the smoke of forest fires. These were burning right down to the east banks of the river. We had to fly just off the water to get through that area. I wanted to reach Colville Lake that day, for it was August 15th, the big feast of the Assumption and the anniversary of the founding of the mission. We made it and were able to celebrate a Mass that evening with all the village. We had been gone nearly two weeks and pretty well circled the Northwest Territories. This was probably the longest flight I would ever make.

❊ ❊ ❊

On the 31st of August, 1995, I arrived at my seventy-fifth birthday, just as Father Mansoz back in Fort Smith had predicted when we had celebrated his seventy-fifth back in 1948. He had seemed ancient to me then, as he told me that I, too, would reach this milestone in such a hurry that I would wonder where all the years had flown so quickly. He was right. Time does fly.

I am glad to state here that my change to a quasi-lay state has not in any way lessened my love for the Church nor my good rapport with my bishop and former missionary associates. I still consider myself an Oblate and am not at all surprised to see mail coming in addressed to "Father Brown." I am still a registered clergyman for the Northwest Territories, so I guess I still rate the title of "Reverend."

People ask if my experience has made me favour a married clergy. As for working in that role in the North, I answered that question when I petitioned Rome for permission to marry. My experience has proved to my satisfaction that for the isolated missionary it can be a wonderful help to have a wife beside him to provide love and companionship and to lighten his load. I can't answer that question, however, when it comes to the clergy living on the home front in large cities. I do believe that celibacy should be made optional. Let the confirmed bachelor clergy remain celibate if they so choose. In my case, I simply was not cut out for that life. It took me twenty-two years to realize this.

Margaret and I celebrated our own twenty-fifth wedding anniversary on July 19th, 1996. I feel so lucky to have a wife like her. She came to me with many wonderful qualities and then built on them. At first she was so quiet I feared that communication might be a problem, but over time this reserve evaporated. She is hardly a chatterbox, which fault would have been annoying for two people together twenty-four hours a day. She is honest to a fault, which provides a check to any exaggeration that might creep into my own conversation.

She welcomes hard physical labour: she is the only woman in the village who keeps gill nets set. This can be hard work when the ice is three feet thick! The sled-dogs in this settlement that belong to Margaret are the lucky ones: they can count on being fed and watered daily and to have mosquito repellent rubbed on them in fly time. This solicitude for animals is a spillover of her care for the sick when she is running the nursing station.

Margaret has filled the role of wife to perfection. It is because of her that I can now state that my married life has been far happier than the unmarried years that preceded it. We have accepted the fact that God chose not to send us children of our own. This may have been a blessing in disguise, however, because we would have been forced to send them away for their education and been separated from them for most of the year. Instead, the mission's common room became a favourite play area for the children of the village, so we have not lacked the patter of little feet.

To be a good cook and seamstress was not number one on my list of priorities for a good wife, but they have surely been a joy to me after my many years as a bachelor. I couldn't run the fishing lodge without her. She generously overlooks my faults and has kept our initial love alive through a quarter of a century. Her presence at church services never fails to inspire me to give thanks to God for the gift she has been to me.

I am not actively promoting optional celibacy in the Catholic Church. I believe that the good Lord in His own time will direct His Church through the Holy Spirit to carry out His will in this regard. I don't think I'll see that day in my own lifetime. In the meantime, I hope to live out my allotted years here at Colville Lake doing essentially the same things that you have read about in these pages.

INDEX

Denis, Father Jean, O.M.I., 25, 26, 29, 30, 34, 39, 52, 74, 75, 76, 524
Deschaines, Sister Rachel, s.g.m., 231, 232
Deschatelets, Father Leo, O.M.I., 363
Desroshier, Johnny, 307
Devitt, Gordon, 250, 251
de Vroom, Hans, 357, 360
Dewer, Ken, 25
Dick, Emma, 279, 280
Dick, Lawrence, 279, 280
Dick, Winnie, 296
Dillon, Ernie, 446
Dillon, Joe and Kapa, 109, 110, 112
Dillon, John, 275, 283
Dillon, Miles, 278, 283
Dillon, Mrs., 283
Dimitroff, Dr. Dan, 534
Dobbin, Colin, 503
Doctor, George, 116
Dolphus, Victor, 118
Douglas, Bob, 255
Douglas, George, 526
Douglas, Ray, 413
Dowler, Dr., D.D.S., 435, 436
Doyles (cousins in Chicago), 514
Drew, Honourable George, 238
Drouart, Father Jean, O.M.I., 224
Duchaussois, Father Pierre, O.M.I., 526
Ducot, Father Xavier, 27
Dunn, Vince, 309, 310
Dunster, Rev., 365
Dupont, Stan, 507, 529, 530
Drury, Commissioner, 272

—E—

Ebner, Father Frank, 204
Echale (See Kochon, Isidore)
Echo Bay, 125
Eden, Carl, 483, 484
Edkins, Stan, 487, 497, 503, 520
Efficially (See Codzi, Frank)
Ekokoolay, 108
Elanik, Jack, 443
Eldorado, 138
Embleton, Tom, 142
Emmott, Florence, R.N., 448
Engle, Bob, 381, 384, 394

Eskimos (Inuit), 27, 46, 49, 118
Ethloleth, 450
Eya, Chief Francis, 63, 83, 95, 100, 115

—F—

Farnham, Eleanor, 476
Farnham, Felix, 495, 496
Faulkner, Dr., 98, 100
Felix, Mona, 495
Ferdinand, Pierre, 225
Ferguson, Pete, 460
Ferris, Don, 123, 125
Fiddler Point, 153, 212
Figney, Jim, 333
Finger Bay, 120
Finto, Tony, 523
Firth, John, 263
Firth, Noel, 245
Fjarnison, Matt, 482, 483
Flett, Charley, 146
Fond du Lac, 137, 139, 158, 159, 161, 166, 193, 202, 203, 215, 216
Foster, John (CBC), 469
Fort Chipewyan, 15, 131, 132, 133, 137, 140, 167, 205, 211
Fort Fitzgerald, 18, 117, 137, 157, 212
Fort Franklin, 33, 57, 62, 63, 71, 72, 76, 82, 87, 90, 99, 103, 104, 108, 122, 124, 147, 164, 170, 176, 203, 204, 213
Fort Good Hope, 45, 52, 77
Fort Liard, 21 n.
Fort McMurray, 15
Fort Nelson, 41
Fort Norman, 1, 2, 25, 27, 28, 32, 36, 42, 51, 52, 53, 54, 55, 57, 62, 72, 73, 76, 77, 104, 110, 116, 119
Fort Providence, 27, 52, 76
Fort Rae, 21, 212
Fort Reliance, 192, 208
Fort Resolution, 20, 146
Fort Simpson, 25, 77, 87
Fort Smith, 16, 18, 23, 52, 111, 120, 192, 212, 213
Fort Wrigley, 77, 123
Fournier, Father Louis, O.M.I., 468
Franche, Father Jean, 49, 251, 270, 296, 297, 507, 524
Franchuk, Magistrate, 373
Franklin (See Fort Franklin)